Understanding and Using Paradox 3.5

Rob Krumm

Brady
New York London Toronto Sydney Tokyo Singapore

Simon & Schuster, Inc.
15 Columbus Circle
New York, NY 10023

DISTRIBUTED BY PRENTICE HALL TRADE

Manufactured in the United States of America

10 9 8 7 6 5 4 3 2 1

Library of Congress Cataloging-in-Publication Data

Krumm, Rob, 1951-
Understanding and using Paradox 3.5 / Rob Krumm.
p. cm.
Includes index.
1. Data base management. 2. Paradox 3 (Computer program)
I. Title.
QA76.9.D3K797 1990
005.75'65—dc20 90-1942
ISBN 0-13-946328-3 : CIP

Limits of Liability and Disclaimer of Warranty

Dedication

For Eric and Jennifer

If you built your castles in the air your work need not be lost;
now put foundations under them . . .

CONTENTS

Introduction

Why Buy This Book?

If you are reading this introduction you are probably standing in a book store in front of shelves filled with dozens and dozens of computer books, many of which include in their titles *Paradox 3*. The obvious, but crucial, question is: Which book should you buy?

❑ **The *Understanding and Using* Goal.** This book is the sixth book in a series. The concept behind all of these books is that true learning takes place only when readers discover how things actually work for themselves. The purpose of this book is not simply to pass on information about Paradox, but to provide a framework that will allow the reader to encounter and comprehend the concepts that underlie Paradox 3.5 and database management in general.

❑ **The *Understanding and Using* Concept.** The concept behind the *Understanding and Using* series is that the best way to learn about a complex application is to choose a single example and demonstrate all of the various techniques, procedures, and applications with reference to the same example. Even though this is a large book, the single example unifies the text in a way that places the emphasis on how different commands, procedures, and techniques affect the same items differently. If a new example is chosen to explain each new idea, it is very hard to see the effect of the new technique.

❑ **The *Understanding and Using* Method.** The information in this book is organized in a *learning* order. Each chapter builds on the concepts discussed in the previous chapters. All of the skills needed to master a given technique are built into the chapters and sections that precede that discussion in a step-by-step manner. The book contains all of the keystrokes, commands, or program instructions needed to carry out the tasks discussed in the book. This means that every reader can reproduce the results illustrated in this text on their computer. By performing the tasks discussed, you will have a chance to discover on your own exactly how Paradox 3.5 really functions.

❑ **What this book is not.** This book is neither a beginner's book nor an advanced user's book. The topics included in this book were selected because they are the ones that most readers will need to know in order to get the benefits from the software. However, the goals, concepts, and methods of this series mean that this book cannot be everything to every reader. Despite its size, this book does not contain *everything* about Paradox. The belief is that by learning the concepts this book has to teach about Paradox you will be able to continue to learn and expand your understanding of the subject long after you have finished this text.

The goals set for this book are not modest goals. It is my sincere belief that the text makes an honest attempt to achieve its goals. I hope that it will serve each reader well.

Rob Krumm

Martinez, California—1990

Part I

Database Fundamentals

1

Organization and Conventions

One of the most important features of the *Understanding and Using* series is that *all* of the procedures, techniques, and operations discussed in this book are documented keystroke for keystroke. This enables each reader to reproduce the examples on their own computer. Experience has shown that this provides a much more compelling educational experience than merely reading about features discussed in isolation from the example. This also creates a book in which the features and operations are learned in a sequence based on what is required to complete a task, in contrast to a book organized by alphabetical or some other arbitrary order. This means that the reader will encounter a number of different types of information in this book, e.g., background text, step by step instructions, keystroke commands, etc.

Special typographical conventions are used to indicate the different types of information. These typographical styles make up the *conventions* used in this book to represent various types of information.

Conventions

Background text is used to inform the reader about the conceptual framework required for a command, operation, or technique. This text is written in paragraph style—of which this paragraph is an example.

Notes supply information that may be of interest to some readers but is not required to understand the concept or procedure being discussed. These notes are written in *italic* text and are enclosed in a box, as shown below.

> *This is a sample of the way notes will appear in this book.*

Step-by-step instructions will follow each of the **background text** sections. The text shown below is an example of how a **step-by-step** instructions section will look:

Heading of Step-by-Step Instructions

All of the text of a step-by-step instruction section is indented from the page margins.

When you need to enter a keystroke the instructions will be written as shown below: indented in bold print. The command below tells you to type in *hello* and then press the ↵ (Return or Enter) key.

hello ↵

Because the PC keyboard contains special keys, it is necessary to use some sort of notation in the text to indicate when you need to enter those keys. The table below shows the symbols that will appear in this text for the special keys on the PC keyboard.

Table 1-1 Notation Used for Keys

↑	up arrow key
↓	down arrow key
←	left arrow key
→	right arrow key
↵	the return or enter key
[backspace]	the backspace key
[Tab]	the Tab key
[Home]	the Home key
[End]	the End key
[Pg Up]	the Page Up key
[Pg Dn]	the Page Down key
[Ins]	the Insert key
[Del]	the Delete key
[Esc]	the Escape key
[F#]	function key F# where # stands for a number 1–10

In addition to the special keys listed in Table 1-1 the PC keyboard uses three keys, Shift, Ctrl(control), and Alt(alternate) to create combinations with other keys. For example, in Paradox the Tab key will generally move the cursor one column to the right. If you hold down the Shift key and then press [Tab], Paradox will typically move one column in the opposite direc-

Table 1-2 Key Combinations

[Shift-*key*]	Hold down Shift when pressing *key*
[Ctrl-*key*]	Hold down Ctrl when pressing *key*
[Alt-*key*]	Hold down Alt when pressing *key*

tion. In this book combinations of the Shift, Ctrl, and Alt keys with the special keys in the previous table will be represented as shown in Table 1-2.

In some cases it is necessary to enter several repetitions of the same key. In that case the number of repetitions will be shown in parentheses following the key. The command below tells you to press the → key three times.

→*(3 times)*

Because some letters may look like numbers, you will see some commands followed by text in parentheses that reminds you to enter a letter not a number—as in the example below. Remember, the text in parentheses is not part of the keystrokes you are supposed to enter.

o(the letter O)

Most of the commands in Paradox require the entry of more than one keystroke. In order to make it easier to follow long sequences of keystrokes they will be broken into short lines as shown below.

[F10 a
example ↵

Exercises

As in the other books in the *Understanding and Using* series, there will be one or two times in a chapter when the text asks you to carry out a procedure on your own. This is done to encourage you to think along with the text and see if you can apply the concept without having to read each keystroke for the commands. The exact keystrokes needed to carry out the exercises are listed at the end of the chapter if you need help. The page on which the answers are found is noted in the text.

Remember that the steps taken in the exercises are needed to complete the example you are working on. Do not skip these exercises if you want to successfully complete the example.

Screen Images

The text is filled with illustrations that show what the screen or report you are working on should look like. This enables you to compare your work with the examples in the book on a step-by-step basis.

In some cases the figure will be a full screen image such as that shown in Figure 1-1.

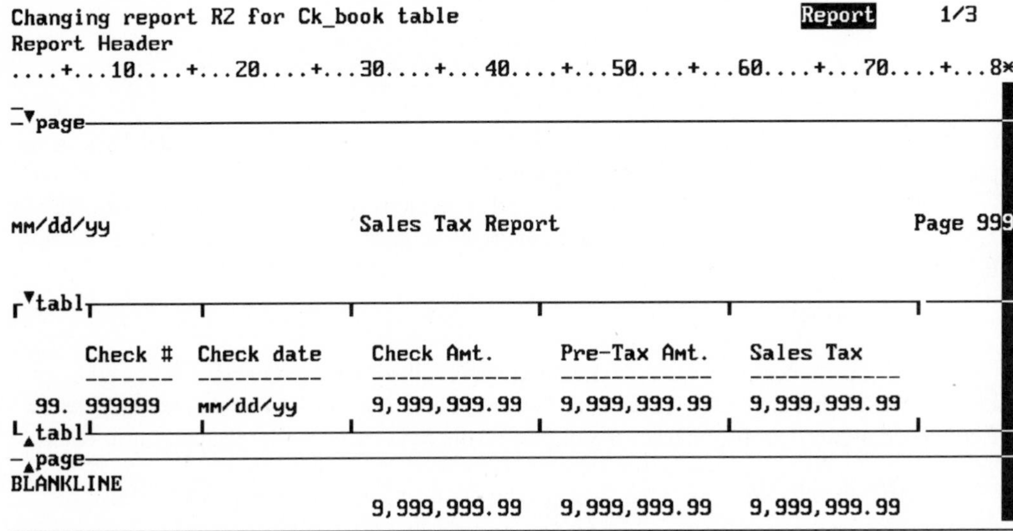

Figure 1-1 Example of a full screen figure.

```
▼tabl
     Check #  Check date    Check Amt.
     -------  ----------    ------------
 99. 999999   mm/dd/yy      9,999,999.99
▲tabl
▲page
BLANKLINE
                            9,999,999.99
```

Figure 1-2 Partial screen figure.

However, because of the difference in the width of a page in a book and the screen of a computer, many of the figures will show only part of the full screen. This has two benefits. First, it isolates the part of the screen that is most significant to the topic being discussed at the moment, and second, it allows that section to be displayed larger than a full-screen image would allow. Figure 1-2 is an example of this type of figure. Note that in these figures, text that will be in **reverse** video on your screen will not appear in **reverse**, i.e., white on black, but merely as bold text.

Selecting or Entering

In Paradox you are often given the option of entering a name, e.g., a file name or a field name, or pressing ↵ so that you can pick the option from a list of file or field names. In writing books such as the *Understanding and Using* series, it is clearer to give instructions in the text for typing in the name rather than for picking it from a list. Look at the two commands below. The first tells you what name to enter while the second tells you to use the → key to highlight and then select a name.

[F10] a
example ↵

[F10] a
→*(6 times)*
↵

The meaning of the first command is unambiguous when read from the text. The instruction that uses the → is less clear.

In this text you will be instructed to enter the name of the file rather than select it. This is done for the sake of clarity. In practice you will probably find that you will prefer to pick the name from a list. Feel free to do so if you prefer.

The Concept of Database Management

Computers were not originally created as data storage devices. The first electronic computers were basically calculating machines used to perform complex mathematical calculations at a high rate of speed, similar to the functions found on a pocket calculator today.

The development of reliable, large-scale devices for storing information electronically, expanded the use of computers as record-keeping devices. The same abilities that made it possible for computers to calculate rapidly also could be used for the storage and retrieval of data that otherwise would have been recorded on paper.

Not only could computers store and retrieve data faster than conventional means of record keeping, but they could also provide summaries and analysis along with the raw data itself. The current generation of desktop computers is capable of handling all the database needs of small businesses, schools, organizations, or work groups within a large company. The key to using this power is in the form of *database management* programs that put the power of the computers to work.

The subject of this book is *Understanding and Using Paradox 3.5*. Paradox 3 is a database management program that combines power, speed, and sophisticated features with a straightforward, visually-oriented command system. Paradox can unlock the power of database management for people with little or no experience with computers or databases.

On the other hand, Paradox contains all the elements needed to create custom-designed database systems programmed using its PAL language.

This book is designed to guide the reader in a step-by-step fashion, through all the areas of database management with Paradox, starting from scratch and moving up to custom-designed programs.

The reader can go as far as he or she desires, or stop once the basics are mastered.

The book is divided into three parts.

I. Database Fundamentals
II. Programming Paradox
III. Using Paradox on a Network

It is important to keep in mind that, because of the nature of learning, the major part of this book is concerned with Part I on the assumption that advanced operations will have no use unless the basics are mastered first.

The topics discussed should lead the reader step by step towards the more advanced and complicated procedures in Paradox because they not only illustrate techniques but teach concepts that will help the reader build upon the examples used in this book. The actual hands-on, step-by-step database course begins in Chapter 2. This chapter is used to explain the basic organization of the Paradox program and the way that various concepts are presented in this text.

The Paradox 3 Program

Paradox 3.5 is a *database management program* designed to run on MSDOS computers.

If you are experienced with computers the terms shown in *italics* in the previous sentence are probably familiar to you. However, it might be a mistake to assume that everyone reading this book is completely comfortable with these terms. It might be useful in the beginning to discuss their meaning with reference to Paradox.

❑ **Program.** The term *program* refers to a set of instructions stored in a file on a disk. This set of instructions is written in a language that the computer can understand but that most humans would find meaningless. Programs are also called *applications* since they apply the power of the computer to a specific task. While stored on the disk the instructions have no effect on your computer. However, if you place the instructions into the *internal* memory of the computer, an area called the RAM, these instructions can be used to control the way the computer behaves. When you *load* or *run* a program you are placing the instructions into the memory and executing them. Once this process begins, the program takes control of the computer. The program controls what appears on the screen and how the computer will respond to the keys on the keyboard.

Each program has the potential to define the layout of the screen and the response of the keyboard in its own way. If you have used a word processing program, e.g., WordPerfect or WordStar, you will find that the screen display and keyboard responses used by those programs are quite different from those used by *Paradox*.

> *Loading a program is technically different than running a program. Loading refers to placing the instructions in memory but not executing them. However, in practice, the terms "load" and "run" are used interchangeably.*

❑ **MSDOS.** MSDOS is an acronym for Microsoft Disk Operating System. It is often referred to simply as DOS because many computer firms, e.g., IBM, Compaq, resell versions of MSDOS under their own company labels. For the most part these versions operate the same way. Each manufacturer may fine-tune DOS to better fit their computers but that does not change the command structure of DOS.

DOS plays a very important role in that it is the master program that controls and organizes all of the basic functions on your computer. For example, all storage of data on the disk is handled by DOS. When an application such as Paradox or WordPerfect is running, it is DOS that actually takes the information from the program and stores it on the disk. Conversely, it is DOS that retrieves that information later on. The application works with DOS at all times. This means that DOS is functioning in the background all of the time you are working with Paradox.

If you are running Paradox on a network, the operating system has been expanded to include operations that allow users to share access to the same information on the disk. The Network Operating System, sometimes called the NOS, is always in the background as well in a network environment.

❑ **Database Management.** Database management is the general name for the type of work done by Paradox. Defined broadly, database management uses the computer to store and retrieve information that would otherwise have to be stored in filing cabinets, notebooks, or other forms of paper records. While computers can produce large amounts of printed material, the basic form of storage is on magnetic disks, both the hard and the floppy kinds. There are many ways to approach the organization of data. The approach taken by Paradox borrows from traditional concepts of data management as well as using its own unique approach. In subsequent chapters you will learn in great detail how Paradox carries out the task of database management.

The Elements of Paradox

The first step in working with any computer application is to run the application. Running a program consists of giving an instruction to DOS to load and execute the instructions stored in the Paradox program files. The exact instructions that you must use will vary with the computer system you are working with. If you are using Paradox at your job you may find that this matter has been simplified for you by the installation of a menu system from which you can simply pick Paradox.

Typically, Paradox is stored in a directory named **\PARADOX3**. To start the program you would have to activate that directory and then enter the name of the program.

Below are two commands. The first tells DOS to activate the **\PARADOX3** directory. The second tells the computer to load and execute the Paradox program. Note that the symbol ↵ is used to indicate that you should press the **Return** or **Enter** key. The ↵ symbol is used because it appeared on the first keyboard for the IBM PC. You may find that your keyboard uses a different symbol or simply the word *Enter*.

cd\paradox3 ↵
paradox3 ↵

As the program begins to load, it displays the Paradox logo, (Figure 1-3) on the screen.

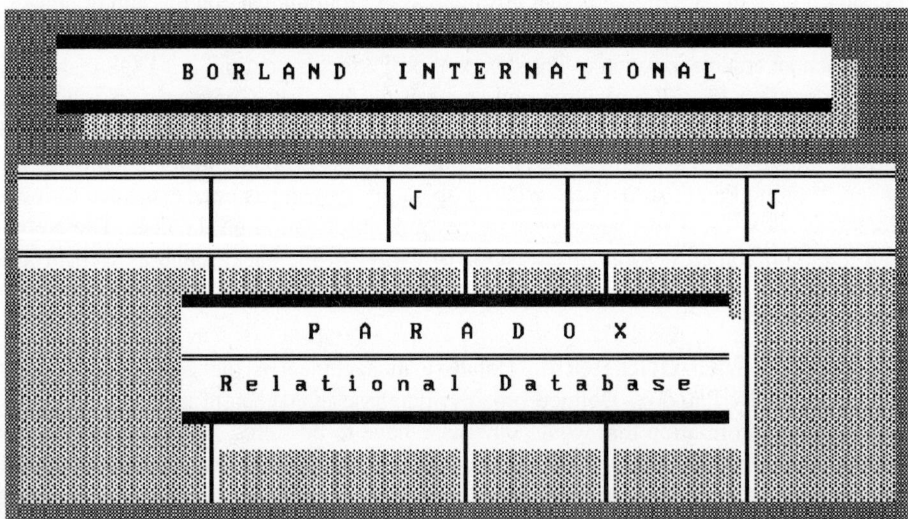

Serial Number: DA233C10639303 Company: Rob Krumm
Contains Licensed Material Copyright (c) Borland International, 1985-1989
All Rights Reserved
Release 3.0 Name: Rob Krumm Publications Loading

Figure 1-3 Paradox logo screen.

The Menu System

When the Paradox program has loaded, the logo is removed from the screen, and Paradox displays its basic user interface. In this mode Paradox divides the screen into three parts.

❑ **Menu.** The menu area takes up the first two lines of the screen display. The top line is the menu bar. It consists of a series of words each one of which represents a command or a category of commands in Paradox. The first item on this menu, **View**, is highlighted in reverse video. The second line displays an explanation of the highlighted item. The message will change when the item which is highlighted changes. The menu that appears when you first start Paradox is called the *Main* menu, Figure 1-4.

```
View  Ask  Report  Create  Modify  Image  Forms  Tools  Scripts  Help  Exit
View a table.
```

Figure 1-4 Main menu.

❑ **Work Area.** The work area is the blank area that appears below the menu. This is the area in which the data and other database objects will appear.

❑ **Message Line.** The message line is the last line on the screen. This line displays explanations and messages about the activities taking place. The opening message summarizes the way that selections can be made from menus. Warning messages appear on the right side of the message line in reverse video.

There are two ways in which you can make a selection from a Paradox menu.

❑ **Highlight.** You can use the ← and → keys to change the position of the highlight on the menu. Each ← or → will move the highlight to the next item in that direction. If you reach the left or right end of the menu, continued movement in that direction will take you to the opposite end of the menu. The [Home] key will move you to the first item in the menu. The [End] key will move the highlight to the end of the menu. If the menu has more items than can be displayed on the screen at one time, an arrow symbol will appear at the end of the menu. If you want to select the item that is currently highlighted, press ↵.

❑ **First Letter.** You can select an item by typing the first letter of the item you want to select. Note that when you type the letter, no ↵ is necessary.

Paradox is organized around *tree-structured* menus. This means that each of the items on a menu can lead to other menus. A single command may require you to enter selections from a series of menus in order to complete the command.

Making Menu Selections

Suppose that you wanted to select Image from the current menu. You can either move the highlight to the word Image and press ↵ or enter **i**, the first letter of Image. Use the arrow key method by entering

→(5 times)
↵

When you select Image Paradox replaces the previous menu with the Image menu, Figure 1-5. This menu lists commands that are related to the original choice, Image.

```
TableSize ColumnSize Format Zoom Move PickForm KeepSet Graph Main
Change the number of records to show in the current image.
```

Figure 1-5 Image menu.

You can make another selection from this menu. For example, you might want to select the Zoom image. Enter the letter this time.

z

This time the menu does not change. Instead, Paradox displays a warning message in the lower right corner of the screen that reads: **There are no images on the workspace**. The message was displayed because Paradox requires certain conditions before it can execute the **Zoom** command. In this case a database table image is required in order to execute the **Zoom** command. Enter a different option, **g** for **Graph**.

g

The reaction is different this time because the **Graph** command can be executed under current conditions.

Canceling a Menu Selection

In working you way through the menu trees, you may find that you have made an incorrect selection. There are two ways to cancel the selection.

❑ **[Esc].** The [Esc] cancels the last menu option you selected and moves you back to the previous menu.

❑ **[Ctrl-break].** This command cancels all menu selections made from the main menu. Note that on most keyboards the *Break* key is labeled *Scroll Lock* with the word *Break* written on the front surface of the key.

Suppose that you wanted to return to the previous menu, the Image menu. Enter

[Esc]

The Image menu appears. You can return to the original menu position, the main menu, by entering

[Ctrl-break]

The Help System

Paradox has a built-in Help system that can be used to get information while you are working in Paradox. There are two ways to access the help system.

❑ **Help.** You can access Help from the main menu by selecting the Help option. The Help option is available from the main menu in any of the major modes in Paradox.

❑ **[F1].** You can directly access the Help system at any time by pressing the [F1] key. Help is context-sensitive, meaning that the information displayed is related to the current activity.

As an example of how to use Help, return to the Graph menu by entering

i g

You can obtain Help by entering the [F1] key.

[F1]

The program displays a screen which explains the options displayed on the Graph menu, Figure1-6. Once it is displayed, there are four actions that you can take.

❑ **[F1].** If you press [F1] while a Help screen is displayed, Paradox displays the Help index. You can browse through the index and select Help items for display. There is also a search feature that locates index entries that contain key words or phrases.

❑ **Paradox.** Each Help screen will show a menu of related topics at the top of the screen. The last item in this list is always Paradox. Selecting Paradox returns you to the program at exactly the point where you were when you pressed [F1] to access the help system.

❑ **Cross References.** The menu at the top of the screen will list topics which are related to the topic being displayed, if any are available. If you select a topic from the menu, Paradox displays the Help screen for that topic.

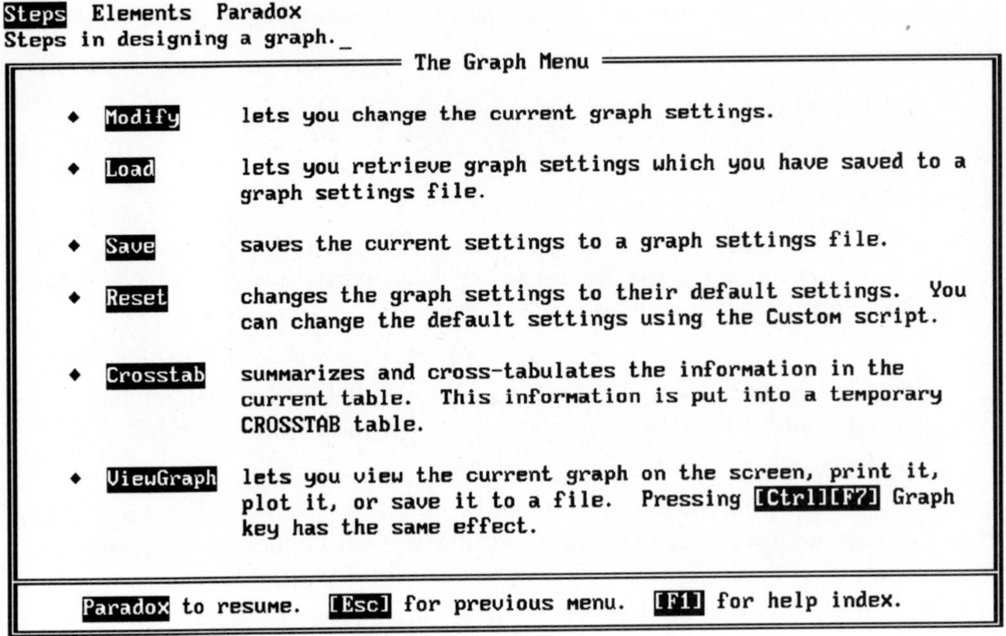

Figure 1-6 Context-sensitive Help screen.

❑ **[Esc].** Pressing the [Esc] key will return you to the previous menu or help topic, if any. For example, if you select one of the menu cross-reference items, e.g., Steps, you can return to the current Help screen by pressing [Esc]. If the current screen is the first item displayed in help, [Esc] will take you back to Paradox—performing the same function as selecting Paradox from the menu.

Using the Help Index

Once Help is activated, you can access help on any available topic by using the Help Index. The index is displayed when you press [F1] while a Help topic is displayed. Enter

[F1]

Paradox displays the Help index, Figure 1-7, shown on page 15. The index consists of a list of topics and subtopics arranged in alphabetical order. You can use the ↑ and ↓ keys to scroll through the list of topics. Pressing ↵ displays the Help screen for the currently highlighted topic.

As an alternative to scrolling through the Help index, you can search the list for topics that contain a key word or phrase using the command [Ctrl-z]. For example, suppose you are interested in pie charts. Enter the search command

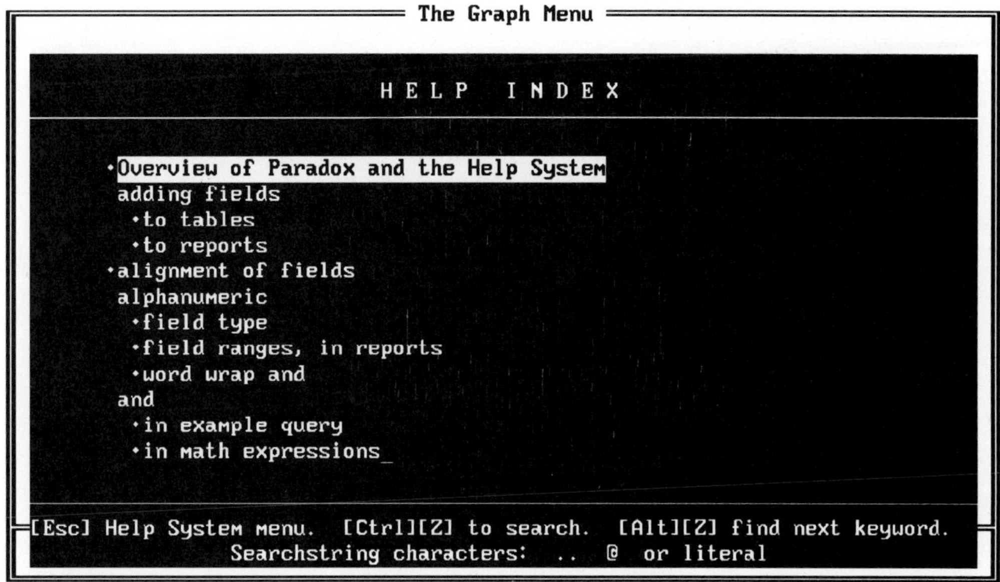

Figure 1-7 Help index.

[Ctrl-z]

A prompt appears at the top of the screen, Figure 1-8, with the word **Value:**. In this case, **Value** refers to the key word or phrase that you want to locate in the Help index.

```
Value:
Enter value or pattern to search for
```

Figure 1-8 Search command in Help system.

Search for topics that contain the word *pie* by entering

pie ↵

Paradox responds by issuing a beep. This tells you that the word *pie* does not appear in any of the topics listed in the Help index. In such a situation you might try to look for a more general term that might include pie charts, e.g., *graphs*. Enter

[Ctrl-z]

Note that the word *pie* appears as the search keyword. In order to search for a different word, you will have to erase the current word by entering

[backspace]*(3 times)*

Enter the new word you want to locate.

graph ↵

The cursor jumps to the topic *graph*. You can display the Help screen for this topic or use the ↑ or ↓ keys to pick the topics listed in this area of the index.

If you want to continue the search for other occurrences of *graph*, use the [Alt-z] command. Enter

[Alt-z]

The highlight jumps to the next item in the index with *graph* in the title.

Return to Paradox by entering

[Esc] p

Return to the Main menu by entering

[Ctrl-break]

You are now back at the main Paradox system menu ready to begin the process of creating and managing databases with Paradox.

Summary

This chapter served as a basic introduction to the organization of this book and the Paradox program.

❑ **Paradox.** Paradox is a computer application designed to help you store and manipulate all types of data. The Paradox screen is divided into three parts: at the top is the menu area, in the center the work area, and at the bottom the message and warning area.

❑ **Database Management.** *Database management* refers to the procedures and techniques needed to manipulate data.

❑ **Tree-structured Menus.** *Tree structure* refers to menus whose options may lead to one or more related subtopic menus. Each command is stored as a separate branch on the menu tree. All of the commands in Paradox begin at the main trunk, which is the main menu displayed when you first load the program.

❑ **Context-sensitive Help.** You can display the Help screen at any time by entering the command [F1]. The screen displayed is related to the current menu or activity. This is called context-sensitive Help. Pressing [F1] a second time displays an index of Help topics. You can use this index to display any of the topics stored in the Help system.

2

Creating Structured Databases

Simply put, a *database* is a block of information stored in a form accessible by a computer. On microcomputers, the database takes the form of a file stored on a hard or floppy disk. A database system usually consists of one or more of these files. It is the job of the database management program to use the raw material to answer questions, print reports, or generate analytical summaries of the data.

There are many ways in which data can be stored in a computer system. For example, the most common use of computer storage—word processing—is an illustration of unstructured storage. Figure 2-1 shows information that could be stored in a computer file. Based on his or her own experiences, a person reading this information should be able to determine the meaning of the data. For example, the letters RI and MA probably represent abbreviations for state names. The numbers 10110 and 01615 probably represent zip codes. Overall, the information appears to be a name and location list of some type.

However, this interpretation of the data can only be made by a human with a sufficient amount of experience to recognize the meaning of the unstructured data. A computer would have no basis for distinguishing one item in the data from the other.

```
Carolyn Rigiero, Providence, RI, 10110
Shrewsbury, Gerri Flynn, MA, 01615
```

Figure 2-1 Unstructured data.

If you want to store data in such a way that the computer can select individual items, the data must be stored in a structured manner. Figure 2-2 shows the same data used in Figure 2-1, displayed in a structured form. The structured form requires that the items be organized as a row-and-column table. Each column represents a specific type of data, e.g., first name, last name, zip code, etc. The columns can be used to determine the classification of the data. For instance, any data in column 4 must be a state name, while any data in column 1 must be a first name. By using the position of the data as its classification, you establish a system that the computer can use to pick out individual data items according to their classification. To simplify references to columns, Paradox allows you to assign column names similar to the names that appear as column headings in Figure 2-2 in **bold** type.

In Paradox each column or classification is called a *field*. In most cases the terms *column* and *field* are synonymous in Paradox databases.

First	Last	City	State	Zip
Carolyn	Rigiero	Providence	RI	10110
Gerri	Flynn	Shrewsbury	MA	01545

Figure 2-2 Structured data.

Another aspect of table structure is that all the data items on the same row are related to one another. For example, if a zip code and city name are found on the same row it implies that the zip code is related to that specific city name. Paradox calls all data items on the same row a *record*. A *record* is a group of data items relating to the same person, place, thing, or event.

A database is composed of *fields* that indicate the data classifications, and *records* that contain a set of related values. The advantage of using a table structure for database organization is that most people have been taught to read and interpret row-and-column tables. When a program displays a table of information, a user with no computer experience can read and understand the data. As much as possible, Paradox attempts to display database information and operations in a table form. Thus the table form of organization is a major theme running throughout Paradox.

> *In Paradox, the terms* table *and* database *are used interchangeably. Some structured database programs, SQL for instance, make a distinction between tables and databases. SQL and Paradox use the term* table *in the same way. However, in SQL a database is a group of related tables. Paradox does not make this distinction.*

The table form of organization implies that a Paradox database will exhibit certain characteristics.

❑ **Define Structure First.** In Paradox you must first define the fields of the database *before* you can enter actual information. Conversely, if you have not created a field for a specific item of information, you cannot enter it until you have modified the structure of the entire database table. For example, the table in Figure 2-2 does not contain a field for the street address. You could not enter a street address for any of the records until you modified the structure by adding an entire new column designated to hold the address information.

❑ **Fixed Length Fields.** In order to organize information from many records into columns, you must select a specific size, in terms of the number of characters, for each field in the table. For example, you might choose 20 characters for the last name field and 5 characters for the zip-code field.

The size of a field sets a limit on the maximum number of characters you can enter for any data item in any of the records. In some cases, such as a zip code field, this is a simple matter to decide, since all zip codes have the same width—five characters. However, many items (such as last names) vary in width. In selecting a field size for these items, you must estimate a size that is likely to satisfy your needs for entering data into that field.

Selecting a field size too large for the data you enter wastes disk space and slows down processing. This is because Paradox saves the field with the maximum number of characters, even if you don't fill the entire column. For example, selecting a last-name field width of 100 characters will result in storing a large amount of unnecessary empty space.

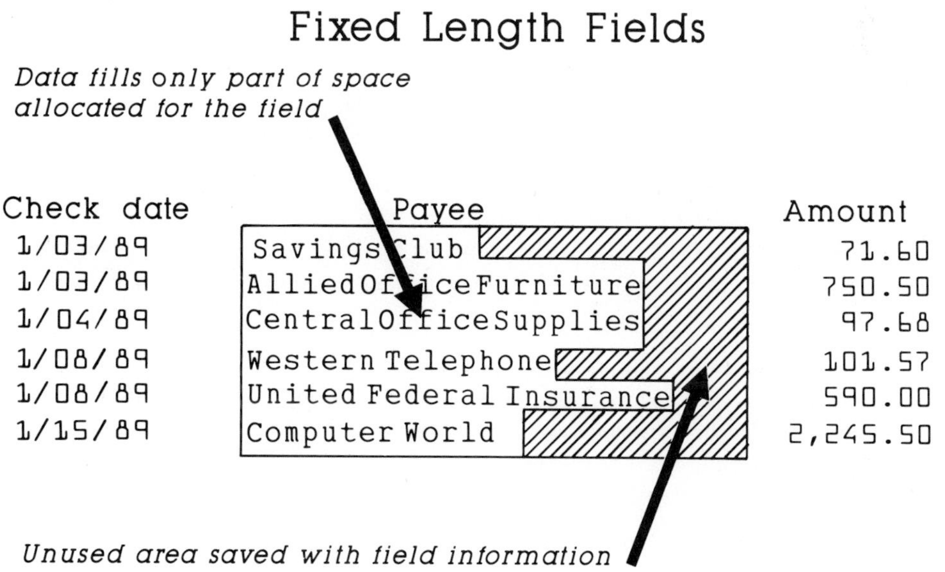

Fixed Length Fields
Data fills only part of space allocated for the field
Check date
Payee
Amount
1/03/89
Savings Club
71.60
1/03/89
AlliedOfficeFurniture
750.50
1/04/89
CentralOfficeSupplies
97.68
1/08/89
Western Telephone
101.57
1/08/89
United Federal Insurance
590.00
1/15/89
Computer World
2,245.50
Unused area saved with field information

Figure 2-3 Fixed length fields.

In this chapter, you will begin working with Paradox by creating a new database table structure.

Creating a New Database Table

Creating the structure of a database table is important because it defines the fields into which the data will be entered. When you create a table, you enter the details that define the table's field names and types.

❑ **Field Names.** You can create a field name up to **25** characters in length. You can use alphabetical, numeric, or other keyboard characters with the exception of the following:

" [ ] { } – +

A field name can contain spaces but cannot begin with a space. Keep in mind that each field name *must* be unique. Paradox prohibits the use of duplicate field names since that would make it impossible to distinguish between table columns with the same name. Examples of valid field names are:

Date of birth
Check #
Last Name

❑ **Field Types.** In order to perform mathematical and chronological operations on numeric and date information, Paradox allows you to specify special field types in addition to fields that contain text information. There are five field types in Paradox:

A **Alphanumeric.** These fields contain text information of any kind. If you enter dates or numbers into an alphanumeric field, they will be treated like text. Alphanumeric fields can be up to **255** characters in length.

N **Number.** Numeric fields can contain values from $\pm\mathbf{10^{308}}$ to $\pm\mathbf{10^{-307}}$ When the number of digits exceeds 15, including the decimal point, the values are stored in rounded, scientific notation form.

$ **Currency.** This field type is the same as the number field, with the exception that numbers are automatically formatted with two decimal places and comma separators. Negative numbers will be displayed in parentheses (standard accounting style.)

Place First Class
Postage Here
Post Office
Will Not Deliver
Without Postage

Brady Books
15 Columbus Circle
New York, NY 10023

ATT: J. Padlad

S **Short Number.** A short-number field is used to hold integer values from **32,767** to **−32,767.** These fields reduce the amount of disk space used to store values that fit within the specified range. Advanced users or program developers may want to use this field type to save disk space when creating large database applications. Since Paradox features such as data entry options and display formatting are not available for this field type, it should be avoided by less experienced users.

D **Date.** Date fields will recognize dates entered in **m/d/yy** (1/10/89) format as a chronological date. You can also enter dates in **dd-mmm-yy** (10-jan-89) or **d.m.yy** (10.1.89) formats. You can enter 3- or 4-digit year values if you want to specify a different century (1/1/2001).

❑ **Limits.** A Paradox table can contain up to **255** fields. However, the total number of characters in all of the fields combined, including date, number, and currency fields, cannot exceed **4,000** characters. This means if you want to enter 255 character alphanumeric fields, a table can hold only 15 of those large fields—3,825 characters.

> *Note that the total number of records that can be entered into a table is 2 billion, a limit that is not of much practical significance on a microcomputer system.*

The Create Command

The process of creating the structure of a new database table is begun from the **Create** menu. Enter

c

Paradox displays a prompt, Figure 2-4, which asks you to enter the name of the table. The name you enter will be used as the file name of the database file that will contain the data. The name must conform to the limits imposed by DOS on file names:

Size. Between 1 and 8 characters.

Characters. File names cannot contain a space bar or any of the following characters: .“/\[ ]|<>+:=;,. You can use an underscore _ character to simulate a space.

```
Table:
Enter New table name.
```

Figure 2-4 Enter new table's file name.

In this example, the database table represents a checkbook database. Name the table CK_BOOK by entering

ck_book ↵

> *Database table files are stored on the disk with a DB extension. For example a table called Ck_book would appear in the directory listing as CK_BOOK.DB.*

Following the entry of the table file name, Paradox displays the *structure* (abbreviated STRUCT) table. This table is used for entering, or later, revising the structure of a database table, Figure 2-5. Since CK_BOOK is a new table, there are no fields listed in the structure display. The right side of the screen displays a summary of the field types available in Paradox. Also, in the upper-right corner of the screen, the word **Create** appears in highlighted video. This is the mode or work area indicator. The indicator shows what type of operational mode Paradox is using at the moment. Knowing the operational mode is important because each mode has a specific range of commands and operations that can be carried out within the context of that mode.

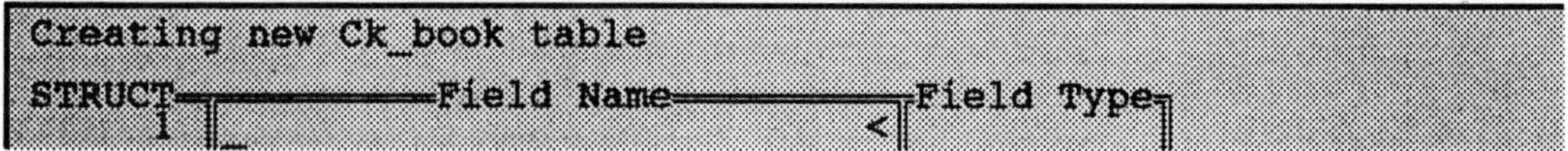

Figure 2-5 Structure table used to enter field specifications.

The checkbook database table requires that you record the same kind of information as you would enter into a check register: check number, date, amount, payee, etc. Use the first field to record the check number. Enter

check # ↵

> *Paradox automatically capitalizes the first character in each field name.*

Since this is a numeric value, specify it as an N type of field. Enter

n ↵

The cursor advances to the next row in the structure table labeled 2. The next field is used for the check date. Enter

check date ↵

Since the information in this field is date information, specify this as a date field by entering

d ↵

The next field is the payee. Because this field contains text, specify it as an alphanumeric field. Note that when you choose type A for a field, you must follow the letter A with the number of characters for the field size. In this case allocate a field size of 25 characters. Enter

payee ↵
a25 ↵

The next entry is the check amount, a currency type field. Enter

amount ↵
$ ↵

You now have a structure that has one of each type of fields, Figure 2-6.

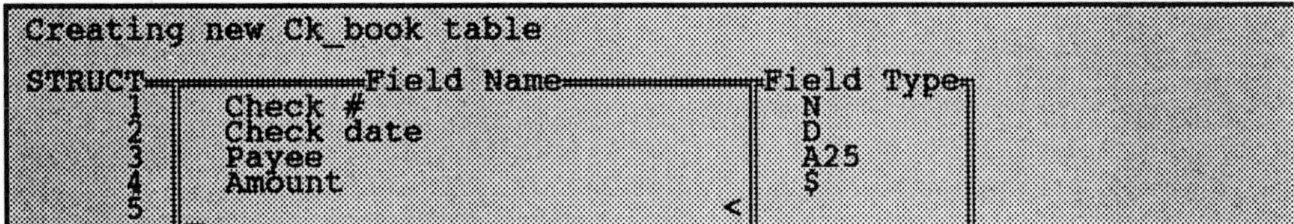

Creating new Ck_book table
STRUCT
Field Name
Field Type
1 Check # N
2 Check date D
3 Payee A25
4 Amount $
5

Figure 2-6 Fields entered into structure table.

In addition to this basic information about the checks you might want to create additional fields such as a memo field, or one that indicates if the check is a tax-deductible expense. Enter

memo ↵
a25 ↵
tax deductible ↵

Fields like *tax deductible* are usually filled out with a *yes* or *no* answer. It is a good idea to limit the field to a single alphanumeric character that can be entered simply as Y or N, or as a single letter code indicating its tax status, such as F for Federal, S for State, and B for both. Using single-letter codes speeds up entry while eliminating inconsistent entries. For example, you might enter Fed or Federal into the field. Keep in mind that you can use Paradox features to convert the single letter codes to words or phrases if the full text is required, e.g., on a printed report. Enter the size as one character.

a1 ↵

Create another small field that holds Y or N, indicating whether or not the check has cleared the bank.

cleared bank ↵
a1 ↵

The table's structure now contains seven fields, Figure 2-7.

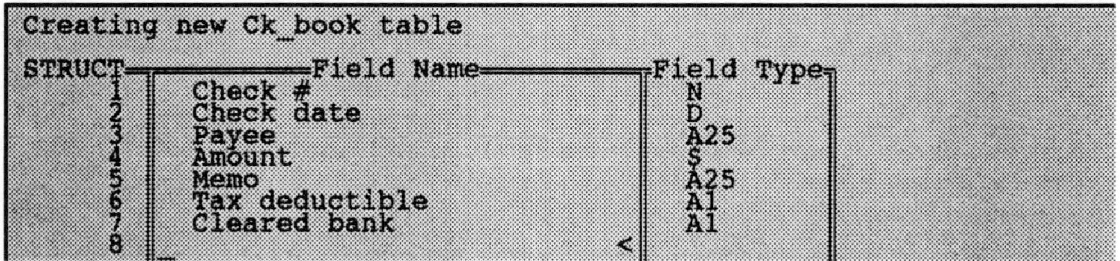

Figure 2-7 Structure table with seven fields defined.

Key Fields

When you are creating or modifying a table's structure, Paradox permits you to designate one or more fields as *key* fields. Fields designated as key fields have the following characteristics, differentiating them from normal fields.

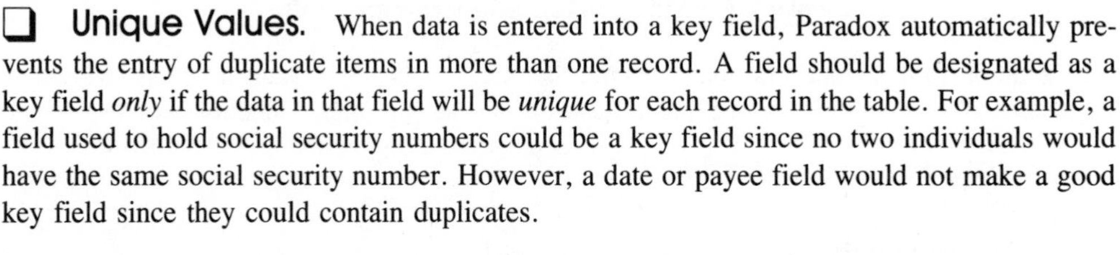

❑ **Unique Values.** When data is entered into a key field, Paradox automatically prevents the entry of duplicate items in more than one record. A field should be designated as a key field *only* if the data in that field will be *unique* for each record in the table. For example, a field used to hold social security numbers could be a key field since no two individuals would have the same social security number. However, a date or payee field would not make a good key field since they could contain duplicates.

❑ **Sequence.** The records entered into the table will be automatically arranged in order, based on the values in the key field. Tables without key fields are arranged in the sequence in which the records were entered, i.e., the *natural* order.

❑ **Primary Index.** When a field is designated as a key field, Paradox maintains a separate file called a *primary index* file. A primary index file stores a copy of the data entered into the key field of the table organized to permit rapid location of specific records. The primary index file has a PX extension, e.g., CK_BOOK.PX. The index file is also used to maintain the table's order by key field.

If you choose to create a key field for a table, the key field must be the *first* field in the structure. In the current example the first field in the structure is *Check #*. This field would fit the criteria for a key field because each check should have a unique check number, and sequencing the records by check number would be logical.

A field is designated as a key field by following the field type specification with an asterisk (*). In this example the *Check #* field would have N* as its type if it were to be designated a key field.

If you wanted to designate a different field as the key field you would have to edit the structure table so that the field you want to designate as the key field is the first one in the structure, and then add the * to the field type specification.

The designation of a key field causes the automatic generation of the primary index file, which has the same name as the database table but a PX file extension.

Designating a Key Field

You can designate the first field in the structure table as a key field by adding an * to the file type. Here, move the cursor to the first field by entering

[Home]

Position the cursor in the Field Type column by entering

→

Designate this as a key field by entering

*

When the file's structure is saved, Paradox will generate both the database table file, DB extension, and a primary index file, PX extension.

> *Paradox allows you to create multiple field keys for database tables. To do so, all of the fields which will be part of the key must be at the beginning of the table's structure. The last field in the key field group must meet all the key field criteria, meaning it must be a unique entry field. For example, suppose you want the checkbook table to be automatically sequenced by payee. Since the payee field potentially contains duplicates you cannot use payee by itself as the key field. However, you could combine payee with other fields, one of which would be unique, such as Check #. For example, using a multiple key of Payee and Check # sequences, the database records by payee. If records with duplicate payees occur, then those duplicates are sequenced within that group according to check number. The check # field serves as a tie breaker. To implement this type of key, you rearrange the table's structure so that the first field name is* Payee *and the second is* Check #*. But fields would have * in their Field Type columns, indicating that they form a multiple key. Note that the total number of characters specified for a multiple field key is 1350 characters.*

Saving the Structure

Once you have entered the desired fields, you can create the database table (and primary index if required) by saving the information. In Paradox, there are two ways to save information when you have completed a design specification.

❑ **Menu Selection.** When you are entering a design specification, such as a table structure or a report design, the operational menu activated with the [F10] key will contain, among other commands, **Do-It!** and **Cancel.** The **Do-It!** command tells Paradox to save the information and perform any operations implied by the specifications. In this case—the creation of a new table—Paradox would create the database table file using the specified structure. If you select **Cancel**, the information is not saved and no operations implied by the information are carried out. Note that if you select **Do-It!** Paradox will ask you to confirm your intention by displaying a menu with the choices **Cancel** and **OK.** This menu gives you a second chance to cancel the operation, or confirm your intention to go ahead by selecting **OK**. Note that the menu highlight will always be placed on the **Cancel** option as a safety precaution.

❑ **Do-It! Shortcut.** The [F2] key is a shortcut for the **Do-It!** menu command. When you press [F2], the design specification is saved and you return to the Paradox work space.

> *Unlike many applications, Paradox does not recognize the [Esc] key as a direct equivalent of the Cancel command in situations that would allow you to perform the Do-IT! command with the [F2]. This is done to ensure that the decision to cancel a design specification is not entered accidentally or carelessly.*

Saving the Table's Structure

In this case you can use the shortcut command, [F2], to save the structure and create the corresponding database and index files. Enter

[F2]

Paradox carries out the operation and returns you to the main work area.

Entering Data

Once you have created the structure of the table, you can enter data into the database table. Paradox provides two basic ways to activate the data entry and editing mode.

❑ **View and Edit.** Paradox allows you to edit a table displayed in the work area. You can display a database table in the work area by using the **View** command on the main menu. The [F9] key will place a selected table into the editing mode allowing you to add or revise records.

❑ **Modify DataEntry.** Another approach to entering new records is to use the **DataEntry** command found on the Modify menu. This command requires you to specify the name of the table to which you want to add records.

DataEntry displays the table in a slightly different mode than does the View and Edit method. **DataEntry** does not display any existing records already entered in the table. Instead, the display restricts entry to the addition of new records only. This is a safety device which prevents you from overwriting existing records while adding new ones. Of course, with a new table, both edit and data entry have the same effect because there are no records in the table at this time.

Using the Data Entry Mode

To add new records to a database table, you can use the **DataEntry** command located on the Modify menu. Enter

m
d

Paradox asks you to enter the name of the table to add records to. If you do not want to manually enter the name of the table, you can display a list of the database tables in the current directory by entering ↵.

↵

The program lists the names of any database table files stored in the current directory, Figure 2-8. You can select a table by using the ← and → keys to position the highlight on the table name and pressing ↵.

```
Table:
Ck_book
```

Figure 2-8 Table names listed.

> *If you have created other database tables in the current directory, they will appear along with the Ck_book table.*

Make sure that **Ck_book** is highlighted and then enter

↵

Paradox enters the data entry mode. As part of the display, Paradox places on the screen an *image* of the database table. An *image* is a visual display of part or all of a table. Figure 2-9 shows the image of the Ck_book table as it appears in the work area. The image shows the fields of the database table as columns and the field names as column headings. Since the screen is not wide enough to display all the fields at one time, the remainder of the fields appear when the screen is scrolled the right.

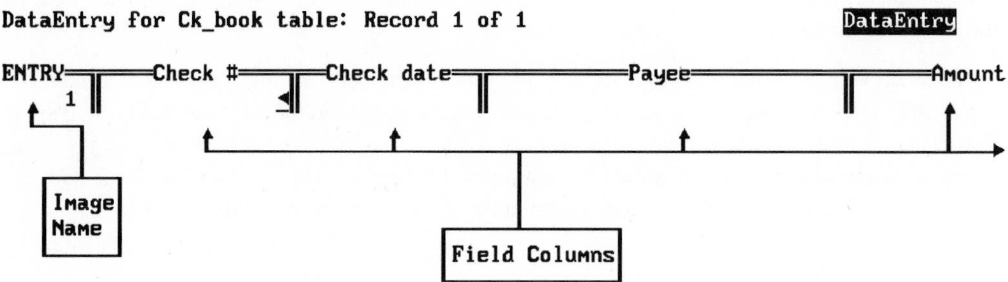

Figure 2-9 Image of Ck_book table in work area.

Each image displayed in the work area is given an image name. In this instance, the image is called ENTRY. You might have expected the image to have been called CK_BOOK because that is the name of the table into which you are making the entries. The reason the image is named ENTRY, not CK_BOOK, is that the DataEntry mode is a *batch* processing mode. When you add records in the DataEntry mode, the records are not immediately added to the selected table. Instead, they are added to a temporary table called ENTRY which has the same structure as the table name you selected. Paradox allows you to enter as many records as you like into this table. When you have finished, the records are treated as a *batch* that can be added to the original table, discarded as a group, or stored as a separate table to be added or discarded at a later time.

> *The batch processing approach used by the DataEntry mode is very handy when operating in a network environment. If the main table is in use by another user you can save the entry batch for inclusion into the main table at another time.*

The cursor is positioned in the *Check #* field of record 1. Enter the check number.

1000 ↵

The cursor moves to the *Check Date* field. You can enter dates in one of three formats:

Table 2-1 Date entry formats

Format	Example
m/d/yy	1/3/89
d-mmm-yy	3-jan-89
d.m.yy	1.3.89

Enter the date using the standard m/d/yy format:

1/3/89 ↵

The cursor moves to the *Payee* field. Enter

Allied Office Furniture ↵

When the cursor moves to the next field, *Amount*, the screen display scrolls the table image to the right, revealing the full width of the *Amount* field but at the same time removing the leftmost field, *Check #*, from the display. Enter the amount:

750.5 ↵

Note that when you enter a value into a currency field it is not necessary to enter trailing zeros. Paradox will fill in one or two decimal place zeros as needed. You need enter only the *significant* figures.

The next field is the memo field. Enter

Desk - 48" by 72" ↵

The next field is used to indicate which items are tax deductible. This type of field requires you to invent a coding system for entires. For example, you might enter Y for deductible items or leave the field blank if the items are taxable. It really doesn't matter what characters you select, so long as you are able to mark the records consistently. In this instance, the item is deductible. Enter

y

The final field is used to indicate if the check has cleared the bank. For now leave this field blank by entering

↵

The cursor jumps back to the first column in the table but now it is positioned in the second row. Fill in a second record. Begin with the check number.

1001 ↵

The Ditto Command

When entering data, you may find that the data in one or more fields is repeated in the next record. For example, check # 1001 might have the same date as the previous check. Such repetitions are very common in databases that contain addresses, where items like city, state, and zip codes repeat quite often.

The ditto command, [Ctrl-d], will copy the data stored in the same field from the previous record, if any.

In this example, you can copy the date from record 1 into the date field of record 2 by entering

[Ctrl-d]

The date from record 1 is copied into record 2. Note that the cursor is positioned at the end of the date so that you can make any editing changes you desire in the copied data. Often it is faster to copy an item and make editing changes than it is to enter the entire item from scratch. Finalize the date by entering

↵

Complete the entry of the record with the following data.

Central Office Supplies ↵
97.56 ↵
Envelopes, folders, files ↵
y ↵ ↵

The ENTRY table now contains two new records as shown in Figure 2-10.

```
DataEntry for Ck_book table: Record 3 of 3                            DataEntry

ENTRY═╦════Check #═╦═══Check date═╦══════════Payee══════════╦════════Amount
    1 ║     1000   ║    1/03/89   ║ Allied Office Furniture ║        750.50
    2 ║     1001   ║    1/03/89   ║ Central Office Supplies ║         97.56
    3 ║            ║              ║                         ║
```

Figure 2-10 Records added in DataEntry mode.

Saving New Records

As mentioned, the DataEntry mode does not add the new records to the selected table as they are entered. Instead, the new records are held in a special table, ENTRY, until you decide to add them as a batch to the selected database table. The command used to save the records as part of the selected table, in this case Ck_book, is the **Do-It!** command which can be executed from the menu, **[F10]d**, or by using the [F2] shortcut key. Here, use the shortcut to save the records.

[F2]

Viewing A Database Table

When you exit the DataEntry mode, Paradox appends the new records onto the selected table. The program then displays the table in the main work area. Note that the mode indicator, upper right corner of the screen, now shows Main. When the indicator shows Main, the program is in the *Table View* mode. The *Table View* mode is used to display database table information in the form of database table images.

If a table is small it is possible to see the entire table—fields and records—on the screen at one time. However, many tables will have more fields and/or records than can be viewed at once. Paradox provides cursor movement keys that move the cursor and scroll the display to reveal different parts of the table.

Table 2-2 Horizontal cursor movement between fields

Key	Movement
[Tab]	next field to the right
→	
[Shift-Tab]	previous field to the left
←	
[Ctrl-→]	one screen to the right
[Ctrl-←]	one screen to the left
[Ctrl-Home]	first field on the left
[Ctrl-End]	last field on the right

Table 2-3 Vertical cursor movement between records

Key	Movement
↑	previous record
↓	next record
[Pg Up]	one screen of records up
[Pg Dn]	one screen of records down
[Home]	first record
[End]	last record

These keys, Tables 2-2 and 2-3, permit you to view information of database tables of any size in view mode images.

Scrolling a View Image

The current display shows the two records entered thus far into the Ck_book table. Since the table is too wide for the screen display, only the first five fields are displayed. Scroll the display one screen to the right by entering

[Ctrl-→]

The screen now shows the next group of fields, Figure 2-11.

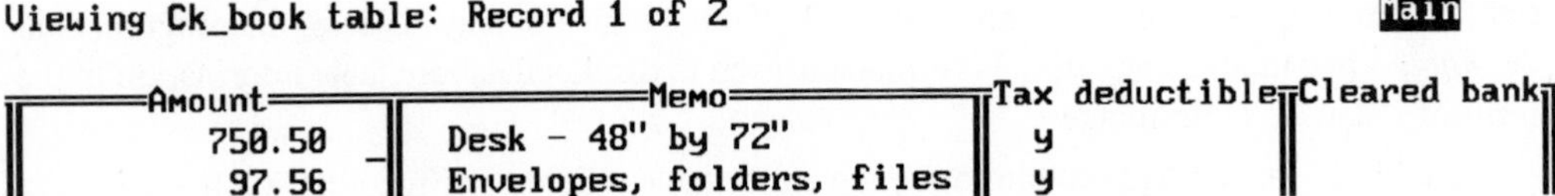
Viewing Ck_book table: Record 1 of 2 Main

Amount	Memo	Tax deductible	Cleared bank
750.50	Desk - 48" by 72"	y	
97.56	Envelopes, folders, files	y	

Figure 2-11 Ck_book table scrolled to the right.

You can move the cursor to the first field in the table image by entering

[Ctrl-Home]

The [Tab] or → keys move the cursor one field at a time. For example, to position the cursor in the *Payee* field, enter

→ (3 times)

You can move to the next or previous records with the ↑ and ↓ keys. For example, to move the cursor to the second record, enter

↓

The cursor is now positioned in the same field, *Payee,* in the second record.

Editing Records and Fields

When a database table image is displayed in the view mode, you cannot make any changes to the data. However, you can activate the Edit mode with the menu command **Modify Edit** or the shortcut key [F9].

The Edit mode allows you to revise any of the fields in any of the records displayed in the table image, add records into the table or delete records from the table.

When adding new records to a table, the Edit mode allows you to insert a new record at any position within the table while the DataEntry mode always appends the new records onto the end of the table.

> *If you have designated a key field for the table, there is no practical difference between appending or inserting records, since the records will be automatically sorted according to the values in the key field.*

When you activate the Edit mode, the indicator changes from Main to Edit. You can append text onto the current field contents by simply entering the characters. In addition, you are able to make changes using the keys listed in Table 2-4.

Table 2-4 Edit mode keys

[Del]	deletes the current record
[Ins]	inserts a new record
[backspace]	deletes 1 character to the left
[Ctrl-backspace]	deletes the current field's contents
[Ctrl-u]	undo field or record change
↵	enters changes, moves to next field

Note that the ← and → keys have the same function in the Edit mode as they do in the View mode, i.e., they move the cursor to the previous or next field. They do *not* position the cursor inside the current field.

Keep in mind that the editing changes made while the Edit mode is active become a permanent part of the database table only if the **Do-It!** command, [F2], is executed at the end of the editing session. You can cancel all changes made during an edit using the command **Cancel** [F10].

While the Edit mode provides the ability to change field information, it would be useful in some cases to be able to change characters in the field without having to backspace and erase all the characters to the right of the character you want to change. Paradox provides the Field View mode to facilitate editing of this type. When the Field View mode is active, you can edit the contents of a field in much the same way as you would edit word processing text. The Field View mode can be activated by entering either [Ctrl-f] or [Alt-F5]. Once activated, the keys listed in Table 2-5 can be used to change the data. Note that while Field View is active, the ← and → keys perform differently than they do in the normal Edit mode.

Table 2-5 Field View editing keys

[Del]	deletes the current character
[Ins]	toggles between insert and overtype
←	positions cursor 1 character left
→	positions cursor 1 character right
[Ctrl-←]	positions cursor 1 word left
[Ctrl-→]	positions cursor 1 word right
[Home]	positions cursor at beginning of field
[End]	positions cursor at end of field
[backspace]	deletes 1 character to the left
[Ctrl-backspace]	deletes the current field's contents
[Ctrl-u]	undo field or record change
↵	enters changes, exit Field View

> *By default, any characters entered in the field view mode are inserted into the field at the current cursor position. The [Ins] key will change Paradox into a typeover mode in which new characters entered will replace existing characters. Pressing [Ins] again will toggle the program back to the insert entry mode. Note that unlike some programs, Paradox does not display an indicator on the screen that shows the current status of the insert mode. If you have lost track of the mode into which you have currently toggled, you can determine the mode only by entering a character to see if it is inserted or if it replaces an existing character.*

Editing a Field

Suppose you found that you wanted to change some of the data in your table. For example, the date in record 2 should really be 1/4/89 and the amount should be 97.68. Changes of this nature can be made by activating the Edit mode and altering the data in the fields. The Edit mode can be activated using the [F9] shortcut key. Enter

[F9]

The mode indicator now shows Edit. You can now change field information. In this example, you want to change the *Amount* field from 97.56 to 97.68. Position the cursor in the amount field by entering

→

Erase the last two characters in the field by entering

[backspace] ***(2 times)***

When you enter the [backspace] character the program shifts the field's contents to the left for editing. Enter the new characters.

68

Editing in the Field View Mode

The next item that needs to be edited is the date of the check. In this case, the only character that needs to be changed is the day number from 3 to 4. However, in the normal Edit mode you would have to backspace over /89 in order to change the character. This means you would have to type three extra characters, /89, in order to complete the editing change. The Field View mode can be invoked in order to permit full editing features that allow you to insert, delete, or replace individual characters any where in the file. The keys [Ctrl-f] or [Alt-F5] will activate the Field View editing mode. Enter

[Ctrl-f]

Activating the Field View mode prompts Paradox to change the cursor to a highlighted block. In addition, the editing keys perform differently, (see Table 2-5 on page 35), than they do in the normal editing mode. For example, you can position the cursor without erasing characters. Move the highlight to the 3 by entering

← ***(4 times)***

Here you want to replace the 3 with a 4. Toggle Paradox into the Replace mode by entering

[Ins]

Replace the 3 with a 4 by entering

4

Once you have made the change or changes desired you can terminate the Field View editing mode by entering ↵. Note that you cannot move to another field or record until you have terminated the Field View mode. Enter

↵

Note that entering ↵ turns off the Field View mode. The program then reverts to the normal Edit mode where you can continue to make changes to the database table.

Adding Records in the Edit Mode

While the Edit mode is active, you can add new records to the database table in two ways. The [Ins] key will insert a new record above the record in which the cursor is positioned. If you want to add a new record to the end of the table, you can simply move the cursor down below the last record in the table. Paradox will add a blank record to the table, which you can then fill with new data.

Since the Ck_book table uses a key field to arrange the records in check number order, there is no particular advantage in inserting records between existing records. Add a new record to the table by entering

↓

The program automatically extends the table one row by adding record 3, a blank record to the table. If you do not fill in any of the fields, Paradox will delete the blank record when you save the editing changes.

You can test the effect of the key field, *Check #*, by entering a record that is out of check number order. Enter

999 ↵
1/3/89 ↵
Savings Club ↵
71.6 56 ↵
Coffee machine ↵

> *Note that you are leaving the deductible field blank to indicate that this expense is not deductible.*

Saving the Changes

Once you have made the necessary changes and additions to the table, you must save these changes with the **Do-It!** command or cancel all the changes with the **Cancel** command when you exit the editing mode.

In this case, use the menu version of the **Do-It!** command to save the changes. Enter

[F10]

The program displays the Edit mode menu. This menu has six options. The last three, Help, Do-It! and Cancel, appear on all mode menus. The first three, Image, Undo, and ValCheck, are specific to the editing mode. You will learn more about these options later.

> *The Undo command listed on the menu is the same as the command key [Ctrl-u]. Selecting this option will undo the* last *change made to the table. In this case, that would be the addition of record 3. The Cancel command eliminates* all *the changes made to the table since the Edit mode was activated. In this case, that would also include the changes to record 2.*

Save the changes by entering

d

When the program saves the changes, it also evaluates the key field to determine the sequence of the records. In this example, the newly appended record is positioned at the beginning of the table since its check number was 999.

The Form View

Paradox displays database tables in the row-and-column table image, such as the one currently on the screen. The table display shows several fields and records at the same time. However, Paradox also has the ability to display data on a full-screen *form*. A form shows the fields from one record at a time. In many cases, all the fields for each record will appear on the screen at once. The [F7] key will toggle the screen display between the table and the form views.

When the Form View is active, you can activate the Edit mode to revise, delete, or add data to the database table. Paradox will automatically generate a form layout by listing the field names down the left side of the screen and with the field's contents displayed next to the field names. This automatically generated form is called the *standard* form. Paradox allows you to customize the standard form or create up to fifteen different form layouts that can be used to display records from a given database table. You will learn how to create and use customized forms in Chapter 6.

When the form view is active, the effect of the special keys is changed somewhat.

Table 2-6 Keys in Form View

[Tab]	next field down
→	
↓	
[Shift-Tab]	previous field up
←	
↑	
[Ctrl-Home]	first field in record
[Ctrl-End]	last field in record
[Pg Dn]	next record
[Pg Up]	previous record

Displaying the Standard Form

The [F7] key will toggle the work area display between the table image display and the form display. Enter

[F7]

The current record, record 1, is now displayed in the form view, Figure 2-12 on the following page. At the top of the screen, the message **Viewing Ck_book table with form F: Record 1 of 3** tells you the name of the table, the name of the form, and which record is being displayed. The letter **F** is used to signify the *standard form.*

Note that the name of the table, Ck_book, and the record number appear in the upper-right corner of the form box.

```
Viewing Ck_book table with form F: Record 1 of 3                    Main  ═▼

                                                          Ck_book   #     1
Check #:                              999
Check date:         1/03/89
Payee:             Savings Club
Amount:                               71.60
Memo:              Coffee machine
Tax deductible: _
Cleared bank:
```

Figure 2-12 Database displayed in the form view.

You can display the next record in the table by entering

[Pg Dn]

The data from record 2 appears in the screen form.

Editing in the Form View

You can use the Edit mode in the Form View in the same way that it was used in the Table View mode. For example, to add a new record, activate the Edit mode and then move the cursor past the last record in the database table. Enter

[F8]
[Pg Dn] ***(2 times)***

The program displays a blank form into which you can enter data. Add a new record to the table by entering

1002 ↵
1/8/89 ↵
Western Telephone ↵
101.57 ↵

Continue by adding another record.

[Pg Dn]

The ditto command, [Ctrl-d], will operate in the Form View just as it does when you are working in the Table View. The only difference is that you cannot see the contents of the previous record when you use the ditto command. In those cases, you can use the ditto command to copy the check number from the previous record. Enter

[Ctrl-d]

Although it is incorrect for two records to have the same value in the key field, there are two reasons why you would want to use the ditto command in this field. First, since the previous check number is not visible, the ditto command will copy it into the new record so that you know what check number is the next one in sequence. Second, since the check numbers are usually consecutive you can save some keystrokes by simply changing the last digit from 2 to 3. Enter

[backspace]
3 ↵

Use ditto again to copy the date from the previous record.

[Ctrl-d] ↵

Complete the record by entering

United Federal Insurance ↵
590 ↵
Policy Number 10012002A ↵
y

Save the changes by entering

[F2]

Validity Checks

The selection of field types provides some measure of control over what data can be entered into individual fields. For example, fields designated as number or currency fields will only accept numeric information. Date fields will only accept date information entered in one of the three allowable formats. However, these restrictions still leave the users with a great deal of latitude in terms of what they may or may not enter into a field. In many cases, you would like to exert more control over the data entry process. For example, you might want to make sure that the check number is never left blank. Or you might want to automatically insert today's date into the check date field as a default value.

Restrictions or limitations placed on what can be entered into a field are called *validity checks*. The **ValCheck** option is found on the menu when the Edit or DataEntry modes are active. This option allows you to set validity checks for individual fields. Paradox allows you to create six different types of validity checks.

❑ **LowValue.** This option allows you to specify minimum value for the field. The restriction includes the value you specify. For example, if you set the LowValue at 100, you could enter a number with a value of 100 or greater. Anything less than 100, e.g., 99.99, would not be accepted.

Although LowValue is typically used with number or currency fields, minimum values can be applied to alphabetical information as well. For example, entering a LowValue of MMM would require that none of the first three letters of the entry used letters A–L.

> *Note that in making judgements about higher or lower values within the alphabet, Paradox uses the ASCII system for ranking characters. In this scheme, the uppercase letters A–Z rank lower than the lowercase letters a–z. Other characters, such as a space, are ranked below the uppercase letters.*

❑ **HighValue.** This option allows you to set a maximum value for the data in a field. It is primarily used for numbers but can also accept alphabetical characters.

❑ **Default.** This option allows you to specify a value, date, or text to be inserted into the field if it is left blank. Default values can be edited if necessary.

❑ **TableLookup.** This option is the most advanced feature among the validity check options. It allows you to link data entry in one table to the data stored in another table. This feature will be discussed in Part 2 of this book.

❑ **Picture.** This option allows you to control data entry by the use of template specifications. The template is used to control the form in which data is entered.

❑ **Required.** This option allows you to specify that a non-blank entry *must* be made in a field before you can continue.

It is possible to specify more than one validity check option for the same field. For example, you could set both a HighValue and a LowValue validity check in order to restrict entry to a specific range of values.

When you create validity check options for fields in a table, Paradox stores those settings in a file with a VAL extension, e.g., CK_BOOK.VAL.

Validity checks can be removed with the **Modify Edit ValCheck Clear** command. You can also erase all validity checks for a table by erasing the VAL file from the disk.

Required Entry

Suppose you wanted to ensure that no records could be added to the Ck_book table unless the *Check #* field was filled in. You could accomplish this by setting a **Required** validity check option.

The first step is to place the table into the Edit or DataEntry modes. Enter

[F9]

Display the Edit menu by entering

[F10]

Select the ValCheck option by entering

v

Paradox displays two options, Define and Clear. To add or revise a validity check option, select Define. To remove one or all validity checks, select Clear. In this instance add a validity check. Enter

d

Paradox allows you to select the field for which you will set the validity check. Since you want to apply this check to the *Check #* field move the cursor to this field by entering

← ***(5 times)***
↵

The menu now lists the six types of validity checks. Select **Required** by entering

r

If you want to create a required entry validity check for this field, select **Yes** by entering

y

Paradox applies the validity check to the field. In the lower-right corner of the screen, the message **Required status recorded** confirms the application of the validity check.

Setting a Value Range

In addition to requiring the entry of a value in the *Check #* field, you may want to set limits on the values that can be entered. Since the values for the check numbers are consecutive, you can avoid accidental mistakes by rejecting the entry of values that would be out of the range of correct values for check numbers. In this example, the first check number recorded is 999. You might make an assumption based on your experience that valid check numbers for the current period would range from 950 up to 1500. Entry of smaller or larger values would probably be the result of a typographical error. You can use the HighValue and LowValue options to restrict the entry to a range of values.

With the Edit mode still active, select the ValCheck option from the menu by entering

[F10] v d

The cursor is still positioned in the *Check #* field. Select that field by entering

↵

To create a restricted range of values for a field, you have to set a LowValue option and then repeat the ValCheck process to set a HighValue option. You cannot do both at the same time in Paradox. Note it does not matter which option, LowValue or HighValue, is set first. Begin with the LowValue option by entering

L
950 ↵

Repeat the process—this time set a HighValue option for 1500. Try this on your own. The correct command can be found on page 55 under Exercise 1.

The *Check #* field now has three validity check options: required entry, low value 950, and high value 1500. These restrictions affect only new records added to the database table. If an existing record is edited, any validity check option created following its entry will apply to the fields when they are edited. For example, suppose one of the existing records has a check number of 800. That entry would be valid until that field was selected for editing. Once opened for editing, the field could not be saved unless the entry was changed to fit the current validity check criteria.

Today's Date

In addition to requiring entry and setting value limits, the ValCheck options allow you to set *default* values for the field. A *default* value is one which is automatically assigned to a field if it is left blank during the data entry process.

Default values are useful when you can anticipate that the same value will be frequently entered into a field. For example, if most of the items entered into the checkbook table are deductible expenses, you might set Y as the value for the *Tax deductible* field.

Paradox also provides a special option that lets you set a date field default as the current date.

> *The date used by this option is drawn from the date used by the operating system. In most AT or 386 computers, the current time and date are maintained by a battery-powered internal clock. However, older PC and XT models did not include an internal clock in their original design, although such clocks could be added through the expansion slots. The date inserted by Paradox will be correct only if the operating system date is correct.*

Suppose you wanted to set a default value for the check date as the current date. Activate the ValCheck definition mode by entering

[F10] v d

Select the date field by entering

→ ↵

Select the Default option by entering

d

The program displays a prompt, Figure 2-13, which asks you to enter the value to use as the default. Note that the value you enter must match the field type, e.g., date values in date fields.

```
Value:
Enter the value to insert if field is left blank.
```

Figure 2-13 Prompt for default value entry.

If the field you are setting the default value for is a date-type field, you can enter the word *today* as a special code, which will insert the current date into the field. Enter

today ↵

The lower right corner of the screen shows the message **Default value recorded** indicating that the operation has been completed.

Using Picture Templates

The Picture option available on the ValCheck menu allows you to control data entry in a wide variety of ways. The name *Picture* is related to the *template* method used to control data entry. A *template* is a series of characters that sets up a model of how the data entered into the field ought to look.

The template recognizes certain characters as symbols for classifications of characters, as shown in Table 2-7.

Table 2-7 Template type matching characters

#	accepts numbers, +, −, and . only
?	accepts letters only
@	accepts any character

The characters can be combined with literal characters to create a template for entry. For example, suppose you have a field that is used for time information, e.g., 12:15am, 09:15pm, etc. All the entries in that field should follow a pattern that can be expressed in the template **##:##??**. The # restricts characters 1, 2, 4, and 5 to numbers. The ? restricts characters 6 and 7 to letters. The colon, character 3, is a *literal*. This means the third character must match the literal, in this instance a comma, exactly.

Creating a picture validity check with the template **##:##??** forces the user to make entries that match the template's pattern. For example, entering **12:45** would not be accepted because the last two characters were left blank. The template requires characters in those positions in order to have a valid entry. The user is constrained to enter characters, hopefully AM or PM, at the end of each time entry.

It is important to understand how Paradox treats the literals used in a picture template. The literal values are automatically entered into the field as the user types in their characters. In the example of the template **##:##??** the third character, :, would be automatically inserted into the field after the user has typed the first two characters. This means that in order to get an entry such as *12:45pm* the user would have to enter only five characters, **1245pm**. This type of template is useful for entry of all sorts of structured data, such as phone numbers or social security numbers.

Another use of template symbols is to control the case of letters entered into a field. The characters in Table 2-8 will automatically convert letters to uppercase as they are entered. For example, the template **&?????????** restricts entry in two ways. First, the fact that there are ten characters in the template limits the entry to ten letters even if the field size is larger than ten characters. Second, the first letter entered is converted to uppercase.

The template **!!!!!!!!!!** allows entry of ten letters or numbers but converts any letters to uppercase.

Table 2-8 Template case conversion characters

!	accepts any character, letters converted to uppercase
&	accepts only letters, letters converted to uppercase

In addition to the special matching characters available for picture templates, Paradox recognizes the characters shown in Table 2-9 which perform special actions during data entry.

Table 2-9 Operational template characters

,	separates alternatives
*#	repeats a character # times
{}	marks group for repetition
[]	optional portion of template
;*c*	designates *c* as a literal

❑ **List alternatives.** You can use this character to create a list of alternative templates. The validity check will allow an entry if it matches any of the listed patterns. For example, fields like *Tax deductible* ought to be limited to Y or N. The template **Y,N** would restrict entry to those two characters.

> *When literal letters are used in a template, the entry is always converted to the case of the literal. For example, using* **Y,N** *as the template automatically converts y or n to uppercase. Conversely, a template of* **y,n** *would convert entries of Y or N to lowercase letters.*

The literals entered into a list can be full words or phrases. For example, you might create a template that reads:

Excellent,Good,Fair,Poor

The effect of this picture template is to restrict the entries in that field to one of the four terms listed in the template. However, the practical effect is to reduce the data entry to the letters E, G, F and P. As soon as you enter one of the letters, Paradox inserts the matching word or phrase. Pressing the [spacebar] in an empty field also prompts Paradox to insert the first item in the list.

> *If you created a picture list that contains words beginning with the same first letter, Paradox would insert the first word in the list that matched the letter you entered. For example, the list* **exit,enter** *would cause* **exit** *to be inserted when E was entered. However, since the word* **enter** *is part of the list, you could edit the inserted word by backspacing over the letters* **xit** *and entering* **n.** *The entry would read* **en** *and prompt Paradox to insert* **enter** *into the field.*

* The * is used to repeat a template character a specified number of times. For example, suppose you wanted to set a 25-character alphabetical field to accept only uppercase characters. Instead of entering **&&&&&&&&&&&&&&&&&&&&&&&&&** you could enter ***25&**.

{} The curly brackets, {}, are used to mark a group of characters for repetition. For example, you can abbreviate a template, such as **###-###-###-##** as ***3{###-}##**.

[ ] These brackets mark an optional portion of the template. For example, the template **[(###)]###-####** would allow phone numbers with or without area codes, so long as they matched the form shown in the template.

; This option permits the use of the special template characters as literals. Suppose you wanted to use the character # as a literal in a template for entry items such as #100, #101, etc. You would use a picture template such as **;####**. The semicolon would cause the first **#** to be interpreted as a literal.

Creating a Picture Validity Check

You can apply some of the options available through the Picture validity check option to some of the fields in the Ck_book table. One obvious use for these functions is in the *Tax deductible* and *Cleared bank* fields.

For example, the entries in the *Tax deductible* field should be Y or N characters only. You can use a Picture template to restrict entry to those two characters. Note that you can also control the case of the letters at the same time since Paradox will convert the letters to match the case used in the Picture template. Activate the ValCheck menu by entering

[F10] v d

Select the *Tax deductible* field by entering

→ ***(4 times)***
↵

Select the Picture option by entering

p

Enter the template which will restrict entry to Y or N.

Y,N ↵

In addition to setting the Picture option, you might also want to create a default value as well. Suppose you believe that the majority of the checks entered will be deductible expenses. You might want to set the default as Y so that the Y would be automatically entered if you pressed Y, [spacebar], or ↵. Keep in mind that you can use more than one type of validity check in each field. Set the default value for *Tax deductible* to Y. Try this on your own. The correct command can be found on page 55 under Exercise 2.

Using Graphic Characters in Validity Checks

The technique just used in the *Tax deductible* field can be applied to the use of special graphics characters as well as to standard keyboard characters. Most MSDOS computers have a character set of 255 characters, only part of which appear on the keyboard. These characters can be entered by using a special keyboard technique. Each of the 255 characters is assigned a numeric value. For example, character number 251 displays a √ character on the screen. To enter a character such as this, you must enter the numeric value of the character on the numeric keypad portion of the keyboard while holding down the [Alt] key. When you release the [Alt] the character that corresponds to the value entered appears. Remember the numbers *must* be entered on the numeric keypad. Thus, entering [Alt-251] will create a check mark on the screen.

> *A full list of the characters available and their ASCII values can be found on page 538 of PAL User Guide supplied with Paradox 3.0.*

You can put these characters to work for you as template characters. For example, instead of using Y and N to indicate if a check has cleared, you might use a √ for cleared and = for not cleared. Using graphic characters may make the data easier to scan for uncleared checks.

The method for creating this type of validity check is the same as you would use for standard characters. Activate the ValCheck menu by entering

[F10] v d
→ ↵

Insert a √ into the Picture option by entering

p
[Alt-251]

Add a dash as the alternative character.

,-

To complete the validity check, set the - character as the default by entering

[F10] v d r
d
- ↵

You have now completed the validity check setup for this database table.

Editing Data with Validity Checks

The purpose of validity checks is to enhance, automate, and control the entry of data into a table. The Ck_book table is currently in the Edit mode. If you look at the *Cleared bank* field you will see that it is empty because you left this field blank when you entered those five records.

However, you have now established a default value for this field. Paradox will insert that value into each of the *Cleared bank* fields that you edit. Enter

↑

What happened? When the cursor was moved up to record 4, Paradox saw that you had left the *Cleared bank* field in record 5 blank. Since the validity check option has been set up to insert - as the default character, Paradox inserts that dash into the field. The same action will occur as you move up the column. Enter

↑ ***(4 times)***

In this case, simply moving the cursor will enter a series of values into a column.
Move the cursor to the *tax deductible* field.

←

Instead of being blank, this field ought to have either a Y or an N. Enter

n ↓

The next two records have lowercase y in the *tax deductible* field. You convert the character to uppercase Y by erasing the current character and allowing the program to insert the default value.

[backspace] ↓

Repeat the operation for the next field.

[backspace] ↓

Complete the column by entering

n ↓

[backspace] [spacebar]

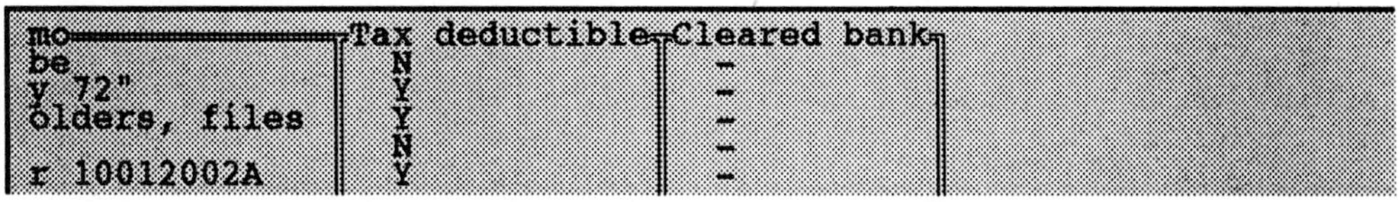

```
mo              Tax deductible  Cleared bank
be                   N               -
y 72"                Y               -
olders, files        Y               -
                     N               -
r 10012002A          Y               -
```

Figure 2-14 Data entered using validity check options.

When you have completed the entry, the *Tax deductible* and *Cleared bank* fields will be filled in, based on the validity check functions as shown in Figure 2-14. Validity check options can be very powerful tools because they allow you to customize many aspects of the data entry and data revision process.

Saving the Validity Check Options

When you add validity checks to a table, the options along with any new or revised data must be saved with the **Do-It!** command. If you choose to **Cancel** the editing session, the validity options and the data modification will be discarded. Save the changes and the validity checks by entering

[F2]

The validity check information is stored in a file, CK_BOOK.VAL in the current directory.

Data Entry with Validity Checks

The validity check options created in the Edit mode will also effect any entry made in the DataEntry mode. Activate the DataEntry mode by entering

[F10] m d

Select the current table by entering

↵ ***(2 times)***

The first field is the *Check #*. Enter

900 ↵

Because the entry does not meet the validity check criteria, Paradox highlights the field and displays a message, **Value between 950 and 1500 is expected**, in the lower-right corner of the screen. Enter a valid check number.

[Ctrl-backspace] 1004 ↵

The next field is the *Check date* field. The Validity Check option used in this field will insert the system date into the field if it is left blank. Enter

↵

The date entered into the field is the current date.

Continue entering data into the record.

Computer World ↵
2245.5 ↵
Turbo 286 Computer ↵

Since the last two fields have default values which you want to accept for this record, enter

↵

Since the cursor is now positioned in the last field in the record, you can terminate your entry at this point by saving the new record, and assume that Paradox will fill in the missing default values. Note that this will work only for the field in which the cursor is positioned. If you do not move the cursor to a field, no default value will be inserted. Enter

[F2]

The program returns to the Main view mode, showing the new record added to the database table.

Removing a Validity Check Option

You may have realized that in terms of following the examples in this book, inserting the actual date as a default value is inappropriate. In this case, it would be necessary to clear the validity check from the date field.

In order to clear a validity check you must be in either the Edit or DataEntry modes. Activate the Edit mode by entering

[F9]

Select ValCheck by entering

[F10] v

This time select the Clear option.

c

The Clear option can be used in two ways. The Field option allows you to remove the validity checks from a specific field. Note that this command removes all validity check options from the field. The All option erases all validity check options in all of the fields, i.e., the VAL file for the table is erased.

> *If you want to remove only one of several validity check options from a field you must first clear all the options and then reenter the options you want to retain. They cannot be cleared selectively.*

Select Field by entering

f

Select the *Check date* field for clearing by entering

← *(4 times)*

Clear the options by entering

↵

The last change that you need to make is to enter a specific date in place of the current date inserted into record 6. Enter

[End]
[Ctrl-backspace]
1/15/89

Save the changed data and validity check options by entering

[F2]

Exiting Paradox

Exit the program by entering

[F10]
e
y

Summary

In this chapter you learned the operations and options used in Paradox for creating, entering, and editing a database table.

❑ **Creating a Table.** All information entered into Paradox is stored in the form of database tables. Tables are organized in columns and rows called *fields* and *records*. Each field contains one item of information about a person, place, thing, or event. All of the fields in one row make up a group of related data items called a record. Paradox stores table information in files with DB extensions. The *Create* command located on the Main Paradox menu is used to design a new database table.

❑ **Field Types.** Paradox recognizes five different types of fields in database tables: *Alphanumeric*, *Number*, *Currency*, *Date*, and *Short Number*.

❑ **Key Fields.** You can designate the first field in the table structure as a key field. The records in the table are automatically sorted according to the values entered into the key field. An index file, PX extension, is created to keep track of the key field values. This file also speeds up searches performed on the key field.

❑ **Do-It!** This command is used to confirm that you want to save the results of the current operation. The [F2] key is a shortcut for entering the **Do-It!** command.

❑ **Data Entry.** Batches of new records can be added to the table using the DataEntry mode. The **DataEntry** command is located on the Modify menu. When using DataEntry, any records already in the table are protected from revision. All records added in the DataEntry mode are added as a batch to the original table when you perform the **Do-It!** command.

❑ **Ditto.** When entering data, the **Ditto** command, [Ctrl-d], will copy the information from the same field in the previous record, if any, into the current field.

❑ **Field View.** The Field View option permits you to have full text editing available when modifying the contents of a field. When Field View is active, you can insert, delete, and replace characters. You can activate Field View for only one field at a time.

❑ **Editing.** The Edit mode allows you to modify existing records and add new records to a table. You can also delete records in the edit mode. The [F9] key activates the Edit mode.

❑ **Form View.** The Form View displays the fields from one record at a time in a full-screen display. Paradox automatically generates a default screen form. The [F7] key toggles the display between the table and the Form Views.

❑ **Validity Checks.** Validity checks are used to control the data entry and editing processes. The validity checks allow you to set minimum and/or maximum values and default values to be inserted if a field is left blank. You can also specify that a field cannot be left blank. Picture options allow you to create a template which controls the individual characters entered into a field. Field contents can also be linked to other data tables. This feature is discussed in Part 2.

Exercises

Exercise 1 from page 44

[F10] v d ↵
h
1500 ↵

Exercise 2 from page 49

[F10] v d ↵
d
Y ↵

3

Viewing Data

Once you have created a database table, entered information, and stored it on the disk in the form of a database table file, DB extension, the next series of tasks you must perform involve viewing the data stored in those files.

As you learned in Chapter 2, Paradox automatically generates a visual display structure called an *image* for every database table that you create. The structure of the image matches the structure of the database table.

In addition to the table image, Paradox also generates a screen form in which individual records can be displayed, one at a time. In this chapter, you will look more closely at how data is displayed on the screen and the options in Paradox that can be used to modify the table image.

Begin by loading Paradox in the usual manner.

The View Command

The first command on the Paradox Main menu is the *View* command. When you first load the program, this command is automatically highlighted. The command is used to display an image of one of the database tables stored on the disk.

Keep in mind that it is not necessary to view a table in order to perform operations such as data entry or editing. The commands **Modify DataEntry** and **Modify Edit** allow you to enter the name of the table.

However, you may fall into the habit of viewing a table before you begin any other operations. This is a good habit because it allows you to view the tables before you begin working with them. Also, it often serves to remind you of the structure and contents of the table.

The command used to display an image of a table stored on disk is the **View** command. **View** is one of the simplest commands in the Paradox system because it has no options or subcommands. Its only function is to display an *image* of a database file. Keep in mind that Paradox can display more than one image at a time.

Viewing a Table

Suppose you want to view the table you created in Chapter 2. Select the **View** command from the Main menu. Note that when there are no table images on the screen, Paradox displays the Main menu. Enter

v

The program displays the prompt **Table:_**. You can enter the name of the table manually or press ↵ to display a list of the available tables. Enter

↵

On the line below the prompt, the program lists the names of all the tables, DB file extension, found in the current directory in alphabetical order. The first table in the list will be highlighted. If you have more than one table stored in the current directory, the Ck_book table will be included in the list. You can select a table from the list using the → and ← keys to highlight the desired table name. If Ck_book is not already highlighted, move the highlight to Ck_book. Display the table by entering

↵

The program displays the image of the database table in the main work area, Figure 3-1.

```
Viewing Ck_book table: Record 1 of 6                                    Main

CK_BOOK╤═══Check #═╤══Check date═╤═══════════Payee═══════════╤═══Amount
     1 ║       999 ║   1/03/89   ║ Savings Club              ║    71.60
     2 ║      1000 ║   1/03/89   ║ Allied Office Furniture   ║   750.50
     3 ║      1001 ║   1/04/89   ║ Central Office Supplies   ║    97.68
     4 ║      1002 ║   1/08/89   ║ Western Telephone         ║   101.57
     5 ║      1003 ║   1/08/89   ║ United Federal Insurance  ║   590.00
     6 ║      1004 ║   1/15/89   ║ Computer World            ║ 2,245.50
```

Figure 3-1 Table image displayed in work area.

Rotating the Table

As you learned in Chapter 2, the number of fields in a table can exceed the screen width of 80 columns. The program will automatically scroll the table to the left or right as you move the cursor from field to field. As an alternative, Paradox allows you to rotate the field columns in the table image without changing the position of the cursor. The ***Rotate*** command is [Ctrl-r].

Each time the [Ctrl-r] command is entered, Paradox moves the column in which the cursor is positioned to the end of the table. All of the columns to the right of the current column are shifted to the left to fill the space formerly occupied by the current column.

If the cursor is in the record number column, as it is when you first display a table image, the rotate command operates on the first column in the table.

For example, if you were to enter the [Ctrl-r] command, the current field *Check #* would be shifted to the end of the table and the other fields would be moved to the right, making the first column in the table *Check date*. Enter

[Ctrl-r]

Check date moves to the first position in the table, Figure 3-2.

```
Viewing Ck_book table: Record 1 of 6
CK_BOOK═╤═Check date═╤════════════Payee═══════
      1 │  1/03/89   │ Savings Club
      2 │  1/03/89   │ Allied Office Furniture
      3 │  1/04/89   │ Central Office Supplies
      4 │  1/08/89   │ Western Telephone
      5 │  1/08/89   │ United Federal Insurance
      6 │  1/15/89   │ Computer World
```

Figure 3-2 Check # field rotated.

To see what happened to the *Check #* field, move the cursor to the end of the table by entering

[Ctrl-End]

The *Check #* field is now the last field in the table. Move back to the beginning of the table by entering

[Ctrl-Home]

You can use the **Rotate** command to arrange the columns so that specific fields are positioned next to other fields. For example, suppose you want the *Cleared bank* field positioned next to the *Amount* field. Currently, the *Memo* field is in that position.

First, position the cursor in the column you want to move—here, the *Memo* field column. Enter

[Tab] ***(3 times)***

Rotate the *Memo* field column to the end of the table by entering

[Ctrl-r]

Repeat the command to rotate the *Tax deductible* column.

[Ctrl-r]

You have now placed the *Cleared bank* field next to the *Amount* field in the current table image, Figure 3-3.

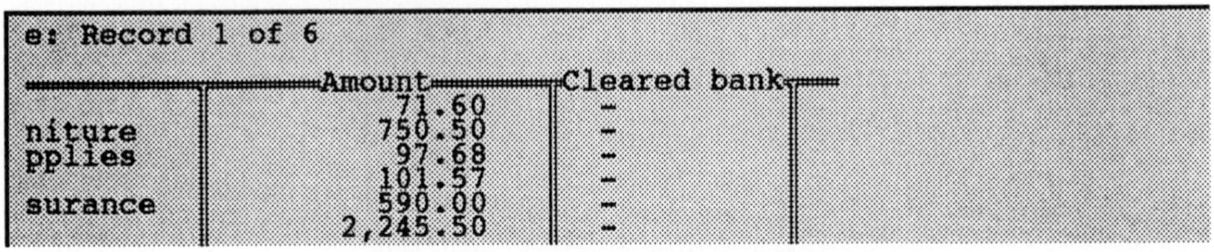

```
e: Record 1 of 6
══════════╤═════════Amount═══════╤Cleared bank╤══
          ║              71.60   ║    -       ║
niture    ║             750.50   ║    -       ║
pplies    ║              97.68   ║    -       ║
          ║             101.57   ║    -       ║
surance   ║             590.00   ║    -       ║
          ║           2,245.50   ║    -       ║
```

Figure 3-3 Column position rotated.

Displaying Another Image

Paradox permits you to display several images of the same table if there is room in the work area. For example, suppose you want to display the original Ck-book table image. You could do this by repeating the **View** command. Since the Main menu is not displayed, enter

[F10]

Select the **View** command.

v

This time enter the name of the table manually.

ck_book ↵

Paradox displays the new image with the Ck_book data in the original column sequence, Figure 3-4.

```
Viewing Ck_book table: Record 1 of 6                                 Main

 Payee                          Amount     Cleared bank   Check #
 Savings Club                    71.60      -              999
 Allied Office Furniture        750.50      -              1000
 Central Office Supplies         97.68      -              1001
 Western Telephone              101.57      -              1002
 United Federal Insurance       590.00      -              1003
 Computer World               2,245.50      -              1004

CK_BOOK  Check #   Check date   Payee                        Amount
   1       999     1/03/89     Savings Club                  71.60
   2      1000     1/03/89     Allied Office Furniture      750.50
   3      1001     1/04/89     Central Office Supplies       97.68
   4      1002     1/08/89     Western Telephone            101.57
   5      1003     1/08/89     United Federal Insurance     590.00
   6      1004     1/15/89     Computer World             2,245.50
```

Figure 3-4 Two images of the same table displayed.

Selecting an Image

You may have noticed that the lines and field names of the new image are displayed in brighter video than the first image. This is done to indicate which of the images is the active image. The *active* image will be affected by any operation you select to perform. Only one of the displayed images can be active.

You can switch the active image by using the [F3] and [F4] keys.

Table 3-1 Activate Image

[F3]	activate previous image
[F4]	activate next image

Activate the first image by entering

[F3]

The bright video moves to the first image indicating that this is the active image. To move back to the second image, enter

[F4]

One of the advantages of having several images of the same table is that you can display the data in different ways. For example, you might rotate the field column differently. Use the

Rotate command to place the *Amount* column next to the *Check date* column. Try this on your own. The correct command can be found on page 74 under Exercise 1.

Removing an Image

The **View** command allows you to place images on the work area. You may find that as the work area gets more crowded you will want to remove an image from it. The command [F8] will remove the currently active image from the work area.

Keep in mind that removing an image from the work area does not erase or delete data. Operations that change table data require you to use the **Do-It!** command to save the changes. The [F8] command simply removes a particular image of the table from the screen. Suppose you want to remove the first image on the screen. Before you can use [F8] to remove it, you must activate that image. Enter

[F3]

The first image is now the active image. Remove it from the display by entering

[F8]

The image is removed from the work area, leaving the second image as the only one displayed.

Image Modifications

When Paradox displays an image on the screen, it uses the table's structure as a guide. The width of the columns is set based on the column type and the field name. For example, character columns are set to the width specified in the structure. The *Memo* field is set as 25 characters, which is the same width as the table column in the image. Note that if the field name is wider than the column, the column width is set so that the entire field name can appear. An example is the *Tax deductible* field. The contents of the field are only a single character in width but the name is 14 characters wide. Paradox displays the data in a column that is 14 characters wide to accommodate the field name.

The table image automatically generated by the view command can be modified in four basic ways using the Image menu.

❑ **Column Width.** You can widen or narrow any of the columns in the image. Character fields can be widened to a maximum of 76 characters or the field width, whichever is larger. If you narrow an alpha column, characters that are too wide for the column will be hidden. Numeric or currency type columns cannot exceed 25 characters. If the column is made too narrow to display the numeric values correctly, the column will show a series of * instead of hiding numbers. This is done to avoid presenting a misleading image of a value by hiding one or more of the digits. Note that displaying the *'s in a numeric or currency field does not erase the values. It simply means that, in the table view, the values are not displayed. Since the column-width setting has no effect on the form view, the values will reappear if you switch to that view.

Date columns are limited to 14 characters in width. If a date column is narrowed, it will hide characters just as an alpha column will.

In data entry or revision, the field view command, [Alt-F5], allows you to scroll a field's content horizontally in a reduced with column. This means data entry or editing is not restricted by the column size, although it may be inconvenient to edit a significantly reduced field.

Use the command **Image ColumnSize**.

❑ **Format.** The format option allows you to change the style in which numeric, currency, or date columns display their information. If the column is numeric or currency, you can select one of four formats.

Table 3-2 Numeric Formats

General	########.##
Fixed	########.00
Comma	##,###,###.00
Scientific	#.00E+00

The General format allows for a floating decimal point that uses the number of decimal places required by the value, if any. The Fixed and Comma formats use a fixed number of decimal places for each value. If that fixed number of decimal places is too small for the decimal position of the value, the value is rounded. Scientific notation uses an exponential format which is useful when storing very large or very small values. There are three types of date formats:

Table 3-3 Date Formats

M/D/YY	1/10/89
D-MMM-YY	1-Jan-89
D.MM.YY	1.01.89

Use the command **Image Format**.

❑ **Table Length.** By default, Paradox will display all of the records in the table as part of the image up to the screen-size limit of 22 rows. If you want to limit the length of the table image to fewer rows, you can specify a table length of 1 to 22 rows. Note that if there are more records in the table than can be displayed in the selected table length, you can scroll the records vertically within the displayed image.

Use the command **Image TableSize.**

❑ **Column Arrangement.** Paradox allows you to change the order of the columns in the table image. The effect is similar to that of the [Ctrl-r] command, except that you can move specific columns to specific locations directly.

Use the command **Image Move.**

Changes made in an image are temporary and remain in effect only until the image is removed from the work area. Paradox offers you the option of saving an image layout as the default layout for the table. This means that each time a new image of that table is displayed on the work area, it will use the custom-designed layout. Note that you can store only one image layout for each table.

Image changes affect only the table view with the exception of numeric or date formats, which appear in both the table and form views.

Changing Column Widths

The default column widths used by Paradox for the table image will often not maximize the number of columns that you can display across the screen. You can use the **Modify ColumnSize** command to change the column width, usually to allow more columns to be visible at one time.

The current table has several fields that could be reduced significantly without hiding any data. For example, the *Tax deductible* and *Cleared bank* fields contain only a single character but the column widths are enlarged to accommodate the full field name. Narrowing these columns to three characters would save a significant amount of screen space.

To change a column width, enter the **Modify ColumnSize** command. You do not have to position the cursor in the column you want to change *before* you enter this command, since you will have an opportunity to specify the column you want to change after the command is activated. Enter

[F10] i c

Paradox displays a prompt, Figure 3-5, which asks you to use the arrow keys to select the column that you want to size.

```
Use ← and → to move to the column you want to resize...
then press ↵ to select it.
```

Figure 3-5 Select column for sizing prompt.

In this case, select the *Tax deductible* column by entering

→ (2 times)

The prompt at the top of the screen changes to indicate that you can now alter the width of the column by using the → key to increase the width, or the ← key to decrease the width, as shown in Figure 3-6. Pressing ↵ will fixed the width at its current size. Press [Esc] to cancel the change and restore the column to its previous width.

```
Now use → to increase column width,  ← to decrease...
press ↵ when finished.
```

Figure 3-6 Change column size prompt.

Narrow the column to its minimum width by entering

← ***(10 times)***
↵

Perform the same operation on the *Cleared bank* field. Enter

[F10] i c

You can use the [Home] and [End] keys as shortcut commands to narrow the column to the minimum or to widen it to the maximum, respectively, when this mode is active. Change the width to the minimum by entering

[Home] ↵

The field now takes up considerably less horizontal space, as shown in Figure 3-7.

```
══Memo══════════════╤Tax═╤Clea╤════════════Paye
achine              │ N ║ -  ║ Savings Club
8" by 72"           │ Y ║ -  ║ Allied Office
s, folders, files   │ Y ║ -  ║ Central Offic
                    │ N ║ -  ║ Western Telep
umber 10012002A     │ Y ║ -  ║ United Federa
o Computer          │ Y ║ -  ║ Computer Worl
```

Figure 3-7 Column sizes reduced.

Changing Column Format

Changing column formats uses a procedure similar to changing column widths. Suppose you want to change the format of the *Check date* field. Enter the **Image Format** command.

[F10] i f

Select the field you want to format. Remember that formats apply only to numeric, currency, or date type fields. Move the cursor to the *Check date* field by entering

← *(4 times)*

Select this field for a format change by entering

↵

The type of menu that appears depends on whether you have selected a numeric or currency field, or a date field. In this instance the Date format menu appears, showing the three format options for date field, Figure 3-8.

```
MM/DD/YY  DD-Mon-YY  DD.MM.YY
All numeric month, day,  year: e.g. 9/23/85.
```

Figure 3-8 Date format menu.

Select the DD-Mon-YY format by entering

→ ↵

The dates in the *Check date* field change to the new format, Figure 3-9.

Keep in mind that even though the date format has been altered, you can still enter dates in the **M/D/YY** form. Paradox will display those entries in the specified format.

```
Check date        Amount
  3-Jan-89          71.60    Coffee
  3-Jan-89         750.50    Desk -
  4-Jan-89          97.68    Envelo
  8-Jan-89         101.57
  8-Jan-89         590.00    Policy
 15-Jan-89       2,245.50    286 Tu
```

Figure 3-9 Date format changed.

Moving Columns

You can use the **Image Move** command to directly place a field column in a new location in the table. This command allows you to specify the new location in contrast to the [Ctrl-r] command that always places the column at the end of the table.

Suppose you would like to place the *Payee* field following the *Amount* field. Enter

[F10] i m

Paradox displays a menu at the top of the screen which consists of the names of the field in the current table, Figure 3-10.

```
Name of field to move:                                                Main
Check #  Check date  Payee  Amount  Memo  Tax deductible  Cleared bank
```

Figure 3-10 Fields listed for column move.

Move the highlight to *Payee* by entering

→ ***(2 times)***
↵

Once you have selected the column to move, use the arrow keys to position it in the table where it should be placed. In order to place the column to the right of the *Amount* field, position the cursor in the *Memo* field by entering

→ ***(2 times)***
↵

Saving the Image Settings

The settings you have selected for the current image are temporary. They will be lost when the image is removed or you exit Paradox.

However, you can preserve the settings as the default layout for a table image by using the **Image KeepSet** command. This command writes the current table settings to a file, e.g., CK_BOOK.SET. Save the current image settings as the default settings for the Ck-book table by entering

[F10] i k

Paradox displays the message **Settings recorded...** in the lower-right corner of the screen to indicate that the .SET file has been written.

The creation of the Settings file means that each time a new image of the file is displayed, it will use the column size, column format, column order, and table size currently specified.

Remove the current image by entering

[F8]

Display an image of the Ck_book table using the **View** command.

↵
ck_book ↵

The table image reflects the saved settings, not the original table structure. Remove the image by entering

[F8]

Sorting a Table

When you designed the current table, you designated the *Check #* field as the key field. This ensured that each entry in the *Check #* field would be unique and that the records would always be ordered by check number.

But suppose you want to list the records in order by some other field, e.g., by *Payee*. Could this be done? How?

Since the Ck-book table is by definition (key field designation) ordered by check number, the trick is to create a new copy of the table that is ordered according to the values in a different field. Paradox performs this action using the **Modify Sort** command.

When this command is used, Paradox generates a new table using the data from the original table but sequencing the records according to the sequence specified as part of the **Sort** command. Note that when the table appears as an image in the word area, Paradox automatically creates a database table file, DB extension, to hold the information from the sorted table. This means that **Sort** first copies the original file and then rearranges the records.

When a table is sorted, Paradox does not copy the key field designation from the original file, since this would defeat the purpose of the sort. In addition, the new table does not copy the table image settings, SET file extension. Instead, the sorted table uses the Paradox default column layout.

> *Note that if the original table did not contain a key field designation, it would be possible to sort the records without creating a new table. The sorted table would simply overwrite the existing table. Note that this means the original sequence of the records, based on the order in which they were entered, will be obliterated if you sort a table on top of itself.*

It is important to keep in mind that any table created with the **Modify Sort** command is the result of a *physical*, not a *logical* sort. A physical sort is used to arrange the existing records into a sort order. If you were to add or insert new records, or modify the data in existing records, Paradox would not make any effort to maintain the sort order. The only way to ensure that these records were in a specific order would be to perform another **Modify Sort** following any additions or changes.

On the other hand, a logical sort is automatically maintained when records are added or modified. This is the type of sort implemented when a key field is designated. Each time an addition or edit is made, the table is automatically resorted to maintain the key field order.

Keep in mind when you sort a table with a key field designation, the new table that results does **not** have a key field. The current sort order of the new table will not be automatically maintained.

Sorting a Table

Suppose you want to create a table based in the Ck_book table sorted by Payee. Enter the **Modify Sort** command.

m s

The program prompts you to enter the name of the table that contains the data you want to sort. In this instance, that is the Ck_book table. Enter

ck_book ↵

The next prompt asks you to enter a name for the new table that will be created when the Ck_book data is sorted. Enter

checks1 ↵

With the name of the source table, Ck_book, and the new table, Checks1, entered, the program displays the Sort Order selection screen, Figure 3-11.

```
Sorting Ck_book table into new CHECKS1 table                    Sort

Number fields to set up sort order (1, 2, etc.).  If you want a field sorted
   in descending sequence, follow the number with a 'D' (e.g., '2D').
       Ascending is the normal sequence and need not be indicated.

_       ◂ Check #
          Check date
          Payee
          Amount
          Memo
          Tax deductible
          Cleared bank
```

Figure 3-11 Sort Order selection screen.

This display lists the fields in the source table. This display allows you to specify the sort key by placing the number 1 next to the field you want to use as the sort key. By default, the program will sort the records in ascending order. If you wish to have a descending order, follow the number with the letter D, e.g., 1D for a descending sort.

If you want to use a multi-level sort key, specify additional levels of sorting by placing numbers 2, 3, etc., next to the secondary key fields. Multilevel sorts are used when the information in a key field is not unique. For example, if the *Payee* field contains repetitions of the same payee name, you might choose *amount* as the secondary key by placing the number 2 next to the field name. This would arrange records by amount if the record has the same payee. Keep in mind that secondary or more sort keys are not required. If you select only a single key, records with duplicate entries in the key field will be listed in the sequence in which they were entered into the table within that group.

In this case, choose *Payee* as the primary sort key. Move the cursor to Payee by entering

↓ ***(2 times)***

Specify this as the primary sort field by entering

1

With the key (or keys) specified, perform the sort by entering the **Do-It!** command.

[F2]

The result of the sort is the creation of a new table, Checks1, with the same data as Ck_book, but arranged according to the payee name, as in Figure 3-12.

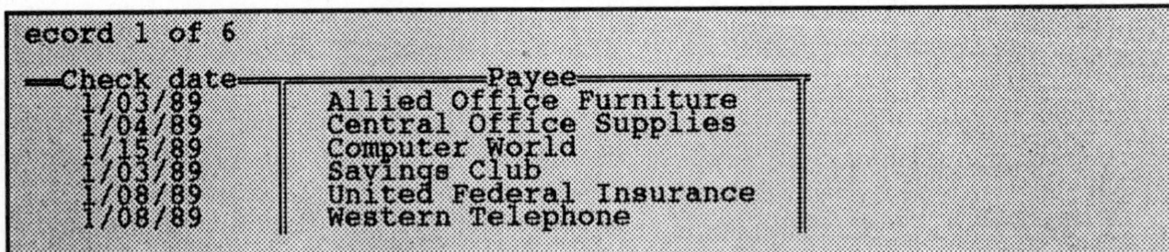

ecord 1 of 6

Check date	Payee
1/03/89	Allied Office Furniture
1/04/89	Central Office Supplies
1/15/89	Computer World
1/03/89	Savings Club
1/08/89	United Federal Insurance
1/08/89	Western Telephone

Figure 3-12 Records sorted by payee name.

Note that the new image does not reflect the customized settings stored for the Ck_book table; instead, it uses the default layout dictated by the table's structure. If you want to change the column layout of the new table, you could do so by using the commands on the Image menu.

Multiple Key Sorts

A *Multiple Key* sort is one in which the primary sort field does not contain unique records. For example, the *Check date* field contains more than one record with the same date. If you sorted by *Check date*, you could then specify a second key by which the records with the same date would be ordered, e.g., *Payee*.

Sort the Checks1 table into order by check date and within checkdate by payee. Enter

[F10] m s

In this example, you can select the current table, Checks1, as the source of the data for the sort. Display a list of tables by entering

↵

Note that the first table name on the list is Checks1, even though Ck_book precedes it in alphabetical order. Paradox automatically places the name of the table, if any, in which the cursor is located at the beginning of a list of tables to select from. This is done to help facilitate selection of the current table. By pressing ↵ a second time you will select the current table. Thus, pressing ↵ twice in succession is a shorthand way of selecting the current table. Enter

↵

Paradox then displays a menu with two options as shown in Figure 3-13. You may recall that this menu did not appear when you performed a sort using the Ck_book table as the source. This is because the Ck_book table contained a key field designation which caused Paradox to automatically sequence records according to the key field, making the table incompatible with any other sort order. In this case, the Checks1 table has no key field, thus it is possible to sort to the same table. This process overwrites the current table order with the new order.

```
Same  New
Place results of the sort in the same table.
```

Figure 3-13 Select destination for sorted records.

Select the same table as the sort destination by entering

s

Here, make the sort order a descending order by *Check date*. A descending date order will place the most recent dates at the top of the table. Enter

↓
1D

Select a second field for the sort order which will be used to order records that have the same *Check date* value. Select *Payee* by entering

↓

2

Execute the sort by entering

[F2]

The table is now sorted in reverse order by date and within duplicate dates by the payee name, Figure 3-14.

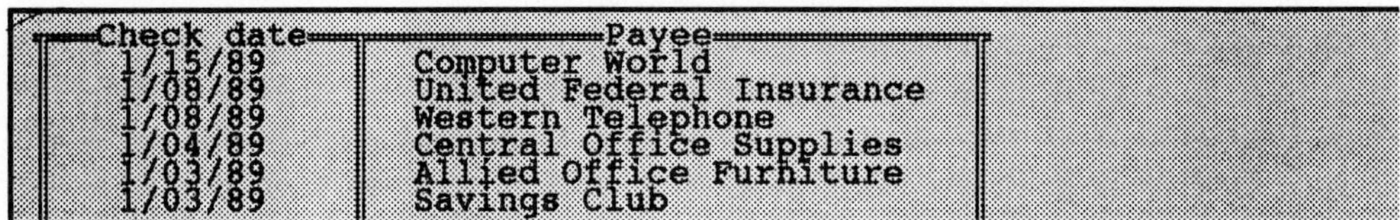

Check date	Payee
1/15/89	Computer World
1/08/89	United Federal Insurance
1/08/89	Western Telephone
1/04/89	Central Office Supplies
1/03/89	Allied Office Furniture
1/03/89	Savings Club

Figure 3-14 Table sorted by multiple field key.

Remove the image from the work area by entering

[F8]

Deleting Files

The two procedures discussed in this chapter, image modification and sorting, create new files. The image modification process can be used to create a settings file, SET extension. Sorting creates new tables, DB extension.

You can remove these files outside of Paradox by using the DOS DEL command. Paradox also contains a **Delete** command on the Tools menu, which can be used to delete the files created by Paradox. For example, suppose you want to delete the Settings file created for the Ck_book table. The result of deleting this file would be that the table image would return to its default settings.

Display the Tools Delete menu by entering

t d

The menu, Figure 3-15, lists the types of files that can be deleted.

```
Table  Form  Report  Script  QuerySpeedup  KeepSet  ValCheck  Graph
Delete a table and its family of forms, reports and indexes.
```

Figure 3-15 The Tools Delete menu.

In this instance, delete the **KeepSet** file for the Ck_book table. Enter

k

The program lists the names of the tables from which you need to select the table whose Settings file you want to delete.

> *Note that all the available tables are listed, even though they do not all have settings files. Selecting a table for which there is no actual settings file on the disk will have no effect.*

Select the Ck_book file by entering

↵

Display the Ck_book table by entering

v
ck_book

The table columns have returned to their original order. Enter

[Ctrl-End]

The column widths have also been restored to the their original widths.

You can delete a table using the same command. Note that when a table is deleted you cannot recover the data. Delete the Checks1 table by entering

[F10] t d t
checks1 ↵

Because deleting a table removes the data permanently from the disk, Paradox displays the Cancel/OK menu to ensure that you do not accidentally delete the table. Enter

o

The table has now been removed from the disk. Exit Paradox by entering

[F10] e y

Summary

In this chapter, you looked at ways in which you could alter the display of table images in the Paradox work area.

❑ **Table Image Settings.** Paradox will automatically generate a column and row table image to use for the display of database table information. The order of the field columns conforms to the order of the field names entered into the table structure. Paradox selects the field widths automatically, based on the field types as entered in the table structure. The **Image** command can be used to change the layout of the table image. You can change the column order, column width, column format (numeric or date fields only), or limit the number of records displayed at one time. These settings are temporary and are discarded when the image is removed or you exit Paradox. The **Image KeepSet** command will write the current table settings into a Settings file, SET extension. These settings can then be used automatically by Paradox to structure the table image for that table each time it is viewed. Each database table can be only one set of table settings.

❑ **[Ctrl-r].** This keystroke is called the **Rotate** command. It automatically shifts the position of the column in which the cursor is positioned to the end of the table.

❑ **Sorting Tables.** The **Edit Sort** command is used to sort the records in a database table into a specific order. If the table you are sorting has a key field designated in the table structure, the **Edit Sort** command creates a duplicate of the table when sorting the record. Tables without key fields can have the sorted record overwrite the existing table.

❑ **Tools Delete.** You can use this command to delete tables, settings, and other Paradox files. Files deleted with this command cannot be recovered.

Exercises

Exercise 1 from page 62

[Tab] ***(3 times)***
[Ctrl-r]

4

Database Queries

A *query* is a question you ask that can be answered using the information stored in a database table. When you create a database table, you probably already have in mind some specific questions you will eventually want to answer using the data entered into that table.

In Paradox, database queries are solicited with the Ask command, which uses a *query by example* approach. For example, suppose you want to retrieve records from the Ck_book table that were tax deductible. In English, a query would be worded as a question or a command: Which records are tax deductible or View all records that are tax deductible.

In keeping with the visual approach of Paradox, a request for such information would be made in the form of an example. Queries are created by using a special form of a work area image called a *query form*. This image is similar to the table image for the database table, except that all the columns are blank. A query is created by entering examples into the column or columns that relate to the query you are entering.

Figure 4-1 shows how a Query by Example is made in Paradox. Records that are tax deductible contain the character **Y** in the *Tax deductible* field. Placing a **Y** in the *Tax deductible* column of a query form shows by example which records should be retrieved.

Figure 4-1 Image expresses Query by Example.

The answer to the query is created when a query form is *processed*. Processing a query form creates a new image called *Answer*. This image contains the information that answers the example specified in the query form.

Queries can be used to carry out five general categories of database operations, as explained below.

❑ **Selection.** One of the major advantages of computer-based database systems over paper-based databases (e.g., filing cabinets) is that the computer can retrieve specific blocks of data from a large database quickly and accurately. This task is called *selection*, because it requires the computer to select a specific part of the stored information. The selection is made on a logical basis. This means that you enter a description of the data you want to retrieve and the computer searches the database for all the records that contain information matching your description. The description is entered in the convention of an example, in a query form.

In addition to selecting records in a query, you can also determine which fields will be included in the answer. Paradox returns only the fields you have selected with a √ as part of the answer image.

❑ **Sequence.** The records returned as part of an Answer image will be sorted according to the values in the first field column selected for Answer image. For example, suppose you ask for the *Payee* and *Amount* fields for all tax deductible records. The Answer image will list the records in order by *Payee*, because that is the first column in the Answer image. If you select *Check date* and *Amount*, the records will be sequenced according to *Check date*.

If you want the answer sequenced by a different field, you can specify a sort field as part of the query form example.

❑ **Analysis.** Queries can be used to obtain analytical information based on the database table, such as arithmetic totals, averages, or record counts. You can also create new field columns defined as calculations, based on the data in the original fields in the database table. Queries can thus be used to create new information implied by, but not contained within, the original database table.

❑ **Updates.** Queries can also be used to carry out updates that affect a group of logically selected records. This type of operation can be used to perform global editing changes similar to the way a word processor can search for a phrase and replace it with another phrase throughout a document. You can also use updates to delete groups of records or to transfer a group of records from one table to another database table.

❑ **Grouping Records.** Grouping is a special form of analysis used to summarize a database table by creating one summary record for each group of records with a unique value. For example, a typical analysis task you might want to perform is to find the total of the

Amount field for all checks written in January or March. A group query could be used to create a total for all the checks for each month. In a table with a full year's worth of records that might produce twelve totals, one for each month.

Paradox queries are the most important single aspect of using Paradox. Queries can vary from very simple to very complex. In this chapter, you will learn the basic techniques involved in making queries and the concepts that underlie Paradox's Query by Example approach to database retrieval.

Begin by loading the Paradox 3.0 program in the usual manner. You will begin with a blank work area and the Main menu displayed.

Searching a Table

The most common use of queries is to select records from the database table. The example table Ck_book is so small that you can locate the information you want by simply reading through the records. However, when a table begins to grow to even a few dozen records, it is no longer practical or reliable to find data by visual inspection. The best way to find information is to rely on Paradox to locate the information you are seeking. Paradox provides two methods for locating data.

❑ **Zoom (Search) Table.** The **Zoom** command can be used to locate information in the Current Table image by positioning the cursor to a specific record or field within a record. **Zoom** is useful when you want to move to a specific place in the table. It is faster and more reliable than moving manually through the database. The **Zoom** command is found on the Image menu. The [Ctrl-z] and [Alt-z] keys can be used as shortcut **Zoom** commands.

❑ **Query form.** You can create a new image based on a query that contains the data you want to locate. A query is a bit more complicated to perform than a **Zoom** but it has a number of advantages. A query displays a new image in which *only* the requested data is displayed. This makes it much easier to work with, since all the extraneous material, which is contained in the original table, is filtered out of the query form. Query forms are created using the **Ask** command.

Searching with Zoom

The simplest, and fastest, way to locate a particular data item is through the use of the **Zoom** command. In order to use **Zoom**, the cursor must be positioned in a table image that you want to search. Begin by displaying an image of the Ck_book table. Enter

v
ck_book ↵

Suppose you wanted to locate the record that contained the payee *United Federal Insurance*. Of course, with a small table image such as Ck_book you could spot the record visually in a moment. For the sake of learning, imagine that the table is much larger and such visual inspection is not practical.

Activate the **Image Zoom** command by entering

[F10] i z

The Image Zoom menu contains three options, Figure 4-2.

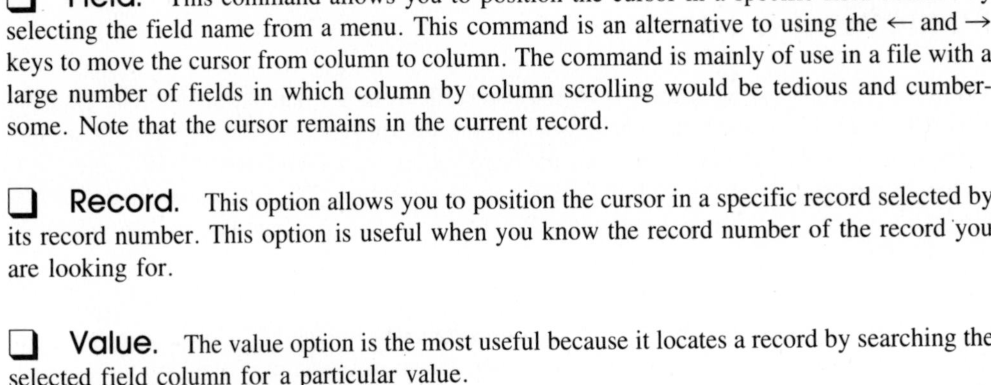

❑ **Field.** This command allows you to position the cursor in a specific field column by selecting the field name from a menu. This command is an alternative to using the ← and → keys to move the cursor from column to column. The command is mainly of use in a file with a large number of fields in which column by column scrolling would be tedious and cumbersome. Note that the cursor remains in the current record.

❑ **Record.** This option allows you to position the cursor in a specific record selected by its record number. This option is useful when you know the record number of the record you are looking for.

❑ **Value.** The value option is the most useful because it locates a record by searching the selected field column for a particular value.

```
Field  Record  Value
Move to a named field.
```

Figure 4-2. Image Zoom menu.

Here, use the **Value** option to locate a record that contains *United Federal Insurance* in the payee field. Enter

v

The program prompts you to select the field column, Figure 4-3, that should be searched.

```
Use ← and → to move to the column you want to search in...
then press ↵ to select it.
```

Figure 4-3 Select search column prompt.

Select the *Payee* field column by entering

→ ***(3 times)***
↵

Next, enter data that the program should search for. It is important to keep in mind that **Zoom** searches are *case sensitive*. This means that the search text and the field text must match exactly, including the use of upper- and lowercase letters. For example, *united federal insurance* would not locate a record that contained *United Federal Insurance* or *UNITED FEDERAL INSURANCE*. Enter

United Federal Insurance ↵

The cursor jumps to the fifth record because its *Payee* field matches the search text.

Zoom Shortcuts

The command [Ctrl-z] can be used as a shortcut for the **Image Zoom Value** command. As a shortcut, the command assumes that the field column in which the cursor is currently positioned is the column that you want to search. For example, suppose you wanted to locate a record with a date of 1/3/89. First, position the cursor in the *Check date* column to indicate that this is the column that should be searched. Enter

←

Activate **Zoom** by entering the shortcut command.

[Ctrl-z]

The program displays a prompt asking you to enter the value to search for. Enter the date you want to locate.

1/3/89 ↵

The cursor is positioned in record 1, which contains a matching date. Paradox always selects the first record in the table image that matches the selection value. However, you can see that in this case there is more than one record with that value. You can use the command key [Alt-z] to continue the search for the next record matching the same value, if any. Enter

[Alt-z]

The cursor moves to record 2 which also contains the date 1/03/89. Enter

[Alt-z]

This time Paradox displays the message **Match not found** in the lower-right corner of the screen. This indicates you have located the last record in the table that matches your criterion value.

Partial Matching

When searching for dates or numeric values, the search value must match the field value exactly. However, when the field contains text, such as the *Payee* or *Memo* fields, it is often useful to be able to match a record on a partial basis. For example, suppose you did not recall the exact name of the insurance company to which you wrote a check. You may want to locate any payee whose name contained the word *Insurance*. You could make the criterion even less specific by locating records with the letters *Ins*, taking into consideration the possibility that you abbreviated the payee's name when making the entry.

Paradox allows you to indicate that you want a partial, not an exact, match by entering . . (2 periods) as part of the search value.

Table 4-1 Matching partial value

xxx..	any field that begins with xxx
..xxx	any field that ends with xxx
..xxx..	any field that contains xxx

In this case use *..ins..* to search for any field that contains those three letters. Also keep in mind that when a partial search value is used the search is *not* case sensitive so that *Ins* and *INS* would also be considered as matching the specified value.

Move the cursor to the *Payee* field column by entering

→

Enter the **Zoom** command.

[Ctrl-z]

Specify a partial match search by entering

..ins.. ↵

The program locates the letter *ins* in record 5, *United Federal Insurance*. Continue the search to make sure that there are no other records that also match this criterion.

[Alt-z]

The message in the lower right corner of the screen, **Match not found**, indicates that you have located the only record in the table that meets your specified criterion.

Remove the current image from the work area by entering

[F8]

Using the ASK Command

The **Zoom** command is useful when you want to change your cursor position with a table image. The **Ask** command provides a far more powerful way of selecting specific records and fields. Unlike **Zoom, Ask** creates a new image containing the fields and records you select.

The **Ask** command involves the use of two images.

❑ **Query form.** The query form is used to enter the example Paradox will use to determine which fields and records should be retrieved from the specified database table file. A query form is displayed when you use **Ask** and select a table to be queried. The query form is a blank table image in which all the fields contained in the table structure are displayed. The information you enter into the query form forms the example that controls what information will appear in the Answer image.

❑ **Answer Table Image.** The Answer image is a table image generated from the query form. Answer contains the records and fields drawn from the specified database table file that matches the examples placed into the query form. Once created, the Answer image operates as a Paradox table. The data can be edited or the image formatted using relevant Paradox commands. The only difference between the Answer table image and other Paradox tables is that the program will overwrite the Answer table image each time a query form is processed. Answer tables are maintained for the duration of the current Paradox session only. Any existing Answer table is automatically erased from the disk when you **Exit** Paradox.

> *You may find that on occasion you would like to retain the Answer image as a database table. This can be accomplished by using the* ***Tools Rename*** *command to change the name of the table from* Answer *to a user-defined file name. This prevents the table from being overwritten when another query is performed.*

Note that it is not necessary to display an image of the original database table in order to create a pair of query/answer images. Paradox will search the database table file on the disk and display only those records and fields needed.

Selecting Fields

The simplest type of query to process is that of selected fields from the original database table, to be displayed in the Answer table. For example, suppose you wanted to create a table that listed only the *Check date*, Payee, and *Amount* fields. This table would be easier to read than the entire Ck_book table.

You can create this table image by using the **Ask** command to process a query. Select the **Ask** command from the main menu by entering

a

The command requests that you enter, or select from a list, a table name. In this case, enter

ck_book ↵

Paradox displays a blank table image with columns that match the fields in the Ck_book table, Figure 4-4.

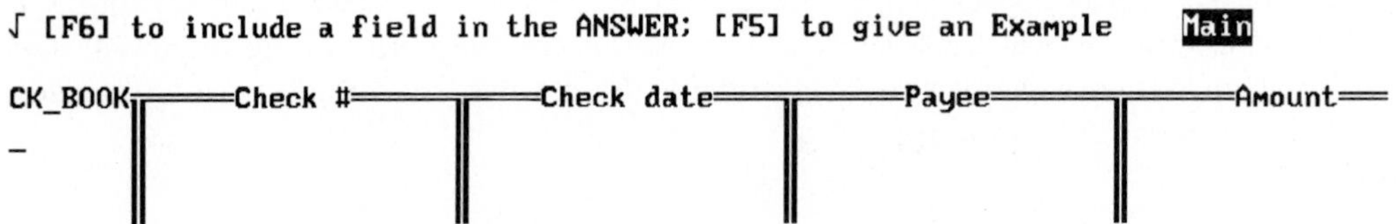

Figure 4-4 Query form created by Ask command.

The table is the query form table. Fields are selected by using the checkmark key, [F6], to place a √ into the field columns. The [F6] is a toggle command, which means that you can deselect a field by pressing [F6] when the field column already contains a √.

In this example you want to select the *Check date*, *Payee*, and *Amount* fields. Enter

→ *(2times)*
[F6]

A √ is inserted into the *Check date* field column, Figure 4-5. This means that the *Check date* information will be included in the Answer image produced when the query form is processed.

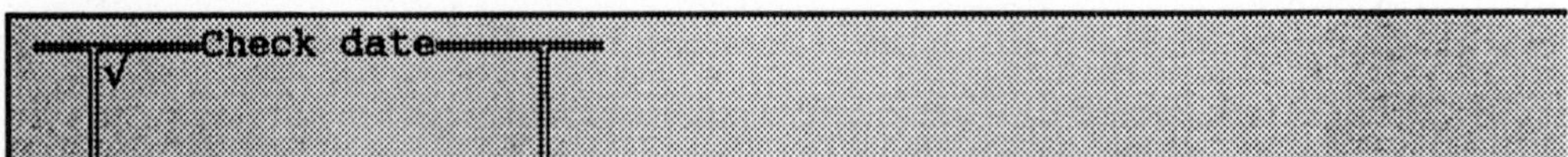

Figure 4-5 Check mark indicates field selected for Answer Image.

Place a √ in the *Payee* field column by entering

→ [F6]

You have now selected two fields to be included in the Answer image. Add the *Amount* field by entering

→ [F6]

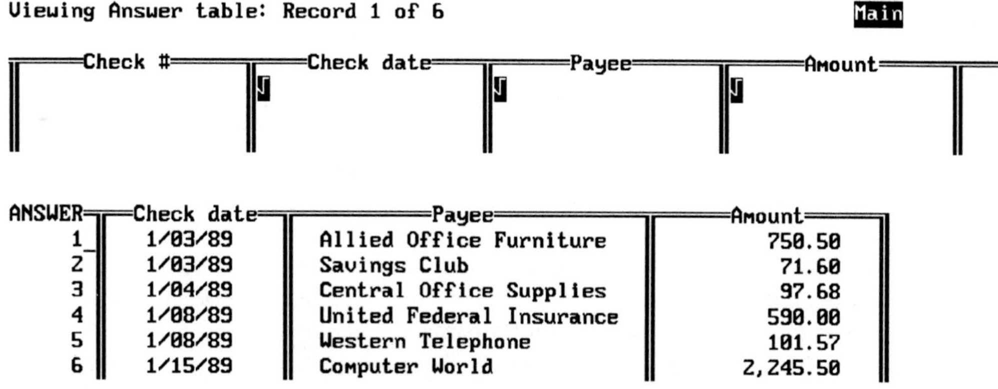
Viewing Answer table: Record 1 of 6 Main

Check # | Check date | Payee | Amount

ANSWER	Check date	Payee	Amount
1	1/03/89	Allied Office Furniture	750.50
2	1/03/89	Savings Club	71.60
3	1/04/89	Central Office Supplies	97.68
4	1/08/89	United Federal Insurance	590.00
5	1/08/89	Western Telephone	101.57
6	1/15/89	Computer World	2,245.50

Figure 4-6 Query form creates Answer image.

Once you have established the query specification, you can *process* the query by entering the **Do-It!** command, [F2].

[F2]

Paradox processes the query by fetching the requested data from the Ck_book database table file and displaying it in an image labeled *Answer*, Figure 4-6.

You can change the fields selected by adding or removing √ from the query field columns. For example, suppose you wanted to eliminate the *Check date* field and include the *Memo* field, instead.

Activate the query form again by entering

[F3]

Use the [F6] command to remove the √ from the *Checkdate* column.

← *(2 times)*
[F6]

Place a √ in the *Memo* field column by entering

→ *(3 times)*
[F6]

Process the modified query by entering

[F2]

When the query is processed, Paradox automatically erases the previous Answer image and then generates a new Answer image based on the most recent query specifications. The new Answer image contains only the three fields that have been checked in the query form.

Selecting Records

In addition to the selection of fields, query forms can be used to pick out records based on the contents of a field or series of fields. The basic technique used in Paradox is to specify records to be selected by entering values you want to match into the query form. When the image is processed, Paradox selects only the records that match the values entered into the field columns in the query form. Keep in mind that the selection of fields based on the √ also takes place at the same time. The result is a table image that contains selected records and fields based on the setup of the Query form. The combination of field and record selection is a very powerful tool for retrieving just the data you need to answer a particular question.

You can select records based on dates, numeric values, or alphabetical text. The simplest type of selection criterion is an exact match. However, Paradox allows you to select records based on partial matches, ranges of values, or relationships such as greater than or less than a value.

Selecting by Date

Suppose you wanted to display the *Payee, Amount*, and *Memo* fields for only the checks written on a specific date, e.g., 1/8/89. The current query form is set to select the three fields but it includes all the records.

In order to narrow the Answer image down to only the records with a *Check date* of 1/8/89, you must enter that date into the *Check date* field column of the query form. The value will be used by Paradox to select the records with that date when the query is processed.

Activate the query form by entering

[F3]

Move the cursor to the *Check date* field column by entering

← ***(3 times)***

To select records for a specific date simply enter the date you want to select by into the column.

1/8/89

Process the query by entering

[F2]

In this case, Paradox selects only two of the records from the Ck_book table for the Answer image because they are the only two records that match the specified date. Note that it is not necessary to include the *Check date* field as part of the Answer image in order to select records based on the *Check date*, Figure 4-7.

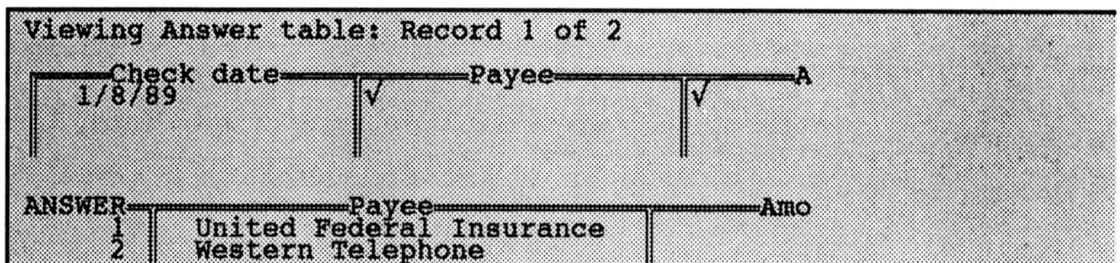
Viewing Answer table: Record 1 of 2

Check date: 1/8/89 | Payee: √ | A: √

ANSWER	Payee
1	United Federal Insurance
2	Western Telephone

Figure 4-7 Record selection for matching check date.

Change the field specifications by removing the *Memo* field and adding the *Check date* field. Enter

[F3]
[F6]
→ *(3 times)*
[F6]
[F2]

This time, because the *Check date* field is included in the Answer, you can see that the records were explicitly selected because the dates match the date in the query form, Figure 4-8.

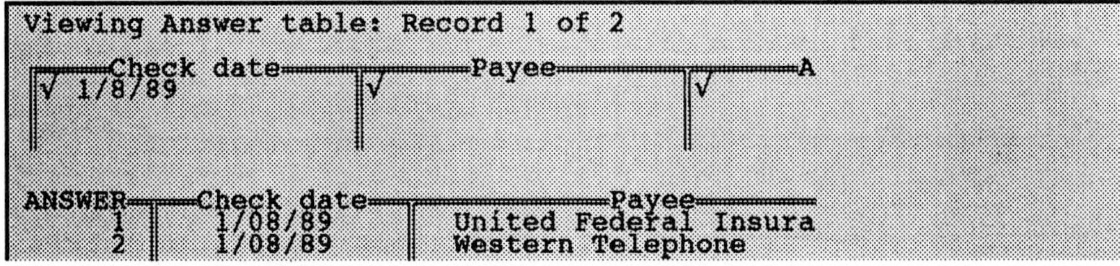
Viewing Answer table: Record 1 of 2

Check date: √ 1/8/89 | Payee: √ | A: √

ANSWER	Check date	Payee
1	1/08/89	United Federal Insura
2	1/08/89	Western Telephone

Figure 4-8 Dates included in Answer image.

Selecting Ranges

In the previous example you selected records that contained a specific date, 1/8/89. Suppose you wanted to select all the records that have a date of 1/8/89 or older, e.g., 1/7/89, 1/6/89, etc. In this case, the date 1/8/89 would be the largest value in a **range** of potential values. Paradox recognizes standard mathematical symbols for range type relationships, Table 4-2.

Table 4-2 Range Operator Symbols

>*x*	greater than *x*
<*x*	less than *x*
>=x	equal to or greater than *x*
<=x	equal to or less than *x*

If you precede a date with one of the range symbols, Paradox will retrieve all the records that fall within that range. In this example, the range **<=1/8/89** would select all the records with 1/8/89 or older in the *Check date* field. Activate the query form by entering

[F3]

Place the cursor in the *Checkdate* column by entering

← ***(3 times)***

The column currently contains the date 1/1/89. Erase the current selection specification by entering

[Ctrl-backspace]

Enter the range specification.

<=1/8/89

Process the query by entering

[F2]

The Answer table shows all the dates that fall into the specified range, Figure 4-9.

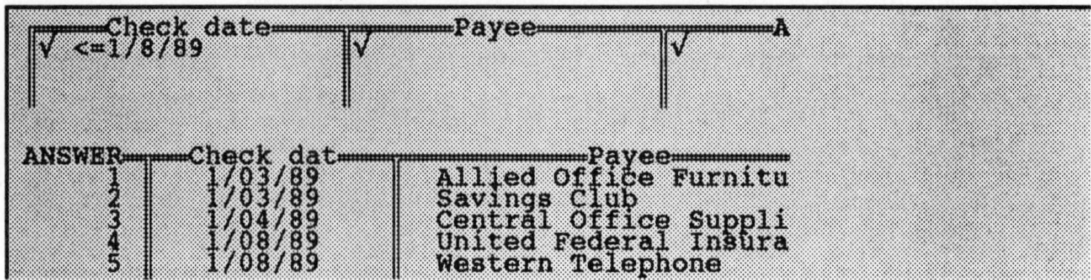

Figure 4-9 Range operator used to select records.

Selecting from a Limited Range

The range specification you entered in the query form created an open-ended range. You restricted the records so that none were more recent than 1/8/89; however, there was no limit on how old a qualifying record could be. In many cases when you want to select a range of values, you will want to set a high and a low value so that you can select all the records that are bracketed by those values. For example, suppose you want to retrieve all checks written between 1/4/89 and 1/10/89. In this case, you would actually need two range specifications: **>=1/4/89** and **<=1/8/89**. Paradox allows you to enter more than one range specifier in a column, as long as you place a comma between the range operators.

Return to the query form by entering

[F3]

Clear the specification from the *Check date* column by entering

[Ctrl-backspace]

This time enter a condition that has a high and a low range specification. It does not matter which item you enter first.

>=1/4/89,<=1/8/89

Process the query by entering **[F2]**

The Answer table shows all the dates that fall into the specified range, Figure 4-10.

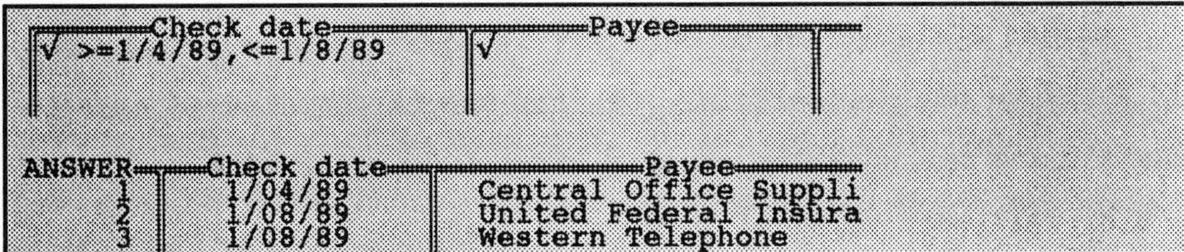

Figure 4-10 High and low range operators used.

Selecting by Numeric Value

Numeric fields operate in a manner similar to date fields when it comes to selecting records. Suppose you want to retrieve any records in which the amount entered was $100. Return to the query form by entering

[F3]

Before you can enter a specification in the *Amount* column you should remove the specification in the *Check date* column. Otherwise Paradox would combine the *Check date* and *Amount* specifications into a single selection criterion. You will see later in this chapter how and why you would enter specifications into more than one column.

Remove the *check date* specifications by entering

[Ctrl-backspace]

Move to the *Amount* field column by entering

→ ***(2 times)***

Enter the value you want to select records by.

100

Process the query by entering

[F2]

The result is an empty Answer image because none of the records in the Ck_book table *exactly* matches $100. While it is possible to select records based on an exact numeric value, it is often not the most practical way to work with numeric fields—especially if the field contains monetary amounts. In most cases, it is better to select a range of values that will probably contain the exact amounts you are looking for. For example, in this case you can look for records that contain amounts between $100 and $150.

Return to the query form and erase the current specification.

[F3]
[Ctrl-backspace]

Enter a range specification

>100,<150

Process the query by entering

[F2]

The use of the range of values provides Paradox with greater latitude in retrieving records. In this instance, the range located a record with an amount of $101.57, which is close to but not exactly $100, Figure 4-11. This is probably the record you were looking for.

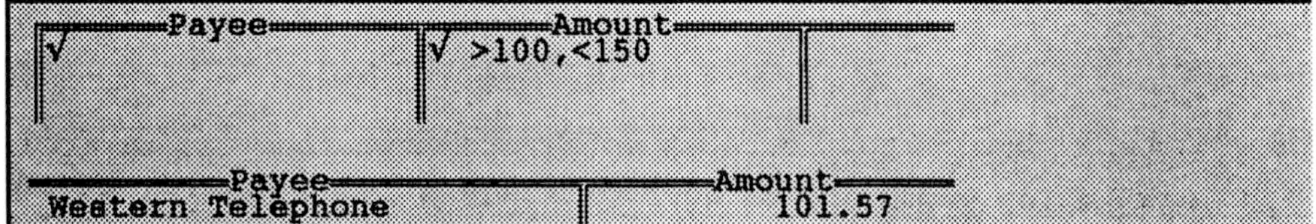

Figure 4-11 Record retrieved with range specifications.

> *Remember that when you enter numeric values in a query column, you should* **never** *include formatting, such as commas or dollar signs, even though the field may display the numbers with those formatting characteristics. For example, in order to retrieve records with values greater than $1,000 you would enter* ***>1000*** not ***>$1,000.00***.

Selecting on Character Fields

You can use the query process to select records based on the contents of the alphanumeric fields, as well as the date or numeric fields. For example, suppose you want to select records that were written to *Computer World.* Activate the query form by entering

[F3]

Remove the *Amount* selection criteria by entering

[Ctrl-backspace]

The query form is empty of selection criteria once again. Place the cursor in the *Payee* field by entering

←

To specify a particular payee simply enter the name into the column and process the query.

Computer World
[F2]

The program retrieves *Check date*, *Payee*, and *Amount* for the record that matches the query specification, Figure 4-12.

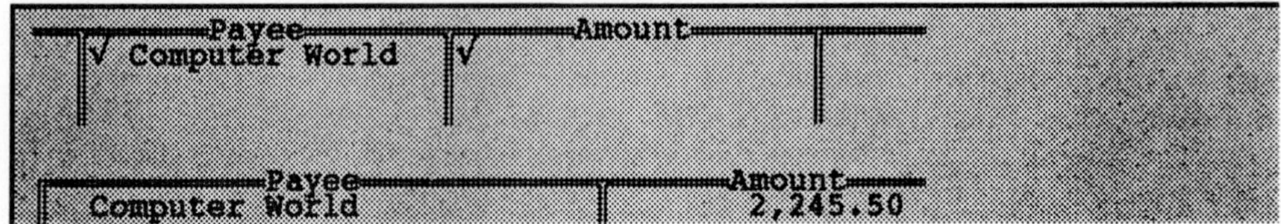

Figure 4-12 Record retrieved by payee name.

Partial Matches

As with dates or numeric values, you may find that searching for an exact match is not the most practical way to locate a record. For example, suppose you wanted to locate records written to the telephone company. You might not recall the exact way in which the payee name was entered. One solution would be to retrieve all the records with the word *telephone* in the *Payee* field. The query form, like the zoom command, will recognize the symbol **..** (two periods) and a wildcard for any character. This means that the specification **..telephone..** will retrieve any record with *telephone* in the *Payee* field. Return to the query form and clear the existing specification.

[F3]
[Ctrl-backspace]

Enter the criterion using the wildcard symbols and process the query.

..telephone..
[F2]

The record retrieved contains the word *telephone* in the *Payee* field, Figure 4-13.

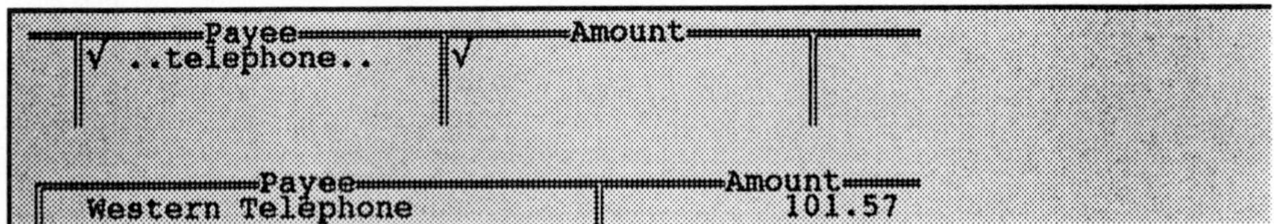

Figure 4-13 Wildcards used to retrieve record by Payee.

Selecting Blank Records

A special case in the area of selection is the selection of records that contain a blank entry in a given field. In order to allow you to retrieve records based on a blank field entry Paradox recognizes **blank** as a special operator which refers to blank field.

For example, suppose you want to locate any record that has a blank in the *Memo* field. Return to the query form and remove the current specification by entering

[F3]
[Ctrl-backspace]

Remove the field selection for the *Amount* field from the query form. Enter

→ [F6]

Select the *Memo* field for inclusion in the Answer table.

→ [F6]

If you want to select only those records that have blank values in this field, enter

blank
[F2]

The Answer table contains one record which is the only one in the Ck_book table that does not contain an entry in the *Memo* field, Figure 4-14.

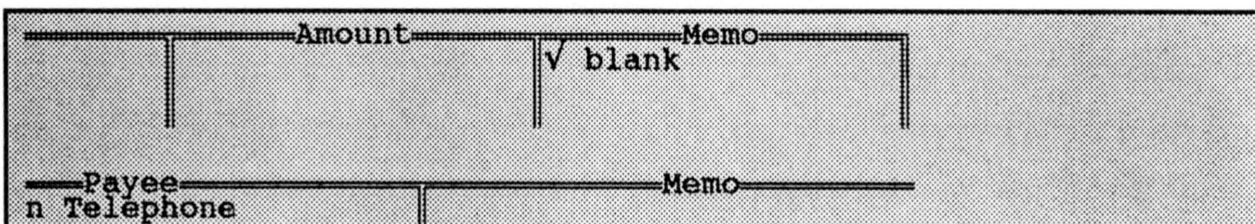

Figure 4-14 Record retrieved for blank field.

The Not Operator

The **not** operator is used to invert the logical meaning of a selection criterion. For example, the **blank** operator selects records that contain blanks in the specified field. However, you could retrieve all records that do *not* contains blanks by placing **not** in front of the **blank** operator, e.g., **not blank.**

Not can also be used with date, numeric, or character selection. For example, **not..telephone..** would retrieve all records that did *not* contain the word *telephone*.

As an example of how this operator works, change the selection in the *Memo* field column to **not blank**. Enter

[F3]
[Ctrl-backspace]
not blank
[F2]

Paradox now retrieves all the records in Ck-book, with the exception of the one record that has a blank *Memo* field, Figure 4-15. The **not** operator allows you to exclude records based on a logical criterion.

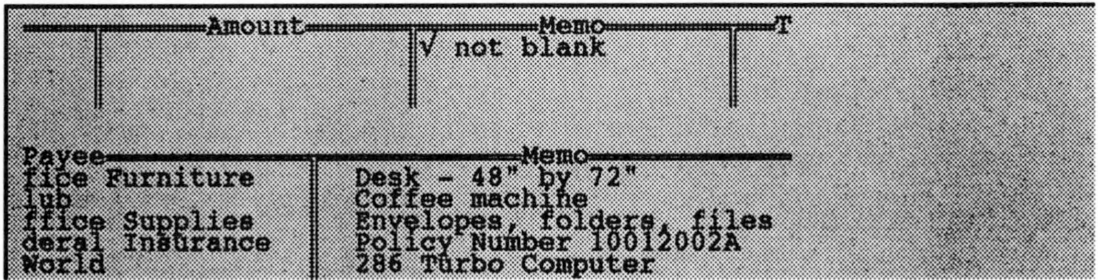

Figure 4-15 Not operator used in query specification.

Summary Operations

Up to this point, all the query operations have concerned the selection of fields and records from the database table, based on some logical criteria. The query form can also be used to calculate summary information, such as totals and averages of numeric fields. Summary calculations are carried out by using the **calc** operator. The use of the operator in a field column is combined with one of the five types of summary calculations available in Paradox.

Table 4-3 Summary Calculations

average	arithmetic average of field values
count	number of records retrieved
max	largest value in field
min	smallest value in field
sum	total values of field contents

To calculate the sum of a numeric field, you would place the operator **calc sum** in the field column.

The way that the calculation is carried out depends upon the field selections. Paradox produces one calculation for each unique group of records in the database table. The *uniqueness* of a record is determined by looking at the data in the selected fields. If the data in two or more records is the same for all the selected fields, Paradox will add together the values for both records into a single total. If the values are unique, i.e., they do not match exactly the data retrieved for the same fields in any other record, a total for that record alone is generated.

This may seem a very complicated and perhaps confusing way to handle summaries. However, when you put this concept into practical application, you will find that it actually makes summary calculations easy to obtain. For instance, if you calculate the sum of the *Amount* field with the *Check date* field selected, Paradox will generate a total for each unique date in the *Check date* field. In the Ck_book table there are six records, but some of the records have the same *Check date* (records 1 and 2 have the check date of 1/3/89). Paradox would add together both records and produce a summary total for 1/3/89.

If you select (√) a field such as *Payee* in which no two records contain the same value, then Paradox would produce one sum for each record. In this case the sum would actually be the same as the amount in the *Amount* field. Conversely, if *no* fields are selected, Paradox would produce a single total for the entire table.

It is important to keep in mind that when you are using a query form to calculate information, the process of field selection serves a different purpose than it does when you are simply retrieving records. When performing summary calculations you would probably want to avoid selecting a field with unique entries, since it would not generate any new information.

Summary calculations are usually performed with no fields selected (in order to obtain values for the entire table) or with fields that can divide the table into groups. For example, the *Tax deductible* field would produce two totals: one for deductible items and one for nondeductible items. The values in each group represent subtotals of all the records that have the same values in the selected field.

> *In most cases, you would probably not select the field upon which the calculations are being made. For example, in Ck_book, most calculations would be made on the* Amount *field. However, this field should not be selected with a √ because it would generate a subtotal for each unique amount. The information produced would be meaningless.*

Calculating Totals

The simplest type of summary information you can generate are calculations that use all the records in the table. For example, suppose you want to find the total of all the check amounts stored in the Ck_book table.

To get a single total that summarizes all the records in the database table you must make sure that there are *no* fields selected in the query form.

You can eliminate the selected fields one by one with [F6]. However, Paradox provides a shortcut for clearing all field and record selection items from a query form. This can be accomplished by placing the cursor in the query form Name column (the first column in the query form) and pressing the [Del] key. Activate the query form for the Ck_book table by entering

[F3]

You can jump to the first column in the query form using the [Ctrl-Home] key combination. Enter

[Ctrl-Home]

Clear the query form of specifications by entering

[Del]

The program removes all the √ signs and any record selection criteria from the query form. The form is now blank, just as it was when you first displayed it.

To find the total of the values in the *Amount* field, move the cursor to that field column and enter the calculation operator. Enter

→ ***(4 times)***
calc sum

Process the query by entering

[F2]

Paradox produces an Answer table image that contains what appears to be a new field entitled *Sum of Amount*, Figure 4-16. The field contains a single value that is the total of all the values in the *Amount* field.

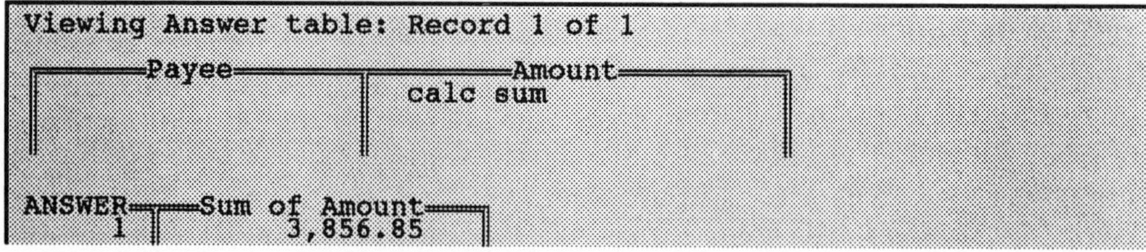

Figure 4-16 Sum of amounts calculated.

You can calculate the average value of the items in the amount field by changing the operator from **sum** to **average.** Enter

[F3]
[backspace] ***(3 times)***
average
[F2]

This time the Answer table contains a field called *Average of Amount* which contains the results of the calculation, Figure 4-17.

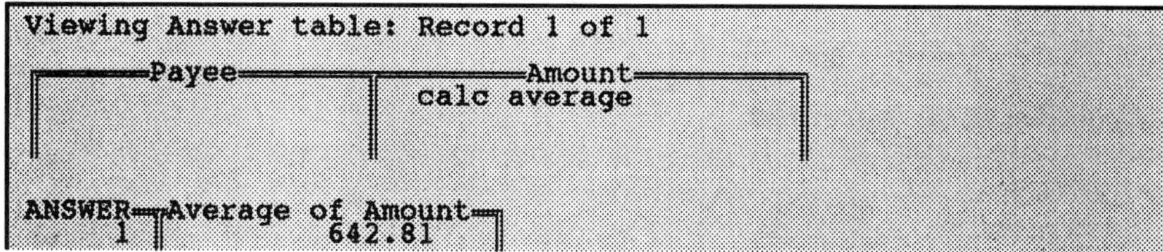
```
Viewing Answer table: Record 1 of 1
   Payee             Amount
                   calc average

ANSWER  Average of Amount
   1          642.81
```

Figure 4-17 Average value of amounts calculated.

A single query can be used to produce several calculated values. This can be achieved by writing more than one calculation instruction into the query form field column. The instructions are separated by a comma. For example, suppose you want to find the maximum and minimum values in the *Check date* field in order to know what range of check numbers has been entered into Ck_book table. In this example, you may want to find both values in a single Answer. Return to the query form and clear the current specifications by entering

[F3]
[Ctrl-Home]
[Del]

Move the cursor to the *Check number* field column by entering

→

The first calculation operator will be **min** to find the smallest value in the field. Enter

calc min

Place a second calculation operator in the same field that will calculate the maximum value for this field. Note that a comma is used to separate the two calculation instructions.

,calc max

The column width automatically expands in order to allow you to enter the second calculation instruction. Process the query by entering

[F2]

The Answer table that results from the query consists of two new columns *Min of Check #* and *Max of Check #*, Figure 4-18. The values returned in those columns show you the low and high values for the *Check #* field from the Ck_book table.

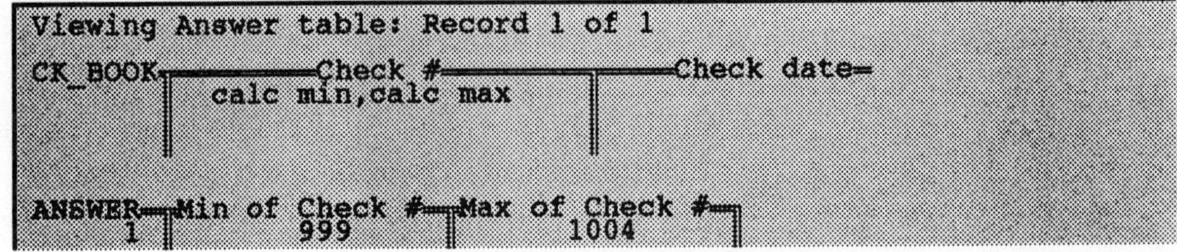

Figure 4-18 More than one value calculated.

The **min** and **max** operators can also be used on date fields to obtain range of dates contained in a date type field. Return to the query form and place the **min** and **max** operators in the *Check date* field. Try this on your own. The correct command can be found on page 117 under Exercise 1.

The result will show the dates 1/03/89 and 1/15/89 as the minimum and maximum dates in the *Check date* field.

Calculating More Than One Field

Paradox does not limit you to performing calculations in a single field. You may place **calc** operators in more than one numeric or date field. For example, suppose you want to know the range of dates in the *Check date* field and also calculate the total number of checks. You can achieve this result by adding a **calc** operator to the *Amount* field while retaining the current operators in the *Check date* field. Enter

[F3]
→ ***(2 times)***

The cursor is now located in the *Amount* field. Enter a **calc** operator that will sum the values in this field.

calc sum

Process the query by entering

[F2]

The Answer table that results contains three columns, one for each **calc** operator entered into the query form. The names of the columns identify the meaning of each of the calculated values, Figure 4-19.

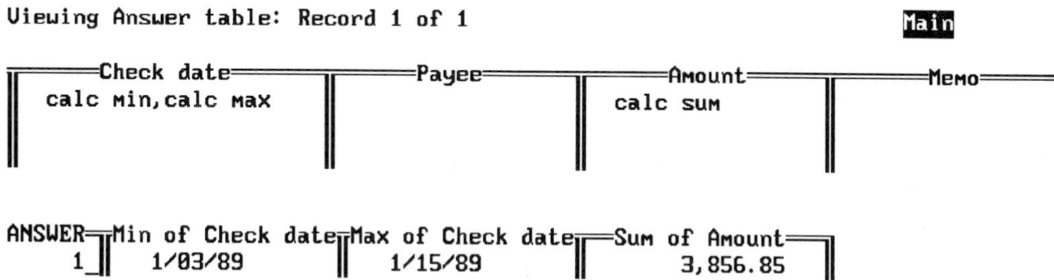

Figure 4-19 Calculations made on more than one field.

Clear the work area by removing both the Answer and query form images. Enter

[F8] ***(2 times)***

Calculating Group Subtotals

As mentioned, the field √'s perform a different function when a query is calculating values. In a record retrieval query, the field √'s select the field columns to be displayed in the Answer table. In a calculation query, the field √'s indicate how group subtotals should be generated. When one or more fields are selected as part of a calculation query, Paradox looks at the values in those fields and groups all records that have the same values in the specified fields together. For example, if you place a √ in the date field, Paradox will produce a subtotal for each unique date in the field. If two or more records have the same date, they will be added together into a single subtotal.

Should you √ more than one field, Paradox will look at all of the values in the √ fields in order to determine if the records should be combined into subtotals. For example, suppose you √ both the *Check date* and *Tax deductible* fields. A record must have the same value in both fields in order to be grouped together for a subtotal. Suppose two records have the date 1/03/89 in the *Check date* field but one is deductible and the other is not. Paradox would generate a separate subtotal for each record because only one of the two √ fields contains the same data.

This means when you are selecting √ fields for a summary calculation your purpose is to select fields that define specific groups into which records can be subtotaled. Fields with unique (*Check #*) or random (*Amount*) values should not be selected as part of a summary calculation query.

A good example of a field you might want to use for subtotals is the *Tax deductible* field. This field will contain either a Y or N dividing the records into two groups. By placing a √ in the *Tax deductible* field, you will automatically generate the total for deductible and nondeductible expenses.

Display a new query form for the Ck_book table by entering

a
ck_book ↵

Place the calculation operator for sums in the *Amount* field by entering

→ *(4 times)*
calc sum

To create subtotals for the deductible and nondeductible checks, place a √ in the *Tax deductible* field column by entering

→ *(2 times)*
[F6]

Process the query by entering

[F2]

The resulting Answer table contains two records, one for each unique entry in the *Tax deductible* field, Y or N, as shown in Figure 4-20.

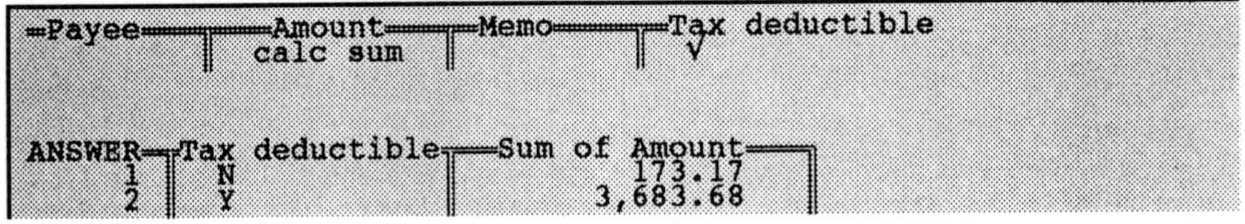

Figure 4-20 Subtotals generated by field selection.

If the √ were removed from the *Tax deductible* field and placed in the *Check date*, field you would generate a subtotal of each day, keeping in mind that some checks were written on the same date. Try this on your own. The correct command can be found on page 117 under Exercise 2.

The resulting Answer table contains four records. The values for the dates 1/03/89 and 1/08/89 are subtotals for the two checks written on those dates.

Remove the current images from the work area by entering

[F8] *(2 times)*

Counting Records

The **count** operator returns a count of the number of records in the database table. If you use a **count** operator in conjunction with a subtotal calculation, you can determine the number for records placed into each group. For example, when you subtotaled the table on the basis of the *Tax deductible* field you could obtain a value for the number for record totals in the Y and N groups. Display a query form for the Ck_book table by entering

a
ck_book ↵

Place two operators in the *Amount* field: one for **sum** and the other for **count**.

→ (4 times)
calc count,calc sum

Select the *Tax deductible* field to create the subtotal groups and process the query by entering

→ (2 times)
[F6]
[F2]

The resulting Answer table shows both the total amount for each group of records and the number of records included in each group, as shown in Figure 4-21.

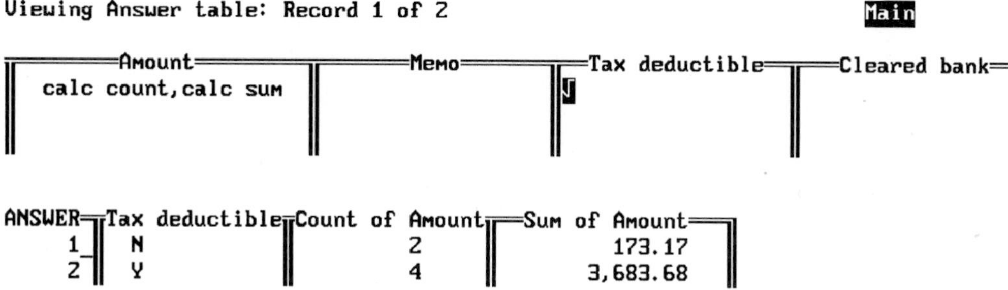

Figure 4-21 Subtotal groups counted and totaled.

Updating Queries

One of the advantages of the Paradox work area approach is that you can work with a variety of images at the same time. Each image represents a specific table, query, answer, or other type of database *object*. The term *object* refers to one of the images in the work area.

> *It is important to understand that the term* **work area** *can refer to a larger area than the area visible on the screen. There can be more images in the work area than can appear on the screen at any one moment. The [F3] and [F4] keys will scroll the display vertically to reveal the other images. Despite the fact that not all these images are visible at the same time, they are still part of the work area.*

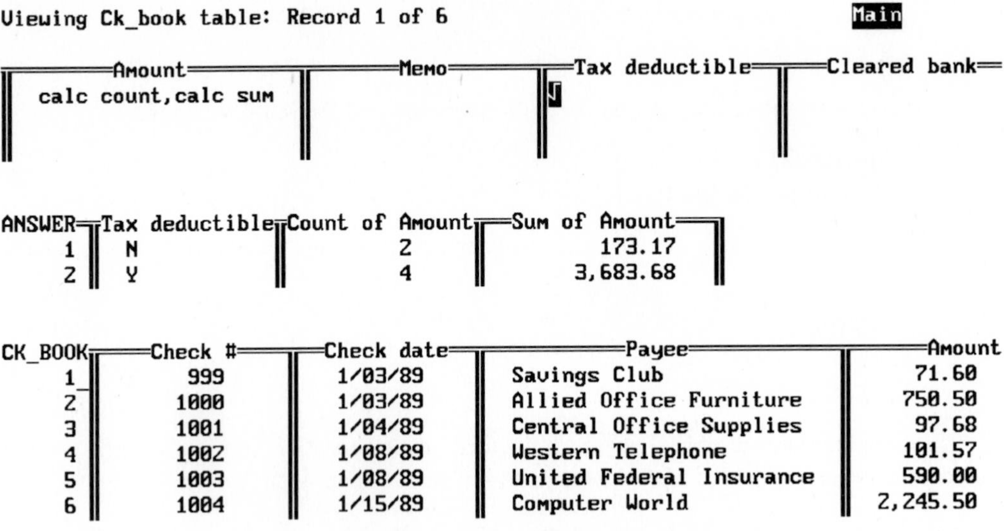

Viewing Ck_book table: Record 1 of 6 Main

Amount	Memo	Tax deductible	Cleared bank
calc count,calc sum		√	

ANSWER	Tax deductible	Count of Amount	Sum of Amount
1	N	2	173.17
2	Y	4	3,683.68

CK_BOOK	Check #	Check date	Payee	Amount
1	999	1/03/89	Savings Club	71.60
2	1000	1/03/89	Allied Office Furniture	750.50
3	1001	1/04/89	Central Office Supplies	97.68
4	1002	1/08/89	Western Telephone	101.57
5	1003	1/08/89	United Federal Insurance	590.00
6	1004	1/15/89	Computer World	2,245.50

Figure 4-22 Table image added to work area.

The Paradox work area concept allows you to view an image of the Ck_book database table along with the query form and Answer images. Use the **View** command to display an image of the entire Ck_book table. Enter

> **[F10] v**
> **ck_book ↵**

The database table image appears in the work area along with the query form and Answer images, Figure 4-22.

You can use the table image to edit or enter data. In this case, add new records to the Ck_book table. Activate the **Edit** mode by entering

> **[F9]**

To add new records, move the cursor to the last record in the file and expand the table using the ↓ key. Enter

> **[End] ↓**

A blank record is added to the end of the table. Fill in the record with the following data.

> **1005 ↵**
> **2/10/89 ↵**
> **Savings Club ↵**
> **157.89 ↵**
> ↵

n ↵
↵

Add another record to the table.

1006 ↵
Western Telephone ↵
237.67 ↵
↵ *(4 times)*

Note that pressing ↵ in the *Tax deductible* and *Cleared bank* field automatically enters the default values for those fields assigned through the use of the validity check settings. Complete the entry process by using the **Do-It!** command to write the new records into the disk file for the current table. Enter

[F2]

Note that changes made to the Ck_book table are not automatically reflected in the Answer table. Update the Answer table by processing the query form again. Enter

[F3] *(2 times)*
[F2]

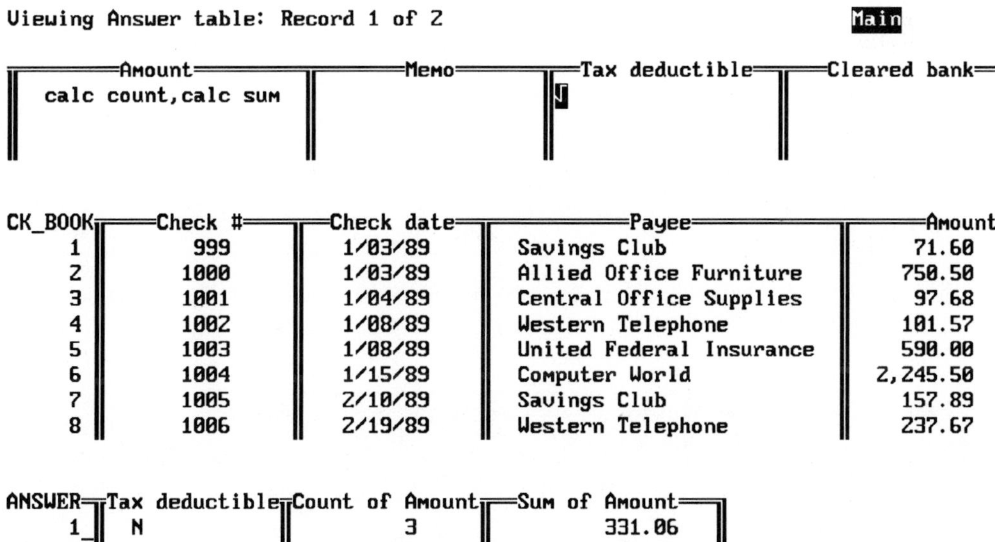

Viewing Answer table: Record 1 of 2 Main

Amount	Memo	Tax deductible	Cleared bank
calc count,calc sum		√	

CK_BOOK	Check #	Check date	Payee	Amount
1	999	1/03/89	Savings Club	71.60
2	1000	1/03/89	Allied Office Furniture	750.50
3	1001	1/04/89	Central Office Supplies	97.68
4	1002	1/08/89	Western Telephone	101.57
5	1003	1/08/89	United Federal Insurance	590.00
6	1004	1/15/89	Computer World	2,245.50
7	1005	2/10/89	Savings Club	157.89
8	1006	2/19/89	Western Telephone	237.67

ANSWER	Tax deductible	Count of Amount	Sum of Amount
1	N	3	331.06
2	Y	5	3,921.35

Figure 4-23 Answer table updated.

The Answer table image is removed from the screen and then replaced at the bottom of the screen with an updated table that reflects the current values stored in the Ck_book table, Figure 4-23.

Remove the images from work area by entering

[F8] ***(3 times)***

Selecting Records for Calculations

The calculations performed up to this point automatically included all the records in the database table. However, you can combine record selection with query calculations. The result is a query that limits the records used in the specified calculation to only those that fill the selection criterion.

Suppose you wanted to calculate the total amount of the checks written to *Western Telephone*. Begin by placing a query form on the work area.

a
ck_book ↵

Enter the selection criterion into the *Payee* field.

→ ***(3 times)***
Western Telephone

Enter **count** and **sum** calculation operators into the *Amount* column. Enter

→
calc count,calc amount

Process the query by entering

[F2]

The Answer table shows that there are two records in the table that match the selection criterion, Figure 4-24. The total for the amounts of those records is $339.24.

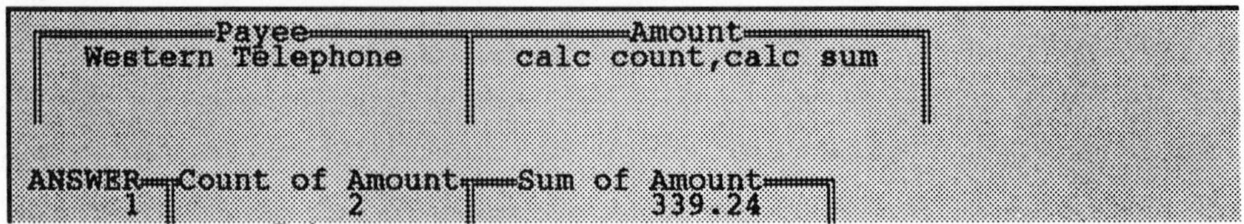

Figure 4-24 Calculation based on selected records.

Selecting by Month

The revised Ck_book table now contains checks written in different months. Suppose you wanted to calculate the total of only those checks written in January.

Selection by month is accomplished by using a partial date as the selection criterion. For example, to select January records you would use **1/..** as the selection so that all the records in month 1 would be selected.

> *Using* **1..** *in place of* **1/..** *will work as long as there are no dates from the months October (10) through December (12). In order to differentiate between 1/1/89 and 11/1/89 the inclusion of the / as part of the specification is necessary.*

Move back to the query form and remove the *Payee* specification by entering

[F3]
← [Ctrl-backspace]

Place the **1/..** specification in the *Check date* column and process the query.

←
1/..
[F2]

The Answer table includes only the six records from January and skips the February records.

Selection can also be combined with subtotal operation. For example, if you placed a √ in the *Check date* column of the query form, Paradox would produce subtotals for each unique date. However, the selection specification would limit the dates to the month of January. Enter

[F3] [F6] [F2]

All the subtotals produced are for dates that fall in the selected month, Figure 4-25.

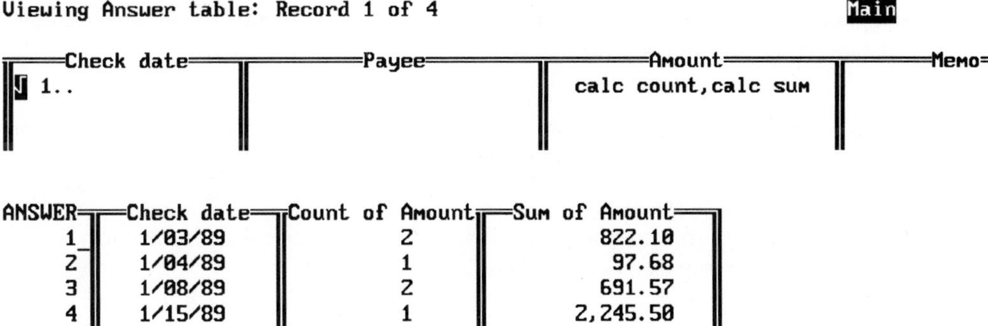

Viewing Answer table: Record 1 of 4
Main
Check date
Payee
Amount
Memo
√ 1..
calc count,calc sum
ANSWER
Check date
Count of Amount
Sum of Amount
1 1/03/89 2 822.10
2 1/04/89 1 97.68
3 1/08/89 2 691.57
4 1/15/89 1 2,245.50

Figure 4-25 Subtotals limited to a single month.

Remove the images from the work area by entering

[F8] ***(2 times)***

Multiple Column Criteria

All the selection operations are carried out with the query forms selected records—based on a single condition—entered into one of the query form columns. However, Paradox is not restricted to making selections based on only one field column at a time. You can enter more than one selection condition into the query form and process records based on a combination of all the selection criteria.

When you use more than a single selection condition, you need to consider the type of relationship you want to establish between the various conditions. There are two types of relations that can exist.

❑ **AND Relationship.** An **and** relationship requires a selected record to meet all the specified criteria. For example, if you specify **1/..** in the *Check date* field and **Western Telephone** in the *Payee* field, in order to be selected a record **must** have both a January date and a payee name of **Western Telephone**. Having one or the other would not be sufficient. **And** relationships are used when you want to narrow the scope of a retrieval.

❑ **OR Relationships.** An **or** relationship allows a record to qualify for selection if it meets **any** of the selection criteria. For example, if you specify **1/..** in the *Check date* field and **Western Telephone** in the *Payee* field, in order to be selected a record may have either a January date or a payee name of **Western Telephone**. **Or** relationships are used when you want to broaden a retrieval to include records that qualify in a number of different ways.

If you have more than two criteria, you may setup combinations of **and/or** relationships. The logic can get quite complicated as more elements are involved.

In keeping with its visual orientation, Paradox uses the row location of a selection specification to indicate the type of relationship.

❑ **Same Row.** If selection criterion are entered in more than one column but on the *same* row, Paradox assumes an **and** relationship between the specifications.

❑ **Different Rows.** If selection criterion are entered in more than one column but on *different* rows, Paradox assumes an **or** relationship.

Query forms can contain as many as 22 rows of specifications. Since each row is treated as having an **or** relationship with the other rows of the query form, the effect of a multiple row query is to add the records selected by each row to the Answer query. Row selection specifications can be entered into the same or different columns in each of the rows added to the query form.

However, Paradox requires that the fields selected be the same for all the rows in the query. This makes sense considering that the result of a query form is an Answer table. It would not be possible to retrieve a field for one record and not retrieve the field for others.

Put another way, when the query form contains more than one row, the fields must be the same for all rows, while the record selection conditions can vary from row to row.

If the same record is retrieved by more than one of the query form rows, it will appear only once in the Answer table.

Using "And" Relationships

Suppose you wanted to retrieve the *Amount* and *Payee* of all the nondeductible expenses in the month of January. This information requires two selection conditions: having **N** in the *Tax deductible* field and having a January date. This is an example of an **and** relationship because both of the conditions must fit a record in order for it to be retrieved.

Display a query for the Ck_book table by entering

a
ck_book ↵

The first entry in the query form will be a specification in the *Check date* column that selects only January records. Enter

→ *(2 times)*
1/..

Next, select the *Amount* and *Payee* fields with the √ command. Enter

→ [F6]
→ [F6]

The final step is to add a second selection condition in the *Tax Deductible* field that will select nondeductible expenses. Enter

→ *(2 times)*
N

Process the query by entering

[F2]

The records selected are the two nondeductible expenses made in the month of January, as shown in Figure 4-26.

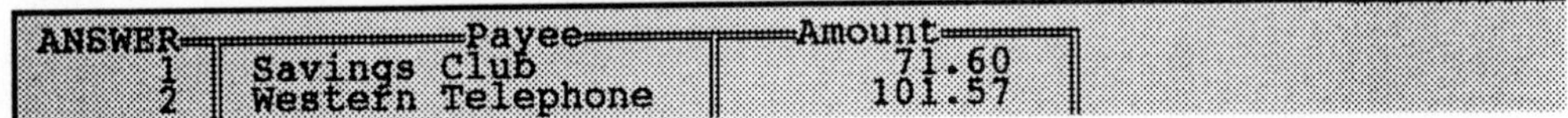

ANSWER	Payee	Amount
1	Savings Club	71.60
2	Western Telephone	101.57

Figure 4-26 Records retrieved based on multiple conditions.

Remove the images from the work area by entering

[F8] ***(2 times)***

"Or" Relationships

Up to this point all the conditions, field selections, and calculations have been entered on a single row of the query form. As mentioned, it is possible to add rows, up to a total of 22 rows, to a query form. What is the purpose of adding rows to a query form? Suppose you wanted to retrieve records for two specific payees, e.g., *Western Telephone* and *Savings Club*. One way to retrieve this data is to perform two consecutive queries, one for *Western Telephone* and another for *Savings Club*. The disadvantage of this approach is that the results of the first query are wiped out by the following query.

A better solution would be to find a way to include both groups of records in the same query. This requires the creation of a query in which there is an **or** type of relationship between two conditions. If both conditions apply to the same field, e.g., *Payee*, you can achieve an **or** relationship by using the **or** operator to separate individual conditions. The **or** is used in place of a comma, which signifies an **and** relationship.

Display a query form for the Ck_book table by entering

a
ck_book

Place the cursor in the *Payee* field column by entering

→ ***(3 times)***

In this instance, you want to select the records with payee names matching *Western Telephone* and *Savings Club*. To be on the safe side, avoiding abbreviations or capitalization differences, you will enter two conditions joined with an **or**. Enter

..tele.. or ..savings..

Select the fields to be retrieved, *Payee* and *Amount*, by entering

[F6] → [F6]

Execute the query by entering

[F2]

The resulting Answer table contains four records. The records are actually the results of two separate selection criterion combined into a single result by the use of the **or** operator, Figure 4-27.

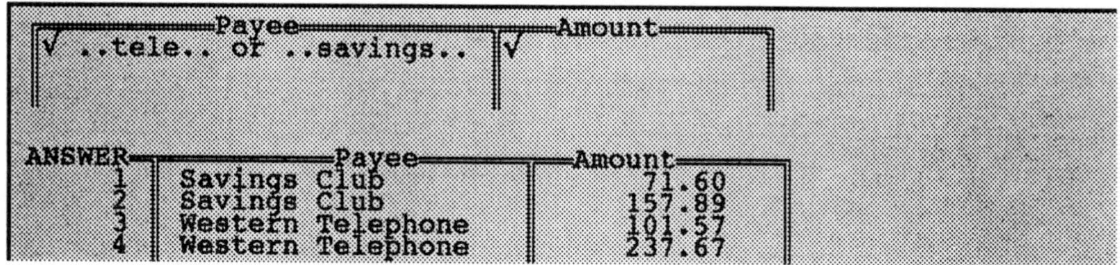

Figure 4-27 "Or" operator used to combine selection conditions.

Calculations with "Or" Relationships

You can use conditions combined with the **or** operator to calculate summary values as well as retrieve records. For example, suppose instead of listing the records you wanted to find the total amounts of the Western Telephone and Savings Club records.

To accomplish this, return to the query form and add a **calc** operator to the *Amount* column. Enter

[F3]
calc sum

Since this is a calculation query, you should remove the √ from the selected fields unless you want to produce subtotals. Remove the √ from the *Amount* and *Payee* fields by entering

[F6]
← [F6]

Process the query by entering

[F2]

The query produces a total for the selected records, $568.73. You can create separate totals for each group of records by placing √ in the *Payee* field. Enter

[F3] [F6] [F2]

The √ causes Paradox to produce one subtotal for each unique payee retrieved according to the selection conditions, as shown in Figure 4-28 on following page.

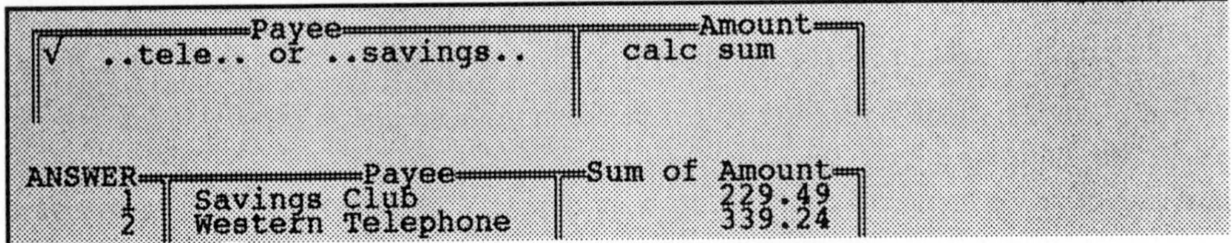

Figure 4-28 Subtotals produced from conditions combined with "or."

Remove the images form the work area by entering

> **[F8]** ***(2 times)***

Multiple Row Selections

The previous selection used the **or** operator to allow selection of records for two conditions within the same field column. But suppose the selection criterion required conditions in different fields to select records for a single query. Imagine you want to list all the nondeductible expenses. You also want the list to include any expenses of $500 or more, regardless of their deductible status.

An Answer table that meets these requirements would have to combine selection conditions that affect two different fields with an **or** relationship.

This type of query requires you to place each condition on a different row of the query form. If they are placed on the same row, Paradox would assume an **and** relationship and retrieve only the nondeductible records with a value of $500 or more. Display a query form for the Ck_book table by entering

> **a**
> **ck_book**

Begin by placing √ in the fields you want to retrieve, e.g., *Payee* and *Amount*. Enter

> **→** ***(3 times)***
> **[F6]**
> **→ [F6]**

You also need to place a condition into the *Amount* field to select records with a value of $500 or greater. Enter

> **>=500**

You have now set one of the two conditions required for the query. The next condition will use the *Tax deductible* field. Move the cursor to the *Tax deductible* column by entering

→ *(2 times)*

The selection criterion for this column is simple, the letter **N**, which selects the nondeductible records. However, since this condition should have an **or** relationship with the condition in the *Amount* column, it *must* be entered on the second row of the query form. Enter

↓

The cursor is now on row 2 of the query form. Enter the condition.

N

The two conditions will be treated as having an **or** relationship because of the different row positions, Figure 4-29.

```
Output  Design  Change  RangeOutput  SetPrinter
Send a report to the printer, the screen, or a file.
```

Figure 4-29 Conditions enter on different rows.

Process the query by entering

[F2]

Instead of producing an Answer table, Paradox displays the message **One or more query rows do not contribute to the ANSWER.** The message is a generic response to a query specification that Paradox cannot make logical sense out of. In this case, the error is related to the field selection √'s. When Paradox encounters conditions on different rows of a query form, it cannot process the query unless there is a common link between the rows which makes it clear how this data should be assembled into a single Answer table.

Generally this link is created by placing √'s in the same field column in all of the rows used in the query form. In this case, you added a condition to row 2 but you did not add the √ to the field columns. While it might seem logical for Paradox to assume that you want to use the fields selected in row 1 for all of the row, Paradox does not make that assumption. It is necessary to explicitly place the √'s in the field columns on all of the rows which contain conditions.

Add the √ characters to the *Amount* and *Payee* fields on row 2 by entering

← *(2 times)*
[F6]
← **[F6]**

With this correction made, process the query again by entering

[F2]

This time, Paradox can successfully process the query. The table that results lists all the records that are selected by either of the conditions, Figure 4-30.

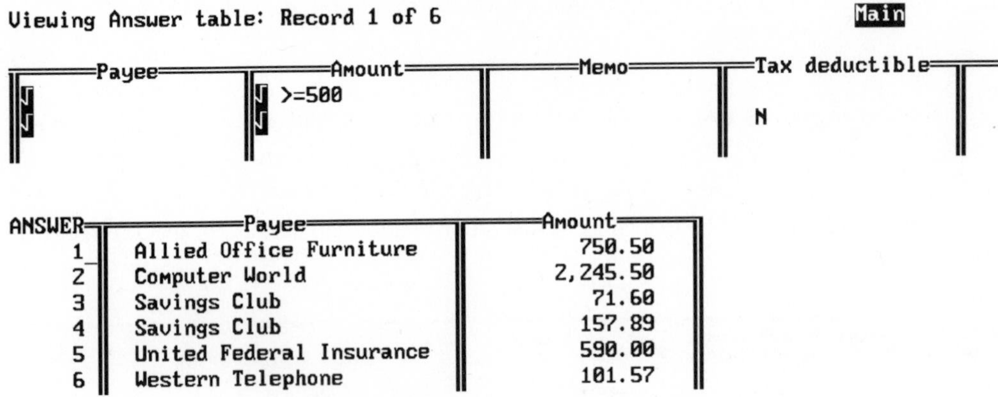

Figure 4-30 Multiple row query retrieves data.

Saving and Printing Answer Tables

In this chapter, you have experimented with queries that retrieve data and create summary information about the records stored in a database table. However, each successive query replaced the previous Answer table with a new Answer table. You may need or desire to save the information generated in a query in a more permanent form.

Paradox allows you to do so in two ways, as explained below.

❑ **Printing the Table.** You can create a printed, hard copy of the information contained within the Answer table. Paradox does not have a specific **Print** command. Instead, tables can be output to a printer through the **Report** command. As part of the **Report** command's options, Paradox includes the ability to send the current table to a printer. The form used to print the table is built into Paradox so that no additional report operations are needed in order to output the table.

> *You also have the option of creating a* text *file that contains the printed output in the form of ASCII compatible characters. Such a file can be loaded into and manipulated by word processing or desktop publishing programs, such as* Word, WordPerfect, Pagemaker, *or* Ventura.

❑ **Save the Answer as a Table.** You will recall that an Answer table generated by a query form is a complete database table in all respects, with the exception of its name, like the Ck_book table you manually created. You can preserve the table by changing its name so that it will not be replaced by future queries. The **Tools Rename** command allows you to change the name of a table—including the Answer table. It is important to understand that Paradox automatically creates a disk file, ANSWER.DB, each time a query is processed. In order to preserve an Answer table, it is not necessary to **save** the table since it is already saved on the disk. What you do need to do to **preserve** the table is to prevent it being overwritten by another Answer table. Hence **renaming** the Answer table has the effect of **saving** the table.

Keep in mind that when you preserve an Answer table, you preserve the data in the Answer table only. You do not preserve the query form which generated that Answer table. To preserve the query form itself, you must use the **Scripts QuerySave** command discussed on page 114.

Printing a Table

Paradox provides a facility through which you can create a printed copy of the data in a selected table. This procedure can be applied to any table including the Answer table generated by a query. All printing takes place through the **Report** command. Display the report menu by entering

[F10] r

This displays the Report menu, Figure 4-31. The simplest way to use this menu is the Output option. This option uses a built-in report form to print the data contained in the selected table.

```
Output  Design  Change  RangeOutput  SetPrinter
Send a report to the printer, the screen, or a file.
```

Figure 4-31 Report menu.

Select the Output option by entering

o

The program asks you to specify the name of the table you want to output. You can enter the table name or select it from the list of table names. Recall that if you want to select the table in which the cursor is currently positioned, enter ↵ twice. Enter

↵ ***(2 times)***

The next menu lists the report forms you can use for the output. Paradox supplies a predesigned report form labeled **R**, Figure 4-32, which can be used to output a table without taking the time to make a custom-designed report form.

```
R
Standard report
```

Figure 4-32 Selecting report forms.

Select the standard form by entering

↵

The final menu determines the destination of the printed report. You can select to send it to the printer, the screen, or store the output in an ASCII compatible text file on the disk. Select the printer by entering

p

The program will send the report to the printer. It should look like Figure 4-33.

```
12/11/89                          Standard Report                        Page  1


Payee                             Amount
-------------------------        ----------------
Allied Office Furniture                    750.50
Computer World                           2,245.50
Savings Club                                71.60
Savings Club                               157.89
United Federal Insurance                   590.00
Western Telephone                          101.57
```

Figure 4-33 Table printed as report.

Saving an Answer Table

If you wish to preserve the information in the Answer table, you can do so by changing the name of the table from Answer to a unique table name. The term *unique* is used to indicate that you can use any valid table name, with the exception of the name *Answer* or a name that is the same as a table that already exists. The **Tools Rename** command is used to alter the name of a table. Enter

[F10] t

The first command on the Tools menu is **Rename**. Select the command by entering

r

You can use this command to change the names of tables, screen forms, report forms, Paradox scripts or Paradox graphs. Enter

t

The next step is to enter the name of the table you want to change. In this case, since the cursor is positioned in the Answer table, you can take the shortcut, ↵ twice, to select that table. Enter

↵ ***(2 times)***

Next, enter the new name for the table.

chk_ans1

The table now has the name CHK_ANS1 (*check answer 1*). Clear the Chk_ans1 table image from the work area by entering

[F8]

You can recall the data in this table using the **View** command. Enter

[F10] v
chk_ans1 ↵

Remove the image again by entering

[F8]

Saving the Query Form

It is important to understand the difference between renaming an Answer table and saving a query form. When you rename an Answer table, you are saving the data generated by a query form. When you retrieve that table, the data is independent of the original table and query form that produced it. If changes have been made to the original table, they are never reflected in the stored Answer table, because Paradox does not establish any links between the renamed Answer table and the table/query form combination that created it.

On the other hand, saving a query form stores not the retrieved or calculated data, but the specifications used to generate the Answer table. The primary advantage of saving the query form is that when the form is retrieved and processed, the answer table it produces reflects any additions, changes, or deletions made in the original table.

Renaming a table saves the results of a query, while saving the query form saves the method used to produce the results. Paradox saves query forms as Paradox *scripts*. A *script* in Paradox is a text file that contains instructions detailing how a Paradox operation should be carried out. Scripts are created in three ways, as explained on page 114.

❑ **Recording.** Scripts can be created by instructing Paradox to **record** all the keys you press while carrying out an operation. When you enter keystrokes into Paradox, the program responds to the data or instructions you enter. When a script record is active, it also stores a list of those keystrokes in a *script* file. The script can then be replayed at a later time when you want the procedure repeated. This process is commonly referred to as *macro recording* in other applications, such as WordPerfect or Lotus 1-2-3.

❑ **Saving Queries.** The specifications used in a query form can be recorded and stored as a script file. The script file can be used to restore the query form image to the work area without having to reenter all the conditions and √'s.

❑ **Direct Entry.** Scripts can be created using a text editor or word processing program by writing instructions in the Paradox Applications Language (PAL). When you create a script directly you are *programming* in the Paradox language. Programming is covered in Part 2 of this book.

If you created a query form you think you will want to use again, saving the query form can save you a great deal of time if you need to retrieve the data. The advantage of saving the query form as opposed to the Answer table is that when the query is processed again it will reflect changes made to the original database table.

Creating a Query Form Script

Suppose you want to save the current query form for reprocessing at some later time. When the cursor is located in the query form you want to save, enter the **Scripts QuerySave** command.

[F10] s q

The program prompts you to enter the name of the script. The script name will be used by Paradox as the file name for the script. This means that script names follow the same naming conventions as table names. Enter

chk_qry1 ↵

The query has been saved as a Paradox script. By using that script, you can create a query form with the exact settings as the current query by playing that script.

Remove the query from the work area by entering

[F8]

To process the query again you must use the **Script Play** command to play the query form script. Enter

s
p

Next, enter or select from a list the name of the script you want to play. In this case, enter

chk_qry1 ↵

The query form appears on the image exactly as it was when you created the script. Process the query by entering

[F2]

The results are processed exactly as they were previously. Exit Paradox by entering

[F10]
e y

Summary

This chapter discussed the basic techniques and procedures used to select fields and records for retrieval from a database table, including the calculation of summary data such as totals and subtotals.

❑ **Zoom.** The **Zoom** command is used to search a table for a specific field, record, or field contents and position the cursor at that location. The command is found on the Image menu. It can also be executed with the shortcut key combination [Ctrl-z].

❑ **Partial Matching.** By default, search or retrieval criteria require exact matches. However, when working with alphanumeric fields, you can specify partial matches using the wildcard symbols (..) or @. The .. matches groups of characters, while @ is a wildcard for a single character.

❑ **Ask.** The **Ask** command is used to perform database table queries. A query selects or analyzes information entered into a database table. Queries are created by entering specifications, instructions, or operators into a query form. When a query form is processed it creates an Answer table that holds the data described by the query form.

❑ **Query Forms.** A query form is a special type of image used for setting up a data retrieval query. The form has the same column setup as the database table to which it is related. The columns are empty when the form is first displayed. You can enter field and record selection specifications or use the query form to perform summary calculations on the database table.

❑ **Field Selection.** Fields are selected by placing a √ into the query form column of the fields you want to include in an Answer table. The [F6] will toggle the √ character on/off for the current column. If you use [F6] in the query form name column, the first column in the query form, all of the field √'s will be toggled. When retrieving records, field selection tells Paradox which fields to include. When the query is processing summary calculations, the field selection determines the creation of subtotal groups.

❑ **Record Selection.** The selection of records for an Answer table is determined by the use of record selection conditions. If no conditions are specified, all the records in the database table are processed by the query. You can use exact-match criterion or inequality operators such as >, <, <=, or >=. In alphanumeric fields, the partial-match wildcard symbols can be used to allow more flexibility in record selection. Note that the field in which a selection condition is entered need not be included in the Answer table display.

❑ **Summary Calculations.** A query form can be used to calculate statistical data such as totals, averages, maximum value, minimum value, or the number of records. The **calc** operator can be placed in any numeric (currency) field. If you are simply counting records, you can place the operator in any field. Calculation queries will recognize any selection conditions in the query and perform the calculations on only those records that qualify for selection. Field selection plays a different role in calculation queries than it does in retrieval queries. A field—or fields—selected in a calculation query is used to group records into subtotal groups. One subtotal is produced for each unique set of values found in the selected field or fields. Selecting a field with unique contents will create a listing of the actual record value since no two records can be combined into a subtotal group.

❑ **And Relationships.** Record selection conditions entered into the same field column and separated by a comma will be treated as having an **and** type of relationship, meaning that all conditions must be true in order to have a record selected. If the conditions are entered into different field columns, they will be treated as having an **and** relationship if they are written on the same row in the query form.

❑ **Or Relationships.** Selection conditions written in the same field column can be treated as having an **or** relationship if the **or** operator is used between conditions. Conditions written into different field columns will be treated as having an **or** relationship if the conditions are written on *different* rows of the query form. Note that each row in the query form must have the same fields selected, √, for the query to be processed correctly.

❑ **Printing.** You can produce a printed output of the contents of a table by using the **Report Output** command. The form of the report is built into Paradox and does not require any report specifications in order to print.

❑ **Renaming Tables.** An Answer table produced by a query is automatically overwritten by the next query processed. To preserve the results of a query as a table, use the **Tools Rename** command to give the Answer table a unique table name. Note that renaming an answer table saves the results of a query, not the query specifications themselves.

❑ **Saving Query Scripts.** You can save the current set of query specifications as a Paradox *Script* by using the **Scripts QuerySave** command. The saved script can be used to recreate the query form at a later date. The advantage of saving a query form is that when it is reprocessed, any changes in the original table will be reflected in the newly generated Answer table.

Exercises

Exercise 1 from page 96

[F3]
[Ctrl-backspace]
→
calc min,calc max
[F2]

Exercise 2 from page 98

Remove *Tax deductible* √.

[F3]
[F6]

Add √ to *Check date* field and process query.

→ ***(4 times)***
[F6]
[F2]

5

Screen Forms

In Chapter 2, you learned that Paradox allows you to display records in either a table or a form view. The Table view shows the fields as columns and the records as rows of data placed into the field columns, seen in Figure 5-1 on the following page. The Form view uses the entire screen for one record. The field names are listed down the left side of the screen with the data placed to the right of each field name, Figure 5-2 on page 121.

> *The screen form is automatically generated the first time you use the command [F7] to display a table in the form view mode.*

The layout of the form used in the forms view mode is automatically generated by Paradox; however, you are not confined to this layout. The advantage of Form view is you can create up to 15 different screen forms for each database table. The forms are numbered 1 through 14. The first form, **F**, is designated as the default form. If you customize this form, it will automatically appear whenever you enter the form view mode, replacing the automatically-generated Paradox form.

Forms have the following advantages:

❑ **Layout.** When you design a form, you have total control over placement of all the information on the screen. You can select the screen location for any of the fields, or choose not to include a specific field in a form. You can also restrict entry into a field by making it a display-only field. The names of the fields are also under your control. You can create whatever type of label you want for each field or omit the field name entirely.

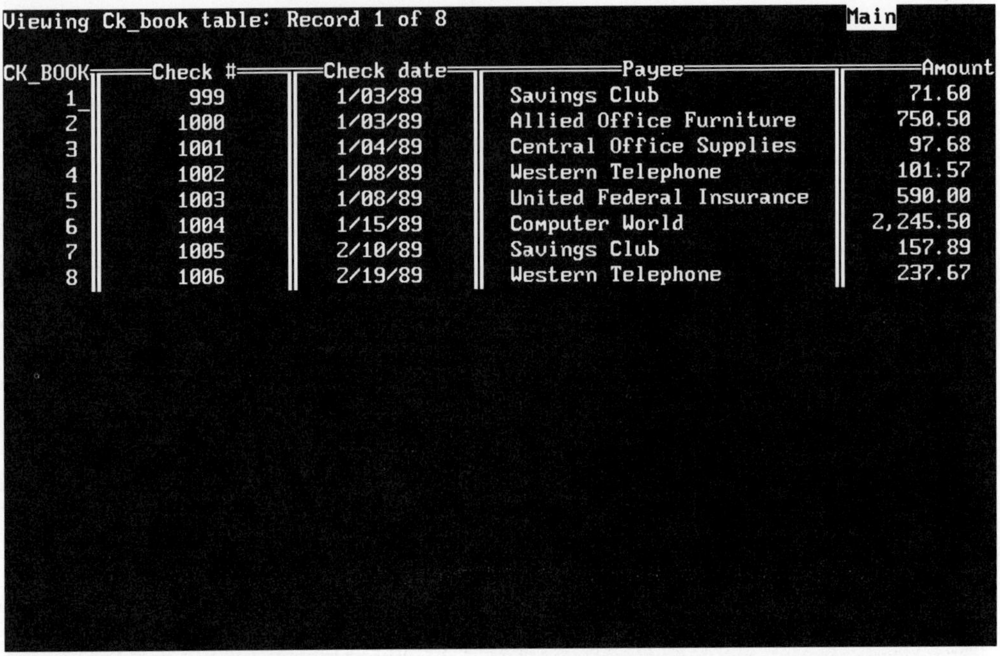

```
Viewing Ck_book table: Record 1 of 8                                Main
```

CK_BOOK	Check #	Check date	Payee	Amount
1	999	1/03/89	Savings Club	71.60
2	1000	1/03/89	Allied Office Furniture	750.50
3	1001	1/04/89	Central Office Supplies	97.68
4	1002	1/08/89	Western Telephone	101.57
5	1003	1/08/89	United Federal Insurance	590.00
6	1004	1/15/89	Computer World	2,245.50
7	1005	2/10/89	Savings Club	157.89
8	1006	2/19/89	Western Telephone	237.67

Figure 5-1 Data displayed in Table view.

❑ **Enhancements.** In addition to fields and field names, you can place a number of enhancements in the display form. This includes explanatory text of any kind, or lines and boxes. You can also control the colors or video attributes of the screen form.

❑ **Calculated Fields.** The only information that appears in the default table or form views is the exact information you entered into the database table fields. However, forms allow you to create calculated fields. These fields can display information calculated from the fields in the original table. For example, you may want to add or multiply the values in two fields to create a third value that would be displayed as part of the record. While calculated fields can operate on numeric values, they can also be used to manipulate dates or alphanumeric fields.

In this chapter, you will learn how Paradox screen forms are designed and used. As part of the example, you will expand the Ck_book table to include information about deposits and service charges so that you can use the table to keep a complete record of all the activity in the checking account.

To begin this chapter, load the Paradox program in the usual manner.

Creating a Screen Form

Screen forms are created using the command **Forms Design.** Existing forms can be modified using the command **Forms Change**. When you begin to design a form, you start with a blank screen. The process of designing a screen form is one in which you place the elements that you want to appear on the screen form, at the locations you desire. There are two basic items that can be placed on a screen form.

❑ **Fields.** In a screen form, a *field* placement is an area in which the data from the current records will be inserted into the form. When designing a form, the field information is not displayed. Instead, the location of the field is indicated by a series of dash marks, one for each character in the field. There are three type of fields that can be placed on a form. 1) A *regular* field displays the contents of the current record for the corresponding field. The data can be edited at this location when the table is in the edit mode. 2) A *display-only* field shows the data but does not allow the field to be edited. 3) A *calculated* field is one whose value is derived by means of a formula that uses values drawn from other fields. Calculated fields are always *display-only* fields.

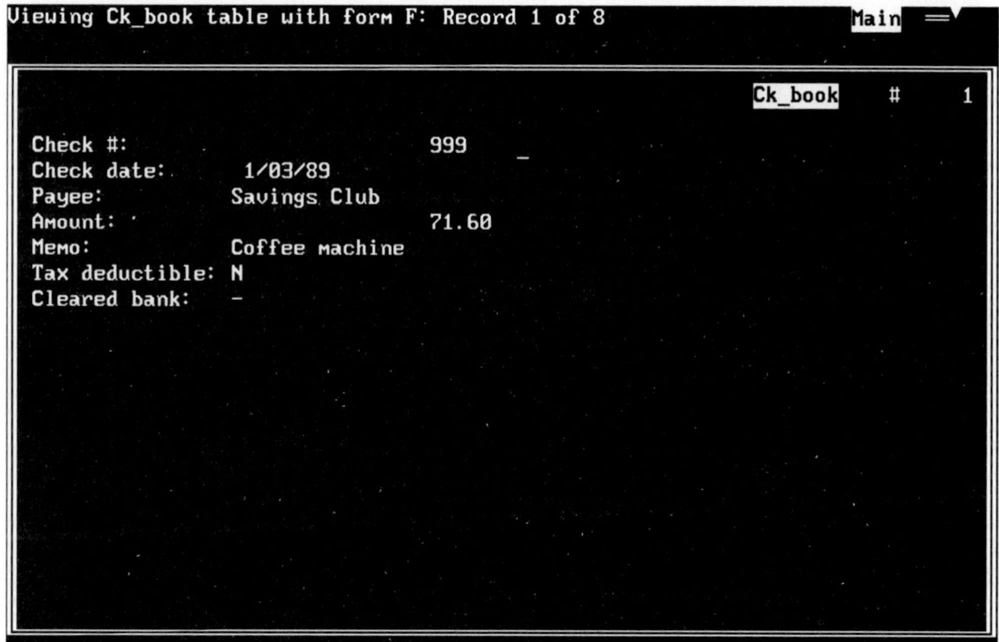

Figure 5-2 Data displayed in Form view.

> *All forms must contain at least one regular field. You cannot create a form that contains all display-only and calculated fields.*

❑ **Literals.** A *literal* is any character or group of characters that are placed onto the form. These characters will appear the same, regardless of what record is selected. The most common use of literal information is to label the field information. Keep in mind that when you place a field in a form, the field name is not placed on the form. If the field information needs to be identified, you must add *literal* text to the form to indicate the meaning of the field data. If the field information is self-explanatory, you may decide not to identify it at all. In addition to labeling fields, you can label text, lines, boxes, or other characters, to enhance the appearance of the form.

If desired, you can create a form that consists of multiple pages. A *page* in this sense is a screenful of information. Multiple page forms allow you to break up the data from one record into a series of screens that can be accessed with the [Pg Up] and [Pg Dn] keys.

As part of the form design you can also specify colors or, on monochrome screens, video attributes for specific areas of the screen.

The overall goal of screen design is to make the data stored in the database table as easy to read and understand as possible. Because forms allow you to control what the user sees, you can use different forms to present the data in different ways specifically designed for different tasks. For example, suppose you wanted to enter both checks and deposits into the Ck_book table. You could create separate screen forms for check entry and deposit entry, showing only those fields relevant to each activity. You might even design a form to use when you are reconciling a bank statement with your checking account.

Screen forms are stored in disk files that use the name of the table to which the form is related, with a file extension of **F#** where # is a number from 1 to 14, e.g., CK_BOOK.F1, CK_BOOK.F2, etc. The default screen form generated automatically by Paradox will have the file extension of **F** alone, e.g., CK_BOOK.F.

The first task will be the creation of a check entry form for the Ck_book table.

Starting a Form Design

All form design in Paradox is based on the structure of an existing table. You cannot create a form for a table that has not been created yet, nor can you place a field in a form that has not been added to the database table. In this way, Paradox can ensure that the form you create matches correctly the structure of the table it is meant to display. If you decide during form creation that you need a new field, you must exit the form design mode and restructure the table before you can place the field in the form.

The **Forms Design** command will display a blank screen form onto which you can place the field and literal information you desire. Enter

f
d

Paradox prompts you for the name of the table to which the form will be related. You can select the table from a list by pressing ↵ or you can manually enter the table name. Enter

ck_book ↵

The next prompt lists the 15 possible forms (1 through 14 plus F) which can be designed for each table, Figure 5-3. Note that this menu always lists the same information. You cannot tell from this display if any of the 15 forms already exists. In this case, the F form has been automatically created by Paradox. If you should select a form that already exits, Paradox will display an additional menu—Cancel Replace—to warn you that you are about to overwrite an existing form.

> *There is no requirement that you create forms in numeric order. You can create form 10 without having created any of the forms 1 through 9. However, since the forms are listed by number rather than by a descriptive name, it is probably best to work in numeric order to keep track of which forms you have used and which remain to be created.*

```
F  1  2  3  4   5   6   7   8   9   10   11   12   13   14
Standard Form
```

Figure 5-3 Select form menu.

Select designing form 1 by entering

→

Note that when the 1 is highlighted, the term *Unused form* appears below the menu. When you create a form, you will have the opportunity to create a descriptive name for the form which will appear in place of *Unused form* the next time the forms menu is displayed. These names are important because they indicate more clearly which forms exist and what their function is. Enter

↵

The next menu asks you to enter a descriptive name for the form you are creating, Figure 5-4.

The descriptive form name can be up to 40 characters.

```
Form description:
Enter description for the new form.
```

Figure 5-4 Enter descriptive form name.

Enter

Check Entry Form ↵

The program now enters the form design mode. As with all Paradox modes, the form design mode has a special type of screen display and a menu of specific commands that relate to this activity. Also keep in mind that nothing you do is saved until you execute the **Do-It!** command.

The Form Design Mode

When you enter the Form Design mode, Paradox presents you with a blank screen, except for the two lines at the top, Figure 5-5. The left side of the top line shows the form and the table being created, **Designing new F1 form for Ck_book**. On the right side, the word **Form** indicates that the form mode is active. The **1/1** indicates you are on page 1 of a 1-page form. On the left side of the second line, Paradox displays the cursor position in a <*line, column*> format. Each page of a form consists of 23 lines and 80 columns. The upper left corner is **< 1, 1>**.

```
Designing new F1 form for Ck_book                          Form      1/1
< 1, 1>
```

Figure 5-5 Form mode display.

In this mode, Paradox behaves like a text editor or word processing program. You can place characters (literals) anywhere on the form by moving the cursor to the desired location with the arrow keys and typing the text.

In this mode, you can use the following special keys:

Table 5-1 Form Design Mode keys

[Home]	move cursor to line 1
[End]	move cursor to line 23
[Ins]	toggle typeover/insert mode
[Del]	delete character
[backspace]	delete character to the left

Note that, in this mode, there is no distinction between using the → key and pressing [spacebar] to move the cursor to the right.

A form consists of literal text and other characters placed on the form along with fields. You can lay out a form in any sequence. For example, you might choose to enter all the field labels first, then place the fields, or visa versa. In many cases you will alternate between literal and field placement. As you gain experience with form design you will probably evolve an approach of your own that reflects your preference.

In this example you will create a form into which you can enter the check data. How should you design this form? One possible answer lies in a *model* of a check form layout you already have, i.e., the check itself. You may want to design your screen form to look as closely as possible like a check. Of course, this is only one of a number of possible approaches. The goal of form layout is to create a form that presents the data so that the reader can quickly and clearly understand the meaning.

If the form is to be used for data entry, you should consider the *source* document from which the information will be entered. In most cases, the data entered into a computer database is being read from a paper document of some type. The document could be an invoice, a check stub, or simply a note written on a pad. The *source* document is important in data entry because the order in which the data is written on the source document is the most logical way to order the fields on the screen form. This allows the person entering the data to work from top to bottom on the screen and the source document without having to jump around.

When possible, it is useful to create screen forms that relate to the source documents people are already used to working with. Keep in mind that because one table can have many forms, you can create special forms for entry and others that are more useful for data retrieval.

> *In rare circumstances data is entered without a source document, e.g., over the telephone and entered directly into the computer.*

Entering Text on a Form

Entering text on a form is quite simple. All you need do is place the cursor at the location where the text will be typed. In this case, begin with the text that will identify the *Check #* field.

move the cursor to 7, 5

Enter

Check No.
[spacebar]

Note that the text used to identify the *Check #* field does not have to match the field name. What is important is for the text to convey to the person reading the screen the significance of the field's contents. In some cases, this would require you to enter an explanation of the field—which could be a sentence or a short paragraph. This flexibility is one of the advantages of creating your own forms.

Placing a Regular Field

To complete the check number section, you need to place the *Check #* field on the form. This requires you to use the **Field Place** command from the Forms Mode menu. Enter

[F10]

Paradox displays the Forms Mode menu, Figure 5-6. The menu displays six options related to form creation.

- ❑ **Field.** This option allows you place, remove, format, or, modify fields in the current form.

- ❑ **Area.** This option is used for moving items to a new location in the form or, erasing a section of the form.

- ❑ **Border.** This option is used for drawing lines and boxes on the form.

- ❑ **Page.** This option creates or deletes additional screen pages.

- ❑ **Style.** This option is used to change the video attributes, such as colors or highlighting.

- ❑ **Multi.** This option is used to link the current form to other forms from other tables. This feature requires the existence of other forms and tables structured to link with the current table.

```
Field  Area  Border  Page  Style  Multi  Help  DO-IT!  Cancel  Form  1/1
Place, erase, reformat, recalculate, or wrap a field.
```

Figure 5-6 Forms Mode menu.

Select **Field** by entering

f

The Field option lists a submenu consisting of five different operations that can be performed on fields, Figure 5-7.

- ❑ **Place.** This option places a field into the form.

- ❑ **Erase.** This option is used to remove a field from a form.

- ❑ **Reformat.** This option is used to adjust the width of a field placed on the form.

- ❑ **CalcEdit.** If the field is a calculated field, this option allows you to edit the formula used to calculate the field's value.

- ❑ **WordWrap.** This option is used to change a long alphabetical field into a series of shorter lines. Paradox will wrap the entry in this field into a paragraph of shorter lines, similar to the way word processing programs wrap lines of text.

```
Place  Erase  Reformat  CalcEdit  WordWrap                Form      1/1
Place a regular, display-only or calculated field on the form.
```

Figure 5-7 Field submenu.

In this example, choose the Place option by entering

p

Paradox next displays the Field Place submenu, Figure 5-8. This menu lists the three types of fields—regular, display only, and calculated—which can be placed on the form. In addition, the #Record option is used to insert a special field that displays the record number of the current record in the form.

> *The #Record option is needed because calculated fields cannot use PAL-Paradox Application Language-functions in a field formula unless you are using Paradox Version 3.5 or later. An example of how to use PAL language functions in s standard screen form is provided in Appendix A of this book. In Part II of this book you will learn how PAL can be used to create screen forms with greater sophistication than can be created through the form design mode.*

```
Regular  DisplayOnly  Calculated  #Record                 Form      1/1
Place a field just as it is seen in the table.
```

Figure 5-8 Field Place submenu.

Here, select a *Regular* type of field by entering

r

Paradox next displays a menu that consists of the field name from the current table, Ck_book, Figure 5-9. You can select the field you want to place by moving the highlight with the ← or → keys to the name of the field you desire and then pressing ↵.

```
Field to place at cursor:                                    Form      1/1
Check #  Check date  Payee  Amount  Memo  Tax deductible  Cleared bank
```

Figure 5-9 Field names listed for placement.

In this instance, the *Check #* field is already highlighted. Place the field into the form by entering

↵

Paradox then displays instructions, Figure 5-10, that tell you to use the arrow keys to position the cursor at the location where the field is to be placed. This option shows that it is not necessary to position the cursor *before* you select the **Fields Place** command.

```
Use ↑↓←→ to move to where you want the field to begin...  Form  1/1
then press  ↵ to place it...
```

Figure 5-10 Select field location.

Place the field at the current location by entering

↵

Paradox inserts a line of 23 dash marks indicating where the field data will be placed. You can reduce or widen the field with ← or → keys respectively. Pressing ↵ will complete the field placement. In this case, reduce the size of the field to eight characters before completing the placement by entering

← ***(15 times)***
↵

The field is now placed into the form alongside the literal text, Figure 5-11. Note that when you press ↵, the dashes change to underscore characters.

```
          Check No. ________
```

Figure 5-11 Field placed into form.

The check date is usually placed in the upper right corner of the check.

move the cursor to 7, 55

When placing fields, it is important to keep in mind how the cursor will travel when this form is used for data entry or editing. When the Edit or Data Entry modes are active, Paradox will move the cursor from field to field. The cursor will start at the field positioned closest to the upper left corner of the form. The cursor will move to the next field down when it is advanced, unless one line contains more than one field. If a line does contain more than one field, Paradox will move to all the fields on that line, starting at the left and moving to the right, before it advances to the next line.

In this example, the *Check #* and *Check date* fields will both be positioned on line 7. The cursor will move first to the *Check #* field, then to the *Check date* field, before it advances to any fields below line 7.

Enter the text and the field for the check date.

Date →
[F10] f p r

Note that on the menu the *Check date* field is automatically highlighted. The *Check #* field does not appear on the menu because you have already placed it on the form. Enter

↵ ***(2 times)***

Shorten the field to eight characters by entering

← ***(3 times)***
↵

The next field to place is the *Payee* field.

***move the cursor to* 9, 5**

Enter the text and insert the *Payee* field by entering

Payee →
[F10] f p r
↵ ***(3 times)***

The form layout will look like Figure 5-12.

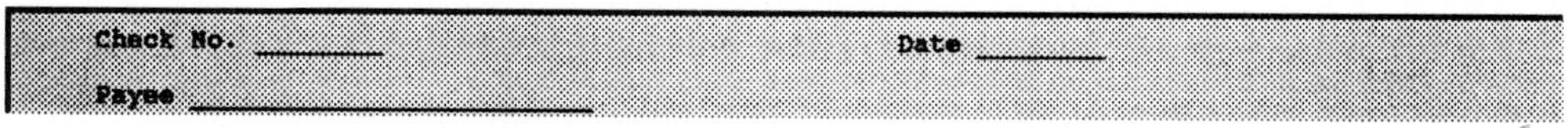

```
Check No. ________                         Date ________
Payee ____________________
```

Figure 5-12 Three fields placed on form.

Adding a Box

The next field to add to the form is the *Amount* field. On an actual check, the amount is usually preceded by a $ and enclosed in a box. You can duplicate that appearance on the screen. Begin by placing the *Amount* field on the form.

move the cursor to 9, 55

Type the label and insert the *Amount* field by entering

$ →
[F10] f p r
↵ *(2 times)*

Shorten the field width to 12 characters by entering

← *(11 times)*
↵

To complete this field draw a box around it. This can be done using the **Border Place** command. Enter

[F10] b p

You have the choice of drawing a single line box, a double line box, or drawing by repetition of a keyboard character. In this case, choose a single-line drawing by entering

s

To begin the drawing, you must move the cursor to the location of one of the corners of the box you intend to draw. Move the cursor to the lower right hand corner of the box you want to draw. Enter

→ *(2 times)*
↓

> *Note that while the border command is active, the line, column indicator is not visible.*

Anchor the corner of the box at this location by entering

↵

From this point on, the arrow keys will draw the box in the direction in which you move the cursor. Enter

↑ *(2 times)*
← *(2 times)*

You have drawn a box that can enclose a single character. Widen the box so that it encloses the entire *Amount* field by entering

← *(13 times)*

Complete the box by entering

↵

The *Amount* field is now enclosed in a box, as shown in Figure 5-13.

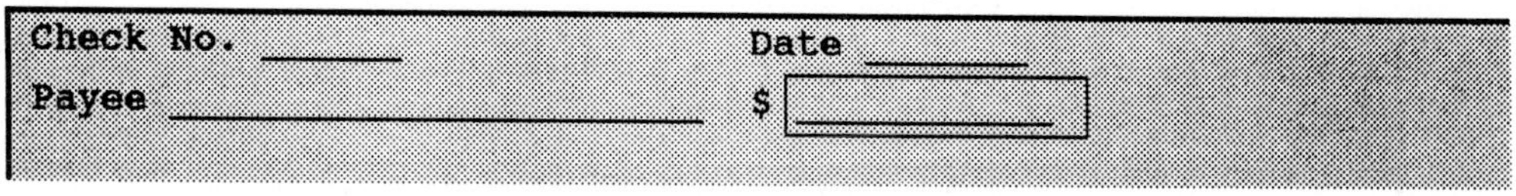

Check No. ______ Date ______
Payee ______________________ $ [__________]

Figure 5-13 Box added to form.

> *When drawing a box around a field, leave at least one space between the end of the field and the right side of the box. The space is needed because Paradox will display the editing mark, a solid <, to the right of the field being edited. If you do not leave the extra space the < will overwrite a line on the right side of the box.*

Wrapped Fields

The next field to be placed is the *Memo* field. Fields like *Memo*, which are designed to contain text notations, will often be quite wide. However, a very wide field may disrupt the symmetry of a form. One solution, shortening the field width, can potentially hide some of the data. Paradox provides another solution in the form of a *wrapped* field. A wrapped field breaks up the field contents into a series of short lines. The operation is similar to the way a word processing program automatically wraps text lines to fit paragraph margins.

In this case, the *Memo* field is only 25 characters wide but it will serve to illustrate the technique. Begin by placing the text for the *Memo* field label on the form.

move the cursor to 11, 5

Enter

Memo →

Place the *memo* field at the current location, but limit the width to 10 characters by entering

[F10] f p r
↵ ***(2 times)***
← ***(15 times)***
↵

At this point, you have limited the *Memo* field to displaying just 10 of the 25 characters. In order to allow the rest of the text to be wrapped onto the lines below the field, you must use the **Field WordWrap** command to designate that the field's contents can be wrapped onto 3 lines (3 times 10 = 30 characters) which will display all of the characters in the field. Enter

[F10] f w

Move the cursor to the field you want to wrap and press ↵. Enter

← ↵

Enter the maximum number of lines for wrapping text. In this case, enter

3 ↵

Enhancing the Form

The form has all of the essential elements needed to enter the check information. However, one advantage of forms is that you can enhance the layout with items that, while not required, can make the form easier to work with. For example, you could use the **Border** command to make the form look more like an actual check. First, draw a double-lined box around the five fields you have placed on the form.

move the cursor to 4, 2

Select the **Border Place** command by entering

[F10] b p

Select drawing a double line by entering

d

Anchor the upper left corner of the box at that location and draw a box around the fields by entering

↵
↓ ***(10 times)***
→ ***(72 times)***
↵

The form now has an appearance similar to an actual check, as shown in Figure 5-14.

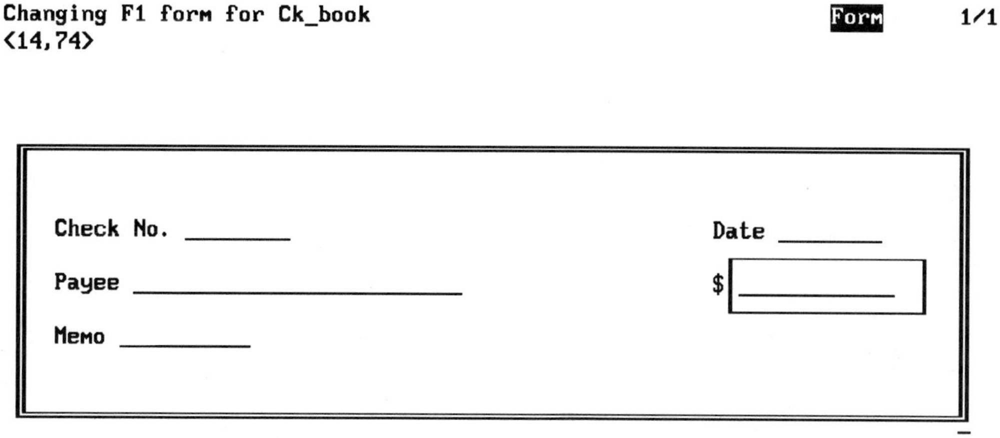

```
Changing F1 form for Ck_book                                    Form        1/1
<14,74>


  Check No. ______                                    Date ______

  Payee ____________________                          $ __________

  Memo ________
```

Figure 5-14 Form designed to look like a check.

Drawing with Special Characters

You could give the check a more three-dimensional look by drawing a *shadow* on the right and bottom sides of the box that encloses the check. In addition to the normal keyboard characters, MSDOS computers can display a number of special characters not shown on your keyboard. These characters are part of the IBM extended-character set. Each character in the set has a numeric value which can be used to enter a character that does not appear on the keyboard.

Table 5-2 Useful IBM extended characters

░	[Alt-176]
▒	[Alt-177]
▓	[Alt-178]
█	[Alt-219]

The characters are entered by holding down the [Alt] key and typing in the numeric value of the character on the numeric keypad. Note that you *must* use the keypad—*not* the number keys on the top row of the keyboard. Also keep in mind that you must hold down the [Alt] key while you type all of the digits in the number, releasing it only when you have entered the complete value of the character.

***move the cursor to* 15, 3**

Activate the border drawing by entering

[F10] b p

The Other option is used when you want to draw a border or line using a character, rather than the single or double lines. Enter

o

Paradox prompts you to enter the character you want to draw with. In this case, use character 178 by entering

[Alt-178]
↵

Draw a line of ▓ characters below the check box by entering

↵
→ ***(71 times)***
↵

Extend the shadow along the right side of the check box by entering

[F10] b p o
[Alt-178]
↵
↑ ***(10 times)***
↵

The shadow, constructed with repetitions of character 178, enhances the effect of the check drawn on the form, Figure 5-15.

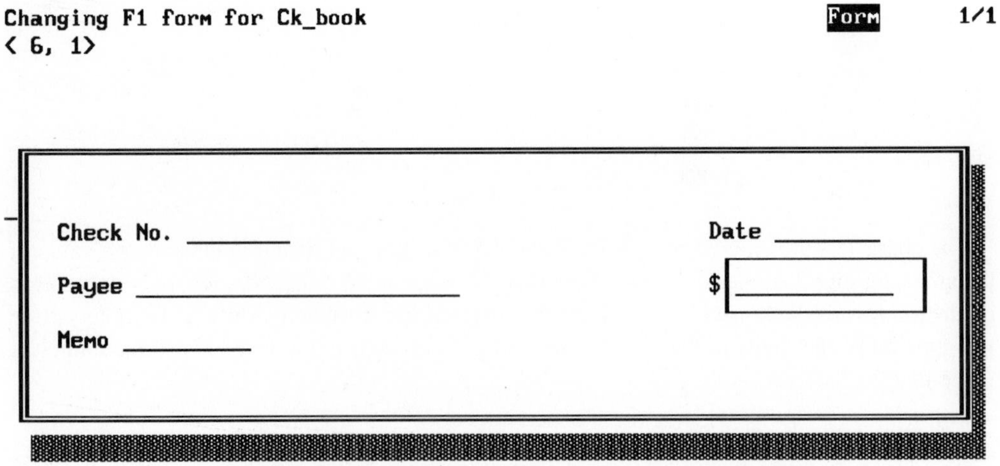

```
Changing F1 form for Ck_book                                  Form      1/1
< 6, 1>

  Check No. ______                                   Date ______

  Payee ____________________                         $ [__________]

  Memo ________
```

Figure 5-15 Shadow effect created on form.

Adding the Record Number

When you create a screen form, Paradox will not display the record number as part of the form. Keep in mind that the status display at the top of the screen will show something like **Viewing Ck_book table with form F1: Record 1 of 10**. However, you may wish to display the record number as part of the screen display. Paradox provides a special option of the Field Place menu which inserts a field that will display the record number of the check.

To add this special field to the current form, begin by placing the cursor at the location where you want the record number to appear.

***move the cursor to* 2, 25**

Enter the following text.

Check Book Database - Record
→

Display the Field Place menu by entering

[F10] f p

The #Record option places the special record number field into the form. Enter

#
↵ ***(2 times)***

Displaying Field Names

When you create a form, the locations of the fields are indicated by the underscore character. If you want to determine what table field is actually placed at those locations, you must move your cursor to the underscores.

***move the cursor to* 7, 60**

When you place the cursor on a field, the type and name of the field appear in the upper right corner of the screen, as shown in Figure 5-16.

```
 Form        1/1
Regular, Check date
```

Figure 5-16 Field identified in upper right corner.

However, you may find times when it would be useful to be able to see at a glance where the fields have been placed on the form. Enter

[F10] s f

The command has two options: Show which will display the field names on the form and hide which displays fields as underscores only. By default, the Form mode operates with the field names hidden. Enter

s

The field names now appear on the form indicating which fields have been placed at what locations on the screen, Figure 5-17.

```
Changing F1 form for Ck_book                                   Form       1/1
< 7,60>                                                   Regular, Check date

                       Check Book Database - Record #____

  Check No. Check #_                              Date Check da

  Payee Payee________________                     $ Amount______

  Memo Memo_____
```

Figure 5-17 Field names displayed on form.

Using Video Attributes

Another element that can be employed to add interest to screen forms is color, or in the case of a monochrome monitor, video attributes such as reverse video. Paradox allows you to change the colors or video attributes of any part of the screen form using the **Style** command. Begin by creating a new field below the check form.

move the cursor to 20, 25

Enter

Is this check tax deductible?
→

Insert the *Tax deductible* field next to this question by entering

[F10] f p r
↵ *(3 times)*

By default, the text and field will appear in normal video.

Suppose, however, that you wanted to enhance this section of the screen by changing the video from normal to a different color combination. Select the **Style** command by entering

[F10] s

The menu displays two options, **Color** and **Monochrome**, which provide means of changing the video attributes of part of the form. If you are using a color display, the **Color** command lets you select from a palette of color combinations. The **Monochrome** option allows you select reverse, bold, bold reverse, or blinking video.

Note that you can use the **Monochrome** option on a color screen. Paradox uses color combination that correspond to the monochrome effects based on the current screen colors.

Since **Monochrome** can operate on any type of screen, select that for this example by entering

m

The program displays two options, **Area** and **Border**. The **Area** option is used when you want to change a rectangular area of the form to different video attribute. The **Border** option will change only the outline of a select rectangular area leaving the interior of the rectangle in the original video. The **Border** option is not related to drawing borders. In this case, select **Area** by entering

a

Select a rectangle to change by entering

↓ ↵
↑ *(2 times)*
← *(32 times)*

The highlight covers the text and fields you have added below the check box. To select the video attribute for this rectangular area, enter

↵

Note that when you enter ↵ the highlight is removed from the screen. This does not mean that the operation is completed. The reason why Paradox removed the highlight, something that would normally be a clue that an operation is complete, is because you have to select the video attribute for the area. This can be done by pressing the ← or → keys. Each time you press one or the other, Paradox changes the video attributes of the selected area. In the upper right hand corner of the screen, Paradox displays the name of the current attribute, e.g., Intense, Blinking, Reverse, etc. The current attribute is **Intense**. See Figure 5-18.

If you are using the **Color** *command to change the area screen attributes in addition to the arrow keys, you can enter [Alt-c] which will display a rectangular palette showing all of the possible color combinations available for the area.*

```
Use → ← to switch between monochrome styles...        Form      1/1
then press ↵ to select the style you want.                  Intense
```

Figure 5-18 Select area video attributes.

Change the attribute to Reverse by entering

→

To make the change a permanent part of the screen form enter

↵

The area surrounding the tax deductible label and field are highlighted in reverse video, Figure 5-19.

```
Changing F1 form for Ck_book                                 Form     1/1
<19,24>

                     Check Book Database - Record #_____

   Check No. Check #_                             Date Check da

   Payee Payee_____________________               $ Amount______

   Memo Memo______


                   Is this check tax deductible?
```

Figure 5-19 Reverse video added to screen form.

Calculated and Display Only Fields

All of the fields you have placed on the form have been *regular* fields. In Paradox, a *regular* field is one that can be used to edit as well as display data. There are two other types of fields that can be placed onto a screen form: calculated fields and display only fields. Both of these types of fields place information on the screen form but cannot be used to edit information. Display only displays fields whose contents you want to protect from editing. Calculated fields are display only fields whose value is determined by an formula. Paradox permits you to create three types of calculated field formulas.

❑ **Arithmetic.** An arithmetic formula is used to perform a mathematical calculation which can include values from numeric (also currency) fields. The arithmetic operations are addition(+), subtraction(−), multiplication(*), and division(/). Paradox also recognizes () as indicating a change in the order of operations. Numbers entered into a formula are treated as literal numeric values. When you want to include a field value in a formula, the field name is entered surrounded by square brackets,[ ]. For example, suppose you wanted to display the value of the *Amount* field multiplied by 2. The formula would read: **[amount]*2**. You can include the names of any of the currency or numeric fields in the table within a formula. When a record is displayed in the screen form the value that apears for the calculated field is based on the values stored in that record.

❑ **Date Arithmetic.** When you are working with date fields, you can perform date addition or subtraction, that is, you can perform date arithmetic on date fields. Date arithmetic consists of date addition and date subtraction. Date addition takes place when you add a value to a date field, e.g., **[Check date]+45**. The field will display a date 45 days from the current date value of *Check date*. Date subtraction can be carried out by subtracting a value from a date or by subtracting two date fields. The formula **[Check date]−45** would yield a date 45 days prior to the value of *Check date*. However, if the table contained more than one date field you could perform subtraction between the dates. In that case, the value that would be returned would not be a date but a value equal to the number of days between the two dates. For example the formula **[date discharged]−[date admitted]** would result in the number of days, i.e., the elapsed time, between the two dates. Note that you cannot add two date fields.

❑ **Text Concatenation.** Concatenation—chaining—is used to combine alphabetical fields into a single display. For example, suppose a table contained the fields *First name* and *Last name*. If you wanted to display the full name as a single display-only field, you would create a calculated field that chains the text from both fields together, using the + sign to indicate concatenation. For example, the formula **[first name]+" "+[last name]** would combine the first and last names into a single field. Note that Paradox automatically trims the field contents to eliminate any blank space in the field not filled with characters. Because there is no blank space between fields, it is necessary to place a literals space between the two fields. Literal text is indicated by quotation marks. The literal " " surround the space with quotation marks. You can place any type of character into a literal. The formula **[last name]+', "+[first name]** inserts a comma and a space between the last name and the first name.

In this case, you will use calculated numeric fields to display additional information about the check amounts. Suppose that all of the purchases have been subject to a 7 percent sales tax. Because checks are written to cover the gross amount including tax, it might be useful to display the amount of sales tax charged to each item and the pre-tax amount of the purchase.

Both these values can be calculated from the *Amount* field assuming that there is always a 7 percent sales tax. First, you can calculate the pre-tax amount by dividing the amount by 1+tax rate, e.g., **[amount]/1.07**

. To find the amount of tax paid, simply subtract the pretax amount from the final amount, e.g., **[amount]-([amount]/1.07).**

Position the cursor in the lower left portion of the form.

move the cursor to 18, 1

Enter the following text:

Sales Tax Information
↵
Pre-Tax Amount ↵

Place the calculated field below the label *Pre-Tax Amount* instead of to the right of the label this time. Select placeing a calculated field by entering

[F10] f p c

The program asks you to enter the formula for the calculated field. Enter

[amount]/1.07
↵ ***(2 times)***

By default, the field width is 23 characters. Shorten the field by entering

← ***(13 times)***
↵

Add the label for the pre-tax amount calculation.

↵ ***(2 times)***
Pre-Tax Amount ↵

Enter the field which will calculate this value.

[F10] f p c
[amount] – ([amount]/1.07)
↵ ***(2 times)***
← ***(13 times)***
↵

The bottom left corner of the screen will look like Figure 5-20.

```
Sales Tax Information
Pre-Tax Amount
[amount]/1

Pre-Tax Amount
[amount]-(
```

Figure 5-20 Calculated fields added to screen form.

Saving the Form

When the form design is complete, e.g., Figure 5-21, you can store the form on disk by using the **Do-It!** command. Enter

[F2]

Paradox writes a disk file, CK_BOOK.F1, which will hold the layout you have created.

Using a Screen Form

Once you have created a screen form, you can use it for the same tasks as you would use the default screen form Paradox generates when Form view is activated with the [F7] key.

When you first activate the form view mode, Paradox will select the F form which it automatically generates. If you want to select one of the custom-designed forms, 1-14, you must use the **Image PickForm** command to select one of the custom-designed forms. When you select a form from the PickForm menu, the list will consist of the form numbers 1 through 14. Note that the list will always show only as many forms that actually exist for a given table. The form numbers need not be consecutive.

In order to aid you in selecting the form you want to use, Paradox will display the descriptive name entered for each form on the second line when you move the highlight to a form number.

```
Changing F1 form for Ck_book                                Form      1/1
<19,24>

                    Check Book Database - Record #____

  Check No. Check #_                          Date Check da

  Payee Payee____________________             $ Amount______

  Memo Memo______

                    Is this check tax deductible?
```

Figure 5-21 Form design complete.

> *If you want to have a custom-designed form appear by default when you press [F7], you need to place your custom design into the F form. This can be done in two ways. One way is to use the* **Forms Change** *command to modify the F form. If you already have a form designed that you want to replace the F form with, you can copy the form to the file name used by the F form. For example, if you wanted the Ck_book form 1(CK_BOOK.F1 file name) to replace the default form, you could use a DOS command to copy that form to the F form file: COPY CK_BOOK.F1 CK_BOOK.F*

In order to select a form with the **Image Pickform** command, you must already have an image of the table displayed on the work area. When the **Image Pickform** command is entered, it displays a list of those forms, if any, created for the table that is related to the active image. If there are no active images in the work area, entering the **Image Pickform** command will generate the message **Form toggle [F7] cannot be used here** in the bottom right corner of the screen. This message, while not stating so directly, means that you cannot pick a form unless you have already displayed an image of the table with the **View** command.

Selecting A Form

In order to display information in a custom-designed screen form, you must first display an image of the table to which the form is related on the work area. Use the **View** command to display the Ck_book table by entering

v
ck_book ↵

When the cursor is positioned in the table image for which you want to select a form, you can enter the **Image PickForm** command to display a list of available forms. Enter

[F10] i p

In this case there are two forms listed on the menu: F, which is the default screen form generated by Paradox and 1, which is the form you have created in this chapter. To display the descriptive name of the form move the highlight to the form number by entering

→

When the highlight is placed on the number **1**, the descriptive name entered into the form appears below the menu, Figure 5-22.

```
F 1
Check Entry Form
CK_BOOK  Check #
   1        999
   2       1000
   3       1001
```

Figure 5-22 Descriptive form name appears in menu.

Select this form by entering

↵

The form is loaded into Paradox and the current record, record 1, is displayed within the custom-designed form, Figure 5-23. Note that the calculated fields in the lower left corner of the form show the values determined by the formula entered into the form.

Also note that the text from the *Memo* field is wrapped into two lines rather than being truncated.

The custom form works like any standard form view display. Move to record 2 by entering

[Pg Dn]

Display the last record in the table by entering

[End]

```
Viewing Ck_book table with form F1: Record 1 of 8                    Main ═▼

                    Check Book Database - Record        1

   Check No.  999  _                                  Date  1/03/89

   Payee Savings Club                                 $      71.60

   Memo Coffee
        machine

Sales Tax Information
Pre-Tax Amount
   66.92                   Is this check tax deductible? N

Pre-Tax Amount
    4 68
```

Figure 5-23 Record displayed in custom designed form.

Editing with Forms

As with the default form generated by Paradox, you can use the custom-designed forms to edit existing records or enter new records. For example, suppose you wante to change the amount of record 8 to 247.67. Place Paradox into the Edit mode by entering

[F9]

The < symbol appears at the end of the *Check #* field indicating that the edit mode is active. Move the cursor to the *Amount* field by entering

Since you only need to change one of the characters in the field, use the Field View mode command [Alt-F5]. Enter

[Alt-F5]
← *(4 times)*
[backspace]
4 ↵

Note that when you changed the value of the *Amount* field, Paradox did not automatically update the calculated fields in the lower left corner of the form. In order to have the program recalculate those fields, you have to make the changes permanent by using the **Do-It!** command. Enter

[F2]

Paradox updates the calculated fields to reflect the new amount values.

You can add new records to the table with the form as well as edit existing records.

> *If you use the* **Modify DataEntry** *command instead of adding records through the Edit mode, Paradox will change the display to the Table view. You can only add new records with the Form view if the Edit view is used.*

Activate the Edit mode and display a new record by entering

[F9]
[End]
[Pg Dn]

Fill in the new record, record 9, with the following information.

1007 ↵
3/5/89 ↵
Fathead Software ↵
378.90 ↵

As soon as you entered the amount, Paradox calculated the value of the calculated fields. Continue the entry.

Spreadsheet Software ↵

Because the *Memo* field is a wrapped field, Paradox wrapped your text into two lines as you entered the memo text. Note that Paradox does not ensure that breaks will occur only between words.

Also pay attention to the fact that validity check settings created for the table operate in all of the forms used for that table. The default value for the *Tax deductible* field, set in the validity check as Y, appears automatically in the current form. Save the new record by entering

[F2]

Using Forms To Control Entry

The Ck_book table contains only one side of the checking account activity. The other side is the deposits made into the checking account. One question that might arise is whether or not the checks and the deposits should be placed into the same table or should they really be two different tables?

The advantage of placing both the checks and the deposits into the same table is that you can use the query operations to calculate the *balance* in the checking account.

The use of forms allows you to display only those fields that relate to a particular activity. In this example, you would add a field to the structure of the table for the deposit amount. To avoid confusion between the *Amount* and *Deposit* fields you would design a form specifically tailored for deposits in which only the *Deposit* field would appear.

The table would then hold both check and deposit information making it possible to calculate the current balance of the checking account.

Restructuring a Table

In order to record both the deposit and checks in the same table, it is necessary to add some new fields to the Ck_book table. You can add, change, or remove fields from a table using the **Modify Restructure** command. Note that when a field is removed all of the data that was contained in that field is lost and cannot be recovered.

In this case, you will add three new fields to the Ck_book table. Two are currency fields, *Deposit* and *Balance*. The third is a text field called *Period*. The *Deposit* field will be used to hold the amount of each deposit made. The other two fields will be used in subsequent chapters to calculate overall and monthly balances.

To modify the structure of the Ck_book table enter

[F10] m r
ck_book ↵

Paradox displays the structure of the table exactly as it was when you created the table in Chapter 2. To add new fields, move the cursor to the bottom of the table and add a new row to the structure by entering

[End]
↓

Add the new fields by entering

Deposit ↵
$ ↵
Balance ↵
$ ↵
Period ↵
A6 ↵

Save the new structure by entering

[F2]

Paradox will save the new structure and then update all of the files that are related to the Ck_book table. If you have modified or deleted a field from the structure, Paradox will remove that field and any calculated fields including that field from related files such as screen forms, reports, validity checks, and table settings. The program then displays the modified table.

The next step is to design a form that can be used for entering deposits.

[F10] f d
ck_book ↵
2

Enter a description for the new form as follows.

Deposit Slips ↵

Begin by drawing a box.

***move the cursor to* 5, 20**

Draw a double lined box using the **Border** command. Enter

[F10] b p d ↵
↓ *(15 times)*
→ *(35 times)*
↵

Add a single line across the top of the box.

***move the cursor to* 7, 21**

Enter the following to draw the box.

[F10] b p s ↵
→ *(34 times)*
↵

Place a title in the small box at the top of the larger box.

***move the cursor to* 6, 30**

Enter

Deposit Slips

The form should look like Figure 5-24.

Figure 5-24 Deposit Slip form.

The information needed on the deposit slip is much simpler than on a check. In this case, all you need to do is enter the date and the amount of the deposit. You will also need to enter a deposit number in the *Check #* field. This is because you have assigned the *Check #* field as a key field. Paradox requires a unique entry in this field in order for the record to be entered. Had you not selected a key field for the Ck_book table, you could simply leave the *Check #* field blank when you enter a deposit.

***move the cursor to* 10, 25**

Place the *Check #* field into the form by entering

Deposit No.
→
[F10] f p r
↵ ***(2 times)***
← ***(15 times)***
↵

The next field to place is the *Check date* field. In this case, you can use the *Check date* to double as the deposit date by simply changing the identifying text.

***move the cursor to* 12, 25**

Place the *Check date* field by entering

Deposit Date:
→
[F10] f p r
↵ ***(3 times)***

Finally, place the *Deposit* field onto the form. You might wonder why it is necessary to have a separate field for the deposit amount when you are using the same number and date fields as you do for the checks. The reason is that, in order to obtain a balance, you will need to have the values for checks and deposits in different fields—since one group must be subtracted from the other.

***move the cursor to* 15, 25**

Place the field by entering

Amount Deposited:
→
[F10] f p r d
↵
← ***(13 times)***
↵

Save the new form by entering

[F2]

Modifying Validity Check Settings

Before you begin the entry of the deposits into the table, you will need to make changes to the validity checks you created for the Ck_book table. First, the validity check setting for the *Check #* field restricts the entry to a range of values between 950 and 1500. In this case, you will want to number the deposits consecutively, 1, 2, 3, etc. This would not be possible so long as the validity check maintained the restricted range of values for the field.

> *Note that default validity check settings such as the one that inserts* Y *automatically into the* Tax deductible *field will not insert the default value unless the field is edited when a new record is added. Since the* Tax deductible *field does not appear on the Deposit form it will remain blank for all new records added using that form.*

In order to allow values between 1 and 1500, you will need to change the validity check for values for the *Check #* field. Begin by placing the table into the edit mode. Enter

[F9]

Select the **ValCheck** command from the Edit menu by entering

[F10] v

If you want to modify an existing validity check setting, select **Define**. Note that **Clear** will erase all of the validity check settings for the selected field. Enter

d

Select the *Check #* field by entering

→ ↵

In this case, you want to change the **LowValue** setting from 950 to 1. Enter

L
[Ctrl-backspace]
1 ↵

The message in the lower right corner, **Low value recorded**, indicates that you have successfully modified the validity check settings. Exit the Edit mode by entering

[F2]

Entering Deposits

Since there is already an image of the Ck_book table on the work area, select the deposit form for display. Try this on your own. The correct command can be found on page 158 under Exercise 1. With the Deposit form displayed, activate the Edit mode and display a new blank record by entering

[F9] [End] [Pg Dn]

Record the following deposits.

1 ↵
1/1/89 ↵
1700 ↵

You have entered the first deposit record. Create more deposits by entering

2 ↵
1/22/89 ↵
860 ↵
3 ↵
2/15/89 ↵
1400 ↵
4 ↵
2/25/89 ↵
900 ↵

Save the new records by entering

[F2]

When you exit the Edit mode the deposit form shows deposit 1. This record is now record 1. This is because the Ck_book table is automatically sorted according to the value in the key field, *Check #*.

The deposit form simplifies the data entry process by eliminating all of the fields that are not needed for the entry of deposits. This eliminates many keystrokes which would be needed to move to the correct field columns in the table view. By reducing the number of fields displayed, you also eliminate the possibility of entering the data into the wrong fields.

Multirecord Forms

One major difference between the form view and the table view is that in the form view only one record at a time is displayed. The form view also allows you to control which fields will appear on the form and at what location on the form. This provides you with a great deal of control about what is seen, what can be edited, and in what sequence.

However, there are circumstances where it would be desirable to be able to display more than one record at a time within a form. The form would still allow you to control the display of fields but you would also be able to place multiple record displays on the screen at one time.

Imagine that you want to reconcile your bank statement with the records in the Ck_book table. Since the table contains a field called *Cleared bank*, you can update the file by checking off the *Cleared bank* for each check or deposit that appears on your statement. While it is possible to perform this operation in either the standard table or form views, there are disadvantages to each method.

In the table view, it is difficult to view all of the necessary fields at once. It is necessary to move the cursor a great deal to reach the required fields. Creating a form would solve many of the problems. Only the fields that needed to be displayed would be displayed. You could protect all but the *Cleared bank* field from entry by making the other fields display only fields. The major drawback to the form method is that you can see and edit only one record at a time. The table view has the advantage that you can move the cursor down a particular column, quickly changing the value in a number of records.

Paradox provides a means by which you can combine the multiple record displays of the Table view along with the custom field layout features of a form. The technique is called a *multirecord* form. In this type of form, you can designate a section of the form to repeat a group of fields several times. When displayed, each repetition will contain the values from a different field in such a way that each row in a table displays values from a different field.

The number of records displayed in a multiple record form depends on how many repetitions of the field can fit onto a single form. One difference between a multiple record form and a table view is that the form can display more than one line for each record, while a table displays all of the fields for each record on the same row.

The next task is to create a multiple record form which will aid in marking the checks and deposits which have cleared the bank.

Creating a Multiple Record Form

Multiple record forms are created in much the same way as any custom-designed screen form. The multiple record quality of a form is an attribute added to the form while you are designing its layout by using the **Multi** command found on the Form menu. Create form 3 for the Ck_book table by entering

[F10] f d
ck_book ↵
3
Reconcile Bank Statement

You can place literal text onto the form just as you would any form.

***move the cursor to* 3, 25**

Enter the following heading

Reconcile Bank Statement

When you create a multiple record form, you begin by laying out the first group of fields which will display the first record. In doing so, you should keep in mind how the final form, with multiple copies of the fields, will appear. For example, you will want to enter column type headings rather than labeling each field individually.

In this case, you will need to place six fields on the form for each record: *Check #, Check date, Payee, Amount, Deposit*, and *Cleared bank.* Keep in mind that all fields with the exception of the *Cleared bank* field are display only fields. The only editable field will be *Cleared bank*. Begin by placing the *Check #* and *Check date* fields on the form.

***move the cursor to* 5, 8**

Place the *Check #* by entering

[F10] f p d
↵ *(2 times)*
← *(15 times)*
↵

Place the *Check date* field next to the *Check #* field by entering

→ (3 times)
[F10] f p d
→
↵ (3 times)

> *When a field is placed as a display only field, Paradox does not remove the field name from the list of fields. Regular fields can only be placed once for each record.*

In order to conserve horizontal space, place the *Payee* field on the line below the *Check date* field.

***move the cursor to* 6, 8**

Place the field into the form by entering

[F10] f p d
→ (2 times)
↵ (3 times)

Next, place the numeric *Amount* and *Deposit fields.*

***move the cursor to* 5, 45**

Enter

[F10] f p d
a ↵
← (12 times)
↵

Place the *Deposit* field next to the *Amount* field by entering

→
[F10] f p d
d ↵
← (12 times)
↵

The last field to place on the form is the *Cleared bank* field. This will be the only regular type field in the form, since it is the only one into which data should be entered.

***move the cursor to* 5, 2**

Place the *Cleared bank* field at this position by entering

[F10] f p r
→ *(6 times)*
↵ *(3 times)*

The form now looks like Figure 5-25.

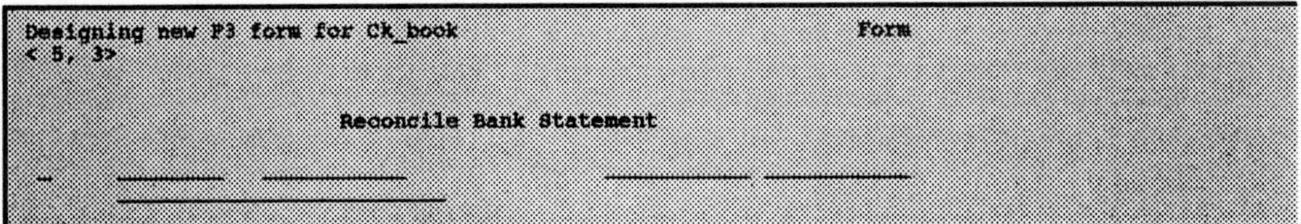
Designing new F3 form for Ck_book Form
< 5, 3>

Reconcile Bank Statement

Figure 5-25 First record placed in form.

Duplicating Field Blocks

Up to this point, the multiple record form has been created using exactly the same techniques and commands that are used to create any form. What makes a multiple record form different is that the initial group of fields placed into the form is duplicated one or more times on the same form. This *duplication* is accomplished with the **Multi Records** command. The command allows you to highlight an area of the current form which you want to duplicate. All of the literal and field information in that form is duplicated as a block.

In this case, you will want to duplicate lines 5, 6, and 7. Line 7, which is blank, is included as a separator between the records that will appear on the form. In some cases, you might choose not to include this extra space in order to get more records on the form.

Begin by entering the **Multi Records** command

[F10] m r

The **Multi Records** command displays a menu with three options: Define, Remove, and Adjust. In order to create duplicate regions you would use the **Define** command. Enter

d

Place the cursor at the beginning of the area that will make up the region to be duplicated. Enter

← *(2 times)*
↵

You can now use the arrow keys to extend the highlight over the area you want to define. In this case, you will want to define the region as all of lines 5, 6, and 7.

As a shortcut, you can highlight the entire line by moving the cursor to the left, not the right. Since the position of the cursor is in column 1, using the ← key to move the cursor will jump the cursor to right end of the line. This is faster than entering 79 → keystrokes. Enter

←
↓ *(2 times)*
↵

The region is now defined. Creating duplicates of this region is now a simple matter of entering the ↓ key. Each time you move down, the region is duplicated. If you make too many duplicates, the ↑ key will remove them one at a time. Add four duplicates of the region by entering

↓ *(4 times)*
↵

The form will now be able to display 5 records at one time. This is less than the 17 that can be displayed in the table view. However, the multiple record form allows you to have control over the field types and placement which will aid in data entry. Save the form by entering

[F2]

Activate the form by entering

[F10] i p 3

The display lists the first five records in the Ck_book table, Figure 5-26.

```
Viewing Ck_book table with form F3: Record 1 of 13

                        Reconcile Bank Statement
          1        1/01/89                                     1,700.00

  -       2        1/22/89                                       860.00

          3        2/15/89                                     1,400.00

          4        2/25/89                                       900.00

  -     999        1/03/89                          71.60
      Savings Club
```

Figure 5-26 Multiple record form display data.

Data Entry in a Multiple Record Form

You can now use the form to go through the table and mark all of the deposits and checks that appear on the bank statement with a √. Recall that the *Cleared bank* field has validity check settings that insert a – by default or a √ when the [spacebar] is pressed. Place the table into the edit mode by entering

[F9]

Suppose that the bank statement shows that deposits 1 through 3 have cleared the bank. Place √ characters into those records by entering

[spacebar] ↵
[spacebar] ↵
[spacebar] ↵

Because all of the fields except *Cleared bank* are display only fields, the cursor travels down the column one record each time you enter ↵.

Display the next group of records by entering

[Pg Dn]

The program display the next group of records using the multiple record form, Figure 5-27.

> *Note that when you use [Pg Dn] or [Pg Up] to display the next or previous screen of records, Paradox begins the listing with the last or first record from the previous screen in order to maintain continuity.*

```
Editing Ck_book table with form F3: Record 5 of 13

                     Reconcile Bank Statement
 -     999         1/03/89                       71.60
       Savings Club

 -     1000        1/03/89                      750.50
       Allied Office Furniture

 -     1001        1/04/89                       97.68
       Central Office Supplies

 -     1002        1/08/89                      101.57
       Western Telephone

 -     1003        1/08/89                      590.00
```

Figure 5-27 Next group of records displayed in multiple record form.

Mark checks 999 as cleared by entering

[backspace] [spacebar] ↵

Note that because the field already contained the character –, it was necessary to delete that character before you could type the [spacebar]. Repeat the action for the next three records. Try this on your own. The correct command can be found on page 158 under Exercise 2.

Skip checks 1003 and 1004 by entering

↓ *(2 times)*

Mark the next two checks as cleared by entering

[backspace] [spacebar] ↵
[backspace] [spacebar] ↵

Save the modified data by entering

[F2]

The multiple record form provides a means by which advantages of both the table and form view modes can be combined. In this example, you were able to speed the process of marking the cleared deposits and checks.

The database table now contains a great deal of information about the activity of the checking account. For example, since the deposit and check amounts are both entered, you should be able to calculate the checking account balance. You should also be able to reconcile the bank statement balance with the checking account balance by totaling all of the deposits and checks that have not been marked as cleared.

In the next chapter, you will learn how to use Paradox to answer these questions which involve more advanced forms of query operations and techniques for automating table processing.

Exit Paradox by entering

[F10] e y

Summary

Custom-designed screen forms allow you to gain control of how information stored in database tables is displayed on the screen. This control allows you to perform the following operations.

❑ **Form Design.** Paradox allows you to create up to 15 different screen forms that can be used to display the data contained in a database table. The F form is the standard screen form, automatically displayed when the form view mode is activated with the [F7] key. Although the F form is automatically generated by Paradox, it can be modified with the **Forms Change** command. Custom-designed screen forms allow you to determine which fields will appear, their width, and their location on the form. You can add literal text and enhancements such as boxes to the form. Forms are stored on the disk with files that use the table name and an extension, F#, e.g., CK_BOOK.F1, CK_BOOK.F2, etc. The standard form F uses the extension F only.

❑ **Field Types.** Fields placed onto a form can be one of several types: regular, display only, calculated, or wrapped. A regular field can be edited when the form is in the Edit mode. A display only field shows the field's contents but does not permit the user to edit the data. Display only fields are useful when you want to protect fields from accidental changes.

❑ **Calculated Fields.** A calculated field is a special type of display only field. Like display only fields, the data display can be seen but not edited. However, the information displayed in a calculated field is the result of a formula that can manipulate the data stored in other fields. Calculated fields can perform arithmetic calculations on numeric (currency) fields such as addition, subtraction, multiplication, and division. They can also carry out date arithmetic or can concatenate alphabetical fields.

❑ **Wrapped Fields.** Long fields can be designated as wrapped fields—fields in which the data is broken into several short lines instead of a single wide field. Wrapped fields are helpful in placing large fields on forms.

❑ **Enhancements.** You can add enhancements such as lines and boxes to the forms you create. Paradox also allows you to change the video attributes (color or monochrome) of specific areas of the screen.

❑ **Multiple Record Forms.** Typically, forms display data from one record at a time. However, you can use forms to create a modified table display in which more than one record appears. Multiple forms repeat a designated region of fields several times on the same form. Each repetition will display a different record. Multiple record forms combine characteristics of both form and table views.

Exercises

Exercise 1 from page 150

[F10] i p 2

Exercise 2 from page 157

[backspace] [spacebar] ↵
[backspace] [spacebar] ↵
[backspace] [spacebar] ↵

6

Query Operations That Change Tables

In Chapter 4, you learned how to use the basic features of the **Ask** command to create query forms that retrieve records, fields, and summary statistical data from stored tables.

In this chapter, you will learn about additional operations that can be accomplished through query forms, such as the ability to generate *calculated* fields and perform mass updates of database tables. These new techniques will demonstrate how you can calculate the checking account balance using the data stored on the Ck_book table.

Load Paradox in the usual manner in order to begin.

Calculated Fields in Queries

In Chapter 5, you were introduced to the concept of calculated fields. These fields were used in custom-designed screen forms, and displayed values based on formulas. You can perform similar operations using query forms to generate calculated fields. Calculated fields in queries can perform the same type of operations—arithmetic, date arithmetic, or text concatenation—as the formulas written for calculated fields on forms.

Query form calculated fields can be combined with other query form operations, such as records selection and summary calculations. For example, you can use a query to find the sum of a calculated field.

The main difference between formulas entered in screen forms and formulas entered in query forms is the way that existing fields are referenced. You will recall that in screen form calculated-field formulas, the names of the fields were surrounded by square brackets, [], when used in a formula.

However, query forms do not allow you to refer to fields by name in your formulas. Query forms use a different technique called an *example*. An *example* in Paradox is a name used to represent some potential value. That value may be a field, a specific value within a file, or the result of a calculation. Examples can be used for many purposes in Paradox to facilitate a variety of operations. Examples often function as *placeholders* within query forms or expressions. When a query is processed, Paradox tries to discern the significance of the example and generates information based on the given examples.

> *An example in Paradox is similar to a variable used in standard computer languages.*

To enter an example name, you must press the Example key, [F5], first. When you type the name, Paradox automatically highlights the example name. The highlighting is terminated when you complete the name. Paradox assumes that the entry of nonalphanumeric characters—a comma, a space, or an arithmetic symbol—indicates the end of the example name. Because of this automatic feature, it is not necessary to press [F5] at the end of each example name.

Example names can include the letters A–Z and the digits 0–9. You cannot include a space in an example name.

Calculated fields are generated from a query form by using the **calc** operator. Instead of using a summary operator, such as **sum** or **average**, you would enter a formula that performs arithmetic operations, such as addition, subtraction, multiplication or division on fields and numeric constants. Note that date arithmetic and text concatenation formulas can also be used, as long as the fields referenced are the correct field types for these operations.

Calculated Fields in a Query Form

In Chapter 5, you used calculated fields in the screen form to calculate the pre-tax value of the *Amount*, and the amount of sales tax included in the *Amount* field. Suppose you wanted to generate those same values through a query form. Begin by displaying a query form for the Ck_book table on the work area.

a
ck_book ↵

The first calculated field will use the formula *pre-tax=amount/(1+rate)* to list the pre-tax values of the amount. Position the cursor in the *Amount* field.

→ *(4 times)*

Select the *Amount* field for display in the Answer table by entering

[F6]

Assigning a Field an Example Name

The calculation requires you to multiply the value in the *Amount* field of each record by 1.07 (used for a sales tax of 7 percent). In the query operations in Chapter 4, you did not need to enter the field names as part of the query specifications. In Paradox query forms, it is the column location of the specifications that indicates which fields should be used. For example, the instruction **calc sum** does not mention which field should be summed. If the instruction is entered into the *Amount* field, Paradox infers that you want to sum the value in the *Amount* field.

However, when you want to create a new field based on a calculation you must make field references more explicit. The method used is to assign an example name to each of the fields you want to include in the formula. The example names can contain any number of alphabetical or numeric characters. However, unlike field names, example names are one word only, i.e., you cannot include a space in an example name.

When selecting an example name, you may want to choose one that is simpler to type than the field name. For example, you might use the name **x** for the *Amount* field. On the other hand, you could use the name **Amount** as the example name in order to maintain continuity with the field name.

> *The use of example names in place of field names may seem confusing. When using calculated fields, it would seem more logical to simply enter the field names—e.g., [amount]—the way they were entered into the formula used for screen displays. The query system in Paradox uses example names for a variety of different types of query operations. In order to fit into that system, it is necessary to assign an example name to each of the fields involved. One advantage of this system is that you can distinguish between fields in different tables with the same name by giving them different example names. This is useful when you are performing complicated queries that use data from more than one table.*

In this case, use the example name **amount**. To assign a field an example name, simply enter the name with the [F5] key. Enter

[F5]
amount

The name is highlighted, indicating it is an example name. Once you have entered this example name, you can refer to the *Amount* field by entering the example name **amount**. Remember that example names must always be entered with the [F5] key each time they are used in the query form.

Writing a Formula with an Example Name

Once you have created the example name for the field you want to include in the formula, you can enter a **calc** operator followed by the formula you want to calculate. It is interesting to note that this formula can be placed into any field column. Summary operations such as **calc sum** depend on the column location to indicate which field to operate on. Since **calc** formulas contain example names, Paradox uses the example name, not the column location, to determine what fields are involved in the calculation.

> *This makes sense when you consider a formula that references two or more fields in the same calculation.*

In this case, you can place the formula in the *Amount* column along with the example name. Separate the formula from the example name by entering

,

Note that the comma appears in normal video. Paradox automatically terminates the example name highlighting as soon as any characters other than A–Z or 0–9 are entered.

The first item in the formula is the **calc** operator, which is then followed by the formula. In this case, the formula will contain a reference to the example name **amount**. This reference is entered with the [F5]. Enter

calc
[spacebar]
[F5]
amount/1.07

The formula has been entered into the query form. The example name **Amount** is used to link the formula with the values stored in the *Amount* field, Figure 6-1.

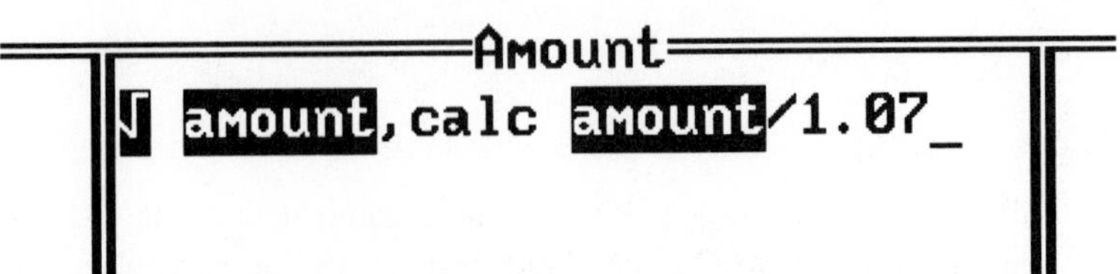

Figure 6-1 Example names used to create field formula.

Process the query by entering

[F2]

The Answer table produced by this query lists two fields: *Amount* and *Amount/1.07*. The *Amount/1.07* field contains the values calculated from formulas entered into the query form, Figure 6-2.

ANSWER	Amount	Amount / 1.07
1	71.60	66.92
2	97.68	91.29
3	101.57	94.93
4	157.89	147.56
5	247.67	231.47
6	378.90	354.11
7	590.00	551.40
8	750.50	701.40
9	2,245.50	2,098.60

Figure 6-2 Calculated field included in Answer table.

Blanks and Zeros

It is significant that there are only nine of the thirteen records in the Ck_book table. This is because the other four records contain deposit information. In those records, the *Amount* field is blank. Records that contain blank values in all of the selected fields will not be included in the Answer table since they would appear as blank lines.

But suppose one of the deposit records contained zero in the *Amount* field. How would Paradox treat that record?

To find the answer, change one of the records that currently has a blank in the *Amount* field to a zero. Enter

[F10] v
ck_book ↵
→ *(4 times)*
[F9]
0
[F2]

Record 1 now has a zero value in the *Amount* field. Execute the query again by entering the **Do-It!** command. Note that you do not have to be positioned in the query form in order to execute the query. Paradox executes the query form or forms currently on the work area whenever [F2] is pressed. Enter

[F2]

The result of this query shows that record 1 with its zero value is included in the Answer table, Figure 6-3.

ANSWER	Amount	Amount / 1.07
1	0.00	0.00
2	71.60	66.92
3	97.68	91.29
4	101.57	94.93
5	157.89	147.56
6	247.67	231.47
7	378.90	354.11
8	590.00	551.40
9	750.50	701.40
10	2,245.50	2,098.60

Figure 6-3 Zero value included in Answer table.

This illustrates that a blank field is treated differently from a field containing a zero value. If the value is zero, the record is included in query operations because zero is treated as a value. A blank field, however, will be ignored because it is seen to have no value. This distinction is important when you make calculations such as averages which would be lower if records with blank fields were included in the average.

It is also an important distinction when you want to process records as part of a query. If you want records with no value in a numeric field to be included, those records should have zeros—not blanks—in those fields.

> *You can use the Validity Check feature to set a default value of zero for a currency or numeric field so that records will not be entered with blanks.*

Change the field back to a blank. Enter

[F3]
[F9]
[Ctrl-backspace]
[F2]

Remove the full table image and reprocess the query by entering

[F8] [F2]

The record no longer appears because the field is now a blank, rather than a zero.

> *If the field is an alphanumeric text field, records with blanks will be included in query processing unless the* not blank *operator is used to exclude them.*

Naming the Calculated Field

When a calculated field is displayed as part of an Answer table, Paradox uses the formula by which the values were calculated as the field name. You can control the name of those field columns by using the **as** operator. The **as** operator allows you to specify a name to be used as the name of the calculated field in the Answer table. Add an **as** operator to the query form by entering

[F3]
[spacebar]
as Pre-Tax

Process the query again by entering

[F2]

The same data appears but the name of the calculated field has been changed to *Pre-Tax*, Figure 6-4.

ANSWER	Amount	Pre-Tax
1	71.60	66.92
2	97.68	91.29
3	101.57	94.93
4	157.89	147.56
5	247.67	231.47
6	378.90	354.11
7	590.00	551.40
8	750.50	701.40
9	2,245.50	2,098.60

Figure 6-4 Field name changed with AS operator.

You can add another calculation formula to the query to calculate the amount of sales tax on each item. Enter

[F3]
,calc
[spacebar] [F5]
amount-(
[F5]
amount/1.07) as Sales Tax

Calculate the query by entering

[F2]

The calculated field displays as part of the Answer table, Figure 6-5.

```
Viewing Answer table: Record 1 of 9                                    Main

═══════════════════════════════════Amount═══════════════════════════════════
√ amount,calc amount/1.07 as Pre-Tax,calc amount-(amount/1.07) as Sales


ANSWER══╤═══════Amount═══════╤═══════Pre-Tax═══════╤═══════Sales Tax═══╗
     1  │         71.60      │          66.92      │           4.68    ║
     2  │         97.68      │          91.29      │           6.39    ║
     3  │        101.57      │          94.93      │           6.64    ║
     4  │        157.89      │         147.56      │          10.33    ║
     5  │        247.67      │         231.47      │          16.20    ║
     6  │        378.90      │         354.11      │          24.79    ║
     7  │        590.00      │         551.40      │          38.60    ║
     8  │        750.50      │         701.40      │          49.10    ║
     9  │      2,245.50      │       2,098.60      │         146.90    ║
```

Figure 6-5 Calculated fields display data in Answer table.

Selecting Records for Calculated Fields

As with other types of queries, you can use a selection criterion to select only specific records for processing. Suppose that you wanted to limit the calculation to tax-deductible checks. To select just the tax-deductible records you need to place a condition in the *Tax Deductible* field. Enter

> → ***(2 times)***
> **Y**
> **[F2]**

This time, only the six tax deductible records are included in the Answer table.

Clear the work area using the [Alt-F8] command. This command removes all of the images currently displayed on the work area with a single keystroke. Enter

> **[Alt-F8]**

Date Arithmetic Formulas

Paradox can perform date arithmetic using the data stored in date fields. There are two types of date arithmetic that can be carried out.

❑ **Date Addition.** Addition can be performed by adding a value to a date. The value added to the date represents the number of days which should be added to the current date. For example, 1/1/89+10 would yield 1/11/89.

❑ **Date Subtraction.** Date subtraction can operate in two ways. If a value is subtracted from the date, the result is the date which is that many days in the past. If you subtract one date from another, the result is a value equal to the number of days that separate the dates. The value will be positive if the first date is newer than the second date, e.g., 1/11/89–1/1/89 = 10, or negative if the older date is first, e.g., 1/1/89–1/11/89 = –10. You can use the **today** operator to use the current system date as part of a formula. For example, the formula **today-date** would yield the number of days between the current date in the computer system and the date stored in the field related to the example name **date**.

Suppose that you wanted to calculate the number of days checks have been outstanding. Create a new query form by entering

a
ck_book ↵

Select the *Check #* and *Check date* fields to be included in the Answer table. Enter

→[F6]
→[F6]

In order to calculate the number of days since the checks have been written you will need to create a field-calculation formula. This formula will require the use of an example name which refers to the *Check date* field. In this case, use the name **written** as the example name of the *Check date* field. Enter

[F5]
written

Since you only want to calculate the days for checks that have not yet cleared the bank, you will want to place a condition in the *Cleared bank* field which will select only those records which have not cleared. Enter

→ *(5 times)*

By default, a dash character is entered into the *Cleared bank* field if the item has not cleared. Enter

-

Process the query by entering

[F2]

Paradox does not process the query. Instead, it displays the message **Expression makes no sense** in the lower right corner of the screen. In this instance, the use of the dash character is ambiguous because the dash also serves as the subtraction operator. In a similar case, by enclosing the character in quotation marks you can indicate that the character, here a dash, is meant as a selection condition, not as an operator. Change the expression by entering

[backspace]
"-"

The last step is to enter a formula that calculates the number of days. In this example, suppose today is 3/21/89. You can enter that date as a literal value into the date formula and subtract the *Check date* values from that date using the example name. Enter

,calc 3/21/89-
[F5]
written as Days

The date formula reads: **calc 3/21/89-written as Days**. Process the query by entering

[F2]

The query selects the four records that have not been marked as cleared and calculates the number of days since they have occurred, Figure 6-6.

ANSWER	Check #	Check date	Days
1	4	2/25/89	24
2	1003	1/08/89	72
3	1004	1/15/89	65
4	1007	3/05/89	16

Figure 6-6 Date arithmetic used in query form calculation.

The **today** operator can be used to automatically insert the system date into the formula. The operator would take the place of the literal date used in the current formula. Modify the formula to use the **today** operator by entering

[F3] [Alt-F5]
[Ctrl ←] ***(5 times)***
[Del] ***(7 times)***
today
[F2] ***(2 times)***

This time the current system date is used to calculate the number of days.
Clear the work area by entering

[Alt-F8]

Concatenation of Text

In addition to normal and date arithmetic, formulas can be used to perform text concatenation. Concatenation takes the text from two or more alphanumeric text fields and combines them into a single text output.

Suppose you wanted to list the payees, memo text, and amounts. Instead of using three fields, you could combine the *Payee* and *Memo* fields into a single field.

Display a new query form by entering

a
ck_book ↵

If you want to combine two fields with a formula, both fields must have example names. In this model, you will use simple example names to make the formula easier to enter. Assign the *Payee* field the name **p** and the *Memo* field the name **m**. Enter

→ ***(3 times)***
[F5] p
→ ***(2 times)***
[F5] m

Select the *Amount* field. Enter

←[F6]

In order to print the combined payee-memo text, you will need to write a **calc** formula that combines the two fields, using the example names assigned to those fields. You will also include literal characters—in this case, parentheses—to separate the payee from the memo text. Enter

calc
[spacebar] [F5]
p+"("+
[F5]
m+")"

The formula reads: calc **p**+"("+ **m**+")". Before you process the query add a condition to the query that eliminates records having no payees, i.e., deposit records. Enter

←
,not blank

Process the query by entering

[F2]

The formula displays the payee and memo information in a single field, as shown in Figure 6-7.

> *Note that calculated fields always appear on the right side of the Answer table following any selected fields. For information about how to control the field and record sequence of a query see Chapter 7.*

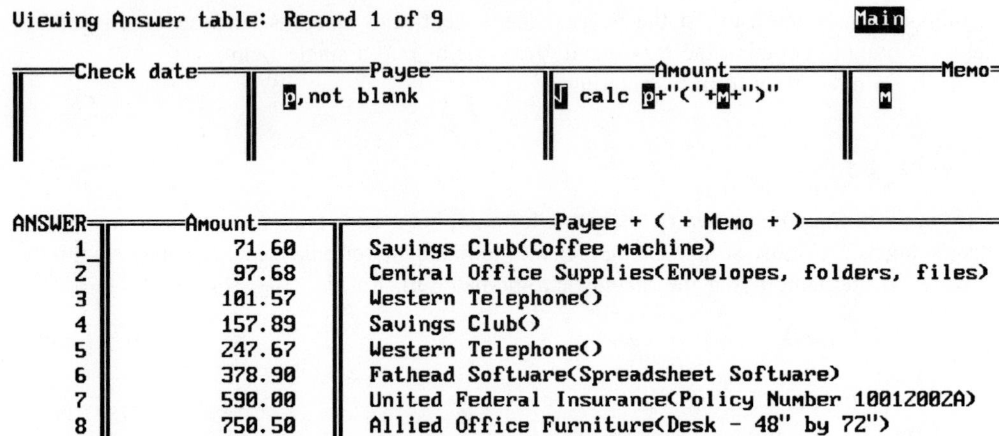

Viewing Answer table: Record 1 of 9 Main

Check date	Payee	Amount	Memo
	p, not blank	calc p+"("+m+")"	m

ANSWER	Amount	Payee + (+ Memo +)
1	71.60	Savings Club(Coffee machine)
2	97.68	Central Office Supplies(Envelopes, folders, files)
3	101.57	Western Telephone()
4	157.89	Savings Club()
5	247.67	Western Telephone()
6	378.90	Fathead Software(Spreadsheet Software)
7	590.00	United Federal Insurance(Policy Number 10012002A)
8	750.50	Allied Office Furniture(Desk - 48" by 72")
9	2,245.50	Computer World(286 Turbo Computer)

Figure 6-7 Concatenated field displayed in Answer table.

Clear the work area by entering

[Alt-F8]

Summarizing Calculated Fields

Suppose you wanted to calculate the total amount of sales tax for all the checks. On page 162, you used a formula to calculate the sales tax amounts for each check in the database table. However, those values were displayed as part of the Answer table. They were generated from, but not stored in, the Ck_book table. How would you obtain the total of a calculated field?

Perhaps you could combine the **calc sum** operator with a field formula. Display a query form by entering

a
ck_book ↵

Place the cursor in the *Amount* field by entering

→ ***(4 times)***

Assign the example name **base** (base value) to the *Amount* field by entering

[F5]
base

Enter a formula that uses the **calc sum** operator to total sales tax amounts. Enter

,calc sum
[spacebar] [F5]
base-(
[F5]
base/1.07)

Process the query by entering

[F2]

Paradox responds by displaying the message **Ambiguous use of example element base** in the lower right corner of the screen. Paradox cannot interpret the formula when the **calc sum** operator is used. While it might seem logical to obtain the sum of a calculated field in this manner, Paradox does not allow this approach.

For now clear the work area by entering

[Alt-F8]

Updates and Changes

How can you obtain information such as the sum of a calculated field? The answer involves the use of a **changeto** operator to make automatic updates and changes in a database table. **Changeto** is used in a query form to insert a value into a field automatically. Unlike manual editing, a single **changeto** operation can affect all the records in the table.

The value placed into the field can be either a literal or the result of a formula. If you want to place the same information in a series of records, you would use a literal value. For example, suppose you wanted to reset the *Tax Deductible* field so all records contained N. You would replace the current entry with a literal value, the letter N.

Using a formula to change values allows you to use information already stored in the records as the basis for the replacement value. This means the that new field information may vary from record to record. For example, you may want to store the sales tax amount in a new field by using a formula similar to *amount–(amount/1.07)*. In each case, the value created by the formula will depend on the value in the *Amount* field.

Also keep in mind that replacements can be done selectively. You might want to calculate the sales tax amount only for those records marked as tax-deductible. In such a query form, you would enter a record selection condition along with the **changeto** formula. The result would be that the change applies only to the records meeting the selection condition. In this way, changes can be applied to individual sections of the database table.

Keep in mind that when you place data into a field, the data and field types must match, i.e., numeric data must be placed into numeric (or currency) fields, dates into date fields, etc.

> *Like the Answer table, the Changed table is automatically deleted from the disk when you exit Paradox. Recovery of data from a Changed table must take place during the current Paradox session.*

The **changeto** operator represents a significant stepup in power. Up to this point, all the operations have concerned data entry and retrieval. The **changeto** operator generates data *indirectly*. Used effectively, the **changeto** operator can eliminate the need to manually enter data that can be created from existing data items.

The goal in any database system is to retrieve as much data as possible from the least possible amount of data entered. While the manual entry of many fields cannot be avoided, good planning can eliminate unnecessary entry, increasing the productivity of the database system.

In this example, your goal is to use the **changeto** operator in conjunction with other query form operations to obtain the checking account balance. However, before you find this answer, you can use the **changeto** operator to locate the total amount of sales tax.

Changing Field Values

On page 170, you saw that Paradox would not permit you to perform both a summary operation, **calc sum**, and a field calculation, **calc** formula, in a single query form. The total amount of sales tax can be found if you break the task into two steps: 1) Calculate the sales tax and store the values in a new field, and 2) calculate the sum of the new field's values.

Step 1 requires the use of the **changeto** operator to store the values in a field. This is in contrast to what happens when you calculate a field with a query form. The data generated by a query form calculation is stored in the Answer table, not the original table. It is important to keep in mind that changes made with a **changeto** operator overwrite data stored in the original database table. This means a **changeto** operation is potentially *destructive*. See page 180 for details about recovering changed data.

To see how this step works, you will use the **changeto** operator to place the sales tax values into the *Balance* field. While the name of the field may not suit the data, you can use this field because it is currently empty and it is the correct type.

Display a query form for the Ck_book table by entering

a
ck_book ↵

First, create example names for the *Amount* field. Enter

→ *(4 times)*
[F5]
base

The **changeto** operator is field column *dependent*. This means that Paradox uses the column location of the **changeto** operator to determine which field is to be changed. If the **changeto** operator is placed in the *Amount* field, it is the amount field that will be changed. In this example, you will want to change the values of the *Balance* field, which requires you to place the **changeto** operator in the *Balance* field column. Enter

→ ***(5 times)***

Next, use the **changeto** operator with the formula that calculates the sales tax amount. Enter

changeto
[spacebar]
[F5]
base-(
[F5]
base/1.07)

Process the query by entering

[F2]

The processing of a **changeto** query is a bit different from that of other queries. Instead of showing an Answer table, the program displays a table called *Changed*. The Changed table contains a copy of each of the records changed by the **changeto** operation, Figure 6-8. Unlike an Answer table, the Changed table contains the *old* information which was stored in the table *before* the **changeto** query modified the table.

> *It is possible to use the* **changeto** *operator to make self-referential changes. A self-referential change is one in which the field used for the* **changeto** *operator is the same field that is referenced in the formula. For example, suppose you wanted to replace all the data in the* Amount *field with pre-tax amounts,* Amount/*1.07. When this type of operation is executed, Paradox takes the current value of the field, uses it in the calculation, and then overwrites the current Amount value with the new calculated value.*

The Changed table serves two functions, as explained below.

❑ **Edited Range.** The records shown in the Changed table indicate which records in the original table were affected by the **changeto** operation. In instances where you use a selection condition as part of the query, this display helps you determine if the proper records were selected for change.

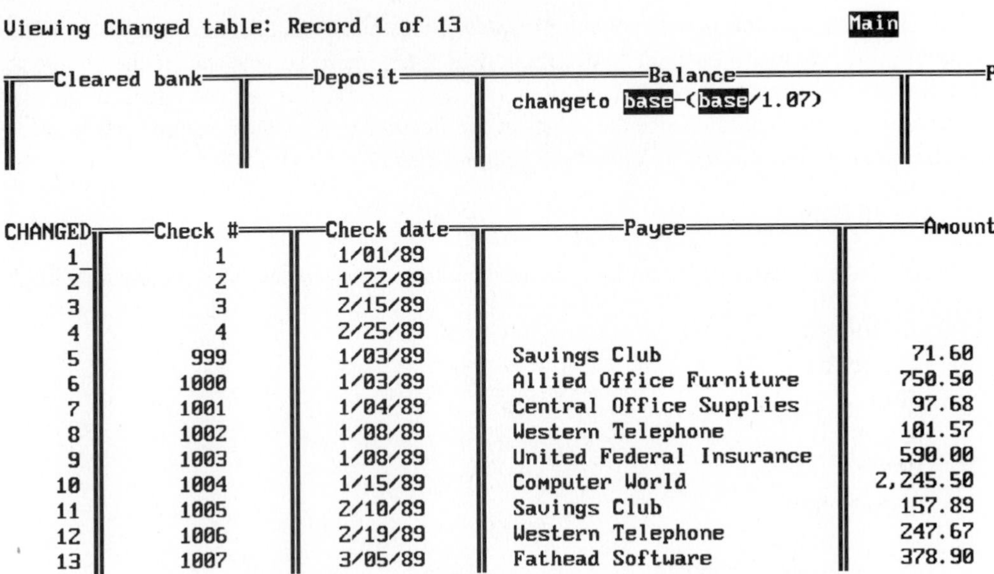

Viewing Changed table: Record 1 of 13 Main

Cleared bank	Deposit	Balance	P
		changeto base-(base/1.07)	

CHANGED	Check #	Check date	Payee	Amount
1	1	1/01/89		
2	2	1/22/89		
3	3	2/15/89		
4	4	2/25/89		
5	999	1/03/89	Savings Club	71.60
6	1000	1/03/89	Allied Office Furniture	750.50
7	1001	1/04/89	Central Office Supplies	97.68
8	1002	1/08/89	Western Telephone	101.57
9	1003	1/08/89	United Federal Insurance	590.00
10	1004	1/15/89	Computer World	2,245.50
11	1005	2/10/89	Savings Club	157.89
12	1006	2/19/89	Western Telephone	247.67
13	1007	3/05/89	Fathead Software	378.90

Figure 6-8 Changed table displayed following a changeto operation.

❑ **Data Recovery.** Since the information in the Changed table is the original data that was in the database table *before* the **changeto** operation, it can be used to recover the original data which was overwritten by the **changeto** query. For details, see page 180.

> *As with the Answer table, Paradox will overwrite the Changed table the next time a* **changeto** *query is processed. Until that time the Changed table will be stored on the disk in the file CHANGED.DB.*

What about the new information generated by the query? That information *does not* appear on the work area although it is *stored* in the database table file. If you want to see the data, you must display the database table with the **View** command. However, there is no necessity to view the changes if you are confident of what your query has done to the table.

In this case, you will use the values in the *Balance* field to find the total of the sales tax. Clear the work area and display a new query by entering

[Alt-F8] a
ck_book ↵

Place a **calc sum** operator in the *Balance* field. Enter

[Ctrl-End] ←
calc sum

Process the query by entering

[F2]

Using the data placed into the *Balance* field, Paradox displays the value that is the total of the sales tax as calculated by the formula you have been using, Figure 6-9.

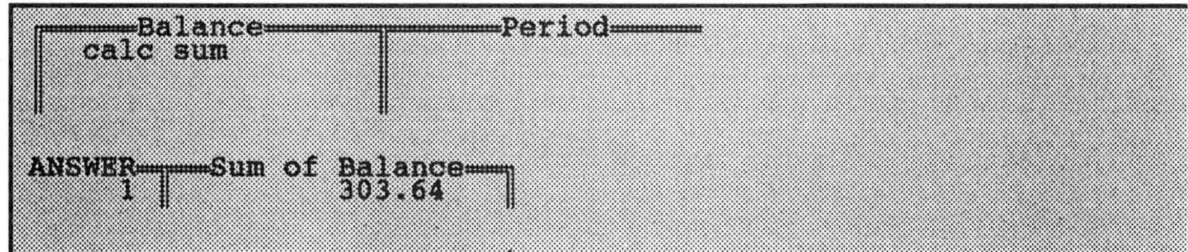

Figure 6-9 Sales tax total displayed.

Thus, in Paradox it is necessary to use a two-step technique to produce the sum of a calculated field. Clear the work area by entering

[Alt-F8]

Calculating the Account Balance

Your next task is to use the facilities of the Paradox query form to obtain the checking account balance. The complication is that the raw data is stored in the *Amount* and *Deposit* fields. While it is possible to calculate the totals of the *Amount* and *Deposit* fields, there is no way of subtracting one total from the other.

The solution is to combine *Amount* and *Deposit* into a single field—e.g., *Balance*—and then total this field. For example, if you applied a formula like *deposit–amount* to all the records, you would generate a series of values. In the deposit records, the value would be the amount of the *Deposit* field since the *Amount* field would be empty. Conversely, in the check fields, the value would be the *Amount* value, since the *Deposit* field would be empty. However, since *Amount* is subtracted from *Deposit*, the values would be negative, e.g., 0–100 = –100.

The *Balance* field would then contain a series of values, positive for deposits and negative for checks, which when totaled would yield the correct checking account balance.

Display a query form for the Ck_book table by entering

a
ck_book ↵

Because the calculation in this example requires data from both the *Amount* and *Deposit* fields, you will need to create example names for both fields. In this instance, use the **c** for the *Amount* field and the **d** for the *Deposit* field. Enter

→ *(4 times)*
[F5]
c
→ *(4 times)*
[F5]
d
→

You can now place a **changeto** operator in the *Balance* field that will subtract the checks from the deposits and store the values in the *Balance* field. Enter

changeto
[spacebar]
[F5]
d-
[F5]
c

Execute the query by entering

[F2]

The Changed table appears, listing all 13 records. This implies that the changes to the table were successful. Examine the new contents of the *Balance* field by viewing the Ck_book table. Enter

[F10] v
ck_book ↵
[Ctrl-End] ←

You may be surprised to see that the *Balance* column is totally blank, Figure 6-10.

What went wrong? The answer lies in the difference between blank and zero values in a numeric field. Recall that no entry was made in the *Deposit* field for checks, or in the *Amount* field for deposits. When the query encountered records with blank values in one of the numeric fields, it placed a blank into the *Balance* field, resulting in an entire column of blanks.

To correct this situation, you *must* replace the blanks with zeros. Doing so will produce the desired results. Clear the work area by entering

[Alt-F8]

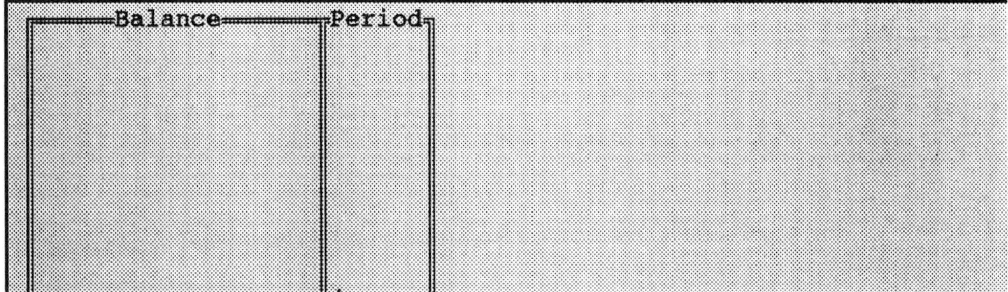

Figure 6-10 Changeto operation fails to calculate balances.

Changing Blanks to Zeros

Before you can proceed with the Balance calculation, you need to place zeros into fields that currently contain blanks. This operation requires the *selective* use of a **changeto** operation. It needs to be selective because the *Amount* and *Deposit* fields both contain data already. You only need to change those records that contain blanks. This means that you need to combine a selection condition with a **changeto** operation.

The task will require two queries: one for each field that contains blanks. Display a new query form by entering

a
ck_book ↵

Begin with the *Amount* field by entering

→ *(4 times)*

Since the only records you want to select are the ones with blank values, enter the **blank** operator into the column as a selection condition.

blank

Next, enter a **changeto** operator that will insert a zero value into the selected records.

changeto 0

Keep in mind that without the selection condition to select specific records, the operator **changeto 0** would overwrite all the *Amount* values. Enter

[F2]

The resulting Changed table lists four records—the deposit records—indicating that you inserted zeros into only the records previously having blank values in the *Amount* field, Figure 6-11.

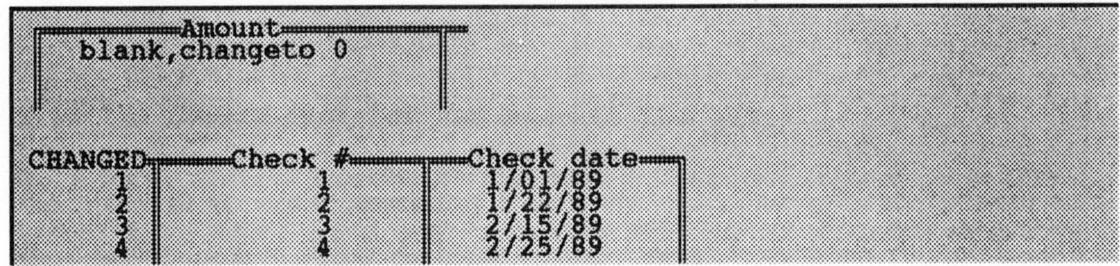

Amount
blank,changeto 0

CHANGED	Check #	Check date
1	1	1/01/89
2	2	1/22/89
3	3	2/15/89
4	4	2/25/89

Figure 6-11 Blanks converted to zero values.

You need to perform the same operation on the blank values in the *Deposit* field. Try this on your own. The correct command can be found on page 191 under Exercise 1.

This operation affects the nine records that were entered as checks. Clear the work area and use a query to display the contents of the *Amount* and *Deposit* fields. Try this on your own. The correct command can be found on page 192 under Exercise 2.

You can see from Figure 6-12 that all the records contain nonblank numeric values in both the *Amount* and *Deposit* fields.

ANSWER	Amount	Deposit
1	0.00	860.00
2	0.00	900.00
3	0.00	1,400.00
4	0.00	1,700.00
5	71.60	0.00
6	97.68	0.00
7	101.57	0.00
8	157.89	0.00
9	247.67	0.00
10	378.90	0.00
11	590.00	0.00
12	750.50	0.00
13	2,245.50	0.00

Figure 6-12 Zero values replace blanks.

You have created the necessary conditions for calculating the account balance. You can now use a query form to place into the *Balance* field the difference between the *Amount* and *Deposit* fields. Enter

[Alt-F8]
a
ck_book ↵

The setup is the same as that described on page 176 which uses the example names **c** and **d** for the *Amount* and *Deposit* fields, respectively. Enter

→ *(4 times)*
[F5]
c
→ *(4 times)*
[F5]
d
→

Enter the **changeto** operator and execute the query.

changeto
[spacebar]
[F5]
d-
[F5]
c
[F2]

All 13 records are listed as changed. The *Balance* field is now ready to be summed. Create a new query form that sums the *Balance* field. Enter

[Alt-F8]
a
ck_book ↵

[Ctrl-End] ←
calc sum
[F2]

Paradox displays the account balance in the Answer table, Figure 6-13.

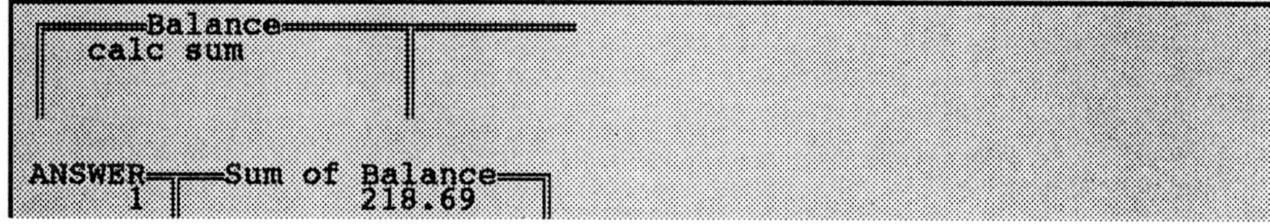

Figure 6-13 Account balance calculated.

Clear the work area by entering

[Alt-F8]

Recovering Changed Data

Changeto operations can overwrite existing data. It is important to know how to recover changed data should you make a mistake using this operator, leading to the unintended destruction of valid data.

Suppose you accidentally overwrote valid data. For example, you placed zero values in the *Amount* field of all records with values greater than zero. How would you recover it?

The solution involves the use of a two-step method.

❑ **Delete Records.** Delete from the table any records that were affected by the **changeto** operation. This can be done manually in the Edit mode, or by using a **delete** operator in a query form.

❑ **Adding Records.** The **Tools More Add** command can be used to insert records from one table into another, assuming corresponding fields. Here you would add to the original table the records contained in the Changed table. This would restore those records eliminated with the **delete** operation.

The final result would be to restore the data originally contained in the table before the **changeto** was performed. Keep in mind that if the original table did not have a key field designated, the restored records may appear in a different order than in the original table.

> *If the **changeto** operation that overwrote your data included all the records in your database table, the Changed table is actually a copy of the original table before the **changeto** was executed. In this circumstance, you could take a shortcut to recovery by renaming the Changed table. Keep in mind that while the Changed table will contain all the original records and fields, the table's structure will not have a key field, even though the original table's structure included a key field. You can designate a key field using the **Modify Restructure*** command.

If the original table has a key field and the changes made by the **changeto** operation do not affect the key field or fields you can take a shortcut method using the Update option of the **Tools More Add** command. Update uses the key field values in the Changed table to locate the matching record in the original database table. Paradox then replaces the current record's field information with the corresponding data from the Changed table. This method requires a key field because by definition key fields always contain unique values. If the key value of the original and Changed tables match, it is certain that they represent two versions of the same record. The advantage of this method is that it eliminates the need to delete records from the original table in order to recover changed data.

Changeto Mistakes

In order to see how mistakenly changed data can be recovered, use a query form to overwrite some of the data in the *Payee* field. Enter

a
ck_book ↵
→ *(3 times)*

Enter query settings that will change to blanks all the payees beginning with the letter M. Enter

S..,changeto blank
[F2]

Note that in this example the changes made by the query are simple enough to be corrected manually. However, as an illustration you will recover the data as if the changes were much greater.

The Delete Operator

The first step in recovering the data is to delete from the Ck_book table the records that were mistakenly changed. The Changed table shows that checks 999 and 1005 were affected by the **changeto** query.

There are two ways to remove records from a table.

❑ **Editing.** In the edit mode you can delete the record in which the cursor is positioned by entering [Del]. Records must be deleted one at a time with this method.

❑ **Delete Operator.** You can use the **delete** operator as part of a query form which will delete one or more records at a time. In addition, records removed with the **delete** operator are stored in a table named *Deleted.* This table can be used to restore records should you accidentally delete the wrong records.

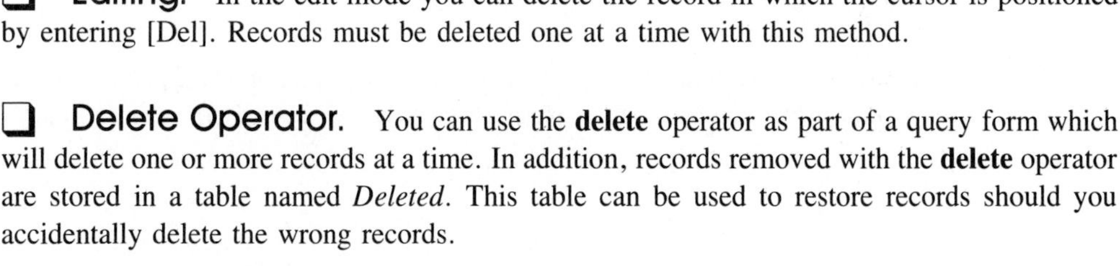

The Deleted table is maintained until you perform another deletion, or exit Paradox. Like the Answer and Changed tables, it is erased at the end of the current session.

In this case, you want to use a query form to delete checks 999 and 1005 from the Ck_book table. Move back to the query form and remove all the current settings.

[F3] [Ctrl-Home] [Del]

The **delete** operator is *always* placed in the leftmost column, the one under the name of the table. Enter

delete

Here, specify check numbers 999 and 1005 for deletion. You can do so by entering the check numbers in the *Check #* column using an **or** operator. The **or** operator is used because records that match either of the numbers should be deleted. Enter

→
999 or 1005

Process the query by entering

[F2]

The result is a new table called DELETED, which contains the two specified records. These records have been removed from the Ck_book table, Figure 6-14.

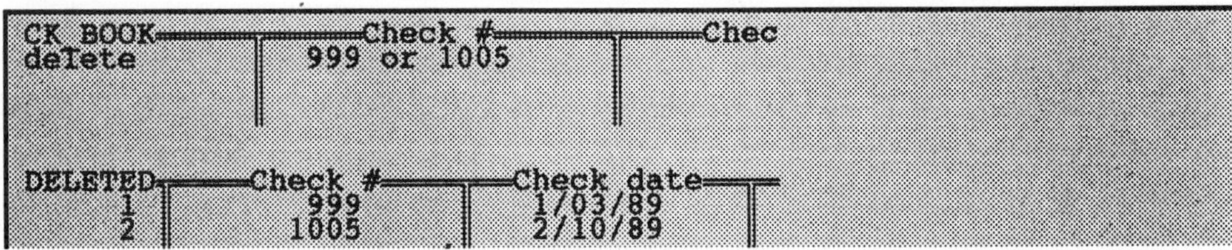

Figure 6-14 Records deleted from table using query.

With the modified records purged from the Ck_book table, you can restore the original records currently stored in the Changed table, using the **Tools More Add** command. Enter

[F10] t m a

Paradox asks you to enter the *Source Table* name. The source table is the one that contains the records you want to add. In this case, it is the Changed table that contains the records that need to be added to the Ck_book table. Enter

changed ↵

Next, you are asked to enter the *Target Table* name. Enter

ck_book ↵

The **Tools More Add** command has two options: NewEntries and Update. NewEntries simply adds the source table to the target table. Update requires that the tables have a common key field. This field is used to match source records with corresponding target records. When matches are made, the target records are updated. In this instance, choose NewEntries by entering

n

The Ck_book table is restored to its original state, Figure 6-15.

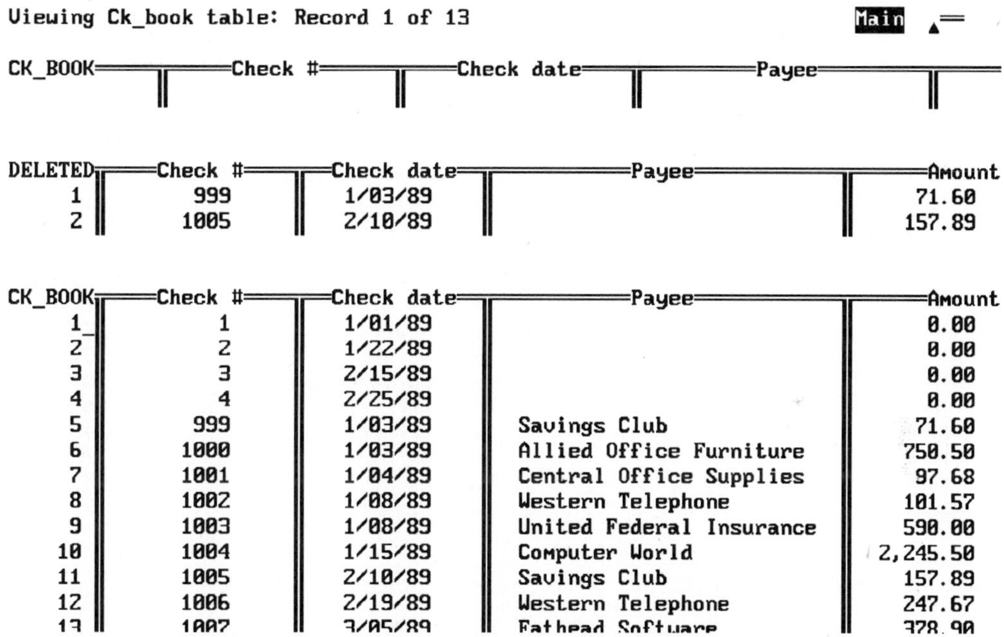

Viewing Ck_book table: Record 1 of 13 Main

CK_BOOK	Check #	Check date	Payee

DELETED	Check #	Check date	Payee	Amount
1	999	1/03/89		71.60
2	1005	2/10/89		157.89

CK_BOOK	Check #	Check date	Payee	Amount
1	1	1/01/89		0.00
2	2	1/22/89		0.00
3	3	2/15/89		0.00
4	4	2/25/89		0.00
5	999	1/03/89	Savings Club	71.60
6	1000	1/03/89	Allied Office Furniture	750.50
7	1001	1/04/89	Central Office Supplies	97.68
8	1002	1/08/89	Western Telephone	101.57
9	1003	1/08/89	United Federal Insurance	590.00
10	1004	1/15/89	Computer World	2,245.50
11	1005	2/10/89	Savings Club	157.89
12	1006	2/19/89	Western Telephone	247.67
13	1007	3/05/89	Fathead Software	378.90

Figure 6-15 Table restored to previous condition.

Restoring Records with Update

As mentioned previously, if the table you are working with uses a key field or fields, and if the changes made to the table do not affect that key field, you can save a step by using the **Tools More Add Update** command to restore information from the Changed table back into the original table.

To illustrate how this shortcut works, change the Ck_book table by blanking all the dates in the month of February. Clear the current query form by entering

[F3] ***(2 times)***
←
[Del]

Set up a **changeto** query that will blank the February dates. Enter

→ ***(2 times)***
2/..,changeto blank
[F2]

The query changes the dates of four records to blanks and stores the original data in the changed table, Figure 6-16.

```
Viewing Changed table: Record 1 of 4                          Main

CK_BOOK  Check #   Check date   Payee                         Amount
   1          1     1/01/89                                     0.00
   2          2     1/22/89                                     0.00
   3          3                                                 0.00
   4          4                                                 0.00
   5        999     1/03/89     Savings Club                   71.60
   6       1000     1/03/89     Allied Office Furniture       750.50
   7       1001     1/04/89     Central Office Supplies        97.68
   8       1002     1/08/89     Western Telephone             101.57
   9       1003     1/08/89     United Federal Insurance      590.00
  10       1004     1/15/89     Computer World              2,245.50
  11       1005                 Savings Club                  157.89
  12       1006                 Western Telephone             247.67
  13       1007     3/05/89     Fathead Software              378.90

CHANGED  Check #   Check date   Payee                         Amount
   1          3     2/15/89                                     0.00
   2          4     2/25/89                                     0.00
   3       1005     2/10/89     Savings Club                  157.89
   4       1006     2/19/89     Western Telephone             247.67
```

Figure 6-16 Dates blanked with changeto query.

Using the Delete and Add methods outlined previously, you would now have to delete the four records from the original table, and then merge the Changed table back into the Ck_book table. But because Ck_book uses the *Check #* field as a key field, you can directly update the Ck_book table with the data in the Changed table using the **Tools More Add Update** command.

Paradox will match up the *Check #* values in the Changed table with the values in Ck_book and replace the current data with the data as it appears in the Changed table, restoring the values mistakenly overwritten. Enter

[F10] t m a
changed ↵
ck_book ↵

This time, choose the update method. Enter

u

Paradox updates the Ck_book table with the corresponding data from the Changed table, restoring the original values, Figure 6-17.

```
Viewing Changed table: Record 1 of 4                              Main

CK_BOOK  Check #   Check date   Payee                          Amount
   1          1    1/01/89                                       0.00
   2          2    1/22/89                                       0.00
   3          3    2/15/89                                       0.00
   4          4    2/25/89                                       0.00
   5        999    1/03/89      Savings Club                    71.60
   6       1000    1/03/89      Allied Office Furniture        750.50
   7       1001    1/04/89      Central Office Supplies         97.68
   8       1002    1/08/89      Western Telephone              101.57
   9       1003    1/08/89      United Federal Insurance       590.00
  10       1004    1/15/89      Computer World               2,245.50
  11       1005    2/10/89      Savings Club                   157.89
  12       1006    2/19/89      Western Telephone              247.67
  13       1007    3/05/89      Fathead Software               378.90

CHANGED  Check #   Check date   Payee                          Amount
   1          3                                                  0.00
   2          4                                                  0.00
   3       1005                 Savings Club                   157.89
   4       1006                 Changed records are shown in CHANGED table
```

Figure 6-17 Table updated.

> *Note that the* ***Tools More Add*** *command can work with any two tables having common fields. You are not restricted to working with special generated tables such as Answer, Changed, and Deleted.*

Clear the work area by entering

[Alt-F8]

Manipulating Text

The **changeto** operator can also be used to insert text or date information into fields of these types. For example, the *Payee* fields of the records used as deposits are currently blank. It may be better to indicate when the *Payee* is a *Deposit*, rather than showing a blank field.

Inserting Deposit in Payee

Display a new query form by entering

a
ck_book ↵

Use the **blank** operator as a selection condition for the *Payee* field. Enter

→ *(3 times)*
blank

Add a **changeto** operator that will insert the word *Deposit* into the records that currently have a blank *Payee*. Enter

,changeto Deposit

Execute the query by entering

[F2]

Paradox selects the four deposit records and makes the change in each *Payee* field. To check the results, display the Ck_book table with the **View** command. Enter

[F10] v
ck_book ↵

The table display shows the deposit records labeled as deposits in the *Payee* field, Figure 6-18.

Clear the work area by entering

[Alt-F8]

Monthly Groups

Suppose you wanted to obtain monthly subtotals for the *Amount*, *Deposit*, and *Balance* fields. Recall that to generate a subtotal you would select a field that contained data which would

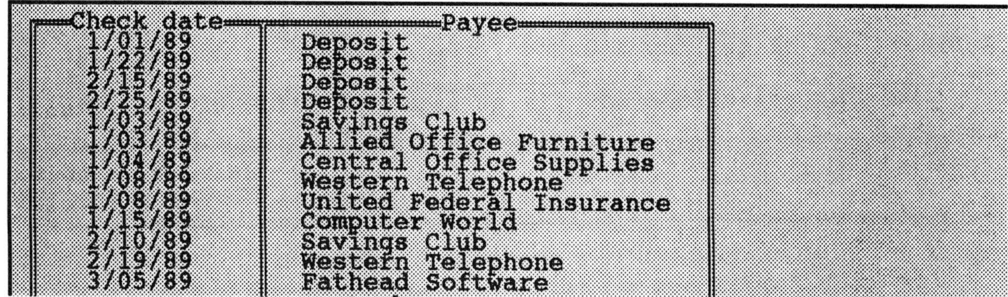

Check date	Payee
1/01/89	Deposit
1/22/89	Deposit
2/15/89	Deposit
2/25/89	Deposit
1/03/89	Savings Club
1/03/89	Allied Office Furniture
1/04/89	Central Office Supplies
1/08/89	Western Telephone
1/08/89	United Federal Insurance
1/15/89	Computer World
2/10/89	Savings Club
2/19/89	Western Telephone
3/05/89	Fathead Software

Figure 6-18 Deposit inserted into Payee field.

group records for subtotals. In the Ck_book table you have a field, *Check date*, which implicitly contains the information needed to group records by month. However, using the *Check date* field to create subtotals would create one subtotal for each unique date, not each unique month. Paradox queries do not allow you to group records according to *partial* field contents. This means that, although a part of the date is the month, you cannot produce subtotals directly from date fields.

How would you overcome this problem? One solution would be to use query forms to enter the name of the month into another field. Recall that when you modified the structure of Ck_book, you added an alphanumeric field called *Period*. You could use **changeto** queries to insert the correct month name based on the date value. For example, if you set as a selection condition **1/..** and place the operator **changeto Jan** in the *Period* field, Paradox will write "Jan" into all the records with January dates. Of course, you will need to repeat the process for each subsequent month. The final result will be a *Period* field that contains names for each financial period—in this case, each month. You can then use this field to generate subtotals for each period.

When generating subtotals based on an alphanumeric field, you must consider the effect of the sort order on the result. By default, the records in an Answer table are always stored according to the field order of the selected fields. Also by default, Paradox maintains the selected fields in the same sequence as they appear in the table structure. For example, suppose you place period names such as Jan, Feb, Mar, etc., in the *Period* field. If you select this field as the subtotal field, the subtotals will be listed in alphabetical order, i.e., Feb, Jan, Mar, etc. In cases such as this where names represent a chronological order of months, it might be better to use some numeric information to help the program list the months in correct chronological order, e.g., 01-Jan, 02-Feb, 03-Mar, and so on. Note that the use of the 0 to hold the place for the 1 that would appear in 10-Oct, 11-Nov, and 12-Dec is necessary because *Period* is an alphanumeric field. In order to get a proper sort sequence, all the numbers must be aligned according to place values.

> *Numeric and date fields automatically take column alignment into consideration so that entry of leading zeros is not required.*

Creating Monthly Periods

The first task in producing monthly subtotals is to have Paradox write the period name into the *Period* field of all of the records that have dates within the same month. This can be done through a series of query forms using **changeto** operators. Display a query form for the Ck_book table by entering

a
ck_book ↵

Begin by inserting **01-Jan** in *Period* for all of the January dates. Place the record selection condition in the *Check date* field by entering

→ *(2 times)*
1/..

Place the **changeto** operator in the *Period* column.

[Ctrl-End]
changeto 01-Jan

Execute the query by entering

[F2]

The Changed table shows that the eight records with January dates have been changed. Return the cursor to the query form and set up the query for February. Enter

[F3] [Ctrl-backspace]
changeto 02-Feb
[Ctrl-Home]
→ *(2 times)*
[Ctrl-backspace]
2/..

Process the query by entering

[F2]

This time the four records with February dates are changed. The last month you need to work with is March. Try this on your own. The correct command can be found on page 192 under Exercise 3.

Clear the work area by entering

[Alt-F8]

Calculating Subtotal Groups

You can now use the *Period* field to find the monthly subtotals for the checks, deposits, and balance. Display a query form for the Ck_book table by entering

a
ck_book ↵

You will want to enter **calc sum** operators into the *Amount, Deposit,* and *Balance* field columns. Enter

→ ***(4 times)***
calc sum
→ ***(4 times)***
calc sum
→
calc sum

In order to group the records into subtotal groups according to month, place a √ in the *Period* field. Enter

→
[F6]

Process the query form by entering

[F2]

The query displays a summary of checking account activity according to month, Figure 6-19.

Save the query form for use at some other time, using the **Scripts QuerySave** command. Note that Paradox displays negative values in reverse video (or red, on color screens). Because the field types are currency, parentheses are used to indicate that the amounts are negative values. Enter

[F10] s q
monthly ↵

The program writes the current query form data into a script file called MONTHLY.SC. Exit Paradox by entering

[F10] e y

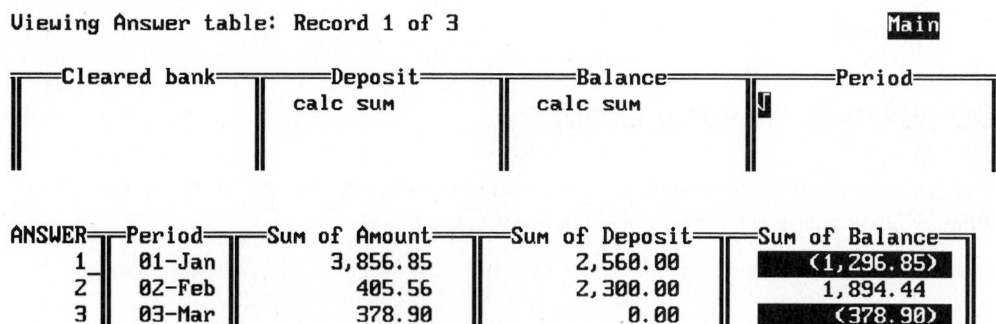

ANSWER	Period	Sum of Amount	Sum of Deposit	Sum of Balance
1	01-Jan	3,856.85	2,560.00	(1,296.85)
2	02-Feb	405.56	2,300.00	1,894.44
3	03-Mar	378.90	0.00	(378.90)

Figure 6-19 Subtotals calculated by month.

Summary

In this chapter, you learned how query form operators can be used to generate information not directly entered into the database table. The information generated is based upon arithmetic, date, or text manipulation of the raw data provided by the table.

❑ **Calculated Field Columns.** The **calc** operator can be used to generate fields based on arithmetic calculation, date arithmetic, or text concatenation. The values are displayed as fields in the Answer tables.

❑ **Examples.** Examples are names assigned to fields. These names can be used in formulas to refer to the contents of specific fields. An example name is created by pressing the [F5] key before entering the example name. Example names, unlike field names, cannot contain spaces. When creating calculated fields, each field used in a formula must have an example name that relates back to the field column.

❑ **As.** This operator is used to assign a name to the field column in the Answer table. The name takes precedence over the one automatically generated by Paradox.

❑ **Changeto.** This operator allows you to use query forms to modify the data stored in the database table. The advantage of **changeto** is that it can use record selection to perform an operation on more than one record at a time. You can use **changeto** to insert literal information or the result of a formula that performs arithmetic, date arithmetic, or text concatenation. The original data from any records that are modified during a **changeto** operation are stored in a table called *Changed*. This table shows which records have been affected by the **changeto** operation. It can also be used to restore the original data to the modified table.

❑ **Delete.** This operator allows you to delete records from a table, using query form selection conditions to select records for deletion. This method has two advantages over manual record deletion performed in the Edit mode: 1) the query can delete multiple records according to a selection condition, and 2) all deleted records are stored in a table called Deleted. The Deleted table can be used to restore records if necessary.

❑ **Restoring Changed or Deleted Records.** Query operations that modify the database table provide a means by which the operation can be undone, i.e., restoring a table to its state prior to the operation. **Changeto** operations generate a Changed table, while **delete** operations generate a Deleted table. The **Tools More Add** command can be used to add the records stored in one table (e.g., Deleted or Changed) to the original database table. If the original table has a key field not affected by the **changeto** operation, you can use the **Update** option to restore records, based on the matching of key field values in the original and Changed tables.

❑ **Zeros and Blanks.** Paradox treats numeric or currency fields containing zero values differently from fields that contain blanks. If a field is blank, the record is not selected as part of a calculated field list or as part of a summary calculation (e.g., average or count). If the field contains a zero value, it is included in all calculations. Note this does not apply to alphanumeric fields where blanks are always included, unless specifically excluded with the **not blank** operator.

Exercises

Exercise 1 from page 178

[Alt-F8]
a
ck_book ↵

→ *(8 times)*
blank,changeto 0
[F2]

Exercise 2 from page 178

[Alt-F8]
a
ck_book ↵

→ *(4 times)*
[F6]
→ *(4 times)*
[F6]
[F2]

Exercise 3 from page 189

[F3]
[Ctrl-backspace]
3/..
[Ctrl-End] [Ctrl-backspace]
changeto 03-Mar
[F2]

7

Column Report Basics

Reports are used to display information stored in database tables. One common way of displaying table data is through column reports. In this respect, they perform a function similar to that of screen forms. However, reports differ from screen forms in several respects.

❑ **Output Only.** A report is used to display or output data. Screen forms, on the other hand, are used for display, editing, and entry of data. Because reports are for output only, you are able to create more complex layouts than is possible with screen forms.

❑ **Pagination.** In contrast to forms, which are set up to fit the 80 x 25 screen display, reports are designed to be printed. Report forms are automatically designed to print data within margins, to break at the end of pages, and to insert page numbers on each page. You can adjust the pagination settings to print data on a variety of different shapes and sizes of paper, including specialized forms such as checks or invoices.

❑ **Calculations.** Reports can include formulas that will generate calculated fields and summary values, such as totals and averages. In addition, reports can generate summary values for calculated fields in a single step. Recall that finding the sum of a calculated field requires two steps when it is done with query forms.

❑ **Groups.** Reports can also be used to create groups of related records and summary values for each group. You have the option of displaying all the details along with group summaries, or simply reporting the group totals.

❑ **Default Layout.** When you decide to design a screen form, Paradox begins with a blank screen. However, Paradox automatically creates a *default* report layout each time you start to design a new report. Paradox assumes that most reports will have the same basic structure. In this case, it is easier and faster to make additions and deletions to the default report layout rather than to start from scratch. This approach works well when the table contains a small number of fields, since most reports probably include most of those fields anyway. Because column reports are limited by the width of the printed page, tables with a large number of fields would probably include only a few related fields in each report form. In this case, it would be necessary to remove many of the fields Paradox automatically inserts into each new report form.

> *Paradox reports can also be used to create non-column, free-form documents, which merge data from tables into mailing labels, form letters or other types of lists and documents. Free-form reports operate much like the mail-merge features found in many word processing programs.*

In this chapter you will learn how column reports are created, what types of options you can exercise in their design, and how to output the reports.

> *Paradox calls column reports* tabular *reports.*

Begin by loading Paradox in the usual manner.

Bands

Another important difference between screen form design and report form design lies in the concept of bands. When you create a screen form, the final form displayed in Paradox corresponds exactly with the layout created in the design form mode. The only difference is that the field locations are filled with field data when the form is used for viewing or editing the table. This direct correspondence is possible because screen forms display only the number of records they are designed to display. Most screen forms display only one record at a time. Multiple record forms display a fixed number of records—two, three, etc.—on each screen.

On the other hand, reports are designed to process all the records in a table. In a report form, the field layout is repeated for each record in the table until all the records have been processed.

Another complication results from the printing process, in which the information generated by the report is placed onto printed pages. There are some items, such as column headings or page numbers, which should be printed each time a new page is started. A report, in fact, actually consists of several different types of items whose printing is triggered by different events, such as the beginning of a new page or the end of the report.

In order to accommodate the different sections of the report in a single form design, Paradox divides the report into a series of *bands*. Each band can contain literal text, fields, or calculated fields. What differentiates one band from another is the *trigger* that causes that band to print.

❑ **Report Header.** The information or text in this band prints once at the beginning of the report, regardless of the number of pages in the report. This band is typically used for printing a report title. The report header is sometimes printed as a cover page, separated from the rest of the report by a page break.

❑ **Report Footer.** This band operates like the report header, except that it prints only once—at the end of the report. This band is typically used to print summary calculations and ending remarks following the report data. Note that if a report ends in the middle of a page, the Report Footer band will print at that position while the Page Footer will print below it at the bottom of the page.

❑ **Page Header.** The information contained in this band will print at the top of every page. This band is used typically to print the page numbers, report date, and other text which should appear at the top of every page.

❑ **Page Footer.** This band prints at the bottom of each page. It is usually used when you want to place the page number at the bottom of the page.

❑ **Table Band.** The Table band prints once for each record in the table. It is the Table band that usually carries the field information from the table. If the report is a tabular (column type) report, the Table band is divided into a series of column specifications. The column specifications consist of three lines: the name of the field, a line of dashes, and the field itself. The field name and dashes print at the top of each page following the Page Header band. Even though these items appear in the Table band, they behave as if they were Page Header information. If the report is a free-form report, all the information in the Table band repeats for each record, including fields and text.

A report is designed by entering the text, fields, or calculated fields you desire into the bands in which they belong, Figure 7-1 shown on page 196.

You can design and store up to 15 reports for each table. As with screen forms, the report named R is the *standard* report. This is the report that is printed if you use the [Alt-F7] command to create an *instant* report to the printer. If you have not designed a standard report when you press [Alt-F7], Paradox will automatically generate one.

Each report can contain up to 255 fields. If the column layout is too wide to fit on a single page, Paradox will split the report horizontally in multiple pages so that all the fields are printed.

(1) Report Band Begin — Print at beginning of report
(2) Page Band — Print on each page
(3) Table Band — Print once for each record
(4) Report Band End — Print at end of report

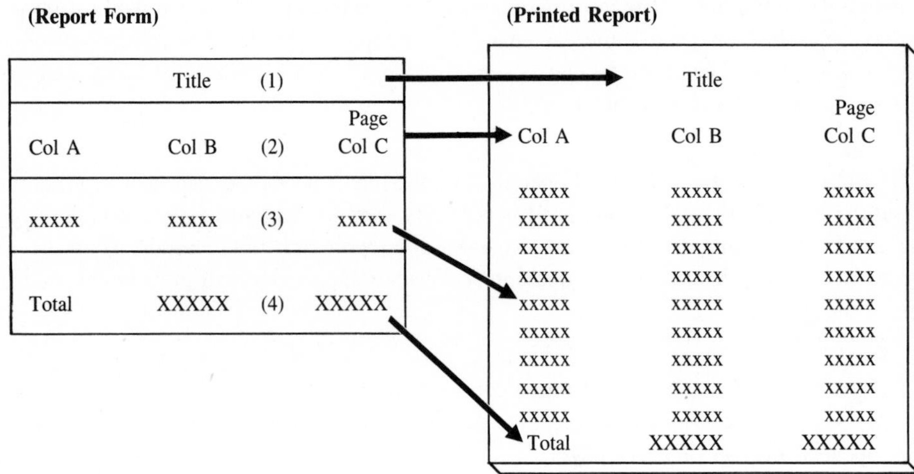

Figure 7-1 Report bands place items on printed report page.

Designing Tabular (Column) Reports

The **Report Design** command is used to create a new report form or overwrite an existing form with a new one. The **Report Change** command allows you to revise an existing report. Create a new report by entering

r d
ck_book ↵

The program lists the 15 report forms (R plus 1–14) which can be designed for each table, Figure 7-2.

```
R 1 2 3 4 5 6 7 8 9 10 11 12 13 14
Standard Report
```

Figure 7-2 Select report to create.

Select report 1 by entering

→ ↵

The program asks you to enter a description of the report, Figure 7-3. This description serves two functions. In addition to identifying the report on the report menu, the text is automatically inserted into the Report Header band of the report form as the title of the report. Keep in mind that you can edit the title in the Report Header band to read differently from the report form description.

```
Report description:
Enter report description
```

Figure 7-3 Enter report description.

Enter the following description for the report.

Checking Account Records ↵

Paradox displays a menu, Figure 7-4, which asks you to select the layout type. **Tabular** reports are column-style reports in which the fields are spread horizontally across the page with the records printing on consecutive lines. In a tabular report form, the Table band is divided into a series of column. Each column contains the specifications for the printing of a column of values from a specific field. **Free-form** reports do not arrange the fields in columns but place the fields on the page in a manner similar to the way in which the fields on screen forms are arranged.

```
Tabular  Free-form
Print the information in rows and columns.
```

Figure 7-4 Select report layout type.

Select **Tabular** by entering

t

Paradox displays the report form design mode. Unlike the screen form report mode, this display is not empty. In fact, it contains all of the specifications needed to print a report, shown in Figure 7-5.

The report automatically uses two bands: the Page Header and the Table bands.

The Page Header contains a field that will print the current system date (**mm/dd/yy**), the title of the report taken from the report description, and a field (**999**) that will print the page number. In addition, there are five blank lines, three above the date/title/page number line, and two below, creating a Page Header that will print six lines at the top of each page. The blank lines in the Page Header and Page Footer bands serve to create top and bottom page margins. If you were to remove all the blank lines from the Page Header and Footer bands, the remaining text would print at the top edge of the page and continue until reaching the bottom edge of the page. In general, it is preferable to leave one or more of these blanks in the Page bands to maintain some white space at the top and bottom of each page.

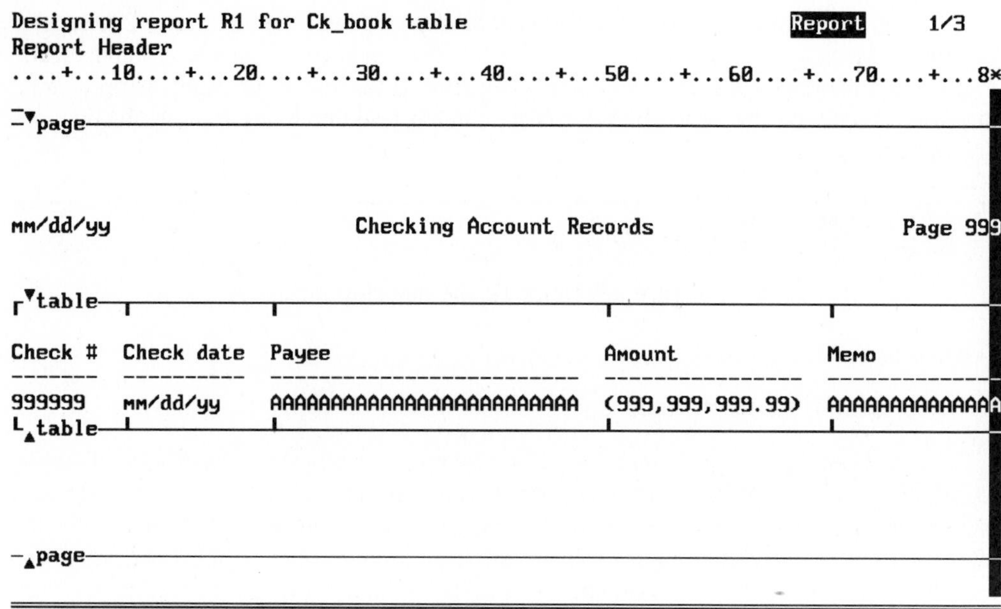

Figure 7-5 Report design mode.

> *Note that there is also, by default, a single blank line in the Report Header band, at the very top of the report. This blank line will print at the top of the first page of the report only.*

The Table band consists of a series of columns, with each column consisting of four lines.

❑ **Blank Line.** The first line in the Table band is a blank line. This line will ensure that there is at least one blank line between the Table band data and the Page Header information.

❑ **Field Names.** Paradox automatically inserts the name of the field as a column heading. The names are literal text, which can be edited or deleted if desired. The names do not need to match the field names as long as they identify the data in the column correctly.

❑ **Separator.** The separators are simply lines of dashes. This text is not required and can be replaced with other characters, or deleted from the report form.

❑ **Fields.** The field indicates where the data from the table will be inserted into the report. By default, Paradox places all the fields in the table in the order in which they appear in the table structure. You can add, erase, or rearrange the field columns. Paradox also permits you to place calculated fields in a tabular report.

In order to aid you in designing the report form, Paradox displays information at the top of the screen, Figure 7-6. The top line shows the name of the form you are working on. On the right side of this line, a fraction appears—here, **1/3**. The denominator of this fraction, 3, tells you the number of pages, horizontally, needed to print the report. In this case, the 3 indicates that in order to print all the fields included in the report form, you will need to print three pages across. Note that this number does not indicate the total number of pages in the report. Page count depends on how many records are printed vertically down the page. The 1 indicates that the cursor is positioned on the first of the three horizontal pages.

The next line displays the name of the band, in this example **Report Header**, in which the cursor is positioned.

The third line is a scale that measures characters. At the far right edge of the scale is an *. Below the * is a vertical highlight that indicates the edge of a page. By default, Paradox assumes a page width of 80 characters.

> *If you have a printer that is capable of printing lines wider than 80 characters, you can change the page width setting using the* ***Setting PageLayout Width*** *command. If you want to change the Paradox default page width, you must use the Custom script discussed in Chapter 8.*

```
Designing report R1 for Ck_book table                    Report     1/3
Report Header
....+...10....+...20....+...30....+...40....+...50....+...60....+...70....+...8*
```

Figure 7-6 Status area at the top of the report design screen.

Changing Field Headings

When Paradox generates the field columns, it uses the information stored in the table structure to determine the column headings and their widths. However, you are free to edit the column headings to read any way that you desire. For example, the *Payee* field will contain both payee and deposit items. It might make more sense to someone reading the report—someone who is not familiar with your field names—if the heading read *Description*, instead. You can edit, add, or remove characters from any of the column headings. First, position the cursor in the Table band by entering

↓ (10 times)

Note that **Table Band** appears in the upper left corner of the screen when you move the cursor to any of the lines in the table band. In tabular reports, the Table band is divided into a series of columns. In this mode, the arrow keys function a bit differently than does the [Tab] key.

Table 7-1 Report Design Mode

→	one character to the right
←	one character to the left
[Tab]	one column to the right
[Shift-Tab]	one column to the left
[Ctrl- →]	one screen to the right
[Ctrl-←]	one screen to the left
[Ctrl-Home]	first column
[Ctrl-End]	last column

Position the cursor in the third column by entering

[Tab]*(2 times)*

Change the heading by entering

[Del]*(5 times)*
Description of Transaction

You can change the position of text by inserting or deleting spaces. For example, you might want the label over the *Amount* column to be positioned in the center of the column. Place the program into the *insert* mode by entering

[Ins]

> *When the* insert *mode is active, the letters* **Ins** *appear next to* **Report** *in the upper right corner of the screen. If* insert *is not active the area is blank.*

Move to the next column by entering

[Tab]

Move the column heading to the right by entering

[spacebar]*(6 times)*

The label is now centered in the column. Column labels in numeric or currency columns will often look better if they are centered or aligned on the right side of the column, since numeric values will be aligned to the right side of the column when they are printed as part of the report.

> *Paradox will remain in the* insert *mode until you press the [Ins] a second time. At this point, the* insert *mode is still active.*

Erasing Fields

As noted, Paradox will automatically include all the fields in the table's structure as part of the report form. If you have over five or six fields in the table, you will often find that you do not want to print all the fields in each report. Reports are more clear when they contain only the fields actually needed.

You can eliminate field columns by using the **Tableband Erase** command. Note that this is different from the **Field Erase** command used to remove just the field from a report form. When **Tableband Erase** is used, Paradox removes the entire column from the report: column heading, separator, and field. In addition, the space occupied by the column is deleted and all the columns to the right move to the left to close up the space. Removing a field, on the other hand, leaves the column where the field had appeared, in place in the report form.

Here, eliminate the *Tax deductible, Cleared bank* and *Balance* columns. Place the cursor in the *Tax deductible* column by entering

[Tab]*(2 times)*

Begin by entering the **Tableband Erase** command.

[F10]

The Report menu lists five commands in addition to **Help, Do-It!** and **Cancel**, which appear on all menus, Figure 7-7 on page 202.

❑ **Field.** This command allows you to place or erase fields from the report form, including calculated fields. You can also reformat and justify fields. The wordwrap option allows you to have a field print on multiple short lines in order to save horizontal space.

❑ **TableBand.** This command is used to manipulate field columns. They can be inserted, erased, resized, moved, or copied.

> *The **Rotate** command, [Ctrl-r], can also be used to rotate the position of the field columns by moving the first column to the right end of the report each time it is entered.*

❑ **Group.** This option is used when you want to include group control breaks within a report.

❑ **Output.** Sends the current report form to the printer, screen, or text file.

❑ **Setting.** This option allows you to change settings that affect the report as a whole including group options, page width, length, and margins. You can also control printer options such as special setup codes or automatic pauses between pages for manual feed printers. The **Setting Setup** command can be used to access printer features such as compressed or landscape printing. You can select from the Pre-defined menu's list of printers or use **Custom** to enter printer codes that match the command set of your printer. The Pre-defined subcommand lists 14 print options support by Paradox.

Table 7-2 Support Printers

Name of Setup	Printer Codes Sent
StandardPrinter*	no codes sent to printer
Small-IBMgraphics	\027W\000\015
Reg-IBMgraphics	\027W\000\018
Small-Epson-MX/FX	\015
Small-Oki-92/93	\015
Small-Oki-82/83	\029
Small-Oki-192	\029
HPLaserJet	\027E
HP-Portrait-66lines	\027E\027&l7.27C
HP-Landscape-Normal	\027E\027&l1O
HP-Compressed	\027E\027(s16.66H
HP-LandscpCompressed	\027E\027&l1O\027(s16.66H
Intl-IBMcompatible	\027\054
Intl-IBMcondensed	\027\054\015

Printer setups are sequences of characters sent to the printer that are recognized by the printer as instructions. The code system can differ from printer to printer, along with the printer's features. Paradox uses the same system of notation to write printer setup code as does Lotus 1-2-3. In this system, all normal alphanumeric characters can be entered literally. Special characters, [Ctrl] combinations, and [Esc], are entered with a \ followed by a three-digit number representing the ASCII value of the character. For example, the [Esc] key would be entered as \027. Printer setup strings can contain up to 50 characters. Note that using an ASCII numeric code, e.g., \027, uses 4 characters out of the 50 allowed. If you want to add a new printer setup, you can edit the printer setup table using the Custom script discussed in Chapter 10.

```
Field  TableBand  Group  Output  Setting  Help  DO-IT!  Cancel Report Ins 1/3
Place, erase, reformat, justify, or wrap fields.
```

Figure 7-7 Main Report menu.

In this instance, you want to use the TableBand option to remove a column. Keep in mind the distinction between erasing a field within a column and removing the entire column from the report. Enter

t

The TableBand menu is displayed. This menu has five operations that can be performed on report columns, as shown in Figure 7-8.

```
Insert  Erase  Resize  Move  Copy
Insert a new column in the table band.
```

Figure 7-8 TableBand menu.

❑ **Insert.** Inserts a blank column into the report form. You would use this option to replace a field column that you had erased, or for the creation of a calculated field column.

❑ **Erase.** Removes all the data, literal text, and fields from the selected column.

❑ **Resize.** Increases or decreases the width of an existing columns. Note that if you want to decrease the width of a column you are restricted by the size of the field, if any, in that column, since the column size cannot be less than the field size. If you want to set the column to a size smaller than the width of the field in that column, you must first use the **Field Reformat** command to reduce the field size and then use **TableBand Resize** to reduce the column width.

❑ **Move.** Changes the location of an existing column within the report.

❑ **Copy.** Copies an existing column and places the duplicate at a different location in the report.

This example requires you to erase a field column. Enter

e

Paradox now allows you to use the ← and → keys to select the column you want to remove.

> *It was not necessary to position the cursor in the column before entering the* ***TableBand Erase*** command. However, the ← and → keys move only one character, not one column, at a time and the [Tab] and [Shift-Tab] keys do not operate in this mode. This means that it is easier to use the [Tab] or [Shift-Tab] keys to select the column before you enter the command.

Since you are positioned in the *Tax deductible* column, enter

↵

The column is removed from the report form. All the columns to the right of the *Tax deductible* column are moved to the right to close up the gap. Repeat the process for the next column, *Cleared bank*. Try this on your own. The correct command can be found on page 237 under Exercise 1.

Move the cursor to the *Balance* field and erase it by entering

> **[Tab]**
> **[F10] t e ↵**

Repeat the **TableBand Erase** command once more to remove the *Period* field. Enter

> **[F10] t e ↵**

You have now reduced the report to the *Check #, Check date, Payee, Amount, Memo,* and *Deposit* fields.

Changing Field and Column Width

Even though you have eliminated a number of fields from the report form, the report is still wider than can fit onto a single page. The highlight running vertically down the screen, Figure 7-9, indicates where the end of the first page is located.

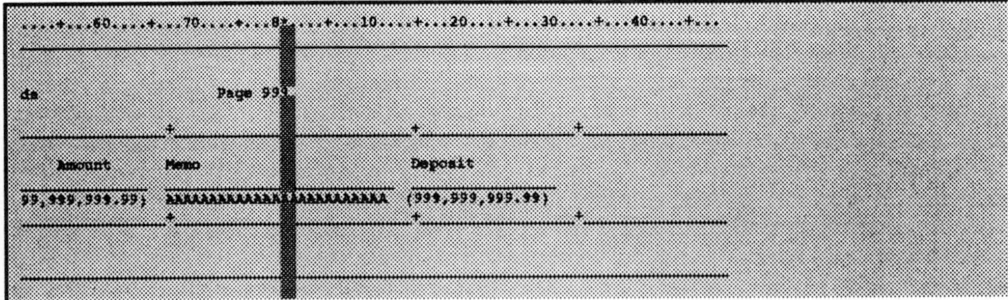

Figure 7-9 Report still wider than a single page.

If you want to print the data from all the current fields but you do not want to print more than a single page width, there are two options to use to reduce the width of the report.

❑ **Reformat/Resize Column.** You can squeeze more fields into a smaller area by reducing the width of the field and the column that contains the field. This is usually a two-step operation in which, first, the field size is reduced with the **Field Reformat** command, and then the column width is reduced using the **TableBand Resize** command.

❑ **Wrap Field.** If you want to reduce the width of a field but still want to be able to display all the information, you can create a *wrapped* field that will expand vertically to print text wider than the specified field length. This option works in a manner similar to the *wrapped* field option used with screen forms. This technique is used primarily with alphanumeric fields.

Changing Column Widths

Notice in the current example that the *Amount* and *Deposit* fields have been formatted to display values as large as 999,999,999.99. In fact, the largest actual value contained in the fields is much smaller than that. You could save space by reducing the fields and columns used for both the *Amount* and *Deposit* fields to 999,999.99, and still have enough space to display the values in those fields.

Note that by default the column width and the field widths are set to match. This means that before you can reduce the column width, the field contained within that column must be reformatted with fewer characters, using the **Field Reformat** command. Enter

[F10] f r

Position the cursor on the field you want to reformat. Here, begin with the *Deposit* field by entering

↓ ***(2 times)***
← ***(3 times)***
↵

When you select a numeric or currency type field, Paradox does not allow you to change the field width using the ← and → keys. Instead, the program displays a special menu that allows you to select formatting options related to numeric values, as shown in Figure 7-10 on following page.

❑ **Digits.** Use this option to enter the number of digits, including decimal places, to be used for the field. This is the option that controls the actual field width.

❑ **Sign-Convention.** Negative numbers can be displayed in mathematical notation, e.g., **–2,900.00** or business notation, e.g., **(2,900.00).** If desired, you can select to have the + sign used for positive numbers, as well as the – sign for negative numbers. Otherwise positive numbers will appear as plain numbers.

❑ **Commas.** This option controls the insertion of commas within the whole-number portion of a value, for the purpose of making large numbers easier to read. The default is to insert the commas. Remember that each comma uses one character of horizontal space. If space is particularly tight, you might select **NoCommas** to save characters.

❑ **International.** This option is used when you want to change from the American style of decimal number display, e.g., **2,900.00** to the European style, e.g., **2.900,00.**

```
Digits  Sign-Convention  Commas  International
Change the number of digits shown.
```

Figure 7-10 Reformat numeric field menu.

Begin by reducing the number of digits from nine to six by entering

d

As soon as you select the digits command, the decimal portion of the current field is removed and a blinking highlight is positioned on the first digit of the whole number, Figure 7-11.

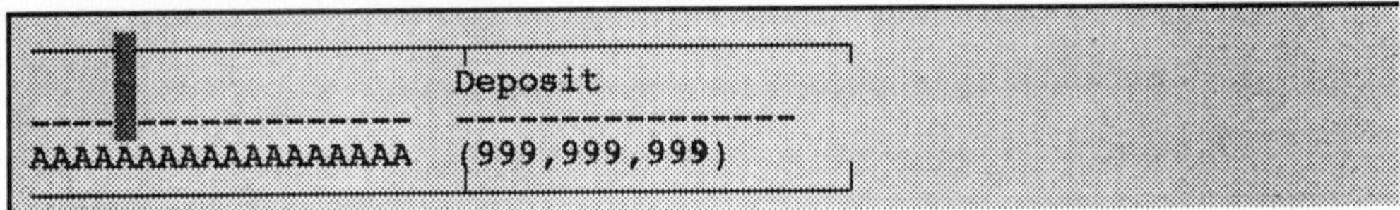

Figure 7-11 Changing digits of a numeric field.

Reduce the field to 6 digits by entering

← ***(4 times)***
↵

Note that you actually save five characters because you eliminate the need for one comma. Paradox next displays the decimal portion of the numeric format. Since *Deposit* is a currency type of field, two decimal places are displayed by default. Accept the two decimal places by entering

↵

You can save an additional character by changing the **Sign-Convention** setting from business, which uses two characters(), to **NegativeOnly**, which uses only a single character to indicate negative numbers.

> *Note that the largest negative number that can be displayed is –9,999.99, since one of the places reserved for a digit will have to be used for the negative sign. If a value in that field exceeds 99,999.99 or is smaller than –9,999.99, Paradox will print ***** characters on the report.*

Enter

[F10] f r ←┘
s n

The field is now six characters smaller.

Reducing the Column Size

Now that the field is smaller than the field column, you can use the **TableBand Resize** command to reduce the width of the column. However, before you attempt to change the column width, you must remove some of the dashes automatically written into the column by Paradox. Paradox will not permit you to make a column more narrow than any of the items, field, or text, located in the column. Delete six of the dashes by entering

↑
[Del]*(7 times)*

The text and fields have now been reduced. You can reduce the column width by entering

[F10] t r ←┘

Paradox does not seem to recognize that you want to reduce the column width. The program displays the message **Cannot split a field during column resize** in the lower right corner of the screen. The message appears because Paradox expects that you would have positioned your cursor at the right edge of the field you want resized. You cannot resize the column with your cursor positioned on a character or field within the column.

In order to perform the resizing, you must move the cursor to the right of the items in the column. Enter

→ ***(9 times)*** ←┘

This time, Paradox accepts the command based on the current cursor position. The → key is used to expand the column width while the ← key contracts the column. Reduce the column by seven characters by entering

← ***(8 times)***
←┘

The report is still too wide but you can reclaim more space by performing the same operation on the *Amount* column. Move the cursor to the *Amount* column by entering

[Shift-Tab] *(3 times)*

Since the cursor is on the dash line, remove six dashes from the column by entering

[Del]*(7 times)*

Recall that you had previously inserted spaces to align the name *Amount* in the center of the column. These spaces count as characters and will prevent you from narrowing the column unless they are removed. Enter

↑
[Del]*(6 times)*

You can now reduce the field size by repeating the operations performed on the *Deposit* field. Enter

↓ ***(2 times)***
[F10] f r ↵
d
← ***(4 times)***
↵ ***(2 times)***

Change the signing convention by entering

[F10] f r ↵
s n

You have now reduced the width of the items in the column. Position the cursor to the right edge of the column by entering

→ ***(9 times)***

Reduce the column width by entering

[F10] t r ↵
→ ***(8 times)***
↵

Wrapping a Field

Reducing the column widths has brought the right edge of the report form closer to the right edge of the page. However, there is still not enough room for all the fields. You can make the final fit by changing the *Memo* field from a horizontal field to a wrapped field. The wrapped field will display the information as a series of short lines wrapped into a narrow column. Keep in mind that the additional lines will be display only if the field contains sufficient text.

Place the cursor in the memo field by entering

[Tab]

The WordWrap option is found on the *Field* submenu. Enter

[F10] f w ↵

The default for WordWrap is 1 line, meaning all the text is printed horizontally across the field. In this case, enter **3** to allow Paradox to create up to 3 lines of text for the field.

[backspace]

3 ↵

Changing a field to *WordWrap* does not, in and of itself, change the field width. However, since the width of the *Memo* field is 25 characters, a field width of 9 characters repeated 3 times would allow the report to display the entire memo using only 9 characters of horizontal space. You can now use the **Field Reformat** command to reduce the field width from 25 to 9 characters. Enter

[F10] f r ↵

Use the ← key to reduce the field to 9 characters from the current 25. Enter

← ***(16 times)***

Before you can narrow the column, the dashes above the field must be reduced. Enter

↑

[Del] ***(16 times)***

↵

The final step is to use the **TableBand Resize** command to narrow the column width. Position the cursor at the right edge of the field. This time, use a shortcut by moving to the next field and then back one character. Enter

[Tab] ←

Reduce the column width by entering

[F10] t r ↵

← ***(17 times)***

↵

The fields now fit onto a single page width, Figure 7-12.

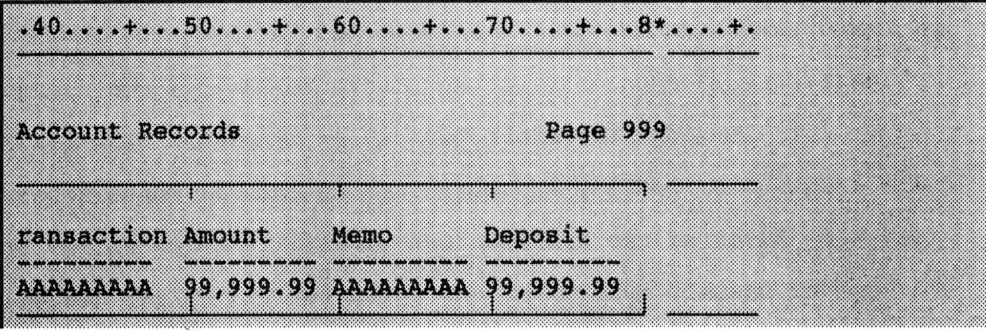

Figure 7-12 Fields manipulated to fit on one page.

Save the report form by entering

[F2]

Print the report using the **Report Output** command. Enter

r o
ck_book ↵
1 ↵

The report will look like Figure 7-13 shown on following page. Note that the text in the wrapped fields will break words between lines if there is no other way to display the text. The more narrow the wrapped field, the more often this will occur.

Moving Columns

The report form just output above used the fields in the order in which they appear in the table structure. The report might look better and be easier to understand if the order of the columns were changed. For example, the *Amount* and *Deposit* columns, both of which contain numeric values, should probably be next to each other, rather than separated by the *Memo* field information.

Paradox makes it easy to rearrange the columns in a report since entire columns, fields, and headings can be moved as a unit. A report can be revised using the **Report Change** command instead of the **Report Design** command. Enter

r c
ck_book ↵
1

1/05/90 Checking Account Records Page 1

Check #	Check date	Description of Transaction	Amount	Memo	Deposit
1	1/01/89	Deposit	0.00		1,700.00
2	1/22/89	Deposit	0.00		850.00
3	2/15/89	Deposit	0.00		1,400.00
4	2/25/89	Deposit	0.00		900.00
999	1/03/89	Savings Club	71.60	Coffee machine	0.00
1000	1/03/89	Allied Office Furniture	750.50	Desk - 48" by 72"	0.00
1001	1/04/89	Central Office Supplies	97.68	Envelopes , folders,	0.00
1002	1/08/89	Western Telephone	101.57		0.00
1003	1/08/89	United Federal Insurance	590.00	Policy Number 10012002A	0.00
1004	1/15/89	Computer World	2,245.50	286 Turbo Com puter	0.00
1005	2/10/89	Savings Club	157.89		0.00
1006	2/19/89	Western Telephone	247.67		0.00
1007	3/05/89	Fathead Software	378.90	Spreadshe et Software	0.00

Figure 7-13 Printed report.

The first item that you can revise, if desired, is the report description. In this case, accept the text of the description as is, by entering

↵

Paradox displays the report exactly as it was when you saved it. In order to change the order of the fields, you must place the cursor in the Table band of the report form layout. Enter

↓ *(9 times)*

The cursor can be positioned in any line within the Table band in order to move a column. In this instance, you want to move the *Memo* column. Position the cursor in this column by entering

[Tab]*(4 times)*

The **TableBand Move** command is used for changing the arrangement of the columns in a report form. Enter

[F10] t m

Select the current column by entering

↵

The new location for the column is selected by moving the cursor with either the ← or → keys. Enter

→ ***(11 times)***
↵

The *Memo* column is moved to the right of the *Deposit* column, allowing *Deposit* to appear next to the *Amount* column. You can output the report directly from the report design mode without having to save the changes, using the **Output** command. Enter

[F10] o p

The report prints with the new arrangement of columns, Figure 7-14.

```
 1/06/90                    Checking Account Records                  Page   1

Check #  Check date  Description of Transaction Amount     Deposit   Memo
-------  ----------  -------------------------- ---------- --------- ---------
      1   1/01/89    Deposit                         0.00  1,700.00
      2   1/22/89    Deposit                         0.00    860.00
      3   2/15/89    Deposit                         0.00  1,400.00
      4   2/25/89    Deposit                         0.00    900.00
    999   1/03/89    Savings Club                   71.60      0.00 Coffee
                                                                    machine
   1000   1/03/89    Allied Office Furniture       750.50      0.00 Desk -
                                                                    48" by
                                                                    72"
   1001   1/04/89    Central Office Supplies        97.68      0.00 Envelopes
                                                                    ,
                                                                    folders,
   1002   1/08/89    Western Telephone             101.57      0.00
   1003   1/08/89    United Federal Insurance      590.00      0.00 Policy
                                                                    Number
                                                                    10012002A
   1004   1/15/89    Computer World              2,245.50      0.00 286
                                                                    Turbo Com
                                                                    puter
   1005   2/10/89    Savings Club                  157.89      0.00
   1006   2/19/89    Western Telephone             247.67      0.00
   1007   3/05/89    Fathead Software              378.90      0.00 Spreadshe
                                                                    et
                                                                    Software
```

Figure 7-14 Columns rearranged in report.

> *The **Output** command allows you to examine the effect of changes before they are saved as part of the report form. You can cancel all changes made to a report by using the [F10] **Cancel** command. The report reverts to the last saved version.*

Summary Calculations

In addition to data from the table, a report can contain summary values such as sums and averages. You can also count the number of records in a field and display the maximum and minimum values.

The most common use of summary fields is in the Report Footer band to print summary totals for numeric or currency columns. Because the summary field is placed into the Report Footer band the value is printed once, at the end of the report.

Summary fields placed into the Report Footer band can perform calculations on fields not included in the other bands. For example, you might want to show the account balance at the end of the report even though the *Balance* field is not included in the table band.

While placing summary fields in the Report Footer band is the most common way to use these fields, they can be placed in any band, report, page, or table. However, it is important to keep in mind that the values printed for the same field will vary depending upon which band they are placed in. For example, if a summary field that sums the values in the *Amount* field is placed into the Report Footer band, it will print once at the end of the report and show the total value of all the records. But if the same field was positioned in the Page Footer band, it would print at the bottom of each page. In this case, the value at the bottom of each page would be the sum of all the records printed up to that point. The value would increase on each page until it reached the final page of the report, where the overall total of all the amounts appear.

A similar effect would take place if the summary field was placed into the table band, except that the field would print each time a record was printed. The value would update for each new record. In general, this would not be very useful, but in some special cases, printing a *running* total might be worthwhile. For example, if the summary field placed into the table band was a **count** operator, it would increase by 1 each time it printed, numbering each of the records consecutively throughout the report.

This reveals something about the way Paradox calculates summary fields in reports. Each summary field used in a report form generates a special area in the memory called an *accumulator*. This area of the memory is used to store the value of the summary field. As each record is processed, the values in the records are used to update the accumulator. Paradox then prints the values in the accumulators when the band where the summary field is located prints.

The accumulator approach to summary fields is quite efficient because all the summary values can be generated in a single pass through the table, i.e., the summary values are accumulated as the records are printed. However, this also means summary fields cannot anticipate the ultimate value they will have at the end of a report or page. For example, suppose you place a summary field that sums the *Amount* field in the Report Header band, rather than the Report Footer band. In Paradox, this will result in a zero value printing, since all the summary field accumulators are zero at the beginning of a report. A similar problem would occur if you place the summary field in the Page Header, rather than the Page Footer band. The total that would print at the top of the page would not be the total of all the records, including that page, but the total of all records from all the previous pages, if any. While there is no technical reason why summary fields cannot be placed in header bands, make sure you understand what the values printed in those headers signify. In most cases you would avoid using summary fields in header bands.

In this report, you will add summary fields that will sum the *Amount* and *Deposit* field, and also print the total number of transactions and the checking account balance at the end of the report.

Column Totals

The most common form of summary field is one that calculates the sum of a numeric or currency field. In this report, you have two such fields, *Amount* and *Deposit*. Field summary totals are usually placed in the Report Footer band so that they will print once at the end of the report.

Begin by creating the summary field for the *Amount* field. Instead of moving directly to the Report Footer band, you may want to position the cursor in the table band first. The reason is that in the table band, the [Tab] and [Shift-Tab] keys can move you quickly from column to column. In the other bands you must position the cursor character by character with the ← and → keys, since they are *not* divided into columns.

Place the cursor at the beginning of the *Amount* field by entering

[Shift-Tab]*(2 times)*

Now move down the screen to the Report Footer band.

↓ *(10 times)*

Report Footer appears in the upper left corner of the screen indicating that the cursor is now positioned in the Report Footer band.

While not required, it is a good idea to enter a line of characters such as - or =, in order to separate the summary field from the table data that will print in the *Amount* column. Keep in mind that the first line of the Report Footer band will print directly after the last record on the last page of the report.

In this case draw a double line by entering

= *(9 times)*

You may have noticed that the Report Footer band is only a single line in height. You can add lines to the band by placing the program in the Insert mode, [Ins], and pressing the ↵ key. Enter

[Ins]
↵

The cursor moves to the beginning of the next line and the height of the Report Footer band is increased to two lines.

Move the cursor back with the → key until it is positioned below the first = in column 49. (The command below shows the actual number of keystrokes needed, but you can probably work faster by eyeballing the cursor movement.)

→ *(48 times)*

To place a summary field in the report, use the **Field Place Summary** command. Enter

[F10] f p s

The program gives you a choice between Regular and Calculated summary fields. The difference between these options may not be apparent from the option names. If you select Regular, you can create the summary field by making menu selections of the field you want to calculate and the type of calculation you want to make. If you select Calculated, you can enter a formula for the summary field. The formulas can duplicate the same calculations that can be made with the Regular option. In addition, you can create formulas that combine several calculations and/or field values. In this case, select a Regular type of summary field. Enter

r

Paradox lists the fields in the table structure. Select the *Amount* field by entering

→ *(3 times)*
r

The next menu lists the five operations, Sum, Average, Count, High, and Low, which can be performed in a summary field, Figure 7-15.

```
Sum  Average  Count  High  Low
Show the total of all values in the field.
```

Figure 7-15 Summary field operations menu.

Here, choose **Sum** by entering

s

The next menu, Figure 7-16, asks you to select Group or Overall summary. Group summaries are used in the Group band to print summary values for the records in a particular group. This means that the memory *accumulator* for the total is reset to zero after each group has printed. Overall summary fields continue to accumulate data throughout the entire report. Note that in reports not using group bands, such as the one you are working on, this distinction has no practical effect.

```
PerGroup  Overall
Calculation for field values within each group.
```

Figure 7-16 Select group or overall summary.

For the sake of form select **Overall** by entering

o (the letter O)

The next option is the placement of the field. Since you have already positioned the cursor in the desired location, you can simply enter

↵

Paradox automatically inserts a numeric output template into the report form. You have the option to increase or decrease the number of digits in the template. In this case, reduce the number of digits to match the number of digits used in the field column.

> *In many cases it is best to have* **more** *digits in the summary field than you use in the field column, since the total value of all records may be a number which has more digits than even the largest number in the table. Because of the small number of records in the sample table, it is not necessary to leave additional space. Keep in mind that when the summary fields are wider than the column fields, the position of the summary field gets a bit tricky. In most cases, you would want the decimal point in the summary field to align with the decimal point in the field column. This means that you should place the start of the summary to the left of the start of the column field so that the decimal place aligns correctly.*

Reduce the number of digits by entering

← ***(7 times)***
↵

By default, the program inserts two decimal places because *Amount* is a currency field. Complete the entry—accepting the two-decimal place—by entering

↵

In order to keep the summary field display consistent with the display of the values in the column, you should change the sign convention format to match the column. Enter

[F10] f r ↵
s n

Repeat the process for the *Deposit* field. Create the separator line by entering

↑
→***(2 times)***
= ***(9 times)***

Place the summary field in the Report Footer band by entering

↓
← ***(9 times)***

The cursor is positioned for the entry of the summary field.

Summary Formulas

The summary field for *Amount* was entered by using the **Field Place Summary Regular** command. The command presented menus from which the field name and the type of summary operation were selected. However, it is possible to create summary fields by writing a **summary** formula using the calculated field option. In report forms, Paradox recognizes special summary operators that can be used to write formulas that perform regular as well as summary arithmetic.

Table 7-3 Report form summary operators

SUM()	sum of a field
AVERAGE()	average of a field
COUNT()	count of records
HIGH()	largest value in field
LOW()	smallest value in field

> *If you have aquired Paradox Version 3.5 you will find that this version greatly expands your ability to perform calculations in a calculated field because it allows you to use PAL language functions, discussed in Part II of the book, in report field formulas. An example of how PAL functions can be used with report forms is supplied in Appendix A.*

Recall from Chapter 5 that field names entered into screen form formulas are surrounded by square brackets, []. By combining fields with summary operators, you can create a formula that will summarize the value of a field. For example, the formula **sum([amount])** would calculate the sum of the *Amount* field exactly as the summary field entered with the **Field Place Summary Regular** command would.

The advantage of writing your own formulas rather than selecting the formula from the menu is that you can create formulas that perform more complex calculations. For example, you could calculate the account balance directly by summing the difference between the *Amount* and *Deposit* fields, e.g., **sum([deposit]–[amount]).**

You can also use more than one summary operator in a formula. For example, suppose you wanted to determine the number of days covered by the report. The formula **high([check date])–low([check date]) uses two operators, high()** and **low()** in order to calculate the number of days between the high and low dates.

Summary formulas can also include literal numeric values which serve as constants. For example, you could calculate the total *pre-tax* value of the *Amount* field with the formula **sum([amount])/1.07** (assuming a 7% sales tax on all amounts.)

> *Note that the ability to calculate summary fields based on more than one field is something that cannot be done using query form calculations.*

If you are comfortable with writing field formulas, you may find that entering formulas is a bit faster than making menu selections. However, when entering formulas you are responsible for any mistakes in syntax or spelling. Paradox will reject any formulas that are incorrect but you must be able to figure out what needs to be corrected.

Writing a Summary Formula

Instead of selecting the summary operation from the Paradox menus, use the Calculated field option to enter a summary formula. Enter

[F10] f p c

The program asks you to enter the *expression* (formula) for the calculated field. Note that a calculated field becomes a summary field when you enter a summary operator. Paradox makes no actual distinction between calculated fields and calculated summary fields. It is only the actual particulars of the formula that determine if the field will use summary calculation. Enter the formula to sum the *Deposit* field.

sum([deposit]) ↵

Place the field by entering

↵

Adjust the number of digits and decimal places by entering

← ***(7 times)***
↵ ***(2 times)***

Change the field format by entering

[F10] f r ↵
s n

You have now placed the fields needed to calculate and display the sum of the *Amount* and *Deposit* fields in the report form, Figure 7-17. In practice, there is no difference between the summary field created with menu options and one created by the direct entry of a formula. The approach you choose is a matter of personal preference.

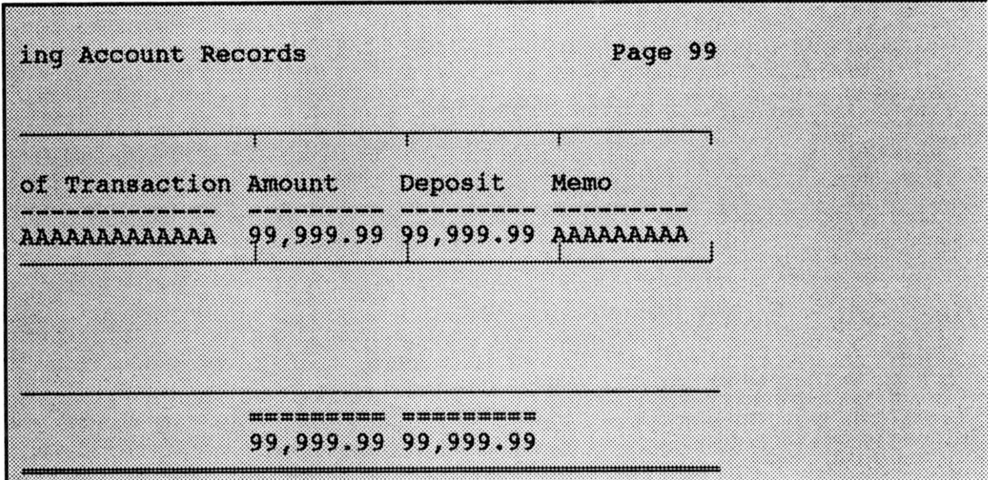

Figure 7-17 Column total fields placed in Report Footer band.

It is important to remember that although you have taken care to place the summary fields below the columns that they summarize, Paradox does not associate these fields with the columns. This means that if you change the column layout by erasing, moving, inserting, or resizing a column, Paradox will *not* automatically change the position of the summary fields to remain aligned with the columns. For example, if you were to move the *Payee* column (called *Description of Transaction* in this report) to the right of the *Amount* and *Deposit* columns the summary fields would remain where they are. Confusion would result as to what the values that appeared in the Report Footer band actually meant, since they would no longer appear directly below the *Amount* and *Deposit* columns. The only way to realign the summary fields with the columns is to manually reposition the fields. This is done using the [Del] key to remove characters to the left of the fields or text—forcing them to move to the left—or, with the insert mode active, enter [spacebar] characters to the left of the items, thus forcing them to move to the right.

Paradox does not provide commands that allow you to directly move fields or text to another position on the report form in a cut-and-paste manner.

For these reasons, it is desirable to add summary fields only after you have arrived at the column layout for the report form. While some changes are inevitable, you should try to plan your work so as to minimize the degree of manual adjustment of summary fields.

Noncolumn Summary Data

The two summary fields that you have just added to the report form use their location, directly below the corresponding field columns, to identify their meaning.

It is possible—and often, useful—to add summary information not directly related to any particular column at the end of the report. For example you may want to print the account balance or the total number of transactions included in the report. Noncolumn summary fields can be placed anywhere in the report form but, considering the way Paradox accumulates summary values, they would usually be employed in Report or Page Footer bands. In addition, it is usually necessary to identify the summary fields with text since there would be no way for a reader to know the significance of the values unless explicitly labeled.

Suppose you want to display the current account balance and the total number of transactions included in the report. You will need to add some extra lines to the Report Footer band. This is done with the ↵ key. Enter

→ ↵

Enter the text that will identify the value.

Account Balance:

You need to insert a calculated field that will compute the sum of the difference of the *Deposit* and *Amount* fields. Enter

[F10] f p c
sum([deposit]-[amount]) ↵

Place the field next to the text by entering

↵ ***(3 times)***

Add another line to the report form by entering

→***(2 times)***
↵

The new line will hold a formula that will count the total number of transactions in the report. Enter

Transactions:
[F10] f p c
count([check #]) ↵
↵ *(3 times)*

Date Fields

Finally, add a new line and place summary formulas that will print the first and last dates contained in the table. This will show the range of dates included in the report. Enter

→ ↵
From
[spacebar]

Place a calculated field at this location that uses the **low()** operator to find the first date in the *Check date* field. Enter

[F10] f p c
low([check date]) ↵

Because the *result* of the formula will be a *date*, Paradox displays a special menu from which you can select 1 of 11 different date formats, Figure 7-18. Note that you can only see the first 5 options on the menu at this time. The display will scroll to the left to display formats 6 through 11.

```
Date format to use:                                        Report Ins 1/3
1) mm/dd/yy  2) M o n t h dd, yyyy  3) mm/dd  4) mm/yy  5) dd-Mon-yy
```

Figure 7-18 Date format menu.

Table 7-4 Report date field formats

No.	Format	Example
1)	mm/dd/yy	1/31/89
2)	M o n t h dd, yyyy	January 31, 1989
3)	mm/dd	1/31
4)	mm/yy	1/89
5)	dd-Mon-yy	31-Jan-89
6)	Mon yy	Jan 89
7)	dd-Mon-yyyy	31-Jan-1989
8)	mm/dd/yyyy	1/31/1989
9)	dd.mm.yy	31.01.89
10)	dd/mm/yy	31/01/89
11)	yy-mm-dd	89-01-31

In this instance, choose format 5 by entering

5 ↵

Continue the item by entering more text and then the high date formula.

[spacebar]
To
[spacebar]
[F10] f p c
high([check date]) ↵
5 ↵

The report form now contains both column and noncolumnar summary fields, Figure 7-19.

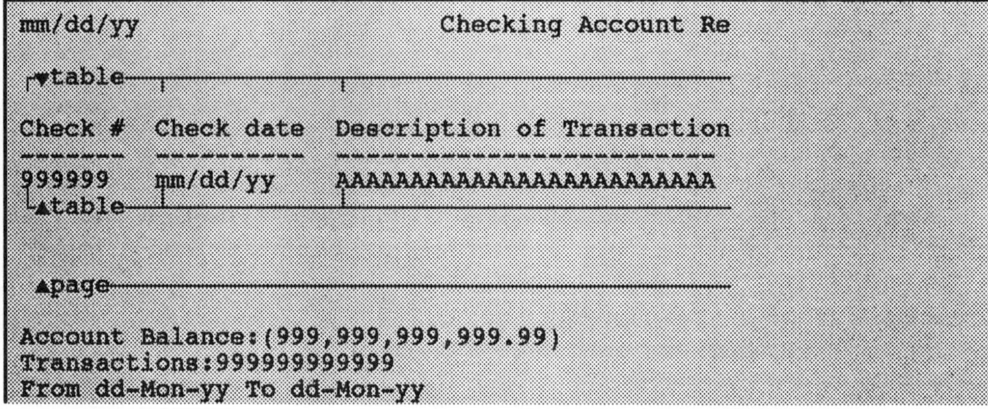

Figure 7-19 Report form with column and noncolumn summary fields.

Save the modified report form and output the report by entering

[F2]
r o
ck_book ↵
1
p

The report will look like the one shown in Figure 7-20.

Calculated Columns

The report just created consists primarily of field data drawn directly from the Ck_book table, with a few summary calculations. You can create reports in which the contents of

```
1/07/90                   Checking Account Records                    Page   1


Check #  Check date  Description of Transaction Amount    Deposit   Memo
-------  ----------  -------------------------- --------  --------  ----------
      1   1/01/89    Deposit                        0.00  1,700.00
      2   1/22/89    Deposit                        0.00    860.00
      3   2/15/89    Deposit                        0.00  1,400.00
      4   2/25/89    Deposit                        0.00    900.00
    999   1/03/89    Savings Club                  71.60      0.00  Coffee
                                                                    machine
   1000   1/03/89    Allied Office Furniture      750.50      0.00  Desk -
                                                                    48" by
                                                                    72"
   1001   1/04/89    Central Office Supplies       97.68      0.00  Envelopes
                                                                    ,
                                                                    folders,
   1002   1/08/89    Western Telephone            101.57      0.00
   1003   1/08/89    United Federal Insurance     590.00      0.00  Policy
                                                                    Number
                                                                    10012002A
   1004   1/15/89    Computer World             2,245.50      0.00  286
                                                                    Turbo Com
                                                                    puter
   1005   2/10/89    Savings Club                 157.89      0.00
   1006   2/19/89    Western Telephone            247.67      0.00
   1007   3/05/89    Fathead Software             378.90      0.00  Spreadshe
                                                                    et
                                                                    Software
                                                ========  ========
                                                4,641.31  4,860.00
Account Balance:            218.69
Transactions:            13
From  1-Jan-89 To  5-Mar-89
```

Figure 7-20 Report includes column and noncolumn summary calculations

the columns is generated by calculations. For example, suppose you want to create a report that displays the sales tax and pre-tax amounts, as calculated in Chapter 6, using query calculations.

Calculated fields can create calculated columns in reports when the field is placed into a report column. You can place any type of valid calculation into a column and produce one value for each record printed. This even applies to summary fields. For example, if the formula **sum([deposit]-[amount])** was placed into a Table band column it would print a running balance for all the records printed up to that point. The value printed for the last record would be the actual report balance.

Copying a Report Form

When you create a new report, Paradox will automatically begin by generating a standard report form layout. In many cases, it is simpler to use one of the reports you have already created as a starting point. Here, it would be better to start the new report by modifying the layout used for report 1, rather than starting with the standard layout that would contain columns for all the fields in the table.

You can use the **Tools Copy Report** command to make a duplicate of an existing report. Enter

[F10] t c r

The **Copy Report** command has two options: SameTable and DifferentTable. In this case, you want to copy a report from the Ck_book to another report name in the same table. Enter

s
ck_book ↵

Choose the report you want to copy. Enter

1

Choose the report number to assign to the copied report. Enter

2

Paradox makes a copy of the report form 1 and stores it under the name of report 2, file name CK_BOOK.R2.

Modifying a Copied Report

To modify the copied report, use the **Report Change** command.

r c
ck_book ↵
2

Change the description of the report by entering

[Ctrl-backspace]
Sales Tax Report ↵

The report form is displayed in the design mode. As expected, this report is a duplicate of report 1.

The first change you will want to make is to the page header title of the report.

> *Because you did not create this report from scratch, Paradox did not transfer the changed report description to the title line in the report form. The title must therefore be changed manually.*

Enter

↓ ***(5 times)***
→***(28 times)***
Sales Tax Report
[spacebar] ***(8 times)***

Next, move to the Table band and remove the columns that will not be needed for this report: *Payee, Deposit*, and *Memo*. Enter

↓ ***(3 times)***

Remove the *Deposit* and *Memo* fields by entering

[Tab]
[F10] t e ↵
[F10] t e ↵

Remove both the *Payee* and *Amount* columns by entering

←
[Shift-Tab]***(2 times)***
[F10] t e ↵
[F10] t e ↵

You may wonder why the *Amount* field was removed, since it is eventually to be included in the final report form. The reason is that the layout of the amount column is constricted so that the entire field can fit onto the a single page in the previous report. In this report, you will have more room and can use a different format for the *Amount* column.

Numbering Records

One special type of calculated column which you might want to use in a report is one that numbers the records as they print. You can create this effect by using a summary field with a **count** operator in the Table band column. The calculated field will begin at 1 and increase by 1 for each record printed, effectively numbering each record with a consecutive number. Insert a column to the left of the report using the **TableBand Insert** command.

Move the cursor to the left side of the form by entering

[Ctrl-Home]

Insert a new column by entering

[F10] t i ↵

Place a calculated field in the new column. Enter

↓ ***(4 times)***
→***(2 times)***
[F10] f p c

The expression you are entering is a summary calculation that will count records. Because it does not matter which field in the table you count, use the *Check #* field. Enter

count([check #])
↵ ***(2 times)***

A two-digit number will suffice, since there are less than 100 records in the table. Enter

←***(10 times)***
↵ ***(2 times)***

As punctuation, place a period after the field. Enter

→
.(period)

The column you inserted was automatically set to a width of 12 characters—wider than is needed for the record numbers. Reduce the width of the column by entering

[Tab]→
[F10] t r ↵
←***(9 times)***
↵

The summary field has now been placed into a column in the Table band, Figure 7-21.

Copying Columns

In order to complete this report, you will need to add three numeric columns. Instead of creating the columns one by one, it may be faster to create one column, copy it twice, and edit its contents. This method is useful when settings such as the field format, column width, and

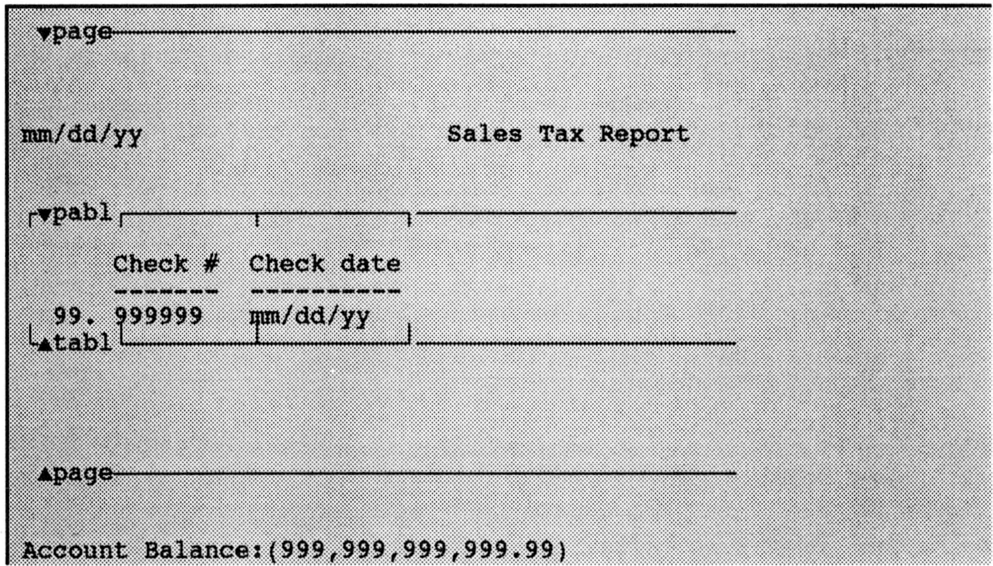

Figure 7-21 Summary field used in Table band.

separator lines remain the same. If each column is composed from scratch, these settings will have to be repeated each time.

Begin by inserting a new column on the right side of the report next to the *Check date* column. It is important to note that when you want to insert a new column, the cursor must be located in one of the current columns in the Table band even though you might want to add the column to the right of the last column in the current layout. Use the **TableBand Insert** command to add a new column to the layout by entering

[F10] t i

Once you have initiated the **TableBand Insert** command, you can move the cursor outside of the current column layout to indicate that the new column should be added to the end of the report form. Enter

→ ***(23 times)***

Paradox adds a blank column to the right side of the report form. Begin by typing the dashes for the separator line. Enter

↑
→***(2 times)***
-(12 times)

Next, insert a calculated field into the column. Enter

[Shift-Tab]
↓
→***(2 times)***

What field or calculation should be placed in this column? Since the report is about the sales tax calculations you need to print the amounts, the pre-tax values, and the amount of sales tax. Thus, you must place the *Amount* field in this column. Should this field be a regular or calculated field? In most cases, you would create a regular field since the contents of this column will simply display the values of the *Amount* field without any arithmetic manipulation. However, part of your goal is to create these three columns without having to start from scratch each time. Paradox has a command that appears on the Field menu called **CalcEdit**. This command allows you to edit the formula used for a calculated field, avoiding the necessity to erase and replace a field if only the formula needs to be changed. If you could place a field in this column that was a calculated field instead of a regular field, you could copy the column and edit the formula without having to go through the trouble of placing a brand new field in those columns. The advantage of editing a copied calculated field is that items in that column, such as field location, format, and the separator lines, do not have to be entered for each column.

This may seem a bit complicated but, in practice, it makes the addition of similar numeric columns much faster. The trick is to enter the field as a calculated field rather than a regular field, since the **CalcEdit** command works only on calculated fields. There is no reason why a calculated field formula cannot consist simply of the field name, e.g., **[amount]**, resulting in the identical information obtained with a regular type of field.

Place a calculated field in this column with a field name as the formula by entering

[F10] f p c
[amount] ↵

Format the field with seven digits and two decimal places by entering

←***(2 times)***
(2 times)

Change the format to

[F10] f r ↵
s n

You have now created a column that is a *generic* numeric column. Its width, field location, format, and separator line can be copied to produce any number of identical numeric columns. All that needs to be done to complete each column is to add the column name and edit the formula of the calculated field.

In this example, your report will contain two more numeric columns. The **TableBand Copy** command allows you to create duplicate columns. Make two copies of the current column by entering

[F10] t c
↵ *(2 times)*
[F10] t c
↵ *(2 times)*

The **copy** command has quickly created a report with three *generic* numeric columns. You can now complete the column by entering the heading and formula details. Begin with editing the formulas. The current column contains the correct formula for that column. Skip that column and edit the formula in the column to its right by entering

[Tab]
→*(2 times)*
[F10] f c ↵

The **CalcEdit** command displays the current field formula at the top of the screen so that it can be edited, Figure 7-22.

```
Expression: [amount]                                  Report    1/3
Calculation from fields in a record -- e.g. [Quan] * [Unit-Price].
```

Figure 7-22 CalcEdit displays field formula for editing.

To change the formula to one that calculates the pre-tax value of the amount, all you need do is to add **/1.07** to the formula. Enter

/1.07 ↵

Paradox displays the message **New expression recorded** in the lower right corner of the screen. All the other attributes of the column remain unchanged.

Move to the next column and modify the formula in it to calculate the amount of sales tax. Enter

[Tab]
→*(2 times)*
[F10] f c ↵

Add the following items to the formula.

-([amount]/1.07) ↵

All three columns now have the correct formulas. The last step is to add the column heading text to all three columns. Enter

[Shift-Tab]*(3 times)*
↑ *(2 times)*
→ *(2 times)*

Enter the headings by typing the following text.

Check Amt.
[Tab]
→*(2 times)*
Pre-Tax Amt.
[Tab]
→*(2 times)*
Sales Tax

The report now contains the numeric columns required to produce the desired data, shown in Figure 7-23. The copy/edit method can simplify the creation of numeric column in reports that contain numeric data. The method is faster and more direct than setting up each column individually.

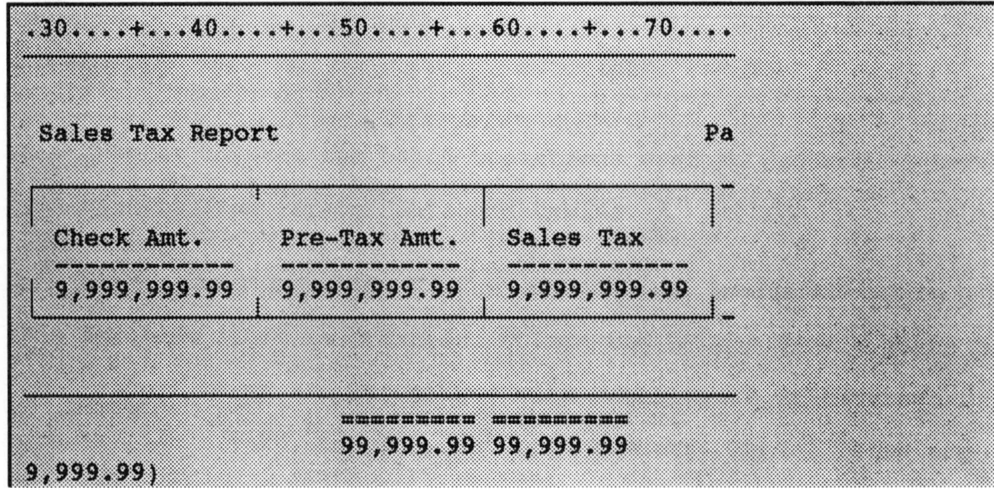

Figure 7-23 Numeric columns created by copying and editing.

Deleting Lines

Unfortunately, the copy/edit method used to speed up the creation of numeric columns cannot be applied to fields in the Report or Page bands, since the **TableBand** commands do not apply to those areas of the report form.

In this report, it would be logical to want to have column sums for the three numeric columns.

The Report Footer band currently contains some calculations that should be removed from the report. You can delete an entire line, and all the text and field items on that line, from the report form by using the command keystroke [Ctrl-y]. Note that to remove an entire line the cursor must be positioned at the beginning of the line, [Ctrl-Home], before the [Ctrl-y] command is entered.

> *Using [Ctrl-y] as the delete line command is compatible with the WordStar editing set. In the early 1980s, WordStar's editing commands were a de facto standard for text editing in many applications and some of those conventions still appear in many applications. Note that [Ctrl-y] is also used in the dBASE IV report editor for the same purpose.*

In addition to removing lines with items inserted, you can use [Ctrl-y] to close up empty lines in the report form. For example, by default, Paradox leaves several blank lines in the Page Footer band. Since this report does not use the page footer band, you can remove those lines. The advantage of removing these lines is that it makes it easier to align the summary field in the Report Footer band with the column in the Table band.

It is important to remember that empty lines in a report form do *not* create *blank lines* on the printed report. Paradox ignores empty lines left in a report form and prints only those lines containing text or field items. If you want blank lines in a report, you must place a special blank line command into the report form.

Close up the unused lines in the Page Footer band by entering

[Ctrl-Home]
↓ *(4 times)*
[Ctrl-y] *(4 times)*

The Report Footer band is now closer to the Table band, making it easier to judge alignment with column items.

The last three lines of the Report Footer contain calculations not needed for this report. Delete those lines by entering

↓ *(3 times)*
[Ctrl-y] *(3 times)*

Moving Existing Fields

As noted earlier, it is usually better to edit existing items than to begin from scratch. This is particularly useful in the Table band where columns can be moved, copied, and edited. In the other report bands you do not have these commands available. However, you can manipulate items using the basic editing tools available in the report design mode.

In this example, you have two summary fields which were used in report 1. These fields are not correctly placed in the report. Note that as you changed the Table band columns, Paradox made no effort to move the summary fields to the new column locations. In Paradox, that operation is completely manual.

Suppose you want to change the horizontal position of the summary field that calculates the sum of the *Amount* field. This is done by inserting or removing spaces to the left of the field. For example, to move the field under the column where the *Amount* field is printed, you must delete spaces. Enter

[Del] ***(19 times)***

Each time the [Del] key was used, it removed one space from the beginning of the line and caused the items on that line to shift one character to the right. Note that both of the fields on the line move together. In order to place the second field under a different column, you must insert or delete spaces between the two fields.

Move the cursor so that it is positioned on the first character in the calculated field with the formula **sum([deposit])**. The exact keystrokes needed are:

→ ***(39 times)***

If you look at the upper right corner of the screen you will see that Paradox displays the formula for the field on which the cursor is positioned, **sum([deposit])**. The formula indicates that this is a calculated field, not a regular field; thus, it can be modified with the **CalcEdit** command.

To move this field to the right, place Paradox into the insert mode and insert spaces into the report form as follows.

[Ins]
[spacebar] ***(5 times)***

While the cursor is positioned on this field, change its formula and its format to match the column under which it is positioned. First, change the formula to calculate the sum of the pre-tax amounts. Enter

[F10] f c ↵
[Ctrl-backspace]
sum([amount]/1.07) ↵

Add two more digits to the format by entering

[F10] f r ↵
d
→*(2 times)*
(2 times)

Make the same formatting change to the summary field for *Amount*. Enter

←*(7 times)*
[F10] f r ↵
d
→*(2 times)*
↵ *(2 times)*

It is interesting to notice that in this band, the addition of digits to the field format causes all the items to the right to be moved to the right thus changing the alignment. In order to restore the alignment of the pre-tax summary field, you now have to delete characters. This would not have been the case in the Table band where each column is distinct from the other columns. Correct the alignment by entering

→
[Del] *(3 times)*

Add a third summary calculation under the Sales Tax column. Enter

[Ctrl-End]
→*(3 times)*
[F10] f p c
sum([amount])-sum([amount]/1.07) ↵
↵
← *(5 times)*
↵ *(2 times)*

The use of a nested parentheses inside of a **sum()** operator would cause a syntax error. For example, according to mathematical notation, the formula **sum([amount]–([amount]/1.07))** ought to yield the same results as **sum([amount])–sum([amount]/1.07)**. However, Paradox scans the formulas entered to determine if the syntax is correct. The use of a () inside of sum() is interpreted as a formula with a missing operator before the () and is rejected by Paradox. If you encounter problems with entering formulas that use () nested within summary operators, try to rework the formula to avoid nesting, e.g., **sum([amount])–sum([amount]/1.07)**.

Change the format of the field to match that of the rest of the report. Enter

[F10] f r ↵
s n

In the previous report, lines of = characters were used to separate the summary fields from the column values. In this case it may be simpler just to insert a blank line above the summary fields to act as a separator. Enter

↑ [Ctrl-Home] [Ctrl-y]

Insert a new empty line into the Report Footer band. (Note that the insert mode is still active from the command [Ins] entered on 232.)

↵ ↑

The report form should look like Figure 7-24.

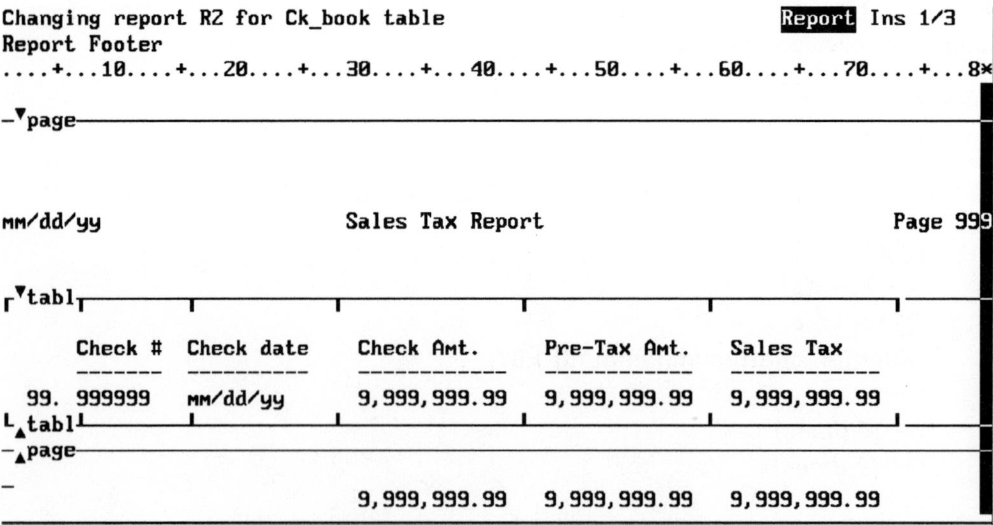

Figure 7-24 Report form with calculated columns.

Output the report by entering

[F10] o p

The report should look like Figure 7-25.

1/08/90 Sales Tax Report Page 1

	Check #	Check date	Check Amt.	Pre-Tax Amt.	Sales Tax
1.	1	1/01/89	0.00	0.00	0.00
2.	2	1/22/89	0.00	0.00	0.00
3.	3	2/15/89	0.00	0.00	0.00
4.	4	2/25/89	0.00	0.00	0.00
5.	999	1/03/89	71.60	66.92	4.68
6.	1000	1/03/89	750.50	701.40	49.10
7.	1001	1/04/89	97.68	91.29	6.39
8.	1002	1/08/89	101.57	94.93	6.64
9.	1003	1/08/89	590.00	551.40	38.60
10.	1004	1/15/89	2,245.50	2,098.60	146.90
11.	1005	2/10/89	157.89	147.56	10.33
12.	1006	2/19/89	247.67	231.47	16.20
13.	1007	3/05/89	378.90	354.11	24.79
			4,641.31	4,337.67	303.64

Figure 7-25 Printer report with calculated columns.

Save the report form by entering

[F2]

Exit Paradox by entering

e y

Summary

This chapter covered the basic operations used to produce column type reports from Paradox database tables.

❑ **Reports.** Reports are used to create formal, paginated outputs from database table information. Unlike the output from a query form, report forms are structured with page layout attributes such as page breaks, margins, and page numbers. Report forms are normally sent to the printer but can be sent to the screen (for previewing) or a text file (for transfer to a word processing or desktop publishing program). Paradox automatically generates an *instant* report form for each database table. This report is stored under the name R, *TABLE_NAME*.R. You can design up to 14 additional report forms for each table. You can also modify the R report form.

❑ **Report Forms.** All new reports created in Paradox begin with the *standard* design layout. The *standard* design for a column report automatically contains columns for all of the fields in the database table. The field names are automatically inserted as the column names. Report design consists of making additions, deletions, or changes to the basic design. If you want to avoid beginning with the *standard* design, you can use the **Tools Copy Report** command to begin a new report with a copy of an existing report form.

❑ **Horizontal Pagination.** In order to accommodate all the fields in a table, Paradox will print additional pages horizontally so that all the fields in the report will print.

❑ **Report Bands.** Report forms are divided into *bands*. A band is a section of the report that prints under specific conditions. The standard design includes five bands. The Report Header and Footer bands print once at the beginning and once at the end of the report. The Report Header is used for introductory information, while the Report Footer is used for summary data such as column or other totals summarizing the entire report. The Page Header and Footer bands will print at the top and bottom of each page. This band is typically used to print page numbers or other data that belongs on each page of the report. The Table band prints the details from the database table. The Table band data prints once for every record in the database table. If a band is left empty it is ignored when the report prints.

❑ **Table Band Columns.** In column type reports, the Table band has a structure that is different from the other bands used in the report. The Table band is divided into distinct columns. The columns allow you to enter column headings, a separator line, and a field (regular or calculated) as a single column unit. Columns, unlike other report items, can be inserted, deleted, copied, and moved as units, i.e., when a column is moved, copied, deleted, or inserted, all of the lines in that column operate together.

❑ **Fields.** Table information is inserted into a report in the form of a field, regular or calculated. Fields can be placed in any of the bands of the report. If you want to print the values of each record, the field should be placed in the Table band.

❑ **Summary Fields.** A summary field is one that calculates summary information about a field or field formula. Summary fields are usually placed in the Report Footer band so that they will print at the end of the report. If they are placed into other bands, the fields will print the values accumulated up to the point at which they print.

❑ **Calculated Fields.** Calculated fields can be used to create a calculated column if placed in the Table band, or to print values if placed in other bands. You can include summary values in a calculated field by using the summary operators, **sum()**, **average()**, **count()**, **high()**, or **low()** in the formula.

Exercises

Exercise 1 from page 204

[F10] t e ↵

8

Report Groups and Report Queries

In Chapter 7, you learned the basic techniques used to create column-type reports in Paradox. The goal of this chapter is to explore some additional techniques that can be used to expand the scope and utility of the basic column reports created in Chapter 7. There are two basic areas that will be covered.

❏ **Reports with Groups.** In addition to the three basic bands used in column reports, Report, Page and Table, Paradox allows you to add *group* bands. Groups bands allows you to create reports in which records can be grouped together according to the values in a specific field. For example, you might want to print a checking account report that groups together all of the deposits and checks for each month. Such reports often will print subtotals for each group in addition to the summary values for the entire report.

❏ **Using Reports with Queries.** When you print a report, Paradox includes all of the records in the table. In many cases, you might war to restrict the records included in a report by some logical condition. In addition, the records in the report always print according to the sort order of the table. It might be desirable to print the records in different record orders depending on the type of report being printed. This can be accomplished by combining report forms with query forms in order to sort and select records which will appear on the reports.

Begin by loading Paradox in the usual manner.

Report Groups

In addition to the three basic bands used in column reports, Paradox allows you to add a fourth band called a *group* band. Group bands are used to break up the records included in a report into a series of record groupings. Each group contains records which contain the same value in the specified group key field. For example, suppose that you selected the *Period* field as the group key field. All of the records that had the same value in the Period field, 01-Jan, 02-Feb, etc. would be grouped together. Summary fields used in the group band would print each time a new group printed. This makes it possible to print subtotals for each group of records. Summary fields that are used to print group subtotals will reset to zero each time a new group starts.

Like the other report bands the group band is divided into a Group Header and a Group Footer band. Text and fields placed into the Group Header band will print prior to the first record in each group. This band usually contains a group heading which is printed to identify the group of records that follows.

The Group Footer band prints after the last record in the group prints. This band usually contains group subtotal summary fields which calculate the totals for each group.

Group bands are always inserted in the Page band unless there is an existing group into which a subgroup band can be nested.

Types of Groups

Groups can be designated in three ways in Paradox using the **Group Insert** command. If a group already exists, you can change its grouping type with the **Group Regroup** command.

❑ **Field.** A group based on a field uses the values contained in a specified field to determine which records should be grouped together. Selecting a field group causes the records in the database table to be sorted in ascending order (unless otherwise specified) according to the values in the group field. All of the records that have exactly the *same* value in the group field are treated as a group. This type of group is referred to as a *control break* report. The name *control break* refers to the fact that the report will print the Group Footer and Group Header each time there is a change in the *controlling* field's value. Logically, group fields should not contain unique values (e.g., key fields). Keep in mind that field groups require **exact** matches in the group field. If you want to group on partial matches use the **Range** option.

❑ **Range.** The range option can be used to form report groups on fields that do not have exact matches but whose values fall into closely assocatied ranges of values. The exact way that the range of values is selected depends on the type of field selected as the group range field. In all three cases, records are sorted in ascending order (unless otherwise selected) when they are printed.

❑ **Date Range.** If the field selected as the range group is a date type of field, Paradox allows you to select one of four chronological categories (day, week, month, or year) by which the records should be grouped. The built-in chronological periods avoid the necessity of having a field like *Period* that isolates the month from the date values. In a group report, this is done automatically by Paradox.

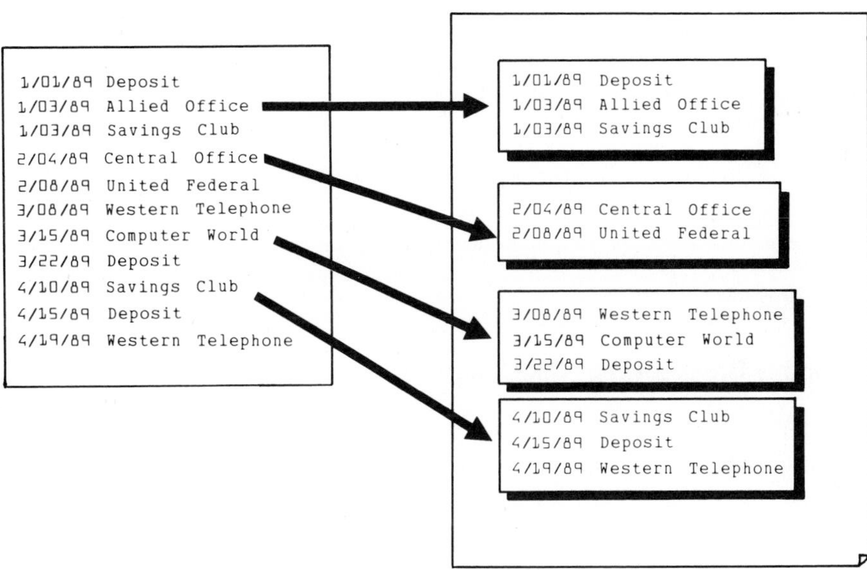

Figure 8-1 Table records grouped by month.

❑ **Numeric Range.** If the field selected at the range group is the numeric (or currency) field, the records are divided into groups according to a range value which you can enter. For example, if you enter 100, all of the records from 0–99 form one group, 100–199 a second group, and so on. This type of grouping is similar to the way that values are categorized in a *frequency distribution* analysis. If no records fall into a given group, the group is skipped.

❑ **Character Range.** If the field selected for the group range is an alphanumeric field, records can be grouped together on the basis of partial matches. You have the option of entering the number of characters, taken from the beginning of the field, which have to match in order to form a group. For example, if you specify **1**, all records that have the same first letter in the group field will be grouped together. If you specify **2**, then the first two characters must match in order to form a group.

❑ **Records.** This type of grouping is the only one in which the contents of the fields is not relevant to the grouping nor are the records sorted differently than in a nongrouped report. In this type of grouping, the user specifies a numeric value for the size of each group. The records are then arbitrarily divided into groups of the specified number of records until all the records have been processed. This type of grouping is often used when you want to break up long columns to make them easier to read or count.

In those cases (all but Record groups) in which the records are sorted before they are printed, you can select to have the sort use descending order instead, by using the **Group SortDirection** command.

Designing a Group Report

Group reports begin like any other type of report. Create a new report for the Ck_book table by entering

r d
ck_book ↵
3
Monthly Breakdown of Checking Account ↵
t

Paradox automatically fills the report form with columns based on the table structure. The report contains the standard Report, Page, and Table bands.

Removing Empty Lines

When Paradox creates the standard column layout for a new report form, it inserts a number of empty lines in the report form. For example, the Report Header band contains a single blank line. The effect of this blank line is that there is an extra blank line printed at the top of the first page of the report. Since you will not be using the Report Header band in this report, it is probably a good idea to remove this blank line. Enter

[Ctrl-y]

The report form also contains a blank line in the Table band. Since there are already two blank lines below the text in the Page Header band, you might want to remove this blank line from the Table band. Enter

↓ *(8 times)*
[Ctrl-y]

Deleting Unwanted Columns

In this report, you will want to print columns for the *Check #, Check date, Payee,* and *Amount* fields. All of the other columns can be erased from the report form. In Paradox, it is necessary to remove the unwanted columns one by one by using the **TableBand Erase** command.

Begin by positioning the cursor in the first of the unwanted columns, the Memo column. Enter

[Tab] ***(4 times)***
[F10] t e ↵

There are five more fields to be removed from the report form. Try this on your own. The correct commands can be found on page 277 under Exercise 1.

Replacing a Field

The current report form consists of four field columns: *Check #, Check date, Payee,* and *Amount*. In this report, the Amount column should show a positive value for each deposit but a negative value for each check. Instead of printing the *Amount* field in the Amount column, you will replace that field with a calculated field.

Because the *Amount* field inserted automatically by Paradox is a *regular* type of field, you cannot change its formula by means of the **Field CalcEdit** command. Instead, you must first erase the current field and then place a calculated field into the column. Move the cursor to the *Amount* field by entering

↓ ***(2 times)***
← ***(2 times)***
[Shift-Tab]

The cursor is now positioned at the beginning of the field. Erase the field by entering

[F10] f e ↵

Insert a calculated field that subtracts the *Amount* from the *Deposit* for each record. Enter

[F10] f p c
[deposit]-[amount]
↵ ***(2 times)***

Shorten the field format by three digits. Enter

← ***(3 times)***
↵ ***(2 times)***

Counting by Group

Up to this point all of the operations which you have carried out would apply to a report with groups. Recall from Chapter 7 how a summary field was used in the Table band to generate numbers for the records that were printed. In that report, all of the records were numbered consecutively. Suppose that you wanted to number each group independently, i.e., starting each group of records with 1 and numbering consecutively within the group.

That type of calculation is called a *group* summary. A group summary is one in which the value accumulator is reset to zero for each new group rather than continuing to accumulate through the entire report.

Group summary fields can be created in two ways.

❑ **PerGroup Option.** When the **Field Place Summary Regular** command is used to insert a summary field, you are given the choice of having the summary operation work in a *PerGroup* or *Overall* manner. If you select PerGroup, the value of the field is reset to zero each time a new group is started.

❑ **Group operator.** If you create creating a calculated summary field, you can select group operation by adding the **group** operator to the formula. For example, the formula **sum([amount]),group** would calculate a separate sum for the *Amount* field for each group in the report. Note that the **group** operator is separated from the formula itself by a comma.

Group summary fields can be placed in any band, but they make the most sense when used in the Group or Table bands, since their printing is logically related to the data in the table.

Counting by Group

Suppose that you wanted to add a group field to the Table band that would number each group of records independently using the menu-command method. Move the cursor to the left side of the Table band by entering

[Ctrl-Home]

Insert a new column into the report by entering

[F10] t i ↵

Select to insert a summary field by entering

[F10] f p s r

Select the *Check #* field by entering

↵

Choose a *Count* operation by entering

c

Paradox now displays the group menu. In this case, select the **PerGroup** option to create a field that starts at zero for each new group in the report. Enter

p

Set the format for a three-digit number by entering

↵
← ***(3 times)***
↵ ***(2 times)***

Add a period for punctutation.

→
. *(period)*

Group Bands

The insertion of a group summary field does not in and of itself create a group report. In order to create a group report, you will need to insert at least one group band into the report.

Paradox allows you to insert up to 16 group bands in one report. When more than one group band is used in a report, it creates a *nested* subgroup within the first group. For example, if you had a group band that grouped records by month, you could nest a group band—inside of the month band—which would create weekly subgroups, Figure 8-2. Nesting subgroups can be based on fields of different types. For example, suppose you grouped records according to their tax-deductible status. That would divide the report into two groups, Y and N. In that case, you might seek to break down each deductible group by month so that each of the two groups would be subdivided into monthly groups.

Group summary fields will follow the logic of the group nesting. In the case of records grouped by month and within month by week, you could place a summary field in each band. The field in the weekly band would generate a new value for each week, while the field in the monthly band would accumulate a value for all of the weeks in a given month.

Groups are added to a report band through the use of the **Group Insert** command. The group band inserted comes in two parts: a Group Header and a Group Footer. The bands are labeled to indicate the value, range, or number of records used to create a group. When first inserted, a group band contains a single blank line in the Group Header and another blank line in the Group Footer. As inserted, the group band would insert two blank lines, one from the Group

Footer and one from the Group Header band, between each group, with the exception of the first and last groups.

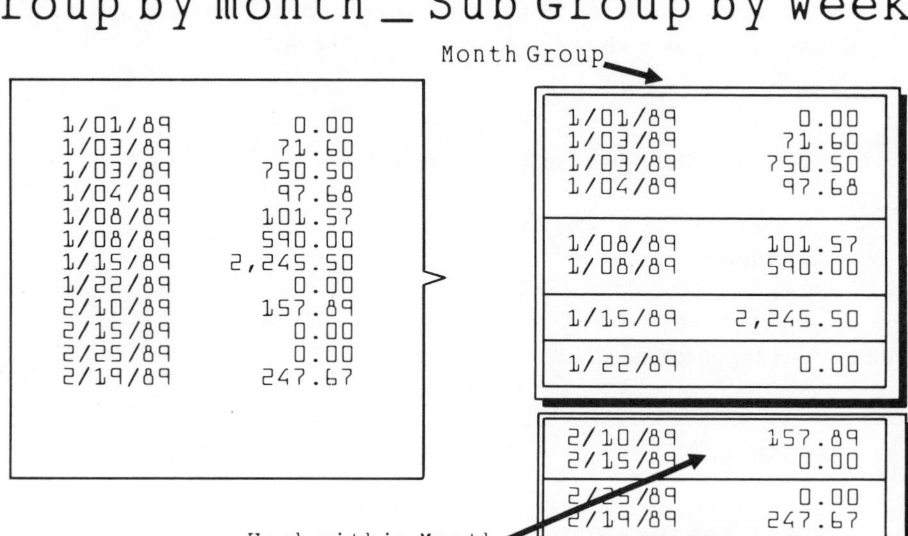

Figure 8-2 Nested group bands created record sub groups.

You can add text, fields, and summary fields to both the Group Header and Group Footer bands. If a field is placed into the Group Header, the value from the corresponding field in the *first* record in the group will print. A field in the Group Header is typically used to insert a value into a group heading.

Conversely, if the field is placed into the Group Footer, it will print the corresponding value in the last record in the group. Group summary fields placed into the Group Footer will produce group subtotals.

In the current report, you will add a group band that will create monthly groups.

Inserting a Group Band

You can insert a group band into a report by using the **Group Insert** command. This command creates the Group Header and Footer bands and also sets the field, range, or record number used to divide the table into groups.

Begin by positioning the cursor in the Page Header band by entering

↑ ***(4 times)***

Insert a new set of group bands by entering

[F10] g i

Grouping dates according to month values is a Range type of group. Select **Range** by entering

r

Paradox displays a menu of the field names. Select the *Check date* field by entering

→ ↵

Because the *Check date* field is a date type of field, Paradox displays a menu of special chronological groups available, Figure 8-3.

```
Day  Week  Month  Year
Form a new group for each day.
```

Figure 8-3 Date grouping options menu.

Select a monthly grouping by entering

m

Once you have selected the type of group you want to create, you are asked to indicate the location for the group. This option has meaning when you want to nest a new set of group bands within an existing group. If there are no group bands in the report, your cursor can be positioned in any part of the Page bands in order to insert a group band. Enter

↵

The program inserts group bands, both Group Header and Group Footer, into the report form, Figure 8-4. The bands display the name of the field and the type of grouping to be used. Note that the group band implies that the records will be sorted by *Check date* order on the report.

Fields in Group Bands

As with the other types of bands used in report forms, you can place fields of any type (regular, summary, overall, or per group) in either of the Group bands. The result of these fields depends on what type of field is placed in which band.

When a group band is inserted into a report it consists of two parts: the header and the footer. The group header is typically used to print a heading which will identify the group of records that will follow. In some cases, you might feel that the records included in the group form a self-explanatory group which needs no further identification. In most cases, it is useful to have a heading that prints before each group in order to clarify the group's significance. A regular type field—regular or calculated, but not a summary field—placed into a group header will print the corresponding field data from the first record in the group.

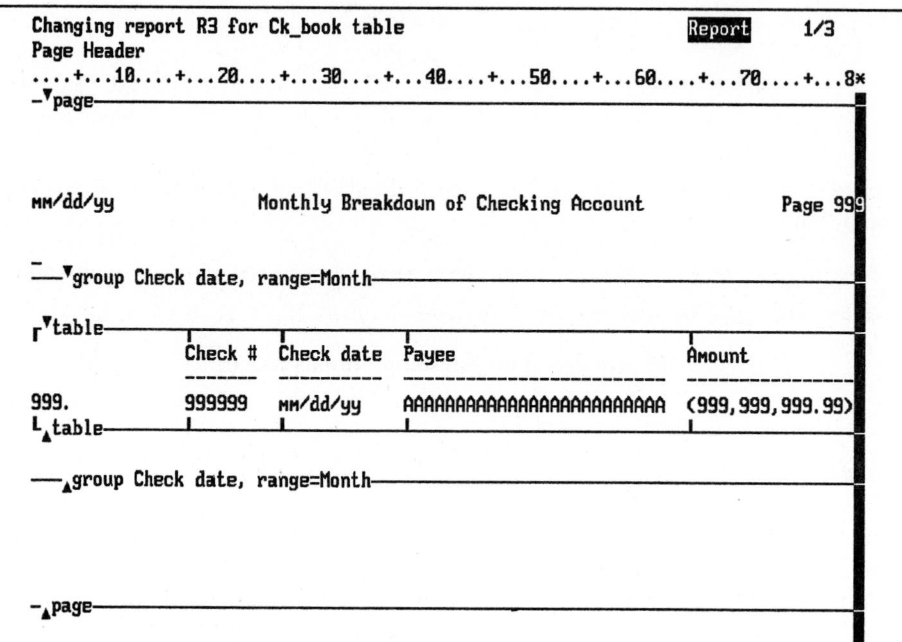

Figure 8-4 Report form with group bands added.

Regular fields placed in the Group Footer will reflect the corresponding values from the last record included in the group. In the case of a table grouped by month, a *Check date* field placed in the Group Header will print the date of the first record in the group while the same field placed into the Group Footer band would display the date of the last record for the current month. Summary fields (regular or calculated) also can be affected by the difference between the Group Header and Footer bands.

An Overall type of summary field placed into a Group Header would reflect the values of all of the records up to that point, including the first record of new group. The same field positioned in the Group Footer would reflect the values of all of the records printed up to that point in the report including all of the record in the current group. This means that entering the same field summary calculation, e.g., **sum([deposit] − [amount]),** placed in the Group Header would result in a different value being printed than if it were placed in the Group Footer band.

Per Group types of summary fields placed into a Group Header would produce the same result as a Regular type of field placed into a Group Header. While it is true that a Per group summary field is reset at the beginning of each group, printing that field as part of the Group Header would still include the values from the first record in the group in the group summary field.

Used in Group Footer, the Per group summary field will reflect the values for all of the records included in the current group. This type of summary field will be reset to zero before the next group of records are processed.

If the summary field is an Overall type summary field it will continue to accumulate values throughout the entire report even through it is positioned in the Group Header or Footer band. However, the value of this field will vary depending on its placement in either the Header or Footer bands. As part of the Group Header an Overall summary field will include all of the records up to that point including the *first* record of the current group. Placed in the Footer, the field would reflect all of the records printed up to that point.

It is important to bear in mind, that fields, in particular summary fields, that print in Group Headers reflect the data in the first record of the new group—a record which has *not* printed yet. Be careful when using fields in headers, since a person reading such a report might not realize that values in group headers include the first record in the group that follows.

Table 8-1 Fields and Group Headers

Field Type	Band Type	Records Included
Field, regular	Group Header	First record in group
Field, regular	Group Footer	Last record in group
Summary Field, overall	Group Header	All previous plus 1st in group
Summary Field, overall	Group Footer	All previous
Summary Field, per group	Group Header	First record in group
Summary Field, per group	Group Footer	All records in group

Fields in Group Headers

Group Header bands are typically used to print information that identifies the group. Since the records in this report will be printed in monthly groups, you might want to use the name of the month as the group heading.

Place the cursor on the first line of the Group Header band by entering

↓ ***(2 times)***

Enter the following text:

Transaction for
→

At this location you can insert a field which will display the *Check date*. The field will display the *Check date* value from the first record in the group that will follow. Enter

[F10] f p r

Select the *Check date* by entering

→
↵

Since *Check date* is a date type of field, you can select one of the 11 date formats available for report form date fields. In this instance, the exact date is not needed or desired. All that you want to display at this location is the month and the year, e.g., Jan 89. Select format 6, **Mon yy**, by entering

6 ↵

The field is inserted into the Group Header band, Figure 8-5.

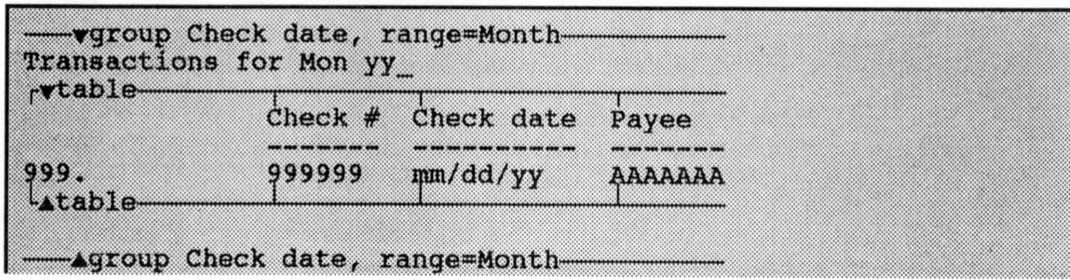

Figure 8-5 Group heading.

Summary Fields in Group Headers

In most cases a summary field would be placed in a Footer band (either report or group) since the value of a summary field depends on the values of the records that *precede* the field. Placed in a header, the summary field would not reflect the values of the records that follow. However, there are some circumstances in which it would be meaningful. For example, in a report dealing with a checking account in which a series of positive and negative cash flows are recorded, each month begins with a balance forward from the previous months and ends with a new balance.

In such a report, a summary field placed into the group header would show the beginning checking account balance for each month. The same summary field placed in the group footer would display a different value, i.e., the balance including the records for that month.

The summary field should be an Overall summary field which will continue to accumulate values throughout the entire report even though the value will be printed as part of the Group Header band. Note that this field would also include the first record of the new group as well. In order to print the starting balance, the formula used will have to compensate for the additional record.

Enter text that will label the field as the starting balance for the current month.

→ ***(5 times)***
Starting Balance:
→

Insert a summary field using the menu method by entering

[F10] f p s

In this instance, the summary field will be a calculated field since the value needed is the current account balance, i.e., deposits minus checks. In addition, the value of the current record, **deposit-amount**, must be subtracted from the sum to get a value equal to all of the previous records. Enter

c
sum([deposit]-[amount])-([deposit]-[amount])
↵ ***(4 times)***

Fields in Group Footers

Summary and regular fields can be placed into a group header to display summary information about the group of records that have just printed. In this report, you will want to print several summary values such as the total checks and deposits for each group, the balance for that month, and the overall balance. Move the cursor to the beginning of the Group Footer band by entering

[Ctrl-Home]
↓ ***(6 times)***

Place Paradox into the insert mode by entering

[Ins]

Enter the text for the summary values you want to display. In each case, you can insert a date field to display the name of the month. Enter

Total Deposits
→
[F10] f p r
→ ↵
6 ↵

Enter the text for the check total.

↵
Total Checks Written
→
[F10] f p r
→ ↵
6 ↵

Next, enter the text for the balance of monthly transactions. Enter

↵
Balance for
→
[F10] f p r
→ ↵
6 ↵

Finally, enter a label for the year-to-date balance. Enter

↵
Balance for Year to date

Add two blank lines to serve as a separator between groups of records.

↵ ***(2 times)***

The labels for the group summary have been added to the Group Footer band, Figure 8-6. Position the cursor under the column labeled *Amount*. In this case, all of the group summary fields will be aligned under this column.

↑ ***(7 times)***
[tab] ***(4 times)***
↓ ***(2 times)***

The first value is a group total for the *Deposit* field. Create this field using the menu method by entering

[F10] f p s r
d
s p ↵

Set the format by entering

← ***(3 times)***
↵ ***(2 times)***

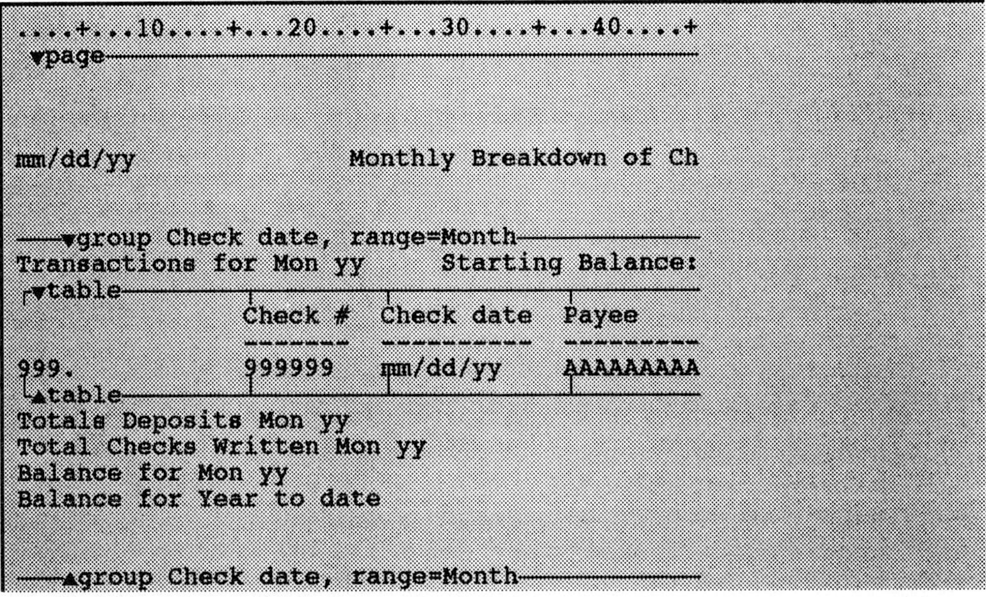

Figure 8-6 Labels entered into Group Footer band.

Move down to the next line and place a field that will summarize the group's check amounts. This time use the formula method. Enter

> ← ***(14 times)***
> ↓

The **group** operator added to a **summary** operator indicates that the formula is a per group type of calculation. Insert the field by entering

> **[F10] f p c**
> **sum([amount],group)**
> ↵ ***(2 times)***

Adjust the number of digits by entering

> ← ***(3 times)***
> ↵ ***(2 times)***

The monthly balance can be obtained by using another field calculation in which the deposits minus the check amounts for the group are summed. Try this on your own. The correct command can be found on page 278 under Exercise 2.

The last calculation in this group is an Overall type of summary field, which will display the overall blance in the checking account. Note that if a summary formula is entered without the **group** operator, it is treated as an Overall summary field. Enter

← *(14 times)*
↓

[F10] f p c
sum([deposit]-[amount])
↵ *(2 times)*
← *(3 times)*
↵ *(2 times)*

There are now four different summary calculations in the Group Footer band, Figure 8-7.

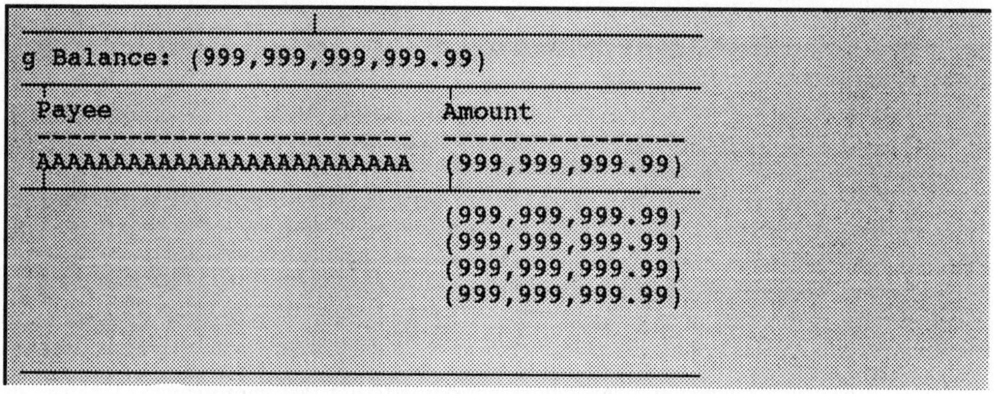

```
g Balance: (999,999,999,999.99)

 Payee                               Amount
 ------------------------            ---------------
 AAAAAAAAAAAAAAAAAAAAAAAA            (999,999,999.99)

                                     (999,999,999.99)
                                     (999,999,999.99)
                                     (999,999,999.99)
                                     (999,999,999.99)
```

Figure 8-7 Summary fields added to Group Footer band.

Before you output the report, you might want to include a separator between the records printed from the Table band and the Group Footer band. In this case, insert a single blank line between the two bands. Enter

[Ctrl-Home]
↑ *(3 times)*

Output the report by entering

[F10] o p

The report should look like Figure 8-8.

```
1/10/90            Monthly Breakdown of Checking Account              Page   1

                 Check #  Check date  Payee                           Amount
                 -------  ----------  ------------------------------  ------------
Transactions for Jan 89      Starting Balance:              0.00
   1.                  1    1/01/89    Deposit                              1,700.00
   2.                999    1/03/89    Savings Club                           (71.60)
   3.               1000    1/03/89    Allied Office Furniture               (750.50)
   4.               1001    1/04/89    Central Office Supplies                (97.68)
   5.               1002    1/08/89    Western Telephone                     (101.57)
   6.               1003    1/08/89    United Federal Insurance              (590.00)
   7.               1004    1/15/89    Computer World                      (2,245.50)
   8.                  2    1/22/89    Deposit                                860.00

Totals Deposits Jan 89                                                  2,560.00
Total Checks Written Jan 89                                             3,856.85
Balance for Jan 89                                                     (1,296.85)
Balance for Year to date                                               (1,296.85)

Transactions for Feb 89      Starting Balance:          (1,296.85)
   1.               1005    2/10/89    Savings Club                          (157.89)
   2.                  3    2/15/89    Deposit                              1,400.00
   3.               1006    2/19/89    Western Telephone                     (247.67)
   4.                  4    2/25/89    Deposit                                900.00

Totals Deposits Feb 89                                                  2,300.00
Total Checks Written Feb 89                                               405.56
Balance for Feb 89                                                      1,894.44
Balance for Year to date                                                  597.59

Transactions for Mar 89      Starting Balance:            597.59
   1.               1007    3/05/89    Fathead Software                      (378.90)

Totals Deposits Mar 89                                                      0.00
Total Checks Written Mar 89                                               378.90
Balance for Mar 89                                                       (378.90)
Balance for Year to date                                                  218.69
```

Figure 8-8 Report with groups.

Group Printing Options

The report you have just created contains all of the basic elements of a grouped report. Paradox provides a number of options that affect various aspects of how the group report will print.

❑ **Group Headings.** Paradox prints the Group Header band at the beginning of each group. In most cases, this is adequate. Suppose that Paradox cannot fit all of the records in a given group on the same page. The remainder of the group will print on the next page. However, since the Header for that group has already printed, the page will begin with the Page Header but no Group Header. If you want to have the current Group Header band repeated at the top of each new page so that the reader does not have to turn back to the previous page to determine which group is starting the page, select the Page option from the Group Headings menu. The Group option, which is the default, prints Group Headers only once at the start of each group regardless of pagination.

❑ **Group SortDirection.** By default, the records in a table are sorted in ascending order according to the group field or range. You can use the **Group SortDirection** command to select a descending order for the group sort.

❑ **Setting Format.** This option is used to control the relationship between the Table band column headings and the Group Header band. The default relationship is what Paradox calls *a table of groups* report. In this type of report, the column headings in the Table band print *once* at the top of the page. The group headers print immedately before each group. Paradox allows you to select the GroupsOfTables option from the Setting Format menu to alter the relationship between these bands so that the column headings from the Table band print *after* each group header so that each group has its own set of column headings. The TableOf-Groups method has the advantage of placing more data on the page but requires the reader to refer to the top of the page to read the column headings. The GroupsOfTables option makes it easier to determine the column names but uses up space on the page with duplicate copies of the column headings, shown in Figure 8-9 on page 257.

❑ **Settings GroupRepeats.** When a group is determined by the contents of a single field, it is obvious that all of the records in the group will have identical values for that field. If a column in the table band is used to print that field, the value will simply repeat for each record in the group. By default, Paradox will print all of the repetitions. You can restrain the printing of these repeated values by selecting the Suppress option from the Settings GroupRepeats menu. If selected, Paradox prints the value for the first record in the group only.

❑ **Separate Pages for Groups.** Paradox allows you to insert a page break instruction into any of the bands in the report. This instruction is typically used in the group bands to force Paradox to begin each group on a new page. The report that results is actually a series of reports, each set of pages belonging to a different group. This type of report is very useful when you want to distribute each group to a different person who needs only that section of the report, e.g., a sales report grouped by sales person. Page breaks are created by inserting the special command word **PAGEBREAK** at the beginning of a blank line in the report.

❑ **Groups Only.** You can create a report that consists of only group summary values by deleting all of the lines in the table band and printing only the Group Footer band. This type of report prints summary information as if they were records in a table.

Printing a Groups of Tables Report

Any group report can be printed in the Groups of Tables style by simply selecting that option from the Setting Format menu. Enter

[F10] s f g

Print the table by entering

[F10] o p

The report should look like Figure 8-10, on page 258.

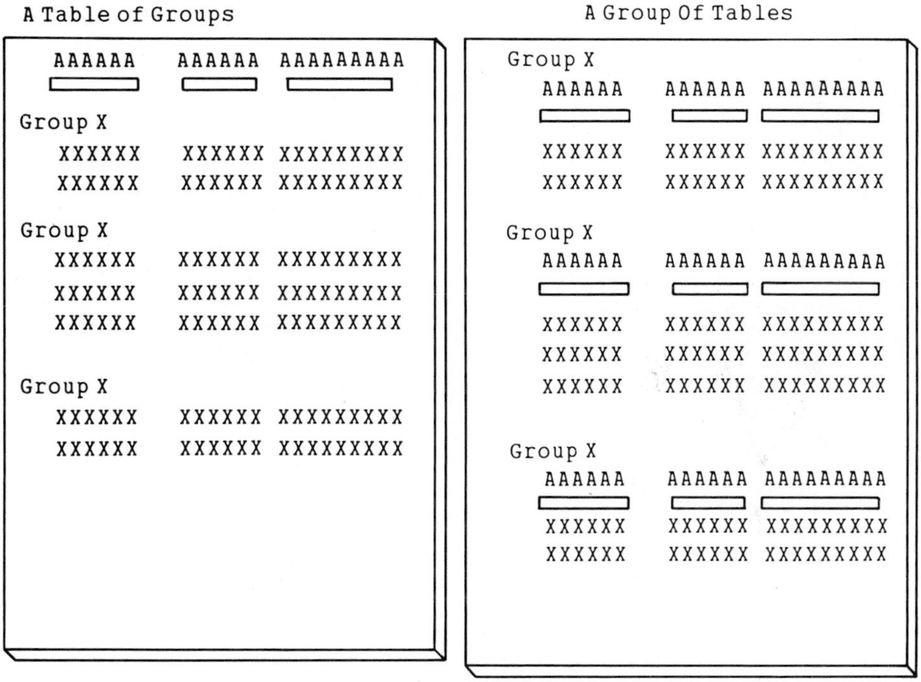

Figure 8-9 Table of groups vs. group of tables.

Groups on Separate Pages

Paradox allows you to *force* a page break at any point in the report form by inserting a line that begins with the word **PAGEBREAK. PAGEBREAK** is a special command word recognized by Paradox as an instruction rather than part of the text to be printed. Note that **PAGEBREAK** must be the first characters on the line. If any other characters, even a space, precede **PAGEBREAK** the command is printed as text. Also note that capitalization is required. Entering **Pagebreak** or **pagebreak** will also cause the command to be treated as normal text.

When used in a Group Footer band, the **PAGEBREAK** command will generate a report in which each group begins on a new page. The **PAGEBREAK** command should be the last line inserted into the Group Footer band.

```
 1/10/90              Monthly Breakdown of Checking Account                Page   1

Transactions for Mar 89      Starting Balance:                 0.00
                  Check #  Check date  Payee                              Amount
                  -------  ----------  ------------------------------  --------------
   1.               1007    3/05/89    Fathead Software                      (378.90)

Totals Deposits Mar 89                                                          0.00
Total Checks Written Mar 89                                                   378.90
Balance for Mar 89                                                          (378.90)
Balance for Year to date                                                    (378.90)

Transactions for Feb 89      Starting Balance:             (378.90)
                  Check #  Check date  Payee                              Amount
                  -------  ----------  ------------------------------  --------------
   1.                  4    2/25/89    Deposit                                900.00
   2.               1006    2/19/89    Western Telephone                     (247.67)
   3.                  3    2/15/89    Deposit                              1,400.00
   4.               1005    2/10/89    Savings Club                          (157.89)

Totals Deposits Feb 89                                                      2,300.00
Total Checks Written Feb 89                                                   405.56
Balance for Feb 89                                                          1,894.44
Balance for Year to date                                                    1,515.54

Transactions for Jan 89      Starting Balance:            1,515.54
                  Check #  Check date  Payee                              Amount
                  -------  ----------  ------------------------------  --------------
   1.                  2    1/22/89    Deposit                                860.00
   2.               1004    1/15/89    Computer World                      (2,245.50)
   3.               1002    1/08/89    Western Telephone                     (101.57)
   4.               1003    1/08/89    United Federal Insurance              (590.00)
   5.               1001    1/04/89    Central Office Supplies                (97.68)
   6.                999    1/03/89    Savings Club                           (71.60)
   7.               1000    1/03/89    Allied Office Furniture               (750.50)
   8.                  1    1/01/89    Deposit                              1,700.00

Totals Deposits Jan 89                                                      2,560.00
Total Checks Written Jan 89                                                 3,856.85
Balance for Jan 89                                                        (1,296.85)
Balance for Year to date                                                      218.69
```

Figure 8-10 Report printed as groups of tables.

To add a **PAGEBREAK** to the current group report, enter

> ↓ ***(5 times)***
> **PAGEBREAK**

Print the report by entering

> **[F10] o p**

The report will print three pages that look like Figure 8-11.
Remove the **PAGEBREAK** command from the report form by entering

> **[Ctrl-Home][Ctrl-y]**

Save the report form by entering

> **[F2]**

```
1/10/90              Monthly Breakdown of Checking Account              Page  1

Transactions for Jan 89      Starting Balance:              0.00
          Check #  Check date  Payee                          Amount
          -------  ----------  ---------------------------    -------------
 1.             1  1/01/89     Deposit                            1,700.00
 2.           999  1/03/89     Savings Club                         (71.60)
 3.          1000  1/03/89     Allied Office Furniture             (750.50)
 4.          1001  1/04/89     Central Office Supplies              (97.68)
 5.          1002  1/08/89     Western Telephone                   (101.57)
 6.          1003  1/08/89     United Federal Insurance            (590.00)
 7.          1004  1/15/89     Computer World                    (2,245.50)
 8.             2  1/22/89     Deposit                              860.00

Totals Deposits Jan 89                                            2,560.00
Total Checks Written Jan 89                                       3,856.85
Balance for Jan 89                                               (1,296.85)
Balance for Year to date                                         (1,296.85)
```

```
1/10/90              Monthly Breakdown of Checking Account              Page  2

Transactions for Feb 89      Starting Balance:         (1,296.85)
          Check #  Check date  Payee                          Amount
          -------  ----------  ---------------------------    -------------
 1.          1005  2/10/89     Savings Club                        (157.89)
 2.             3  2/15/89     Deposit                            1,400.00
 3.          1006  2/19/89     Western Telephone                   (247.67)
 4.             4  2/25/89     Deposit                              900.00

Totals Deposits Feb 89                                            2,300.00
Total Checks Written Feb 89                                         405.56
Balance for Feb 89                                                1,894.44
Balance for Year to date                                            597.59
```

```
1/10/90              Monthly Breakdown of Checking Account              Page  3

Transactions for Mar 89      Starting Balance:            597.59
          Check #  Check date  Payee                          Amount
          -------  ----------  ---------------------------    -------------
 1.          1007  3/05/89     Fathead Software                    (378.90)

Totals Deposits Mar 89                                                0.00
Total Checks Written Mar 89                                         378.90
Balance for Mar 89                                                 (378.90)
Balance for Year to date                                            218.69
```

Figure 8-11 Groups printed on separate pages.

Summary Reports

A variation on the idea of group reports is a *summary* report. A summary report is one in which *only* the group bands print. This is accomplished by deleting the Table band lines completely from the report. The result is that none of the individual record details appear, leaving only the summary data. The effect is similar to that achieved in a summary query in which a field is also selected, Chapter 6.

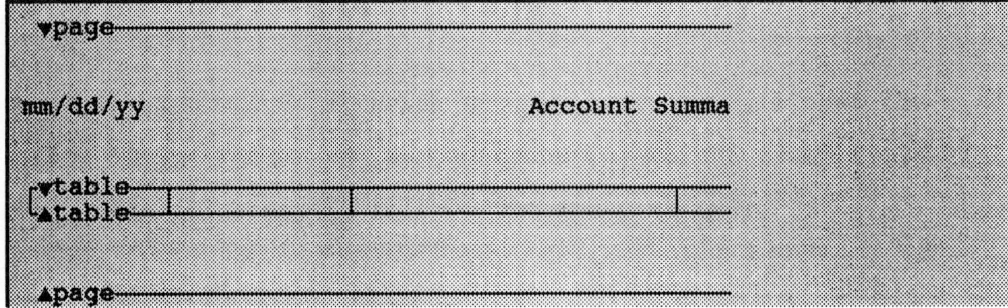

Figure 8-12 Table band deleted from report.

For example, suppose that you wanted to print a report that lists four items: the month, the total checks written, total deposits, and account balance. This report requires summary information but no record details.

Begin by creating a standard column report. Enter

r d
ck_book ↵
4

Enter the report description.

Account Summary ↵
t

Since this is going to be a summary report only, delete all of the lines in the Table band by entering

↓ *(9 times)*
[Ctrl-y] *(4 times)*

The Table band is closed up so that it will print no information on the report, Figure 8-12. Note that the band marks still appear in the report form. This allows you to use the Table band, if you desire, by inserting lines.

With the Table band removed from the report, you will have to use the Page and Group bands to print all of the information. In this type of report, column information will be output by the Group Footer band while the column headings will be printed through the Page Header band.

Next, insert a group band into the report that will group records by month. Enter

[F10] g i r
→ ↵
m
↓ ↵

The group bands are inserted with a single blank line in the header and footer bands. In this type of report, you will not use the Group Header band since the column headings will be generated at the top of the page by the Page Header band. Delete the line in the Group Header band by entering

[Ctrl-y]

You can create what will appear to be a column report by placing group summary totals in the Group Footer band. Begin with a field that will print the month and year of each summarized group. Enter

↓ ***(2 times)***
[F10] f p r
→ ↵
6 ↵

Move the cursor to the right two spaces and insert a group summary field that will total the deposits for each group. In this case, the calculation formula method will be used to create the group summary value. Enter

→ ***(2 times)***
[F10] f p c
sum([deposit],group) ↵
↵ ***(3 times)***

Repeat the procedure in order to create a field that will print the group total for the checks written. Enter

→ ***(4 times)***
[F10] f p c
sum([amount],group) ↵
↵ ***(3 times)***

The next field is one that calculates the balance, **deposit-amount,** for the group. Try this on your own. The correct command can be found on page 278 under Exercise 3.

With the fields placed into the Group Footer band, you can enter the text of the column headings into the Page Header band. In most cases, it is better to place the field before you write the headings because the field locations will show you where the headings should go. Enter

[Ctrl-Home]
↑ *(4 times)*
Month
→ *(14 times)*
Deposits
→ *(13 times)*
Withdrawals
→ *(12 times)*
Balance

Insert a blank line below the headings to separate them from the rest of the report. Enter

[Ins] ↵

The last step would be to add overall summary fields which will calculate the grand totals. These fields should be placed into the Report Footer band so that they will print only once, at the end of the report.

Position the cursor in the Report Footer band by entering

↓ *(11 times)*

Add a blank line before the summary totals to separate them from the group totals. Enter

↵

Label the line as *Totals* by entering

Totals

Insert an overall summary field for the total of the deposits. Enter

→ *(2 times)*
[F10] f p c
sum([deposit]) ↵
↵ *(3 times)*

Repeat the process for summary fields for *Amount* and *Deposit-Amount*. Try this on your own. The correct command can be found on page 000 under Exercise 4.

The final report form, shown in Figure 8-13, is one that does not use the Table band at all but relies on the Report Footer, Page Header, and Group Footer bands to generate a summary report.

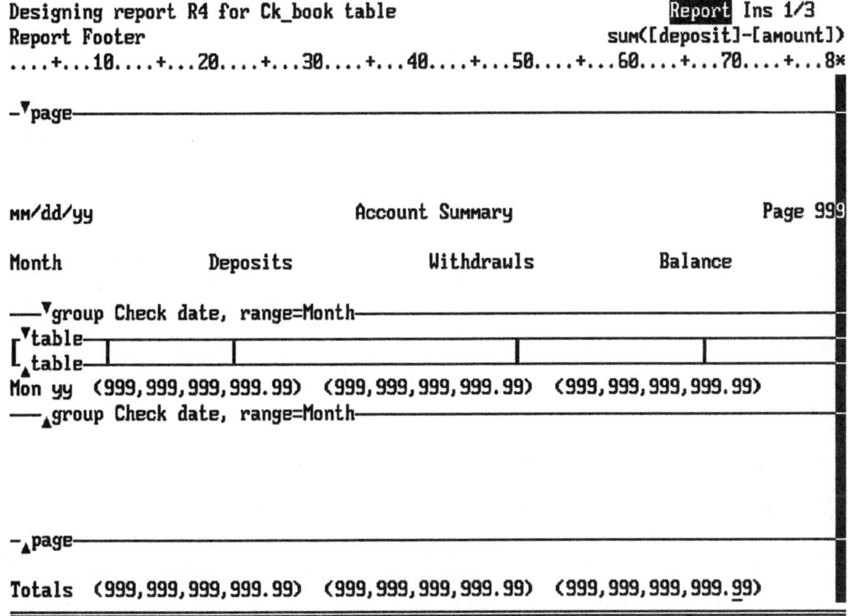

Figure 8-13 Report form that prints summary values only.

Output the report by entering

[F10] o p

The report will look like Figure 8-14.

```
1/11/90                 Account Summary                 Page   1

Month          Deposits           Withdrawals        Balance

Jan 89         2,560.00           3,856.85           (1,296.85)
Feb 89         2,300.00             405.56            1,894.44
Mar 89             0.00             378.90             (378.90)

Totals         4,860.00           4,860.00              218.69
```

Figure 8-14 Summary only report.

Save the report by entering

[F2]

Using Groups for Sorting Only

One of the byproducts of using groups in a report is that the records in the report are sorted according to the group field or range. This is necessary in order to group records.

In reports that do not use groups, the records are always printed in the order in which they appear in the database table related to the report form.

It is possible to employ the sorting effect of a group band with a report that otherwise would not use groups, in order to change the sort order of the records. For example, you might take an ordinary column report, such as the report 1 created for Ck_book and alter the sequence of the records by adding a group band. If you delete all of the lines from the group band, no additional information would print but the sequence of the records would be changed to match the grouping field or range.

Sorting with Group Bands

Begin by making a copy of an existing column report that does not use groups, by using the **Tools Copy Report** command. In this case, use report 1. Enter

[F10] t c r

Since you are going to use the report with the same table, choose **SameTable** by entering

s
ck_book ↵

Copy report 1 to report 5 by entering

1 5

Load the copied report form into the report form design mode by entering

r c
ck_book ↵
5

Modify the title of the report to indicate that this report will also sort the records. Enter

[spacebar]
Sorted ↵

Suppose that you wanted to print the report with the records listed in alphabetical order by *Payee* name. Create a Group band that uses the *Payee* field as the grouping field. Enter

[F10] g i f

Select the *Payee* field by entering

→ (2 times)
↵

Place the field into the Page band by entering

→ (2 times)
↵

The Group Header is inserted into the report form. By default, Paradox places a blank line in the Group Header and Footer bands. These lines would divide the records into groups for each unique payee name if they were left in the report. However, in this case you don't want the records divided into groups by blank lines. Remove the blanks form the group bands by entering

↓ (7 times)
[Ctrl-y]
↓ (6 times)
[Ctrl-y]

When you print this report, the records will appear exactly as they do in report 1—with the exception that the sort order of the records will be according to the *Payee* field, not the *Check #* field. Recall that since *Check #* is the *key* field in the table, all reports that do not contain groups are printed in that sequence. Enter

[F10] o p

The report will look like Figure 8-15. The records print in the same format as the original report 1 form but the nonprinting group band causes the records to be listed in *Payee* order.

Using Multiple Sort Groups

You can use nested group bands to sort the records by multiple keys. For example, suppose you wanted to list the records by *Payee* in two groups—those that cleared the band and those that did not. This could be achieved by placing the *Payee* group bands within a group band which uses the *Cleared bank* field to group records. When nesting groups, the priority of each group is determined by which band is inserted inside of the other. Figure 8-16 shows two bands nested inside one another. The left side of the figure shows *Payee* nested inside of *Cleared bank,* which would produce a sort order in which records would be sort by *Cleared bank*. If records had duplicate *Cleared bank* values, they would be sorted within those groups by *Payee*.

```
 1/11/90                      Checking Account Records                   Page   1

Check #  Check date  Description of Transaction Amount      Deposit   Memo
-------  ----------  -------------------------- ---------- ---------- ---------
   1000    1/03/89   Allied Office Furniture        750.50       0.00 Desk -
                                                                      48" by
                                                                      72"
   1001    1/04/89   Central Office Supplies         97.68       0.00 Envelopes
                                                                      ,
                                                                      folders,
   1004    1/15/89   Computer World               2,245.50       0.00 286
                                                                      Turbo Com
                                                                      puter
      1    1/01/89   Deposit                          0.00   1,700.00
      2    1/22/89   Deposit                          0.00     860.00
      3    2/15/89   Deposit                          0.00   1,400.00
      4    2/25/89   Deposit                          0.00     900.00
   1007    3/05/89   Fathead Software               378.90       0.00 Spreadshe
                                                                      et
                                                                      Software
    999    1/03/89   Savings Club                    71.60       0.00 Coffee
                                                                      machine
   1005    2/10/89   Savings Club                   157.89       0.00
   1003    1/08/89   United Federal Insurance       590.00       0.00 Policy
                                                                      Number
                                                                      10012002A
   1002    1/08/89   Western Telephone              101.57       0.00
   1006    2/19/89   Western Telephone              247.67       0.00
                                                ========== ==========
                                                  4,641.31   4,860.00
Account Balance:              218.69
Transactions:            13
From  1-Jan-89 To  5-Mar-89
```

Figure 8-15 Reports sorted by non-printing group band.

The right side of the chart shows the bands, and subsequently the sort order, reversed—creating a primary sort by *Payee* and a secondary sort by *Cleared bank.*

The key to how the bands are arranged is the cursor location. If the cursor is placed inside of an existing group band, the new group is nested inside of the existing groups as a secondary group. Conversely, if the cursor is positioned in the Page band outside any existing group bands, the existing group is nested inside the new group.

In this example, you want to nest the existing group band, *Payee,* within the new band, *Cleared bank.* Enter

[F10] g i f
→ *(6 times)*
↵

Before the field is inserted, position the cursor in either the Page Header or Footer bands outside the existing group band. Enter

↓ ↵

The new band, *Cleared bank,* encloses the existing band, *Payee.* Note that both new bands have a blank line which will print unless it is removed. In this case, remove the blank line from

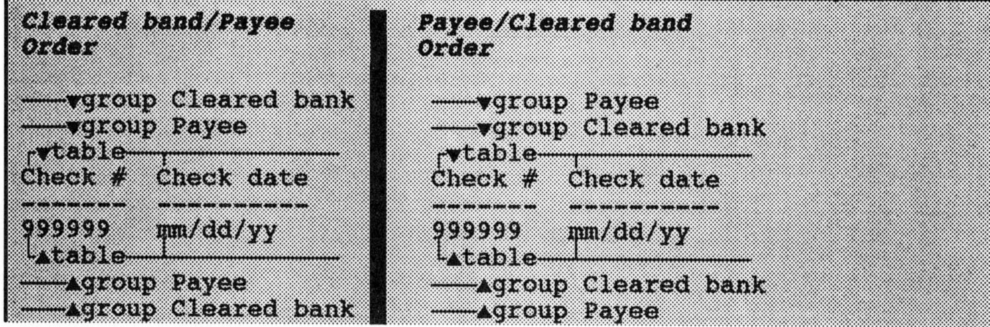

Figure 8-16 Nesting of group bands indicates sort order.

the Group Footer but leave the blank line in the Group Header so that it will separate the cleared transactions from the outstanding transactions on the report. Enter

↓ *(2 times)*
[Ctrl-y]

Print the report by entering

[F10] o p

The report should look like Figure 8-17, on page 268. The first four transactions are outstanding while the remainder of the report prints the cleared items. Note that using a blank line to separate the two groups, between 1003 and 1000, is not very clear. In this example, you might want to add a more visible group header to indicate the two groups of records.

Save the report form by entering

[F2]

Selecting Report Records with Query Forms

One feature that is not directly supported by report forms is the selection of records to be included in a report. Paradox reports will automatically include all of the records in the table. In many circumstances you might want to print a report using only some of the records in a table. For example, the sales tax report, report 2 created in Chapter 7, would make more sense if the deposit records were not included in the report.

You have already learned that query forms can be used to select groups of records from an existing table and to place the data into the Answer table. But query form processing cannot

```
 1/11/90                  Checking Account Records                 Page    1


Check #  Check date  Description of Transaction Amount     Deposit    Memo
-------  ----------  -------------------------- ---------- ---------- ----------

   1004    1/15/89    Computer World               2,245.50       0.00 286
                                                                       Turbo Com
                                                                       puter
      4    2/25/89    Deposit                          0.00     900.00
   1007    3/05/89    Fathead Software               378.90       0.00 Spreadshe
                                                                       et
                                                                       Software
   1003    1/08/89    United Federal Insurance       590.00       0.00 Policy
                                                                       Number
                                                                       10012002A

   1000    1/03/89    Allied Office Furniture        750.50       0.00 Desk -
                                                                       48" by
                                                                       72"
   1001    1/04/89    Central Office Supplies         97.68       0.00 Envelopes
                                                                       ,
                                                                       folders,
      1    1/01/89    Deposit                          0.00   1,700.00
      2    1/22/89    Deposit                          0.00     860.00
      3    2/15/89    Deposit                          0.00   1,400.00
    999    1/03/89    Savings Club                    71.60       0.00 Coffee
                                                                       machine
   1005    2/10/89    Savings Club                   157.89       0.00
   1002    1/08/89    Western Telephone              101.57       0.00
   1006    2/19/89    Western Telephone              247.67       0.00
                                                 ========== ==========
                                                   4,641.31   4,860.00
Account Balance:             218.69
Transactions:            13
From  1-Jan-89 To  5-Mar-89
```

Figure 8-17 Report using multiple bands to create sort order.

produce formatted reports generated from custom-designed report forms. The trick is to combine the report forms you design for the source table, e.g., Ck_book, with the records selected by query form as they appear in the Answer table. You can accomplish this trick by using the **Tools Copy Report** command to copy a report designed for one table, e.g., Ck_book, to the Answer table. The report can be printed using the records selected for the Answer table.

> *If all you need to print is a standard report using the selected records, you can take a shortcut by using the [Alt-F7], instant report command to generate a standard report and report form from the Answer table. Keep in mind that standard reports do not include summary fields for column totals. That requires a custom-designed report form.*

Printing Reports from the Answer Table

As an example of how queries can be used to print reports with selected records, imagine that you want to print the sales tax report but you only want to include the checks—not the deposits.

The first step is to create a query form Answer table that contains the records you want to select. Enter

a
ck_book ↵

In order for this procedure to work, you must include all of the fields in the original table in the Answer table. This is because Paradox will only copy a report from one table to another if both tables contain the same fields. If you were to select only some of the fields from Ck_book for the Answer table, Paradox would not permit you to copy Ck_book reports to the Answer table.

When the cursor is positioned in the leftmost column of the query form, you can select all of the fields in the table for query processing by entering

[F6]

Note that √ characters appear in all of the field columns. The next step is to enter the selection condition. There are several ways in which Paradox could distinguish between check and deposit records: amount greater than zero, Payee not equal to *Deposit,* or even deposit equal to zero. In this case, you will use the *Payee* field column with the condition **not Deposit** to select all records that do not show **Deposit** as the *Payee*. Enter

→ *(3 times)*
not Deposit

> *Note that capitalization is significant when selecting an Alpha-type field. The word* Deposit *must be written exactly as shown or the records will not be selected properly.*

Process the query by entering

[F2]

The query form produces an Answer table that contains *only* the check records, nine in all.

Sorting the Answer Table

One advantage of printing from the Answer table rather than directly from the original table is that the Answer table does not have a key field. The Ck_book table is always ordered by *Check #* because that field was designated the *key* field in the table's structure.

Although Answer is currently sorted by *Check #,* the same as Ck_book, it can be re-sorted using the **Modify Sort** command. For example, you might want to print the sales tax report in descending order by *Amount.*

To sort the current table, Answer, enter

[F10] m s
answer ↵

The Sort menu displays two options, Same and New. The new option must be used when the source table has a key field. In this case, you can use Same to simply rearrange the Answer table because Answer does not have a designated key field. Enter

s

The program then displays a full screen menu listing all of the fields by which the table can be sorted. Enter the number **1** next to the field that is the primary sort key, in this case *Amount.* Enter

↓ ***(3 times)***
1

To make the sort a descending sequence add the letter **d** to the number, making the sort specification **1d.** Enter

d

Execute the sort by entering

[F2]

The Answer table is rearranged into descending order by *Amount.*

Transferring a Report

With the Answer table selected and sorted, the next step is to transfer a copy of the desired report from the original table, Ck_book, to the Answer table. This is done using the DifferentTable option of the **Tools Copy Report** command. Enter

[F10] t c r

Select the **DifferentTable** option by entering

d

Paradox asks you to enter the name of the table from which you want to copy a report, in this instance Ck_book.

ck_book ↵

Paradox then lists all of the existing reports, F and 1–5, for Ck_book. If you are not sure which report is the one you want, use the cursor to move the menu highlight to the various report numbers. As you do, the description which you entered for each report will appear on the second line of the menu. Enter

→ (2 times)

The menu displays the description for report 2, Sales Tax Report. Select this report by entering

↵

Paradox asks for the name of the *Target* table. This is the table to which the copied report will be attached. Recall that the table entered at this point must have a structure that includes all of the fields contained in the source table (Ck_book.) Enter

answer ↵

The final selection is the report number for Answer, under which the report form will be stored. This option usually is not important because all reports stored for the Answer table will be deleted from the disk the next time a new Answer table is generated or when you quit Paradox. In this case, store the report under the standard form **R**. Enter

r

The advantage of using the standard report **R** is that you can take advantage of the instant report shortcut key [Alt-F7] to print the standard report for the table in which the cursor is currently positioned. Print the report by entering

[Alt-F7]

The report will look like Figure 8-18.

Using a Dummy Table

The **Tools Copy Report** command allows you to transfer a report from the original table to the Answer table without having to design a report. However, as soon as another query of any type is processed, Paradox will erase the existing Answer table and any reports associated with that table.

For example, suppose that you decide that you want to restrict the records in the sales tax report to those records marked as tax-deductible. Move the cursor back to the query form by entering

[F3]

```
1/11/90                      Sales Tax Report                          Page   1


       Check #  Check date    Check Amt.    Pre-Tax Amt.    Sales Tax
       -------  ----------    ----------    ------------    ---------
  1.    1004     1/15/89        2,245.50        2,098.60       146.90
  2.    1000     1/03/89          750.50          701.40        49.10
  3.    1003     1/08/89          590.00          551.40        38.60
  4.    1007     3/05/89          378.90          354.11        24.79
  5.    1006     2/19/89          247.67          231.47        16.20
  6.    1005     2/10/89          157.89          147.56        10.33
  7.    1002     1/08/89          101.57           94.93         6.64
  8.    1001     1/04/89           97.68           91.29         6.39
  9.     999     1/03/89           71.60           66.92         4.68

                                4,641.31        4,337.67       303.64
```

Figure 8-18 Report form copied to Answer table for output.

Add a selection criterion to the *Tax deductible* field which will select records that contain a **Y** in that field. Enter

→ ***(3 times)***
Y

Process the revised query by entering

[F2]

Print the Answer table report.

[Alt-F7]

What is the result? The report that printed was not the Sales Tax Report but the default standard report. This is because Paradox erased the report that you copied when the query form was reprocessed.

Since it is likely that in some cases you might want to process the query and the report several times, you need to find a way to maintain the copied reports when you reprocess the query. The solution is to create a *dummy* table onto which you can copy the reports.

The first step is to create the summary table. There are a number of ways to do this. The simplest way at this juncture is to use the **Tools Rename** command to change the name of the Answer table. Enter

[F10] t r t

Use the Answer table as the source table. Since your cursor is located in the Answer table, you can insert that name into the command by entering

↵ ***(2 times)***

Enter the name for the new table.

temp ↵

Once you have created the Temp table, you can transfer all of the reports from the Ck_book table by using the JustFamily option of the **Tools Copy** command. JustFamily copies all of the files related to a specified table, screen form, report forms, etc., but does not copy the table data itself. Using this command with Temp would enable you to copy all of the reports from Ck_book to Temp at one time. Enter

[F10] t c

Choose the JustFamily option.

j

Enter the name of the source table, in this case Ck_book.

ck_book ↵

Enter the name of the table you want to copy the files to.

temp ↵

Confirm your intention to overwrite any files associated with Temp by entering

r

You now have two tables with the same structure and the same set of screen and report forms, Ck_book and Temp.

How would you use the two tables to print reports with selected and sorted groups of records generated from a query form? As an example, suppose that you wanted to print report 1, Checking Account Activity, with only those records in the month of February sequenced in date order. The first step is to create an Answer table with just those records in the desired order. Return to the query form by entering

[F3]

Clear the form of √'s and conditions by entering

[Ctrl-Home]
[Del]

Select all of the fields for the query by entering

[F6]

Enter a selection condition in the *Check date* field which will select only the February records. Enter

→ *(2 times)*
2/..

Process the query in order to obtain the Answer table. Enter

[F2]

The Answer table is generated by the query form. Next, use the **Modify Sort** command to sequence the four records in the Answer table in date order. Enter

[F10] m s
↵ *(2 times)*
s
↓
1
[F2]

Substituting Table Records

The records in the Answer table have been correctly selected and sorted. However, you need to place the records that you have selected and sorted into the Temp table so that you can use the report forms assocatied with Temp.

The problem is that Temp probably contains records from a previous query. Your task is to get Temp to have the same contents, no more and no less, than the current Answer query. This can be accomplished with a two-step process: 1) use the **Tools More Empty** command to remove all of the records currently stored in the Temp table, and 2) use the **Tools More Add** command to copy the records in the Answer table into the Temp table without overwriting the table or its family of screen and report form files.

Execute the first step by emptying all of the records from Temp. Enter

[F10] t m

Choose the **Empty** command by entering

e

Enter the name of the table you want to empty.

temp ↵

Confirm your intention to empty the table by entering

o *(the letter O)*

The Temp table is now empty. Use the **Add** command to place copies of the Answer table's records into Temp. Enter

[F10] t m a
answer ↵
temp ↵

The Temp table now matches the contents of the Answer table. However, unlike Answer, the reports copied to the Temp table are still intact. Print report 1 using the records in the Temp table. Enter

[F10] r o
↵ *(2 times)*
1
p

The report will look like Figure 8-19.

The use of a dummy table to hold sections of the original table enables you to print reports with selected records. Exit Paradox by entering

[F10] e y

Summary

This chapter has covered the use of group bands in reports. It also explains how query forms can be used to print selected sections of a database table through a report form.

```
 1/11/90                    Checking Account Records                 Page   1


Check #  Check date  Description of Transaction Amount     Deposit   Memo
-------  ----------  -------------------------- ---------- --------- ---------
  1005    2/10/89    Savings Club                   157.89      0.00
     3    2/15/89    Deposit                          0.00  1,400.00
  1006    2/19/89    Western Telephone              247.67      0.00
     4    2/25/89    Deposit                          0.00    900.00
                                                ========== =========
                                                    405.56  2,300.00
Account Balance:              1,894.44
Transactions:               4
From 10-Feb-89 To 25-Feb-89
```

Figure 8-19 Report printed from Temp table.

❑ **Group Bands.** Group bands are added to report forms through the **Group Insert** command. A group band is used to print the records from a database table as a series of groups based on a common field or range value. All of the records in the table are sorted using the group value as the sort key. Groups can also be defined by a fixed number of records. A group band has two parts: Group Header and Group Footer. The header prints before each group and the footer print following each group.

❑ **Grouping by Field.** Records can be grouped together according to a value which they have in common in a specified field. In this type of grouping, a single field is selected as the group field. The table is sorted using that field as the sort key. Records which have identical values in the group field will be printed as a group, i.e., they will be preceded by the Group Header and be followed by the Group Footer. Keep in mind that the values must be exact matches in order to form a group. The actual appearance of a group depends upon what is entered, if anything, into the group bands.

❑ **Grouping by Range.** The range option allows you to form groups based on partial as opposed to exact matches in a particular field. Date fields can be grouped by chronological factors such as records that have the same year, month, week, or day. Numeric fields can be grouped based on a fixed range of values. For example, you can select to group by 100 which will form groups of records that have values 0–99, 100–199, 200–299, etc. Alpha fields can be grouped using the first one or more characters from the field as the basis for grouping records.

❑ **Grouping by Records.** Groups can be created by arbitrarily clustering records in a group with a fixed number of records. You can select the number of records in each group. The group bands print automatically following each group of the specified number of records. Note that, with this type of grouping, the records are not sorted but appear in the same order in which they are stored in the table.

❑ **Group Summary Fields.** In addition to regular, calculated, and summary fields (all of which can be used in any report form), group reports allow you to create summary fields that calculate values for each group in the report independently. Group summary fields can be selected using the Per group menu option or designed in a summary formula by adding the **group** operator to a summary function. Group summary fields are reset to zero following the printing of a Group Footer band.

❑ **Queries.** A query form can be used to select records from a table. If the Answer table produced by the query form contains the same fields as the original table, a report can be copied from the original table so that the selected records can be printed.

❑ **Copying Reports.** Reports are linked to specific tables. In order to print a report with a selected group of records, a query form is used to produce an Answer table or copied into a third table. Reports from the original table can be copied to the new tables one at a time with the **Tools Copy Report** command or as a group with the **Tools Copy JustFamily** command.

Exercises

Exercise 1 from page 243

Repeat the following five times:

[F10] t e ↵

Exercise 2 from page 254

← ***(14 times)***
↓

[F10] f p c
sum([deposit]-[amount],group)
↵ ***(2 times)***
← ***(3 times)***
↵ ***(2 times)***

Exercise 3 from page 262

→ ***(4 times)***
[F10] f p c
sum([deposit]-[amount],group) ↵
↵ ***(3 times)***

Exercise 4 from page 263

→ ***(4 times)***
[F10] f p c
sum([amount]) ↵
↵ ***(3 times)***

→ ***(4 times)***
[F10] f p c
sum([deposit]-[amount]) ↵
↵ ***(3 times)***

9

Linking Supporting Tables

Up to this point all the work you have done in Paradox, and it has been quite an amount, has been done with a single small table called Ck_book. This simple database table has been transformed in a variety of ways through the use of the main operational modes in Paradox: query modes (Ask command), form view mode, and the report form mode.

Paradox, however, is capable of working with more than one table at a time in any of those operational modes. Why would you want to work with more than one table?

There are two ways in which multiple table operations can be useful.

❑ **Supporting Tables.** A supporting table is one that contains a list of items or values that are related to the items in the master table. Many times, in order to simplify data entry, fields will contain abbreviations or codes rather than a full item. For example, the *Tax deductible* field contains the letters Y or N instead of more elaborate entries such as *Deductible* and *NotDeductible*. The advantage of Y and N is that you save time and eliminate typing errors using the simplest possible entries. However, the more elaborate forms *Deductible* and *Not Deductible* would be much more explicit and unambiguous, especially when the data is being read by people less familiar with the structure of your table than you are. A supporting table enables you to link the codes and abbreviations used in a field with a list of more elaborate items in another table. As shown in Figure 9-1. Paradox can look up one item (Y or N) and place a corresponding value into a screen form, report form, or even an Answer table.

❑ Cross-Referencing Tables. Cross-referencing is similar to supporting tables in that records in different tables are linked by common values. However, with cross-referencing, the relationship between the tables involved can be more complicated than a simple lookup. These relationships will be covered in more detail in a later chapter.

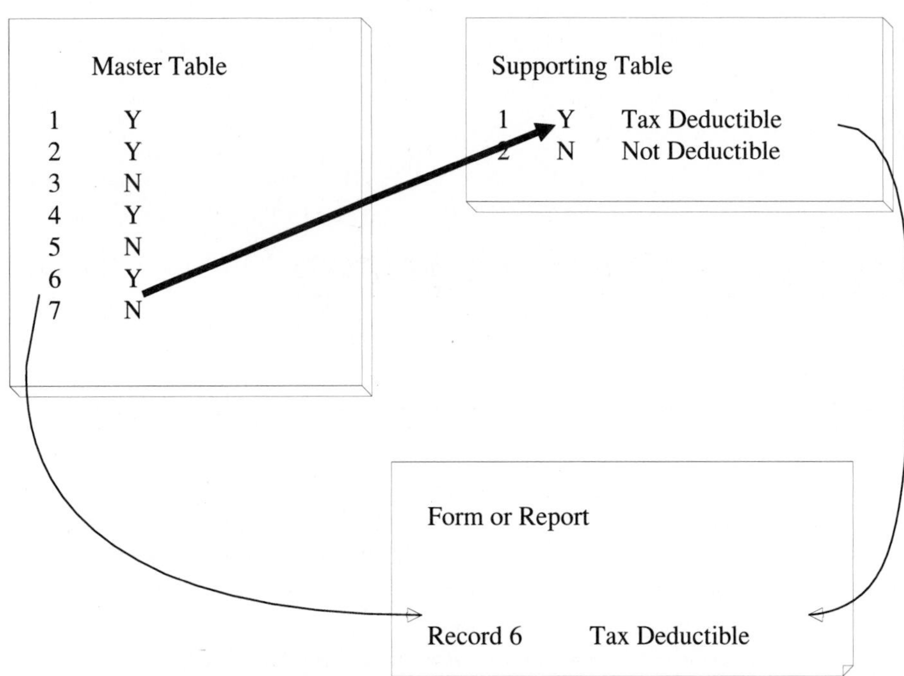

Figure 9-1 Supporting table supplies linked item.

In this chapter, you will learn how to link supporting tables with the fields in a master table in query, screen forms, and report forms. The subject also serves to introduce the concepts used in the more advanced type of cross-reference linking that Paradox can perform.

Begin by loading Paradox in the usual manner.

Creating Supporting Tables

Before you can create links between tables, you must create the tables you want to link. Supporting tables are typically used to relate short entries, abbreviations, and codes placed into the master table to more elaborate items. For example, you could create a table that would link the

Y and N characters entered into the *TaxDeductible* field to terms such as *Deductible* and *Non-Deductible*. A supporting table might link general ledger account numbers to the descriptive name of the general ledger account, or link a customer's name to the address, phone, and social security number.

All these operations are examples of *lookup* operations. A lookup operation is one in which a value from the master table is used as a search key in a supporting table. The operation returns a value or corresponding values from the matching record in the supporting table.

There are several advantages in using supporting tables.

❑ **Improved Data Entry.** The use of supporting tables allows you to minimize the amount of data that needs to be entered into the master table. As in the *Tax deductible* field example, the actual entry is reduced to a single character, Y or N. You could also use other letters to indicate that deductions could be S for State or F for Federal. The entry is merely an abbreviation for some longer term. By storing the full text in the supporting table, you reduce the effort required to fill out each new record.

❑ **Improved Accuracy.** Using codes, abbreviations, and other forms of shorthands not only improves the speed of data entry but improves the accuracy. The fewer characters required for each, the fewer chances for mistakes. The full value or text needs to be entered only once in the supporting table.

❑ **Flow-through Changes.** Supporting tables also allow you to change the full text or value used for a given code or abbreviation and have the change appear on related objects such as report forms.

❑ **More Efficient Storage.** Because the items in supporting tables are entered only once, using supporting tables to add supplementary material to a master file takes up less disk space then entering full text or values as part of each record in the master table.

❑ **One-to-Many Relationships.** Supporting tables usually have a *one-to-many* relationship with the master table. This means the values stored in any *one* of the records in the supporting table can be related to *many* records in the master table. When a link is forged between a supporting and a master table, the data output can be greater than the data stored in either table. Relating values in tables allows you to *output* more information than you actually *input*, creating a gain in productivity.

The key problem with supporting tables is that their use requires foresight and planning. When you create a database table, you need to think about relationships between various data items. In fields where the entries are selected from a finite number of possibilities, you might consider using abbreviations or codes and listing the full name or value of the item in a lookup table. The larger the master table, the greater the benefit of this planning.

Supporting the Tax Deductible Field

As a first example, suppose you want to create a supporting table for the codes you use in the *Tax deductible* field. Create a new table called Tax by entering

c
tax ↵

This table will have three fields.

❑ **Tax Code.** This field will be the *common* field with the master table. It will contain one example of each code that might appear in the *Tax deductible* field of the master table. It is not necessary for the common fields to have the same name in both the master and supporting tables. The only requirement is that they be the same data type (numeric, date, or alpha.)

❑ **Tax Status.** This field is an alpha field containing the full description for each tax code.

❑ **Percent Allowed.** This field is a numeric field containing a value indicating what percent of the *Amount* is deductible. For example, an N record would have 0 as the percent while a Y record would have 1 (100 percent). These values could be used to calculate the amount of deductible expenses at some later point.

Create the field for this table by entering

Tax code ↵
A1 ↵
Tax status ↵
A15 ↵
Percent allowed ↵
N

Save the new table by entering

[F2]

Filling in the Support Table

Use the **DataEntry** command on the Modify menu to add the data to the Tax table. Enter

m d
tax ↵

Fill out the record for the Y tax code by entering

Y ↵
Deductible ↵
1 ↵

The number 1 is equal to 100 percent.

The next entry is the N code. Enter

N ↵
Not Deductible ↵
0 ↵

Add two more codes not currently in use in the file, which you may want to use at a later time. Enter

F ↵
Federal only ↵
.75 ↵

S ↵
State only ↵
.5

There are now four codes entered in the Tax table. Save the data by entering

[F2]

Linking Tables with a Query Form

You have now created a table that is designed to support the master table Ck_book. You can put this table to use by linking it with the master table. The simplest way to link information between tables is with a query form. In a query form, example names are used to indicate fields in different tables that should be linked. For example, suppose you want to list the *Payee, Amount,* and the *Tax Status* information as listed in the Tax table.

There are two tables involved in this operation and you will have to display query forms for both. The *order* in which the query forms are displayed is significant because it indicates how the linking will function. Here, use the value in the *Tax deductible* field of the Ck_book table to locate the record in the Tax table that contains a matching value in the *Tax code* field. The goal is to join the information stored in the *Tax status* field of this record with the *Payee* and *Amount* fields from the Ck_book table. The resulting Answer table will have three fields, two from Ck_book and one from Tax. The Answer table will list all the records from Ck_book only once since it is the master table. However, the values drawn from the Tax table will repeat whenever the *Tax deductible* field value repeats in Ck_book.

In traditional database management terms, this operation is called a *join* or a *lookup*. *Join* refers to data from both files joining to create a new table that is a combination of both tables. *Lookup* means that it is the field in the master table that supplies values to be looked up in the supporting table.

Using Multiple Query Forms

The work area currently has an image of the Tax table. Remove this image and place two query form images onto the work area—the first for the Ck_book file and the second for the Tax table. Enter

[F8]
a
ck_book ↵
[F10] a
tax ↵

There are now two query form images on the work area at the same time. Move the cursor back to the Ck_book query form by entering

[F3]

Select the *Payee* and *Amount* fields for inclusion in the Answer table by entering

[Tab] ***(3 times)***
[F6]
[Tab]
[F6]

Linking Tables

In Paradox, links are created by placing example names in the fields you want to link. There is *no* specific **link** command. This is interesting because you have already seen that example names can be used for other functions. Paradox is designed to figure out the meaning or significance of an example name by analyzing all the items in all the query forms on the work area.

To indicate that two fields in different tables are linked, you would place the same example name in the corresponding field columns in both query forms. It doesn't matter what name you use, as long as it is the same name in both field columns.

In this case place the example name **link** in the Ck_book *Tax deductible* field and also in the *Tax code* field of the Tax table. Paradox will interpret this as a link between the tables. Since Ck_book is the top query form, the *Tax deductible* field will be treated as the master field. The *Tax code* field will be used as the lookup field.

Place the example name in the *Tax deductible* field column by entering

[Tab] ***(2 times)***
[F5]
link

Move the cursor to the Tax query form by entering

[F4]

To create a link between the tables, insert the example name **link** into the *Tax code* field column.

[Tab]
[F5]
link

The final setup in the query form setup is to place √'s in the field columns you want to join to the fields selected in the Ck_book table. In this instance, it is the *Tax status* column that should be selected. Enter

[Tab] [F6]

Process the query by entering

[F2]

The Answer table produced by the query forms consists of nine records and three fields—two fields from Ck_book and the *Tax status* field from Tax operating as a lookup field, as shown in Figure 9-2. Since the link is made on the *Tax deductible* field, any records in the master table with blanks in that field will not be included in the Answer table. In this example, those records are the deposit records you would logically want to exclude from the answer to this query.

Also, notice the order in which the records and fields appear in the Answer table. Since the first query form is treated as the master table form, the fields from Ck_book come first, followed by the field from Tax. The sort order of the records is, therefore, the sequence according to the first selected field from the master table, *Payee*. Save the current query form setup for future use with the **Scripts QuerySave** command. Enter

[F10] s q
tax_stat ↵

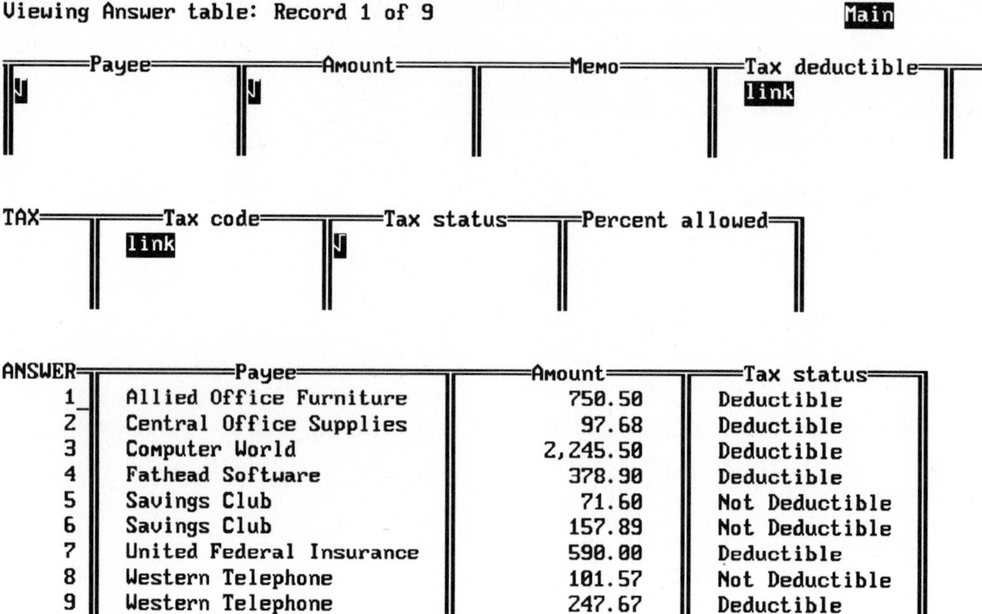

ANSWER	Payee	Amount	Tax status
1	Allied Office Furniture	750.50	Deductible
2	Central Office Supplies	97.68	Deductible
3	Computer World	2,245.50	Deductible
4	Fathead Software	378.90	Deductible
5	Savings Club	71.60	Not Deductible
6	Savings Club	157.89	Not Deductible
7	United Federal Insurance	590.00	Deductible
8	Western Telephone	101.57	Not Deductible
9	Western Telephone	247.67	Deductible

Figure 9-2 Lookup link created between master and supporting table.

Clear the work area by entering

[Alt/F8]

Revising Codes

Recall that you entered four codes in the Tax table, although the Ck_book table has made use of only two of the codes. You may want to go back through the table and see if some records could be more correctly identified by the S or F codes instead of Y or N. Place the Ck_book table into the Edit mode by entering

[F10] m e
ck_book ↵

Move the cursor to record 5, then to the *Tax deductible* field by entering

↵ *(4 times)*
[Tab] *(6 times)*

> *Note that care was taken not to move the cursor through the* Tax deductible *field in records 1 through 4, which are currently blank. Recall that you created a default entry for this field as part of the Validity Check settings stored for this table. If you were to move the cursor through this field it would automatically insert the default value in the field. If this happens there is no way to directly enter a blank. The only way to preserve the blank status is to use the* **Cancel** *command to negate all changes made during the editing session, or save the changes and use a* **Changeto blank** *command in a query form to insert a blank value. Data inserted into a field with* **Changeto** *will not be affected by the default value setting.*

Change some of the values in this field by adding some S and F codes. Enter

s

Paradox beeped when you attempted to enter the letter S. The reason is that you had set up validity check restrictions that limited the entries to Y or N. This was done by using the ValCheck Picture option on the Edit menu to enter a list of acceptable values for the field. (See "Creating a Picture Validity Check" in Chapter 2.) If you want to expand the code letters that can be used in this field, you must remove or modify the validity check settings.

Revising Validity Check Settings

Since the Edit mode is currently active, you can access the **ValCheck** command from the Edit menu. Enter

[F10] v

You can use the Define option to revise the current validity check, or Clear to remove all validity checks from the specified field. In this case, you will revise the existing check. Enter

d

Select the *Tax deductible* field by entering

↵

The check option used to limit entries to a specific list of values is the Picture option. Enter

p

The program displays the current Picture validity check for this field, shown in Figure 9-3 on page 288.

```
Picture:  Y,N
Enter a PAL picture format (e.g. ###-##-####).
```

Figure 9-3 Existing validity check displayed for revision.

Add to the list the other code letters F and S. Enter

,F,S ↵

Paradox displays the message **Picture specification recorded** in the lower right corner of the screen, indicating that the validity check revision has been accepted. You can now enter the additional code letters.

[backspace]
s
↓ *(2 times)*
[backspace]
f
↓ *(3 times)*
[backspace]
f

Save the revised table by entering

[F2]

The changes in the codes listed in the *Tax deductible* field will be reflected when you process the Tax_stat query again. Process the query using the **Scripts Play** command. Enter

[F10] s p
tax_stat ↵
[F2]

The Answer table now shows all four types of tax status associated with the single-letter codes, Figure 9-4 on page 289.

Clear the work area by entering

[Alt-F8]

Linking More Than Two Tables

The concept of master and supporting tables can apply to more than two tables at a time. You may want to link several fields, each to a different supporting table. For example, the *Cleared bank* field

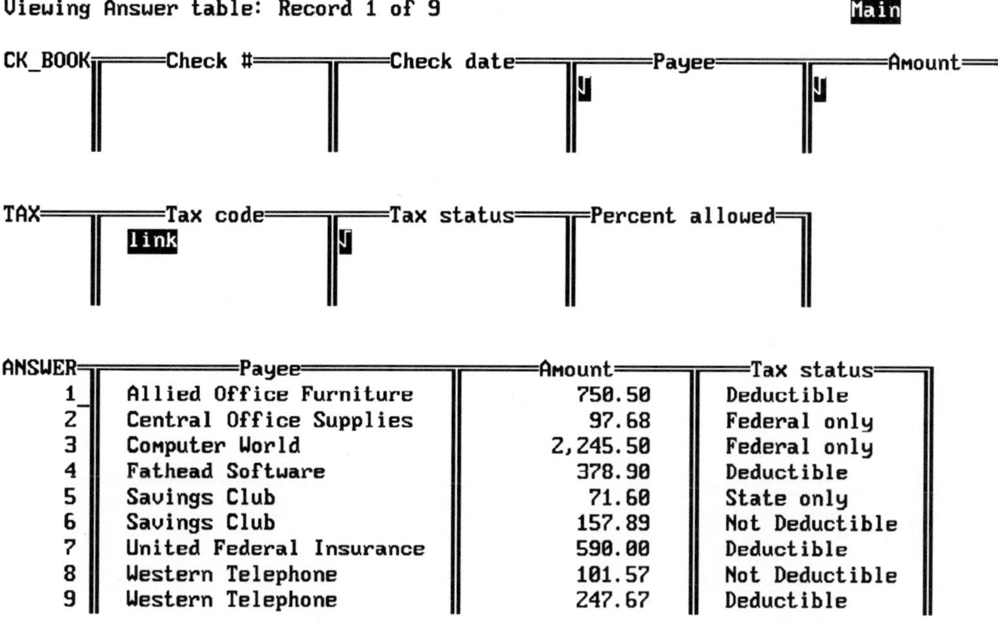

ANSWER	Payee	Amount	Tax status
1	Allied Office Furniture	750.50	Deductible
2	Central Office Supplies	97.68	Federal only
3	Computer World	2,245.50	Federal only
4	Fathead Software	378.90	Deductible
5	Savings Club	71.60	State only
6	Savings Club	157.89	Not Deductible
7	United Federal Insurance	590.00	Deductible
8	Western Telephone	101.57	Not Deductible
9	Western Telephone	247.67	Deductible

Figure 9-4 Query links four different tax codes to tax status.

also contains the single-character codes, √ and −, which indicate whether the item has cleared the bank or not. Create a new table called Bank to act as a supporting table for the *Cleared bank* field.

c
bank ↵

The table will have two fields, the linking field *Bank code,* and a descriptive field, *Bank status*. Enter

Band code ↵
A1 ↵
Band status ↵
A15

Save the new structure by entering

[F2]

Fill in the table with two records, one for the √ code and the other for the − code. Place the Bank table in the Edit mode by entering

m e
bank ↵

Enter the record that matches the − code.

- ↵
Outstanding

Recall that in order to enter a √ character, you must use the [Alt—*keypad*] method where you type the character set value on the *numeric* keypad while holding down the [Alt] key.(See "Using Graphic Characters in Validity Checks" in Chapter 2.) Enter

[Alt-251] ↵
Cleared

Save the new table by entering

[F2]

Clear the work area by entering

[Alt-F8]

The next step is to modify the Tax_stat query form to link the Bank table to the Cleared band field. Begin by recalling the stored query form. Enter

s p
tax_stat ↵

Move the cursor to the Ck_book query form by entering

[F3]

In order to display all of the field on a single screen width, making the example easier to follow, add a √ to the *Check #* field and remove the √ from the *Payee* field. Enter

[Tab] [F6]
[Tab] *(2 times)*
[F6]

Move the cursor to the *Cleared bank* field by entering

[Tab] *(4 times)*

Enter an example name to use as the linking name to the Bank table. Keep in mind that the name in itself has no significance and can be anything. In this case, use **banklink** as the example name. Enter

[F5]
banklink

In order to establish a link between this field and the corresponding field in the Bank table, you need to display a third query form on the work area, a query form for the Bank table. Enter

[F10] a
bank ↵

Create the link between Ck_book and Bank by placing the same example name used in the *Cleared bank* field of the Ck_book table into the *Band code* field of the Bank table. Enter

[Tab] [F5]
banklink

The purpose of the link is to retrieve the matching text from the *Bank status* field. To include the *Bank status* field in the Answer table place a √ in that field.

[Tab] [F6]

The query now consists of three tables. The Tax and Bank tables are supporting fields within the Ck_book table, Figure 9-5.

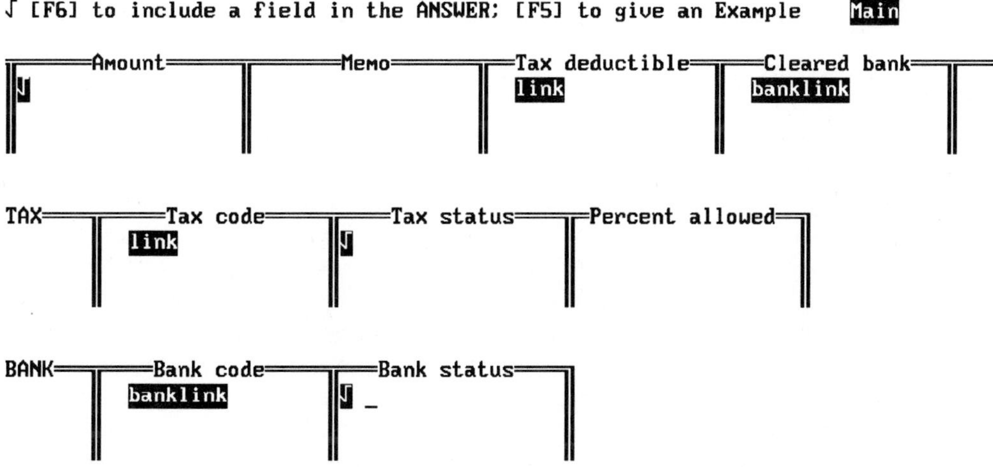

Figure 9-5 Three tables linked in a single query setup.

The Answer table produced by the query forms contains nine records and four fields. The *Tax status* and *Bank status* fields are created by performing lookup operations on the support tables Tax and Bank, Figure 9-6 on page 292.

The resulting Answer table uses the supporting tables to generate a table whose meaning is much less ambiguous than the master table, which used abbreviations and codes to repre-

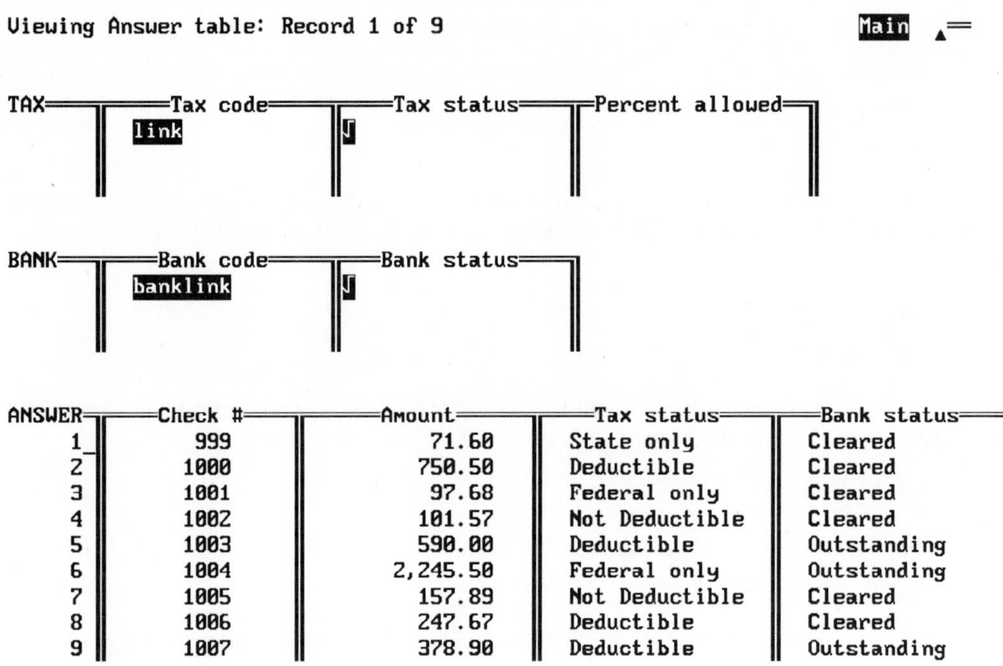

ANSWER	Check #	Amount	Tax status	Bank status
1	999	71.60	State only	Cleared
2	1000	750.50	Deductible	Cleared
3	1001	97.68	Federal only	Cleared
4	1002	101.57	Not Deductible	Cleared
5	1003	590.00	Deductible	Outstanding
6	1004	2,245.50	Federal only	Outstanding
7	1005	157.89	Not Deductible	Cleared
8	1006	247.67	Deductible	Cleared
9	1007	378.90	Deductible	Outstanding

Figure 9-6 Answer table combines data from three tables.

sent the tax and band status of the transactions. The supporting tables allow the elaborated table to be produced with a minimum of extra entry. Also keep in mind that once the supporting tables have been established, they will furnish this data with no additional effort no matter how large the master table grows. When the database system is used in this manner, the amount of effort needed to generate the data is *not* proportional to the size of the tables involved. On the other hand, methods requiring the user to make longer manual entries in each field are proportional to the size of the database. The goal in any database system is to use nonproportional methods wherever possible. In the short run non proportional techniques, such as the use of supporting tables, may seem more difficult and complicated than simply entering data. However, the long-run benefits of these approaches are very significant, because they employ the power of the computer to a much greater degree than do the more obvious but less automated approaches.

The Include Operator

You may have noticed that the Answer table generated by the current query form setup includes the nine check records from the Ck_book table. The four deposit records in the table are ignored because the first linking field, *Tax deductible*, is blank for the deposit records.

> *The* Tax deductible *field controls record selection because it is the* first *linking field in the master table. If only the Cleared bank field was used to link to the Band table, all the records would be included because all the records in Ck_book have a nonblank value in the* Cleared bank *field.*

In some cases, you may want to ensure that all the records in the master table are included in the Answer table, even though they may contain blank values in the link field. Since the current query displays the *Bank status* as well as the *Tax status*, you may want to include all records in the Answer, not just those having nonblank entries in the *Tax deductible* field.

This can be activated by using the **inclusion** operator. The **inclusion** operator, entered as a **!**, tells Paradox to include all the records found in that field in the Answer table.

The current query form setup can be made to generate a full list of records by adding the **!** operator to the example name in the *Tax deductible* field. Enter

[F3] ***(3 times)***
[Shift-Tab]
!

The **!** is placed beside the example name in the *Tax deductible* field as shown in Figure 9-7 in order to indicate to Paradox to include all records in the linking process.

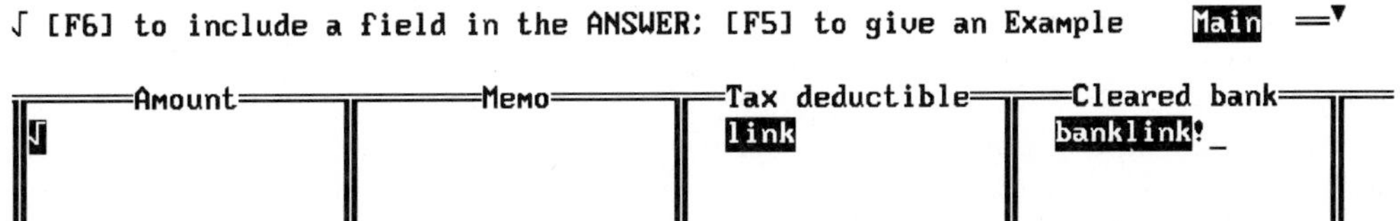

Figure 9-7 Inclusion operator, !, added to query form.

Execute the query by entering

[F2]

The resulting Answer table lists all 13 records. Note that the *Tax status* field is left blank for any items which do match a record in the lookup table Tax. Save the revised query setup under the name Tax-stat by entering

[F10] s q
tax_stat ↵

Since there is already a script file with the name Tax_stat, Paradox asks if you want to replace the existing script with the new query setup. Confirm your intention to overwrite the existing query form script by entering

r

Clear the work area by entering

[Alt-F8]

Budget Category

One very common use of supporting tables in financial databases is the coordination of a chart of accounts with individual transactions. While the Ck_book table is not a general ledger of accounting transactions, it might be useful to link various records with specific accounts. Create a new table called Accounts by entering

c
accounts ↵

The first field in this table will be the *Account #* field. Enter

Account # ↵
n ↵

Next, create an alpha field for the name of the account. Enter

Account Name ↵
a20 ↵

Save the new table by entering

[F2]

Fill in the chart of the Accounts table with the following account information.

[F10] m d
accounts ↵
100 ↵
Cash in Bank ↵
500 ↵
Office Furniture ↵
600 ↵
Office Supplies ↵
650 ↵

Office Equipment ↵
700 ↵
Utilities

Save the data by entering

[F2]

The records should look like Figure 9-8.

```
Viewing Accounts table: Record 1 of 5

ACCOUNTS═╤══Account #═╤═══Account name══════╗
    1    │     100    │ Cash in Bank        ║
    2    │     500    │ Office Furniture    ║
    3    │     600    │ Office Supplies     ║
    4    │     650    │ Office Equipment    ║
    5    │     700    │ Utilities           ║
```

Figure 9-8 Account information entered into Accounts table.

The next step is to add a new field to the Ck_book table to hold the account number for each record. Changes in table structure are made using the **Modify Restructure** command. Enter

[F10] m r
ck_book ↵

Paradox displays the current table structure and allows you to add, delete, or modify the field designated in the structure.

> *If you modify existing fields, you can create a situation in which there can be some potential loss of data if you shorten the length of an alpha field or convert date or number fields to alpha. If Paradox encounters a problem fitting the existing field entry into the modified structure, the program will display a special menu. The Trimming option tells Paradox to truncate characters that will not fit into the field. The Non-trimming option copies all problem records into a table called Problems for further analysis. The Oops! option cancels the Do-It! and returns you to the Restructure Editing mode.*

You can add a new field at any position in the structure by positioning the cursor and pressing [Ins]. When [Ins] is pressed, the current field definition is moved down one row and a blank row is inserted at the cursor position. In this instance, place the account number field following the *Check #* field. Enter

↓ [Ins]

Enter the field definition.

↵
Acct # ↵
n

Save the modified structure by entering

[F2]

When you modify the structure of an existing table, Paradox will update other files in the table's family such as screen or report forms, validity checks, or image settings. Fields that have been deleted from the structure, or field types that have been changed, are automatically deleted from any screen or report forms. Calculated fields containing a reference to a delete or a type-changed field will also be removed. This will allow you to display or print the existing forms without encountering an error, but with missing fields.

This does not apply to saved query forms. Such forms are unaffected by changes in the table structure. Thus, when you attempt to replay a query save script, you may encounter an error caused by a script containing the name of a deleted field.

Use the Edit mode to fill in the account numbers for each of the records. Enter

[Tab] ***(2 times)***
[F9]
100 ↓
100 ↓
100 ↓
100 ↓

Enter the account numbers for the check items.

600 ↓
500 ↓
600 ↓
700 ↓
600 ↓
650 ↓
600 ↓
700 ↓
600

Save the revised data by entering

[F2]

The new data should look like Figure 9-9.

Clear the work area by entering

[Alt-F8]

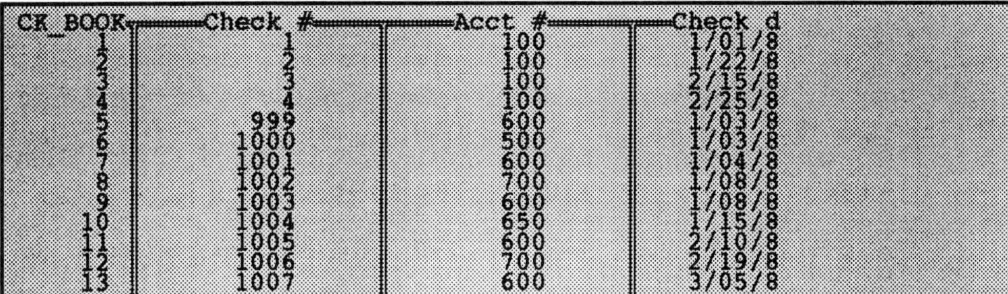

CK_BOOK	Check #	Acct #	Check d
1	1	100	1/01/8
2	2	100	1/22/8
3	3	100	2/15/8
4	4	100	2/25/8
5	999	600	1/03/8
6	1000	500	1/03/8
7	1001	600	1/04/8
8	1002	700	1/08/8
9	1003	600	1/08/8
10	1004	650	1/15/8
11	1005	600	2/10/8
12	1006	700	2/19/8
13	1007	600	3/05/8

Figure 9-9 Account numbers added to Ck_book table.

Query Form Order

In the previous multiple table query form layouts, the Ck_book table has always been the first query form. In this position, the Ck_book table controls the order in which records are displayed in the Answer table.

What would happen if a different table, e.g., Accounts or Tax, was used as the first table in the query layout? One difference would be that the first field selected in that table would control the order of the records in the Answer table. For example, suppose you use the Accounts table as the first table. Instead of listing the records by *Check #* order (the key field in Ck_book) the records in the Answer table would be listed by account number or account name.

If you use the Tax or Bank tables as the leading table, the items in those tables would control the order of the records. Used in this way the lookup tables function as a way of listing records by group, based on the items in the lookup table.

Listing by Account Number

Suppose you want to produce a table that lists the records in order of account number. In this example, you would place the Accounts query form on the work area first, followed by the Ck_book form. Enter

a
accounts ↵

Select both fields and place an example name into *Account #* to be used to link to the *Acct #* field in Ck_book. Enter

[Tab] [F6] [F5]
link
[Tab] [F6]

Place a Ck_book query form on the work area by entering

[F10] a
ck_book ↵

Place the **link** example name into the *Acct #* field in order to establish the link between the two tables. Enter

[Tab] ***(2 times)***
[F5]
link

From this table choose the *Payee* and *Amount* fields. Enter

[Tab] ***(2 times)***
[F6] [Tab]
[F6]

Selecting Records in Multiple Table Queries

You may also want to select records as part of this query setup. For example, limit the records listed to checks, not deposits, because the deposit records have a zero value in the *Amount* field. Add a selection condition to the *Amount* field that will prompt the query to skip any records with a value of zero in this field. Enter

>0

Process the query by entering

[F2]

The program lists the nine check records in order of their account numbers, Figure 9-10.

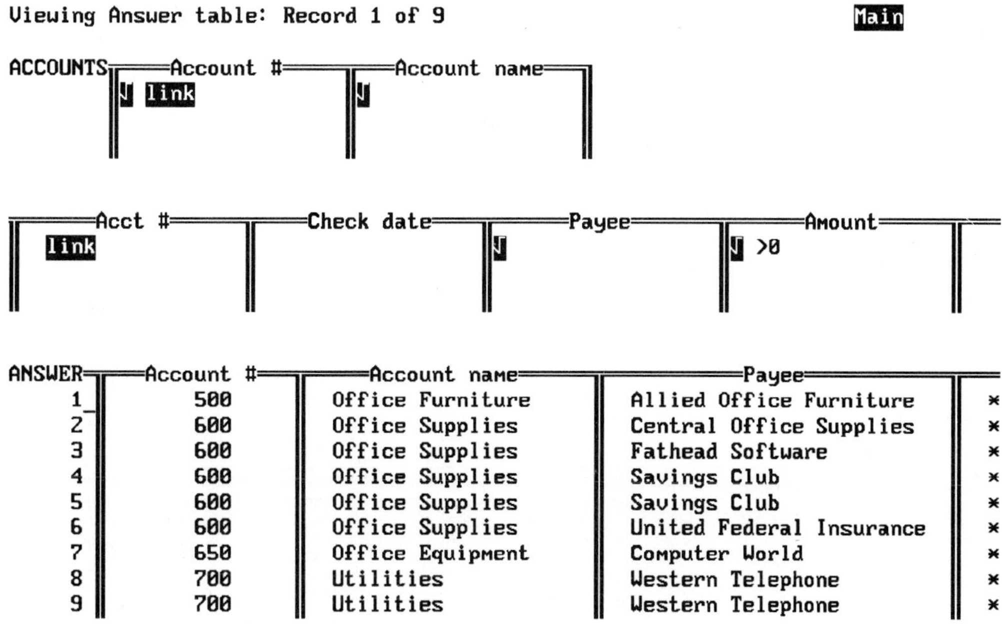

ANSWER	Account #	Account name	Payee	
1	500	Office Furniture	Allied Office Furniture	*
2	600	Office Supplies	Central Office Supplies	*
3	600	Office Supplies	Fathead Software	*
4	600	Office Supplies	Savings Club	*
5	600	Office Supplies	Savings Club	*
6	600	Office Supplies	United Federal Insurance	*
7	650	Office Equipment	Computer World	*
8	700	Utilities	Western Telephone	*
9	700	Utilities	Western Telephone	*

Figure 9-10 Records organized by Accounts table.

You can, in turn, link the records in the query to the Bank table, in order to list the bank status along with the account information, Figure 9-11.

Move the cursor back to the Ck_book query form by entering

[F3]

To simplify the Answer table, remove the *Payee* field by entering

← [F6]

Place an example name in the Cleared bank field column to use as a link to the Bank table. Enter

[Tab] ***(4 times)***
[F5]
linkbank

Add a query form for the Bank table to the work area by entering

[F10] a
bank ↵

Place the **linkbank** example name into the *Bank code* field to establish the link between the Ck_book and Bank tables. Enter

[Tab] [F5]
linkbank

Add the *Bank status* field to the Answer table by entering

[Tab] [F6]

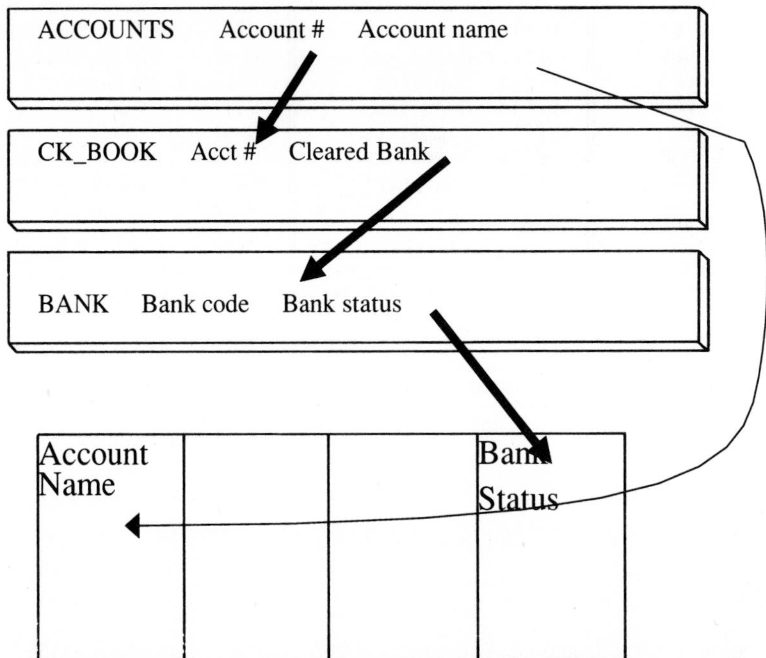

Figure 9-11 Supporting table forms placed before and after master table form.

Execute the query by entering

[F2]

The Answer table, Figure 9-12, lists the records in order of account number. Note that the only field that directly displays information from Ck_book is the *Amount* field. All others are a result of a lookup link operation.

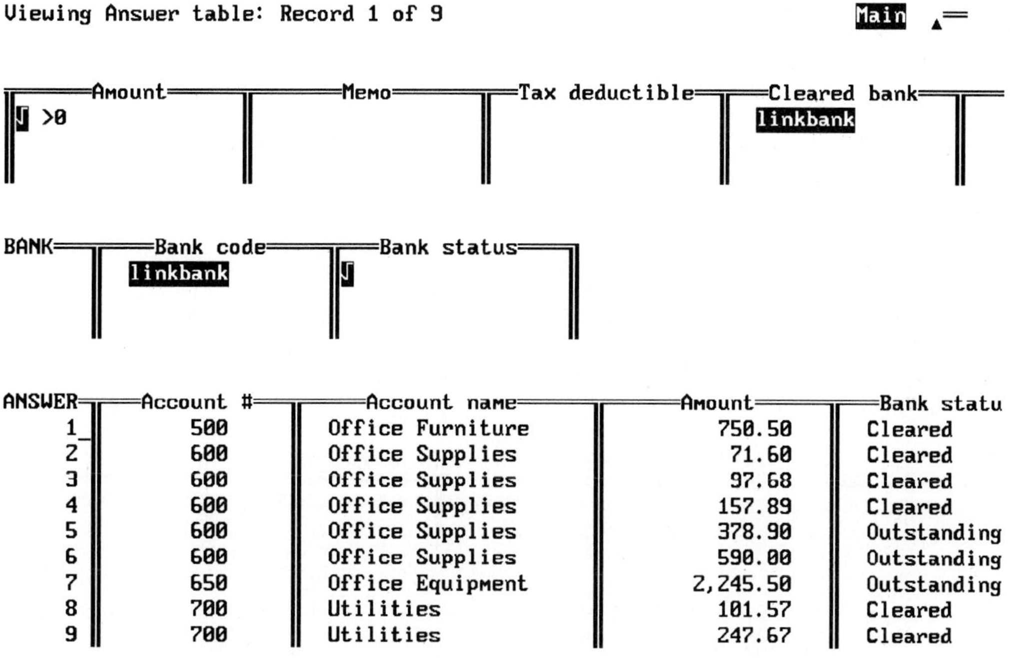

ANSWER	Account #	Account name	Amount	Bank statu
1	500	Office Furniture	750.50	Cleared
2	600	Office Supplies	71.60	Cleared
3	600	Office Supplies	97.68	Cleared
4	600	Office Supplies	157.89	Cleared
5	600	Office Supplies	378.90	Outstanding
6	600	Office Supplies	590.00	Outstanding
7	650	Office Equipment	2,245.50	Outstanding
8	700	Utilities	101.57	Cleared
9	700	Utilities	247.67	Cleared

Figure 9-12 Query uses Account number table to control record sequence.

You can use the same logic to list records according to the Bank or Tax status. Clear the work area by entering

[Alt-F8]

Display a query form for the Tax table by entering

a
tax ↵

Place an example name in the *Tax code* field column and select the *Tax status* field column for display in the Answer table by entering

[Tab] [F5]
link
[Tab] [F6]

Place a query form for Ck_book on the work area.

[F10] a
ck_book ↵

Select the *Payee* and *Amount* fields for display by entering

> **[Tab]** ***(4 times)***
> **[F6] [Tab] [F6]**

Link the Ck_book table to the Tax table by placing the example name in the *Tax deductible* field column. Try this on your own. The correct command can be found on page 330 under Exercise 1. Execute the query by entering

> **[F2]**

The query lists the *Payee* and *Amount* data organized according to the tax status of each record, Figure 9-13.

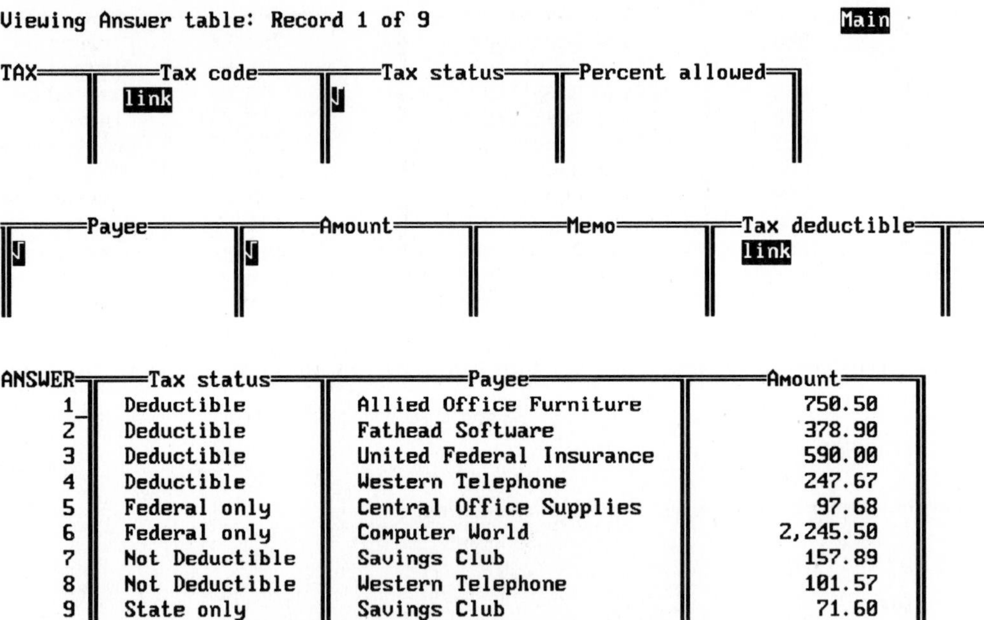

Viewing Answer table: Record 1 of 9 Main

TAX	Tax code	Tax status	Percent allowed
	link	✓	

	Payee	Amount	Memo	Tax deductible
	✓	✓		link

ANSWER	Tax status	Payee	Amount
1	Deductible	Allied Office Furniture	750.50
2	Deductible	Fathead Software	378.90
3	Deductible	United Federal Insurance	590.00
4	Deductible	Western Telephone	247.67
5	Federal only	Central Office Supplies	97.68
6	Federal only	Computer World	2,245.50
7	Not Deductible	Savings Club	157.89
8	Not Deductible	Western Telephone	101.57
9	State only	Savings Club	71.60

Figure 9-13 Records organized by tax status.

Clear the work area by entering

> **[Alt-F8]**

Calculations with Lookup Tables

The records contained in a supporting lookup table often represent a list of values by which the records in the master table can be grouped. The Tax table was used, Figure 9-13, to divide the records into four different groups according to tax status. You can perform summary calculations in linked tables in a similar manner to the way in which you performed them for individual tables. The advantage of using linked tables is that you can use the data from the additional fields contained in the linked tables.

Summary by Lookup Group

As an example, if you wanted to calculate the total amount for each tax status category, the Tax table should be first on the work area. Display a query form for the tax table by entering

a
tax ↵

As with the previous query, place an example name in *Tax code* to use for linking the table to Ck_book, and a √ in the *Tax status* field. Try this on your own. The correct command can be found on page 330 under Exercise 2.

Next, add a query form for Ck_book.

[F10] a
ck_book ↵

Place a **calc sum** operator in the *Amount* field. Enter

[Tab] ***(5 times)***
calc sum

Link the Ck_book table to the Tax table by placing the example name in the *Tax deductible* field column.

[Tab] ***(2 times)***
[F5]
link

The query will link the tables according to the *Tax code*, Figure 9-14.

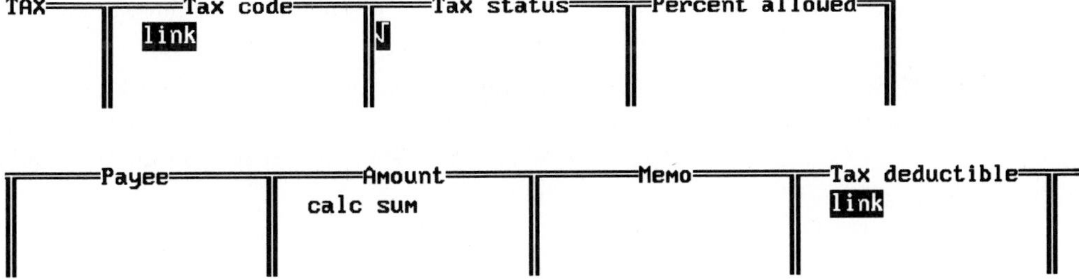

Figure 9-14 Linked tables producing group totals.

Calculate the group totals by processing the query form.

[F2]

The Answer table displays four records, one for each of the tax status codes, and the total of the records in those categories, Figure 9-15.

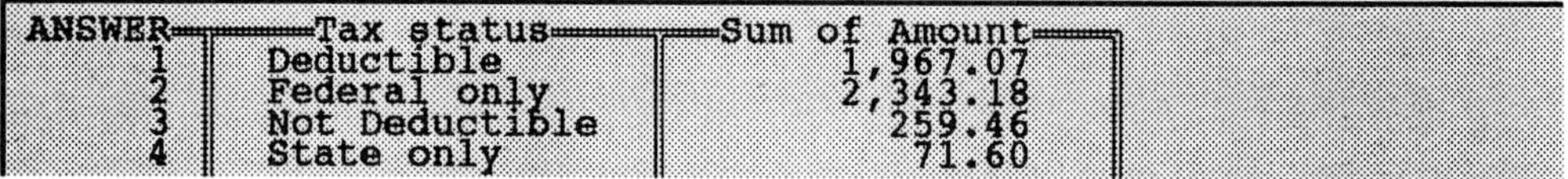

ANSWER	Tax status	Sum of Amount
1	Deductible	1,967.07
2	Federal only	2,343.18
3	Not Deductible	259.46
4	State only	71.60

Figure 9-15 Amounts totaled by tax status.

Clear the work area by entering

[Alt-F8]

Calculating with Lookup Values

Another way to use information stored in lookup tables is to perform calculations using values from the master and lookup tables. The Tax table contains a field called *Percent allowed.* This field holds values that correspond to the percentage of the actual amount that can be deducted. The idea is that in addition to having a full text description for each tax code, you can also have values stored in the table that would be used in calculations.

For example, record 4 in the Tax table, code S for State only, has the value .5 in the *Percent Allowed* field. You would want to multiply the *Amount* by .5 for each record that had S for the tax code. On the other hand, records with the code Y would have 100 percent of the *Amount* deductible. The *Percent Allowed* for that code is 1, which is the same as 100 percent.

The linking processes allow you to lookup the appropriate percentage for each of the records based on the tax code. In setting up queries to perform this calculation, you will use example names for two different purposes. One example will be used to link the tables through the *Tax deductible* and *Tax code* fields.

The other examples will be used to identify the values from the *Amount* and *Percent allowed* fields, which will be used to calculate the deductible amounts. Begin by placing the Ck_book query form on the work area. Ck_book is used first to allow the first field in the Ck_book table to control the sequence of the Answer table.

a

ck_book ↵

Begin by placing √ in the *Account* and *Amount* fields. Enter

[Tab] ***(2 times)***
[F6]
[Tab] ***(3 times)***
[F6]

The cursor is now in the *Amount* field. Because this field will be used in the calculation of the deductible amount, it is necessary to assign the field an example name. Enter

[F5]
base

The formula that will calculate the deductible amount is ***Amount*Percent allowed***. The example name for *Amount* has just been entered as **base**. In this case, you need to plan ahead by entering the example name you intend to use for the *Percent allowed* field in the Tax query form. Here, use **rate** for that field. Enter the calculation formula as follows.

,calc
[spacebar] [F5]
base*
[F5]
rate

Add one more item to this column whose purpose is to select only records that have amounts greater than zero. Enter

,>0

The final entry in the Ck_book query form is the example name that will link the records in the two tables according to tax code. Place an example name in the *Tax deductible* column by entering

[Tab] ***(2 times)***
[F5]
link

Display a query form for the Tax table by entering

[F10] a
tax ↵

Insert the linking example name into the *Tax code* field.

[Tab] [F5]
link

Next, select the Tax Status field as part of the Answer table by entering

[Tab] [F6]

Lastly, place the example name **rate** into the *Percent allowed* field to relate those values to the formula. Enter

[Tab] [F5]
rate

The query layout is set to calculate a value that depends on values drawn from the linked lookup table, Figure 9-16.

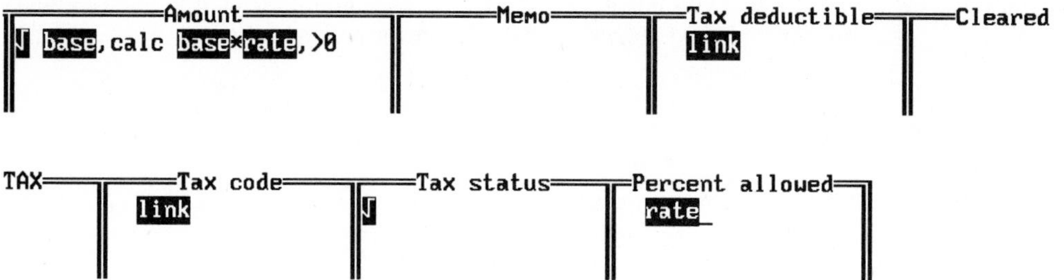

Figure 9-16 Formula uses values from linked tables.

Execute the query by entering

[F2]

The Answer table produced by the query includes a column labeled *Amount*Percent allowed*, which shows the results of the formula, Figure 9-17. If you examine the values, you will see that the percentage of the *Amount* allowed matches the tax status of each record. The Lookup link was able to find and use the proper value based on the link between the tables.

Save this query form by entering

[F10] s q
ded_perc ↵

Clear the work area by entering

[Alt-F8]

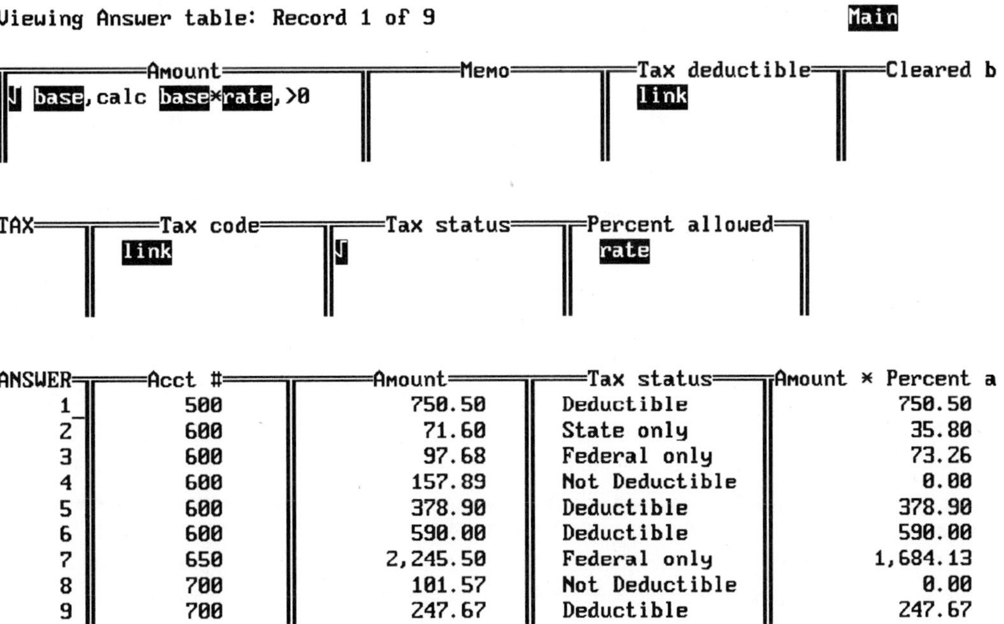

Figure 9-17 Formula calculates using values from linked tables.

Linking Tables to Data Entry

As discussed in the previous section, supporting lookup tables can be used to combine information from more than one table into a single Answer table.

In those examples, the values found in the supporting table are inserted into an Answer table at the point of *output*, i.e., as the Answer table is being generated.

An alternative approach is to use a supporting table to directly enter information into the current table during data entry and editing. This can be accomplished by using the TableLookup option of the Edit ValCheck menu, and can be used in three basic ways.

❑ **Check entry against list.** In its simplest application, the first field in the lookup table can function as a list of acceptable values for the current field. In this regard, the lookup table performs a similar function to the Picture validity check option that can also hold a list of acceptable values. Using a lookup table for this purpose has the advantage of making it much simpler to add, delete, or revise the list of values, since they are actually records in the lookup table. You might also create the values in the lookup table by drawing them from some other table by way of a query form.

❑ **Display table as help.** The lookup table linked to a particular field can be used as a popup help listing. For example, suppose the Tax table was linked as a lookup to the *Tax deductible* field. When you wanted to make an entry into the *Tax deductible* field, you would have the option of entering a value or pressing [F1]. [F1] would display the image of the Tax table, in which you could use the ↑ and ↓ keys to select a record that contained the value you wanted to enter. Pressing [F2] would return you to the master table, having copied the value from the first field of the lookup table into the master table field.

❑ **Copy data from corresponding fields.** If the master and lookup tables have fields with the *same* names, Paradox will copy data from the lookup into the master table. For example, suppose you added a field to the Ck_book table called *Tax status*, matching the name used in the Tax table. Each time a value was entered into the *Tax deductible* field, Paradox would find the record in the lookup table with the matching code and insert the value in the *Tax status* of that record into the master table's *Tax status* field. The feature can also be combined with the Help type of display so that when a selection is made from the Help table the copying takes place.

Keep in mind that when a lookup table is linked to a field, the link will automatically use the *first* field in the lookup table as the link field. This is less flexible than the query form operation in which you can place the example names in any field. You must make sure that the lookup table has the common field as the first field in the table before you attempt to link the fields.

> *When the ValCheck TableLookup option is used, the field in the master table being linked and the first field in the Lookup table must be the same type. This means if you are linking two alpha fields, the length of the fields must be the same. For example, if the master table field is A1 and the Lookup table field is A15, Paradox will refuse to create the link. The message* **field not appropriate type** *will be displayed. On the other hand, currency and numeric fields are treated as the same type because they differ only in the area of display format, not actual field structure.*

This method has the advantage of immediate feedback to the user at the point of data entry or revision. The lookup table, used in the Help type mode, can help a user decide what ought to be entered. On the other hand, since the data is copied into the master table, the amount of disk storage needed is increased.

Displaying Lookup Values During Edit

The use of account numbers with the records in the Ck_book table is important because it enables you to classify transactions according to accounting categories. However, as the number of accounting categories increases, it can be difficult to remember the account numbers associated with the various accounts.

One solution is to use the Accounts table as a Help type of lookup table. This allows you to enter the account numbers manually when you recall the account number you need, or to display the Accounts table when you need help in recalling the correct account number.

Lookup tables can be linked to fields through the **ValCheck** command on the Edit menu. Place the Ck_book table into the Edit mode by entering

m e
ck_book ↵

Display the ValCheck menu by entering

[F10] v

Select the Define option by entering

d

In this case, you want to define a new validity check for the *Acct #* field. Enter

→ ***(2 times)***
↵

Tables are linked to fields with the **TableLookup** command. Enter

t

Paradox asks you to enter the name of the table to which the field will be linked. In this instance the link will be made to the Accounts table. Enter

accounts ↵

Paradox displays a menu with two options, JustCurrentField and AllCorrespondingFields, Figure 9-18.

❑ **JustCurrentField.** This option limits the interaction between the master and supporting tables to the *current* field in the master table and the *first* field in the supporting table.

❑ **AllCorrespondingFields.** This option allows Paradox to relate fields in the supporting table to fields in the master table if they have the same names. If you select this option, Paradox will copy values from the selected record in the lookup table into the current record in the master table.

```
JustCurrentField  AllCorrespondingFields                              Edit
Check entered values in current field against stored values in lookup table.
```

Figure 9-18 Menu controls which fields are affected by lookup.

In this case, you are only concerned with the *Acct #* field and do not want to copy values from other fields into the master table. Select JustCurrentField by entering

j

This selection leads to another menu, Figure 9-19. The purpose of this menu is to select the type of lookup operation you want to have.

❑ **PrivateLookup.** This option prompts Paradox to locate the entered value in the first field of the lookup table. If the value can be located, no action is taken. If the value cannot be located, then the message **Not one of the possible values for this field** is displayed. You can edit the value until you make a valid entry or leave the field blank. This option prevents any values other than the ones listed in the first field in the lookup table to be entered in the field.

> *If you have also selected the* Required *entry validity check option for the same field that you have designed as a* PrivateLookup *field, you must enter an acceptable value since Paradox will not allow a blank space in this field. The combination of* Required *and* TableLookup PrivateLookup *should be used only when you are sure that the user will know how to make a valid entry.*

❑ **HelpAndFill.** Like PrivateLookup, this option requires that a valid entry, i.e., one that matches one of the values in the first field of the lookup table, be made in the current field. However, this option also provides the possibility for the user to display the lookup table by pressing the [F1] key. The user can then select a value using the ↑, ↓ or [Ctrl-z](the zoom key) to search the first field in the lookup table. Pressing [F2] inserts the value from the selected record into the master table.

```
PrivateLookup  HelpAndFill                                            Edit
Check entered values against stored values; prevent access to lookup table.
```

Figure 9-19 Select type of lookup relationship.

Here, choose the **HelpAndFill** option to allow the Accounts table to function as a Help screen reference for data entry.

h

Paradox confirms the linking of the table with the message **Table lookup recorded** in the lower right corner of the screen.

To see how this new validity check option works, add a new record to the table by entering

[Ctrl-Home[[End] ↓

Enter the check number.

1008 ↵

The cursor is now in the *Acct #* field. The message **Press [F1] for help with fill-in** appears at the top of the screen, Figure 9-20, indicating that a Lookup table can be displayed for this field.

```
Editing Ck book table: Record 14 of 14
Press [F1] for help with fill-in
```

Figure 9-20 Press [F1] appears, indicating lookup table available for this field.

Display the lookup table by entering

[F1]

The screen display changes from showing the Ck_book table to one that displays the Accounts table. All the accounts are listed so that you can select, rather than manually enter, the account number you deem appropriate.

> *You can use the → and ← keys to move the cursor to different fields. However, when you press [F2] to select a record, the value in the* first *field is the one that is copied, regardless of the field in which the cursor is positioned.*

In this case select the last record in the lookup table, account 700, by entering

[End] [F2]

The account number 700 is copied into the *Acct #* field. Complete the record by entering

↵
3/10/89 ↵
Interstate Power & Light ↵
175.49 ↵
↵
s ↵
↵
[F2]

Copying Data to Corresponding Fields

Another variation of editing with lookup tables is the insertion of data into fields in the master table that have matching fields in the lookup table. For example, suppose you inserted into the Ck_book table a field called *Tax status*. You could automatically fill in the *Tax status* field if you attached Tax as a lookup to the *Tax deductible* field.

The first step is to add a new field, *Tax status*, to the Ck_book table with the **Modify Restructure** command. Enter

[F10] m r
ck_book ↵

Insert the new field following the *Tax deductible* field by entering

↓ *(7 times)*
[Ins]

Enter the field name so that it is exactly the same as the name of the field in the lookup table you want copied. Enter

→
Tax status ↵

Enter the field type.

A15

Save the modified table by entering

[F2]

Paradox examines all the files in the Ck_book family as part of the process that restructures the table according to the modified structure. When the process is complete, you are returned to the Ck_book table image.

The next step is to attach the Tax lookup table to the *Tax deductible* field. Activate the Edit mode. Enter

[F9]

Define a new validity check by entering

[F10] v d

Select the *Tax deductible* field by entering

→ *(7 times)*
↵

Choose **TableLookup** by entering

t

Enter the name of the lookup table, Tax.

tax ↵

In this instance, you want to copy data from corresponding fields. Enter

a

A submenu appears with two options, Figure 9-21.

```
FillNoHelp  HelpAndFill                                              Edit
Check values, no access to lookup table, fill values in corresponding fields.
```

Figure 9-21 Corresponding fields options.

❑ **FillNoHelp.** This option will cause Paradox to fill the corresponding fields automatically once the data is entered into the linked field. However, this option does not permit the display of the linked table with the [F1] key. This means that you could allow linking to tables that contain fields with sensitive material. Since the user cannot display the entire table with [F1], only the corresponding data will be known.

❑ **HelpAndFill.** This option will automatically fill the corresponding fields and allow you to select values from a Help table displayed when you press [F1].

In this case, select the HelpAndFill option. Enter

h

Paradox records the new validity check lookup table. Add a new record to the table by entering

[Ctrl-Home] [End] ↓
1009 ↵

Display the lookup table for *Acct #* by entering

[F1]

Select *Office Supplies* by entering

↓ ***(2 times)***
[F2]
↵

Continue entering fields, as follows:

3/12/89 ↵
Central Office Supplies ↵
36.89 ↵
↵

You are now located in the *Tax deductible* field. You have the option to enter a tax code, or lookup all the tax codes with the [F1] key. Enter the tax code directly.

y ↵

The lookup table automatically inserts **Deductible** into the *Tax status* field when you entered Y into the *Tax deductible* field, Figure 9-22.

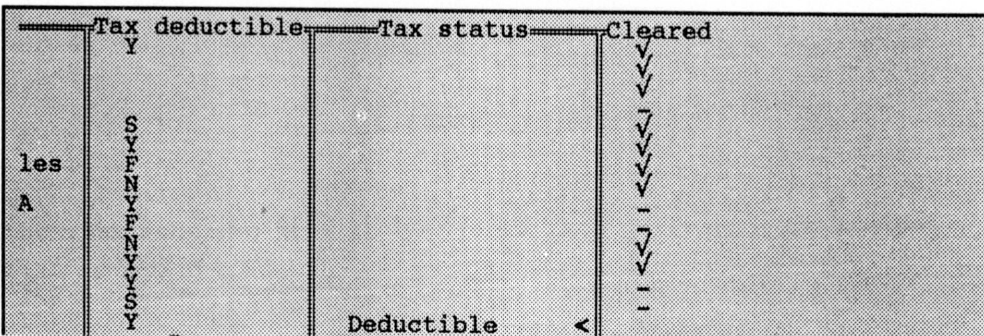

Figure 9-22 Value inserted in corresponding field.

Complete the record by entering

↵ *(2 times)*
[F2]

Clear the work area by entering

[Alt-F8]

Lookup with Changeto

In the two previous procedures, the lookup tables were used to insert data into the master table as records were being entered or edited. In the *Tax status* field only, the record that was edited is updated to show the tax status. The remainder of the records, entered before the lookup table was linked to the field, remain blank.

You can combine the logic of a lookup table with the query form **changeto** operator to automatically fill in the values in the *Tax status* field in a single command.

To perform a **changeto** operation, it is necessary to create a query form layout that will indicate which records and fields should be changed and in what way.

Begin the query layout by displaying a query form for the Tax table. Enter

a
tax ↵

Why begin with the Tax table rather than the Ck_book table? It is important to keep in mind that most of the records in Ck_book upon which you want to operate are currently blank records. By default, Paradox would exclude records with blank values from the query operation. If you were to place Ck_book into the master table position, i.e., the first query form on the work area, the blank records would not be affected, defeating your purpose. By placing Tax first, you begin with a master table that has values in all the fields. The result will be that all the records in Ck_book having a tax code will be changed.

In this example, you will need to create two example names. The one placed in the *Tax code* field will serve to link the records in the Tax table to the records in the Ck_book table. Enter

[Tab] [F5]
link

The next example name will be placed into the *Tax status* field. Its purpose is to create a way to refer to the contents of the *Tax status* field in the Tax table. Since that is what you will want to insert into the *Tax status* field of the Ck_book table, you will need to use the name as part of the **changeto** operator. Use the example name **status**. Enter

[Tab] [F5]
status

The second part of the query uses a Ck_book query form. Enter

[F10] a
ck_book ↵

Link the records to the Tax table by placing the **status** example name in the *Tax deductible* field. Enter

[Tab] ***(7 times)***
[F5]
link

The **link** example name shows Paradox how to decide which records in each table should be associated with each other. The **status** example name will be used with the **changeto** operator to indicate what action Paradox should perform on each pair of corresponding records. The instruction **changeto status** will tell Paradox to insert the *Tax status* value from Tax into the field indicated by the **changeto** operator. Enter

[Tab]
changeto
[spacebar]
[F5]
status

The query is now set to fill in the *Tax status* field with data linked from the Tax table, Figure 9-23.

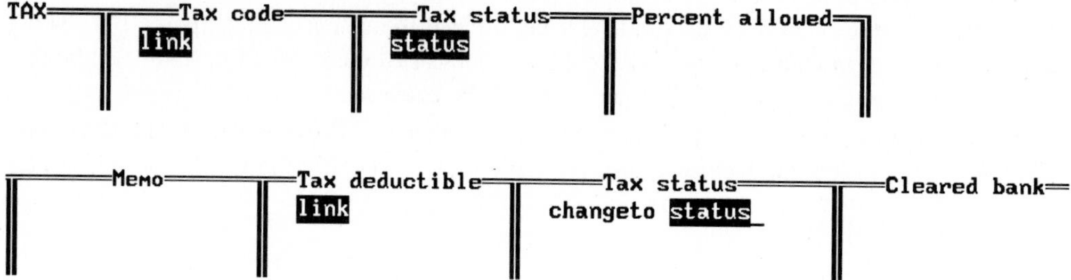

Figure 9-23 Query changes records using linked tables.

Execute the query by entering

[F2]

The program generates a table called **CHANGED**. As you will recall from Chapter 6, this table shows the records changed by the **changeto**. The 11 records indicate that all 11 check records were affected by the operation. If you want to see the actual changes made to the Ck_book table, you need to place that table in the View mode. Enter

[F10] v
ck_book ↵

Move the cursor to the *Tax status* field by entering

[Tab] ***(8 times)***

The field now contains the tax status names that match each of the tax status codes in the *Tax deductible* field, Figure 9-24.

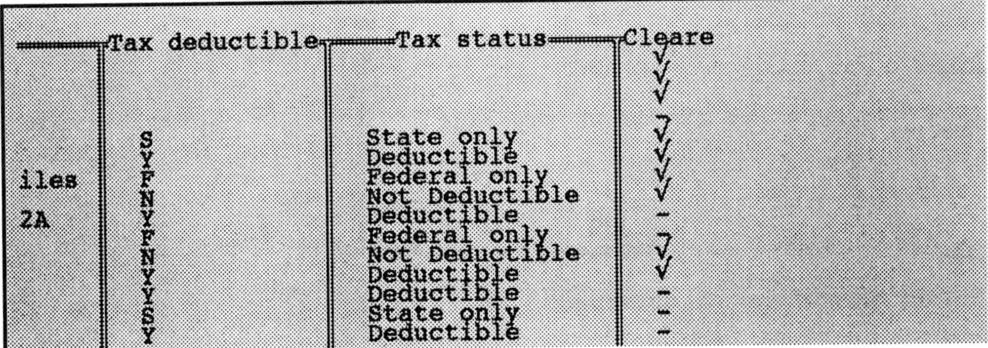

Figure 9-24 Table shows values inserted with linked changeto operators.

Clear the work area by entering

> **[Alt-F8]**

Lookup Tables in Report Forms

Data from supporting lookup tables can be used with Paradox reports. While the basic logic of linking tables remains the same, the procedure used in report forms is a bit different.

Supporting Tables Need Key Field

In the previous lookup techniques, the supporting tables did not have key fields designed in the structure of the table. If you want to link a supporting Lookup table in a report form, the supporting tables *must* have the first field designed as a key field. The reason has to do with the amount of time it takes to locate matching records in a lookup table.

In Paradox, you are not required to understand the mechanics Paradox uses to carry out operations such as linking tables. However, upon reflection it is obvious that Paradox must search the lookup table once for each value in the master table that needs to be linked. When a field is designed as a key field, Paradox creates a special file called an *index file* which is used to maintain the records in the table in order by the key field. In Ck_book, the *Check #* field is the key field. In addition to keeping the table sequenced, the index file has another function that may be even more important than merely sequencing records. The index file makes it possible to search a table for a record with a specific value in the key field in less time than it would take to perform the same search on a nonkey field that did not have an index file.

The performance improvement is achieved by the organization of an index file. The values stored in the key field are maintained in the index file in a logical order. This logical order enables Paradox to search without having to look at each record, using a binary type search approach. A binary search is one in which you can make assumptions about the values that are higher or lower than a given value. For example, if you are looking for a value of 1000 in a key field, you might begin by looking at the middle record in the table. If that record has a value of 400 you could assume that all the records from the beginning to the middle would not contain the record you were looking for, since all the records are arranged in ascending order. It is not necessary to examine each of the records in order to eliminate them from the search.

Conversely, the nonindexed fields in the table have the field data arranged randomly in the order in which they were entered. Searching these fields for a particular value requires that you start at the first record and examine each record until you find a match or you reach the end of the table. This type of search is called a sequential search and the amount of time needed to perform it rises in proportion to the overall size of the tables involved.

For this reason, Paradox requires that reports work only with lookup tables that have key fields.

Field Pointers

When a lookup table is linked to a report form, it has no immediate affect on the report. What does happen is that the field list available to the report is extended to include the fields that are in the linked tables. The list of fields will show a **pointer** that represents a linked lookup table. A pointer is the name of the linked table enclosed in square brackets and followed by the characters **->**. For example, if a report form is linked to the Accounts table, a pointer, **[Accounts->]**, will appear in the field list menu. If you select this, the menu then changes to a list of the fields in the lookup table.

Pointers can also be used in calculated field formulas to refer to fields in the lookup table. For example, if you wanted to multiply the *Amount* field by the *Percent allowed* field in the linked table Tax you would refer to the field as **[tax->percent allowed]** in the formula. The entire formula would look like this: **[amount]*[tax->percent allowed]**.

Preparing the Lookup Tables

Before you can create reports that use lookup tables, you *must* make sure that the tables you want to link the report to have key fields. In this case, none of the supporting tables—Tax, Accounts, or Bank—has key fields.

A key field is designated in the table structure. If you want to add a key field to a table, you must use the **Modify Restructure** command. A key field is designated by placing an * next to the field type. Note that the key field must be the first field in the table structure. If you want to designate a multiple field key, then the fields must be consecutive at the beginning of the structure.

To prepare the Accounts table for use as a lookup table in a report form, you must begin by displaying the structure. Enter

m r
accounts↵

Add an * next to the field type by entering

[Ctrl-End]
*****
[F2]

The Accounts table is restructured. During that process, Paradox creates an index file for the table called ACCOUNTS.PX. The records in the table are sorted into order by the *Account #* field. Since the records were entered in this order to begin with, there will be no apparent change in the table when it is displayed. Repeat the same procedure for Tax table assigns the first field as a key field. Try this on your own. The correct command can be found on page 331 under Exercise 3.

Remove the Accounts and Tax images from the work area by entering

[Alt-F8]

Reports with Lookup Tables

Suppose you want to print a report that summarizes the Ck_book table in terms of the general ledger account numbers. You could arrive at this report by creating a report that groups records by the *Acct #* field.

However, suppose you wanted to print the name of the account along with the account number. The names could be added to the report form by linking the report to the Accounts table. Begin by creating a new report form for the Ck_book table. Enter

r d
ck_book ↵
6
General Ledger ↵
t

Paradox displays the default report form generated from the table's structure. Since this is going to be a summary only report, i.e., group totals only, you can delete all of the lines in the Table band section of the report. Enter

↓ *(9 times)*
[Ctrl-y] *(4 times)*

Add a group band to the report that will group the records according to the *Acct #* field. Enter

[F10] g i f

Paradox lists all the fields contained in the structure of the Ck_book table for your selection.

Narrowing a Menu List

In the report form menus, and in other Paradox menus, the program will often display a list of items—e.g., table name, field names—from which you can select the item you want to work with. The most common way to work with a list menu is to use the → and ← keys to position the highlight on the item that you want, and press ↵ to select it.

However, there is an alternative way to make a selection. You can select an item by typing the first letter. For example, to select the *Memo* field you would enter **M**. But in a list of table names or field names, there is no guarantee that all the items will have a unique first letter. For example, the current field list contains *Acct #* and *Amount*. If you type A, which one would be selected?

The answer is that if you enter a letter for which there is more than one match in the list, Paradox creates a **sublist**. The sublist consists of only those items that match the letter you entered.

In this example, you want to select the *Acct #* field. Enter

a

The list of fields is now reduced to only those fields that begin with the letter A, Figure 9-25. This technique will work on all list menus. It can make it much easier to locate the item you are looking for. Note that once a list is narrowed, you must then move the highlight to the desired item and press ↵.

```
Name of field to group on:
Acct #  Amount
```

Figure 9-25 List narrowed to items that begin with the letter A.

Select *Acct#* by entering

↵

Place the cursor in the Page band in order to insert the group bands. Enter

↓ ↵

Since you will be printing only a single line for each group, remove the blank line in the Group Header band by entering

↑ [Ctrl-y]

Insert the *Acct #* field into the Group Footer band. Enter

↓ *(2 times)*
[F10] f p r
→↵
↵ *(3 times)*

Linking a Lookup Table

The next item in the report will be the name of the account. The field that contains that name, *Account name*, is located in the Tax table. In order to print the name that corresponds to the account number, you must link the report form to the Accounts table. The command to create a link between the current report form and a lookup table is **Field Lookup**. Keep in mind that this command does not change any part of the report form. It simply makes the fields in the lookup table available for placement on the report form with the **Field Place** command. Enter

[F10] f

Select the **Lookup** command by entering

l

The Lookup menu has three options as shown in Figure 9-26.

❑ **Link.** This option establishes a link between the current table and the lookup table.

❑ **Unlink.** This option cuts the link between the report and a lookup table. This command will also cause any regular or calculated fields that draw data from the lookup table to be removed from the report form.

❑ **Relink.** This option is used when you want to revise the link between the master table and the lookup table without having to delete all the fields, as would be the case if you used **Unlink**. The command allows you to change the name of the master table field to which the lookup table is linked. The command would be of use only if the master table contained several fields to which the lookup table could be related.

```
Link  Unlink  Relink                                          Report
Set up a link to include records from another table in this report.
```

Figure 9-26 Field Lookup menu.

Select the Link option by entering

l

Enter the name of the table to link to.

accounts ↵

Paradox displays a menu, Figure 9-27, that lists the master table fields. The first line of the menu shows the name of the lookup table and the key field (*Account # in ACCOUNTS*) onto which the link will be made.

```
Select CK_BOOK field to match Account # in ACCOUNTS.          Report    1/3
Check #  Acct #  Check date  Payee  Amount  Memo  Tax deductible  Tax status
```

Figure 9-27 Select master table field to link with lookup table.

Select the *Acct #* field as the linking field.

→ ↵

The link is now established between the two tables. Note that this link does not immediately make any changes in the layout of the report. The only change that you will see will appear when you list the fields for placement. Paradox will show the name of any linked tables, in the pointer format, at the end of the field list.

Placing a Linked Field

In order to more clearly identify the accounts in the report, you will want to place the *Account name* field next to the *Acct #* field. Enter

→ (2 times)
[F10] f p r

The field name menu is displayed. Since you want to select a field from a lookup table, you will have to select the *pointer* for that table. Table pointers are located at the end of the field list. Enter

[End]

The pointer **[Accounts->]** appears at the end of the list, Figure 9-28.

```
Field to place                                             Report    1/3
  Tax status  Cleared bank  Deposit  Balance  Period  {Accounts->}
```

Figure 9-28 Table pointer appears on field menu.

Select the pointer by entering

↵

The selection of a lookup field pointer changes the field list menu to show the fields contained in the lookup table. See Figure 9-29.

```
Field to place
Account #  Account name
```

Figure 9-29 Menu shows lookup table fields.

Select and place the *Account name* field in the report form.

→ ↵

↵ ***(2 times)***

The field is placed into the Group Footer band. If you look at the upper right corner of the screen, you will see the name of the field, **[Accounts->Account name]**, displayed. The pointer, **Accounts->**, indicates that the field **Account name** comes from a lookup table. Complete this simple report by inserting a field that will calculate the total value for each account. Recall that in the Ck_book table, the values for a record are entered in either the *Amount* or the *Deposit* fields. In order to arrive at the correct totals, the field that should be summarized is really the sum of **Amount + Deposit**.

Create a group summary calculated field by entering

[F10] f p s c

Enter the expression to calculate.

[amount] + [deposit] ↵

Select a Sum calculation by entering

s

Select **PerGroup** totals by entering

p

Place the field into the report by entering

→ *(2 times)*
↵ *(3 times)*

The report form contains fields from both the master and the lookup table, Figure 9-30.

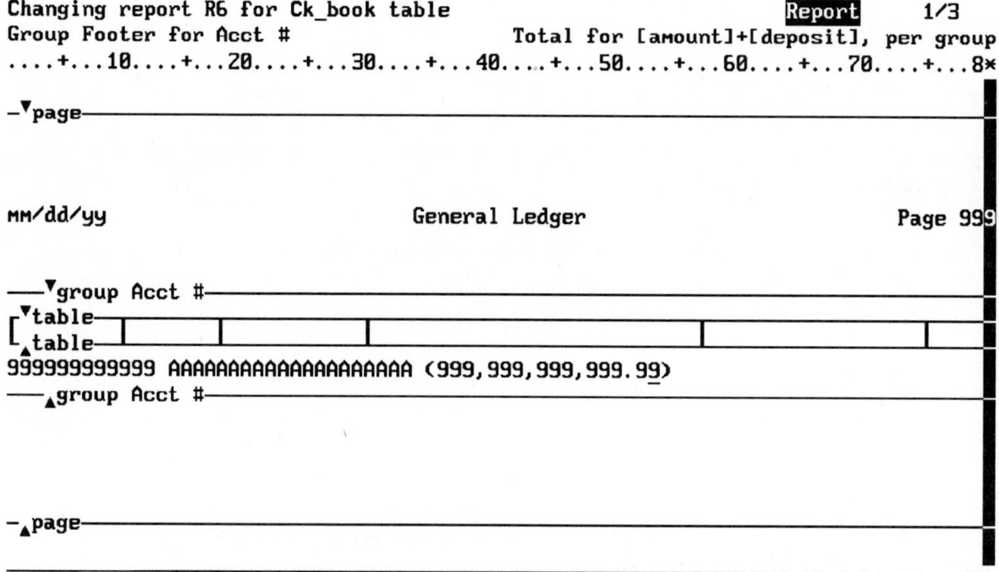

```
Changing report R6 for Ck_book table                              Report      1/3
Group Footer for Acct #                       Total for [amount]+[deposit], per group
....+...10....+...20....+...30....+...40....+...50....+...60....+...70....+...8*
-▼page

MM/dd/yy                          General Ledger                          Page 999

——▼group Acct #
▼table
▲table
999999999999 AAAAAAAAAAAAAAAAAAAA (999,999,999,999.99)
——▲group Acct #

-▲page
```

Figure 9-30 Report form with lookup table field.

Print the report by entering

[F10] o p

The report should look like Figure 9-31.

```
1/24/90                     General Ledger                    Page    1

          100 Cash in Bank                     4,860.00
          500 Office Furniture                   750.50
          600 Office Supplies                  1,296.07
          650 Office Equipment                 2,245.50
          700 Utilities                          349.24
```

Figure 9-31 General Ledger report includes lookup table information.

Save the report form by entering

[F2]

Calculations Using Lookup Values

Data stored in lookup tables can be used to create calculations in reports. For example, the Tax table contains values for the percentage of the amount which can be deducted for each category. You might want to create a report that calculates the deductible and nondeductible portions of each transaction.

Begin by creating a new report for the Ck_book table.

r d
ck_book ↵
7
Deduction Report ↵
t

Once again, the program generates a standard report form. The first task is to delete all the field columns that are not needed. Enter

↓ *(9 times)*
[Tab] *(2 times)*

Delete the *Check date* and *Payee* field columns from the report form with the **TableBand Erase** command. Enter

[F10] t e ↵
[F10] t e ↵

Move the cursor to the *Memo* field column.

[Tab]

Delete the rest of the field column. Try this on your own. The correct command can be found on page 331 under Exercise 4.

Insert two columns into the table layout. The first column will show the deductible portion of each amount while the second will show the nondeductible portion. Enter

[F10] t i ↵
[F10] t i ↵

Enter the text to use as the column headings.

↓
→ *(2 times)*
Deductible
→ *(4 times)*
Non Deductible

Move the cursor to the position where you want to insert the field formula for calculating the deductible portion of the amount.

[Shift-Tab] *(2 times)*
↓ *(2 times)*
→

Writing Formulas with Lookup Values

The formula you will want to write into this column will multiply the *Amount* by the value in the *Percent allowed* field of the Tax table. This means you must first establish a link with the Tax table. Enter

[F10] f l l
tax ↵

Link the lookup table to the *Tax deductible* field. Enter

t ↵

You now have the fields available for writing the formula. Enter

[F10] f p c

The formula for this field will use a pointer format, **[tax->percent allowed]** to refer to the field in the lookup table. Enter

[amount]*[tax->percent allowed] ↵

Place the field and shorten the format to fit into the column by entering

↵
← *(3 times)*
↵ *(2 times)*

Move the cursor to the next column and begin the entry of a calculated field in that column.

[Tab] →
[F10] f p c

The formula in this field will find the nondeductible portion by subtracting the deductible portion from the total amount. Once again, the lookup field will be indicated by using the pointer format.

[amount]-[amount]*[tax->percent allowed] ↵

Place and shorten the field by entering

↵
← ***(3 times)***
↵ ***(2 times)***

The final step is to write calculated fields for the column totals. Move the cursor into the Report Footer band by entering

[Shift-Tab] ***(2 times)***
↓ ***(7 times)***
→

Insert a calculated field by entering

[F10] f p c

This formula is the same as the one used in the column, except that it is an overall summary calculation. Enter

sum([amount]*[tax->percent allowed]) ↵

Place and size the entry.

↵
← ***(6 times)***
↵ ***(2 times)***

The next summary calculation belongs in the *Non Deductible* column. Enter

→ ***(5 times)***
[F10] f p c

Once again the expression is identical to the one used in the Table band except that it is now nested inside a **sum** operator. Enter

sum([amount]-[amount]*[tax->percent allowed]) ↵

Complete the entry by placing and sizing the field.

↵
← ***(6 times)***
↵ ***(2 times)***

Print the report by entering

[F10] o p

The report should look like Figure 9-32.

1/24/90 Deduction Report Page 1

Check #	Acct #	Amount	Deductible	Non Deductible
1	100	0.00		
2	100	0.00		
3	100	0.00		
4	100	0.00		
999	600	71.60	35.80	35.80
1000	500	750.50	750.50	0.00
1001	600	97.68	73.26	24.42
1002	700	101.57	0.00	101.57
1003	600	590.00	590.00	0.00
1004	650	2,245.50	1,684.13	561.38
1005	600	157.89	0.00	157.89
1006	700	247.67	247.67	0.00
1007	600	378.90	378.90	0.00
1008	700	175.49	87.74	87.74
1009	600	36.89	36.89	0.00
			3,884.89	968.80

Figure 9-32 Report calculates amounts using lookup table values.

Save the report by entering

[F2]

Exit Paradox by entering

e y

Summary

The entry of data into a table is the most time-consuming and error-prone area of database management. In many cases, data entry can be made simpler, faster, and more accurate by reducing field entries to abbreviations or codes.

While codes and abbreviations can improve data entry, they may be hard for people not familiar with database tables or the Paradox system to understand when displayed on the screen or printed in a report.

This chapter covered the use of support tables that can be used to overcome the disadvantages of code or abbreviated entries without requiring substantial additional entry.

Supporting tables can be linked to fields in the master database table, providing an efficient means of elaborating upon the raw data stored in a database table for query forms, data entry, or report form production.

❑ **Supporting and Master Tables.** A master table is one that contains raw data, often in the form of a code or abbreviations. A supporting table contains information that can be related to a number of records in the master table. The master and supporting table must have at least one field in common. This field is used to link the records in the master table to specific records in the supporting table. When a supporting table is linked to a master table, Paradox performs a lookup operation in which the values from one table are used to search for matching values in a supporting table. Once established, a link can display related information or allow related values to be used in calculations.

❑ **Linking Fields.** Links can be established between fields in different tables so long as the fields have the same data type. They do not have to have the same field name. If the link is made as part of a validity check the linking field must be the first field in the table. If the link is made in a report form the first field in the supporting table must be a key field.

❑ **Links in Query Forms.** You can create query forms that process data from more than one table by displaying query forms for each table involved and creating links between the tables using example names. When a query is processed, Paradox treats the table related to the first query form on the work area as the master table. The value in the linked field is searched for in the corresponding linked field in the supporting table. Value or data from the record in the supporting table can be included in the Answer table generated by the query.

❑ **Linking Example Names.** In query processing, fields are treated as linked if the same example name appears in the field columns. The example name used does not matter so long as the exact same name appears in the field columns to be linked in the supporting and master query forms.

❑ **Inclusion Operator.** The inclusion operator, !, is used to ensure that records that contain blank values in the linked field of the master table will be included in the Answer table. Normally, Paradox ignores records that have blank values in the linking field or the first linking field if there is more than one link.

❑ **Links in Validity Checks.** Supporting tables can be linked to a master table through the validity check option found on the Edit menu. When linked with this option, supporting tables can be utilized during the data entry and revision process. Tables can be used to restrict entries in a field to those that are contained in a supporting table. In addition, you can set up the supporting table as a Help reference that is displayed during data entry if the user presses [F1]. The supporting table is displayed and the user can select their entry from the supporting table's records.

❑ **Copying Data.** The validity check technique can also be used to copy data and values from the supporting table into fields in the master table that have the same field names. Note that the linking fields do not have to have the same field names, only the additional fields you want to use for copying data.

❑ **Links in Report Forms.** Linking supporting tables to a report form enables you to use the fields from the supporting table in report fields and calculations. Note that links in reports can be established to supporting tables only if those tables have a key field.

❑ **Pointers.** A pointer is a special symbol used to represent the name of a table linked to a report form. The pointer appears on the field list menus, once a supporting table has been linked. You can also enter a field name in a pointer format in a calculated field formula. This enables you to use values from the supporting table in report form calculations.

❑ **Key Fields.** Key fields are designated in the table's structure by placing an * after the field type. The key field must be the first field in the table.

Exercises

Exercise 1 from page 302

[Tab] ***(2 times)***
[F5]
link

Exercise 2 from page 303

[Tab] [F5]
link
[Tab] [F6]

Exercise 3 from page 319

[F10] m r
tax ↵
[Ctrl-End]
*****
[F2]

Exercise 4 from page 325

Repeat the following 7 times:

[F10] t e ↵

10

Automating Paradox with Scripts

In the first nine chapters of this book, you have learned how to perform a wide variety of database management tasks. You have created tables, queries, screen forms, and reports. In many cases a given task requires you to perform a combination of tasks. For example, in Chapter 8 you learned how to print a selected group of records in a report by using a *dummy* table. The process involved a series of steps.

- *Generate an Answer table.* Use a query form to select the records you want to work with.
- *Empty out the dummy table.* Remove any existing records from the dummy table.
- *Add records.* Copy the records from the Answer table to the dummy table.
- *Print report.* Print the report from the dummy table.

All of the steps require specific selections from menus, cursor movements, etc., each time that you want to process the report. In a sense, this book is like a script, in that all of the keystrokes needed to carry out the various operations have been recorded in the pages of this book. The instructions written in the text are read by you and you in turn enter the keystrokes into the computer. If the process goes smoothly, the computer reproduces the effects documented in this book.

When you create script files, you eliminate the middle person by providing a means by which the computer can directly read the list of instructions.

In this chapter, you will look at methods by which multi-step operations can be automated using Paradox scripts.

Begin by loading the Paradox program in the usual manner.

What Are Scripts?

When working with a computer you will find that there are two different operational modes.

❑ **Immediate Execution Mode.** The Immediate Execution mode is one in which the computer carries out each instruction as it is entered. For the most part this is how you have been working with Paradox. Each command or command keystroke you enter is immediately carried out. For example, the **Do-It!** key, [F2], causes Paradox to immediately perform the action, e.g., process a query or save an edited table, at the exact moment that you enter it.

❑ **Deferred Execution Mode.** In contrast to the immediate execution mode, deferred execution, as the name implies, involves a delay between the time that a command is entered and the time that it is executed by the computer.

What is the advantage of deferring execution? The answer is that in order to defer execution of a command you must find some way to store that command or series of commands until such time as you are ready to have them executed. You might write down a series of commands which need to be carried out on the last day of each month, e.g., print a summary report calculating sales tax. In immediate execution, you would have to enter the necessary commands at the end of each month. On the other hand, a deferred execution mode would allow you to write down the commands as a sort of *things to do* list for the computer. When the end of the month arrives you simply tell the computer to read the list and carry out the instructions. Of course, even though the same task is carried out each month, you would need to write the list only *once*. Each month, you would simply tell the computer to read and carry out the same list of commands.

A *script* in Paradox is a list of Paradox commands stored in a file. The file contains text, just like a word-processing document. The only difference is that a Paradox script contains, not paragraph text, but lists of Paradox commands. When you instruct Paradox to play a script, it reads the commands written in the script file and executes them just as if you were entering the commands from the keyboard.

Using scripts to carry out Paradox tasks has a number of significant advantages.

❑ **Speed.** When Paradox reads and executes the instructions written into the script file, it does so at the fastest rate your computer can operate. While the speed will vary from computer to computer, it is always much faster than you would be able to enter the commands yourself.

❑ **Accuracy.** When you need to enter a complicated sequence of commands, it is quite easy to make typing mistakes that create errors. The commands stored in the script will always execute the same way, assuming that the script was written correctly.

❑ **Repetition.** Scripts maker it simple to repeat complex operations because all of the details can be stored in the script and replayed whenever needed.

❑ **Easy to Use.** A complicated series of operations, such as that needed to print a report with a summary table would ordinarily be beyond the ability of users who have not worked much with Paradox. However, it is easy to teach people to play a script. You can create scripts that will simplify operations for other users and therefore make Paradox even easier for them than it is for you, increasing overall productivity.

❑ **Modification.** Since scripts are simply text files, you can use a text editor or word processor to make changes, additions, or deletions to the script. You can make copies of a single script and modify each one to operate slightly differently.

Scripts provide the means by which Paradox can move from an immediate execution tool to a fully automated database environment.

Scripts and Macros

The term *macro*, or *keystroke macro*, is used in many computer applications to describe files that contain sequences of keystrokes that can be played back at a later time. In Paradox, keystroke macros are stored in *script* files. There are two ways in which scripts can be created.

❑ **Writing.** A script can be created by writing out a list of commands and storing them in a script file. A script file is a standard DOS text file with the file extension of SC. Paradox contains an editor which allows you to create these files. However, there is no reason why you could not create or modify any script file with popular word processing programs such as Word or WordPerfect. (See page 373.)

❑ **Recording.** An alternative to writing out a script is to record one. Paradox can be placed into a recording mode, in which a written record is made of each keyboard entry that you make while the recording mode is active. Paradox then saves this recording as a script file. Scripts created by the recording method are saved as text files that can be modified by editing.

Recording a script is the simplest way to create a script, because the key sequence is automatically written for you. However, if you make a mistake during the recording process Paradox will include those keys in the script and the mistake will replay each time you play the script.

Writing scripts takes more planning and patience because you must visualize the menus and screen layouts upon which the script keys will be entered.

One way to get started with scripts is to record scripts and then modify them with the Paradox script editor. This combines the automatic writing feature of recording with the ability to make additions, deletions, and changes offered by direct script writing. In Paradox, there is no strong distinction between recorded macros and written scripts.

Recording Scripts

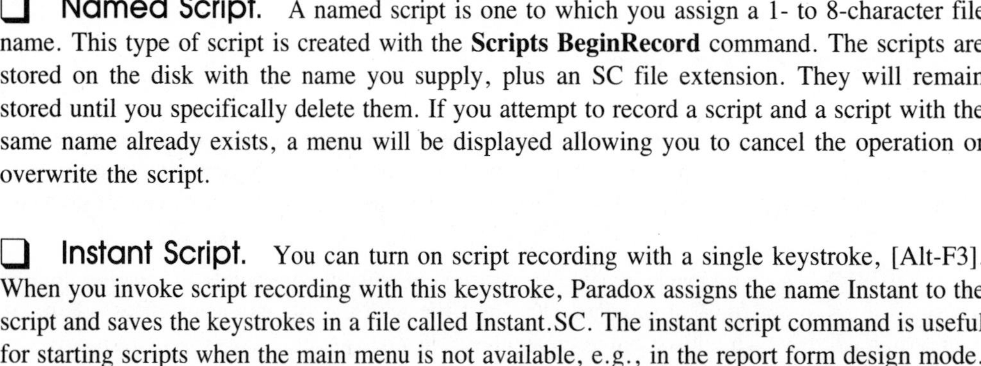

The best way to get started working with scripts is to use the *record* and *play* method. When you *record* a script, Paradox automatically writes a record of all of the key commands you enter while the recording is active. When you stop recording, a script file, SC extension, is written on the disk. When you select to *play* a script, Paradox reads the keys written in the file and treats them as if they were being entered from the keyboard. When the recording mode is active, the letter **R** will appear in the upper right corner of the screen.

There are two ways to create a recorded script.

❑ **Named Script.** A named script is one to which you assign a 1- to 8-character file name. This type of script is created with the **Scripts BeginRecord** command. The scripts are stored on the disk with the name you supply, plus an SC file extension. They will remain stored until you specifically delete them. If you attempt to record a script and a script with the same name already exists, a menu will be displayed allowing you to cancel the operation or overwrite the script.

❑ **Instant Script.** You can turn on script recording with a single keystroke, [Alt-F3]. When you invoke script recording with this keystroke, Paradox assigns the name Instant to the script and saves the keystrokes in a file called Instant.SC. The instant script command is useful for starting scripts when the main menu is not available, e.g., in the report form design mode.

> *Because Paradox always assigns the same name, INSTANT, to all scripts recorded with the [Alt-F3] command, each new recording will overwrite the previous instant script. Note that unlike most instances where a file is overwritten, Paradox will* not display a warning *message when you overwrite an instant script. Instant scripts can be preserved by using* **Tools Rename** *or the DOS Rename command to change the name of the file from INSTANT.SC to a unique script file name.*

Script recording can be terminated in two ways.

❑ **Scripts End-Record.** This command, available from the main menu, terminates the macro recording.

❑ **[Alt-F10].** The command [Alt-F10] displays the Paradox Applications Language (PAL) menu. This menu can be used to end the recording of a macro without having to display the main menu, such as when you are recording in the report form design mode.

Recording a Script

The primary value of scripts is that they allow you to repeat an operation without having to enter all of the detailed keystrokes each time. In the first nine chapters of this book you have learned a large number of procedures and techniques. Each one consisted of a sequence of commands and entries that accomplished a task. One example of a complicated operation was the one discussed at the end of Chapter 8, the use of a dummy table to print reports with only a group of selected records. That task required four separate tasks, outlined beginning on page 272. Each of the four tasks consists of several commands and entries.

By using a script to record some or all of the operations you could reduce the amount of effort needed to carry out that operation.

While it might be ideal to have a single script to carry out the whole operation, it is often best to begin the creation of a large or complicated script by making small scripts that cover distinct parts of the overall task. It is difficult to record a long and complicated script without making a mistake or a typographic error. If you record small scripts you can later use special techniques to combine them into the larger script you had in mind.

The first stage of the dummy report operation is to create an Answer table with the desired records. Begin by creating an Answer table with records for the month of January only. Enter

a
ck_book ↵

Enter the condition which will select the records you desire.

[Tab] ***(3 times)***
1/..

You have now reached a very important point in the process. Once you have entered the selection condition, the next several steps are automatic, i.e., they will be the same no matter what selection condition you have entered. The goal is to transfer the selected records to the dummy table. Recall that in Chapter 8 you created a table called Temp to act as the dummy table for report processing.

To speed up the task of getting the selected records into the Temp table, you can record the processing in a script. Since the main menu is available, you can use the **Scripts BeginRecord** command to start the script recording. Enter

[F10] s b

Paradox asks you to enter the name of the script. In this instance, name the script *trans* for transferring record.

> *Script names follow the same file name conventions as tables, screen forms, and report forms.*

Enter

trans ↵

When you return to the main work area display, you will notice that the letter **R** appears in the upper right corner of the screen. This letter indicates that script recording is active. The first step in this process is to place √'s in all of the fields in the table. Enter

[Ctrl-Home] [F6]

Next, process the query by entering the **Do-It!** command.

[F2]

With the Answer table created, you will use the **Tools More Empty** command to remove any records currently stored in the Temp table. Enter

[F10] t m e
temp ↵

Select OK by entering

→ ↵

The next step is to add the records in the Answer table to the now empty Temp table using the **Tools More Add** command. Enter

[F10] t m a
answer ↵
temp ↵
n

The Temp table is now filled with the same contents as the Answer table. The final step is to select the report you want to print. Enter

[F10] r o
temp ↵

You have now reached the point where you can select the report form to print. It is here that the *automatic* sequence ends, because you may not always want to print the same report. To allow that flexibility you will want to stop the recording at this point. Since you are currently in a menu, you cannot use [F10] to display the Scripts menu. You can however use the PAL menu command, [Alt-F10], to terminate the script recording. Enter

[Alt-F10]

The command displays the menu for terminating the script recording, as shown in Figure 10.1. If you select the **Cancel** option, you are actually selecting to continue recording.

```
Cancel  End-Record
Stop script recording without keeping it.
```

Figure 10-1 [Alt-F10] displays stop recording menu.

Terminate the macro by entering

e

Paradox flashes a message in the lower right corner of the screen, telling you that the script has been saved. However, since this message appears for only the time it takes to save the script, you may not have a chance to read it. Cancel the current command and clear the work area by entering

[Ctrl-Break]
[Alt-F8]

Playing a Script

The script you have just created will automate the part of the process involved in printing a report with a selected group of records. Suppose that you wanted to select only check records from the month of February. Begin by creating the query form selection conditions needed for that operation.

a
ck_book ↵
[Tab] ***(3 times)***
2/..
[Tab]
not Deposit

Instead of entering the rest of the commands, you can simply play the script you recorded. Enter

[F10] s

Choose the **Play** command.

p

Enter the name of the script.

trans ↵

Paradox seems to pause for a few moments while the script is being played. When the script has completed, the work area shows the Answer and Temp tables with the selected records and the report selection menu displayed in the menu area, Figure 10-2.

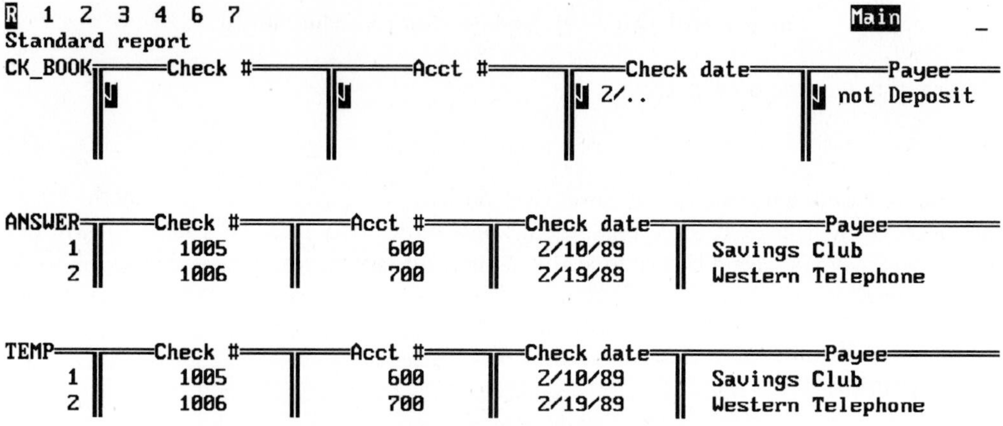

Figure 10-2 Script performs transfer operation.

The script has carried out all of the operations needed to get from the selection conditions to the report form selection.

Cancel the activity by entering

[Ctrl-Break]
[Alt-F8]

Chaining Scripts

The Trans script that you have just created carries out the middle part of the selective report process. The first and last parts of the operation are still performed manually. Suppose that you find that you need to print selective reports for the checks from each month on a regular basis. It would make sense to have scripts to carry out as much of the process as possible, in order to eliminate repetitive work on your part.

How would you go about creating these scripts? One method would be to create a new script and record the entire process from query form to printed report. However, you already have a script, Trans, that carries out the middle section of processing. Instead of creating a new script from scratch, you could *chain* the Trans script to a new script. The advantage of chaining the existing script is similar to the advantage in using the script by itself, i.e., you avoid having to reenter the keys needed to transfer the records. You could play the Trans script as part of a new script you are recording.

For example, suppose you decide to create a script called Janrpt (January report) which sets up a query form for the January checks and then executes the Trans script. Begin by turning on the script recording mode.

s b
janrpt ↵

The script recording mode is now active. Note that while the main menu is displayed, you cannot see the **R**(ecording) indicator displayed. Set up the query form you want to process.

a
ck_book ↵
[Tab] *(3 times)*
1/..
[Tab]
not Deposit

It is at this point that you want to *chain* the Trans script to the one you are currently recording by playing that script. Enter

[F10] s p
trans ↵

The Trans script plays. When it is finished the cursor is positioned in the **Report Output** menu, waiting for you to select the report you want to print, Figure 10-3.

Choose report 1 by entering

1

Select the output device, in this case the printer, to which the report should be sent.

p

To complete the operation, clean up the work area by entering

[Alt-F8]

You have returned to a clear work area. You can now stop the recording by entering

[Alt-F10] e

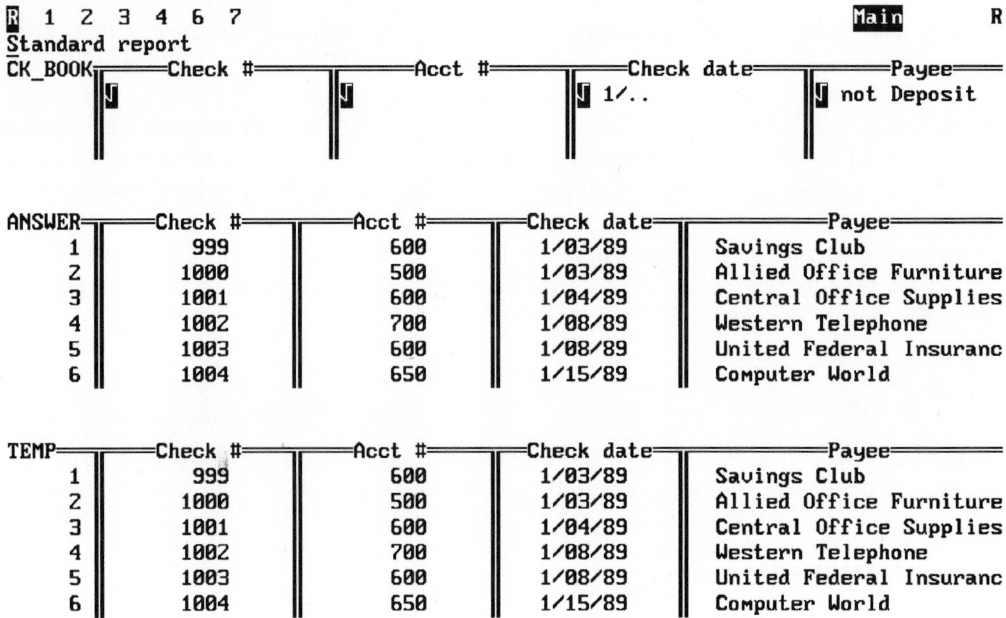

R 1 2 3 4 6 7 Main R
Standard report

CK_BOOK	Check #	Acct #	Check date	Payee
			1/..	not Deposit

ANSWER	Check #	Acct #	Check date	Payee
1	999	600	1/03/89	Savings Club
2	1000	500	1/03/89	Allied Office Furniture
3	1001	600	1/04/89	Central Office Supplies
4	1002	700	1/08/89	Western Telephone
5	1003	600	1/08/89	United Federal Insuranc
6	1004	650	1/15/89	Computer World

TEMP	Check #	Acct #	Check date	Payee
1	999	600	1/03/89	Savings Club
2	1000	500	1/03/89	Allied Office Furniture
3	1001	600	1/04/89	Central Office Supplies
4	1002	700	1/08/89	Western Telephone
5	1003	600	1/08/89	United Federal Insuranc
6	1004	650	1/15/89	Computer World

Figure 10-3 Trans script plays while recording a new script.

The Janrpt script is a complete set of instructions that include the creation and processing of a query form, the transfer of records from one table to another, and the printing of a report form. To reproduce the report, all you need to do is play the script. Enter

[F10] s p
janrpt ↵

The report should look like Figure 10-4.

You might have noticed that when the Janrpt script was executing, the screen remained completely blank. By default, Paradox does not update the screen display while a script is playing. In this example, none of the query forms or menus used by the script were shown on the screen. When the script is finished, Paradox returns the screen display to normal. In this case, only the main menu is displayed because the last command in the script is the [Alt-F8] which clears the work area.

Instant Scripts

An Instant script is one that is created by using the [Alt-F3] command. This command turns on script recording and automatically assigns the name Instant to the script. The advantage of an Instant script is that you can replay the script with a single key command [Alt-F4]. The disad-

```
1/25/90                    Checking Account Records                    Page   1


Check #  Check date  Description of Transaction Amount     Deposit   Memo
-------  ----------  -------------------------- --------- --------- ---------
  1004    1/15/89    Computer World              2,245.50      0.00 286
                                                                    Turbo Com
                                                                    puter
  1003    1/08/89    United Federal Insurance      590.00      0.00 Policy
                                                                    Number
                                                                    10012002A
  1000    1/03/89    Allied Office Furniture       750.50      0.00 Desk -
                                                                    48" by
                                                                    72"
  1001    1/04/89    Central Office Supplies        97.68      0.00 Envelopes
                                                                    ,
                                                                    folders,
   999    1/03/89    Savings Club                   71.60      0.00 Coffee
                                                                    machine
  1002    1/08/89    Western Telephone             101.57      0.00
                                                ========= =========
                                                 3,856.85      0.00
Account Balance:          (3,856.85)
Transactions:                  6
From  3-Jan-89 To 15-Jan-89
```

Figure 10-4 Report generated by Janrpt script.

vantage of instant scripts is that Paradox can have only one instant script at a time. Each time [Alt-F3] is used the previous instant script is overwritten with no warning message.

Instant scripts are useful when you think you might need to quickly repeat a sequence of keystrokes but do not plan to use the script again.

For example, Paradox automatically creates new tabular report forms with columns for each of the fields in the table's structure. As you saw in Chapters 8 and 9, a report may use only a few of the fields listed in the table's structure. In order to remove the columns from the report, you must repeat the **TableBand Erase** command once for each column that you want to remove. You could speed up the process by creating an instant script. As an example, create a new report for the Ck_book table. Enter

r d
ck_book ↵
8 ↵
t

Move the cursor to the table band by entering

↓ ***(9 times)***

In looking at this report, you decide that of the current field columns you want to delete all but the *Check date, Payee,* and *Amount* columns. Since the command to erase each column is exactly the same, you can make an instant script which will speed up the operation. Turn on the instant script recording mode by entering

[Alt-F3]

Note that the letter **R** is displayed in the upper right corner of the screen, indicating that this command keystroke has activated the script recording mode. Enter the command to remove the current column from the report. Enter

[F10] t e ←┘

To terminate the script use the [Alt-F10] command.

[Alt-F10] e

The script has been saved in a file called INSTANT.SC. The advantage of this script over a named script is that you can execute the script with a single keystroke, [Alt-F4]. Enter

[Alt-F4]

The single keystroke removes the current column. Move the cursor to the *Memo* field column and remove it with the instant macro. Enter

[Tab] ***(3 times)***
[Alt-F4]

Repeated Playing

The instant script that you have created allows you to execute a command with a single keystroke. In this example, you have six more field columns to remove using the instant script. Paradox allows you to enter a command that will automatically *replay* a given script a specified number of times. In this case, you could complete the deletion of columns by repeating the instant script six times.

The command which repeats a script can be found on both the Scripts menu and the [Alt-F10] menu. Since you are currently in the Report form design mode, where the Scripts menu is not available, you can use [Alt-F10]. Enter

[Alt-F10]

The [Alt-F10] script menu is displayed at the top of the screen, Figure 10-5.

```
Play  RepeatPlay  BeginRecord  Debug  Value  MiniScript
Play a script.
```

Figure 10-5 [Alt-F10] script menu.

The second command on the menu is the **RepeatPlay** command. This command enables you to repeat a script automatically. Enter

r

Paradox asks you to enter the name of the script. In this case, the name of the script is *instant* because you want to repeat the instant script. Enter

instant ↵

Paradox next asks you to enter the number of times to repeat the script. Enter

6 ↵

The program pauses for a brief moment while the macro repeats. When it is done, all six remaining columns have been removed. Cancel the current report form and return to the main menu by entering

[F10] c y

Saving an Instant Script

As mentioned, the instant script created with the [Alt-F3] command will be overwritten the next time the command is used to create a new instant script. However, you can preserve the current instant script by changing its file name to something other than *instant*. In this example, you might want to change the name of the instant script to Delcol (delete column). You can accomplish this using the **Tools Rename** command. Enter

t r

Select **Scripts** by entering

s

Enter the name Instant to select the instant script.

instant ↵

Enter the new name for the script.

delcol ↵

The script INSTANT.SC has been changed to DELCOL.SC. Delcol will remain on the disk until it is deleted or specifically overwritten.

Editing Scripts

The recording of scripts is a good way to get started using scripts to automate operation. One of the great advantages of scripts is that the key commands stored in the script files are actually written in a text format. This means that you can access the scripts with a text editor. You can add, delete, or modify existing scripts.

On the most basic level, the ability to edit the contents of scripts allows you to fine tune the scripts and make minor changes in the way they operate. However, you are not limited to making small changes. By editing, you expand the power of the script by writing instructions in the Paradox Application Language, PAL. Part 2 of this book will deal with writing PAL programs in detail. In this chapter, you are concerned with the basic editing skills that allow you to modify existing scripts or even create scripts from scratch.

Paradox is supplied with an editing mode in which text files, such as scripts, can be edited. An *editor* is a simple type of word-processing program. As with most word-processing programs, you can enter, delete, and insert characters and lines. Unlike word-processing programs, the Paradox editor cannot perform operations such as copy, cut-and-paste, or search-and-replace.

> *For simple scripts, the Paradox editor is adequate. If you are writing large complicated scripts, you may find that you may want to replace the built-in Paradox editor with one of your own choosing, e.g., the Norton Editor from Peter Norton Computing. You can select a different editor using the Custom script, discussed on page 366.*

When you are working in the script editor, you will find that the editing keys are the same as those used in other design modes such as the screen and report form design mode, Table 10-1.

Table 10-1 Script Editor keys

↓	down one line
→	right one character
↑	up one line
←	left one character
[Pg Up]	scroll half screen up
[Pg Dn]	scroll half screen down
[Ins]	turn on/off insert mode
[Home]	first line in script
[F10]	Edit menu
[F1]	help
[End]	last line in script
[Del]	delete character at cursor
[Ctrl-y]	delete to end of line
[Ctrl-v]	shows vertical ruler
[Ctrl-Home]	beginning of line
[Ctrl-End]	end of line
[Ctrl-→]	scroll screen right
[Ctrl-←]	scroll screen left
[backspace]	delete character left of cursor

Editing a Script

While recording scripts is a very easy way to create automated procedures, editing scripts can be very beneficial. For example, the script you created called Janrpt prints a report for all of the checks written in the month of January. But suppose you wanted to create a script that performed the same operation, only using the records from the month of February instead. If you relied on the recording method, you would have to record a new script just as you did when you created the Janrpt script. It is interesting to note that the January script which is stored in the JANRPT.SC file and the February script you want to create will differ by only a single character: the change of month number from 1 to 2. The most direct solution would be to simply change the 1 to 2 and you would have the script you need.

This is exactly the type of change that can be made using the script editor.

In this example, since you want to have both the existing script, Janrpt, and a new script for February, you can begin by making a copy of the script, with the **Tools Copy Script** command, and then editing the copy. Enter

t c s
janrpt ↵
febrpt ↵

To edit a script you must use the **Scripts Editor Edit** command. Enter

s e e

Enter the name of the script you want to edit.

febrpt ↵

The program displays the contents of the script in the script editing mode, Figure 10-6.

```
Changing script D:\paradox3\febrpt                                 Script
....+...10....+...20....+...30....+...40....+...50....+...60....+...7
{Ask} {ck_book} Tab Tab Tab "1/.." Tab "not Deposit" Menu
{Scripts} {Play} {trans} {1} {Printer} Down ClearAll
```

Figure 10-6 Script loaded into script editor.

Reading a Script

Displaying a script in the script editing mode reveals that a script is composed of a series of notations that represent the keys and commands entered while the script was being recorded. The script contains three different types of representations.

❑ **Names.** Names appear in scripts enclosed in curly brackets, {}. Names are used to record the selection of an item from a Paradox menu. For example, the name {**Ask**} represents the selection of the **Ask** command on the main menu. Names of files (tables, report forms, scripts) or field names are also enclosed in brackets if they are selected from a list menu. Note that if you select to type in the file or field name instead of picking it from the list menu, Paradox still encloses the name in {} in the script file.

❑ **Special Keys.** Special keys are those nonalphanumeric keys used in Paradox for cursor movement, ←, →, [Tab], etc., or shortcut commands such as [F2] or [Alt-F8]. Paradox has special names for each of those keys. For example the [Alt-F8] key is written in the script as **ClearAll** and the [Tab] key as **Tab**. Note that special key names are not surrounded by quotations or brackets.

Table 10-2 Function Key Names

[F1]	HELP
[F2]	DO-IT!
[F3]	UPIMAE
[F4]	DOWNIMAGE
[F5]	EXAMPLE
[F6]	CHECK
[F7]	FORMKEY
[F8]	CLEARIMAGE
[F9]	EDITKEY
[F10]	MENU
[Alt-F3]	INSTANTRECORD
[Alt-F4]	INSTANTPLAY
[Alt-F5]	FIELDVIEW
[Alt-F6]	CHECKPLUS
[Alt-F7]	INSTANTREPORT
[Alt-F8]	CLEARALL
[Alt-F9]	COEDITKEY
[Alt-F10]	PAMENU

❑ **Literal Key Sequences.** These are sequences of alphanumeric keys which are entered into Paradox exactly as they appear in the script. All literal information is enclosed in quotation marks.

It is important to understand that Paradox scripts are not an exact recording of each key that was pressed during the recording. In some cases, Paradox records the essence of the keystrokes rather than the keystrokes themselves. For example, you can select the **Ask** command from the main menu by entering → ↵ or the letter **a**. In order to avoid confusion about what is actually being recorded, Paradox places the name of the item selected, {**Ask**}, into the script. Paradox records *what* was selected, not *how* it was selected.

The conversion of menu selections from keystrokes to item names is very important because it makes Paradox scripts much easier to understand. Below are three sequences of keys. The first shows the actual keys that have been entered. The second is similar to the first but in that case the keys entered were arrow and ↵ keys. The third shows how Paradox would represent those keys in a script.

1) [F10]sptrans↵
2) [F10]→→→→→→→→↵↵↵→→→→→→→→→↵
3) Menu {Scripts} {Play} {trans}

You can see that reading the Paradox script is far more clear than simply reading a sequence of keystrokes. The Paradox names make it easy to visualize the menu selections being made. The third example above clearly shows the command **Scripts Play** executed from the main menu and selecting the Trans script file.

The script displayed in the editor is divided arbitrarily into two lines. The division of a script into lines is not significant and has no effect on the way in which the script is played. Paradox divides scripts into lines which are about 60 characters in length to make the scripts easier to read. You can divide the script into any number of lines you desire and still achieve the same result. In Figure 10-7, the Febrpt is rearranged into four lines in which each line more closely corresponds to one part of the overall task. The change in arrangement will have no effect on the way that script plays because the key commands are still arranged in the same order.

```
Changing script D:\paradox3\febrpt
....+...10....+...20....+...30....+...4
{Ask} {ck book}
Tab Tab Tab  "1/.." Tab  "not Deposit"
Menu {Scripts} {Play} {trans}
{1} {Printer} Down ClearAll
```

Figure 10-7 Script divided into several short lines.

Changing a Script

In order to change the current script from a January report to a February report you need to make only one change. The change needed is to change the number in the key sequence "**1/..**" to "**2/..**". Use the → key to position the cursor on the **1**. The exact keystrokes needed are:

→ ***(30 times)***

Since the editor is not in the insert mode, you can type over the 1 and change it to 2. Enter

2

The script has been altered to produce a report for February instead of January. Save the revised script, using the **Do-It!** command.

[F2]

Execute the edited script by entering

[F10] s p
febrpt ↵

The result is a report that looks like Figure 10-8.

```
 1/26/90                    Checking Account Records                  Page   1


Check #  Check date  Description of Transaction Amount     Deposit   Memo
-------  ----------  -------------------------- --------- --------- ---------
   1005    2/10/89    Savings Club                 157.89      0.00
   1006    2/19/89    Western Telephone            247.67      0.00
                                                ========= =========
                                                   405.56      0.00
Account Balance:            (405.56)
Transactions:                  2
From 10-Feb-89 To 19-Feb-89
```

Figure 10-8 Report generated by edited script.

Script editing allows you to make modifications to existing scripts, even those created by script recording. In this case, the change of a single character was able to generate an entire new report.

You can repeat the procedure and create a third script called Marrpt which will print the records for the month of March. Try this on your own. The correct commands can be found on page 372 under Exercise 1.

When you have completed your modification, you can print the report using the new script. Enter

s p
marrpt ↵

The report will look like Figure 10-9.

```
 1/26/90                    Checking Account Records                  Page   1


Check #  Check date  Description of Transaction Amount     Deposit   Memo
-------  ----------  -------------------------- --------- --------- ---------
   1009    3/12/89    Central Office Supply         36.89
   1007    3/05/89    Fathead Software             378.90      0.00 Spreadshe
                                                                    et
                                                                    Software
   1008    3/10/89    Interstate Power & Light     175.49
                                                ========= =========
                                                   591.28      0.00
Account Balance:            (378.90)
Transactions:                  3
From  5-Mar-89 To 12-Mar-89
```

Figure 10-9 Report generated by Marrpt script.

Writing a New Script

While editing scripts is useful, you can create a script entirely from scratch by writing the key commands directly into a blank script file.

At this point, you have created three scripts, Janrpt, Febrpt, and Marrpt, to print reports for their respective months. Suppose that you wanted to create a script that would execute all three of the scripts as a single operation. One way to accomplish this is to record a new script while you execute the three report scripts.

On the other hand, you can create this script by directly entering the commands you want in the Edit mode. Since recording the new script would require you to print all three reports, you could save time by writing the instructions directly into a script file.

To create a new script use the **Scripts Editor Write** command. Call this script Monthsum (monthly summary). Enter

s e w
monthsum ↵

You now have a blank file into which you can enter script commands. When writing a script, you need to keep in mind the situation in Paradox at the time the script will start. In this case, you will assume that the work area is clear and that the main menu is displayed.

The commands in this script will each play a different script. In that respect, all of the commands will be the same except the name of the script that is played in each case.

To play a script from the main menu, you would enter the **Scripts Play** command followed by the name of the script. In script notation, the menu options are written surrounded with { }. Enter

{**Scripts**} {**Play**} {**janrpt**}

Note that each of the key commands is separated by a blank space. Paradox is not fussy about the amount of space between commands since it will ignore any additional spaces that might be inserted between commands.

The next command in the script is a repeat of the first command but with a different script name. You could continue writing the command on the same line or start a new line to make the script easier to read. In this case, place the second command on the next line. Enter

↵
{**Scripts**} {**Play**} {**febrpt**}

Complete the script with the third **Play** command, which will play the Marrpt script. Enter

↵
{**Scripts**} {**Play**} {**marrpt**}

The script should now look like the one in Figure 10-10.

```
Designing script D:\paradox3\monthsum
....+...10....+...20....+...30....+...40....+.
{Scripts} {Play} {janrpt}
{Scripts} {Play} {febrpt}
{Scripts} {Play} {marrpt}
```

Figure 10-10 New script will play three existing scripts.

The Go Command

Once you have completed the script you will want to save the script and then play it. This would normally involve two commands: [F2] and then **Scripts Play** *script_name*. Since saving and executing a script is a common operation, Paradox provides a command on the Scripts Editor menu that will perform these actions in a single step. The command is called **Go.** Display the menu for the Scripts mode by entering

[F10]

The menu contains the standard options (*Help, Do-It!*and *Cancel*) as well as three commands specific to the Scripts editor, Figure 10-11.

```
Read  Go  Print  Help  DO-IT!  Cancel                              Script
Read contents of another script into this script starting at the cursor.
```

Figure 10-11 Scripts editor menu.

❑ **Read.** This option reads into the current script, the contents of another script or text file. The text is inserted into the current script at the current cursor location. This option is useful when you want to combine scripts. Once read in, the text of the script can be edited as if you had typed in the entire script.

❑ **Go.** This command saves the current script and immediately plays the script once it is saved.

❑ **Print.** This option prints the contents of the script editor. This gives you a printed copy of the script.

Save and execute the current script by entering

g

The script will produce a copy of all three of the reports as part of the playing of the script.

Subroutines and Modular Design

The Monthsum script you created is an example of how a script can be constructed by using other scripts to carry out parts of the operation. In Figure 10-12, you can see that the Monthsum script accomplishes its task by playing the Janrpt, Febrpt, and Marrpt scripts. These scripts in turn rely on the Trans script to complete part of their functions.

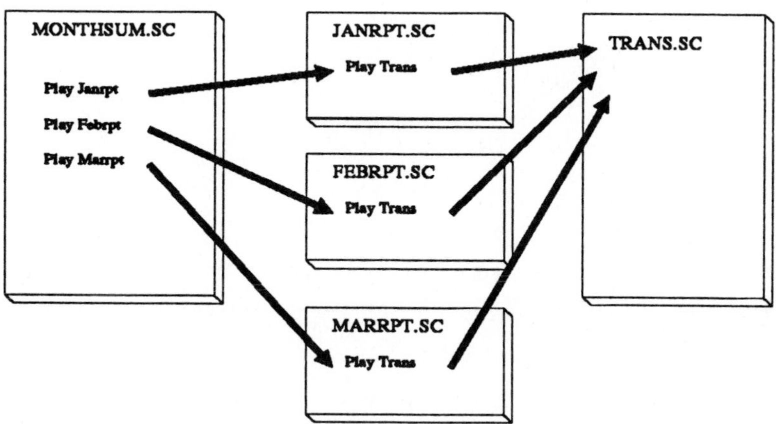

Figure 10-12 Scripts play subroutine scripts as part of their execution.

The use of scripts in this manner is called *chaining*. The scripts that play within other scripts function as *subroutines* to the master script which is the one that you specified in the **Scripts Play** command. In this example, the subroutines have subroutines of their own, e.g., Janrpt uses Trans as a subroutine.

The advantage of subroutines is that one routine can be used by a number of different scripts. The Monthsum script uses the Trans script three times when it executes. Breaking up a large task into a series of small scripts that function as subroutines is referred to as a *modular* approach to automating tasks. This is in contrast to creating a single large script that contains all of the key commands in a single long sequence. When a subroutine script is completed, Paradox returns to the script which plays the subroutine and continues with the next key command, Figure 10-13.

PAL Commands Versus Script Key Commands

The Monthsum script uses Paradox key command names to carry out the **Scripts Play** command. The key commands follow the sequence of menu selections you need to make in order to carry out a task. For example, to play a particular script you would enter three key names corresponding to the menu selections you would have to make.

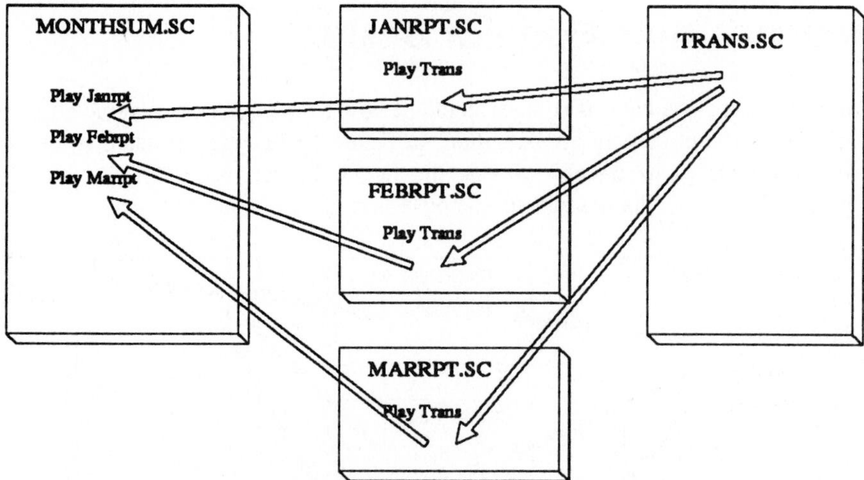

Figure 10-13 Subroutine scripts return to playing script when complete.

```
{Scripts} {Play} {script_name}
```

If you wanted to print a particular report you would have to enter a command that looks like the following:

```
{Report} {Output} {table_name} {report_#} {output}
```

In addition to the key command name shown above, Paradox scripts can also contain PAL (Paradox Application Language) commands. The advantage of PAL commands in scripts is that they can often express the same command operation in a more concise way. Most of the Paradox commands that you select from the Paradox menus have equivalent PAL command *verbs*. A command *verb* is a word that represents some Paradox operation in a similar way that a verb, in the English language, stands for an action.

For example, PAL uses the command verb **PLAY** to represent the **Script Play** command. The PAL command verb **REPORT** is the equivalent of the **Report Output Printer** menu command.

Of course, as in English, often a command verb by itself does not describe a complete action. For example, if you want to play a script, you must specify the name of the script you want to play. Printing a report requires the name of the table and the report number. These additional pieces of information are called *arguments*. The **PLAY** command requires the script name as the argument. The PAL command shown below specifies the Janrpt script as the script to be played.

```
PLAY "janrpt"
```

The syntax of a PAL command is a bit different from that used by script key commands. PAL command verbs are not enclosed in { }. On the other hand, names of tables, scripts, or fields are enclosed in quotation marks.

PAL commands have the advantage of expressing Paradox operations in a much more direct and concise manner. It is usually easier to remember the PAL command than it is to remember the exact sequence of menu selections, especially when the menu has a large number of options.

A script can contain any type of mixture of key name and PAL commands. Paradox will recognize key commands and PAL commands in the same script. While it is not required that you use PAL commands, you will find that they are far superior for writing scripts than are the key name commands.

The PAL language contains commands that allow you to create full-blown applications in Paradox. In Part 2 of this book, you will learn how structured programs are written in the PAL Language.

Writing a Script with PAL Commands

The Monthsum script can be written entirely with PAL commands instead of script key names. Create a new script that will overwrite the Monthsum script by entering

s e w
monthsum ↵
r

The script will consist of three **PLAY** commands. Enter

PLAY "janrpt" ↵
PLAY "febrpt" ↵
PLAY "marrpt"

The PAL commands express the same operations in a more compact and lucid way. When you read the script, it is quite clear what the script will do. Save and execute the script by entering

[F10] g

The new version of the script produces the exact same results as the original key-name version of the script.

> *In order to help you differentiate PAL commands from other text in scripts, all PAL commands will be written in uppercase letters in this text. Keep in mind that Paradox does not care about capitalization in PAL commands and will accept them in any style of upper or lowercase letters.*

QuerySave Scripts

In Chapter 4, you learned how to use the **Scripts QuerySave** command to store a query for use at a later time. The query forms were saved in script files with SC file extensions. Now that you are more familiar with scripts, you might be interested in exactly how query forms are saved and how you can integrate those forms with scripts that you create with the script editor.

Query forms are a major part of Paradox operations. You may recall that in Chapter 6 a series of query form operations were needed to calculate the current balance of the checking account based on the records in the Ck_book table.

Done with query forms alone, the process required several steps. However, you could create a script that would perform all of the tasks needed to find the account balance with a single command. One way to accomplish this is to go through the process described in Chapter 6 and record all of the operations in a script. However, by using script editing, you can create a script that will perform the operations without having to record the entire process.

Before you begin to create this script, it would be useful to understand how Paradox saves query forms when the **Scripts QuerySave** command is used. As an example, create one of the query forms needed for the account balancing and save it using **Scripts QuerySave**. In Chapter 6, you used a **changeto** operator to fill in the *Balance* field with the difference between the *Deposit* and *Amount* fields. The *Balance* field would then contain negative values for all check amounts and positive values for all deposits. When you summed the *Balance* field, you would arrive at the current balance in the checking account.

The process was complicated by the fact that Paradox would only perform the **changeto** operation on records that contained values in both the *Deposit* and *Amount* fields. If one of the fields was a blank, Paradox would skip that record. Of course, when you entered data, the *Amount* field would be blank for all deposits while conversely the *Deposit* field would be blank for all checks. In order to fill in the *Balance* field, it was necessary to make sure that all of the blank *Deposit* and *Amount* fields were changed to a zero numeric value. To accomplish all of that, you needed to execute four different query forms.

1. **Convert blank Amounts to zeros**
2. **Convert blank Deposits to zeros**
3. **Fill in the Balance field**
4. **Calculate the sum of Balance**

You can automate the entire process with scripts, and you can construct many of the scripts by writing them instead of recording them.

How Query Forms Are Saved

The first step in the creation of a script that will calculate the account balance is to understand how query forms can be manipulated through scripts. As an example, lay out a query form that will fill in the *Balance* field with the difference between *Deposit* and *Amount*. Enter

a
ck_book ↵

In order to carry out this calculation, you will need to create example names for the *Deposit* and *Amount* field. Enter

[Tab] ***(5 times)***
[F5]
checks

Move to the *Deposit* field column and create another example name. Enter

[Tab] ***(5 times)***
[F5] deposits

Place the **changeto** formula in the *Balance* field. Enter

[Tab]
changeto
[spacebar]
[F5]
deposits-
[F5]
checks

In normal circumstances, you would use the [F2] key to process the query operation you had specified. In this case, you are interested in what happens when this query form is saved as a script with the **Scripts QuerySave** command. The query script will be called Updtbal (update balance field). Enter

[F10] s q
updtbal ↵

Load the script that you just created into the script editor.

[F10] s e e
updtbal ↵

The script loaded into the scripts editor, Figure 10-14, is not a duplicate of the query form displayed in the work area, but like the key name commands, it is a distillation of the meaning of the query form. What Paradox saves is a *model* of the actual query form.

The first word in the script is the PAL command **QUERY** while the last word in the script is **ENDQUERY**. These two commands work as a pair. They indicate that all of the information following **QUERY** until **ENDQUERY** is reached makes up the query form information.

The query form itself is represented by lines of text that approximate a query form. Note that only the field columns that actually contain information are included in the query form model.

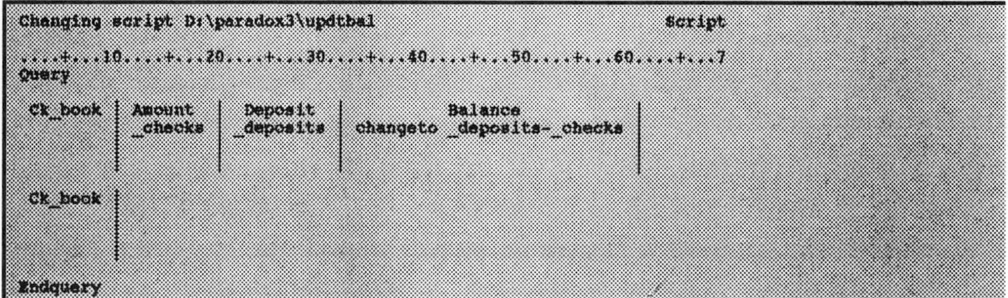

```
Changing script D:\paradox3\updtbal                                    Script
....+...10....+...20....+...30....+...40....+...50....+...60....+...7
Query

 Ck_book | Amount  | Deposit   |          Balance            |
         | _checks | _deposits | changeto _deposits-_checks  |
         |         |           |                             |

 Ck_book |
         |
         |

Endquery
```

Figure 10-14 Script representation of saved query form.

The first line of the model contains the table and field names. The second line contains the data type entered into the query columns. One difference between the script text and query form display is that example names are marked with a _ (underscore) character in front of the name. The | (vertical line) characters are used to mark off one field column from another.

It is important to understand that the query form model is text and it can be edited in any way that you like so long as you preserve the basic structure of the query form model. (See page 363.) Because a query form is saved in a script file, you can add key name or PAL commands to the script. For example, query form scripts will redisplay the saved query form. But you still must enter the [F2] **Do-It!** command to process the query. You can add the **Do-It!** command to the script, creating a script that will set up and then process the query.

Move the cursor to the end of the script by entering

[End] [Ctrl-End]

Add a new line to the script by entering

↵

The PAL command equivalent of the [F2] key is entered as **DO_IT!**. Enter

DO_IT!

Save and execute the script by entering

[F10] g

The script sets up and then executes the query form producing a Changed table. Recall that **changeto** query operations produce a Changed table instead of an Answer table because the query operation directly effects the original table.

Combining Scripts

Adding the PAL command **DO_IT!** to the QuerySave script transforms the saved query form into a script that carries out a procedure. However, the task of finding the current checking account balance requires four query operations. Recall that the **changeto** operation will only be accurate if all blanks have been eliminated from both the *Amount* and *Deposit* fields. This means that you should precede the **changeto** operation with queries that eliminate the blanks.

The query operation needed to eliminate blanks from the *Amount* field uses the **blank** operator to select blank records and a **changeto** operator to insert a zero value in the selected records. The same operation can be used to eliminate the blanks in the *Deposit* field with the exception that the operators will be placed in the *Deposit* field column.

Create a query form which is set up to eliminate blanks in the *Amount* field. Enter

[Alt-F8]
a
ck_book ↵

Move the cursor to the *Amount* field.

[Tab] ***(5 times)***

Enter the operators needed for this task.

blank,changeto 0

Once again, you do not want to execute the query but merely to save the setup in the form of a script. Enter

[F10] s q
blanks ↵

You now have two query forms saved in different scripts, Blanks and Updtbal. You can use the **Read** command on the Scripts mode menu to combine these scripts into a single script. Create a new script called Balance. Enter

[F10] s e w
balance ↵

The first command in this new script will be the key command equivalent for [Alt-F8], the command that clears the work area. That key command is **CLEARALL**. This command should be placed in the script in order to assure that the script will begin from a clear work area. Enter

CLEARALL ↵

The next part of the script should be the query form stored in the Blanks script file. The **Read** command allows you to insert a copy of an existing script into the script being edited. The script is inserted at the current cursor location. Insert a copy of the Blank script by entering

[F10] r
blanks ↵

The text of the entire Blanks script, which consists of a QUERY/ENDQUERY layout, is added to the current script as in Listing 10-1.

Listing 10-1

```
CLEARALL

Query

      Ck_book | Amount              |
              | blank,changeto 0    |
              |                     |

ENDQUERY
```

The next step is to add the **DO_IT!** command following the query form so that the query is automatically executed as part of the script.

Move the cursor to the end of the script and insert the DO_IT! command by entering

[End] [Ctrl-End] ↵
DO_IT! ↵

Adding Another Copy of a Script

The current script is now set to perform the task of converting all of the blank *Amount* fields in the table to zero values. The same operation needs to be repeated in the *Deposit* field.

If you were working in the work area, you would need to delete the items from the *Amount* field column in the query form and reenter then in the *Deposit* field column. However, the structure of the **QUERY/ENDQUERY** command suggests that there is a much simpler method available to you using script editing.

If you look at the **QUERY** command inserted from the Blanks script, you will notice that the only way the field column is identified is by the name *Amount* entered on the first line of the script. If you change *Amount* to *Deposit*, the query would operate on the *Deposit* field column.

In this instance, you do not want to change the **QUERY** command currently in the script since it is needed to convert blanks in the *Amount* field. Instead, you can use the **Read** command to insert another copy of the Blanks script and edit the field column name in that copy of the **QUERY** command.

Begin by entering another **CLEARALL** command so that the second **QUERY** command will also begin on a blank work area.

CLEARALL ↵

Read in another copy of the Blanks script. Enter

[F10] r
blanks ↵

You now have two copies of the Blanks script contained in the script you are editing, Listing 10-2.

Listing 10-2

```
CLEARALL

Query

Ck_book    |      Amount      |
           | blank,changeto 0 |
           |                  |

Endquery
DO_IT!
CLEARALL

Query

Ck_book    |      Amount      |
           | blank,changeto 0 |
           |                  |

ENDQUERY
```

The Vertical Ruler

When you are writing scripts, it is often useful to be able to reference individual lines in the script by line number. Paradox will display a *vertical* ruler which shows the numbers of each of the lines in the script. The vertical ruler can be turned on or off using the command [Ctrl-v].

Turn on the ruler by entering

[Ctrl-v]

The vertical ruler now lists the line numbers of each line in the script down the left side of the screen, Figure 10-15. The ruler display has no effect on the script but is useful when you want to refer to specific lines in the script.

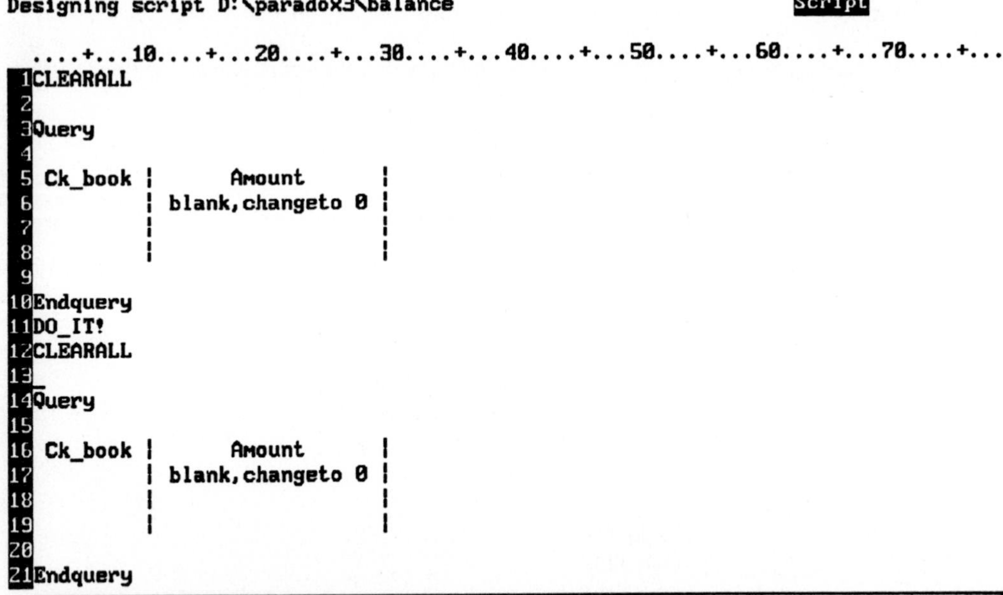

```
Designing script D:\paradox3\balance                                  Script

  ....+...10....+...20....+...30....+...40....+...50....+...60....+...70....+...
 1CLEARALL
 2
 3Query
 4
 5 Ck_book |        Amount      |
 6         | blank,changeto 0   |
 7         |                    |
 8         |                    |
 9
10Endquery
11DO_IT!
12CLEARALL
13
14Query
15
16 Ck_book |        Amount      |
17         | blank,changeto 0   |
18         |                    |
19         |                    |
20
21Endquery
```

Figure 10-15 Vertical ruler numbers lines in script editor.

Editing a Query

The second copy of the Blanks script must now be changed so that it affects the *Deposit* columns. Change the name of the field column in line 16 from *Amount* to *Deposit*.

Old line 16	→	Ck_book |	Amount	|
New line 16	→	Ck_book |	**Deposit**	|

The **QUERY** command will now operate on the *Deposit* field instead of the *Amount* field. The script now carries out two of the four query operations necessary to arrive at the checking account balance. Move to the end of the script and add a **DO_IT!** command for this **QUERY** command. Enter

[End] [Ctrl-End] ↵
DO_IT! ↵

Add a **CLEARALL** command to establish a blank work area for the next step.

CLEARALL ↵

The next step is to perform the **changeto** operation carried out by the Updtbal script. You have two ways to combine the scripts: use a **PLAY** command to execute Updtbal as a subroutine or **Read** to add a copy of Updtbal to the current script. In this case, use the **Read** method. The reason is that Updtbal would probably be needed only once in the script and would not benefit from being saved as a distinct subroutine. Enter

[F10] r
updatbal ↵

The script is added to the Balance script. Note that the cursor remains on line 24. Move the cursor to the end of script by entering

[End] [Ctrl-End] ↵

You can see that the contents of Updtbal have been added to the Balance script. With this addition, the Balance script accomplishes three of the four steps needed to find the account balance.

Writing a Query Form Model

In general, **QUERY/ENDQUERY** commands are best created or revised using the work area query form display and the **Scripts QuerySave** command. Minor changes, such as the field name which you changed on page 362 are the type of changes you would typically make in a Query model.

However, it is possible—and in some cases, desirable—to write a query model entirely from scratch. The purpose of the next **QUERY** command in the script is to calculate the sum of the *Balance* field which, thanks to the three previous queries, contains the positive and negative values needed to calculate the account balance.

It makes sense to create the query form from scratch in this case, since the model needed is quite simple, consisting of a **calc sum** operator in the *Balance* field column.

A Query command begins with the command word **QUERY.** Enter

QUERY ↵

The query model created by the **Scripts QuerySave** command is written so that the items line up in vertical columns. This is not absolutely necessary although it makes the model easier to read. Below are two examples of QUERY commands. The first uses the spacing in the same manner as Paradox does when it creates a script using **QuerySave**. The second example contains all of the same information, but the spacing needed to align the items in a vertical column is omitted.

Listing 10-3

```
QUERY

Ck_book    | Balance  |
           | calc sum |
           |          |

ENDQUERY
```

Listing 10-4

```
QUERY

ck_book|balance|
|calc sum|

ENDQUERY
```

Paradox will not see any difference between the scripts because all the additional spacing used in the first example will be ignored when the script is executed. The only spacing that is *required* is the blank line following **QUERY** and the blank line preceding **ENDQUERY**. The | (vertical line character) is used to separate the items horizontally. Note that omitting the spacing makes the query difficult to read, easy to make a mistake. Entering all of the spacing is quite tedious. This means that, unless the query operation is a simple one to write, you should use **QuerySave** to create the model.

In this example, the model is simple enough to be entered without any additional spacing. Enter

↵

ck_book | balance | ↵

| calc sum | ↵

ENDQUERY ↵

The screen will look like Figure 10-16.

```

Query

 Ck_book | Amount  | Deposit   |               Balance               |
         | _checks | _deposits | changeto _deposits-_checks          |
         |         |           |                                     |
         |         |           |                                     |

 Ck_book |
         |
         |
         |

Endquery
DO_IT!
QUERY

ck_book|balance|
|calc sum|

ENDQUERY

```

Figure 10-16 Query form model entered directly in script.

Add the DO_IT! command for this query.

DO_IT! ↵

One final touch can be added to this script. If you follow the logic of the script with your mind's eye, you should be able to picture the work area display at this point. There will be two images: the query form and the Answer table with the account balance. While it is not crucial to the outcome of the script, it might be neater to clear the query form image so that only the Answer table appears on the work area.

If you were working manually you would enter the [F3] key to move the cursor back to the Query form image and then [F8] to clear that image from the work area. In a script, these keystrokes would be entered by using the key names for those keys, **UPIMAGE** and **CLEARIMAGE** respectively. Enter

UPIMAGE CLEARIMAGE

The script is now complete. (See page 374 for the complete listing) Save and execute the script by entering

[F10] g

The script will take a few moments to execute. When it completes, the screen will show a single image containing the balance of the checking account, as shown in Figure 10-17.

```
Viewing Answer table: Record 1 of 1
ANSWER═╤══Sum of Balance══╗
     1 ║         6.31     ║
```

Figure 10-17 Results of Balance script.

The script makes it possible to obtain the current account balance at any time by issuing a single command, i.e., playing the balance script.

The Custom Script

The *Custom* script is a script supplied with Paradox. This script is designed to function as a *configuration* program for Paradox. A configuration program is one that is used to establish or change the default values or options used by Paradox. These options concern hardware-specific settings such as screen colors, the use of Expanded memory (EMS), or the length and width paper used in your printer. Other options allow you to customize certain Paradox operations to fit your specific needs.

The file PARADOX3.CNF is used to hold the configuration settings for Paradox. The Custom script allows you to change those settings and store the results in an updated copy of the PARADOX3.CNF.

When playing the Custom script, you will find that is looks and feels as enough you were operating in Paradox because the script displays menus just like those in Paradox. In fact, you can use the Custom script without knowing anything about Paradox scripts.

> *This tells you that the PAL Language has commands that enable you to create applications with the look and feel of Paradox. See Part 2 of this book for instructions in using the PAL language.*

The Custom script displays eight items on its main menu. Below is a brief summary of what changes can be made using the Custom script.

❑ **Tune.** This option will appear only if you are using version 3.5 of Paradox. Its function is to provide control over protected mode operation. Paradox can take advantage of protected mode operation on computers that have a 386 or 486 microprocessor. In most cases this option is not needed because Paradox 3.5 will automatically implement protected mode operation. In order to aid in the diagnosis of problems, the ***Tune*** option has a ***MachineInfo*** selection that can produce a basic or detailed analysis of your computer's operating environment. A sample of the basic hardware report is shown below:

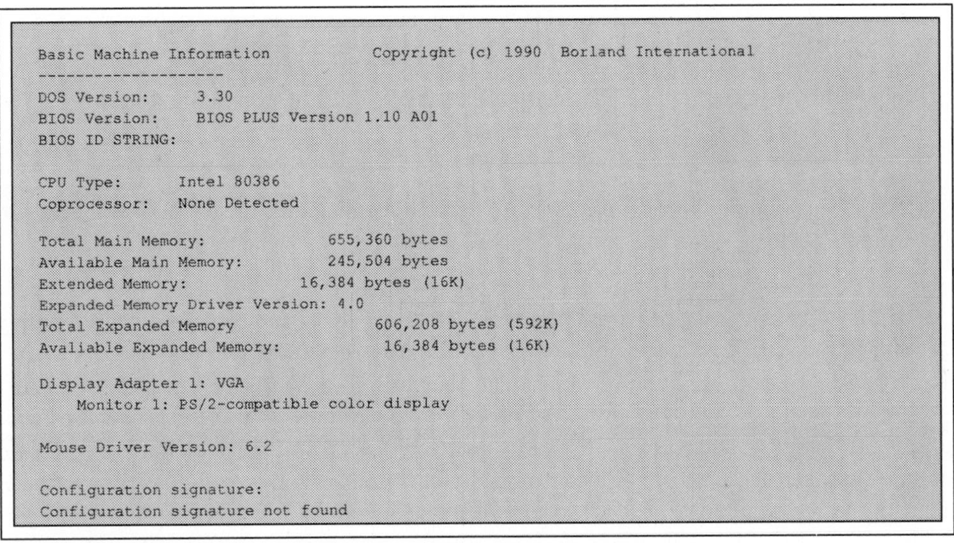

```
Basic Machine Information          Copyright (c) 1990  Borland International
--------------------
DOS Version:      3.30
BIOS Version:     BIOS PLUS Version 1.10 A01
BIOS ID STRING:

CPU Type:        Intel 80386
Coprocessor:     None Detected

Total Main Memory:              655,360 bytes
Available Main Memory:          245,504 bytes
Extended Memory:             16,384 bytes (16K)
Expanded Memory Driver Version: 4.0
Total Expanded Memory                606,208 bytes (592K)
Avaliable Expanded Memory:            16,384 bytes (16K)

Display Adapter 1: VGA
    Monitor 1: PS/2-compatible color display

Mouse Driver Version: 6.2

Configuration signature:
Configuration signature not found
```

❑ **Video.** Use this menu to set the default video display characteristics, including colors if available, for Paradox to use. For example, the **NegativeColors** option allows you to choose the color in which negative values will appear.

❑ **Reports.** This option sets the default page widths and lengths, margins, group settings, and printer controls for reports. Keep in mind that you can specify different values for these settings in each report form, if necessary. You would use this option only when you want to start each report automatically with a different set of values than Paradox would normally use.

The Reports Setups option displays a Paradox table, in the edit mode, which contains three fields: *Name, Port* and *Setup String*. You can modify existing printer setup or add new steps to this table. These changes can then be accessed from the Report Setting Setup Pre-defined menu during the design of a report form.

❑ **Graphs.** Graphs changes the current graph settings, and sets printer, and screen specifications for graphics.

❑ **Defaults.** This option allows you to set special options that affect the way in which Paradox operates.

❑ **Int'l.** This option stands for *international*. The options presented allow you to set the default date and number formats for reports, forms, and images to operate as American or European style displays.

❑ **Net.** Use this option to set your user name, private directory name and location, and the interval between screen image updates that Paradox will use if running in a network environment.

❑ **PAL.** This option allows you to specify operations related to the creation of PAL programs within Paradox.

❑ **ASCII.** Use this option to specify default delimiters and separators, treatment of empty fields, and decimal indicators for ASCII files use for data import and export.

If you run the Custom script and save changes that you make to the system setup, the Custom script automatically exits Paradox when you exit the Custom script. This is because Paradox loads the default values from the PARADOX3.CNF file only at the beginning of a session when you first load the program. Custom forces you to reload Paradox after you have made changes in the configuration.

Aside from hardware-specific options, e.g., screen and printer selections, there are three options that are of general interest to Paradox users.

❑ **Defaults QueryOrder.** When a query form is processed, Paradox will list the field columns in the Answer table in the same order in which the field names appear in the table's structure. This will be the case even if you have used the **Rotate** command, [Ctrl-r], to change the order of the field columns in the query form. This is called *TableOrder*.

Using the Custom script, you can change the way Paradox processes queries so that the Answer table will follow the field sequence as shown in the current query form image rather than always going back to the order in the table's structure. This is called *ImageOrder*. Making this change allows you to get Answer tables that are sorted in orders which would not be possible without manually sorting the Answer table after it has been created.

For example, the Ck_book table lists the *Check date* field before the *Payee* field. If both of those fields are included in an Answer table, the records will always be sorted according to *Check date*. If you select *ImageOrder* in the Custom script, you can control the sort order by changing the order of the fields in the query form. For example, placing the cursor in the *Check date* field and entering [Ctrl-r] will shift that field to the end of the query form image causing *Payee* to precede *Check date*. If the query was processed, the Answer table would be sorted by *Payee*.

❑ **Defaults Blank=Zero.** This setting controls the way that blank values in numeric (or currency) fields are treated. As discussed earlier in this chapter, Paradox will normally treat blank numeric fields differently than it will numeric fields with zero values. The idea is that the meaning of a blank numeric field is not obviously the same as a value of zero. By default, Paradox will ignore records that have blank values but will operate on records that have zero values. In the previous example, the formula **changeto Deposit – Amount** would skip any records that has blank values in either the *Deposit* or *Amount* fields. The solution used was to insert zero values into these fields.

If you wish to have Paradox automatically assume that a blank numeric field is a zero value, select the Yes option under **Defaults Blank = Zero**. Keep in mind that selecting this option changes all operations carried out in Paradox.

❑ **Defaults AutoSave.** Editing changes or new records added to tables are stored in the internal RAM memory of the computer until you enter the **Do-It!** command. If the power to your computer is cut off during an edit or data entry session, it is possible to lose some of the changes or data because it had not been transferred to the disk. The AutoSave feature tells Paradox to automatically write all changes to the disk more frequently than would be normally required. Note this setting has no effect on the **Cancel** or **Undo** commands.

> *Paradox employs virtual memory management which balances the use of internal memory and disk space automatically. When working with large tables, Paradox may need to transfer data from the RAM memory to the disk even though you have not entered* **Do-It!**.

Using the Custom Script

If you need or desire to make changes in the Paradox configuration, you can execute the Custom script by entering

s p
custom ↵

The Custom script displays its own screen logo and then shows a main menu which lists the eight configuration topics.

Suppose that you wanted to change the Defaults settings for **AutoSave**, **Blank = Zero,** and **QueryOrder**. Begin by selecting the Defaults option. Enter

→ *(4 times)*
↵

Begin with the **QueryOrder** setting. Enter

q

The default setting, TableOrder, is currently highlighted. Select ImageOrder by entering

iNext select Blank=Zero by entering

b

In this case, change the setting to **Yes** to have blanks treated as zeros.

y

Turn on the **AutoSave** feature by entering

a y

Return to the main menu by selecting the Return option. Enter

r

Adding a Printer Setup

If you want to add or modify the predefined printer setups listed in Chapter 7, you can do so using the **Reports Setups** command from the Custom script main menu. Enter

r s

Unlike the other menu settings, this option displays a table, Figure 10-18. The table can be edited or you can add a new printer setup. For example, the IBM Proprinter (and compatibles) has a near-letter-quality mode that is activated with the sequence [Esc] X 1. Suppose that you wanted to add this setting to the predefined printers.

```
Press: [F1] - Help; [F2] - save changes; [F7] - Form Toggle; [Esc] - cancel.
To choose a default, place an asterisk at the end of name of desired string.
PRINTER ========Name========== Port ================Setup String===========
    1   StandardPrinter*        LPT1
    2   Small-IBMgraphics       LPT1   \027W\000\015
    3   Reg-IBMgraphics         LPT1   \027W\000\018
    4   Small-Epson-MX/FX       LPT1   \015
    5   Small-Oki-92/93         LPT1   \015
    6   Small-Oki-82/83         LPT1   \029
    7   Small-Oki-192           LPT1   \029
    8   HPLaserJet              LPT1   \027E
    9   HP-Portrait-66lines     LPT1   \027E\027&l7.27C
   10   HP-Landscape-Normal     LPT1   \027E\027&l1O
   11   HP-Compressed           LPT1   \027E\027(s16.66H
   12   HP-LandscpCompressed    LPT1   \027E\027&l1O\027(s16.66H
   13   Intl-IBMcompatible      LPT1   \027\054
   14   Intl-IBMcondensed       LPT1   \027\054\015
   15   _
```

Figure 10-18 Printer setup table.

The cursor is automatically positioned at the end of the table, ready for you to add a new printer setup. Enter

IBM-Pro-NLQ ↵

Enter the printer port. In most cases, this is LPT1. Use the Ditto key to copy the Port from the previous record.

[Ctrl-d]
↵

The last entry is the actual code sequence to send to the printer. The [Esc] key would be entered as ASCII numeric value \027. The **W1** would be normal characters entered as literals. Note that the **W** must be upper case, since **w** has a different ASCII value. Enter

\027W1

> *When reading the printer manual, take care to note the difference between the characters 0 or 1 and the ASCII decimal values of 0 or 1. In older printers, such as the Epson MX series, some commands use the value 1 or 0—not the characters. Those values would be entered as \000 or \001. The character 0 and 1 have ASCII values of \048 and \049 respectively. In most newer printers, the code sets have been rewritten to use characters 0 and 1 in hopes of avoiding this confusion.*

Save the new refined printer setup table by entering

[F2]

Return to the main Custom menu by entering

r

Saving the New Configuration

Save the revised configuration by entering

[F2]

Paradox gives you a choice of saving the changes for a single-user **HardDisk** system or a multiuser **Network** system. The Network option is used if you want to store different configuration files on the network server so that each user can operate Paradox with their own configuration. Enter

↵

When you save a new configuration file, Paradox automatically exits so that you will be forced to restart the program with the new configuration.

Summary

This chapter covered the creation and use of scripts to automate operations in Paradox.

❑ **Scripts.** Scripts allow you to store sequences of Paradox commands which can be executed by playing the script. Scripts allow you to record multiple keystroke operations or compose complete applications using the PAL languages. All scripts are stored as text files with SC file extensions. The files can be edited using the built-in Paradox editor or any ASCII compatible text editor or word processing program.

❑ **Recording Scripts.** The simplest method for creating scripts is to record the script. When recording is active, all of the keystrokes and commands entered into Paradox are also written into a script file. The file can then be replayed, causing Paradox to read the commands in the script file instead of the keyboard. Script recording can be activated using the **Scripts BeginRecord** command from the main menu. Recording can be stopped with **Scripts End-Record.** If the main menu is not available, as when you are operating in the Report Design mode, you can use the [Alt-F10] command to display the PAL menu which has options for starting and stopping script recording.

❑ **Instant Scripts.** The [Alt-F3] key will place Paradox into the instant script recording mode. The instant script is always assigned the name INSTANT.Sc. The script can be executed with a single key command, [Alt-F4]. Each new instant script overwrites the previous instant script. To preserve an instant script, you must rename it or copy it to a new file name before using [Alt-F3] again.

❑ **Repeat Play.** The **Scripts RepeatPlay** command allows you to play a selected script a specific number of times automatically.

❑ **Editing Scripts.** Since scripts are stored in text files, they can be edited like a word processing document. Paradox has a built-in script editor accessed through the **Scripts Editor** command. You can edit an existing script file or create a new script from scratch. The **Read** command allows you to copy the contents of existing scripts into the script you are editing. The **Go** command saves the current script and immediately plays it.

❑ **Key Names.** Scripts created by recording contain special key names which represent menu choice and special Paradox key commands. Menu options are written within { }.

❑ **PAL Commands.** PAL stands for the Paradox Application Language. Scripts can contain both key names and PAL commands in any combination. PAL language commands often express operations in more concise syntax than the key names needed to execute the equivalent operation.

❑ **Custom Script.** Paradox is supplied with a special script called Custom which is used to modify the PARADOX3.CNF configuration file. This file holds the settings for hardware, e.g., screen and printers, as well as the default options for Paradox operations.

Text Editing with Word Processors

All Paradox scripts are standard DOS text files, also called ASCII (American Standard Code for Information Interchange) files. The built-in editor in Paradox creates standard text files. You can, if desired, create or modify scripts using word processing programs such as *Microsoft Word, WordPerfect,* or *WordStar*. Note that all of these programs store word processing documents in a non-text format. However, by using specific commands, you can create text files.

WordStar

In *WordStar* you can read and write text files. To ensure that documents edited or created with *WordStar* are stored in text format, use the N command from the main menu when you edit or create a file. Note that *WordStar* does not impose a default file extension on new files created with the program. If you create a script in *WordStar*, you must add the SC file extension to the file name or it will not be recognized by Paradox as a script file.

Microsoft Word

All versions of *Word,* 1.0 to 5.0, will allow you to edit existing text files. *Word* automatically recognizes a text file when it is loaded and no special conversion is needed.

If you want to create a script text file with *Word*, you must take two actions not needed when you are creating a word-processing document. These actions take place after you have created the text and are using the **Transfer Save** command to store the text in a disk file.

First, *Word* will automatically add a DOC extension to a new file. To create a script file you must enter the file extension, SC, along with the file name, when you use the **Transfer Save** command. Second, you must select the text format option on the Transfer Save menu in order to designate the file format as text rather than the standard *Word* word-processing format. In Version 1.0 through 4.0, this is done by selecting **No** under the Format option. In Version 5.0, the Format option lists several file format types. To save the document as a text file, select the Text-only option.

If you are using the *Windows* version of *Word*, you will have to follow a different procedure since *Windows/Word* requires conversion to and from text. Text files can be created using the **File Save As** command in contrast to **File Save,** which automatically uses *Word* file format. In order to save a document as text file, you must remember to specify the SC file extension in the file name and then select **Options** from the **File Save** dialog box. This will reveal the **File Format** options box which will display a list of file formats from which you can choose Text Only.

WordPerfect

WordPerfect text file handling differs slightly with the version you are working with. In Version 4.2, the [Ctrl-F5] command displays a menu that loads and saves text files. Option 2 is used to load a text file and option 1 saves the current document as a text file. You can also retrieve text files using the subcommand **5** (Text In) from the List Files, [F5], directory display. In Versions 5.0 and 5.1, the command to save a text file is [Ctrl-F5] **DOS Text Save**. You can retrieve a text file with [Ctrl-F5] **Dos Text Retrieve** (CR/LF to [HRt]) or [F5] **Text In.**

In Version 5.1, you can load a text file from the pulldown menus using [Alt-=] **File Text In DOS Text.** The pulldown command for saving a text file is [Alt-=] **Text Out DOS Text.**

Scripts

Listing of BALANCE.SC

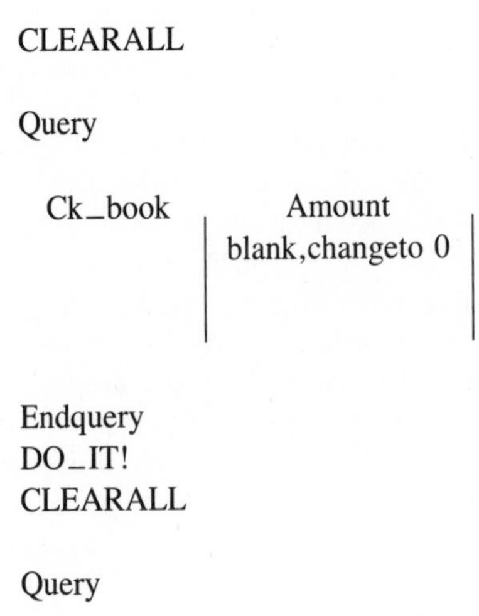

```
CLEARALL

Query

  Ck_book | Amount             |
          | blank,changeto 0   |
          |                    |

Endquery
DO_IT!
CLEARALL

Query
```

Ck_book	Deposit blank,changeto 0

Endquery
DO_IT!
CLEARALL

Query

Ck_book	Amount _checks	Deposit _deposits	Balance changeto _deposits-_checks

Ck_book

Endquery
DO_IT!
QUERY

ck_book | balance |
| calc sum |

ENDQUERY
DO_IT!
UPIMAGE
CLEARIMAGE

Exercises

Exercise 1 from page 350

Step 1. Copy Janrpt script to Marrpt

t c s
janrpt ↵
marrpt ↵

Step 2. Load Marrpt into the script editor

s e e
marrpt ↵

Step 3. Edit the script

→ ***(30 times)***
3
[F2]

11

Creating Graphs

If you have a video adapter that can display graphics, you can create standard business graphs of the information stored in your Paradox tables. The graphs can display information as bars, lines, shade areas, or slices of a pie. You can also control detailed aspects of the graph, such as labels, the color or patterns used to represent data, or the scale of the graph. In this chapter, you will learn the basic procedures used to create, modify, save, and output graphs on Paradox.

Begin by loading Paradox in the usual manner.

Displaying Graphs

Graphs are drawings that represent relationships between values. They have the ability to instantly convey a summary of large amounts of information in a form that highlights broad characteristics of the data stored in a table. Graphs can reveal trends, tendencies, or patterns in the data in a way that you cannot obtain by simply viewing the database information in a table of values.

Graphs are primarily a summary tool since their style of data representation tends to obscure the details contained in individual records. In many cases, you will find that a database table contains too much unorganized data to create a meaningful graph. In such instances, you can use a query form to organize and summarize the table and then base the graph on the Answer table rather than on the raw data in the original table. The ability of Paradox to quickly summarize tables makes it an ideal applications in which to create graphs (although most database application on the market today do include graphs.)

Paradox supports graphs usually classified as *standard business graphs*. Business graphs are designed to show the relative magnitude of various items. Most graphs are rectangular in shape, Figure 11-1. The left side of the rectangle is called the *Y* or *value* axis. The Y axis shows a scale of values with the smallest at the bottom, increasing in even increments to the largest value at the top. The Y axis is used to indicate the value of the bars in the chart. The bottom side of the rectangle is the *X* or *category* **axis. This axis lists the various items represented by the bars. The X axis can contain any type of information such as dates, numbers, or names. While you may want to arrange the categories in chronological or alphabetical order, there is no requirement that the categories be in any particular order.**

> *The terms X and Y come from the designations used in coordinate geometry for the horizontal and vertical axis. Paradox uses the X and Y terminology but it may be more helpful in terms of business graphics to think of the Y axis as the scale of values that measures the items organized by category along the X axis.*

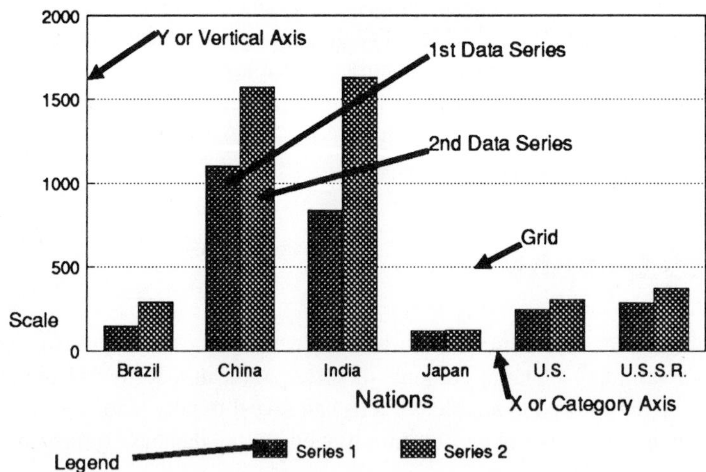

Figure 11-1 Basic business graph.

Paradox permits each item listed in the category axis to have up to six values. As shown in Figure 11-1, each value appears as a separate bar grouped at the same category item but differentiated by color or shade from another. Each set of values is called a *data series*. The *legend* is added to a graph to identify the meaning of the data series that appears on the graph by associating a label with each color or shade used.

Paradox has a number of different *predefined* graph layouts built into the program. All you need to do to produce a graph is to indicate where the value and category information is stored, and Paradox takes care of the details needed to generate the graph. The data used for graphs is supplied as a field. The categories that appear on the chart are the items entered in the key field of the table you are graphing. If no key field is designated, Paradox selects the first non-numeric field in the table as the category listing.

The bars are generated by using the values in the numeric fields of the table. Each numeric field, up to a maximum of six, is treated as a data series. All the values in the same series appear in the same color or shade.

The rules by which Paradox selects fields to act as categories or data series mean that many database tables may not be suitable for graphing directly. In those cases, you may want to generate an Answer table that contains the desired fields and records in the desired order.

Types of Graphs

Paradox can create four types of graphs.

❑ **Bar Graphs.** Bar graphs, Figure 11-2, are the most traditional type of business graph because they directly represent individual values. In a bar chart, each data item is represented

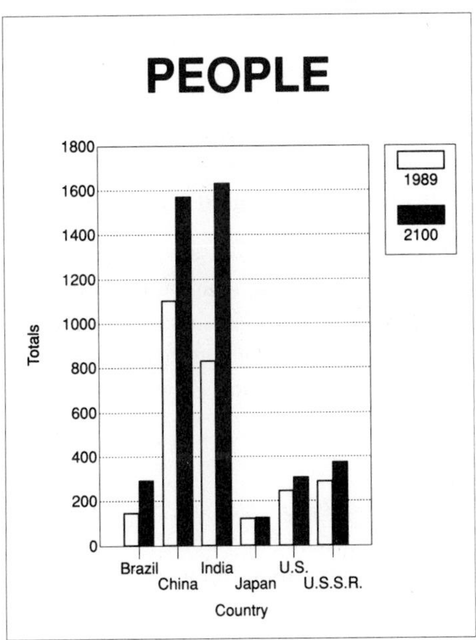

Figure 11-2 Bar graph.

by a separate bar. This means there is one bar generated for each record in the table. All the bars generated by a single numeric field make a data series. You can place up to six data series, representing six different numeric fields, on a bar graph at the same time.

❑ **Rotated Bar.** This type of graph rotates the X and Y axis so that the values are written horizontally, while the categories are listed vertically, Figure 11-3.

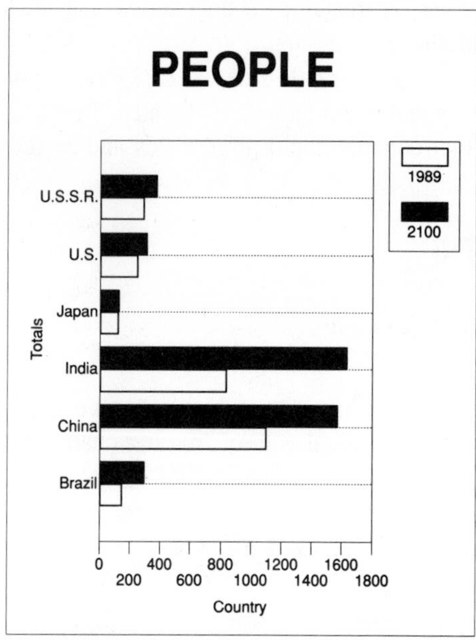

Figure 11-3 Rotated bar graph.

❑ **3-D Bar.** This graph is similar to the standard bar graph with the exception that a *shadow* is added to each bar to give a three dimensional effect, Figure 11-4, to make each bar stand out more clearly. This effect works best when there are relatively few bars on the chart, since each 3-D bar requires more room and the 3-D effect is lost when too may bars are crowded together.

❑ **Stacked Bar.** A stacked bar graph is an alternative method of displaying a bar chart having more than one data series. A stacked bar graph displays the all the bars from all the data series for a given category, stacked on top of one another, Figure 11-5. A stacked bar is used to show the cumulative effect of the data series. For example, if each series represents a quarterly value, the entire stacked bar represents the entire year. By looking at the different shades in each bar you can estimate the contribution to the whole of each data series part.

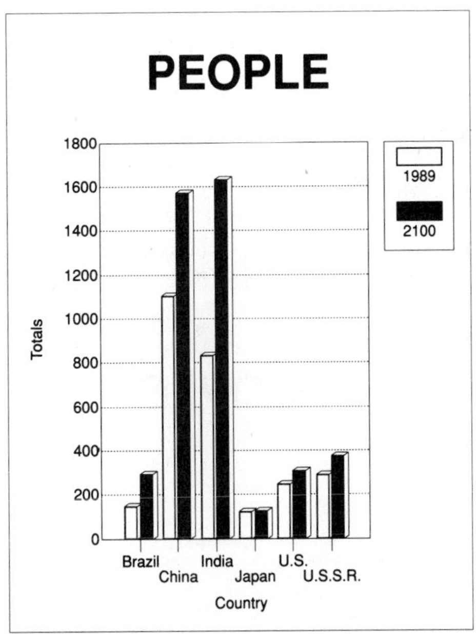

Figure 11-4 3-D bar graph.

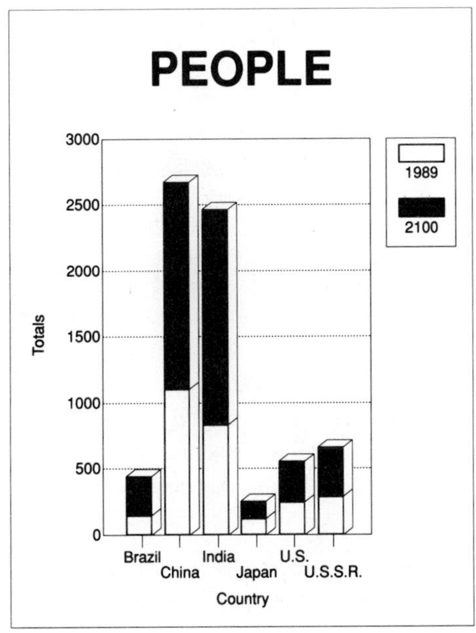

Figure 11-5 Stacked bar graph.

❑ **Line Graphs.** Line graphs are used to draw attention to patterns or trends revealed by a series of values, Figure 11-6. In a line graph, each value appears as a point above each item on the category axis. The point's height is determined by the magnitude of the value. The points are then jointed by lines to indicate the trend of the change between one point and another. Line charts tend to deemphasize the magnitude of individual points and highlight the general trends, up or down, between points. Line charts typically use chronological items, days, months, years, as the X axis items, since trends are usually measured against the passage of time.

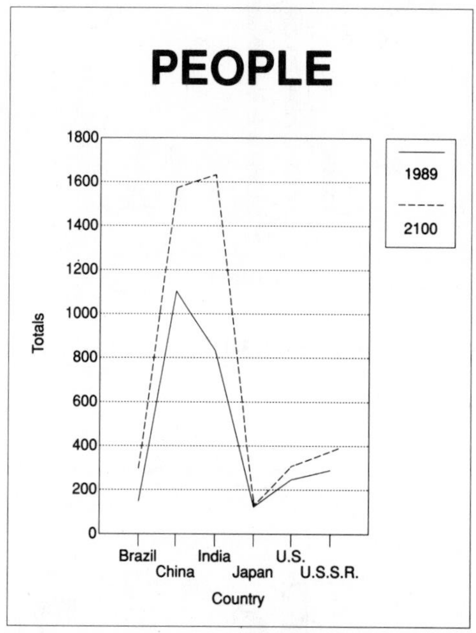

Figure 11-6 Line graph with pointer markers

❑ **Marker Only.** You can display the data from a line chart as pointer markers only if desired. This type of display is used to show a *scattergram* of data points, Figure 11-7. This option is used when the X axis items are not arranged in a random order. The goal of the graph is to show any patterns in the way data points are clustered. If lines were added to such a chart, they would zigzag in all directions, confusing the display.

❑ **Line Only.** This type of chart shows the lines drawn between data points but removes the pointer markers themselves, Figure 11-8. This style places the emphasis on the trend of the line and stresses that individual data points are not significant. Line graphs are useful when you want to contrast the trends indicated by different data series.

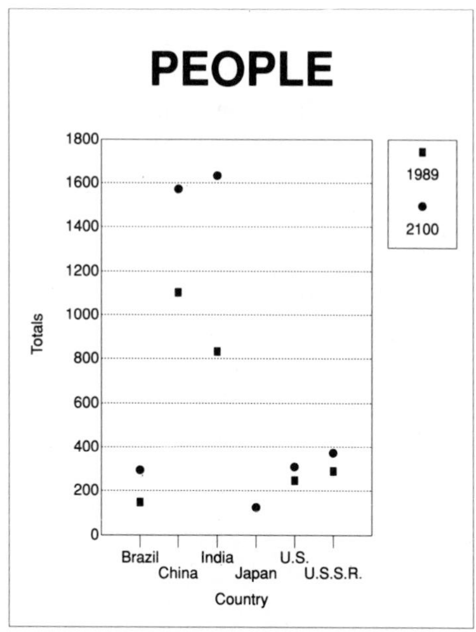

Figure 11-7 Marker only graph.

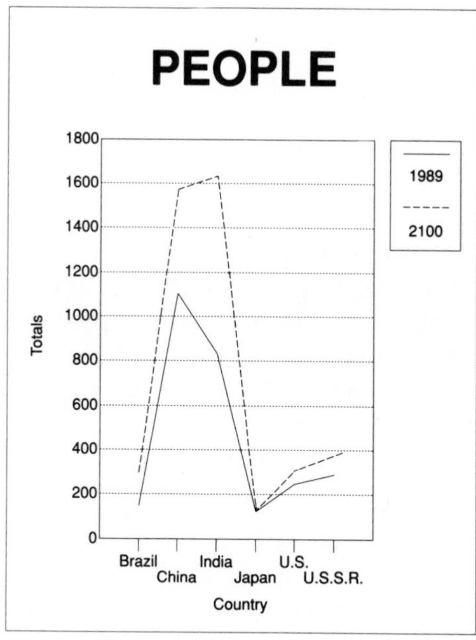

Figure 11-8 Line only graph.

❑ **X-Y Graphs.** An X-Y graph is one that draws a trend line based on using a numeric series for both the X and Y axis. An X-Y graph uses the values in two numeric fields to obtain the data points. The pair of values that appear in each record produces a single point on the chart by using the first field as the X value and the second field as the Y value, Figure 11-9.

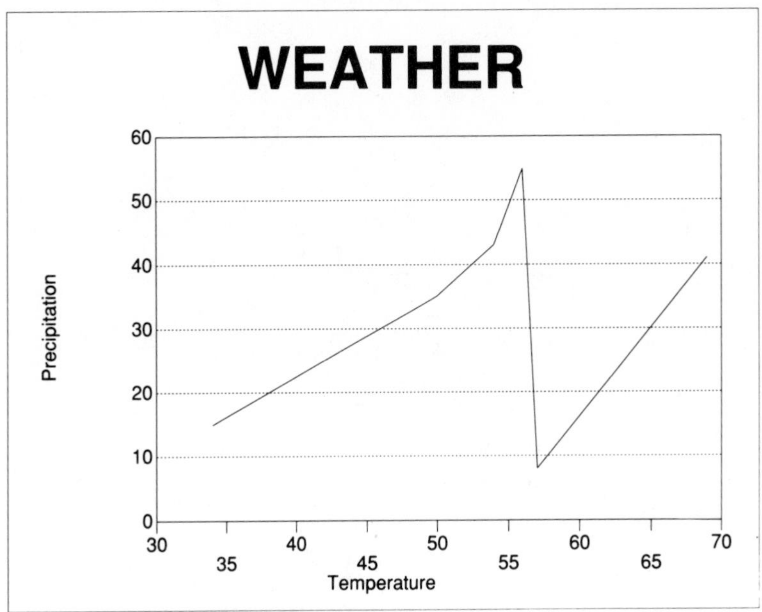

Figure 11-9 X-Y type of graph.

The first field should hold the values of the independent variable, while the second field should be the dependent variable. For example, if you have a table with fields for sales revenue and advertising expense, you might want to produce an X-Y graph that shows the relationship between money spent for advertising and the subsequent sales revenues generated. In this case, advertising is the independent variable and revenue the dependent variable, because the assumption is that sales depend in some degree on advertising. Note that when you create an X-Y type chart, the X axis series is the first numeric field, in contrast to other types of graphs in which the X axis is the first non-numeric field.

❑ **Area Graphs.** An area graph is similar to both line graphs and stacked bar graphs. In an area graph, each data series is represented by a line that connects each of the data points in the field. However, in this type of graph, the area under the line is filled with a color or shade. If there is more than one series, the area displays are stacked on top of each other so that all the areas taken together represent the total of all the data series. The area graph shows the cumulative effect of several data series, e.g., monthly totals adding up to a quarter of year. They also indicate general trends across a data series, e.g., up or down trends from month to month. Area charts are not useful when you want to contrast data series, such as comparing the same months in different years.

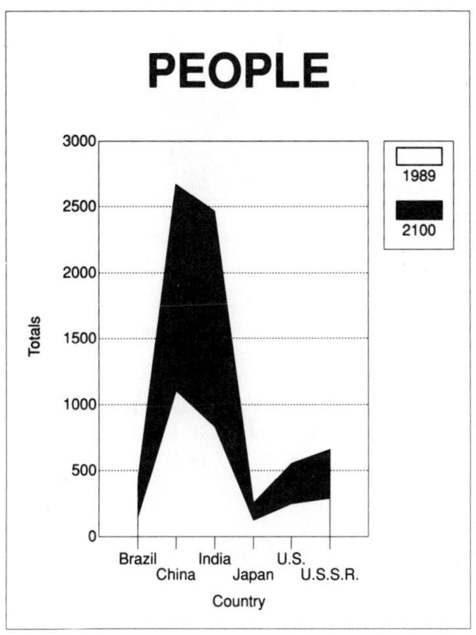

Figure 11-10 Area graph.

❑ **Pie Charts.** Pie charts are different from other graphs in two important respects. First, rather than plotting points, bars, or lines on a rectangular grid, pie charts are circular—showing each data item as a slice of the pie, Figure 11-11. Second, because of their shape, pie charts can show only one data series at a time. Pie charts are used to show the relative size of values in the same series. Pie charts tend to hide the actual value of an item and emphasize the percentage that each item is of the total for the entire series. Pie charts stress comparisons rather than magnitudes.

❑ **Mixed Types.** Rectangular graphs that plot each data item individually, and non-stacked bar or line charts can permit the mixing of line, marker, and bars in a single graph, Figure 11-12.

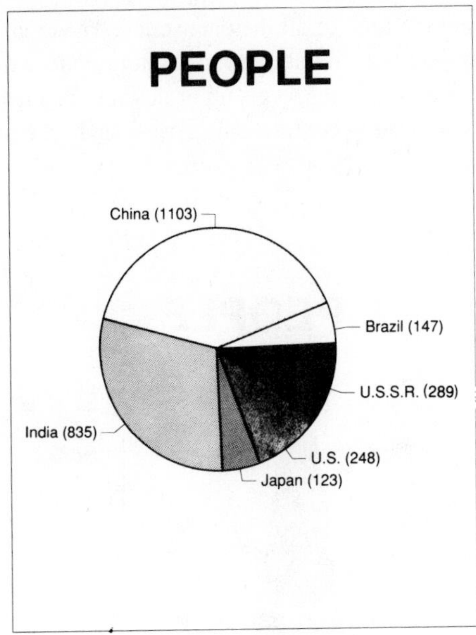

Figure 11-11 Pie chart.

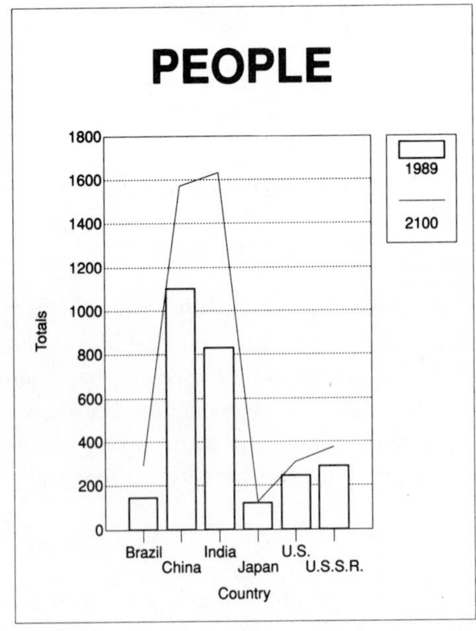

Figure 11-12 Mixed format graph.

Instant and Custom Graphs

In keeping with the theme of simplicity, Paradox can generate graphs instantly from the work area display, with the command [Ctrl-F7]. [Ctrl-F7] is the **instant graph** command. It uses the cursor position to determine the table to be graphed and the values in the table to be used as the X and Y series for the chart. The selection process follows the rules discussed on page 378, by which Paradox picks out the fields for the chart. When creating an instant chart, you prepare the graph by manipulating the table so that it contains the proper fields in the proper order. In many cases, this requires you to create an Answer table that contains selected fields or subtotals. Answer tables can also be arranged in different sort orders from the original table, and the fields can be rotated to change their order as well. The rules for graph creation follow.

❑ **Stacked Bar Graph.** By default, the graph produced by [Ctrl-F7] is always a stacked bar type graph. You can change the graph type using the command **Image Graph Modify Type.**

❑ **X Axis Series = First Non-numeric Field.** When a graph is created Paradox selects the first non-numeric field in the table to use as the X axis series. The values in that field are listed along the bottom of the graph or—in the case of pie charts—show as slice labels.

❑ **X Axis = Key Field.** If the table contains a key field, it is selected as the X axis series even if it is numeric.

❑ **X Axis Title = Field Name.** The title of the X axis that appears on the graph is the name of the field selected as the X axis series.

❑ **Y Axis Series = First 6 Numeric Fields.** Paradox uses numeric fields, up to as many as six, as data series for the Y axis values in the chart. Pie charts use only the first series, since they can display only one series of values at a time.

❑ **Legends = Field Names.** Paradox automatically generates a legend that uses the field names to identify the data series. The legend is always produced even when there is only one data series being graphed. If you are using subtotals stored in an Answer table, you may want to use the **as** command in the query form to assign new field names to the calculated fields.

❑ **Pie Chart Labels = X Series Field + Value.** Pie charts, since they do not have axes, label each slice of the pie with the value from the first non-numeric field. The value used to determine the size of the slice is shown in parentheses.

❑ **Graph Title = Table Name.** The main title of the graph is the name of the table. If you are using an Answer table, the title would always be Answer. The **Tools Rename** command can be used to change the name of the Answer table to one that better fits the graph. Note that by using table name as the title, you are limited to an eight-character title for the graph.

❑ **Y Axis Title = "Totals".** The Y axis is always labeled *totals*.

The automatic settings listed as part of the *rules* used by Paradox can be changed on two levels.

❑ **Image Graph Modify.** The Image command contains the Graph options that can be used to alter settings for the current graph. Under **Graph**, the **Modify** command gives you access to commands that control all the details used to create the graph, including chart type, labels, legends, color and shades, data series, and more. You can save the settings in a special Graph Settings file that can be stored on the disk for later use.

❑ **Change Defaults with Custom Script.** The default settings for graph type, colors, and other options can be changed using the Custom script and selecting the Graph option.

In general, the fastest way to create a graph is to generate a table that contains the desired records and fields in the sort and field order that you desire, and then use [Ctrl-F7]. If further modifications are needed, you can use the Image Graph options to fine tune the graph image.

Creating an Instant Graph

The information in the Ck_book table, in and of itself, would not make a meaningful chart. This is often the case with tables that contain raw data about financial transactions. However, it is possible to use a query form to create a summary table that would gather together data to make a meaningful chart. For example, suppose you calculated the totals for each of the accounts listed in the *Acct#* field. Begin by creating the query form needed to generate the summary table. Enter

a
ck_book ↵

Select the *Acct#* field as the subtotal field for the Answer table by placing a √ in that field. Enter

[Tab]*(2 times)*
[F6]

In addition, use an **as** operator to change the name of the field to *Account*. Enter

as Account

You will recall that Account #100 contains deposits rather than checks. In this case, exclude the deposits by placing a selection operator in the *Acct#* field that will exclude Account 100 records. Enter

,>100

The last step is to place the **calc sum** operator in the *Amount* field. Enter

[Tab] *(3 times)*
calc sum as Amount

Process the query by entering

[F2]

The result is a two-field Answer table as shown in Figure 11-13.

ANSWER	Accounts	Amount
1	500	750.50
2	600	1,332.96
3	650	2,245.50
4	700	524.73

Figure 11-13 Summary table created.

In order to generate a graph with the [Ctrl-F7] command, you need to place the cursor in a numeric field column. Enter

[Ctrl-End]

Display the graph by entering

[Ctrl-F7]

This command causes Paradox to create a graph based on the current table. It may take Paradox a few moments to generate the graph that it will automatically display, Figure 11-14. Paradox writes two temporary files to the disk that are used to generate the instant graph. These files are automatically erased when you have finished viewing the graph.

> *The exact appearance of the graph will vary slightly depending upon the type of screen display you are using. Paradox will attempt to automatically detect the type of screen display you have attached to the computer and use a screen display driver that matches the display type. If you are using an unusual type of monitor, e.g., a high-resolution desktop publishing monitor such as the Wyse 700, Paradox will use a standard type of display mode, typically CGA, since it will probably not have a driver built in that will work with the high-resolution mode on these specialized monitors.*

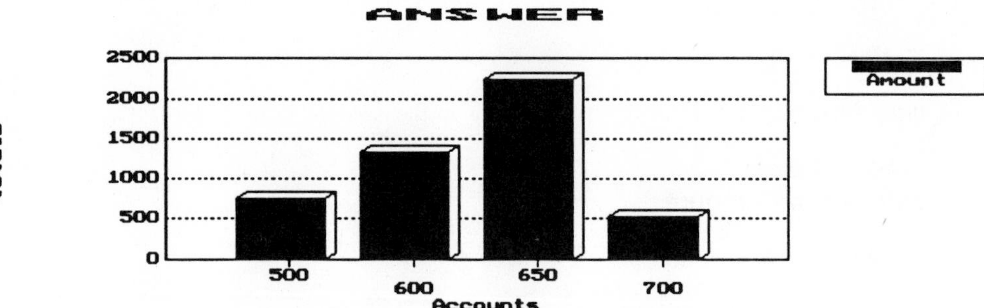

Figure 11-14 Graph created by instant graph command [Ctrl-F7].

Note that the graph has the title of *Answer* because it was generated from the Answer table. You can change the title name by renaming the table. You can remove the image from the screen by pressing any key. Enter

↵

The screen shows the work area again. Use the **Tools Rename Table** command to change the name of the Answer table to *Expenses*. Enter

[F10] t r t
↵ *(2 times)*
expenses ↵

Notice that when you rename the table, the cursor position is changed. You will need to move the cursor before you can redisplay the graph. Enter

[Ctrl-End] [Ctrl-F7]

The graph has the title *Expenses* instead of *Answer*. Clear the work area by entering

[Alt-F8]

Chart, with Multiple Series

The chart you have just created displays values for only a single data series, the totals of the *Amount* field. However, Paradox charts can graph up to six different series of values. An obvious example is a graph that charts the *Amount* and *Deposit* fields.

Suppose you used a query form to generate totals for the *Amount* and *Deposit* fields for each month of the year. That can be done by using the *Period* field to group records together by monthly period.

In order to use the *Period* field, you must remember to fill in the *Period* field for each record. In this example, there are two new records added to the table that did not have their period fields filled out. Correct that now by entering

v
ck_book ↵
[Ctrl-End] End]

Enter 03-Mar into the two records that are blank for the *Period field.*

[F9]
03-Mar ↑
03-Mar
[F2] [F8]

With the table updated, you can use a query form to summarize the *Amount* and *Deposit* fields by month. Enter

a
ck_book ↵

Begin by selecting the *Period* field with a √ by entering

[Ctrl-End] [F6]

Enter **calc sum** operators in both the *Amount* and *Deposit* fields. Use **as** operators to name the fields. Keep in mind that without an **as** operator, the field would be named *Sum of Amount* and *Sum of Deposit.*

← *(2 times)*
calc sum as Deposit
← *(5 times)*
calc sum as Checks

Execute the query by entering

[F2]

The resulting Answer table, shown in Figure 11-15, list totals for checks and deposits for each month.

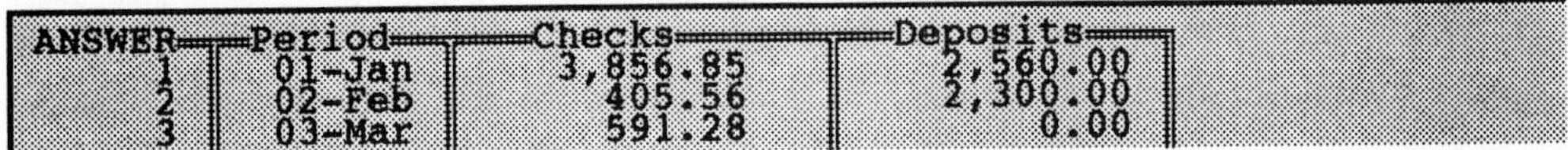

ANSWER	Period	Checks	Deposits
1	01-Jan	3,856.85	2,560.00
2	02-Feb	405.56	2,300.00
3	03-Mar	591.28	0.00

Figure 11-15 Table summarize activity by month.

Create a chart from this table by placing the cursor in a numeric field and using the instant graph command.

[Tab] ***(2 times)***
[Ctrl-F7]

Paradox generates a stacked bar graph, the default graph type, Figure 11-16.

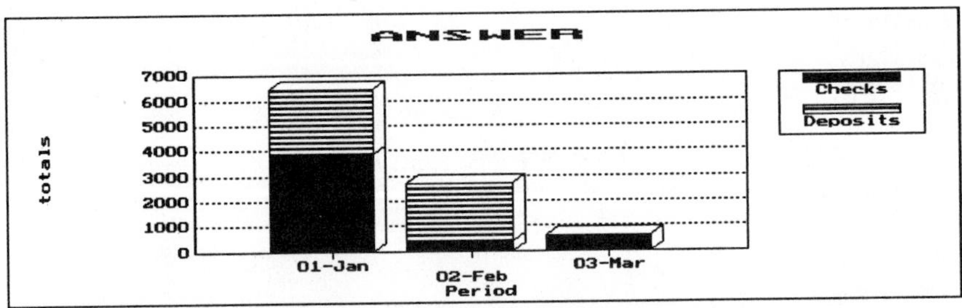

Figure 11-16 Graph shows two data series as stacked bar segments.

Changing Graph Types

The stacked bar graph that Paradox generates is not an appropriate form in which to display the data in the Answer table. The stacked bar format joins the checks and deposits for each month into a single bar with different segments for each value series. Adding together the checks and deposits does not create a meaningful value. These data series would be better represented if the bars were placed side by side instead of stacked.

In order to change the type of graph displayed you must use the **Image Graph Modify** command. Enter

↵

[F10] i g m

When you elect to modify a graph, Paradox displays a full screen menu that temporarily covers the work area display. The display is the Graph type menu, Figure 11-17.

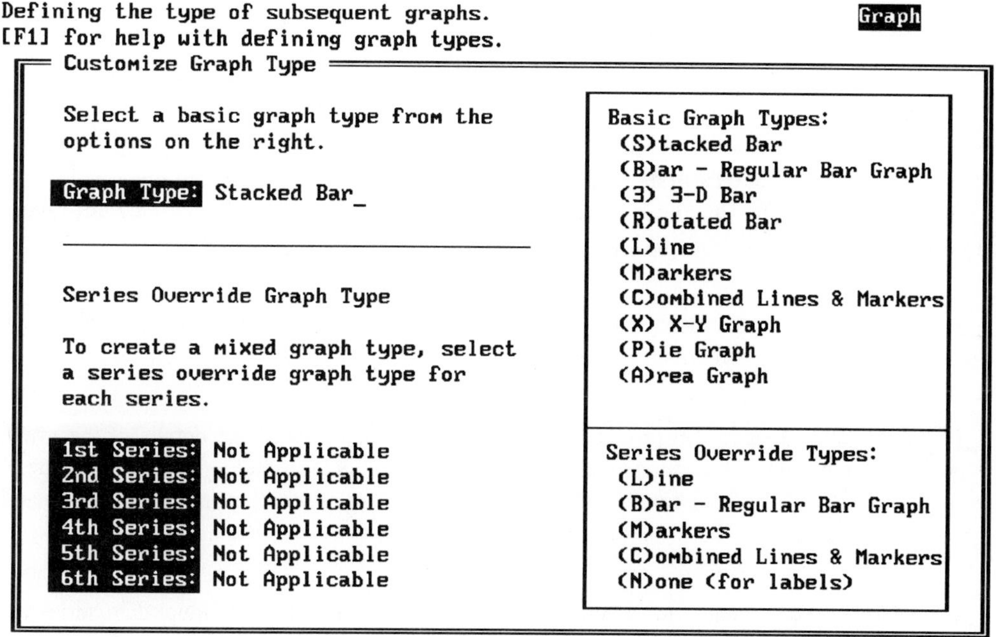

Figure 11-17 Graph type menu.

The menu consists of three parts.

❑ **Graph Type.** The graph type selection controls the overall format of the graph.

❑ **Series Overrides.** Some graph types allow different data series to be displayed in different formats. For example, it is possible to display some data series as bars while others are lines. You can create this mixed type of graph. If this cannot be done with the current graph type, **Not Applicable** appears in the series overrides.

❑ **Options List.** The right side of the display lists a menu of graph and series overrides.

In this case, change the graph type to a regular, i.e., nonstacked bar graph. Enter

b

As soon as you type the first letter of your choice, Paradox writes the entire name into the graph type entry area.

Viewing a Modified Graph

When you are working in the graph modifications menu, you can view the results of the changes you are making to the graph without having to exit the entry mode. This is done by selecting the **ViewGraph** option from the **Graph** menu. Enter

[F10]

Paradox displays the **Graph** menu that appears only when you have entered the graph modification mode using the **Image Graph Modify** command from the main Paradox menu, Figure 11-18. There are five options listed on the menu.

❑ **Type.** This is the menu that is currently displayed. It is used to select the basic graph format and any series style overrides available.

❑ **Overall.** This option provides you with options that control the details of the graph type you have chosen. The options include graph titles, colors and shading, the scale of the X and Y axes, the grid layout for rectangular graphs, print size, location and orientation, and printer selection. All of these options affect the overall style of the graph.

❑ **Series.** This menu allows you to control details of how the individual data series are displayed including legends, colors, and shadings.

❑ **Pies.** This menu has options specifically oriented towards pie charts, such as the Exploding slices option.

❑ **ViewGraph.** This option allows you to display the graph on the screen, send it to the printer, or capture it in a printer output file. Note that you cannot output the graph to the printer or a printer file until you have selected your graphics printer, discussed on page 412.

```
Type  Overall  Series  Pies  ViewGraph  Help  DO-IT!  Cancel
Change the currently specified graph type.
```

Figure 11-18 Modify graph menu.

In order to display the graph on the screen enter

v

You are given three options: Screen, Printer, and File. Place the graph on the screen by entering

s

The screen displays the graph, Figure 11-19. In this new format, the bars are displayed side by side rather than stacked. This format is more appropriate for the data being presented.

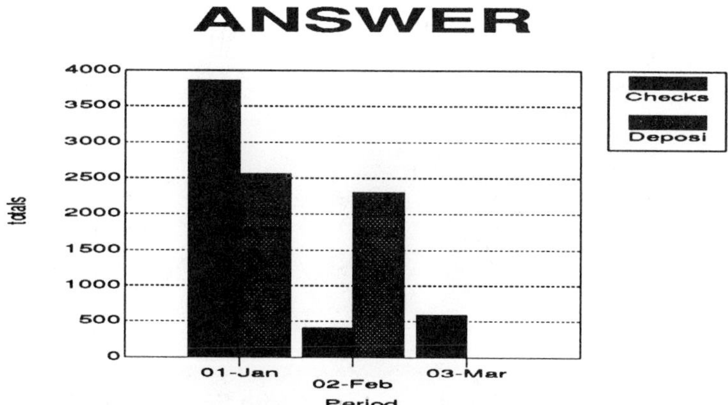

Figure 11-19 Graph changed to regular bar graph.

Return to the type menu by entering

↵

Overriding the Basic Format

When you select a new graph type, the series override options will all show the same graph type or **Not Applicable** for charts that can display only one type of series. In a standard bar graph, you have the option to vary the way each series is displayed by using the Series Override list to change the bars to lines, markers, or lines with markers. Note that you also have the option of suppressing the display of a series by using the None options.

Here, change the first data series, checks, to a line with marker form of representation. Enter

↵
c

Paradox writes the name **Combined Lines & Markers** onto the line for the First Series override. This means that your graph will be a combination of bars and lines with markers. Display the modified chart by entering

[F10] v s

The graph now shows a mixture of bars and lines with markers, Figure 11-20.

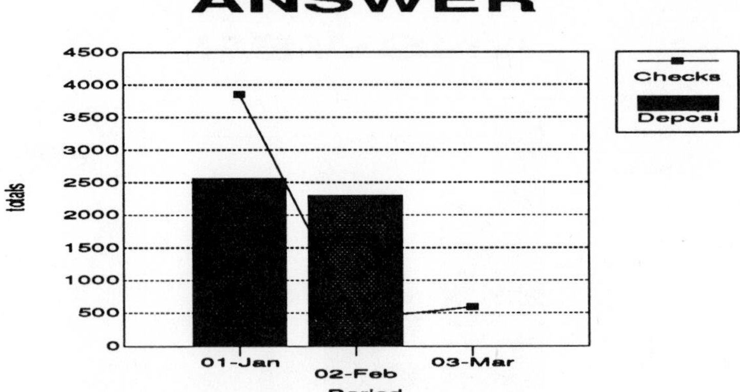

Figure 11-20 Graph uses bars mixed with lines and markers.

Return to the Graph type menu by entering

↵

Change the graph to a 3-D bar graph by entering

↑
3

When you change the graph type, the entire series is reset to match the option available with the selected graph type.

Changing Graph Details

When you create a graph, most of the details that make up the graph are automatically filled in by Paradox. In most cases, these selections will satisfy most users. However, there may be areas where you will want to *fine-tune* specific aspects of the graph. These options can be found on the Overall menu. This menu divides the graph into seven menus of graph options.

❑ **Titles.** Titles controls the text that is displayed above the data area of the graph and besides the X and Y axes. You can enter a main and subtitle that will appear centered at the top of the graph. You can also specify titles for the axes as well. The menu permits you to select the size of the characters used in the titles the font used.

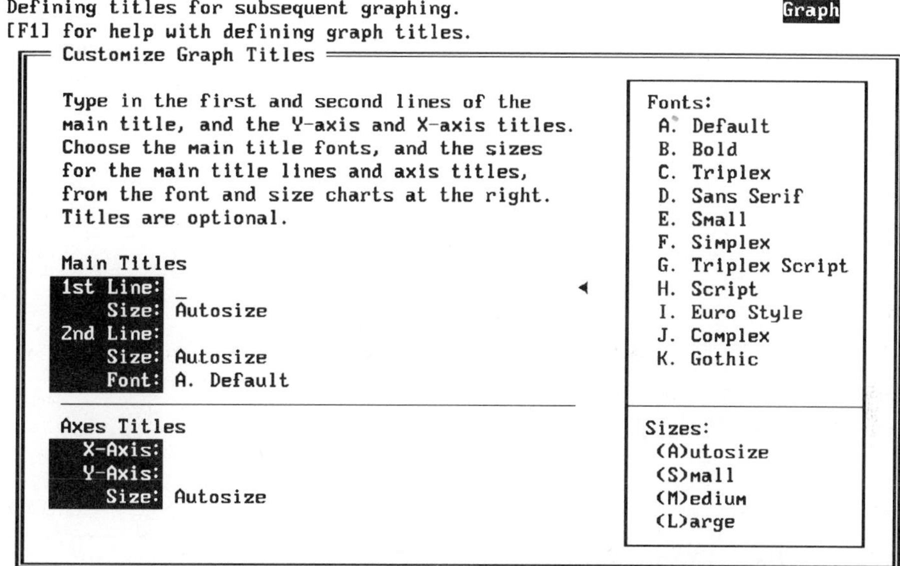

❑ **Colors.** This option can be used to control the colors on parts of the graph, such as the graph background, the titles, and the data series elements. You can select colors for screen and printer if you have a printer that can print in colors other than black and white.

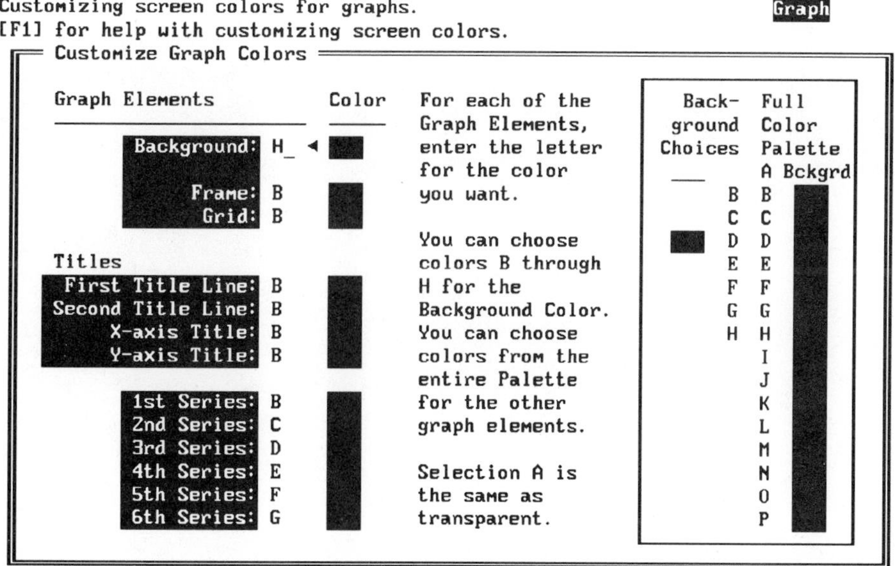

❑ **Axes.** This option is used to control the axes that border the graph area. If desired you can manually set the scales of the axes and control the frequency with which items and tick marks appear on the axis. The scaling of the axes is set by default to automatic scaling. Paradox creates a scale that will accommodate the largest and smallest values found in all of the data series.

```
Customizing axes for subsequent graphing.                                Graph
[F1] for help with customizing graph axes.
 ═ Customize Graph Axes ═══════════════════════════════════════════════════════
                                                        
                         X-Axis        Y-Axis           Set Axis Scaling:
      ─────────────────────────────────────────
         Set Axis Scaling: Automatic_   Automatic         (A)utomatic
                      Low:      0           0             (M)anual
                     High:      0           0
                Increment:      0           0           Low, High, and
                                                        Increment values
                                                        only with manual
                                                        scaling.
      ─────────────────────────────────────────
        Format of Ticks: Fixed         Fixed            Tick Formats:
     Decimal Places (0-15):        0            0
                                                          (F)ixed
     Number of Minor Ticks:        0            0         (S)cientific
          Alternate Ticks? Yes                            (C)urrency
                                                          (,)Financial
      ─────────────────────────────────────────           (G)eneral
      Display Axis Scaling? Yes                           (P)ercent
      Enter (Y)es or (N)o
```

❑ **Grids.** This menu allows you to control the grid lines that are displayed on the plot area of the graph. You can display horizontal or vertical grids, or suppress the grid entirely. You can also select the type of line to be used and the color.

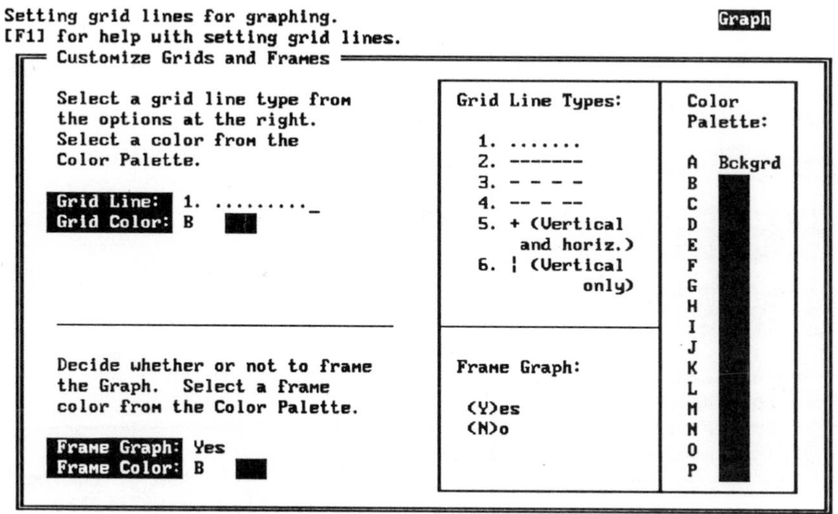

❑ **PrinterLayout.** Printer layout refers to how the graph will be printed. By default, Paradox will print a full-page graph rotated in a landscape orientation. Landscape means that the width of the graph will print across the widest side of the paper. On an 8.5″ by 11″ page, the X axis would print across the 11″ side, allowing the most room for items in a data series.

Defining the layout of the graph for printing. Graph
[F1] for help with defining the layout of the graph printing.

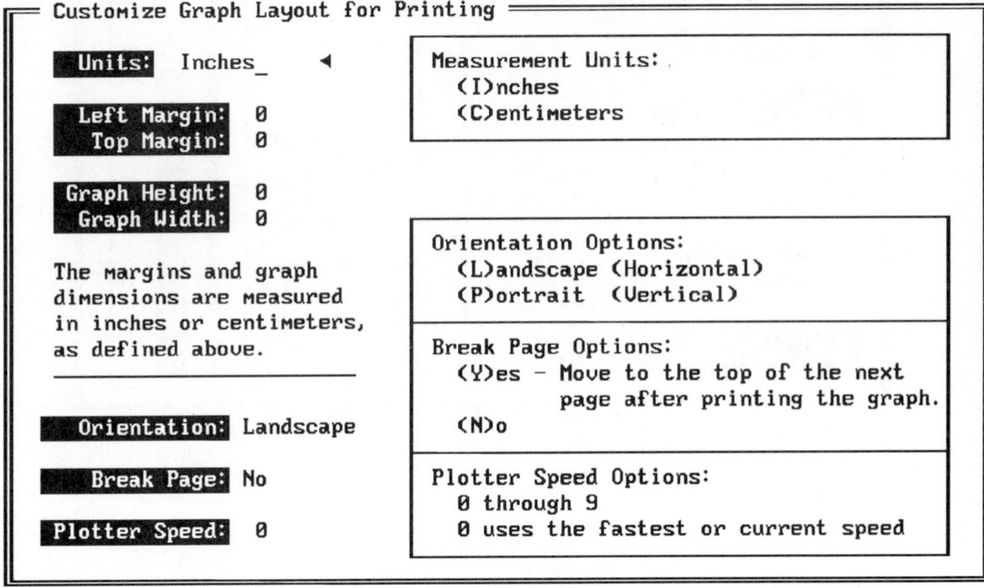

❑ **Device.** In order to print graphs you must display the Custom script and select the graph printer from the printer graphics library. From the Device menu, you can select up to four different devices to which you can output graphs. Note that until you install a graphics printer with the Custom script, you cannot print a graph.

❑ **Wait.** This option allows you to set Paradox switches from graph display to normal display. By default, Paradox will wait until a key is pressed before removing the graph from the screen. As an alternative, you can specify a duration time, in seconds, for graph displays. When a graph is displayed, Paradox will wait the specified number of seconds, then automatically return to the previous menu or work area display. Using the Duration option allows you to view scripts that display graphs in a *slideshow* manner.

Graph Titles

As you recall, graphs generated from Answer tables are automatically given the title of Answer. You can change the title by changing the name of the table, or by using the Overall

Titles menu. This menu allows you to change the title, as well as create a subtitle, and titles for the X and Y axis. Enter

[F10] o t

The Titles menu shows blanks for the main and axes titles. This means that Paradox will use the table name for the main title, the field name for the X axis title, and the word *totals* for the Y axis title. Create a new main title by entering

Checking Account Activity

Below the first line of the main title is a line for Size. The Autosize option allows Paradox to select the size of the characters used for the title automatically, depending on the amount of text in the title. You can override this by specifying Small, Medium, or Large characters. Note if you select Large, part of your title may be truncated because it will not fit across the width of the graph.

You can also select a font for the title. Fonts are styles of type that vary in the ways the letters are formed. Add titles for the X and Y axes by entering

[Tab] ***(5 times)***
Financial Periods ↵
Dollars

Changing the Axis

The information displayed along the X and Y axis can also be modified using the Overall menu. Select the Axes option menu by entering

[F10] o a

The Axes menu controls the scale of the axes and the format used to display the items. These items are set by default to be automatically generated.

The scale of the values displayed on the Y axis will be automatically calculated to include the highest and lowest value in any of the data series.

Also by default, the format of the values on the Y axis is set as Fixed. Since the values are dollar amounts, you might want to use the Currency or Financial formats. The format of the X axis is not relevant because the field used for the X axis, *Period*, is not numeric. Change the format to Financial by entering

→
↓ ***(4 times)***
, ***(comma)***

The menu refers to *ticks* and *minor ticks*. A tick is placed on the axis where a value is displayed and a horizontal grid line drawn across the graph. A *minor tick* is an additional mark placed on the axis between values. The minor ticks do not have values displayed beside them, and grid lines are not drawn across the graph at those marks. Adding minor ticks to an axis reduces the frequency of values displayed along the axis and the number of horizontal grid lines drawn across the graph. In the current graph, each tick indicates a value of 500 dollars—listing values 500, 1000, 1500, and so on. If you add one minor tick to the axis, every other tick will be a minor tick with no value or grid line. The major ticks will then be numbered by thousands, 1000, 2000, and so on. Add a minor tick to the axis by entering

↓ ***(2 times)***

1 ↵

Display the modified graph by entering

[F10] v s

The graph will now look like Figure 11-21.

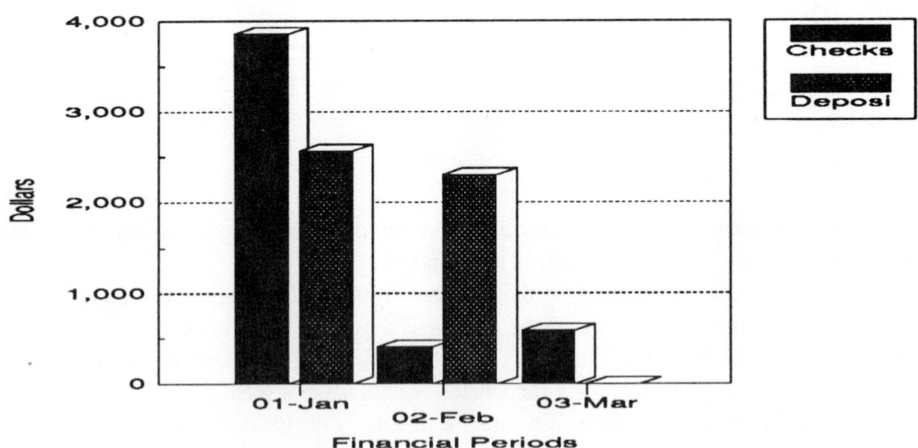

Figure 11-21 Modified graph.

Return to the menu by entering

↵

Saving Graph Settings

When you make modifications to the default settings for a chart, you may want to save those settings. Saving graph settings is different from saving other types of settings, such as screen or report forms, in some very significant ways.

When you create a report form or a screen form the form is directly linked to a specific table, i.e., the table selected when you created the screen or report form. Graph settings are not related to any particular table or list of fields. Keep in mind that all the settings you can choose when modifying a graph are defined in terms of the overall graph or some data series.

When you display the graph, Paradox follows a specific set of rules about which fields are selected for the X and Y axes series. This means you can apply any type of graph setting to any table that has at least one numeric field. While you may wish to use a specific graph setup with a specific table, you are by no means required to always use the two together.

When you save a graph, you are saving a group of graph setting modifications. There are two levels by which those settings can be saved.

❑ **Changes to the Current Graph.** The *current* graph refers to the settings that Paradox will apply when the instant graph command, [Ctrl-F3], is used. When you use the **Image Graph Modify** command to alter the current graph you are making changes to the settings used by [Ctrl-F7]. If you select the **Do-It!** command from the Graph Modify menu, all the graphs created with [Ctrl-F7] from that point on will use the settings specified in **Graph Modify** instead of the original default settings. Because graph settings are not linked to any specific database table, they are not affected by images displayed or removed from the work area.

For example, if you change the graph type to pie, all the graphs you create with [Ctrl-F7], regardless of the table being used, will be pie charts. The pie charts will continue until you exit Paradox, at which time the **Graph Modify** changes will be discarded. If you want to return to the default settings without exiting Paradox you can do so by executing the **Image Graph Reset** command.

❑ **Storing Changes in Graph Settings Files.** If you want to preserve the current set of graph settings, you can store them on the disk in a file with a G extension. The command used to store the settings is **Image Graph Save**. You can restore the settings stored in a graph file to the current graph by using the command **Image Graph Load.**

Keep in mind that graph settings not specifically saved to a file will be lost when you exit Paradox.

Saving the Current Graph Settings

When you are satisfied with the layout, style, and format of the elements in your graph, save the settings by entering

[F2]

Paradox returns you to the work area. The cursor is positioned in the Answer table. Change the name of the table to Monthly by entering

[F10] t r t
↵ *(2 times)*
monthly ↵

Clear the work area of all images by entering

[Alt-F8]

You may not realize it, but the graph settings you created for the Answer table are still active in the memory of the computer. If you were to create an instant graph with any table, Paradox would use those settings. Display the Expenses table and create an instant graph.

v
expenses ↵
[Ctrl-End] [Ctrl-F7]

The graph displayed uses the same settings that you specified for the Monthly table. The values in the Expenses tables are reflected in the graph but the settings for type, titles, and axes remain the same, Figure 11-22. The current graph settings will be used for each new graph created, no matter which table is selected. This is very different from report and screen forms that are linked to specific tables.

It is important to note that certain graph settings can be applied to almost any table while others tend to be specific to a particular table. For example, the selection of the *comma* format for the values on the Y axis could apply to almost any table. On the other hand, entering specific titles, such as *Financial Periods* for the X axis title, would be applicable only to tables that actually have a field corresponding to that title. When you store a graph setting, you should consider how narrowly or broadly you want to make the settings. If you add table specific items, such as titles, or restrict the scale of the Y axis to a range of values, the graph settings will apply only to a limited number of tables. On the other hand, you may want to create a graph setting file containing only changes that could be generally applied to a wide variety of tables.

Return to the work area display by entering

↵

Saving Graph Settings

The current graph settings can be stored in a file on the disk. Once this is done, you can retrieve the settings any time you want to use this particular graph layout with a table. If you do not save these settings they will be lost when you exit Paradox. The command used to save graph settings is **Image Graph Save**. It is important to understand that when you save graph

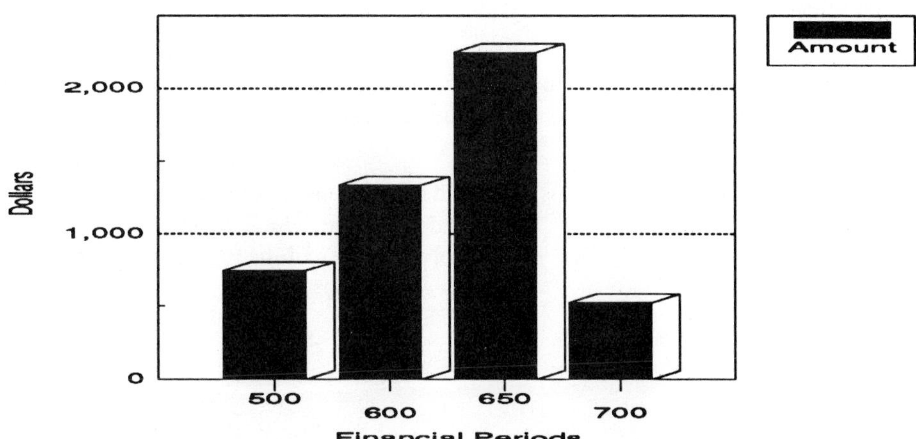

Figure 11-22 New tables graphed with current settings.

settings you are *not* saving the image of the graph itself, only a set of graph options that can be used to create graph images.

In this example, save the current settings under the name Monthly to match the table with which you originally used the settings. Because the current bundle of graph settings contains table specific titles, you will probably only use the settings with the Monthly table, or one that has a very similar structure. Enter

[F10] i g s
monthly ↵

Note that, unlike screen and report forms, graph files do not allow you to write a description of the contents to help you recall what they are used for. Like scripts, the only clue as to the use of the file is the file name that is limited to a maximum of 8 characters. The settings are now stored in a file called MONTHLY.G.

Resetting the Graph

Saving the graph settings in a file does not alter the current graph settings. Enter

[Ctrl-F7]

The graph displayed is exactly the same as the one shown in Figure 11-22 on page 412. These settings will stay in place until one of the following actions is taken.

❑ **Image Graph Modify.** You can use this command to make further alterations in the graph settings.

❑ **Exit.** When you exit Paradox, all the graph settings are lost. When you run the program again, the graph settings will return to the default settings.

❑ **Image Graph Reset.** This command has the same effect on graph settings as exiting Paradox. The current graph settings are discarded and the default settings are reestablished. The advantage of this command is that you are not forced to exit the program in order to return to the default settings.

Enter

[F10] i g r
o *(the letter O)*

Display the instant graph by entering

[Ctrl-F7]

The graph displayed now shows the default settings reflected in changes in the titles and in the Y axis display, Figure 11-23.

Return to the work area display by entering

↵

Restoring Stored Settings

Once a graph setting file has been stored, you can recall the settings with the command **Image Graph Load.** When this command is used, the settings stored in the selected file are transferred to the memory of the computer and become the active settings until they are modified, reset to the default, or another group of settings is loaded.

Suppose you want to display the Monthly graph again. First, display the table that contains the records and fields for the graph on the work area. Enter

[F10] v
monthly ↵

Place the cursor in a numeric field.

[Ctrl-End]

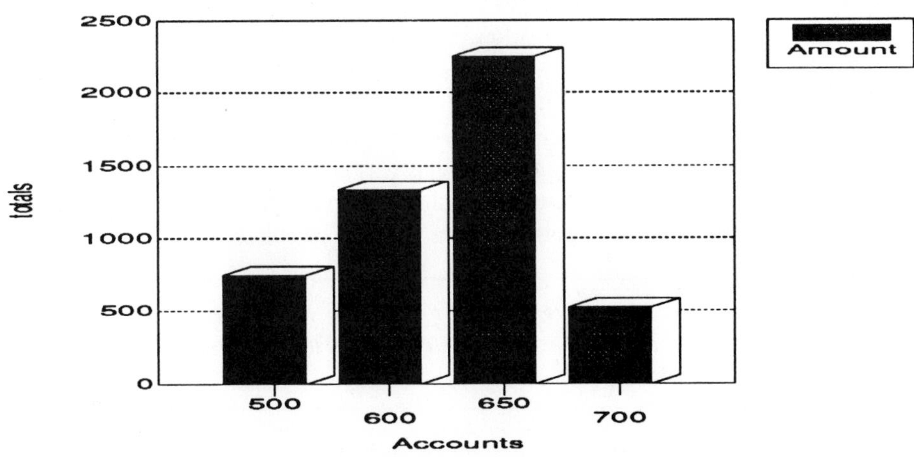

Figure 11-23 New tables graphed with current settings.

Load the graph settings that go with this table.

[F10] i g l
monthly ↵

Note that the loading of graph settings has no visible effect on the work area display. Use the instant graph command to generate a graph display.

[Ctrl-F7]

The graph produced is identical to the one in Figure 11-22 on page 405 demonstrating that you have recalled the graph settings from the file.

Return to the work area by entering

↵

Printing a Graph

Printing a graph requires that you play the Custom script and select the device or devices on which you want to print the graph. The most common device is a printer, but you can also select to output graphs to pen plotters or to special file formats.

Paradox allows you to select up to four devices for graph printing. This allows you the option of printing on a different printer or plotter without having to run the Custom script each time you want to change devices.

It is important to note that graphics output is more printer-specific than is text output. Text printing in Paradox is rather simple in that all the output is standard ASCII text. Paradox does not allow you to mix text styles, point sizes, or typeface fonts, such as you can in word processing programs. For that reason, most printers will operate correctly for text printing without having to make any sort of selection from the Custom script. Graph printing is quite another matter since there is no standard, such as ASCII, for graphics printing. Different printers can—and often do—use incompatible systems of printing graphics. For this reason you *cannot* print a Paradox graph unless you make a selection from the Custom script list of graphics printers. If your printer is not listed among the printers, there is no guarantee that you will be able to print graphs.

> *Many printers are designed to emulate the command set of popular printers. If your printer is not listed, check the printer manual to see if it emulates any other printers that do appear on the list.*

Graph Output Files

Paradox provides a means by which graphs can be output to a disk file. When you output a graph to a disk file you create a file, that contains the instructions needed for the selected printer to create the graph you see on the screen, more or less. Keep in mind the difference between a graph settings file created with the **Image Graph Save** command and a graph output file created with the **Image Graph ViewGraph File** command. The graph output file contains information about the actual graph image while the graph settings file contains a list of settings but no actual graph image. Most printers take much longer to print graphs than they do text. One advantage of creating graph output files is that you can store them on disk and send them to the printer at a later time, using a DOS utility such as PRINT.

However, in three cases, the output files can be used to transfer the image of a graph to another program such as a word processing or desktop publishing application that can integrate text and graphics. This occurs because the output file contains instructions in a graphics output language that can be understood by other applications. The three options follow.

❑ **Lotus PIC output.** If you select this option as one of the graph output devices, you can create a file containing a graph description in the *Lotus* PIC format. This is the same format as created by the *Lotus 1-2-3* command **Graph Save**. This file cannot be sent directly to a printer. It can, however, be read by programs that can display, manipulate, and print *Lotus 1-2-3* PIC graphs. Examples of such programs are *Microsoft Word 5.0, WordPerfect 5.0* and *5.1, Ventura Publisher* and *Aldus Pagemaker*.

❑ **Apple Laserwriter.** This selection causes Paradox to print graphs using the Postscript page description language. Postscript output can be send directly to a Postscript printer, such as an Apple Laserwriter. If output is to a file instead of to a printer, you can use that file as an EPS (encapsulated Postscript) graphics file. This file can be imported into programs such *Microsoft Word 5.0, WordPerfect 5.0* and *5.1, Ventura Publisher*, and *Aldus Pagemaker*. Note that EPS files created with graph file output from Paradox do not contain a bit-mapped image of the graph. This means that applications such as *Ventura Publisher* will display a blank frame when the graphic is viewed on the screen. The graph will appear correctly on the printed page.

❑ **HPGL Plotter.** Hewlett-Packard plotters use the HPGL (HP Graphics Language) to communicate with Hewlett-Packard plotters. *Microsoft Word 5.0* and *Ventura Publisher* can both read output files that are written in the HPGL format as graphics files.

Paradox offers you two ways to output graphic files in the PIC and EPS formats. One way is to select these options are printer devices and using the **Image Graph ViewGraph File** to output the graph to a file. Paradox also has a built-in command **Image Graph Modify Overall Device File** that allows you to choose output to an EPS or PIC file format. In terms of Postscript output, both methods create identical EPS files. If you want to use files in HPGL, you must define one of your printers as an HP plotter and output the printer format to the graphics file.

Note that the orientation of the page, found on the Overall PrinterLayout menu, will affect graphics output files. If you intend to integrate a Paradox graph in a desktop publishing document you should take into account the orientation of the document. For example, if you are using portrait-oriented pages in the desktop publishing application, you will probably want to output the Paradox graphs in a portrait orientation so that the top of the graph faces towards the top of the page when it is imported into the desktop application.

Selecting a Graph Printer

In order to print graphs, you must play the Custom script and select a graphics printer. Enter

[F10] s p
custom ↵

The Custom script asks if you are using a black and white or color monitor. Enter

y

Select **Graphs** from the main menu.

g

To select a printer, pick **Printers** by entering

p

Paradox displays a menu that lists four devices, 1stPrinter, 2ndPrinter, 3rdPrinter, and 4thPrinter, which you can define. Begin with 1stPrinter since this will be the default printer. Enter

1

Each printer has two options.

❑ **TypeOfPrinter.** This is the selection of the actual printer to be used from the list of available printers.

❑ **Settings.** This option allows you to select the input/output port for the printer and to select whether the printing should pause before starting a new page in order to allow you to place a new sheet of paper in the printer. By default, the printer port is LPT1 with continuous printing.

Display the list of printers by entering

t

Paradox lists the printers that it supports in a column on the right side of the screen, Figure 11-24. Select your printer by using the ↓ key to move the cursor to the name matching your printer, and press ↵. Paradox then displays a list of the models under the manufacturer that are supported. Select your model from the list if available and press ↵. Since many graphics printers can print graphs in several quality or density modes, Paradox will display a list of mode options, if available. Mode options are sometimes listed showing the dots-per-inch (dpi) rating, e.g. 120 x 72 dpi. Keep in mind that the higher the dpi, the finer and more detailed the graph. On the other hand, higher dpi generally increases the time required to print the graph. If your printer supports multiple density modes, you may want to define 1stPrinter as low density and 2ndPrinter as high density so that you can choose modes from the graph menu.

When you have completed the selection, you are returned to the menu. To save your printer selection, enter

r *(3 times)*
→ *(9 times)*
↵

If you are working on a network, select the Network option. Otherwise, enter

↵

Since you have made a change in the program configuration, Paradox exits to the operating system. To continue, you must now reload Paradox. Enter

paradox3 ↵

```
Move to the MANUFACTURER to be selected
Press [Enter] to select the MANUFACTURER; Press [Esc] for previous screen
 Selecting a Graphics printer
   PRINTER 1                             ALPS_
                                         Apple
   Choose a graphics printer from the    C. Itoh
   list at the right of the screen.      Calcomp
   First find the company that makes     Canon
   your printer, then the printer        Citizen
   model, and finally the mode.          Epson
                                         Fujitsu
   The current selection is listed       HP Printers
   in the fields below.                  HP Plotters
                                         IBM
                                         Lotus .PIC Output
   Manufacturer:                         Mannesmann Tally
   Apple                                 NEC
                                         Okidata
   Model:                                Olivetti
   Laserwriter                           Panasonic
                                         Quadram
   Mode:                                 Star Micronics
   PostScript                            Tandy
                                         Texas Instruments
                                              Press [PgDn] for more choices
```

Figure 11-24 Graphics printer selection menu.

Printing a Graph

With the printer selected, you can now print a graph. In this case, print the Monthly graph. First display the Monthly table and then load the matching graph settings. Enter

v
monthly ↵
[F10] i g l
monthly ↵

Place the cursor in a numeric field column by entering

[Ctrl-End]

Print the graph by entering

[F10] i g v p

Paradox outputs the graph to the printer. using the printer you selected during the Custom configuration.

Slide Show Scripts

Paradox charts can be displayed in an automatic sequence like a slide show by using a script to select tables and graph settings in order to display a series of graphs. You can use the **Wait** command to automatically display the graph for a specified number of seconds before going on to the next graph so that no keystrokes are needed when viewing the slide show.

Creating a Slide Show

As an example of this type of script, you can use the two tables created earlier in this chapter—Expenses and Monthly—as the basis of a slide show. Begin by defining graph settings for the Expenses table.

Place the Expenses table on the work area by entering

[F10] v
expenses ↵

Place the cursor in the numeric field by entering

[Ctrl-End]

In the slide show, you will show this table in two different ways: as a bar chart and as a pie chart. Begin with the bar chart by changing the graph type to 3-D bar. Enter

[F10] i g m
[F10] t 3

In order to make the slide show automatic, select a display duration of five seconds using the **Overall Wait** command. Enter

[F10] o w

By default, the graph is displayed until a keystroke is entered. In this case, set the display for a **Duration** of five seconds. Enter

d 5 ↵

The next step is to create a graph settings file that will store the current batch of graph settings. Enter

[F2] [F10] i g s

Call these settings EXP_BAR (expenses bar graph).

exp_bar ↵

Note that it is not necessary to display the graph during this process. If you are not sure of what the graph will look like you may want to view it at some point in the process.

Change the graph type to a pie. Enter

[F10] i g m
[F10] t p

Save this graph setting in a file called EXP_PIE (Expenses pie graph) by entering

[F2] [F10] i g s
exp_pie ↵

The Monthly table already has a graph settings file. However, you will want to load and modify that file so that it will use a five-second duration instead of waiting for a keystroke to clear the screen. Keep in mind that you can make changes to the Monthly graph settings file without having the Monthly table on the work area. Recall that there is no actual link between the settings and the table. They are related only because you have decided that they should be used together as a pair. Paradox is not involved in that relationship. Load the Monthly settings file by entering

[F10] i g l
monthly ↵

Set this graph for a five-second display duration by entering

[F10] i g m
[F10] o w d
r ↵

Save the modified graph settings by entering

[F2] [F10] i g s
monthly ↵

Because MONTHLY.G already exists, Paradox asks if you want to replace that file with the current graph settings. In this case you do, so enter

r

The stage is now set to create a slide show. You have three graphs that you want to present. Each is set to display for five seconds, making the overall duration of the slide show fifteen seconds.

Writing a Slide Show Script

The slide show is actually created by a script. In this case, you will create the script from scratch by writing in all of the commands needed to display the three graphs. The script will be called SLIDESHW. Enter

[F10] s e w
slideshw ↵

As with most scripts, you will want to begin with a clear work area. Begin with the CLEARALL command.

CLEARALL ↵

You are ready now to display the first graph. In this case, display the Monthly graph. The first step in displaying a graph is to place the table that you want to use as the data for the graph onto the work area. Tables can be displayed using the PAL command **VIEW** followed by the name of the table. In this case, the table name is *Monthly*. Note that in PAL commands, file names are entered in quotation marks. Also remember that you need to place the cursor in a numeric field in order to display a graph for that table. The command word **CTRLEND** performs the action of the [Ctrl-End] key. Enter

VIEW "monthly" CTRLEND ↵

Note that you can put more than one command on a line if you desire. The ↵ at the end of the line is entered only to make the script easier to read.

Before you display the graph, you must load the graph settings file from the disk. PAL does not have a specific command for this action so you can enter it as a series of key commands. Recall that menu options or file name selections are enclosed in { }. Enter

MENU {image} {graph} {load} {monthly} ↵

Display the graph by using the PAL equivalent of the [Ctrl-F7] key, **GRAPHKEY. Enter**

GRAPHKEY ↵

The script should now read as follows:

```
CLEARALL
VIEW ''monthly'' CTRLEND
MENU {image} {graph} {load} {monthly}
GRAPHKEY
```

The next graph requires you to view the Expenses table. Place the table on the work area and move the cursor to the last field by entering

VIEW "expenses" CTRLEND ↵

The first graph will be the bar graph of expenses. Load that graph settings file.

MENU {image} {graph} {load} {exp_bar}

Display the graph with the next command.

GRAPHKEY ↵

The last graph is the pie chart. Since it uses the current table, Expenses, all you need to do is to change graph settings files. Enter

MENU {image} {graph} {load} {exp_Pie}
GRAPHKEY ↵

The next command is a **CLEARALL** command to remove the tables from the work area.

CLEARALL

There is still one operation left to perform. The current set of graph settings are those loaded from the EXP_PIE file. It is always a good habit to return the program to the state that it was before the script began. This means that you should reset the graph to the default values using the **Image Graph Reset** command. Enter

MENU {image} {graph} {reset} {ok}

The script now reads as follows:

```
CLEARALL
VIEW "monthly" CTRLEND
MENU {image} {graph} {load} {monthly}
GRAPHKEY
VIEW "expenses" CTRLEND
MENU {image} {graph} {load} {exp_bar}
GRAPHKEY
MENU {image} {graph} {load} {exp_pie}
GRAPHKEY
CLEARALL
MENU {image} {graph} {reset} {ok}
```

Save and play the script by entering

[F10] g

The graphs are displayed for five seconds each. Following the last graph, the empty work area is displayed.

Cross Tabulations

A *cross tabulation* is really a special type of table that summarizes a table in a way that is not easily achieved through query form operations. Cross tabulations are associated with graphs because they summarize tables in a way that fits well with the X and Y axis orientation of graphs. However, a cross tabulation may be performed for its own sake in order to produce a summary database table.

A cross tabulation is a special type of summary because it generates values based on the intersection of two classifications. This may sound complicated but an example will make the operation more clear. You have noticed that certain fields are included in a table in order to summarize the records in the table. The *Period* field allows you to generate summary values based on the monthly periods such as those stored in the Monthly table. On the other hand, the *Acct#* field can generate totals based on the accounts assigned to each check. But suppose you wanted to cross reference the *Acct#* and the *Period* field so that you would get monthly summary for each of the account numbers. The best way to express this type of summary would be to create a table in which the each field represented a specific account number and each record began with the name of a month, Figure 11-25. The table produced by a cross tabulation is similar to a table in a financial spreadsheet application such as *Lotus 1-2-3* in which the significance of the value is determined by its row (record) and column (field) position.

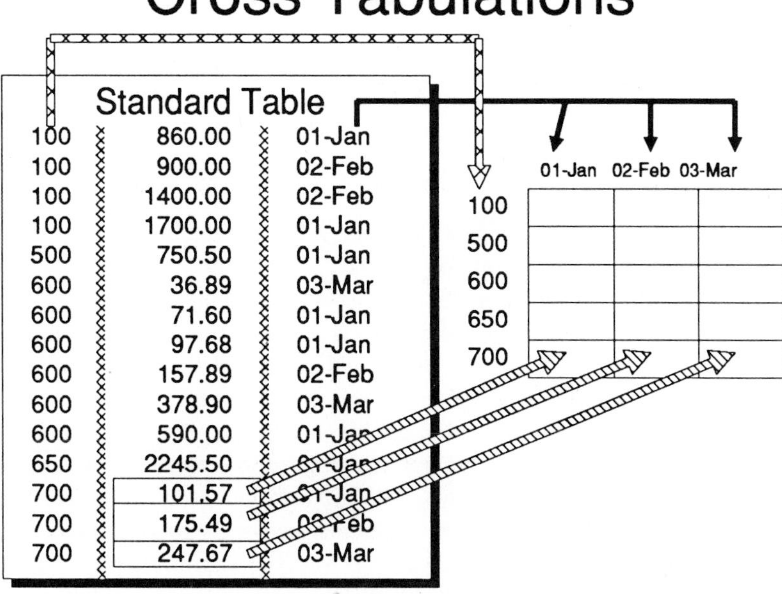

Figure 11-25 Cross tabulation type table generation.

A cross tabulation uses three fields from the original table to construct the CROSSTAB table generated by the **Image Graph Crosstab** command. One field is assigned as the *row labels* and another as the *column labels*. These fields can be date, alpha, or numeric. They should also be fields that contain repetitive values that are summarized in the cross tabulation.

The third field must be a numeric field because it is one that will be summarized in the cross tabulation table. Paradox can summarize values by sum, count, or average. Cross tabulation can also be used to select the highest or lowest values in each category.

The size and structure of a cross tabulation table will be different from the original table. The cross tabulation table will have one row for each unique value in the *row label* field. The field selected as the *column labels* will be used to generate the field in the cross tabulation table. There will be a new field added for each unique value in the *column label* field.

For example, suppose that the *Acct#* field was selected as the row label field and the *Period* field was selected as the *column label* field.

The cross tabulation table created would contain five rows: one for each unique account number (100, 550, 600, 650, and 700.) Paradox automatically designates the row label field as a key field in the CROSSTAB table.

The table would contain four fields. The first field would be the *row label* field, in this case *Acct #*. The remainder of the fields would be generated by the unique values in the *Period* field: 01-Jan, 02-Feb, and 03-Mar.

Paradox would then generate fifteen values, five rows by three columns, based on all of the possible combinations of account number and period. If there were no records for a particular combination the field would contain zero, not a blank.

Cross tabulations assume that the field designated as the *row label* field is positioned to the *right* of the fields that you will select for the *column label* and *value* fields for the cross tabulation. Further, Paradox assumes that all of the fields to the left of the *row label* field should be included as part of the row label designation. This is not always the case. In order to prepare for a cross tabulation, it may be necessary to change the order of the fields using the [Ctrl-r] command. It may also be necessary to create an Answer table that contains only selected fields in order to produce the cross tabulation you desire.

If you have a key field designated in the table, it will have a significant effect on the cross tabulation. Key fields are automatically included in cross tabulation tables because they are by definition placed to the left of all of the other fields in a table, and will automatically be included as part of the row label designations. The result will always be that the Crosstab table will have the same number of records as the original table because the key field in any table *must* contain unique values. In most cases you would need to create an Answer table, which does not include the key field, and generate CROSSTAB from it rather than the original table.

If you are working with a table that contains raw data such as Ck_book, chances are that you will have to create an intermediate Answer table before you can effectively perform a cross tabulation.

Cross tabulations are associated with graphs because they conform to the horizontal and vertical axes of a graph. The row labels, beginning in the left most field in the CROSSTAB table become the X axis categories. Each of the remaining fields becomes a data series in the graph.

As a general rule, you should select fields in a cross tabulation that generate a table that has more rows than columns. This is because a Paradox graph is limited to six data series, i.e., six columns of numeric field information. Graphs tend to be easier to read when there are more data points than data series.

In preparing a cross tabulation table that will be used to generate a graph, it is important to keep in mind that the function of the graph is to communicate an idea visually, one which is not as apparent when you simply read the values from a table. With that in mind, your steps in preparing a cross tabulation should be planned to produce as simple a graph as possible that contains the desired information. The more complicated the graph, the less likely a reader will be to understand what it is you are trying to illustrate.

As a general rule, graphs cannot convey as much detailed information as can tables of figures. For example, fields that include values that are of widely different orders of magnitude are difficult to graph well. A field that contains values from 1 to 10,000 would have a Y axis scale of 0 to 10,000. Such a scale would make values under 1,000 so small that they would not appear at all. This may create an incorrect impression. If possible, it might create a better graph if you consolidated some of the categories with small values into a single category called Other that would show up on the overall scale of the graph.

You can use Paradox query form operations to manipulate the raw data in your tables into a form that will make an effective graph presentation.

Keep in mind that it is possible to generate Crosstab tables that have more than six value columns. This means that you will have to select the values that you want to appear on the graph.

> *Cross tabulation operations are usually associated with graphs. However, there is no reason why you would not use cross tabulation tables in printed reports without graphs. Cross tabulations often eliminate the need to transfer data into a spreadsheet program such as Lotus 1-2-3, since the CROSSTAB table resembles a financial spreadsheet.*

The CROSSTAB table is a temporary Paradox table that will be overwritten the next time you perform a cross tabulation. The table is automatically erased when you exit Paradox. To preserve the table, use the **Tools Rename Table** command to give the table a unique name.

Preparing a Cross Tabulation

In most cases, it will be necessary to prepare a table for cross tabulation processing. The preparation can be achieved by creating a query form that will process the raw data from the table into a form that will fit well into the constraints imposed on cross tabulation processing. In some cases, you may have to use several stages of processing to get the organization you desire. The example in this case would be a graph expressing the cross tabulation of the *Acct #* and *Period* fields. There are two problems that you need to overcome in order to create the cross tabulation table for graphing.

❑ **Consolidate Deposits and Amounts.** In the Ck_book table, values for account 100 appear in the *Deposit* field while all of the rest of the accounts use the *Amount* field. In the cross tabulation, it is not necessary to distinguish between positive (deposits) and negative (check) amounts. What is needed is a single field for all values.

❑ **Eliminate Key Field.** The Ck_book table uses *Check #* as the key field. Any cross tabulation generated directly from this table would automatically include the *Check #*, causing Paradox not to consolidate rows based on the row label field, e.g., *Acct #*, but to produce one row label for each check number.

This cross tabulation process must begin with a query form that will draw only the required data from the Ck_book table. Enter

a
ck_book ↵

Include the *Acct #* field in the Answer table by placing a √ in that field column. Enter

[Tab] ***(2 times)***
[F6]

Add the *Period* field by entering

[Ctrl-End] [F6]

What field should be used to supply the values? The answer is that the values must come from a combination of the *Amount* and *Deposit* fields. This can be accomplished by writing a calculation formula.

Since the formula will need values from the *Amount* and *Deposit* fields, you will need to create example names for those fields. In this example call *Amount* **y** and *Deposit* **x.** Enter

← ***(2 times)***
[F5] x
← ***(5 times)***
[F5] y

The formula for the sum of the fields would be **calc x+y.** Enter

,calc
[spacebar] [F5]
x+
[F5] y

Process the query by entering

[F2]

The result is an Answer table that contains just the information required to create the cross tabulation, Figure 11-26.

ANSWER	Acct #	Period	Deposit + Amount
1	100	01-Jan	860.00
2	100	01-Jan	1,700.00
3	100	02-Feb	900.00
4	100	02-Feb	1,400.00
5	500	01-Jan	750.50
6	600	01-Jan	71.60
7	600	01-Jan	97.68
8	600	01-Jan	590.00
9	600	02-Feb	157.89
10	600	03-Mar	36.89
11	600	03-Mar	378.90
12	650	01-Jan	2,245.50
13	700	01-Jan	101.57
14	700	02-Feb	247.67
15	700	03-Mar	175.49

Figure 11-26 Table prepared for cross tabulation.

Generating the CROSSTAB Table

Once you have organized a table that contains the data you wish to cross tabulate, you can generate the CROSSTAB table in two ways.

❑ **Image Graph Crosstab.** This command is used to generate the cross tabulation table by making selections from menus. You begin by selecting the type of cross tabulation calculation (sum, count, max, or min) that you want to carry out. You next indicate by cursor movement the fields to be used for row labels, column labels, and values.

❑ **[Alt-x].** This key command allows you to generate a cross tabulation with a single keystroke, assuming that you have a table in which the fields are properly arranged. First, the cursor is positioned in a field that will be used for the row labels. The field that contains the values to be cross tabulated *must* be the *last* field in the table. In addition, column label field *must* be the field to the *left* of the last field. Note that the current Answer table fits these conditions. Keep in mind that this shortcut always produces **sum** calculations.

Because of the arrangement of the Answer table, you can use the shortcut method, [Alt-x]. Position the cursor in the field, *Acct #*, that will be used to generate the row labels. Enter

[Tab]

Generate the cross tabulation table by entering

[Alt-x]

Paradox generates a cross tabulation table with five records, one for each unique value in the *Acct #* field, and four fields. The last three fields begin the cross tabulation values for each unique value in the *Period* field, Figure 11-27.

CROSSTAB	Acct #	01-Jan	02-Feb	03-Mar
1	100	2,560.00	2,300.00	0.00
2	500	750.50	0.00	0.00
3	600	759.28	157.89	415.79
4	650	2,245.50	0.00	0.00
5	700	101.57	247.67	175.49

Figure 11-27 CROSSTAB table generated.

Note that the cursor is not positioned in the record number column but in the first numeric column. This adjustment is automatically made by Paradox to facilitate the creation of a graph. In this case, use the instant graph command to generate a graph with the default settings. Enter

[Ctrl-F7]

The graph, stacked bar by default, displays the data generated by the cross tabulation process. See Figure 11-28.

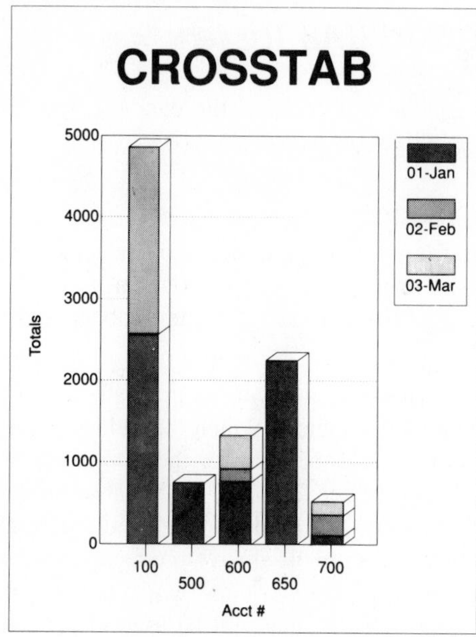

Figure 11-28 Graph of CROSSTAB table.

Exit Paradox by entering

[F10] e y

Summary

This chapter discussed the creation and modification of graphs based on data stored in Paradox tables.

❑ **Graphs.** A graph is a pictorial representation of information. Paradox can create standard business graphs such as bar graphs, line graphs, area graphs, and pie charts based on the data stored in Paradox tables. Not all tables are suitable for graphing. Paradox follows a built-in set of rules that it uses to interpret a table in the form of a graph.

❑ **Instant Graphs.** Paradox will generate a graph from the data in the current table when you enter the command [Ctrl-F7]. The cursor must be in a numeric field when the command is entered. Paradox uses the first non-numeric field or the key field as the X axis categories. The numeric fields are used to create up to six data series that are plotted against the Y axis of the graph. Pie charts can display only one data series at a time. If there are more than six numeric fields in a table, only the first six are displayed on the graph.

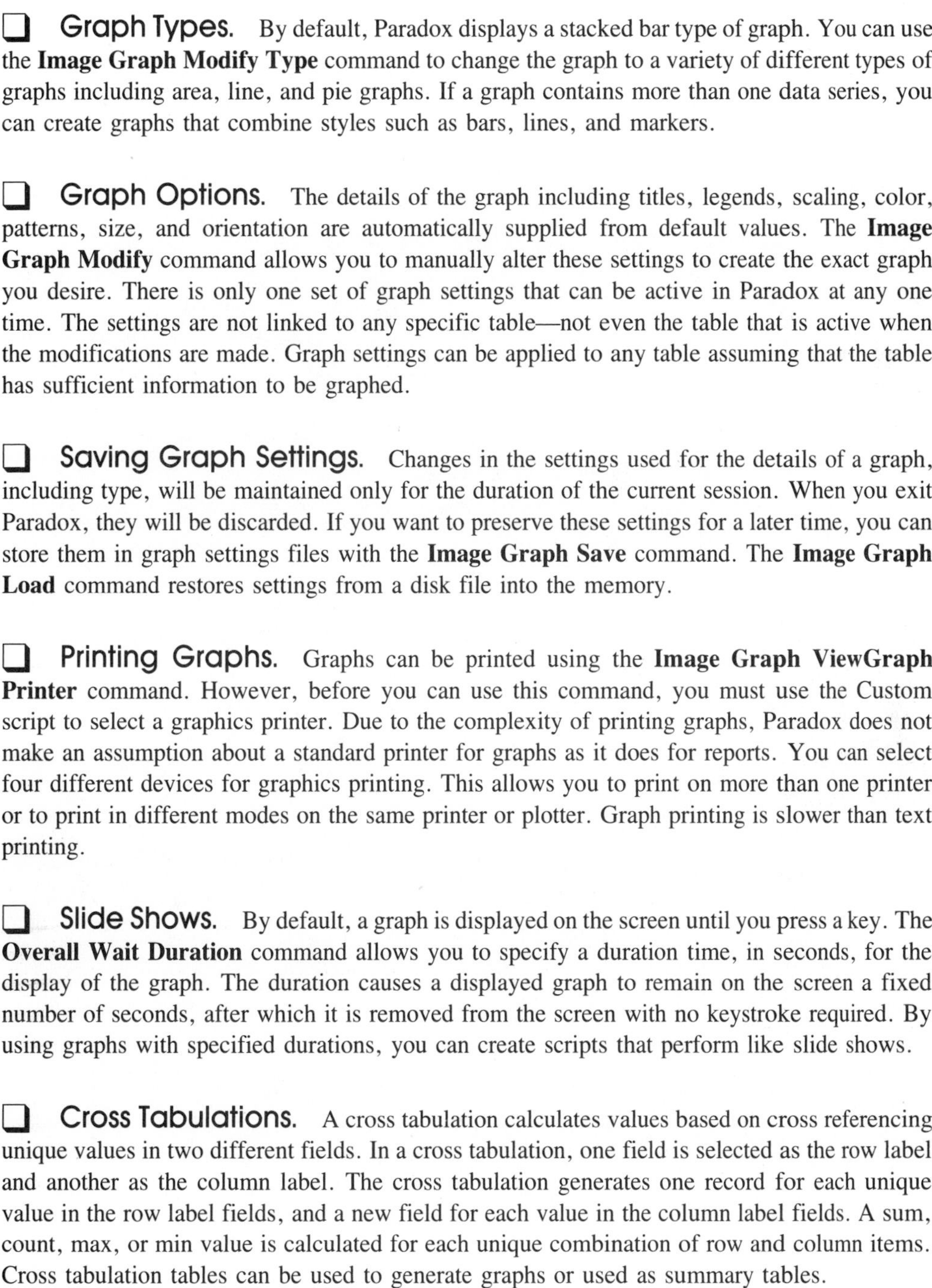

❑ **Graph Types.** By default, Paradox displays a stacked bar type of graph. You can use the **Image Graph Modify Type** command to change the graph to a variety of different types of graphs including area, line, and pie graphs. If a graph contains more than one data series, you can create graphs that combine styles such as bars, lines, and markers.

❑ **Graph Options.** The details of the graph including titles, legends, scaling, color, patterns, size, and orientation are automatically supplied from default values. The **Image Graph Modify** command allows you to manually alter these settings to create the exact graph you desire. There is only one set of graph settings that can be active in Paradox at any one time. The settings are not linked to any specific table—not even the table that is active when the modifications are made. Graph settings can be applied to any table assuming that the table has sufficient information to be graphed.

❑ **Saving Graph Settings.** Changes in the settings used for the details of a graph, including type, will be maintained only for the duration of the current session. When you exit Paradox, they will be discarded. If you want to preserve these settings for a later time, you can store them in graph settings files with the **Image Graph Save** command. The **Image Graph Load** command restores settings from a disk file into the memory.

❑ **Printing Graphs.** Graphs can be printed using the **Image Graph ViewGraph Printer** command. However, before you can use this command, you must use the Custom script to select a graphics printer. Due to the complexity of printing graphs, Paradox does not make an assumption about a standard printer for graphs as it does for reports. You can select four different devices for graphics printing. This allows you to print on more than one printer or to print in different modes on the same printer or plotter. Graph printing is slower than text printing.

❑ **Slide Shows.** By default, a graph is displayed on the screen until you press a key. The **Overall Wait Duration** command allows you to specify a duration time, in seconds, for the display of the graph. The duration causes a displayed graph to remain on the screen a fixed number of seconds, after which it is removed from the screen with no keystroke required. By using graphs with specified durations, you can create scripts that perform like slide shows.

❑ **Cross Tabulations.** A cross tabulation calculates values based on cross referencing unique values in two different fields. In a cross tabulation, one field is selected as the row label and another as the column label. The cross tabulation generates one record for each unique value in the row label fields, and a new field for each value in the column label fields. A sum, count, max, or min value is calculated for each unique combination of row and column items. Cross tabulation tables can be used to generate graphs or used as summary tables.

12

Printing Labels and Free-Form Reports

This chapter deals with a special problem in Paradox, relating to printing information in forms other than column-oriented reports or graphs. The example discussed involves printing mailing labels and mailing lists. However, the concepts introduced in this chapter can be applied to a variety of printing problems that require you to print data in forms other than report formats.

Creating the Mail List

In order to understand the printing of forms, including mailing labels, you must create a new table called Mail. Begin by loading Paradox in the usual manner.

Making the Mail List Table

Create the new table by entering

> **c**
> **mail** ↵

Enter the fields for this table as follows.

Last ↵
A15* ↵
First ↵
A15 ↵
Title ↵
A3
Street ↵
A30 ↵
Apt ↵
A20 ↵
City ↵
A20 ↵
State ↵
A2 ↵
Zip ↵
A5 ↵

The structure should look like Figure 12-1.

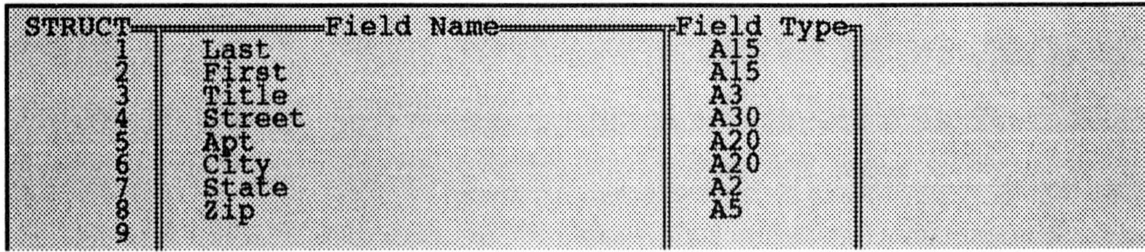

STRUCT	Field Name	Field Type
1	Last	A15
2	First	A15
3	Title	A3
4	Street	A30
5	Apt	A20
6	City	A20
7	State	A2
8	Zip	A5
9		

Figure 12-1 Structure of Mail table.

Save the structure by entering

[F2]

Adding Records

The next step is to enter the records. In this example, you will enter five records into the table. Because this is only an example, you can duplicate the effect of a larger mailing list by simply duplicating the records a number of times.

Activate the data entry mode for the Mail table by entering

m d
mail ↵

Enter the following five records.

Record 1
Last Flynn
First Gerri
Title Mrs
Street 18 Corsica Drive
Apt Suite 2000
City Concord
State MA
Zip 01602

Record 2
Last Kurnick
First Sarah
Title Ms
Street 12000 Washington Pike
Apt
City Tuscon
State AZ
Zip 85717

Record 3
Last LaFish
First Walter
Title Mr
Street 4830 Milano Way
Apt Apt. 45
City Walnut Creek
State CA
Zip 94596

Record 4
Last Litman
First Ira
Title Mr
Street 1790 Woodpark Lane
Apt
City Philadelphia
State PA
Zip 19115

Record 5
Last Waldov
First Joan
Title Mrs
Street 45 Pleasant Hill Road
Apt
City Shrewsbury
State MA
Zip 01680

Save the table by entering

[F2]

Multiple Records

In order to create a larger table without having to take the time to enter more records, use the **Copy** and **Add** commands on the Tools menu to add duplicates of the first five records to the current table. Begin by creating a duplicate of the current table using the **Tools Copy Table** command.

[F10] t c t
↵ *(2 times)*
dup ↵

The next command adds the records in the Dup table back into the Mail table, doubling the number of records from five to ten. Since you will want to repeat this command several times, record it as a script. Turn on the script recording

[Alt-F10]
b
dup ↵

Enter the command that copies records from the Dup table to the Mail table. Enter

[F10] t m a
dup ↵
mail ↵

The size of the Mail table doubles. Stop the script recording by entering

[Alt-F10] e

You can use the **Scripts RepeatPlay** command to execute the Dup script a specified number of times. In this case, run the script six times by entering

[F10] s r
dup ↵
6 ↵

The result is a Mail table that now contains 40 records. You now have a database from which you can design mailing labels. Clear the work area by entering

[Alt-F8]

Mailing Label Design

In Paradox, mailing labels are printed using a *free-form* report. In free-form reports, the Table band is not organized in columns but has fields placed in it at any location, just as you can place fields or text at any location in other bands.

Free-form reports can be used to generate a wide variety of printed material, only one of which is mailing labels. Labels are interesting because they are the most common output from databases. They also illustrate how reports can be altered to print data on forms or pages that are not simply 8.5″ by 11″ sheets of paper.

The task of printing mailing labels differs from the column reports created in Chapter 7 in two fundamental respects.

❑ **Free-Form Layout.** A free-form layout is one in which the fields and text are not arranged in column and row format. The fields and text can be spread horizontally or vertically to any location on the page.

❑ **Nonstandard forms.** Information printed in label form can be printed on standard sheets of paper. However, often the printing is performed on nonstandard forms such as continuous sheets of prepasted labels. In these reports, you will need to learn how to alter the form width and height factors to achieve the desired output.

Since the actual type of form being used in the printer has a significant effect on how you construct a label report, you will create two types of label reports. The first is for dot matrix printers that can use continuous form labels. The second is for laser printers that use full-sheet copier labels.

Continuous Form Labels on Dot Matrix Printers

The first type of label report to create is one for continuous form labels, typically used with dot matrix (or daisy wheel) printers. These labels are supplied on a continuous form paper that has tractor feed pinholes punched through the backing so that it can be accurately feed through the printer. The most common size of mailing label is 3.5″ by 15/16″. The height of 15/16″ may seem a very odd size for a label. However, when labels are placed on this type of backing, it is not the height of the label that counts but the distance between the top of one label and the top of the next. That distance is one inch, Figure 12-2.

Since most printers will print six lines per vertical inch, this means that each mailing label consists of six lines: five that can contain information and a sixth that includes the 1/16″ gap between the bottom of one label and the top of the next label.

> *If your printer is not equipped with a tractor feed mechanism, you will find that continuous form labels will not feed accurately using the friction feed rollers. The rollers are sufficient to feed individual sheets of paper but will not be able to maintain an accurate alignment for more than a dozen or so labels.*

Creating a Free-Form Report

Begin the process of creating a mailing label report by selecting the Free form option from the Report Design menu. Enter

r d
mail ↵
→ ↵
Mailing Labels ↵

Select a free-form report by entering

f

Paradox generates the default free-form report layout, Figure 12-3. Like the column type report, it is divided into bands: Report Header and Page Header. Instead of a Table band, free-form reports have a Form band.

The Page Header band contains six lines, of which all but the fourth are blank. The fourth line contains the current date, the title of the report, and the page number.

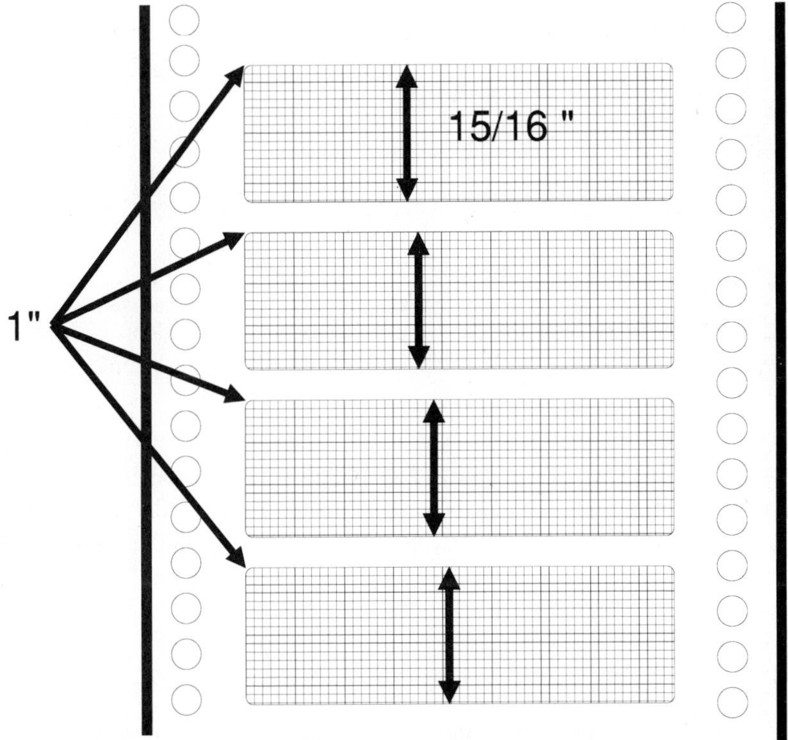

Figure 12-2 Mailing labels on continuous form backing.

By default, this band contains what looks like a list of fields. The name of each field is written in the order of the table's structure, down the left side of the Form band. The name is followed by a colon and the output area for the corresponding field.

What sort of report would this current layout generate? The answer is that the information from the fields would print repeatedly on each page until it was filled with records, Figure 12-4.

The current report is inadequate for printing labels for several reasons.

❑ **Form Band Too Large.** The Form band uses one line for each field and adds a blank line before the first and after the last record. Since the label form is limited to a specific number of lines—in this example, six—the fields must be rearranged to fit into the space.

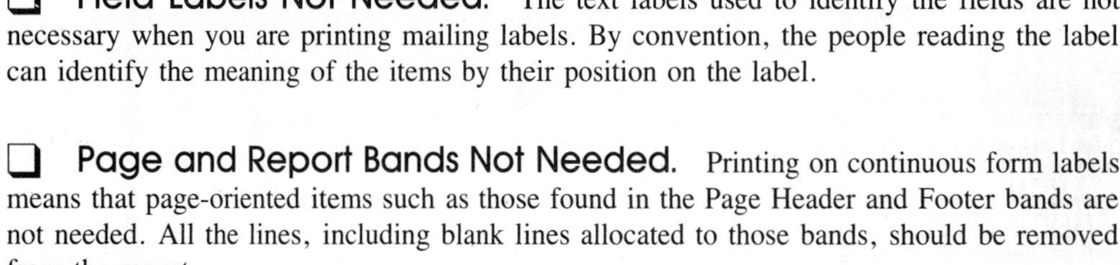

Figure 12-3 Default free-form report layout.

❑ **Field Labels Not Needed.** The text labels used to identify the fields are not necessary when you are printing mailing labels. By convention, the people reading the label can identify the meaning of the items by their position on the label.

❑ **Page and Report Bands Not Needed.** Printing on continuous form labels means that page-oriented items such as those found in the Page Header and Footer bands are not needed. All the lines, including blank lines allocated to those bands, should be removed from the report.

Compressing the Report

The first task is to delete all the lines in the default report layout since they do not apply to the type of report you want to generate. Begin by removing the blank line in the Report Header band by entering

[Ctrl-y]

Move to the Page Header band and remove the lines from this band.

↓
[Ctrl-y] ***(6 times)***

Move next to the Form band and remove all the fields and text. Enter

↓ ***(2 times)***
[Ctrl-y] ***(8 times)***

```
2/13/90                          Mailing Labels                        Page    1


Last: Flynn
First: Gerri
Title: Mrs
Street: 18 Corsica Drive
Apt: Suite 2000
City: Concord
State: MA
Zip: 01602


Last: Kurnick
First: Sarah
Title: Ms
Street: 12000 Washington Pike
Apt:
City: Tuscon
State: AZ
Zip: 85717


Last: LaFish
First: Walter
Title: Mr
Street: 4830 Milano Way
Apt: Apt. 45
City: Walnut Creek
State: CA
Zip: 94596


Last: Litman
First: Ira
Title: Mr
Street: 1790 Woodpark Lane
Apt:
City: Philadelphia
State: PA
Zip: 19115


Last: Waldov
First: Joan
Title: Mrs
Street: 45 Pleasant Hill Road
Apt:
City: Shrewsbury
State: MA
Zip: 01680
```

Figure 12-4 Report generated by default layout.

This leaves the report with two blank lines in the Form band. Since the mailing label height is effectively one inch, i.e., six lines, fill out the rest of the Form band by inserting four blank lines. Recall that you must place Paradox into the Insert mode to add the blank lines.

> **[Ins]**
> ↵ ***(4 times)***

The Page and Report footer bands still contain additional blanks. Remove these lines by entering

↓ ***(2 times)***
[Ctrl-y] ***(4 times)***
↓
[Ctrl-y]

The report bands are now adjusted to printing continuous form labels, Figure 12-5.

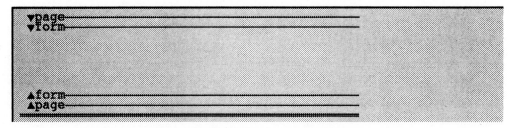

Figure 12-5 Bands adjusted to print continuous form labels.

Continuous Form Page Length

When you are printing reports on non-page-oriented continuous forms such as mailing labels, the page-length settings should be changed from a value, e.g., 66 lines, to the letter C indicating that the printing will be continuous without the need for page breaks or form feeds. This is accomplished with the **Setting PageLayout** command. Enter

[F10] s p

Select the **Length** option.

l *(the letter L)*

The default value is 66 lines. Note that in Paradox the length of the page is defined not in inches but in the number of lines printed on the page. The assumption is made that your printer is printing 6 lines per vertical inch, making an 11″ sheet of paper 66 lines in length.

> *It is rare, though possible, that your printer is set to print at a different number of lines per inch, e.g., 8 lines.*

In this example, you will want to set the page length to C for continuous printing. Selecting C turns off the Page break options. Enter

[Ctrl-backspace]
c ↵

The C option for page length would cause the Page Header or Page Footer bands, should they be used, to print only once at the beginning and the end of the report—in effect, operating the same way as the Report Header and Footer bands.

Placing the Fields

The next task is to place the fields into the form band in the format that matches the way mailing labels should be structured. With mailing labels, the structure is determined by custom—in which the name, address, city, state, and zip codes are always placed onto a label in the same way.

> ↑ ***(7 times)***

There are eight fields in the Mail table. All of the fields of the mailing labels will be placed onto the report without the addition of labels for the field. This means a series of eight **Field Place Regular** commands will place one field each time. In order to speed this process, use the Instant script feature to assign the **Field Place Regular** command to the [Alt-F4] key.

The first field to place in the mailing label is the *Title* field. Turn on the Instant script record mode by entering

> **[Alt-F3]**

Enter the **Field Place Regular** command.

> **[F10] f p r**

Before selecting the field to place, stop the Instant script recording at this point. Use the PAL menu, [Alt-F10]. Enter

> **[Alt-F10] e**

Complete the current command by selecting the field to place. In this example, select *Title* by entering *T* because it is the only field on the list beginning with this letter. Enter

> **t**
> ↵ ***(2 times)***

Adding Literals

The *Title* field contains the abbreviation of the person's title, e.g., Mr., Mrs., Dr., or Ms. The period that follows the abbreviation was not entered in the *Title* field but it can be added as part of the label form. The period is a constant literal value that will appear on each label following the *Title* field. Items like the period are best added as part of the label form, not as part of the database table field, since you would have to enter the period in each record in contrast to entering it once on the label report form.

The same is true of other constants. For example, if your mailing list includes only residents of a single state, e.g., California, there would be no purpose in having a *State* field since you could enter the state, CA, as part of the label form. In some cases, the same may be true of the zip code and it can be placed on the label rather than in a field.

Add the period to the label form by entering

→
. *(period)*

Place the *First* field next to the *Title* field separated by a single space. Enter

→

Instead of entering the **Field Place Regular** command, use the instant script by entering the [Alt-F4] command.

[Alt-F4]

You are now at the Field Selection menu. Select the *First* field by entering

f
↵ ***(2 times)***

Repeat the process to add the *Last* field to the same line of the label report form.

→ ***(2 times)***
[Alt-F4]
l *(the letter L)*
↵ ***(2 times)***

You have now placed the *Title, First,* and *Last* fields on the first line of the label. Place the street address on the second line.

[Ctrl-Home]
↓
[Alt-F4]
→ ***(4 times)***
↵ ***(3 times)***

The next line in the label is for the *Apt* field. Enter

[Ctrl-Home]
↓
[Alt-F4] a
↵ ***(2 times)***

The remainder of the fields, *City*, *State,* and *Zip* will be placed on the next line of the label form. Enter

[Ctrl-Home]
↓
[Alt-F4] c
↵ ***(2 times)***

The *City* field should be followed by two literal characters, a comma and a space, which separate the city from the state. Enter

→
, *(comma)*
[spacebar]

Insert the *State* field next.

[Alt-F4]
[End] ←
↵ ***(3 times)***

Finally, place the *Zip* field next to the *State* field.

→ ***(2 times)***
[Alt-F4] z
↵ ***(2 times)***

You have now placed the fields into the proper locations on the report form, Figure 12-6. Note that there are still two blank lines at the bottom of the form. These blank lines are impor-

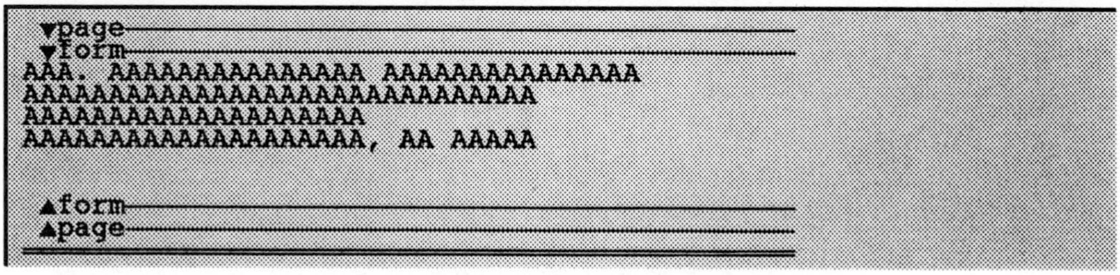

```
 ▼page
 ▼form
AAA. AAAAAAAAAAAAAAA AAAAAAAAAAAAAAA
AAAAAAAAAAAAAAAAAAAAAAAAAAAAAA
AAAAAAAAAAAAAAAAAAAA
AAAAAAAAAAAAAAAAAAAA, AA AAAAA

 ▲form
 ▲page
```

Figure 12-6 Fields placed in label form report.

tant because they will cause the label to move a full six lines, i.e., one inch vertically, for each record that prints, ensuring that the next record is printed beginning at the top of the next label.

Output a sample of the label form to the screen in order to evaluate the label report form. Enter

[F10] o s

The screen displays the first of several records that will print as a result of the report form, Figure 12-7.

In looking at the report as shown on the screen, notice that the labels may not appear as you expect them to. The fields appear too spread out both horizontally and vertically. This is a result of two factors.

❑ **Trailing and Leading Blanks.** Most fields, especially those used in mailing label type applications, are seldom filled completely. This means that in alpha fields there will be *trailing* blanks that fill up the remainder of the field. These trailing blanks will appear as gaps between the fields. In column arrangements, trailing blanks serve to maintain column alignment. In free-form reports, these gaps are often undesired since they make the labels *look* as though like they were generated by a computer.

> *If you are using numeric fields in a label report, the blanks will appear to the left of the numeric field. These are called* leading *blanks.*

```
Now Viewing Page 1 of Page Width 1
Press any key to continue...
Mrs. Gerri           Flynn
18 Corsica Drive
Suite 2000
Concord              , MA 01602


Ms . Sarah           Kurnick
12000 Washington Pike

Tuscon               , AZ 85717


Mr . Walter          LaFish
4830 Milano Way
Apt. 45
Walnut Creek         , CA 94596


Mr . Ira             Litman
1790 Woodpark Lane
```

Figure 12-7 Label report form output on screen.

❑ **Blank Lines.** The *Apt* field is used as an optional line in the address. Many labels can be filled in without this additional line since the *Apt* field is blank. However, since you have placed the *Apt* field on a line by itself in the report form, Paradox will print a blank line when the field is blank. This creates a gap on many of the labels between the street address and the city, state, and zip line.

Exit the screen display of the labels by entering

[Ctrl-break] ***(3 times)***

Suppressing Trailing Blanks

In order to produce acceptable mailing labels, you will need to suppress the unwanted spacing. You can suppress the printing of trailing (and leading) spaces by using the **Setting RemoveBlanks** command. The **FieldSqueeze** option eliminates all the trailing and leading blanks, trimming the size of the printed field. Enter

[F10] s r

Select the **FieldSqueeze** option by entering

f y

Output the report to the screen by entering

[F10] o s

This time, the trailing blanks are removed from the report so that each of the field items prints next to the previous field without the gaps caused by trailing (or leading) blanks, Figure 12-8.

```
Now Viewing Page 1 of Page Width 1
Press any key to continue...
Mrs. Gerri Flynn
18 Corsica Drive
Suite 2000
Concord, MA 01602

Ms. Sarah Kurnick
12000 Washington Pike

Tuscon, AZ 85717

Mr. Walter LaFish
4830 Milano Way
Apt. 45
Walnut Creek, CA 94596

Mr. Ira Litman
1790 Woodpark Lane
```

Figure 12-8 Label report printed with trailing blanks suppressed.

Stop the display by entering

[Ctrl-break] ***(3 times)***

Note that on the second line of the screen the words **Form Band, Field Squeeze** appear, indicating that trailing and leading blanks will be suppressed.

> *Note that the RemoveBlanks options affect only the fields printed in the Form band. When Field Squeeze is active, fields printed in the Page or Report bands will still exhibit trailing and leading blanks.*

Suppressing Blank Lines

Removing blank lines has two possible meanings in Paradox reports. The **Setting RemoveBlanks LineSqueeze** command has two options.

- **Fixed.** The Fixed option removes blank lines that fall in between lines with actual text. However, the total number of lines printed remains the same, no matter how many blank lines are suppressed. In effect the blank lines are not removed but printed following the last line of text. This option is used when continuous form printing is in effect; the blank lines serve to define the length of each label or form.

- **Variable.** This option actually suppresses the printing of blank lines. The effect is that each record will print only the number of lines actually containing text. This option is useful when you have a form of a specific length in line and you are using the Pagebreak option to skip to the next form after the text lines have printed.

In this case select the **Fixed** method of handling blank lines. Enter

[F10] s r l y
f

Output the labels to the screen once again by entering

[F10] o s

The labels now take on the appearance you would expect from mailing labels, Figure 12-9. Exit the screen display by entering

[Ctrl-break] ***(3 times)***

Save the label form by entering

[F2]

```
Now Viewing Page 1 of Page Width 1
Press any key to continue...
Mrs. Gerri Flynn
18 Corsica Drive
Suite 2000
Concord, MA 01602

Ms. Sarah Kurnick
12000 Washington Pike
Tuscon, AZ 85717


Mr. Walter LaFish
4830 Milano Way
Apt. 45
Walnut Creek, CA 94596

Mr. Ira Litman
1790 Woodpark Lane
Philadelphia, PA 19115
```

Figure 12-9 Blank lines printed below text.

Range Output of Continuous Form Reports

In order to test the effectiveness of the label form, print out the labels. However, instead of testing the label report form by printing all the records in the label, print only some of the records to make sure the data is properly placed on the label forms.

> *It is not necessary to load labels into your printer to test the report form. Continuous form paper will suffice. You can check the printing by measuring the distance between the first line of any two labels. If the report form has been created properly, that space will measure exactly 1 inch. After printing label forms on standard paper, you will need to realign the paper in the printer for normal page printing.*

Suppose you want to print just the first five records in the Mail table. Select the RangeOutput option from the Report menu. Enter

r r

Enter the name of the table.

mail ↵

Select the report form you have just created, report 1, by entering

1

Select the printer by entering

p

The program prompts you to enter the first page number. Page 1 is entered by default. Accept this page by entering

↵

You are now asked to enter the ending page number. It may occur to you that since the page length is set to continuous form printing, page numbers are no longer relevant. In fact, with continuous form printing each page is actually a single line. If you want to print 5 records of 6 lines each, you would enter 5 times 6 = 30 lines in order to restrict the print to the first 5 records. In order to stop the printing before the first line of the 6th record, subtract 1 from the total number of lines, making the entry value 29. Enter

29 ↵

The program prints the first five records from the table in label format.

Making an Alignment Test Script

In most cases, printing mailing labels requires you to change the type of form in the printer. Many people use continuous 8.5″ by 11″ pages in their printers and change when they want to print labels, rather than using two different printers.

When you remove the pages and feed the labels into the printer, it is inevitable that you will need to test the alignment of the label forms to insure that you have positioned the labels correctly. The best way to do this is to print one or two labels as a test before starting to print the entire table.

You can use the **Report RangeOutput** command to test the first label. If the label was not properly placed on the form, you would manually adjust the forms in the printer and perform the test again. By repeating this process, you will eventually arrive at the proper alignment, allowing you to print the entire table.

You can automate this task by recording or writing a script to carry it out. In this case, record the script by entering

s b
align ↵

Enter the following sequence of commands that will print a single label. Enter

r r
mail ↵
1
p ↵
5 ↵

The program outputs only the first labels. End the script by entering

s e

You can print another test label by replaying the Align script. Enter

[Alt-F10] p
align ↵

Multiple Column Labels

In addition to the label described in the previous section, continuous form labels are also supplied on wide backings that allow you to have two or three columns of mailing labels next to each other, Figure 12-10. The advantage of these mailing labels lies in the fact that most printers will move faster when printing horizontally than when feeding forms through the printer vertically. If you are printing a large number of labels, you may find that you can decrease the time it takes to print those labels by using two- or three-column forms instead of the more common single-column label forms. Note that these multi-column label forms tend to be more expensive than the single-column labels.

Suppose you wanted to print mailing labels across label forms that have three columns of 15/16″ by 3.5″ labels. Since most printers default to printing at 10 characters per inch, the 3.5″ width of the label is 35 characters wide. Typically the multi-column label forms are separated horizontally by a space equal to 2 characters in width. This means that the labels are separated by 1″ vertically and 37 columns horizontally.

Creating a Multi-Column Label Form

Instead of starting from scratch to create a multi-column label form, begin with a copy of the first label form you created. Use the **Tools Copy Report** command to create report 2, copied from report 1. Enter

t c r s
mail ↵
1 2

Load report 2 into the report design mode.

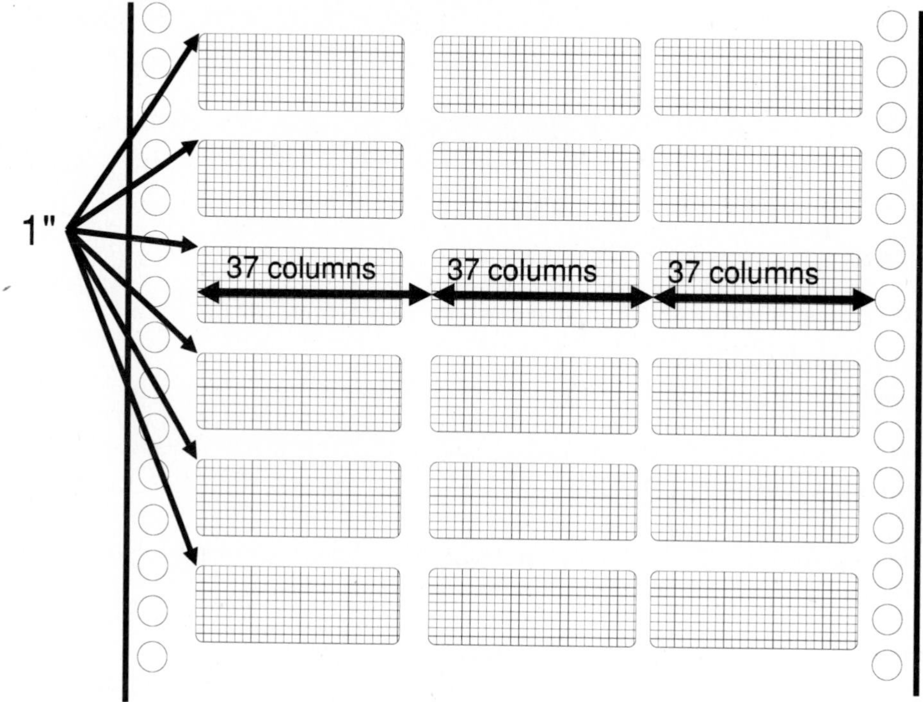

Figure 12-10 Multiple column label forms.

r c

mail ↵

2

Change the title of the report by entering

[spacebar] 3 labels across ↵

Setting the Page Width

There are two basic changes that need to be made in order to change the single column label report into a multi-column label report.

❑ **Page Width.** The page width of the report should be changed to match the width of a single column, in this case 37 characters wide. You would then add page widths so that there were the same number of page widths, i.e., three, on the report, as there are on the multiple column label form.

❑ **Labels Columns.** The **Setting PageLayout** command has a Labels option. This option causes the report to print duplicates of the form layout in the first page width, in all the page widths in the report. For example, if there were three page widths with a label form only in the first width, this option would create a three-column label output.

The first step is to set the width of the report page to the width of the label columns on the form. Recall that the 3.5″ label is equal to 35 columns but that a 2-character gap is left between each column of labels, making the effective width of each column 37 characters.

It is important to remember that in setting up a multi-column label form, all the fields must fit into the first-column width. The widest line in the current report is the first line in the label, which is 36 characters wide. If one of the lines exceeds 37 characters, you would have to reduce the width of the fields so that all of the label can fit onto the first page width.

In this case, set the page width to 37 characters by entering

[F10] s p w
[Ctrl-backspace]
37

The change in page width results in the creation of a report that contains three page widths, each 37 columns wide, Figure 12-11. Each page width is marked by a vertical highlight.

Paradox creates three widths because the original page width was 80 columns, which when divided into blocks of 37 is 2.16. Paradox always adds a full column if the current page width does not divide evenly by the new page width. Keep in mind that you can add or delete page widths from a report, using the **Setting PageLayout Insert** or **Delete** commands.

> *If you had selected a width of 40, then Paradox would have generated only 2 page widths.*

The Labels Options

Now that the report has been divided into three page widths you can designate the page width as label columns. As the report currently stands, the only page width that actually contains items to print is the first page. Page widths 2 and 3 are blank and would not be printed.

The goal in this case is to print a copy of the label form currently entered in the first page width in page widths 2 and 3 using a different record in each page width.

This can be accomplished simply by taking advantage of a command built into the Setting menu for this exact purpose, called Labels. In order to use the Labels options, all page widths—with the exception of the first—must be blank. If that is the case, selecting Labels and

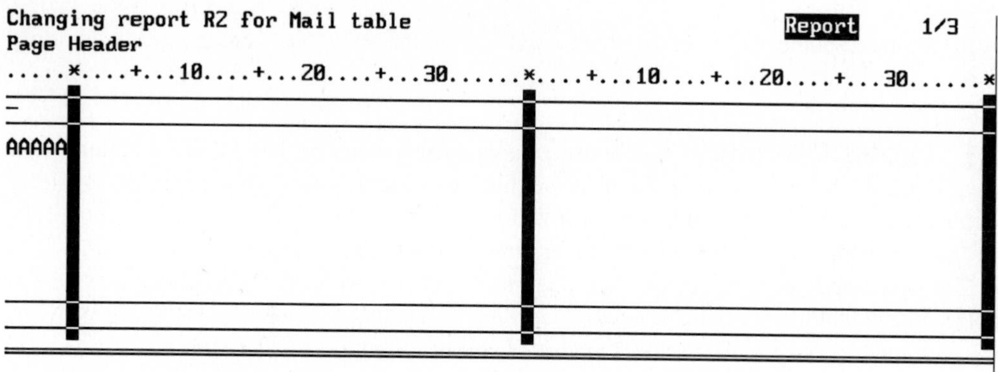

Figure 12-11 Report with three 37-column page widths.

turning the Labels feature on will cause the labels to be printed in as many columns as there are page widths. Enter

[F10] s l y

The message **Label status has been recorded** that appears in the lower right corner of the screen is the only sign that the format of the printed report will be a multi-column label format. Save the report by entering

[F2]

To print this report you must have paper or label forms of an adequate width in your printer. If so, you can print the report using the following command:

r o
mail ↵
2
p

If you do not, display the report on the screen using the command:

r o
mail ↵
2
p

Press any key to continue the screen display until you have seen the entire report.

The printed labels will look like Figure 12-12. The figure shows only a portion of the labels printed.

```
Mrs. Gerri Flynn            Ms. Sarah Kurnick           Mr. Walter LaFish
18 Corsica Drive            12000 Washington Pike       4830 Milano Way
Suite 2000                  Tuscon, AZ 85717            Apt. 45
Concord, MA 01602                                       Walnut Creek, CA 94596

Mr. Ira Litman              Mrs. Joan Waldov            Mrs. Gerri Flynn
1790 Woodpark Lane          45 Pleasant Hill Road       18 Corsica Drive
Philadelphia, PA 19115      Shrewsbury, MA 01680        Suite 2000
                                                        Concord, MA 01602

Ms. Sarah Kurnick           Mr. Walter LaFish           Mr. Ira Litman
12000 Washington Pike       4830 Milano Way             1790 Woodpark Lane
Tuscon, AZ 85717            Apt. 45                     Philadelphia, PA 19115
                            Walnut Creek, CA 94596
```

Figure 12-12 Labels printed three across.

Altering the Number of Page Widths

Paradox automatically created a three-page-width report when you reduced the report form page width from 80 characters to 37 characters. In that particular case, that was exactly the type of page width layout required.

However, it is possible that you would need a different number of page widths, i.e., columns of labels, depending on the particular forms you wish to load into your printer.

Paradox allows you to manually insert or delete page widths from a report so that you can contract or expand the number of labels columns to match the form that you are using. For example, in addition to the single and three-column label forms, you can also purchase two-column label forms. The two-column forms have the advantage of fitting onto narrow-width, 8.5″ printers. Suppose you wanted to create a report that printed only two columns of labels. In this case, you can start with the three column report you have just created and adjust the number of column widths.

Use the **Tools Copy Report** command to make a duplicate of the three-column report, report 2. Enter

t c r s
mail ↵
2
3

Report 3 is now a duplicate of the three-column report. Load report 3 into the report form design mode by entering

r c
mail ↵
3

Change the description of the report to a two-column report by entering

[Ctrl-backspace]
Two-column label report ↵

The report form is now displayed in the design mode. You can determine the total number of page widths included in the report by looking at the fraction that appears in the upper right corner of the screen. Here, that fraction is **1/3**. The **1** tells you that the cursor is positioned in the first page width of the report. The **3** tells you that the report form contains a total of three page widths. Because this report has been set up to use the **Setting Labels** option, each page width in the report will function as a column of labels. To change this report from a three-column output to a two-column output requires you to delete one of the page widths. When you insert a page width, Paradox adds that new page width to the right end of the report. Conversely, when you delete a page width, Paradox removes the last page width on the right side of the report. This means that the location of the cursor is not significant when inserting or deleting page widths.

In this instance, you wish to delete the last page width from the report. Enter

[F10] s p

The PageLayout menu has two commands, **Insert** and **Delete**, that apply to the page width, Figure 12-13.

```
Length  Width  Insert  Delete
Change the length of the printed report page.
```

Figure 12-13 Insert and Delete page width commands.

Remove a page with by selecting the **Delete** command.

d
o *(the letter O)*

If you look at the fraction in the upper right corner of the screen, it now shows **1/2**, indicating that the report has been reduced to two page width, i.e., a two-column label report. Output the report to the screen to examine the results of the change.

[F10] o s

The screen will show the data in a form similar to Figure 12-14.

Exit the report display by entering

[Ctrl-break]*(3 times)*

Save the report form by entering

[F2]

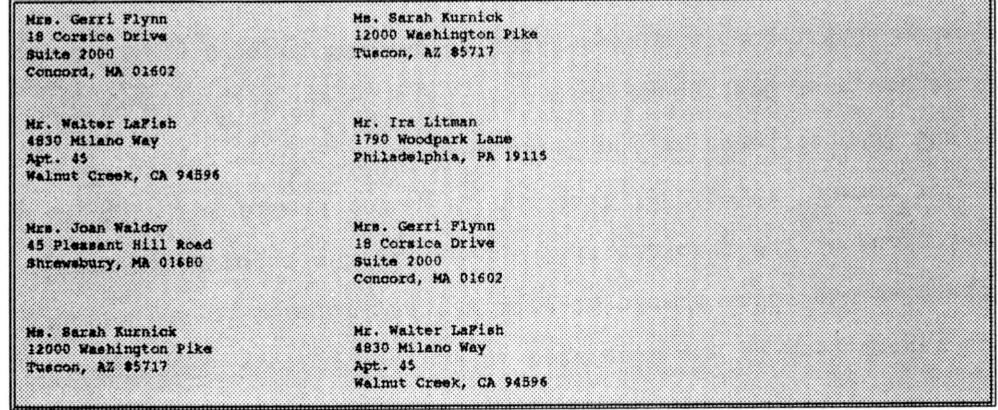

```
Mrs. Gerri Flynn                    Ms. Sarah Kurnick
18 Corsica Drive                    12000 Washington Pike
Suite 2000                          Tuscon, AZ 85717
Concord, MA 01602

Mr. Walter LaFish                   Mr. Ira Litman
4830 Milano Way                     1790 Woodpark Lane
Apt. 45                             Philadelphia, PA 19115
Walnut Creek, CA 94596

Mrs. Joan Waldow                    Mrs. Gerri Flynn
45 Pleasant Hill Road               18 Corsica Drive
Shrewsbury, MA 01680                Suite 2000
                                    Concord, MA 01602

Ms. Sarah Kurnick                   Mr. Walter LaFish
12000 Washington Pike               4830 Milano Way
Tuscon, AZ 85717                    Apt. 45
                                    Walnut Creek, CA 94596
```

Figure 12-14 Two-column label report.

Printing Labels on a Laser Printer

If you are using a laser printer to print reports, in this case multiple-column label reports, you will need to organize the report in a different way than you do when you print labels on a dot matrix printer using continuous forms.

Laser printers feed only individual sheets of paper. You can use the *copier* type of label supplied on 8.5″ by 11″ sheets of prepasted labels. The labels on these sheets are 1″ in height, the same as standard continuous form labels, but because they must fit across an 8.5″ sheet, the width of each label is reduced to approximately 2.75″. The labels are arranged in three columns on the sheet. Since this is the only way to feed labels through a laser printer, all laser-printed label reports are three column label reports. This means that there are 33 labels on each page. Since most laser printers default to a 10-character-per-inch monospaced typeface, this means the labels are wide enough for about 25 or 26 characters. This is a reduction of 30 percent in the width of the label. You will need to compensate for this reduction in the way that you place the fields onto the labels, since the current full field widths for the Mail table reach a width of 37 characters.

It is also important to keep in mind that laser printers cannot reach the entire page area. Because of the way paper is fed through these printers, a small area at the top, bottom, and the sides, about a quarter-inch, is a *nonimage* area. In order to be safe, the first row of labels on each page should be left blank. This means that, even through there are 33 labels on each sheet, you will print only 30 labels.

In this section, you will create a report form that will print labels on prepasted 8.5″ by 11″ sheets.

Formfeeds versus Linefeeds

Before you attempt to print labels on a laser printer, you must make sure that Paradox is set to use *formfeeds* instead of *linefeeds* when printing. Formfeeds and linefeeds refer to two ways of filling out the remainder of each page. By default, Paradox is set to print with the linefeed method. This means that when the last line of actual text on a given page has printed, Paradox will print a series of blank lines to fill out the full length of the page. The formfeed method uses a different approach to the same task. When the formfeed method is active and the program has printed the last line of text on the page, a single command called a formfeed (ASCII character 12) is issued to the printer. The command tells the printer that printing for the current page is complete and the page should be fed through the printer and a new page started.

The difference between the linefeed and formfeed methods is that in the linefeed method, the computer controls the pagination process by issuing explicit commands about how many lines to skip to reach the top of the next form. In the formfeed method, the computer relies on the printer's built-in programs to know how to start the next page.

Most dot matrix printers can work with either approach, although some older printers require the use of the linefeed method. Laser printers usually work best with the formfeed method because they cannot actually print on the entire 11″ length of the page. Printing with the linefeed method on a laser printer can cause problems because the computer is trying to print more lines, 66 by default, on the page then a laser printer can actually print. The printer will usually hold over the last several lines on the page and print them at the top of the next page. However, once again, the computer will send another 66 lines for the second page. As this process continues, the printed material will begin to *slip* down the page as each successive page is printed, Figure 12-15. If you have experienced reports that start a little lower on the page as each successive page prints, you are probably using the linefeed method on a printer that would work better with the formfeed method.

Selecting the Formfeed Method

To change Paradox from the linefeed to the formfeed method of advancing pages, you must play the Custom script and select the Formfeed option on the Reports menu. Play the Custom script by entering

s p
custom ↵

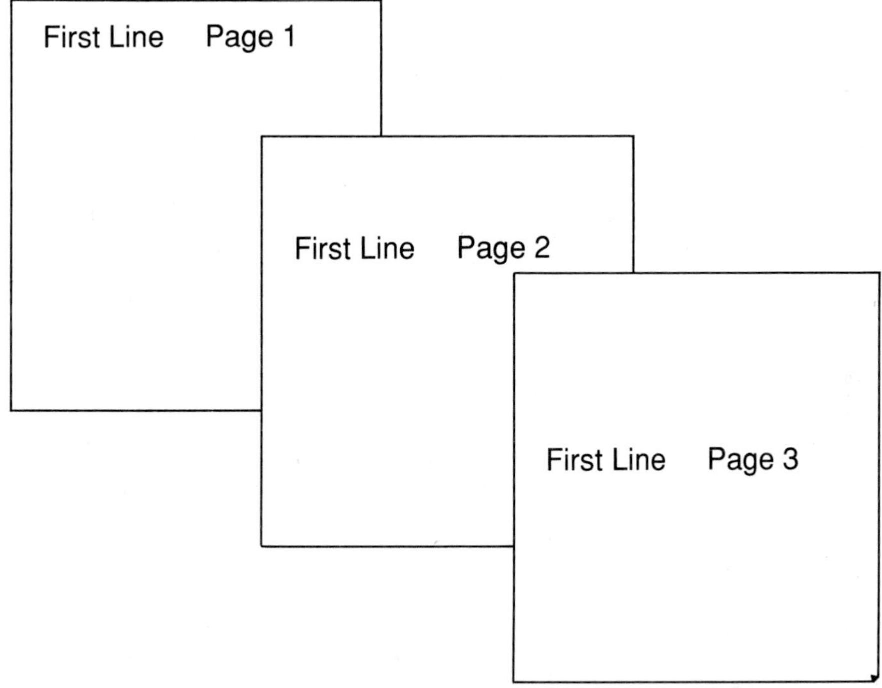

Figure 12-15 Too many linefeeds cause top of page to slip.

Enter the appropriate response for the type of monitor you are using, e.g., Y if you are using a noncolor monitor.

y

Select the Reports menu by entering

r

Select the Formfeed option by entering

f

This selection can be answered in two ways: Yes or No. The No option, active by default, tells Paradox to use the linefeed method. Selecting Yes activates the formfeed method. Enter

y

Save the modified configuration by entering

r d
→ ↵
↵

As you will recall from Chapter 10, Paradox exits to DOS when you save a new configuration. Restart the program by entering

paradox3 ↵

Laser Labels

Create a new report form for the Mail table in which you will design a report that will print the mailing information on sheets of prepasted labels. Enter

r d
mail ↵
4
Laser printer labels ↵
f

The first step in this process is to remove all the lines from the Report Form bands, with the exception of the six blank lines in the Form band. Enter

[Ctrl-y]
↓
[Ctrl-y] ***(6 times)***
↓
[Ctrl-y] ***(9 times)***

Insert five more blank lines into the Form band. Enter

[Ins]
↵ ***(5 times)***

Delete the blanks from the Page and Report footer bands.

↓ ***(2 times)***
[Ctrl-y] ***(4 times)***
↓
[Ctrl-y]

Concatenation of Fields

You are ready to lay out the fields for the label form. With laser printer labels, there is an additional concern in that the width of these labels is 30 percent shorter than the standard label. In this instance, limit the width of the label to 25 characters.

In the previous label reports, you placed the three fields, *Title*, *First*, and *Last*, on the same line—allocating the full width of the field for each item. The **FieldSqueeze** option was used to eliminate trailing spaces.

But the current report does not have enough space to place the fields on the form in the way that you did in the other reports. One solution would be to use the Formatting option to reduce the width of the fields so that they would fit into the 25 character columns needed on this report. However, this approach raises a problem. If you shorten the *First* or *Last* fields, you may end up truncating part of the first or last name. The irony is that if you combined the *Title*, *First*, and *Last* fields, most of the entries in the table would probably fit into the 25 characters because long last names may be paired with short first names, or the other way around. Shortening the field size is not a very flexible way to reduce the width.

A better solution would be to create a calculated field using a *concatenation* formula. A *concatenation* formula combines text and data from alpha fields into a formula that prints the combined text as a single field. The formula below would combine the *Title*, *First*, and *Last* fields into a single output.

```
[title]+[first]+[last]
```

> Concatenation *means a chaining together of a series of items. When a + appears between two alpha fields, it does not mean arithmetic addition but concatenation of the two items into a single text item.*

The advantage of this formula is that Paradox automatically eliminates trailing blanks from each field as part of formulating the result of the formula. This means that the output would use only as many characters as needed for each field, without including the blanks. You can add punctuation to the formula in the form of text literals enclosed in quotation marks. The formula below adds the period and proper spacing to the formula.

```
[title]+". "+[first]+" "+[last]
```

Using a formula like the one above ensures that you will get the maximum benefit from the 25 characters you allot to each line in the label.

Move the cursor to the first blank line in the Form band by entering

↑ *(7 times)*

Instead of placing a Regular field into the form, create a calculated field by entering

[F10] f p c

Enter a concatenation formula that will combine the text from the *Title*, *First* and *Last* fields. Take care to enter spaces where indicated by the _ characters.

[title]+"._"+[first]+"_"+[last]
↵ *(2 times)*

Paradox shows a field width of 39 characters. Reduce it to 25 by entering

← *(13 times)*
↵

Place the *Street Address* field on the next line of the Form band by entering

↓ [Ctrl-Home]
[F10] f p r
→ *(3 times)*
↵ *(2 times)*

This field must also be limited to 25 characters. Enter

← *(5 times)*
↵

Place the *Apt* field on the next line of the Form Band.

↓ [Ctrl-Home]
[F10] f p r a
↵ *(2 times)*

Move the cursor to the beginning of the next line.

↓ [Ctrl-Home]

This line should contain the *City*, *State*, and *Zip* fields. In this instance, you should create a calculated field that will concatenate the three fields into a single item. Enter

[F10] f p c

Enter the formula. Note that spaces are represented by _ characters.

[city] + ",_" + [state] + " + _"[zip]
↵ *(2 times)*

Shorten the width to 25 characters by entering

← *(7 times)*

The label form should look like Figure 12-16.

```
 ▼page──────────────────────────────────
 ▼form──────────────────────────────────
AAAAAAAAAAAAAAAAAAAAAAAAA
AAAAAAAAAAAAAAAAAAAAAAAAA
AAAAAAAAAAAAAAAAAAAA
AAAAAAAAAAAAAAAAAAAAAAAAA

 ▲form──────────────────────────────────
 ▲page──────────────────────────────────
```

Figure 12-16 Label form with concatenated field formulas.

Creating the Columns

With the basic label form established, you can now lay out the columns for the report. Begin by reducing the page width to 25 characters. Enter

[F10] s p w
[Ctrl-backspace]
25 ↵

Because the result of 25 divided into 80 is more than 3, Paradox sets the report to four page widths as indicated by the fraction in the upper left corner of the screen. However, in this case you want only three columns. Eliminate one of the page widths by entering

[F10] s p d
o *(the letter O)*

The report is now reduced to three page widths. Convert the page widths to columns by activating the Labels option. Enter

[F10] s
l *(the letter L)*
y

Activate the LineSqueeze option by entering

[F10] s r
l *(the letter L)*
y f

Adding a Top Margin

The report is complete with the exception of one item. As mentioned, most laser printers will not be able to print on the very top of the page in an area extending about one-quarter inch from the top of the page. In order to eliminate problems with this nonimage area, you will want to skip the first row of labels on each page. This can be done by adding six blank lines to the Page Header band. Move the cursor to the Page Header band by entering

↑ ***(4 times)***

Note that to insert a new line the cursor must be at the left edge of the report. Enter

[Ctrl-Home]

Paradox should still be in the Insert mode, activated on page 457. Enter the blank lines.

↵ ***(6 times)***

The report form will look like Figure 12-17.

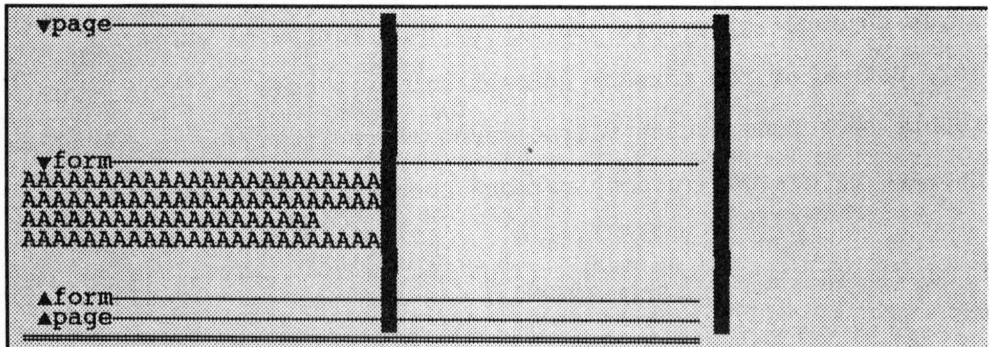

Figure 12-17 Three column laser printer labels report.

Save the report form by entering

[F2]

Print the report by entering

r o
mail r
4
p

The labels should look like Figure 12-18.
Exit Paradox by entering

e y

```
Mrs. Gerri Flynn          Ms. Sarah Kurnick         Mr. Walter LaFish
18 Corsica Drive          12000 Washington Pike     4830 Milano Way
Suite 2000                Tuscon, AZ 85717          Apt. 45
Concord, MA 01602                                   Walnut Creek, CA 94596

Mr. Ira Litman            Mrs. Joan Waldov          Mrs. Gerri Flynn
1790 Woodpark Lane        45 Pleasant Hill Road     18 Corsica Drive
Philadelphia, PA 19115    Shrewsbury, MA 01680      Suite 2000
                                                    Concord, MA 01602

Ms. Sarah Kurnick         Mr. Walter LaFish         Mr. Ira Litman
12000 Washington Pike     4830 Milano Way           1790 Woodpark Lane
Tuscon, AZ 85717          Apt. 45                   Philadelphia, PA 19115
                          Walnut Creek, CA 94596

Mrs. Joan Waldov          Mrs. Gerri Flynn          Ms. Sarah Kurnick
45 Pleasant Hill Road     18 Corsica Drive          12000 Washington Pike
Shrewsbury, MA 01680      Suite 2000                Tuscon, AZ 85717
                          Concord, MA 01602

Mr. Walter LaFish         Mr. Ira Litman            Mrs. Joan Waldov
4830 Milano Way           1790 Woodpark Lane        45 Pleasant Hill Road
Apt. 45                   Philadelphia, PA 19115    Shrewsbury, MA 01680
Walnut Creek, CA 94596

Mrs. Gerri Flynn          Ms. Sarah Kurnick         Mr. Walter LaFish
18 Corsica Drive          12000 Washington Pike     4830 Milano Way
Suite 2000                Tuscon, AZ 85717          Apt. 45
Concord, MA 01602                                   Walnut Creek, CA 94596

Mr. Ira Litman            Mrs. Joan Waldov          Mrs. Gerri Flynn
1790 Woodpark Lane        45 Pleasant Hill Road     18 Corsica Drive
Philadelphia, PA 19115    Shrewsbury, MA 01680      Suite 2000
                                                    Concord, MA 01602

Ms. Sarah Kurnick         Mr. Walter LaFish         Mr. Ira Litman
12000 Washington Pike     4830 Milano Way           1790 Woodpark Lane
Tuscon, AZ 85717          Apt. 45                   Philadelphia, PA 19115
                          Walnut Creek, CA 94596

Mrs. Joan Waldov          Mrs. Gerri Flynn          Ms. Sarah Kurnick
45 Pleasant Hill Road     18 Corsica Drive          12000 Washington Pike
Shrewsbury, MA 01680      Suite 2000                Tuscon, AZ 85717
                          Concord, MA 01602
```

Figure 12-18 Labels printed on pre-pasted label sheets.

Summary

This chapter discussed the use of free-form reports to print labels in a variety of formats and on both dot matrix and laser printers.

❑ **Continuous Form Labels.** Continuous form labels can be used with printers, primarily dot matrix printers, that have the ability to use tractors to pin feed forms that are not 8.5″ by 11″ sheets. Labels are supplied on a continuous form backing. They can have single- or multiple-column labels on a single backing.

❑ **Laser Labels.** Laser printers can feed only sheets, not continuous forms. Labels, designed for copying machines, are prepasted on 8.5″ by 11″ sheets in three columns.

❑ **Free-Form Reports.** Free-form reports are report forms that do not contain a column-oriented Table band. Instead, they contain a Form band in which fields can be positioned in any way desired within the band. Free-form reports are more flexible than column reports and can be used to print information on a variety of forms, including mailing label forms.

❑ **Continuous Page Length.** When printing on continuous forms that are not divided into individual pages, such as mailing label forms, you can set Paradox for continuous-form printing. This suppresses the printing of the Page Header and Footer Bands and other page-oriented features on all but the first and last pages.

❑ **Suppressing Blanks.** Fields placed on the same line of the Form band will normally print their full formatted length, including any trailing or leading blank spaces. You can suppress these blanks with the RemoveBlanks SqueezeFields option.

❑ **Suppressing Blank Lines.** If the fields specified for a given line in the Form band are blank because the fields in a particular record are blank, Paradox will still print that line. If you want to suppress these blank lines, you can select the **LineSqueeze** option. **LineSqueeze** can operate in a fixed mode in which blank lines print at the bottom of the Form band, or in a variable-length mode in which blank lines are not printed at all.

❑ **Page Widths.** In most reports, the page width is set to match the actual width of the form in the printer. Reports that print labels in columns use page widths that match the width of the column of labels. Additional page widths can be used to produce multiple-column label printing. When you reduce the width of the page, Paradox automatically adds as many page widths as would have fit on the overall page width before you changed it. You can use the Setting PageLayout menu to insert or delete pages widths.

❑ **Multicolumn Form Printing.** Multicolumn label printing is accomplished by selecting the Labels option from the Setting menu of a report form that has multiple page widths. When selected, the Form band in the first page width will automatically be printed in each of the other page widths in the report creating multiple column printing. Note that if the Labels option is used, all the page widths, with the exception of the first, must be blank.

❑ **Alignment Tests.** Continuous-form labels often require the printing of one or more labels to test the alignment of the label forms in the printer. Once you have created a report form for label printing, you can use the Report RangeOutput option to print a selected number of labels as an alignment test.

❑ **Formfeeds and Linefeeds.** Paradox can use one of two methods for feeding the remainder of a form at the bottom of a page. The linefeed method, the default, prints blank lines until the total page length, e.g., 66 lines has been reached. The alternative method, formfeed, uses the form-feeding routine built into the printer to move to the top of the next form. Some older printers cannot use formfeeds and require the linefeed method. Other printers, such as laser printers, cannot actually print a full 66 lines on a page. They work best with the formfeed approach. You must play the Custom script to select the alternate method.

❑ **Concatenation Formulas.** You can combine several fields as well as text literals into a single calculated field by using concatenation formulas. Paradox automatically trims trailing blanks from fields within a concatenation formula.

Part II

Programming with the Paradox Application Language

13

Basic Programming with PAL

Part 2 of this book is designed to introduce the reader to the creation and design of custom applications through the use of Paradox Application Language, PAL.

The PAL language was introduced in Chapter 10 under the discussion of scripts. Scripts can contain any combination of keystroke command names and PAL language commands. As noted in Chapter 10, PAL commands express Paradox operations more simply and clearly than do lists of command keystrokes.

Writing scripts that include PAL language commands and techniques is a subject that users may feel is beyond their capabilities. In most instances, this is not true. Since PAL is really an extension of the basic set of commands accessed from the Paradox menu system, you will find it is often easier to work out complicated tasks as a script program than it is to enter them directly through the menus. Why? When you are trying to carry out a task that has multiple steps, entering a mistake in some part of the procedure may require you to start over again. Not only is this frustrating but it wastes a lot of time. You may even lose data. When you write a script that carries out the task, any mistake in the script can be corrected by editing. All the correct commands remain in the script to be used again and again, without requiring you to reenter them.

Part 2 of this book is designed to teach you the concepts and techniques needed to begin writing scripts and to continue to enhance and improve those scripts. The text will not make you a master programmer; that will come only with experience. But it will illustrate how the PAL language can be used to carry out tasks that are common to almost every application you want to design. As with Part 1, these chapters are written in an ascending order of complexity, each building on the ideas presented in the previous chapter.

In this chapter, you will learn more about PAL and the advantages it offers to Paradox users. The goal of this chapter will be to explore the basic concepts and techniques used to create Paradox applications with PAL.

Programs and Scripts

In Chapter 10, you learned that you could create a Paradox script by recording an operation, directly writing the commands into a script file or some combination of the two. What is the difference between programming a PAL application or writing a script?

The answer is that there is no actual difference in kind between a *script* and a *program*. In Paradox, the two terms have virtually the same meaning. The difference is one of emphasis. When you talk about *scripts* you are generally referring to a way of automating a series of actions that accomplish a task, e.g., calculating the balance of a checking account. A *program* suggests that the goal is to create something that not only automates individual tasks but coordinates and organizes a variety of tasks related to a given activity. However, even though a program is usually larger and more complicated than a simple script, both are constructed out of the same materials—i.e., they are text files that contain a list of PAL instructions and/or keystroke command names.

Structured Programs

Granted that a program is an expanded type of script, the concept of programming implies the existence of *structures* with a script or group of related scripts. Structures are elements of a program used to coordinate and organize the individual tasks carried out by the scripts. For example, in Part 1 you created one script that would calculate the checking account balance and another script that would display a slide show of graphs illustrating checking account activity. How would you organize individual, task-specific scripts into a larger program? One obvious answer is to do what Paradox itself does, which is to create a menu of some sort that lists the available scripts and allows the user to make a selection as to which activity to carry out.

A *menu* is a structure that helps tie together individual activities. If you think about how a menu operates you will realize that it possesses a number of qualities that the scripts you created in Part 1 do not.

❑ **Interactive Dialog.** Menus, prompts, and other similar structures enable a program to carry on a dialog with the person using the computer. The dialog takes place when the menu or prompt is placed on the screen. The program, instead of carrying out a task such as displaying a graph, must pause and wait until the user reacts to the information on the screen. The user then reacts by pressing a key or a series of keys. The program may respond by placing a new menu or prompt on the screen, requesting a further response from the user. This back-and-forth game of message and response is a dialog between the program and the person using the program. If you are to design a program, you must learn how to create and control the interactive dialog between the program and the person using the program.

❑ **Memory Variables.** An interactive dialog creates the conditions necessary for the program to receive the instruction from the person using the computer in the form of keystrokes entered. But if these keystrokes are to have use within the program, they must be stored somewhere in the computer's memory. A dialog would not lead to useful action if the keystrokes went in one ear and out the other. The program must have some way of storing the responses made by the user in order to know what actions to take. The storage areas used for this type of information are called *memory variables.*

❑ **Conditional Structures.** Keystrokes entered in response to a menu or prompt constitute a different type of entry than does data entered into a table field. The user enters the keystrokes in order to select an option or an alternative. When the user makes that selection there must be a structure in the program that can *evaluate* the entry. This type of structure is called a *conditional* structure. It allows programs to evaluate and respond to users' requests.

Interactive dialog, memory variables, and conditional structures are the basic tools out of which programs are created. In Paradox these elements can be combined with the tables, screen forms, report forms, and other objects that are part of the way Paradox manages data.

It is the addition of these elements to scripts that changes them from simple sequences of commands to actual programs.

Controlling What Appears on the Screen

The most obvious difference between a program and a simple script such as the ones created in Part 1 of this book is the ability of a program to control what appears on the screen. If you recall, the scripts written in Part 1 did not display any information on the screen while they were running, with the exception of the instant graph command, **Graphkey**, which displayed the graph during the script. When the script was complete, the work area display returned.

The reason this happens is that Paradox maintains two different types of screen displays.

❑ **Work Area Screen.** The work area screen is the display you see when you are working with Paradox at all times, with the one exception of the time during which a script is being played. The PAL canvas remains inactive all the while the normal screen display appears.

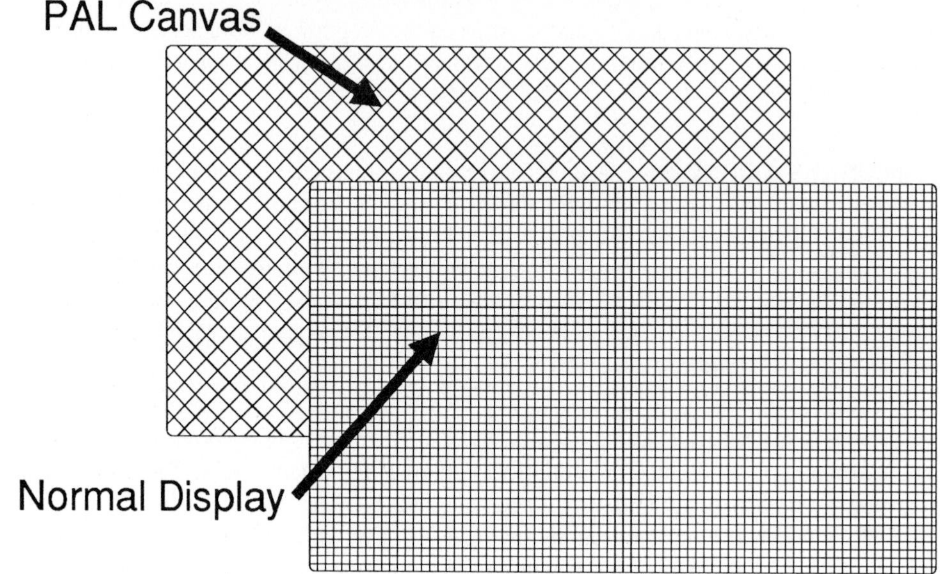

❑ **PAL Canvas.** When a script is played, the normal work area screen display is suppressed and only the information placed on the PAL canvas screen, if any, appears. When the script terminates, Paradox returns to the normal screen display.

Why does Paradox make a distinction between the two types of screen display? The answer has to do with the visual approach to database management that Paradox uses. When you load a database table, it immediately appears on the screen in the form of a *table image*. Query operations are executed in the form of a *query form image* that generates an *Answer table image*. All these images are automatically formatted and displayed by Paradox. This approach makes database management tasks easy to carry out once you become familiar with Paradox images.

On the other hand, one of the primary goals of writing programs is to control very carefully what information appears on the screen display. In order to resolve the conflict between the visual approach to database operations and a programmer's need to control what appears on the screen, Paradox uses the dual display mode system just described. When a script is *not* being played, all of the visual images appear on the screen. As soon as a script begins to play, the screen images are suppressed until the script is complete.

The scripts you created in Part 1 took advantage of this dual display mode system to perform the query-processing operations in the *background* while the script was running. Recall the Balance script which performed several query form processing operations before it revealed the final Answer table that contained the checking account balance. None of the images created to obtain the balance appeared on the screen because the PAL canvas, which is blank, covered the work area where the images were being processed. By the end of the script, the **CLEARALL** and **CLEARIMAGE** commands (the PAL equivalents of [Alt-F8] and [F8]) removed all of the images, except the last Answer table. When the script ended and the work area became visible again, the Answer table appeared.

The dual display mode created the *illusion* that only one table, the Answer table with the account balance, was generated by the script. This *illusion* is useful because the user would be distracted or confused by seeing all of the images from the intermediate steps flash on and off the work area. By controlling the amount of information displayed, the script conceatrates the users attention on the important data, i.e., the checking account balance.

Placing Data on the PAL Canvas

The dual display modes have the advantage of automatically suppressing the images that appear as the script's processing takes place, due to the display of the blank PAL canvas for the duration of the script.

The key to displaying information on the PAL canvas is the **?** command. The **?** command can be followed by one or more *expressions*. Expressions are formulas similar to the ones that you used in report forms to generate calculated fields. Expressions can contain fields, text literals, and arithmetic calculations. Note that field names are enclosed in [ ].

> *If you have used the BASIC programming language, the ? command is similar to the PRINT command also abbreviated as ? in BASIC.*

Displaying Data on the PAL Canvas

Suppose you wanted to place text on the PAL canvas. To do so you would have to use the **?** command from a script. The command would be followed by the item or items you want to display. As a simple example, place the word *Hello* on the PAL canvas. Create a new script called Show by entering

s e w
show ↵

Enter the **?** command into the script.

? "Hello"

Execute the script by entering

[F10] g

What happened? It appears that the script has no effect at all. Execute the script again using the PAL menu, [Alt-F10].

[Alt-F10] p
show ↵

Once again, nothing appears on the screen. Why? The answer is that the screen you are looking at is the work area display—not the PAL canvas. You can tell that this is the case because the main menu is displayed, something that happens only on the work area screen.

But why didn't the script display the word you entered? The answer is that it did, but it did so on the PAL canvas—not the work area display. Since the script is only two commands long, the script terminates only a fraction of a moment after it begins. The work area display covers the PAL canvas so quickly you don't get a chance to see the effect of the commands.

There are several solutions to this problem. The one you will use here—the **SLEEP** command—is the simplest. The **SLEEP** command performs a similar function to the **Overall Wait** command on the Graph Modify menu in that it causes Paradox to pause a specified length of time before it goes on to the next operation. The **SLEEP** command requires that you specify a duration in 1/1000 of a second. For example, the command **SLEEP 1000** would create a one-second delay. In this case, adding a **SLEEP** command to the end of the script will pause the script long enough for you to see the text placed on the PAL canvas.

Modify the script by entering

s e e
show ↵

Add the **SLEEP** command to end of the script by entering

[Ctrl-End] ↵
SLEEP 5000

Execute the script by entering

[F10] g

This time the screen clears and the single word *Hello* appears in the upper right corner of the screen. The word will remain there for five seconds, due to the delay caused by the **SLEEP** command. After the five seconds elapse, the script ends and Paradox overlays the PAL canvas with the work area display, obscuring the text.

Horizontal and Vertical Position

The **?** command places text at the beginning of the next available line on the PAL canvas. When you start to play a script, the cursor is automatically positioned in the upper right corner of the screen. The first **?** places text beginning in the corner. Subsequent **?** commands would continue down the screen until all the lines were filled. Further **?** commands would *scroll* the entire display up one line to make room for the new text.

But how would you display the word *Hello* in the center of the screen instead of the upper left corner? The answer lies in PAL commands that are specifically designed to place information at specific locations on the PAL canvas screen. The two commands that form the basis of all PAL canvas displays follow:

❑ **??.** The **??** command is similar to the **?** command in that it places data onto the PAL canvas. However, **??** places the text starting at the current cursor position. The **??** command does not start a new line before it displays the item.

❑ **@.** The @ command controls the location of the cursor on the PAL canvas. The PAL canvas is organized as a grid of 25 rows and 80 columns. The rows are numbered from 0 to 24 and the columns from 0 to 79, Figure 13-1. The @ command is followed by two numeric values that indicate the row and column location on the grid where the cursor should be positioned.

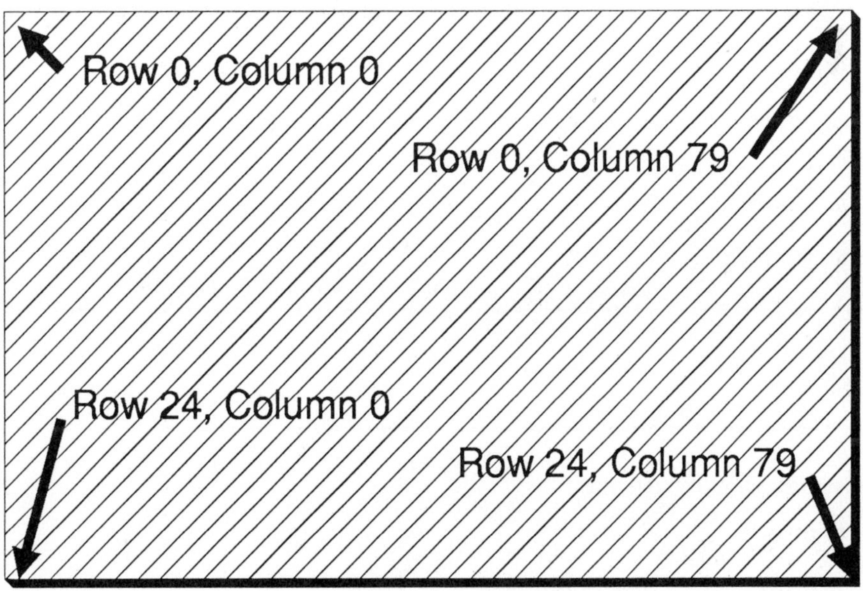

Figure 13-1 PAL canvas grid.

The two commands can be used together to place the contents of a field, a text literal, or the result of a calculation at any position on the PAL screen. The @ command is typically used first to position the cursor. The **??** command that follows places the first character of its first expression at the row/column location specified by the @. For example, the commands below would place the word *Hello* at row 11/column 36, approximately the center of the screen.

```
@ 11,36
?? "Hello"
```

PAL commands do not have to be written on separate lines. You can write as many commands on the line as you wish. With the @ and **?** commands, you might write them on a single line as shown below.

```
@ 11,36 ?? "Hello"
```

Controlling Locations

You can modify the Show script so that the text is displayed at a specific location rather than at the upper left corner of the screen. Enter

s e e
show ↵

Place the Paradox script editor into the insert mode by entering

[Ins]

Use the @ command to position the cursor at row 11/column 36 and then the **??** command to place the word on the PAL screen. Enter

@ **11,36 ??**

The script now reads:

```
@ 11,36 ?? "Hello"
SLEEP 5000
```

Execute the script by entering

[F10] g

This time the word appears in the center of the screen for five seconds before the program returns to the work area display.

Displaying Table Fields

The scripts that you created in Part 1 of this book demonstrated that activities that place images on the normal work area display are hidden from view while the PAL canvas is displayed. This creates the effect by which Paradox operations take place in the background while the foreground display, the PAL canvas, remains unchanged.

It many cases it would be useful to be able to transfer data from a hidden work area image to the PAL canvas. This can be done by using the **?** or **??** commands to display the contents of a field from a table image currently on the work area to the PAL canvas which is visible while a script is playing.

Field names can be included in the expression or list of expressions following a **?** or **??** command, by enclosing the field names in []. The command below would display the contents of the *Check date* from the current work area table image on the PAL canvas.

```
@ 11,36 ?? [check date]
```

Pointing at a Record

When you display the contents of the *Check date* during a script, what data will actually be displayed? Afterall, the Ck_book table contains a number of records. Which particular *Check date* will appear when the command **?? [check date]** is executed?

The answer is determined by the position of the cursor in the table image at the time that the **?? [check date]** command is encountered. If the cursor is positioned in the first record in the table, the check date for that record will appear. If the cursor is positioned in the last record in the table, then a different date—the one stored in that record—will appear when a reference is made to **[check date]** in an expression.

The cursor location serves to *point* at the record which will be used to fill in any field references. In programming terms, the cursor position is called the *record pointer*.

From working with Paradox table images, you know how the cursor is positioned when a table image is placed onto the work area and how that cursor position can be changed. It is important to keep in mind that even though the work area images do not appear when the PAL canvas is active, any operational instructions that are relevant to table operations will affect the table—including changes in cursor position.

For example, the cursor is always positioned in the first record when a table image is first displayed. You also know that the [End] key will move the cursor to the last record in the table. The script below displays the *Check date* field from the Ck_book table twice. The first time, the cursor is positioned in the first record. The second time, the cursor has been moved by the **End** command to the last record in the table.

```
VIEW "ck_book"
@ 5,25 ?? [Check date]
END
@ 6,25 ?? [Check date]
```

Note that only the @ and **??** commands affect the display of the PAL canvas. The script will simply place two dates on the screen.

Tables and the PAL Canvas

Suppose you wanted to use a script to display the beginning and ending dates in the *Check date* field of the Ck_book table. Create a script called Range by entering

s e w
range ↵

The first command in the script will be a **CLEARALL** command. In most cases you would want to begin a program with this command so that you can be sure that only the images generated by your program will be on the work area display.

CLEARALL ↵

Place an image of the Ck_book table on the work area using the **VIEW** command. Keep in mind that while the script is being played the user will not see this image reflected on the PAL canvas.

VIEW "ck_book" ↵

The cursor is now positioned in the first record in the table. Use the @/**??** commands to display the *Check date*. Since the PAL screen is blank at this point you will want to include some text literals to identify the meaning of the date.

@ 5,25 ?? "Checking Account Records" ↵
@ 7,25 ?? "Beginning Date",[check date] ↵

The second **??** command uses a comma to separate two items: ''Beginning Date'' and [check date]. This is called an *expression list*. Remember that each item in an expression list is separated by a comma. Paradox will display the items in the list one after the other on the same line.

The next command will change the position of the cursor in the table but will have no effect on the PAL screen.

END ↵

With the cursor now positioned in the last record of the table you can use @/**??** to display the *Check date* field from that record.

@ 9,25 ?? "Ending Date",[check date] ↵

Pause the display for 10 seconds with a **SLEEP** command. Add a **CLEARALL** command at the end of the script to remove any images created during the script from the work area.

SLEEP 10000 CLEARALL

The entire script (RANGE.SC) reads as follows:

```
CLEARALL
VIEW ''ck_book''
@ 5,25 ?? ''Checking Account Records''
@ 7,25 ?? ''Beginning Date'',[check date]
END
@ 9,25 ?? ''Ending Date'',[check date]
SLEEP 10000 CLEARALL
```

Execute the script by entering

[F10] g

The PAL canvas shows the text plus the dates from the first and last records, Figure 13-2.

```
Checking Account Records

Beginning Date1/01/89

Ending Date3/12/89
```

Figure 13-2 Display generated by Range script.

Spacing Between Items

The display generated by the Range script uses **??** commands with items lists. The result was that two items, the text and the dates, were displayed one after the other with no spacing between them, e.g., **Beginning Date1/01/89**. In most cases, you would want to have a space between items on the list. This can be accomplished by adding an extra space to the text literal. For example, instead of using **"Beginning Date"** you would use **"Beginning Date▌"** where ▌ stands for a [spacebar] character. Note that this character *must* be entered inside the quotation marks in order to be a part of the text displayed by the command. Spaces entered outside the quotation marks are ignored by Paradox.

Load the Range script into the editor by entering

s e e
range ↵

You will need to make two changes to this script on lines 4 and 6. You can display a vertical line number ruler by entering [Ctrl-v]. Also note that if you want to insert characters in a script you must activate the Insert mode by pressing [Ins]. Otherwise, you will type-over existing characters. When the Insert mode is active, **Ins** appears in the upper right corner of the screen. Make the following changes to the script. Note that ▌ is used to indicate where a space should be added.

Old line 4 @ 7,25 ?? "Beginning Date",[check date]
New line 4 @ 7,25 ?? "Beginning Date▌",[check date]

Old line 6 @ 9,25 ?? "Ending Date",[check date]
New line 6 @ 9,25 ?? "Ending Date▌",[check date]

Execute the revised script by entering

[F10] g

This time the text and the dates are separated by a space, improving the appearance of the display, Figure 13-3.

```
Checking Account Records
Beginning Date 1/01/89
Ending Date 3/12/89
```

Figure 13-3 Spaces added to text literals.

Vertical Alignment

When items are displayed from a list of expressions following a **??** command, the items are placed on the screen immediately following each other. This is called *relative* placement because the end of the first item dictates the location where the second item begins.

In the Range script, this process has the effect of printing the dates at different horizontal locations because the text that precedes them is different lengths.

It might improve the appearance of the display if both dates were positioned so that they aligned vertically, one above the other. There are two ways to achieve this effect.

❑ **Pad with Spaces.** You can achieve vertical alignment by simply adding enough spaces to the ends of each of the text literals so that all of the text literals are the same length. An example of *adding* is shown below where the ▮ stands for the spaces.

```
@ 7,25 ?? "Beginning Date▮        ",[check date]
@ 9,25 ?? "Ending Date▮▮▮         ",[check date]
```

❑ **Specific @ commands.** The alternative method would use separate **??** commands preceded by @ commands to ensure that items align vertically. Below is an example of this approach.

```
@ 7,25 ?? "Beginning Date" @ 7,42 ?? [check date]
@ 9,25 ?? "Ending Date" @ 9,42 ?? [check date]
```

The padding technique is simple but can be a bit confusing unless you align the commands in the script in vertical columns so that you can easily gauge the length of the text items. The @/**??** method is more accurate because it allows you to specify the exact location for each of the items you want to display.

Aligning Text Vertically

Modify the Range script so that the two dates that print will align vertically. Enter

s e e
range ↵

Make the following changes.

Old line 4 @ 7,25 ??"Beginning Date ",[check date]
New line 4 @ 7,25 ?? "Beginning Date " @ 7,42 ?? [check date]

Old line 6 @ 9,25 ?? "Ending Date ",[check date]
New line 6 @ 9,25 ?? "Ending Date " @ 9,42 ?? [check date]

> *It is not necessary to place spaces between commands or elements in a command if you do not want to do so. For example, the command @* **9,42 ?? [check date]** *could just as well be entered as* **@9,42??[check date]**. *Paradox would be able to pick out the distinct elements in the command without the additional spaces. However, it is much harder to read scripts without spaces. In general, you should use as much space as necessary to write your commands in a format that is easiest for you to read. Most scripts undergo a long process of edit and revision before they are finalized. Scripts that are hard to read are also hard to edit.*

Execute the modified script by entering

[F10] g

This time the dates are aligned to form a vertical column. This is a much easier display to read, Figure 13-4.

```
Checking Account Records
Beginning Date    1/01/89
Ending Date       3/12/89
```

Figure 13-4 Items aligned vertically.

Using the Answer Table

The Range script uses the dates in the first and last records to find the range of dates contained in the Ck_book table. While it is possible that this will yield accurate results, there is no certainty that the first and last records will yield the low and high dates in the field. A better approach would to be use a query to find the actual minimum and maximum values in the *Check date* field and display those values.

Create a new script called RANGE1 by entering

s e w
range1 ↵

Begin the script by entering **CLEARALL**. In addition, the command **CLEAR** is used. **CLEAR** erases any text that may be on the PAL canvas at the time. The combination of these two commands ensures that the script starts with a blank in both the canvas and work areas.

CLEARALL CLEAR ↵

You need to create an Answer table that will contain the high and low date values based on a query calculation. This can be accomplished by using a **QUERY/ENDQUERY** command. Since there is no QuerySave script already stored which performs this operation, you can create a **QUERY** setup from scratch. Enter the query command shown below. Remember that you *must* leave blank lines following **QUERY** and preceding **ENDQUERY**. You do not have to add all the spaces shown below in order to make the column align vertically although it is probably best to enter the query setup that way because it is much easier to read.

```
QUERY

ck_book     |     check date     |
            | calc max,calc min  |

ENDQUERY
DO_IT!
```

Once the query has been processed you will have created and displayed an Answer table with two fields: *Max of Check date* and *Min of Check date*. It is these fields that you want to display on the PAL canvas.

> *If you wanted to work with simpler field names, you could use the* **as** *operator to assign a shorter name to the Answer table fields.*

Functions

The next part of the script will use **@/??** commands to display the information stored in the Answer table. In this case, both of the items are dates. By default, dates are displayed in the m/dd/yy format. In images, report, and screen forms, you can use options to change the format in which dates or numeric values are displayed.

You can use the same type of formatting options in scripts by using the **FORMAT()** function. A *function* is a special command word that can be used in Paradox expressions. The **function** provides additional information in several ways.

❑ **Provide Information.** These functions provide information about Paradox operations. During normal operation, many of these values are obtained by looking at the images on the work area. However, in scripts you may need to use functions to determine files names (FIELD()), record numbers (RECNO()) or the current date (TODAY())

❑ **Mathematical.** These functions perform special calculations on the supplied values. An example of mathematical functions is LOG(), which calculates the logarithms to the base 10 of a specified value.

❑ **Transformation/Conversion.** These functions are used to change data from one form to another. In some cases the process converts data from one type to another, e.g., STRVAL() converts numbers to alpha text. Transformations can affect only the appearance of the data. For example the UPPER() function causes text to appear in all uppercase letters.

Functions are always followed by an *argument*. The *argument* is a Paradox value or expression enclosed in parentheses. The argument indicates what value or expression the function should operate on. For example, if you wanted to find the logarithm to the base 10 of the number 1000, you would use the function LOG() with 1000 as its argument, e.g., LOG(1000).

It is important to keep in mind that a function does not constitute a command. The function LOG(1000) is a value. In order to have a command you must tell Paradox what you want to do with that value. If you wanted to display that value on the PAL canvas you would combine the function with the ? command forming a complete Paradox instruction, e.g., **? LOG(1000).**

> *Some functions do not require a value or expression as an argument. For example, the TODAY() function is used with only an empty pair of parentheses () as the argument. This is called a* null *argument because the parentheses enclose nothing.*

Using the Format Function

The FORMAT() function is particularly useful for displaying data on the PAL canvas. This function allows you to impose a stylistic format on the dates, numbers, or alpha text placed on the canvas with **?** or **??** commands.

The FORMAT() function requires two arguments.

❑ **Format Code.** The format code is a two-character code that tells Paradox how you want the item to be formatted. The format code is always the first argument and it is enclosed in quotation marks, e.g., **? FORMAT("d2",[check date])** displays the *Check date* field in date format #2. Note that case is not significant when it comes to entering a format code. In some cases, where formats are not incompatible, you can specify a list of codes. For example, you can use the width code along with the alignment code in order to print an item centered on the screen, e.g., **?FORMAT("w80,ac,d2",[check date])** displays the *Check date* field in date format #2 in the center of the screen. The width is set at 80 because that is the width, in characters, of the screen display.

Table 13-1 Width

W#	set width of item—pad with spaces
W#.#	set width and decimal places

Table 13-2 Date Format Codes

D1	mm/dd/yy
D2	month dd, yyyy
D3	mm/dd
D4	mm/yy
D5	dd-Mon-yy
D6	Mon yy
D7	dd Mon yyyy
D8	mm/d/yyyy
D9	dd.mm.yy
D10	dd/mm/yy
D11	yy-mm-dd

Table 13-3 Text Format Codes

AL	align left
AR	align right
AC	align center
CU	convert to all uppercase
CL	convert to all lowercase
CC	first letter each word uppercase

Table 13-4 Numeric Format Codes

E$	floating $
EC	commas added as separators
EZ	print leading zeros
EB	no leading zeros
E*	use * to fill leading spaces
EI	international format
ES	scientific notation format

❑ **Data Items.** The data item is the item which will be formatted. This can be a literal value, a field name, or an expression.

Centering Items on the Screen

You can use the FORMAT functions to augment the items displayed on the PAL canvas. In the script you are currently working on, you have arrived at a point where you will want to display information on the canvas. The first item will be a title explaining the rest of the display. Titles are often displayed centered on the screen.

Finding the right location at which to place an item so that it appears centered can be tricky. For example, suppose you wanted to print the word *Hello*, horizontally centered on a line. You begin with the knowledge that the screen has 80 columns. The word you want to print will take up five of those columns. That leaves you with 75 columns of blank space. To center an item the blank space should be evenly divided with half placed before the text and half afterwards. Half of 75 is 37.5. This means that you would place the first character at the 37th column on the screen. Recall that Paradox numbers the column beginning with zero, not one, so that the 37th column is column 36. The result of this calculation would be a command like this: **@ 5,36 ?? "Hello".**

The FORMAT() function can be used to achieve the same result without having to count characters and perform arithmetic. The use of FORMAT() is also important because in some cases it is *not* possible to know the number of characters you are printing when the command uses field names. Suppose that you substituted a field for the word *Hello*, e.g., **@ 36 ?? [payee].** This command would work only if you were sure that all of the *Payee* fields contained exactly five characters.

Using FORMAT() allows you to create a command that allows Paradox to perform the calculations necessary to arrive at the correct location, e.g., **"? FORMAT(w80,ac","Hello")** or **? FORMAT("w80,ac",[payee])** would accurately center the text.

The command below positions the cursor at the beginning of the desired line and then prints a centered heading. Add the following command to your script:

```
@ 5,0 ? FORMAT("w80,ac","Checking Account Records")
```

The next set of commands uses the FORMAT() function to display the dates in the Answer table in the D2 date style. Recall that the fields in the Answer table have been assigned the field names *Max of Check date* and *Min of Check date.*

```
@ 8,10 ?? "Beginning Date"
@ 8,30 ?? FORMAT("d2",[min of check date])
@ 10,10 ?? "Ending Date"
@ 10,30 ?? FORMAT("d2",[max check date])
SLEEP 5000 CLEARALL
```

Execute the script by entering

[F10] g

The script displays the dates in the month name, day, and year format due to the effect of the FORMAT() function, Figure 13-5.

```
                    Checking Account Records
Beginning Date           January  1, 1989
Ending Date              March 12, 1989
```

Figure 13-5 Format function used to display data.

Finding the Account Balance

You can expand the operation of the RANGE1 script to include finding the current checking account balance. Load the script into the editor by entering

s e e
range1 ↵

The first change is to expand the query form to include other calculations, such as the sum of the *Amount* and *Deposit* fields. Below is the modified query form with the changes in **bold**. Make these changes in your script.

QUERY

ck_book	check date	**amount**	**deposit**
	calc max,calc min	**calc sum**	**calc sum**

ENDQUERY
DO_IT!

Decimal Alignment

The additions to the query form will generate two additional fields in the Answer table, *Sum of Amount* and *Sum of Deposit*. You can use those fields to display the totals of the *Amount* and *Deposit* fields. You can also find the checking account balance by displaying the result of a formula that subtracts *Sum of Deposit* from *Sum of Amount*. You will need to insert some additional commands following line 13 in the script. Remember to place Paradox in the Insert mode by pressing **[Ins]**. You can insert a new line following line 13 by placing the cursor at the end of line 13 and entering ↵.

In this case, you will want to display three values, representing the total deposits, total checks, and the account balance. When printing values such as this, it is best to place the values so that they align correctly in terms of decimal places. Suppose you entered the following commands into the script.

```
@ 10,10 ?? [sum of amount]
@ 11,10 ?? [sum of deposit]
@ 12,10 ?? [sum of deposit]-[sum of amount]
```

Since all the commands print at column 10, the values generated by the expressions should be aligned correctly. However, the command would result in a display that looks like the one in Figure 13-6.

```
4853.69
4860.00
6.31
```

Figure 13-6 Numeric values aligned to the left.

While it is true that the values are aligned vertically, they are aligned vertically to the *left*. Numeric values must be aligned to the *right* so that the decimal places of values with different numbers of figures can align vertically.

One solution is to use a FORMAT() function to set a fixed width with a fixed number of decimal places, e.g., **W10.2,** for each item and use **AR** (align right) to align the value to the right side of the display area. You should choose a width value that you are sure is large enough to hold the values that will be generated by the query form. In addition, you can use the **EC** format code to insert commas, where needed, in the numbers. Add the commands shown below in **bold** following line 13 of the script. Note that for the vertical alignment to work properly you must use the same format codes for each value.

@ 10,30 ?? FORMAT(''d2'',[max of check date])
@ 12,10 ?? ''Total Deposits''
@ 12,30 ?? FORMAT(''w10.2,ar,ec'',[sum of amount])
@ 14,10 ?? ''Totals Checks''
@ 14,30 ?? FORMAT(''w10.2,ar,ec'',[sum of deposit])
@ 16,10 ?? ''Current Balance''
@ 16,30 ?? FORMAT(''w10.2,ar,ec'',[sum of deposit]-[sum of amount])
SLEEP 5000 CLEARALL

Execute the script by entering

[F10] g

The script displays the numeric values, including the checking account balance, correctly aligned according to decimal place value, Figure 13-7.

The RANGE1 script will be accurate each time it is run because it will query the table so that any new entries will be included in its processing. Add a new deposit to the table. Enter

```
                Checking Account Records
Beginning Date        January  1, 1989
Ending Date           March 12, 1989
Total Deposits          4,853.69
Totals Checks           4,860.00
Current Balance             6.31
```

Figure 13-7 Totals and balance aligned on decimal point.

m d
ck_book ↵
5 ↵
100 ↵
3/22/89 ↵
Deposit ↵
↵ *(5 times)*
875.90

Save the new record by entering

[F2]

To find the new balance run the RANGE1 script by entering

[F10] s p
range1 ↵

The program immediately reflects the change made to the Ck_book table by showing a new ending date, total deposit, and balance values, Figure 13-8.

```
                Checking Account Records
Beginning Date        January  1, 1989
Ending Date           March 22, 1989
Total Deposits          4,853.69
Totals Checks           5,735.90
Current Balance           882.21
```

Figure 13-8 Script updates results.

Questions and Answers

The scripts that you have created so far are examples of *monologues* rather than *dialogs*. The RANGE1 script carries out a one-way conversation with the user, in which all of the information flows from the program to the user in the form of screen output on the PAL canvas. In this respect, the function of these scripts is the same as of those created in Part 1.

The next step in sophistication is to create script programs that allow for a two-way conversation, a *dialog*, between the user and the application. This dialog takes a question-and-answer form. At one or more points in the script, the program will pause to ask the user to enter a response. The pause can be used to ask the user a question, to request the entry of data, or to allow the user to state a preference.

Adding dialogs to scripts is significant for several reasons.

❑ **Interactivity.** Scripts that pause for user input are more interesting to work with because the user is involved in the operations instead of simply being a passive reader of information.

❑ **Flexibility.** The responses entered by the user can be used to change the way the rest of the script operates. For example, instead of using the **SLEEP** command to pause a script for a predetermined length of time, the script might pause until the user presses a key. This allows the user to control the length of time rather than having it built into the program.

❑ **General Application.** When a script allows the user to enter responses, the script can be designed to carry out tasks in a more *generalized* way. For example, suppose you wanted to have scripts that would summarize each month in a manner similar to the way RANGE1 summarized the entire account. One way would be to create specific scripts for each month. An alternative would be to create a single script that would ask the user what month he wanted to summarize and use the response to carry out the operations for the selected month. By using user responses in this way, a single script can be substituted for a number of scripts with fixed parameters.

Variables

The key concept in program dialogs is the concept of a *variable*. When a script pauses to allow the user to enter a response, Paradox must have some way of storing the response so that it can be integrated into the rest of the script.

Up to this point all data has been stored in database tables. A *variable* is an area in the memory of the computer in which data can be stored without having to place it into a field in any of the existing database tables. The term *variable* refers to the fact that the value of a variable is subject to change.

In many ways, variables in Paradox perform a role similar to variables used in mathematical formulas. They can be used to *hold the place* of some actual value (which is yet to be determined) when you are writing commands in a script. In this respect, they function like field names. The primary difference is that unlike fields, variables are not associated with a particular table, record, or field.

Variables in Paradox have the following characteristics.

❑ **Names.** A variable name can be up to 132 characters in length but unlike a field name it *cannot contain spaces*. Underscores can be used to create variable names that appear to be composed of several words, e.g., *your_choice*.

❑ **Types.** Variables have the same types as fields. However, variables behave differently than fields in that a variable's type is not fixed. When you create a variable, it takes on a data type based on the contents use to define the variable. If you store a numeric value for a variable, that variable will behave like a numeric data item. If you redefine the variable at a later point as a different data type, e.g., date or text, the variable will then change types.

❑ **Duration.** Once a variable is created, it will remain in the memory until you exit Paradox. This makes variables *global* in their accessibility in contrast to fields which have meaning only when the table in which the field is contained is available on the work area. Once defined in a script, a variable remains in memory until you exit Paradox. In order to avoid confusion, you will probably want to erase all variables from memory when you no longer need the values. The **RELEASE VARS ALL** command, usually placed at the end of a script, clears all variables from memory.

How Variables Are Created

Variables can be created in two basic ways.

❑ **User Input.** Variables can be created as a result of a user's response to a prompt displayed during a script. The most direct method is to use the **ACCEPT** command. This command pauses the execution of a script in order to allow the user to enter a data item. The item that is entered is assigned to a variable. The command shown below pauses a script and waits for a user response. After the user has entered a response and pressed ↵, the command assigns the response to the variable named *last_name*. The variable is now available to other commands such as **?** and **??** for output.

```
ACCEPT "A20" TO last_name
```

Note that the data type of the variable is determined by the data type code **A20** (alpha 20) used in the **ACCEPT** command.

❑ **Direct Definition.** You can create a variable by writing a statement that looks a bit like a mathematical equation. The command below creates a variable called *sales_tax_amount* that contains the result of the formula **[amount]*1.07** in which the field *Amount* is multiplied by 1.07. In this example, the data type of the variable is determined by the type of expression assigned to it—here, numeric.

```
sales_tax_amoount=[amount]*1.07
```

While the command looks like an equation, the = should be understood to mean *is defined as*. This type of command assigns the value of the expression to the right of the = sign to the variable name written to the left of the = sign. The command could be read as meaning: *sales_tax_amount* **is defined as the value of [amount]*1.07**. It is important to keep this in mind when you are looking at commands that assign a value from one variable name to another. Below are two commands that transfer data from one variable name to another. Command {1} takes the current value of *customer_name* and copies it to a new variable called *last_name*, while command {2} does just the opposite.

```
{1}  last_name=customer_name
{2}  customer_name=last_name
```

Direct assigning of values to variables allows you to manipulate the value of variables behind the scenes.

Dialogs are created by combining prompts created with the **?** or **??** commands with an **ACCEPT** command. The example below uses **?** to display the prompt *Enter your last name:* before the script is paused for the user's input.

```
? "Enter your last name;" ACCEPT "A25" TO last _name
```

Editing versus Inputting

The use of memory variables has much in common with the use of fields. However, it is important to keep in mind that Paradox provides more flexibility when it comes to editing fields than it does to entering responses to **ACCEPT** commands.

Data entry and editing of fields takes place in a *full screen editing* mode. This means you can move back and forth among all the fields displayed and make changes in the values as many times as you desire. The [Alt-F5] command can be used to edit items within a field using the field Edit mode.

This is not the case with entries made to **ACCEPT** variables. Once you press ↵ the value is passed to the variable and cannot be revised unless you execute another **ACCEPT** command for the same variable. This is true even though the value you entered is still displayed on the screen. Paradox does not permit you to move the cursor **back** to that entry area as you could in the table Edit mode.

Also note that when you use **ACCEPT** to enter a value, the current value, if any, of the variable is not displayed.

If you design a program that calls for a large amount of data entry, you may find that it is better to create a table for the entry of the values instead of using individual variables. This approach is discussed in more detail later in Part 2.

The ACCEPT Command

The **ACCEPT** command consists of four basic items as shown below. The *type_code* is a character string which uses the same system as the field type entries, i.e., N for numeric, D for date, and A# for text of # number of characters.

```
ACCEPT type_code TO variable_name
```

In addition to this basic usage, you can add the following options to the **ACCEPT** command. *Options* are additional key words that can be used with a PAL command to control various aspects of its operation with features similar to the ValCheck option found on the Edit menu.

❑ **PICTURE.** This option acts in a similar manner to the Picture options in the ValCheck menu. You can use the picture to control the format of input. Example:

```
ACCEPT "a8" PICTURE "###-####" TO phone_number
```

❑ **MIN *value*, MAX *value*.** These options are used to restrict the entry to a range of values. In the example below, these options limit the entry to a value between 99 and 1.

```
ACCEPT "n" MIN 1 MAX 99 TO interest_rate
```

❑ **DEFAULT *value*.** This option inserts a default value into the input area. The value can be accepted with ↵ or edited.

```
ACCEPT "n" DEFAULT 10 TO interest_rate
```

❑ **LOOKUP *table_name*.** This option allows you to use the values stored in the first field of a specified table as a validity check in the entry. If used, the value entered must match one of the values in the first field of the specified table or the entry is rejected by Paradox.

❑ **REQUIRED.** This option causes Paradox to require an entry for a variable that should not be left blank.

You can use one or more of these options in combination, if desired.

When using **ACCEPT** commands, take care to take the size of the variable into account when writing data on the screen. For example, creating a numeric input with an accept, e.g., **ACCEPT "n" TO value**, would create an input area 23 characters wide, beginning at the cursor location and extending to the right. The input area would overwrite any text already located at that position. The commands shown below both place text on line 10.

```
@ 10,0 ?? "aaaaaaaaaabbbbbbbbbbccccccccc"
@ 10,0 ACCEPT "n" TO x
```

The result of these commands is shown in Figure 13-9 in which the first 23 characters on line 10 are overwritten by the **ACCEPT** command. If the **ACCEPT**command was displaying a date entry, only the first eight characters would be overwritten. The size of alpha input areas would correspond to the size specified in the type code.

```
                         ccccccc
```

Figure 13-9 Input area overwrites text.

Because input areas have the same color as the PAL canvas background, their size is not apparent. However, if you are placing input areas on the same lines as text, you need to be aware of what text will be overwritten by the input areas generated by the **ACCEPT** commands.

Writing Script Dialogs

When you add dialogs—between the program and the user—to a script, you can create scripts of all types. You can even create scripts that perform tasks not directly related to manipulation of database tables.

For example, you can create *calculator* programs which manipulate user input to perform calculations. Paradox contains a number of mathematical and financial functions that can produce special values, such as standard deviations or the monthly payment on a loan. As an example, create a script that will calculate the monthly mortgage payment based on the input of the user. Calculator-type programs have three sections.

❑ **User Input.** The program begins by asking the user to enter a value or values. This is done with **ACCEPT** commands.

❑ **Processing.** Once the user has entered the required values, the program, behind the scenes, calculates the values resulting from the user's input. This section often makes use of special functions to perform complex calculations. The resulting values are assigned to memory variables.

❑ **Output Results.** Once the processing section has created the information and stored it in the memory variables, the information can be displayed on the screen.

Begin by creating a new script called MORT by entering

s e w
mort ↵

Begin the script with the **CLEARALL** and **CLEAR** commands.

```
CLEARALL CLEAR
```

Display a title in the center of line 5. Note that the **?** command always begins at the *next*, not the *current*, line. Therefore, to print on line 5, you would use @ **4,0 ?** since **?** skips to the next line or @ **5,0 ??**.

```
@ 4,0 ? FORMAT("w79,ac","Calculate Monthly Mortgage Payment")
? FORMAT("w80,ac","30 Year Fixed Rate Mortgages")
```

Ordering Prompts and Inputs

The next section of the script will be used to acquire from the user values that are needed to perform the calculation, such as the cost of the house and the interest rate charged on the loan. There are two ways to approach this section. Both sets of commands below contain exactly the same instructions, i.e., display two prompts and accept entry into two variables. The difference is in the order in which the commands are listed. In Example 1 the **PROMPT** and **ACCEPT** commands are executed in matching pairs. The second example executes the two **PROMPT** commands first, followed by the **ACCEPT** commands.

Example 1

```
@ 7,10 ?? "Amount to Borrow" @ 7,40 ACCEPT "n" TO loan
@ 8,10 ?? "Interest Rate"    @ 8,40 ACCEPT "n" TO rate
```

Example 2

```
@ 7,10 ?? "Amount to Borrow"
@ 8,10 ?? "Interest Rate"
@ 7,40 ACCEPT "n" TO loan
@ 8,40 ACCEPT "n" TO
```

The difference is significant because each **ACCEPT** command *pauses* the script at that point. The next command will not execute until an entry is completed. This would mean that Example 1 would display the *Interest Rate* prompt only after the amount was entered. Example 2 would display both prompts *before* the program paused for user input. In most cases, it is desirable for the user to have some idea how many different values he will be asked to enter before beginning entry, instead of having the prompts pop up only after each entry is made.

In most cases, the method shown in Example 2 is preferable. Enter the following section into the script.

```
@ 7,10 ?? "Cost of Home"
@ 8,10 ?? "Down Payment"
@ 9,10 ?? "Interest Rate"
@ 7,40 ACCEPT "n" TO price
@ 8,40 ACCEPT "n" TO down
@ 9,40 ACCEPT "n" TO rate
```

Calculating the Results

Once you have obtained the input from the user, you can now manipulate the data to arrive at the answer you desire. The first calculation would be to find the amount of the loan by subtracting the down payment from the price. This can be done by defining a new variable, *loan*, as the result of that calculation. The = command can be used to directly define the new variable. Enter the following command.

```
loan=price-down
```

The calculation to find the monthly payment is a bit complicated. However, Paradox simplifies the operation with a built-in function that performs the calculation automatically. The PMT() function can calculate the monthly payment given three arguments.

PMT(*loan_amount,rate,periods*)

The *rate* is the rate of interest charged per period. Since interest rates are normally quoted as annual rates you will need to divide the rate by the number of periods per year if more than one payment is made per year. On the other hand, *periods* refers to the total number of payments. For example, a 10 percent annual rate for 30 years would require you to divide the rate by 12 and multiply the years by 12 to get the periods. Also, in this case you assume that the interest rate will be entered as a whole number. In order to convert that whole number to a percent it must be multiplied by .01.

> *Note that PMT() applies to a standard loan calculation on which interest is paid only on the unpaid balance each month. This means that the principal declines some amount with each payment. Loans made for cars or other consumer loans often use special loan contracts in which all interest charges are paid first without decreasing the principal with each payment.*

Use this function to derive the monthly payment amount.

```
payment=PMT(loan,rate*.01/12,360)
```

You now have the payment value assigned to a variable. You might want to use that value to generate other values. For example, you could find the total amount of interest paid over the life of the loan by using the *payment* variable. Add the following commands. Note that in this case, both commands are entered on a single line.

```
total_payments=payment*360 total_interest=total_payments-loan
```

Displaying the Results

The last part of a calculator program is the display of the results. In this case, you will display the values stored in the variables *loan, payment, total_payments,* and *total_interest*. You can use functions, such as FORMAT(), to control the format of the numbers. Add the following section to the script.

```
@ 12,10 ?? "Loan Amount"
@ 12,40 ?? FORMAT("w12.2,ec",loan)
@ 13,10 ?? "Monthly Payment"
@ 13,40 ?? FORMAT("w12.2,ec",payment)
@ 14,10 ?? "Total Payments"
@ 14,40 ?? FORMAT("w12.2,ec",total_payments )
@ 15,10 ?? "Total Interest"
@ 15,40 ?? FORMAT("w12.2,ec",total_interest)
```

Pausing Scripts with GETCHAR

The final part of the program must contain a command that pauses so the user can read the results on the screen. In the previous scripts, a **SLEEP** command was used to pause a specified number of seconds. In many cases, the **SLEEP** command is not an adequate way to pause the script because it is hard to know in advance the correct amount of time needed to maintain the pause. In the current example, a better solution would be to pause the display until the user decides he has finished with the screen. There are two ways to create this pause.

❑ **ACCEPT.** You can pause a script by using an **ACCEPT** command. In this usage, the actual value entered is not important. The user can simply press ↵ to terminate the pause. The commands below display the prompt *Press Enter to Continue...* at the bottom of the screen, along with a pause which waits for the user to enter ↵. Note that the width of the format is set at 79 characters to allow room for the input area at the end of the line, which is the lower right hand corner of the screen. The input area is set at a single character with the "a1" type code.

```
@ 24,0 ?? FORMAT("w79,ac","Press Enter to Continue...")
ACCEPT "a1" TO x
```

❑ **GETCHAR() Function.** The GETCHAR() function operates differently from most Paradox functions in that it causes the script to pause and wait for a user response, in much the same manner as the **ACCEPT** command. The primary difference between **ACCEPT** and **GETCHAR()** is that **GETCHAR()** stores only one keystroke and then automatically releases Paradox to continue the script. In addition, the character is not stored in alpha text format but as a numeric value equal to the ASCII decimal value of the key that is pressed. The example commands below shows how **GETCHAR()** would be used in place of **ACCEPT** to pause a script.

```
@ 24,0 ?? FORMAT("w79,ac","Press any key to continue...")
x=GETCHAR()
```

> *If the key pressed is not one of 128 standard ASCII keys, e.g., special IBM keyboard keys such as [Home] or [End], the value stored is a negative number. The number stored for each special key is determined by the Paradox extended keycodes found on pages 507-508.*

The advantage of **GETCHAR()** is that it will terminate the pause as soon as *any* key is pressed, in contrast to the **ACCEPT** command which will terminate the pause only when the ↵ key is pressed. In most cases, the **GETCHAR()** method is more comfortable for the user.

Creating a Keystroke Pause

Add the following commands to the end of the script to create a pause which will be terminated as soon as the user presses any key.

In addition to the pause, two other commands appear at the end of the script, **RELEASE VARS ALL** and **RETURN**. These commands perform housekeeping functions. The **RELEASE VARS ALL** command erases all the variables from the memory. The **RETURN** command marks the end of the script by telling Paradox to return to the previous script or the work space display. To a great degree, these commands are superfluous in this simple example. For example, Paradox will return to the main work area when it runs out of script commands even if you don't use the **RETURN** command. However, the commands represent good programming habits that will pay off when you are writing more complex scripts.

```
@ 24,0 ?? FORMAT("w79,ac","Press any key to continue...")
x=GETCHAR()
RELEASE VARS ALL
RETURN
```

The entire MORT script should now read:

```
CLEARALL CLEAR
@ 4,0 ? FORMAT("w79,ac","Calculate Monthly Mortgage Payment")
? FORMAT("w80,ac","30 Year Fixed Rate Mortgages")
@ 7,10 ?? "Cost of Home"
@ 8,10 ?? "Down Payment"
@ 9,10 ?? "Interest Rate"
@ 7,40 ACCEPT "n" TO price
@ 8,40 ACCEPT "n" TO down
@ 9,40 ACCEPT "n" TO rate
loan=price-down
payment=PMT(loan,rate*.01/12,360)
total_payments=payment*360 total_interest=total_payments-loan
@ 12,10 ?? "Loan Amount"
@ 12,40 ?? FORMAT("w12.2,ec",loan)
@ 13,10 ?? "Monthly Payment"
@ 13,40 ?? FORMAT("w12.2,ec",payment)
@ 14,10 ?? "Total Payments"
@ 14,40 ?? FORMAT("w12.2,ec",total_payments )
```

```
@ 15,10 ?? "Total Interest"
@ 15,40 ?? FORMAT("w12.2,ec",total_interest)
@ 24,0 ?? FORMAT("w79,ac","Press any key to continue...")
x=GETCHAR()
RELEASE VARS ALL
RETURN
```

Execute the script by entering

[F10] g

The script displays the text and places the cursor on the *Cost of Home* line waiting for you to enter a value, Figure 13-10.

```
Calculate Monthly Mortgage Payment
                30 Year Fixed Rate Mortgages
Cost of Home
Down Payment
Interest Rate
```

Figure 13-10 Display generated by MORT script.

Enter 150,000 as the amount.

150000 ↵

Errors in Scripts

What happened? When you entered the amount, Paradox encountered an error in the script. Paradox displayed the message **Script error - select Cancel or Debug from menu** in the lower right corner of the screen. In the upper left corner a menu is displayed, Figure 13-11, that lists two options.

❑ **Cancel.** This option immediately cancels the script and returns you to the main work area.

❑ **Debug.** This option places Paradox into the debugging mode. In this mode, Paradox displays the commands being executed as the script plays. This enables you to associate directly the action taking place with the commands in the script. In addition, when an error occurs, Paradox displays a message indicating what is wrong with the command that is causing the error.

```
Cancel  Debug
Stop playing script.
```

Figure 13-11 Script error menu.

In this case, since you are probably not aware of what is causing the error, it is best to activate the Debug mode by entering

d

Once activated, the Debug mode immediately reacts to the error by displaying, Figure 13-12, information about the cause of the error.

```
                                        Syntax error: Expecting a variable name

Script: MORT  Line:   8                     Type Control-Q to Quit
@ 8,40 ACCEPT "n" TO  ▶ down
```

Figure 13-12 Error messages in debug mode.

The last line on the screen shows the command, **@ 8,40 ACCEPT "n" TO down**, which caused the error. Above that line, Paradox identifies the script and the line number in which the offending command appears: **Script: MORT Line: 8.**

In addition, Paradox displays a message that explains what is wrong with the command. In this case, the message is **Syntax error: Expecting a variable name**. If you look at the command shown on the last line of the screen, you will see that there is a flashing arrow pointing at the word **down** indicating it is the source of the problem.

Syntax errors are mistakes made in the writing of Paradox commands. Since these errors are so basic to script execution, Paradox permits you only two options.

❑ **Quit.** The command [Ctrl-q] will terminate the script at the current line and return you to the main work area. Note that any tables or other items generated by the script will be left in the exact position they are in when the error in the script was encountered.

❑ **Edit.** The command [Ctrl-e] will immediately activate the script editor mode and place the cursor at the line in the script that caused the error.

Use the Edit option by entering

[Ctrl-e]

The mode changes to the script editor and the cursor is positioned at the beginning of line 8. You can now correct the error.

Reserved Words

You are now in a position to correct the error, assuming that you know what caused the error. The message displayed by Paradox when it encountered the error was **Syntax error: Expecting a variable name**. The arrow was pointing at the word **down** as the source of the problem. But what is wrong with the command? Isn't **down** the name of the variable you want to use?

The answer is that Paradox does not recognize **down** as the name of a variable. But why? The word seems to fit the rule for variable names. However, there is another restriction placed on variable names. The names cannot be the same as PAL commands or function names. The word **DOWN** is the PAL command that corresponds to the ↓ key. These words are called *reserved* because they belong to the Paradox language and therefore cannot be used as variables. In this case, Paradox sees **down** as a command. This leaves the **ACCEPT** command without a variable name, resulting in the error.

Correcting the Script

The solution to this problem is to change the name to something other than **down**. For example, the name **down_payment** would be acceptable. Begin by changing the current line.

Old line 8 @ 8,10 ACCEPT "n" TO down
New line 8 @ 8,10 ACCEPT "n" TO down **_payment**

Remember that you will have to change every command in the remainder of the script that uses the **down** variable as well. Move the cursor to line 10 and make the change in the variable name.

Old line 10 loan=price-down
New line 10 loan=price-down**_payment**

Play the revised script by entering

[F10] g

Enter the value of the house.

150000 ↵

This time, the program goes on to the next input area without an error. Enter the down payment amount.

25000 ↵

Finally, enter the interest rate.

10 ↵

The program responds by calculating and displaying the information about the loan, Figure 13-13.

```
                Calculate Monthly Mortgage Payment
                    30 Year Fixed Rate Mortgages
       Cost of Home                 150000
       Down Payment                 25000
       Interest Rate                10
       Loan Amount                    125,000.00
       Monthly Payment                  1,096.96
       Total Payments                 394,907.21
       Total Interest                 269,907.21

              Press any key to continue...
```

Figure 13-13 MORT script calculates mortgage information.

The script pauses, waiting for you to enter a key. Enter

[space bar]

The script terminates and Paradox returns to the main work area. Run the script again to see what the difference would be if the interest rate was 11 percent. Enter

s p
mort ↵
150000 ↵
25000 ↵
11 ↵

This time, the monthly payment is $1,190.40—an increase of 93.44 over the 1,096.96 required for a 10 percent mortgage. Complete the program by entering

↵

Passing Input to Queries

The ability to create programs with dialogs greatly expands the utility of scripts. In the calculator-type script MORT, you used the dialog to allow the user to specify the specific values they wanted to use for the mortgage calculation. This is an important change in the way that you have been using scripts. The MORT script differs from all of the others you have created in that its result is determined by the interaction of the user with the script.

The same techniques can be applied to scripts that work with tables, including those that use query forms to generate data. Recall that the Ck_book tables have assigned a ledger account number to each of the transactions in the table. Suppose you wanted to create a script that summarized the activity in a specified account. This script would require you to combine the query form processing used in the RANGE1 script with the dialog techniques illustrated in the MORT script.

The key to linking these two techniques is called a *tilde variable*. A *tilde variable* is a variable inserted into a query form. In order to indicate that the item is a variable name instead of a literal item in the query form, a ~ (tilde) character is placed in front of the variable name. The ~ tells Paradox to perform a symbolic substitution in which the variable name is replaced with the current value of the variable, Figure 13-14.

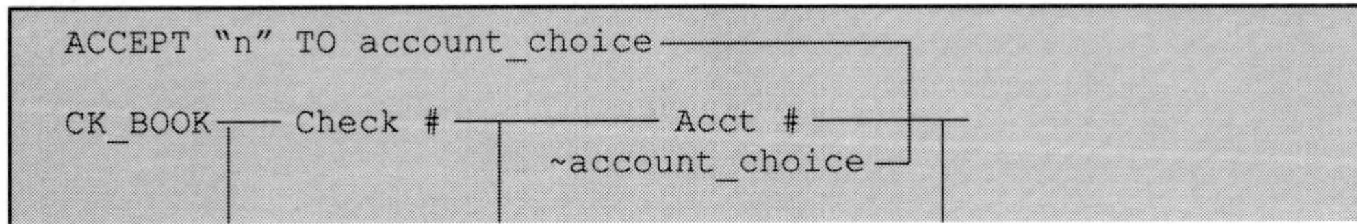

Figure 13-14 Tilde variable passes user entry to query form.

Using Tilde Variables

As an example of how this approach works, create a script that allows the users to enter the account number of the account they want summarized. Create a new script by entering

s e w
actsum ↵

Begin with the clear commands.

```
CLEARALL CLEAR
```

Display a title on the screen that identifies the program's function.

```
@ 4,0 ?? FORMAT("w79,ac","Summarize Ledger Account")
```

Create a prompt and an input area that will allow the user to enter the account number. In this case, the account numbers should be restricted to those valid account numbers listed in the Accounts table. This can be done easily by using the LOOKUP option with the **ACCEPT** command. LOOKUP requires that the data entered by the user match one of the values in the first field of the specified table. In this case, the first field in the Accounts table contains the valid account numbers.

```
@ 7,20 ?? "Enter Account to Summarize: "
ACCEPT "n" LOOKUP "accounts" TO choice
```

Adding Comments

As the complexity and length of the scripts you create increases, a need arises for you to *document* the programs you are writing. The term *document* refers to the insertion of text comments into the program file. These comments are used to explain the purpose of various commands or groups of commands within your program. At first, the addition of comments may seem like a waste of time since you are aware of why you are entering the commands. The value of the comments is that they will serve as reminders when you return to the program at a later time. They also serve as a guide to other users who might need to understand how your program functions.

You can add comments to any part of a script by placing a semicolon in front of the comment text. The semicolon tells Paradox that the text that follows is not part of the program's commands.

Comments can be written on separate lines or added at the end of a line that contains a command. Add a comment to this script that indicates that the next section of the program will be a query form which that on the user's input.

```
; insert variable choice into query form
```

In this book, most of the programs are written without many comments. This is because the text of the book serves to document the function of the program's commands and to cut down on the amount of lines you are requested to enter into a script. However, in your own programs, comments should be added to identify each major portion of your program. While this may seem to slow down the program writing process, comments often become your only link to the purpose of the commands in the script. It is a good programming habit to document your scripts.

Query Forms with Tilde Variables

The next section of the program is a query form in which the user's input is passed to the query in the form of a *tilde variable*. The query form shown below uses the variable **choice** in the *Acct #* field to select records that match the user's input for account number. Note that the **count** function was placed into *Check #* because that is a key field which—by definition—contains unique values. This will ensure that you get an accurate count of records that match the specified account number. Add the query form to the script.

```
QUERY

Ck_book    | Check #    | Acct #   | Amount   | Deposit  |
           | calc count | ~choice  | calc sum | calc sum |

ENDQUERY
DO_IT!
```

Capturing Answer Table Values

In the RANGE1 script, the summary values included in the Answer table were displayed on the screen by using **??** commands which specified the field names used in the Answer table.

This method will work correctly, as long as the Answer table remains unchanged. However, suppose that in this script you want to display the name of the specified account along with the other information. The name of the account is stored in the Accounts table. You could use another query form operation to retrieve the name associated with the account number.

The problem with a second query operation is that it would replace the current Answer table with a different answer table, which, as a result, would erase the values calculated during the first query.

One solution to this problem is to transfer the values from the first Answer table to memory variables. Once stored in variables, you are no longer dependent on the Answer table to supply the values. With this approach, you can process as many query forms as you desire and still have all of the values available for output.

The following commands transfer the values from the current Answer table into memory variables. Once that is accomplished, you can feel free to clear or overwrite the Answer table without having to be concerned about losing the values.

```
; pass field values to variables
transactions=[count of check #]
total=[sum of amount]+[sum of deposit]
```

Finding the Account Name

You can find the account name by processing a query form which uses the Accounts table. The goal of this query is to obtain the account name related to the account number entered by the user. Once again the *tilde* variable is inserted into a query form. Since **choice** is a memory variable, it can be used in any number of query operations. Add the following query form to the script.

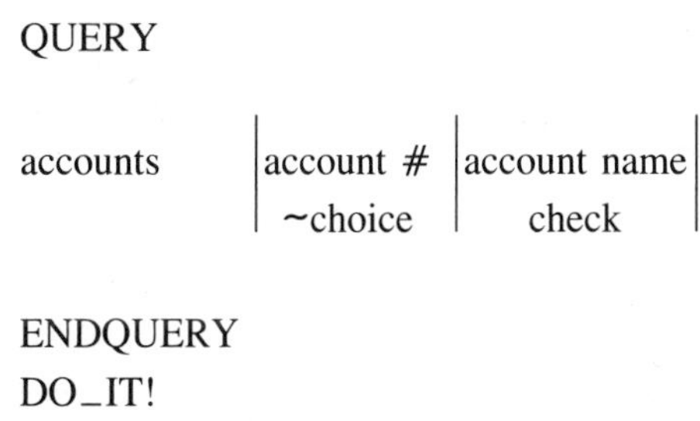

```
QUERY

accounts    | account # | account name |
            | ~choice   | check        |

ENDQUERY
DO_IT!
```

Complete the script with an *output* section in which all of the values related to the account number are displayed. At the end of the section, the GETCHAR() function is used to pause the script and the **RELEASE** command is used to erase the memory variables from memory.

```
; display calculated values
@ 10,10 ?? ``Summary of Account: '',choice,'' – '',[account name]
@ 12,10 ?? ``Number of Transactions''
@ 12,40 ?? FORMAT(``w12,ec'',transactions)
@ 14,10 ?? ``Total of Transactions''
@ 14,40 ?? FORMAT(``w12.2,ec'',total)
@ 16,10 ?? ``Average Transaction''
@ 16,40 ?? FORMAT(``w12.2,ec'',total/transactions)
@ 24,0 ?? FORMAT(``w79,ac'',``Press any key to continue...'')
x=GETCHAR()
RELEASE VARS ALL CLEARALL
RETURN
```

A full listing of the script can be found on page 509.
Execute the script by entering

[F10] g

The program asks you to enter an account number. Enter

200 ↵

Paradox responds by displaying the message **Not one of the possible values for this field** in the lower right corner of the screen. The message is generated because the LOOKUP option used with the **ACCEPT** command restricts entry to values that match the account numbers in the Accounts table. Change the entry

[Ctrl-backspace]
500 ↵

This time the account number is accepted. Paradox completes the processing and displays the summary data, Figure 13-15.
Complete the script by entering

[spacebar]

Execute the script again and enter a different account number.

s p
act_sum ↵
100

This time the information displayed summarizes account 100, Figure 13-16.

```
              Summarize Ledger Account

         Enter Account to Summarize: 500

Summary of Account: 500 - Office Furniture

Number of Transactions                   1

Total of Transactions               750.50

Average Transaction                 750.50
```

Figure 13-15 Account 500 summarized by script.

```
              Summarize Ledger Account

         Enter Account to Summarize: 100

Summary of Account: 100 - Cash in Bank

Number of Transactions                   5

Total of Transactions             5,735.90

Average Transaction               1,147.18
```

Figure 13-16 Account 100 summarized

Complete the script by entering

[spacebar]

The Act_sum script combines a user dialog with Paradox query processing in a way that allows the script to carry out its processing based on the input of a user. The program is a generalized routine for summarizing activity in any of the ledger accounts.

Summary

This chapter discussed the basic techniques involved in creating Paradox scripts that exhibit the characteristics of programs in contrast to the scripts created in Part 1, which simply replay standard Paradox operations.

❑ **PAL Canvas.** When Paradox executes scripts, it displays the PAL canvas instead of the normal work area display. The PAL canvas is a screen display mode that suppresses the elements (table images, menus, messages) which appear on the work area display as you execute Paradox operations. The PAL canvas displays only information specifically placed onto the canvas with commands such as **?** and **??**. The elements displayed by ongoing Paradox operations, such as query forms, cannot be seen while the PAL canvas is active. Conversely, the PAL canvas disappears as soon as a script terminates.

❑ **?/??.** These commands display information such as text literals, fields, Paradox expressions, or variables, on the PAL canvas. The **?** or **??** command is followed by one or more items in a list for display. The **?** command displays the items beginning at the left end of the next row available on the screen. The **??** command displays the items at the current cursor location.

❑ **@.** The @ command positions the cursor on the PAL canvas. The command is followed by two numeric values. The first value indicates the row number while the second value indicates the column number of the position on the screen where the cursor should be located.

❑ **Functions.** A function is a special Paradox PAL language element used to perform special operations such as data conversion or mathematical calculations. Functions are followed by arguments enclosed in parentheses. A function may accept one or more arguments. Some functions, e.g., GETCHAR(), require no arguments.

❑ **FORMAT().** This function allows you to control various aspects of the way data are displayed on the PAL canvas. This function allows you to apply formatting options such as those available from the ValCheck option on the Edit menu, to items displayed on the PAL canvas.

❑ **Dialog.** A dialog refers to a process by which the program displays a prompt, pauses for a user input, and then stores the response in a memory variable so that it is available for further manipulation and analysis by the remainder of the program. Dialogs allow scripts to become more like applications since they can be written in a more generalized fashion that responds to the user's input.

❑ **ACCEPT.** The **ACCEPT** command pauses a script and allows the user to make an entry. The entry is then stored in the memory variable specified in the **ACCEPT** command. The command can use optional clauses **PICTURE**, **MIN**, **MAX**, **LOOKUP**, **DEFAULT**, and **REQUIRED**, which duplicate the input options available from the ValCheck menu of the Edit mode.

❑ **GETCHAR().** When it is necessary to define the value of a variable, this function stores the key code value of the first key pressed to the specified variable name. The advantage of entering a key with GETCHAR is that no ↵ is needed.

Tilde Variables. You can cause Paradox to insert a value stored in a variable within a query form by preceding the variable name with a ~ character.

DEBUG. Paradox has a special operational mode in which data about script commands is available while the script is executed step by step. This mode is used to resolve errors in scripts. When Paradox encounters an error in a script, it gives you the option to enter the Debug mode.

Scripts

Listing of ACT_SUM.SC

```
CLEARALL CLEAR
@ 4,0 ?? FORMAT("w79,ac","Summarize Ledger Account")
@ 7,20 ?? "Enter Account to Summarize: "
ACCEPT "n" LOOKUP "accounts" TO choice
; insert variable choice into query form
QUERY

Ck_book     | Check #    | Acct #  | Amount   | Deposit  |
            | calc count | ~choice | calc sum | calc sum |

ENDQUERY
DO_IT!
; pass field values to variables
transactions=[count of check #]
total=[sum of amount]+[sum of deposit]
QUERY

accounts    | account # | account name |
            |  ~choice  | check        |
ENDQUERY
DO_IT!
; display calculated values
@ 10,10 ?? "Summary of Account: ",choice," - ",[account name]
@ 12,10 ?? "Number of Transactions"
@ 12,40 ?? FORMAT("w12,ec",transactions)
@ 14,10 ?? "Total of Transactions"
```

```
@ 14,40 ?? FORMAT(‘‘w12.2,ec’’,total)
@ 16,10 ?? ‘‘Average Transaction’’
@ 16,40 ?? FORMAT(‘‘w12.2,ec’’,total/transactions)
@ 24,0 ?? FORMAT(‘‘w79,ac’’,‘‘Press any key to continue...’’)
x=GETCHAR()
RELEASE VARS ALL CLEARALL
RETURN
```

ASCII and Extended Keycodes

The following tables list the ASCII and Paradox extended keycode values returned by the GETCHAR() function.

Table 13-5 ASCII keycode values

Value	Key	Value	Key
1	[Ctrl-a]	33	!
2	[Ctrl-b]	34	‘
3	[Ctrl-c]	35	#
4	[Ctrl-d]	36	$
5	[Ctrl-e]	37	%
6	[Ctrl-f]	38	&
7	[Ctrl-g]	39	’
8	[Ctrl-h], [backspace]	40	(
9	[Ctrl-i], [Tab]	41	)
10	[Ctrl-j]	42	*
11	[Ctrl-k]	43	+
12	[Ctrl-l]	44	,
13	[Ctrl-m], ↵	45	-
14	[Ctrl-n]	46	.
15	[Ctrl-o]	47	/
16	[Ctrl-p]	48	0
17	[Ctrl-q]	49	1
18	[Ctrl-r]	50	2
19	[Ctrl-s]	51	3
20	[Ctrl-t]	52	4
21	[Ctrl-u]	53	5
22	[Ctrl-v]	54	6
23	[Ctrl-w]	55	7
24	[Ctrl-x]	56	8
25	[Ctrl-y]	57	9
26	[Ctrl-z]	58	:
27	[Esc]	59	;
28	[Ctrl-\	60‹	
29	[Ctrl-]	61	=
30	[Ctrl-6]	62	›
31	[Ctrl--]	63	?
32	[spacebar]	64	@

65	A	97	a
66	B	98	b
67	C	99	c
68	D	100	d
69	E	101	e
70	F	102	f
71	G	103	g
72	H	104	h
73	I	105	i
74	J	106	j
75	K	107	k
76	L	108	l
77	M	109	m
78	N	110	n
79	O	111	o
80	P	112	p
81	Q	113	q
82	R	114	r
83	S	115	s
84	T	116	t
85	U	117	u
86	V	118	v
87	W	119	w
88	X	120	x
89	Y	121	y
90	Z	122	z
91	[	123	{
92	\	124		
93	]	125	}
94	^	126	~
95	_	127	[Ctrl-←]
96	`		

Table 13-6 Extended keycode values

Value	Key	Value	Key
-3	Null	-36	[Alt-j]
-15	↵	-37	[Alt-k]
-16	[Alt-q]	-44	[Alt-z]
-17	[Alt-w]	-45	[Alt-x]
-18	[Alt-e]	-46	[Alt-c]
-19	[Alt-r]	-47	[Alt-v]
-20	[Alt-t]	-48	[Alt-b]
-21	[Alt-y]	-49	[Alt-n]
-22	[Alt-u]	-50	[Alt-m]
-23	[Alt-i]	-59	[F1]
-24	[Alt-o]	-60	[F2]
-25	[Alt-p]	-61	[F3]
-30	[Alt-a]	-62	[F4]
-31	[Alt-s]	-63	[F5]
-32	[Alt-d]	-64	[F6]
-33	[Alt-f]	-65	[F7]
-34	[Alt-g]	-66	[F8]
-35	[Alt-h]	-67	[F9]

-68	[F10]	-102	[Ctrl-F9]
-71	[Home]	-103	[Ctrl-F10]
-72	↑	-104	[Alt-F1]
-73	[Pg Up]	-105	[Alt-F2]
-74		-106	[Alt-F3]
-75	←	-107	[Alt-F4]
-76		-108	[Alt-F5]
-77	→	-109	[Alt-F6]
-78		-110	[Alt-F7]
-79	[End]	-111	[Alt-F8]
-80	↓	-112	[Alt-F9]
-81	[Pg Dn]	-113	[Alt-F10]
-82	[Ins]	-114	[Ctrl-PrtSc]
-83	[Del]	-115	[Ctrl-←]
-84	[Shift-F1]	-116	[Ctrl-→]
-85	[Shift-F2]	-117	[Ctrl-End]
-86	[Shift-F3]	-118	[Ctrl-Pg Dn]
-87	[Shift-F4]	-119	[Ctrl-Home]
-88	[Shift-F5]	-120	[Alt-1]
-89	[Shift-F6]	-121	[Alt-2]
-90	[Shift-F7]	-122	[Alt-3]
-91	[Shift-F8]	-123	[Alt-4]
-92	[Shift-F9]	-124	[Alt-5]
-93	[Shift-F10]	-125	[Alt-6]
-94	[Ctrl-F1]	-126	[Alt-7]
-95	[Ctrl-F2]	-127	[Alt-8]
-96	[Ctrl-F3]	-128	[Alt-9]
-97	[Ctrl-F4]	-129	[Alt-0]
-98	[Ctrl-F5]	-130	[Alt--]
-99	[Ctrl-F6]	-131	[Alt-=]
-100	[Ctrl-F7]	-132	[ctrl-Pg Up]
-101	[Ctrl-F8]		

14

Designing Menus

In Chapter 13, you learned how to create scripts that do more than replay a sequence of keystrokes. You were able to use PAL commands in script files to create screen displays on which only the exact information you desired appeared. Further, you were able to create scripts that would carry on a dialog with the user in the form of pauses, allowing the user to enter information which in turn is integrated into the remainder of the script. In this chapter you will learn more about how the types and styles of dialogs can be included in your Paradox script programs.

The User Interface

These features create the *user interface* of the program. In a broad manner, the term *user interface* refers to the way in which the user and the program communicate with each other. In many ways, the dialog that takes place is only the tip of the iceberg. A large number of instructions entered into a script program do not actually place information on the screen. They execute behind the scenes without the user even being aware of what their functions are. When you write a program, you are always making a specific decision about what information the user sees at any given point in the program.

To a great degree the art of writing programs is to know how much information and what kind of information should be placed on the screen at any given moment. To know the answer, you must try to place yourself in the position of someone using the program you are writing. What can you assume that they understand or know and what do you need to tell them? The answer to these questions should be reflected in the *user interface* you create for your program. When it comes to the dialog portion of your program there are three ways in which the dialog can be carried out.

❑ **Direct Entry.** Direct entry is the type of question and answer dialog created by using prompts and ACCEPT commands, as discussed in Chapter 13. The approach allows users to fill in a response of their own choosing each time the script is paused with an **ACCEPT** command. The user is free to enter anything wanted. The entry may be rejected because of restrictions placed on the entry by data type, MAX, MIN, or LOOKUP options, but users are free to try to enter anything they can think of.

❑ **Menus.** Menus represent a list of possible options from which the user can make a selection. Paradox menus consist of horizontal bars across the top of the screen from which you can make selections. Menus have two advantages: they list all the possible options for the user and by their nature limit the user's response to a selection of one of the items on the current menu. Menus provide a tighter control on what the user can select.

❑ **Full-screen Editing.** Full-screen editing refers to a screen display that allows the user to make direct entry into a number of input areas. Full-screen operations allow the user to enter and edit a number of items at one time. When all the entry and editing changes have been made, the user signals the program with a special command. In Paradox, full-screen editing screens are usually related to tables, and their displays are controlled by screen forms. The standard completion signal is the **DO IT!** command.

All three of these approaches have strengths and weakness. Programs will typically use various combinations of dialog depending upon the situation and the desired response. The key issues in designing a user interface involve how much control you should allow the user to have over the flow of the program. In the calculator program Mort, which you created in Chapter 13, the user was restricted to entering values one at a time. The user was unable to go back and edit a value after it was entered. Is this the best way to carry out this type of dialog? What alternatives are available?

In the previous chapter, you learned the basic technique used to create *direct entry* with the **ACCEPT** command. In this chapter, you will learn to use a more complicated style of user interface to enhance the appearance and operation of scripts.

User-Defined Menus

The most common form of user interface in Paradox is the tree structure bar menu which appears at the top of the screen in the major Paradox work modes, e.g., Main, Report, Graph, etc. These menus are built into the Paradox program and are suppressed when the PAL canvas is activated during the execution of a script. However, PAL includes a command called

SHOWMENU which allows you to create user-defined menu bars that can be integrated into the operation of your script programs. The **SHOWMENU** command requires two items of information.

❑ **Menu Items.** The items that appear on the bar menu are defined by a list of text items written in pairs. Each pair consists of a menu item followed by a comma, and then the text that will appear on the second line of the menu when the highlight is placed on the item. The example below would create a menu option that reads **Add**. When Add is highlighted, the text **Add more records** would appear on the second line of the menu.

```
"Add":"Add more records"
```

The menu is made up of a series of menu specifications like the one above separated by commas. The script pictured in Figure 14-1 shows a **SHOWMENU** command that will have three items: Add, Delete, and Quit. Note that no comma is used after the last menu item in the list. The text for the second line is required. If you do not want to display text on the second line, you must enter a null item, as shown below.

```
"Add":""
```

The menu bars generated by this command will function just like the built-in Paradox menu bars. This means that if the menu contains more items than can fit across a single screen, the program will scroll the menu options left and right as you move the highlight past either end of the menu. You can make selections from user-defined menus by typing the first letter of the option, so long as you do not have more than one menu item with the same first letter. If you do, pressing that letter will redisplay the menu with only items with the matching letter, exactly as would occur on a built-in Paradox menu with more than one item with the same first letter.

❑ **Variable Name.** Following the list of menu items, the **SHOWMENU** command uses the additional **TO** to store the results of the user's selection in a memory variable. The results of a menu selection is always an alpha type of field that contains the name of the menu item selected. For example, if the user selected the Add option from the sample menu shown in Figure 14-1, a variable called option would be created that contained the text *Add*. Note that the data type of the variable will be an alpha type of variable that matches the exact length of the menu item. Selecting Add would define the option as an A3 type of variable while selecting Delete would define the variable as A6.

It is important to keep in mind that *all* selections from menu bars create alpha-type variables, even if the option text contains numbers. The command below would display a menu with the options **100** and **200**.

```
SHOWMENU "100":" ","200":" " TO account
```

```
....+...10....+...20....+...30....+
SHOWMENU "Add":"Add new record",
"Delete":"Erase a record",
"Quit":"Terminate Program"
TO option
```

```
Add  Delete  Quit_
Add new record
```

Figure 14-1 SHOWMENU command creates bar menu.

However, either selection would define **account** as an A3 type of variable. If you wanted to use the menu selection as a numeric value, the NULVAL() function can be used to convert numbers stored in an alpha field or variable into a numeric variable. The command below defines **account_value** as a numeric variable based on the text in the alpha variable **account**.

```
account_value=NUMVAL(account)
```

The same would be true of a date value. The example below shows a menu from which the user can select a text date. The DATEVAL() function then defines the variable **start_date** as a D type of variable which can be used, for example, as a title variable in a date field within a **QUERY** command.

```
SHOWMENU
"1/1/90":"First day of Year",
"12/31/89":"Last day previous year"
TO option
start_date=DATEVAL(option)
```

Adding a Menu to a Script

In Chapter 13, you created a script, ACT_SUM, which would summarize a specified account from the Ck_book table. The script could be modified to operate using a user-defined menu in place of the direct input method currently used. Begin by making a copy of the ACT_SUM script called BAR_SUM (bar menu summary). Enter

t c s
act_sum ↵
bar_sum ↵

Load the new script into the script editor by entering

s e e
bar_sum ↵

In the current version of the script, lines 3 and 4 contain the commands that make up the direct entry prompt and pause for user input. Remove those two lines by entering

↓ ***(2 times)***
[Ctrl-y] ***(2 times)***

Place Paradox into the Insert mode by entering

[Ins]

You have now removed the commands which allowed users to enter the account number they desired. You will want to replace those commands with a menu bar that allows them to select the account number they want to summarize. This requires the entry of a **SHOWMENU** command. Enter

SHOWMENU ↵

The next section of the command will be a list of the menu options. In this case, that would consist of the account number—with the name of the account as the message for the second line of the menu. An example is shown below:

```
"100":"Cash in Bank"
```

Transferring Table Data to a Script

To create a complete menu, you would have to enter one menu item definition for each of the five accounts currently in use with the Ck_book tables. In looking at the contents of the menu, you might recall that exactly this information is stored in the Accounts table. It might make the writing of this command simpler if there was a way to extract the text stored in Accounts tables and place it into the script, using the **Read** command. Once the account numbers and names were copied into the script, it would be a simple matter to add punctuation (commas, quotation marks, and colons) needed to make the data into a menu.

Paradox contains a utility which will convert table values into ASCII text. This type of text can be added to and edited as part of scripts. The feature is part of the **ExportImport** command on the Tools menu.

Here, converting the Accounts table has two benefits. First, it saves you the time and effort of entering all of the account numbers and names in the script. Second, it ensures that the menu you are creating is an accurate reflection of the accounts actually used in the table.

To take advantage of this shortcut, you must exit the Script Editing mode for now. Enter

[F2]

Select the **ExportImport** command found on the Tools menu by entering

t e

In this instance, you want to *export*, draw data from, a Paradox table. Enter

e

The Export menu lists eight different file formats into which Paradox table data can be copied: *Quattro, 1-2-3, Symphony, dBASE, Pfs, Reflex, Visicalc*, and *ASCII*. Since a script is an ASCII text file, the ASCII option is the proper one to select. Enter

a

The ASCII option has two ways in which to convert table data into ASCII text.

❑ **Delimited.** Delimited text refers to a text file in which the fields are written as items in a list—separated by commas—on a single line. Data stored in alpha fields is automatically enclosed in quotation marks. Numeric data is entered without quotations. All leading and trailing blanks are eliminated. There will be one line in the file for each record in the table.

❑ **Text.** This format creates a file in which each record is a single line of text. All of the fields in a given record are printed on a single line as text, just as they appear in the fields including all leading and trailing blanks. No characters are inserted to indicate where one field ends and another begins. Neither of the ASCII text formats includes any information about the table structure, such as the names of the fields. Only the contents of the records are included.

In this case, the Delimited option would be the most useful because it eliminates the leading and trailing blanks and it encloses text items in quotations. This will create a text file that is close in structure to the way that it needs to appear inside the **SHOWMENU** command. Select Delimited by entering

d

Enter the name of the table from which to copy the data.

accounts ↵

The next prompt asks you to enter the name of the ASCII text file that will be created by the **Export** command. It is important to make sure that you add an SC extension to the file name so that Paradox will recognize it as a script file. Otherwise, ASCII text files are given a file extension TXT. While the structure of the file is compatible with any script, Paradox script commands will not recognize any file that does not have an SC file extension. Enter

accts.sc ↵

You have now copied the Accounts table information into a file that can be read by the **Scripts Read** command. Return to the BAR_SUM script by entering

s e e
bar_sum ↵

Move the cursor to the point in the script, just below the **SHOWMENU** command, where the account information should be placed. Note that text read into a script is automatically inserted, regardless of the status of the insert mode, and it is placed on the line below the current cursor position. Enter

↓ ***(2 times)***

Use the **Read** command to load a copy of the text in ACCTS.SC into the current script. Enter

[F10] r
accts ↵

The script now reads as shown below.

```
CLEARALL CLEAR
@ 4,0 ?? FORMAT(''w79,ac'',''Summarize Ledger Account'')
SHOWMENU
100,''Cash in Bank''
500,''Office Furniture''
600,''Office Supplies''
650,''Office Equipment''
700,''Utilities''
; insert variable choice into query form
QUERY
```

The text imported from the table contains most of the information needed to form a menu. You need to make the following changes to the text in order to format the information so that it will appear as a user-defined menu.

- Add quotation marks around the account numbers.
- Change the commas after the account numbers to colons.
- Place commas after each of the first four menu items.

Turn on the insert mode in order to avoid overwriting any of the text.

[Ins]

Make the changes shown below to the text in order to format it properly as a menu.

```
SHOWMENU
"100":"Cash in Bank",
"500":"Office Furniture",
"600":"Office Supplies",
"650":"Office Equipment",
"700":"Utilities"
; insert variable choice into query form
```

The final step in creating the menu is to add the **TO** clause. This is the clause that tells Paradox what variable to assign the selected menu value. In this case, assign the entry to a variable called **account**. This may seem odd because the remainder of the program requires a value called **choice** to carry out the summary operations. However, because all menu selections are stored as text, there needs to be an in between step in which the menu selection is converted to a numeric value through the use of the NUMVAL() function.

Move the cursor to the beginning of line 9 and insert the **TO** clause by entering

TO account ↵

Add another command that converts the **Account** variable into a numeric value and stores that value in the variable **choice.** Once **choice** contains the numeric value equal to the account number you want to summarize, the remainder of the script will function exactly as it did in the ACT_SUM script. Enter

choice = NUMVAL(account) ↵

The modified section of the script should read as follows.

```
CLEARALL CLEAR
@ 4,0 ?? FORMAT("w79,ac","Summarize Ledger Account")
SHOWMENU
"100":"Cash in Bank",
```

```
"500":"Office Furniture",
"600":"Office Supplies",
"650":"Office Equipment",
"700":"Utilities"
TO account
choice=NUMVAL(account)
; insert variable choice into query form
```

Execute the script by entering

[F10] g

The script produces a menu at the top of the screen that lists the account numbers to summarize, Figure 14-2.

```
100  500  600  650  700_
Cash in Bank

                         Summarize Ledger Account
```

Figure 14-2 User-defined menu generated by script.

Select account 600 by entering

→ ***(2 times)***
↵

The program summarizes account 600 using the value selected from the menu to control the remainder of the program as shown by the result in Figure 14-3.

```
            Summarize Ledger Account


Summary of Account: 600 - Office Supplies
Number of Transactions                     6
Total of Transactions               1,332.96
Average Transaction                   222.16
```

Figure 14-3 Menu selection controls program operations.

Complete the program by entering

↵

Run the script again but summarize account 500 this time. Enter

s p
bar_sum ↵
→ ↵

This time the program summarizes the selected account, account 500. Complete the program by entering

↵

Controlling the Flow of Programs

The BAR_SUM program illustrated how a user-defined menu bar could be used in a script program to provide the user with a type of user interface. However, there is something missing from the way this script operates that you would expect from a Paradox menu. You will recall that after you have made your selection from the menu, the menu display is removed from the PAL canvas. Following the display of the summary information, the program terminates. If you want to summarize another account, you must execute the script and make a different selection.

It might seem more logical for the menu to continue to be displayed, allowing you to summarize as many accounts as you desire until you decide you have finished. The difference between the way the program might work and the way it currently does work is the difference between *linear* programs and *structured* programs. A *linear* program is one in which the commands are read and executed in exactly the order they appear in the script, i.e., starting at the top of the script and going to the bottom. When the script reaches the bottom of the file, it terminates because there are no more commands to execute. In order to allow the user to read the PAL canvas display, you had to place a special command at the end of the script to pause or delay its termination.

A *structured* program is one that uses special script structure commands. These commands have the effect of creating logical structures within a script. These structures are actually special commands that can redirect Paradox to read, skip, or reread certain sections of the script. Placing structure commands within a script changes the *flow* of execution. This means that the script will not necessarily execute the commands in the order in which they are written. Instead of processing in a straight line—beginning to end—the program may skip certain commands or go back and reread and execute commands that have already been read and executed.

The two most common types of structures in programs are:

❑ **Conditional Structures.** Conditional structures are used to cause Paradox to skip or ignore a command or group of commands within a script. Of course, if you didn't want the commands in your script you could erase them. A conditional structure skips the command *only under certain conditions.* The command may execute if the circumstances are right. Whether or not the commands are skipped is determined by a logical expression. A logical expression is a form of Paradox formula. Instead of resulting in a value, a logical formula evaluates as either true or false. Conditional structure use logical expressions to determine if the conditions are right for the execution of the specified command or group of commands, Figure 14-4.

The advantage of conditional structures is that you can create programs that can react differently to different circumstances making the program a much more flexible tool which can react differently depending on how it is being used.

A Conditional Program Structure

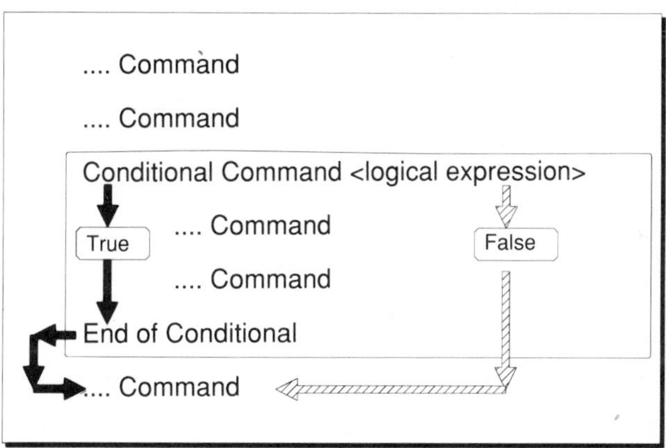

Figure 14-4 Conditional structure redirects program flow.

Paradox includes two sets of commands that create conditional structures in scripts.

❑ **IF THEN/ENDIF(ELSE).** This type of structure is used to determine if a set of commands should be included in the execution of the script or ignored. The Else option sets up an alternative set of commands to execute if the initial set is ignored. If the Else option is used one of the two sets of commands is always executed.

❑ **SWITCH/ENDSWITCH(OTHERWISE).** This conditional command is used when you want to evaluate more than two possible alternatives. Note that anything that **SWITCH** can do can also be done with **IF THEN**; however, **SWITCH** makes it much simpler to set up a series of alternative actions.

Loop Structures. A loop structure is used to determine if Paradox should stop executing commands in a linear fashion and jump backwards in the script and reexecute a section of the script again. The loop will continue until the condition that controls the loop no longer applies. At that point, the program moves to the command following the loop structure and continues executing commands at that point, Figure 14-5.

The advantage of loop structures is that by repeating a given group of commands, a script can process more work without requiring you to lengthen the number of commands in the script. Loops allow programs to operate for an indefinite length of time by simply repeating a small set of commands over and over. Programs with loop structures can be set to repeat until the user explicitly decides to leave.

A Loop Program Structure

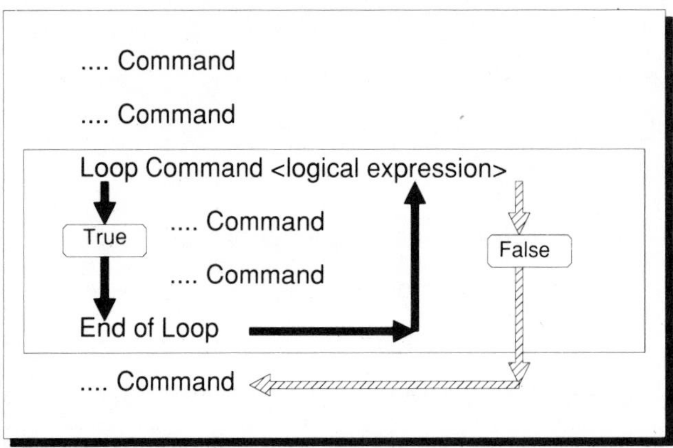

Figure 14-5 Loop structures cause a section of a program to repeat.

Paradox supports three different command sets that create loops within a script program.

FOR/ENDFOR(FROM/TO/STEP). This type of loop is used when you want to control a loop based on a specific number of repetitions.

WHILE/ENDWHILE. This structure is used to create a more general type of loop that repeats until a specific condition occurs.

SCAN/ENDSCAN(FOR). This type of structure is used when you want to relate the processing of a loop to the number of records contained in a specific table.

The addition of structures such as conditional structures and loops to a script greatly raises the level of sophistication of the script program.

Logical Expressions

Loops and conditional structures have one basic ingredient in common: the use of a *logical expression* to control the flow of commands in a program. A *logical expression* is one that compares two values. In contrast, an *arithmetic expression* calculates a value. Logical expressions can compare values for the following qualities using the indicated symbols.

Table 14-1 Logical Comparison Operators

A=B	A equals B
A>B	A is greater than B
A<B	A is less than B
A>=B	A is greater than or equal to B
A<=B	A is less than or equal to B
A<>B	A is not equal to B

The commands that control the flow of the program use logical expressions to perform *tests* at various points in the program. For example, you will recall that in the Ck_book table all of the items with *Account #* 100 are deposits while the rest of the accounts represent some type of expense. You could use a conditional structure to print all accounts except 100 as negative numbers. Below is an example of how such a structure might appear in a script.

```
IF choice=100
        THEN ? [amount]
        ELSE ? [amount]*-1
ENDIF
```

The command structure begins with a test formulated with the **IF** command followed by a logical expression. In this case the expression, **choice=100**, tests the value of the variable **choice** compared to the value 100. The expression can be either true or false. If it is *true*, the command or commands following **THEN** are executed and the command or commands following **ELSE** are ignored. On the other hand, if **choice** is not equal to 100 it is *false* and the opposite action would take place.

In the previous chapter, you learned that you could vary the values used by a script to carry out its operation by allowing the user's input, stored in the form of a variable, to be integrated with the rest of the script. For example, in the ACT_SUM and BAR_SUM scripts, the account number—entered or selected by the user—is passed to the query form as a tilde variable.

Conditional structures make it possible to know not only the values used by script commands but which commands will execute. Up to this point, each script has contained commands which carry out a single type of calculation or operation. The only variance has been in the exact values used. With conditional structures, it is possible to have more than one type of operation in the script. Users can decide which operation they want to carry out by entering a choice, or by selecting one from the menu. This means that it is possible to create a single script that carries out a number of different but related functions. In other words, scripts with conditional structures can react with different sets of operations to different conditions.

Scripts with Conditional Structures

Suppose you wanted to create a script that would calculate the total amount of the checks written to a given payee. In such a script, the user would enter the name of the payee. The script would then use that name to sum all the records that matched the user's entry and display the total of those records. Create a script called Find that will carry out this task by entering

s e w
find ↵

Begin the script with the usual **clear** commands followed by an **ACCEPT** command that allows the user to enter the name of the payee he wants to summarize. In this example the user's input is stored in a variable named **key.** It is the text entered into the **key** variable that will be the basis of the search.

```
CLEARALL CLEAR
@ 10,10 ?? "Total checks written to? "
ACCEPT "a20" TO key
```

Once the user has made the entry, the value in **key** can be used as a tilde variable in a query form which will count and total the records that match the payee. In order to allow partial matches the **..** (double period) operator is used with the tilde variable. This means that entering *Western* will match records with *Western Telephone* or any other record that begins with the word *Western.* Note that the search performed by the query will not be sensitive to differences in capitalization. Entering a search key such as *western* will match *Western, western*, or *WESTERN* in the payee field. Add the query form command to the script.

```
QUERY

ck_book   | payee            | amount   | check #    |
          | ~key..           | calc sum | calc count |

ENDQUERY
DO_IT!
```

The **DO_IT** command will produce an Answer table with the summary values. Display those values on the screen with the following commands.

```
@ 12,10 ?? ''Checks:'' @ 12,30 ?? [count of check #]
@ 13,10 ?? ''Amount:'' @ 13,30 ?? [sum of amount]
@ 24,0 ?? FORMAT(''w79,ac'',''Press any key when done'')
```

The final section of the script pauses the script until a key is pressed. When pressed, the key releases the script to clear the memory and work area before ending the script.

```
x=GETCHAR( )
RELEASE VARS ALL
CLEARALL
RETURN
```

The entire script is listed on page 560. Run the script by entering

[F10] g

Enter *central* as the search key.

central ↵

The script will display the values for the matching record, the key *central*, as shown in Figure 14-6.

```
Total checks written to? central

Checks:                 2
Amount:                 134.57
```

Figure 14-6 Script calculates totals for matching records.

Exit the script by entering

↵

Run the script again, but this time total all of the *deposit* entries.

s p
find ↵
deposit ↵

The results of the script show the correct number of records, 5, but a value of zero for the total. Why? The answer is that all the records that have *Deposit* in the *Payee* field have zero values in the *Amount* field. The deposit records use the *Deposit* field instead. The script finds the correct records but it totals the wrong field as shown in Figure 14-7.

```
Total checks written to? deposit

Checks:                5
Amount:                0.00
```

Figure 14-7 Script fails to calculate deposits correctly.

This problem has come up many times before in this book. It results from the fact that deposit records ought to be treated differently from check records. This is something a human could easily adjust to but a computer program would fail to recognize. In the past, you have used various methods to get around this problem such as creating a third field, e.g., *Balance*.

Exit the script by entering

↵

Using the IF Command

Conditional structures make it possible to build into a script program instructions that will allow the script to treat deposits differently from checks. This can be accomplished by adding an IF THEN/ELSE/ENDIF structure to the script. The structure would test to see if the **key** variable matched *deposit*. If it did, the script would carry out the calculation on the *Deposit* field. If not, the calculation would be carried out on the *Amount* field.

Load the FIND script into the script editor by entering

s e e
find ↵

For reference you may want to turn on the line numbering ruler by entering

[Ctrl-v]

Where in the current script should the conditional structure be placed? There are two basic ways in which you could approach the problem.

❑ **Different Queries.** One way to change the script is to use a conditional structure to execute one of two different query forms based on the entry made to the **key** variable. For example, one query form would use **calc sum** in the *Amount* field while the other would use the operator in the *Deposit* field.

❑ **Different Displays.** Another approach would be to calculate the sum of both the *Amount* and *Deposit* fields every time. The conditional structure would be used to determine which value was displayed.

The second method is the one that you will use in this example—for two reasons. First, controlling the screen display portion of the script would require less modification of the script. Second, in order to display the correct value, you would have to have a conditional structure in the display area, anyway, to decide if the value to be displayed is the *Sum of Amount* or *Sum of Deposit*.

The first step in modifying this script is to add another column to the query form which will calculate the sum of the *Deposit* field. Change the query form section of the script, lines 4 through 9, to read as follows.

```
QUERY

ck_book   |payee     |amount   |check #    |deposit  |
          |~key..    |calc sum |calc count |calc sum |

ENDQUERY
```

The script now has two potential values to display. The conditional structure will decide which field, *Sum of Amount* or *Sum of Deposit* is actually displayed. The conditional structure will affect lines 11 and 12 of the script. If the search has been for deposits, line 11 should read *Deposits* instead of checks and line 12 should display *Sum of Deposit*.

Move the cursor to the beginning of line 11 and insert the following commands. Note that you will need to turn on the insert mode by entering

[Ins]

Add the following commands, shown in **bold** to the script. Note that in addition to the group of commands beginning on line 12, the **ENDIF** command is also added on line 18 to mark the end of the conditional structure.

```
IF key="Deposit"
THEN
@ 12,10 ?? "Deposits" @ 12,30 ?? [count of check#]
@ 13,10 ?? "Amount" @ 13,30 ?? [sum of deposit]
ELSE
@ 12,10 ?? "Checks:" @ 12,30 ?? [count of check #]
@ 13,10 ?? "Amount:" @ 13,30 ?? [sum of amount]
ENDIF
```

The conditional structure commands enclose both sets of display commands so that they will function as alternate procedures based on the veracity of the logical expression **key="Deposit"**. Test the changes by entering

[F10] g
Deposit ↵

This time the program is able to display a meaningful total for the deposits, Figure 14-8, because it was structured to process deposits differently from checks.

```
Total checks written to? deposit

Deposits            5
Amount:             5735.90
```

Figure 14-8 Script program treats deposits differently than checks.

Exit the script by entering

↵

Test the script to see that it still works correctly for checks. Enter

s p
western ↵

The script displays the information for the specified payee. Note that the prompts show the word *Checks*, indicating that the conditional structure selected the correct set of commands. Exit the script by entering

↵

Case Sensitivity in Logical Expressions

In the Find script, the logical expression **key="Deposit"** controls which set of commands is used to display the data on the screen. Note that the value used in the logical expression is **Deposit**. What would happen if you forgot to capitalize the first letter of the entry, i.e., you entered **deposit**?

Run the script and find out by entering

s P
find ↵
deposit ↵

The results of the script show that failing to enter the key with the exact capitalization used in the **IF** command causes the script to select the wrong set of commands for display, Figure 14-9.

```
Total checks written to? deposit

Checks:               5
Amount:               0.00
```

Figure 14-9 Logical expression is case sensitive.

Exit the script by entering

↵

How can you protect the logic of your script from differences in case, i.e., how can the script be made case *insensitive*? One way is to use a PAL function to convert the entry to all lower or all upper case and use a literal value that matches the conversion. PAL includes the functions **UPPER( )** which converts text to all uppercase values and **LOWER( )** which converts text to all lowercase values. The two commands below use the function to create case insensitive logical expressions.

```
IF UPPER(key)="DEPOSIT"
or
IF LOWER(key)="deposit"
```

Either approach will have the same effect; however, you must keep in mind that the text literal to which you compare the variable must match the conversion function, i.e., upper to upper and lower to lower. The command shown below would always be false because it compares a variable converted to upper case and a literal that is written in lower case.

```
IF UPPER(key)="deposit"
```

Load the Find script into the script editor and make the change needed to formulate the script as a case insensitive search. Enter

s e e
find ↵

The change should be made to line 11 of the script.

Old line IF key=''Deposit''
New line IF **UPPER** (key)=''**DEPOSIT**''

Save and execute the revised script by entering

[F10] g
deposit ↵

The script executes properly because it is no longer sensitive to variations in the case of the search key. Exit the script by entering

↵

Nesting Conditional Structures

Suppose you enter a key value for which there are no matching records. How would the program react? Run the script again and enter a key value that will not match any of the existing records.

s p
find ↵
test ↵

The results, Figure 14-10, show a zero value for number of checks and a blank for amount. This is the logical result of generating an Answer table with no records in it. However, it is not the clearest way to communicate with someone using this program. It might be better if, instead of the results shown in Figure 14-10, the program displayed a message stating that no matching records were found for the specified key.

```
Total checks written to? test

Checks:                  0
Amount:
```

Figure 14-10 Results when no match is found.

Exit the script by entering

↵

The program could be improved if you used a conditional structure to test the results of the query processing. If the Answer table did not contain any records you would want to display a message telling the user that no matching records were found.

In such a script, you would use a conditional structure to control whether or not the current conditional structure was used at all, or whether a **not found** message would be displayed. In other words, the current IF THEN/ELSE/ENDIF structure that distinguishes between checks and deposits would be itself an alternative inside a larger IF THEN/ELSE/ENDIF structure that would test to see if the key value matched any record at all in the table.

When a conditional structure is placed inside another conditional structure it is called *nesting*. The diagram in Figure 14-11 illustrates how conditional structures can be nested within each other. In the diagram, there are two sets of **IF THEN/ELSE/ENDIF** commands labeled {1}and {2}. Note that the entire {2} structure is positioned within the ELSE/ENDIF section of structure {1}. Proper nesting requires that the nest structure be completely contained within a section of the larger structure, in order to be *properly nested*.

Nested Conditional Structures

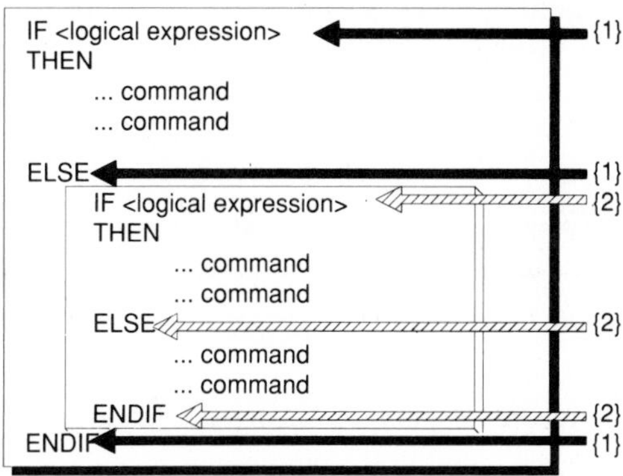

Figure 14-11 Conditional structures nested within one another.

In terms of the script you are working on, structure {1} would use a logical expression to determine if the Answer table contained a record or was blank. If it were blank, a message would be displayed. If it were not blank, the structure would activate the nested structure {2}, which would determine if the Answer table was reporting deposits or checks.

Note that the diagram shows the use of indenting to more clearly indicate the layout of the program structure. Indenting can be used when you write scripts to help you keep track of which commands are contained in what structures. In this book the scripts will show indenting in all scripts that used structures. The indents are optional, because PAL ignores all extra spaces in a script.

> *The PAL editor does not support indents with the [Tab] key. All indents in the PAL editor must be made by inserting spaces at the beginning of the line. If you want to speed up the indenting process, you might create an instant script with the [Alt-F3] command that types in 5 spaces. Each time you want to indent, you would enter [Alt-F4] to insert 5 spaces with a single keystroke. If you use a different text editor to write scripts, indents created with [Tab] will be recognized by PAL and the PAL editor.*

Load the Find script into the script editor by entering

s e e
find ↵

Since the purpose of the new structure is to test the number of records in the Answer table, the **IF** command should follow the **DO_IT!** command. The structure should be inserted (Insert mode *on*) beginning at line 11.

The first question you run into is how would you perform such a test? Recall that when you entered a nonexistent payee, *test,* the value for the *Count of Check #* field was zero. You could use an expression such as **[count of check #]=0** to test the results of the query. If that expression is true, you will want to display a message warning the user that he has entered a nonexistent payee. If it is false, you can assume that some records have been selected for summation and that the program should next process the second conditional structure to determine if the records are checks or deposits.

Insert the following commands. Note that the indenting is optional.

```
IF [count of check #]=0
THEN
    @ 12,10 ?? "**No records matching "+key+" found.**"
ELSE
```

Lines 15 through 22 remain the same since they make up the conditional structure that will distinguish between checks and deposits. In order to properly nest this structure inside the new structure, insert on line 23 the **ENDIF** command that marks the end of the **[count of check #]=0** structure. This means there will be two consecutive **ENDIF** commands in the program. Paradox will be able to logically match the **ENDIF** to the corresponding **IF**. However, in order to make it easier for you to keep track of which structural commands are related to which, you can add a comment after the command to identify its function. The comment is added to the end of the command line by inserting a semicolon followed by the text of the command. Add the command shown below.

```
ENDIF; test for empty Answer table
```

The complete listing of the current version of the Find script can be found beginning on page 561.

Execute the script by entering

[F10] g
test ↵

This time the script displays a message telling you that no matching records were found for the specified key, Figure 14-12.

```
Total checks written to? test
**No records matching test found.**
```

Figure 14-12 No records found that match key expression.

Exit the script by entering

↵

Loops

A *loop* is a conditional structure used to repeat part or all of a script. Repeating a section can have a wide variety of uses. One of the most fundamental uses of a loop is to repeat a procedure until the user requests to exit.

For example, the FIND script will perform a single search, pause while you read the results, and then exit. Each time you want to make another search, you must execute the script again with the **Script Play** command.

It might make more sense to structure the script so that you have the option of exiting or repeating the script. You can use a loop to create this type of structure. The loop structure would cause Paradox to repeat the FIND script over and over, rather than having users run the script each time they want to perform a search.

Automatic Loops

One of the simplest and most commonly used types of loops is called an *automatic loop*. An *automatic loop* is one that is set up to repeat continuously the commands enclosed in the loop. Automatic loops have two distinguishing features.

❑ **The TRUE Operator.** Loop structures, like conditional structures, require the use of a logical expression to control the loop. In order to create an automatic loop you would use a logical expression that would always be true. For example, you might select a self evident mathematical expression such as **2+2=4**. This would mean that the loop should continue until **2+2=4** is not true, i.e., continue forever. However, while an expression like **2+2=4** will work perfectly well for creating an automatic loop, it may be confusing to read, since it is in no way related to the purpose of the program. Paradox provides specials operators, **true**and **false**, which can be used in place of a logical expression when you want the outcome to be always true or always false. The most common use of this operator is with the **WHILE** loop command. The command **WHILE true** is commonly used to start an automatic loop.

❑ **The QUITLOOP Command.** The concept of an automatic loop raises one very important question: If the loop will repeat automatically forever, how can you ever stop the script? The answer is found in the **QUITLOOP** command. The **QUITLOOP** command functions as a *break* instruction. When encountered, it causes Paradox to immediately jump out of the current loop and continue the script with the next command following the **ENDWHILE**, if any. For the **QUITLOOP** command to function, it *must* be inserted between the **WHILE** and **ENDWHILE** commands.

But if **QUITLOOP** automatically breaks the execution of a loop, then the loop will never repeat if a **QUITLOOP** command is included inside the loop. In order to make the **QUITLOOP** command practical, you must enclose it in an **IF/ENDIF** conditional structure as shown in Figure 14-13.

The **QUITLOOP** command will be ignored, and the loop will repeat, until the logical expression used with the **if** command evaluates as true. When that happens, the **QUITLOOP** command breaks the execution of the loop and the program continues with the commands found after the **ENDWHILE**.

The most common way to use this automatic loop structure is to control the use of the **QUITLOOP** command with a user input. On page 537 is a fragment of a script that shows the basic elements used in an automatic loop. Lines {1} and {7} establish the range of the automatic loop. Lines {2} and {3}pause the program and ask the user to enter Y or N. Immediately following the entry the IF command on line {4} tests to see if the user entered N. If so, the **QUITLOOP** command terminates the loop; if not, the loop continues.

```
WHILE true                                          {1}
   @10,10 ?? "Continue? (Y/N)"                      {2}
   ACCEPT "A1" DEFAULT "Y" TO more                  {3}
   IF UPPER (more) = "N"                            {4}
        THEN QUITLOOP                               {5}
   ENDIF                                            {6}
ENDWHILE                                            {7}
```

The main advantage of an automatic loop is that the **QUITLOOP** command will immediately terminate the loop. Loops that are controlled with actual logical expressions are a bit more complex and require somewhat more planning—as you will see in subsequent chapters.

The automatic loop is an easy way of turning scripts such as the Find script into scripts that will run continuously.

Adding an Automatic Loop

Suppose that you wanted to add an automatic loop to the FIND script in order to have it repeat its operation until specifically terminated. Begin by making a copy—called FINDLOOP—of the FIND script.

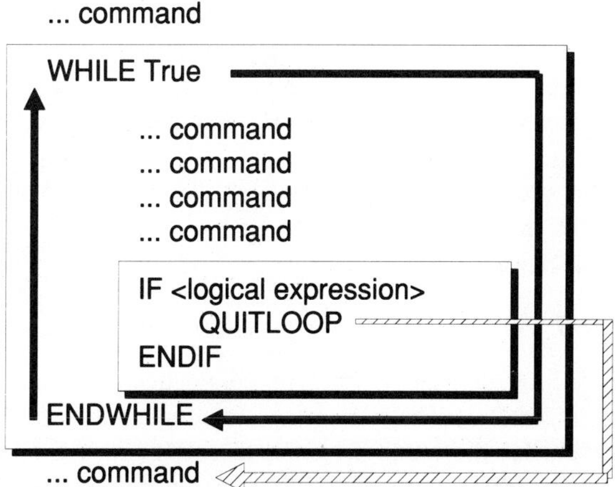
An Automatic Loop
... command
WHILE True
... command
... command
... command
... command
IF <logical expression>
QUITLOOP
ENDIF
ENDWHILE
... command

Figure 14-13 Automatic loops uses IF/ENDIF with QUITLOOP.

t c s
find ↵
findloop ↵

Load the Findloop script into the script editor.

s e e
findloop ↵

The first step in adding a loop is to decide where in the script the loop should begin. In this case, you can insert the **WHILE** command on line 1 of the script. This will cause the **CLEAR** and **CLEARALL** commands to be part of the loop—meaning that the work area and display will be cleared each time you begin a search.

> *In some circumstances, you might want to leave previous tables or display items on the screen at the beginning of the loop.*

Turn on the Insert mode and add the following line at the beginning of the script.

[Ins]
WHILE true ↵

The next place where you would want to add commands is at the bottom of the script after the data has been displayed, line 25. Currently, lines 25 and 26 create a pause that stops the script until the user presses a key. In the modified version of this script, the pause should still take place at this point. However, the key that the user enters is now significant. The user must make a choice between repeating the loop or exiting the program.

This can be accomplished with direct entry through the **ACCEPT** command or **GTECHAR( ) function or with a SHOWMENU** command. The **SHOWMENU** command has the advantage of ensuring that the user makes a valid selection since the menu limits their choices. It also gives the program a comfortable feel, since the user can simply press ↵ to accept the highlighted option.

Delete the current lines 25 and 26 by entering

[Ctrl-y] ***(2 times)***

Insert the following section into the script. The commands create a menu from which the user can select to *Continue* or *Quit*. The response is stored in a variable called **program_flow**. An IF structure then evaluates the menu selection to determine if the loop should be terminated. Note that the **ENDWHILE** command marks the end of the section of the script controlled by the automatic loops

```
SHOWMENU ''Continue'':''Search for another Item'',
''Quit'':''End Program''
TO program_flow
IF program_flow='Quit''
    THEN QUITLOOP
ENDIF
ENDWHILE; end of loop automatic loop
```

A full listing of the FINDLOOP script can be found on page 562. Execute the modified script by entering

[F10] g

The script operates exactly as it did before, by displaying a prompt which asks you to enter the search key. Respond by entering

deposit ↵

The display is the same as before except that instead of the message at the bottom of the screen, a menu appears at the top of the screen, Figure 14-14.

Select to continue, i.e., repeat the script, by entering

↵

```
Continue  Quit_
Search for another Item




          Total checks written to? deposit

          Deposits                  5
          Amount                    5735.90
```

Figure 14-14 Menu provides option to repeat procedure.

The screen clears and once again you are asked to enter the search item. This time enter

savings
↵

The program finds two matching records with a total of $229.49. The menu appears again. To stop the program, you need to select the Quit option from the menu. Enter

q

The script now terminates and you are returned to the main program menu. The automatic loop changes the character of the script from a keystroke macro command into that of a small program that continues to operate until you exit. This also means that the running of a single script can generate a large amount of work, because the loop recycles the commands as many times as you desire.

Subroutines

The FINDLOOP script illustrates how a loop structure can be added to a script to allow the script to automatically reappear until it is specifically terminated by the user. In this example script. almost the entire original FIND script was enclosed in the loop structure. In a sense, you can reduce the logic of the loop by representing all the commands from the original FIND script as an instruction that reads "*perform Find script*". The example below displays a *pseudocode* listing that shows the basic structure used in the FINDLOOP program.

```
WHILE true
      ...perform Find script
      IF <logical expression>
            QUITLOOP
      ENDIF
ENDWHILE
```

Pseudocode refers to a listing that mixes actual PAL commands with elements of text that make sense to people reading the code but are not written in the actual PAL syntax. Pseudocode is useful in working out the logic of a program without having to write the exact PAL commands required in the final version.

If you look at the logic of the pseudocode, you can see that any number of scripts could be substituted in the "*perform Find script*" position. The loop structure is not particularly concerned with what goes on inside the loop. Its task is simply to decide when to repeat or stop the execution of the script.

PAL contains a command that allows you to execute a script from within a script. The command is **PLAY**. **PLAY** has the same effect within a script as **ScriptsPlay** does from the menu. You can substitute the **PLAY** command for "*perform Find script*" in the example listing and arrive at the outline of a program that would perform the same function as FINDLOOP, but without requiring any editing changes to the FIND script.

```
WHILE true
      PLAY <script_name>
      IF <logical expression>
            QUITLOOP
      ENDIF
ENDWHILE
```

When you are entering the actual name of a script file as a parameter of the PLAY command, the name should be written as a text literal, i.e., enclosed in quotation marks.

When a script is executed from another script, it is referred to as a *subroutine*. The **PLAY** command allows you to execute a script as a *subroutine* of the current script. When **PLAY** is used, control is passed to the specified subroutine script which retains control until it runs out of commands or a **RETURN** command is encountered, Figure 14-15.

Scripts Used as Subroutines

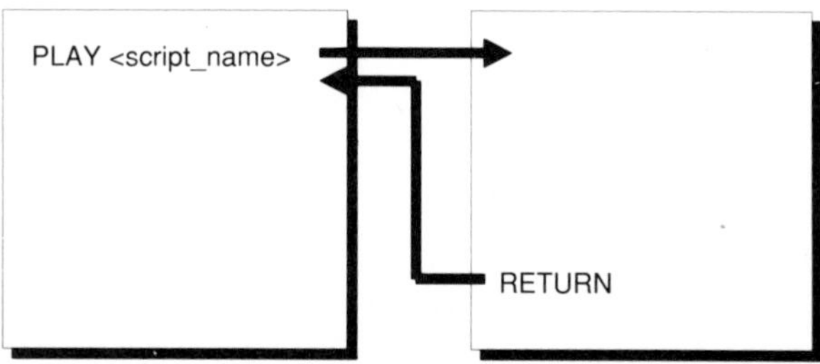

Figure 14-15 Script uses PLAY to execute subroutine.

Recall that earlier you were told it is good form to always make the last command in a script a **RETURN** command. This makes sense when you consider the possibility that the script might be used as a subroutine of another program.

Creating programs by using subroutines has two primary advantages.

❑ **Modularized Applications.** The *modular* approach to creating an application is one in which a large application is broken down into a series of scripts, each of which handles one part of the overall application. Each *module* can be written and tested independently before being assembled into a single application. Modules also have the advantage of being accessible by different applications so that a single subroutine may be used by several different applications or used in several different places by the same application.

❑ **Simpler Scripts.** When applications and tasks are broken down into small modules, the scripts are simpler to write, debug, and revise. This aids in the development of larger applications.

Using Subroutines

Suppose you wanted to create a script that would use the FIND script as a subroutine, instead of requiring you to change the commands of the FIND script. Begin by creating a new script called CK_DATA. This script will contain an automatic loop routine that executes the FIND script as a subroutine.

This approach separates the flow control routine, which will be contained in CK_DATA, from the specific task routine, e.g., summarizing records from the Ck_book table, which will continue to be stored in FIND. The FIND script can then be used exactly as it was before and still serve as part of the CK_DATA script.

Create the new script by entering

s e w
ck_data ↵

Enter the commands of the script as shown below. The script consists of the commands added to the FINDLOOP script, plus the **PLAY** command which executes the FIND script as a subroutine.

```
WHILE true
      PLAY "find"
      SHOWMENU
      "Continue":"Search for another Item",
      "Quit':'End Program"
      TO program_flow
      IF program_flow = "Quit"
          THEN QUITLOOP
      ENDIF
ENDWHILE
RELEASE VARS ALL
RETURN
```

Execute this script by entering

[F10] g

When the script executes, the first item displayed on the screen is the prompt generated by the FIND script running as a subroutine. Enter the item you want to summarize.

west ↵

The summary data is displayed. Note that the script is paused with the **Press any key when done** prompt, which is still part of the FIND script. Enter

↵

When you press ↵, the FIND script terminates. However, because FIND is a subroutine of CK_DATA, you return not to the main work area but to the remainder of the CK_DATA script. The result is that CK_data now displays the Continue/Quit menu, Figure 14-16.

As with the FINDLOOP program, you have the option of continuing with the operation or quitting. Run the routine again and find the total for Fathead software.

↵
fat ↵

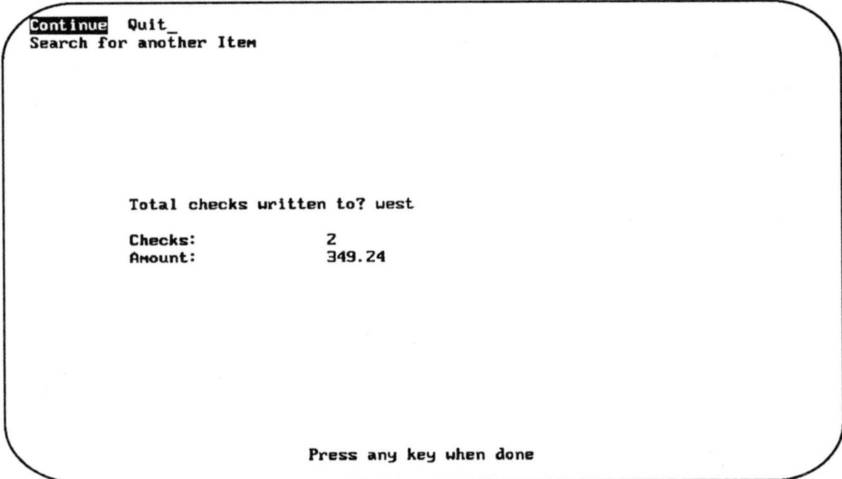

Figure 14-16 Ck_data screen display.

In this case, there is one check for $378.90. Quit the script by entering

↵

q

The selection of the Quit option from the menu returns you to the main Paradox work area. The function of the CK_DATA program, with the exception of the additional pause, is identical to the FINDLOOP program even though no modifications were required to the FIND program.

Running a Different Subroutine

The general nature of the CK_DATA script means that it could be used to execute any number of scripts as subroutines. For example, the BAR_SUM script created at the beginning of this chapter could be substituted for the Find script in the **PLAY** command. Load the CK_DATAS script into the editor.

s e e
ck_data ↵

To use the script to execute the BAR_SUM script repeatedly, simply change the name of the script specified in line 2 from Find to BAR_SUM.

Old line PLAY "find"
New line PLAY "bar_sum"

Execute the revised script by entering

[F10] g

The result is that the script now displays the menu of accounts used in the BAR_SUM script. Select account 700 by entering

7

The script shows a summary of that account's activity. Enter

↵

When you press ↵, the subroutine script terminates and the Continue/Quit menu from the CK_DATA script is displayed. Suppose you wanted to summarize account 500. Select Continue by entering

↵

Summarize account 500 by entering

5

The CK_DATA program performs the same flow-control function for this script as it did when the FIND script was specified as the subroutine. Exit the program by entering

↵
q

The CK_DATA script now terminates the loop and allows you to return to the main Paradox work area.

Using Multiple Subroutines

The routine used in CK_DATA is capable of coordinating the execution of a number of different scripts, e.g., FIND or BAR_SUM. In fact, it is possible to adapt the structure of CK_DATA to create a program that links a series of subroutines together as menu options. For example, you have four scripts (FIND, BAR_SUM, RANGE1, and MORT) which could be combined into a single application. Instead of having a menu that simply listed two options, Continue/Quit, you could expand the menu to have options that would execute any of the four scripts, plus an option to quit. Create a new script called MULTI by entering

s e w
multi ↵

Begin this script with an automatic loop. Enter

```
WHILE true
```

This program is bit different from CK_DATA in that you do not know at this point what subroutine should be executed. In order to determine that, it is necessary to display a menu listing the options. Add a **Showmenu** command that will display the options, including Quit, that are available. Add the following to the script.

```
SHOWMENU
"Balance":"Summarize checking account",
"Account":"Summarize by account number",
"Item":"Summarize by Item",
"Mortgage":"Calculate Mortgage Payment",
"Quit":"Exit program"
TO program
```

The Switch Structure

At this point in the application, the user will have made a selection from the menu. The variable **program** will contain the text of the menu item selected. How will you go about transforming the menu select to the execution of matching subroutine?

The situation calls for a conditional structure of some type. The IF THEN/ELSE/ENDIF structure does well when you want to evaluate one or two alternative actions. However, in the current circumstance you are presented with the task of selecting one action among five possible options. One way to solve this problem is to list a series of IF THEN commands, each of which would be triggered by one of the menu options as shown below.

```
IF program ="Balance"
        THEN PLAY "range1'
ENDIF
IF program ="Account"
        THEN PLAY "bar_sum"
ENDIF
IF program ="Item"
        THEN PLAY "find"
ENDIF
IF program ="Mortgage"
        THEN PLAY "mort"
```

```
ENDIF
IF program ="Quit":
        THEN QUITLOOP
ENDIF
```

The series of IF THEN/ENDIF structures do the job, but there is a great deal of overhead involved in creating a conditional structure for each option that needs to be evaluated. An alternative is provided by PAL in the form of the SWITCH/CASE/ENDSWITCH structure. SWITCH is specifically designed to allow you to create a structure which selects *one* of a number of possible options. A single SWITCH structure can accommodate any number of options entered in the form of a *case*. A *case* is a shorthand way of writing a conditional structure requiring the word CASE followed by the logical expression and a list of commands to execute if the expression evaluates as true. Using Switch, the series of options shown above in IF THEN format would translate to the following.

```
SWITCH
        CASE program ="Balance":PLAY "range1'
        CASE program ="Account":PLAY "bar_sum"
        CASE program ="Item":PLAY "find"
        CASE program ="Mortgage":PLAY "mort"
        CASE program ="Quit":QUITLOOP
ENDSWITCH
```

The SWITCH structure is much simpler to write and read, expressing more clearly a list of alternatives. Should you want to follow each case with more than a single command, you can place as many commands as you like following each case statement as shown below in pseudocode.

```
SWITCH
        CASE <logical expression>:
                ...command,command,command
                ...command,command,command
        CASE <logical expression>:
                ...command,command,command
                ...command,command,command
ENDSWITCH
```

The SWITCH structure can also use an option clause called OTHERWISE. The OTHERWISE clause is always the last option listed in a structure and it set ups a *default* option. OTHERWISE, unlike the CASE clause, does not use a logical expression. Instead, the commands listed under OTHERWISE will execute if *all* of the CASE options are *false*. The example below shows that the **QUITLOOP** command will be executed if none of the previous cases prove to be true.

```
SWITCH
        CASE program ="Balance":PLAY "range1'
        CASE program ="Account":PLAY "bar_sum"
        CASE program ="Item":PLAY "find"
        CASE program ="Mortgage":PLAY "mort"
        OTHERWISE:QUITLOOP
ENDSWITCH
```

When the selection to be evaluated comes from a menu, an OTHERWISE clause is not generally needed because the only options available are those listed on the menu. OTHERWISE is important when it is possible to have a random value entered for the variable.

There is one additional difference between IF THEN and SWITCH. The SWITCH structure will select the **first** case that evaluates as true. This means that even if more than one of the CASE expressions is true, only the first one encountered will be selected and all of the others will be ignored. When a series of IF THEN structures is used, it is conceivable that all of the structures will evaluate as true and execute the commands contained within the structure.

Evaluating a Menu

A SWITCH structure is the most common way to evaluate the results of a menu selection. In this script, the SWITCH structure will play a different script. Add the following section to the script.

```
SWITCH        CASE program =''Balance'':PLAY ''range1''
      CASE program =''Account'':PLAY ''bar_sum''
      CASE program =''Item'':PLAY ''find''
      CASE program =''Mortgage'':PLAY ''mort''
      OTHERWISE:QUITLOOP
ENDSWITCH
```

Complete the program by closing the loop with the **ENDWHILE** command, clearing the variables, and adding **RETURN** to mark the end of program.

```
ENDWHILE
RELEASE VARS ALL
RETURN
```

A listing of the entire Multi script can be found on page 563. Execute the script by entering

[F10] g

The program displays the five options as a bar menu. Select the Balance option by entering

↵

The balance script executes as a subroutine displaying the summary data. At the end of that script the menu reappears at the top of the screen, Figure 14-17.

```
Balance  Account  Item  Mortgage  Quit_
Summarize checking account



                               Checking Account Records

          Beginning Date         January  1, 1989

          Ending Date            March 22, 1989

          Total Deposits           4,853.69

          Totals Checks            5,735.90

          Current Balance            882.21
```

Figure 14-17 Menu selects subroutines to execute.

This time select the Account option by entering

a

The main menu is replaced by the account menu. Summarize account 100 by entering

1

Return to the menu by entering

↵

Exit the MULTI script by selecting the Quit option.

q

The script terminates and returns you to the main program menu. The MULTI script illustrates how a series of scripts each designed to perform a specific function or operation can be coordinated by a single menu and a SWITCH structure. This type of script is the basis for building custom-designed applications with the PAL language.

Using Tables to Make Selections

Allowing users to make selections from menus has several advantages over asking the user to make a direct entry. First, the user does not need to remember the options since they are listed on the menu. Second, the user does not have to worry about making an invalid entry because only valid options appear on the menu. Third, menu selection cuts down on mistaken entries because the user does not have to enter the text. This also eliminates problems caused by differences in case.

However, not all situations lend themselves easily to the use of bar menus as implemented with the **SHOWMENU** command. The biggest limitation is that in order to create a menu with **SHOWMENU**, you must know in advance the number and names of the items you want to display. For example, the Find script summarizes all the transactions related to a given *Payee*. The Find script requires that you directly enter the name or part of the name of the *Payee* you want to summarize. The direct entry method used in that script has all the drawbacks associated with direct entry. First, the user must remember the names of all the payees, as well as the spelling used for those names in the Ck_book table. This approach places the memory burden on the user, not on the computer. It would be much better if you allowed the user to pick a payee from a menu or a list.

But creating a menu that lists the names in the *Payee* field presents a problem. If you wanted to use **SHOWMENU**, you would have to write one menu item for each of the unique names in the *Payee* field. Even if you had that information handy when you were writing the script, there is no guarantee that the list would remain valid. As soon as a new payee was added to the Ck_book table, the script would be out of date since you would have no menu option to match the new entry.

A solution to this problem can be found in the **WAIT** command. The **WAIT** command is designed to integrate direct access to Paradox tables with a script program. When **WAIT** is used in a script it has the following effects.

❑ **Work Area Displayed.** When the **WAIT** command is invoked, the work area, normally hidden by the PAL canvas—becomes visible. This means any tables currently on the work area will appear during the execution of the script.

❑ **Limited Access to Tables.** The **WAIT** command allows the user to have limited access to the table on the work area which is currently active when the **WAIT** command is executed. Access to the table is controlled by two factors. First, the table is accessed in a Read-Only mode unless the **WAIT** command is preceded by an **EDIT <table_name>** command in which case the user is permitted to edit the fields in the table. Second, cursor movement within the table can be restricted to the current field or the current record by using the Record or Field options. If the Table option is specified, the user can navigate through the entire table.

❑ **Keylist.** The **WAIT** command maintains the current table as the active work area until one of the keys specified in a special key list. As soon as one of the keys is pressed, the program continues with the command following the **WAIT** command in the script. The **WAIT** command provides a means of integrating the contents of a table, either in table or form mode, along with script operations.

The Answer Table as a Menu

The **WAIT** command allows the user to have *limited* access to a table while a script is running. But how will this help solve the problem of creating menus?

The solution is related to the use of the Answer table to generate specific lists of information from the main table. For example, you could use a query form to create a list of all the unique payee names. Place a query form for the Ck_book table on the work area by entering

a
ck_book ↵

Place a √ in the *Payee* field by entering

→ *(4 times)*
[F6]

Process the query by entering

[F2]

The result is an alphabetized list of the unique names that appear in the *Payee* field, Figure 14-18. This list could be looked at as a type of menu. Because it is a table, you can use the arrow keys to move the cursor to any location just as you would move the highlight in a menu.

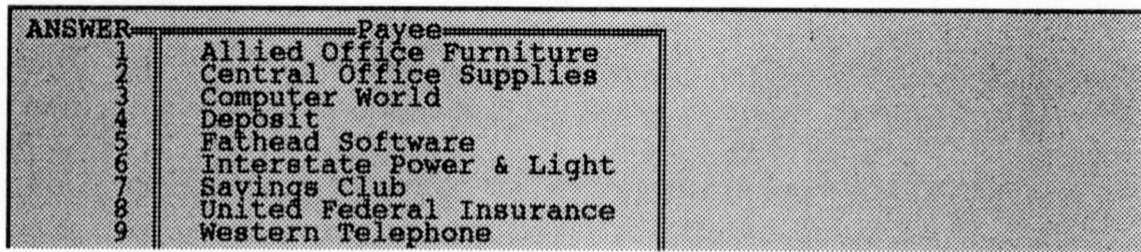

ANSWER	Payee
1	Allied Office Furniture
2	Central Office Supplies
3	Computer World
4	Deposit
5	Fathead Software
6	Interstate Power & Light
7	Savings Club
8	United Federal Insurance
9	Western Telephone

Figure 14-18 Answer table is a list of payee names.

The **WAIT** command provides the controls needed to display a table such as this one during the execution of a script, allowing users to move the cursor to the item they want to summarize. The keylist feature makes it possible to set up the table access so that pressing a key such as ↵ will terminate access to the table.

What is important to keep in mind is that the table location of the cursor, when access is terminated, remains active as the program proceeds. You can therefore use the cursor location to draw from the table the payee name from that record. Once obtained, the name can be passed, as a memory variable to a subroutine such as Find, which will summarize the records related to that name. Clear the work area by entering

[Alt-F8]

Preparing a Menu Table

This approach may seem complicated at first, but as you work out the details, the method will become more clear. The first task is to see how the **WAIT** command will enable you to use a table as a type of menu from which the user can make a selection. Create a new script called Vertmenu (vertical menu) by entering

s e w
vertmenu ↵

Begin, as usual with the clearing commands to ensure that you begin the script with a clean slate.

```
CLEARALL CLEAR
```

The first task to accomplish is to generate a table that contains just the items from which the user is to make a selection. In this example, that would be a table that lists the unique names in the *Payee* field. Create a query form command that will generate an Answer table with the desired data. Note that the **as** operator is used to change the name of the field from *Payee* to *Choices* so that the items will appear under the column heading of *Choices* when the table is displayed as a menu. Add the following to your script.

```
QUERY

ck_book      |payee             |
             check as Choices   |

ENDQUERY
DO_IT!
```

Clear the work area of table images. Remember that once created, an Answer table remains on the disk until another query is processed or you exit Paradox. The current Answer table is still available for other operations.

```
CLEARALL
```

In order to make the Answer table look more like a menu, you might want to rename the table. In this case, use the **RENAME** command (the PAL equivalent of **Tools Rename Table**) to change the name of the Answer table to Menu.

```
RENAME ''answer'' ''menu''
```

Now place the renamed table on the work area. Keep in mind that all of this activity is hidden during the execution of the script by the PAL canvas.

```
VIEW ''menu''
```

You are now ready to display the table as a vertical menu. You might want to position the cursor in the *Choices* field of the Menu table. You can do this in two ways.

❑ **Cursor Movement Commands.** The **LEFT, RIGHT, UP** and **DOWN** commands duplicate the effect of the ←, →, ↑, and ↓ keys. Positioning with these commands requires that you anticipate the cursor location and the exact topography of the table in order to know what direction to move the cursor.

❑ **Moveto.** The **MOVETO** command allows you to place the cursor in a specific field, record, or work area image, directly. For example, the command **MOVETO [Choices]** will place the cursor in the *Choices* field. You do not need to know how far that field is to the left or right of the current field. If there is more than one image on the work area, you could select a table, e.g., the Answer table, with the command **MOVETO ''answer''**.

Use **MOVETO** to place the cursor in the *Choices* field.

```
MOVETO [choices]
```

Using WAIT

The next section of the program is the one that actually displays for the user to work with the Menu table. All the commands issued in the script so far have been work area operations. During a PAL script, the canvas hides these activities from the user's view. It is at this point in the program that the **WAIT** command is used to display the table as a vertical menu and to allow the user to select, by cursor movement, the item on the menu he wants to use as the key value.

The **WAIT** command requires two parameters and supports two optional parameters.

❑ **TABLE <access_type>.** The **TABLE** command is always followed by one of three access-type key words: FIELD, RECORD, or TABLE. The Field option is the most narrow access code limiting the user to the current field and record. When Field is selected, the user is not permitted to move to any other field or any other record. The Record option permits left to right movement to other fields in the current record but no up or down movement to other records. The Table option is the least restrictive, allowing the user to move the cursor to any record or field in the table.

❑ **PROMPT <text> (*optional*).** The Prompt option can be used to create a one or two line display in the menu area at the top of the screen. The text displayed with the Prompt option is used to inform the user about what to do in the table display, in particular noting the exit key defined under the UNTIL parameter.

❑ **MESSAGE <text> (*optional*).** The Message option allows you to display a highlighted message in the lower right corner of the screen. The message has the appearance of the warning messages used in Paradox.

❑ **KEYLIST <key_names>.** This parameter establishes what key or keys will terminate the **WAIT** command and allow the script to continue execution of the next command, if any. Keys are specified by entering the Paradox key names as text literals (enclosed in quotation marks.) For example, the key list **"Enter","F10","F2"** would cause the **WAIT** command to terminate if ↵, [F2], or [F10] was pressed. You must specify at least one key name.

In this case, you will want to specify the ↵ key, written as "Enter", as the key that terminates the WAIT command. In addition, the **PROMPT** command is useful in indicating how the user should proceed. In the command shown below, the prompt is designed to include special symbols for the ↑ and ↓ keys. This is done by using the ASCII value of those characters in the IBM extended screen character set. Character 24 displays on the screen as ↑ while character 25 displays as ↓. The CHR() function is used to convert the character number into the screen character. Add the following **WAIT** command to the script.

```
WAIT TABLE
     PROMPT "Select Item to Summarize",
     "Use "+CHR(24)+" or "+CHR(25)+" to position cursor"
     "+" then press Enter"
UNTIL "Enter"
```

During the **WAIT** command, the user is free to position the cursor to any record in the table. The contents of the *Choices* field in the record in which the user positions the cursor is the key value that should be used to summarize all transactions for that payee. You can store the value indicated by the cursor position to a variable. Once that is accomplished, the selected value can be used independently from the Menu table.

In this script the value in the *Choices* field is stored as the memory variable **key.** Note that **key** is used so that it will be easy to tie this script to the processing commands used in the FIND script that also use the variable **key**. Once the value is stored in a variable, you no longer need to maintain the Menu table image so that the **CLEARIMAGE** command can be used to remove it from the display.

```
key=[choices]
CLEARIMAGE CLEAR
```

Note that when **WAIT** is used to display the work area during a script, the table images displayed become part of the PAL canvas display and will remain on the screen unless you use the **CLEAR** command to wipe clean the PAL canvas.

At this point, if the script works as planned, you will have stored in memory the key value selected by the user. Before you complete the script, add a temporary command which displays the **key** variable and pauses the script.

```
@ 10,10 SAY key+ "selected by user"
x=GETCHAR()
RETURN
```

Before you complete the script with the commands that summarize the transactions, test the first part of the script to see if it does successfully transfer the user's selection to the memory variable. A full listing of the script can be found on page 563. Enter

[F10] g

The script executes for a few moments without anything appearing on the screen. What is going on in the background is the creation of the Menu table. The length of time will vary with the speed of your computer system. When done, the script will display the menu table, with the two line prompts at the top of the screen and the cursor positioned in the first name in the *Choices* field, Figure 14-19.

```
Select Item to Summarize
Use ¡ or » to position cursor then press Enter
MENU ──────────── Choices ──────────┐
      1   Allied Office Furniture   │
      2   Central Office Supplies   │
      3   Computer World            │
      4   Deposit                   │
      5   Fathead Software          │
      6   Interstate Power & Light  │
      7   Savings Club              │
      8   United Federal Insurance  │
      9   Western Telephone         │
```

Figure 14-19 Table displayed as menu.

If you wanted to summarize *United Federal Insurance* you would move the cursor to that item in the menu and press ↵. Enter

↓ ***(7 times)***
↵

When the ↵ key is pressed, the **WAIT** command terminates. The script then displays the text passed to memory variable **key**, Figure 14-20.

```
United Federal Insurance selected by user.
```

Figure 14-20 Key value matches menu selection.

> *Note that when an alpha field is stored as a memory variable, all trailing spaces are omitted.*

Exit the script by entering

↵

Run the script again and make a different selection to test if that key will always correspond to the selected item. Enter

[F10] s p
vertmenu ↵

Select the *Deposit* item by entering

↓ *(3 times)*
↵

The prompt shows that *Deposit* is now the key value, indicating that the vertical menu table is able to pass the selection to a memory variable just as **SHOWMENU** does with menu bars. Exit the script by entering

↵

Completing the Processing

The last step in this process is to combine the summarization performed in the FIND script with the vertical menu selection method implemented in the VERTMENU script. The **Script Read** command can be used to load a copy of the FIND script into the VERTMENU script. You can then simply delete the user input section of the FIND script and allow the processing portion to carry out the same operations. This is possible because the VERTMENU program stores the search item to the same variable name, **key.** Load the VERTMENU script into the editor.

s e e
vertmenu ↵

The last two lines of the script, lines 21 and 22, were added only for testing the effect of the **WAIT** command. They can now be deleted by entering

[End]
↑
[Ctrl-y] *(2 times)*

Use the **Read** command to add a copy of the FIND script to the end of the current script. Enter

[F10] r
find ↵

The FIND script is appended onto the end of the current script. To make the two scripts work correctly as a single program, you will need to do some editing.

↓
[Ctrl-y] *(3 times)*

The remainder of the commands added from the FIND script can remain exactly as they are. The full listing of the script can be found beginning on page 564. Execute the script by entering

[F10] g

Select the payee to summarize by moving the cursor. In this case, select *Computer World* by entering

↓ ***(2 times)***
↵

The program locates the one transaction for that name and displays the amount, Figure 14-21.

```
Computer World selected by user.
Checks:               1
Amount:               2245.50
```

Figure 14-21 Vertmenu script uses table as menu successfully.

Exit the script by entering

↵

The advantage of the vertical, i.e., table, type menu is that the items will always accurately reflect the actual choice available in the table. As records are added, revised, or deleted from the table, the vertical menu will automatically reflect those changes. Vertical (table) menus can be used in applications where bar menus are simply not practical while enabling the script to still allow user selection rather than direct input of items. This is particularly useful when the selection is going to be used as a search key since it eliminates the possibility of the user entering an invalid search key.

Summary

This chapter covered the use and design of menus in Paradox PAL language scripts.

❑ **User Interface.** User interface refers to the way in which dialogs between an application and the person using the application are designed.

❑ **Menus.** A menu is a list of options from which a user can make a selection. Menu entry is an alternative to direct user entry as implemented with the **ACCEPT** command. Menu entry has several advantages including ease of use and the elimination of invalid entries.

❑ **SHOWMENU.** You can create user-defined menu bars that function like the menu built into Paradox. The command lists the menu options that will be displayed and the name of a memory variable that will be defined when a selection is made from the menu. The variable will contain the text of the menu item selected from the menu.

❑ **Programming Structures.** A programming structure refers to the use of special sets of commands to control the flow of command execution during the playing of a script. By default, Paradox executes script commands in exactly the order they were written or recorded. Programming structures alter the sequence by skipping over or repeating a command or group of commands.

❑ **Conditional Structures.** These structures are used to skip the execution of a command or group of commands when circumstances do not meet a specified condition. These structures allow scripts to be more flexible since not all the commands entered into a script will be used all of the time. The script's operation will adjust to the environment in which it is executing by means of the logical expressions used in the conditional Structures.

❑ **IF THEN/ELSE/ENDIF.** IF THEN structures are used to skip a command or group of commands if a logical condition is not satisfied. The Else option allows you to specify an alternative set of commands to execute should the condition evaluate as false.

❑ **SWITCH/ENDSWITCH.** SWITCH is used when you want to evaluate more than two possible conditions. The SWITCH structure allows you to list as many cases as desired. The script will execute the commands related to the *first* case, if any, that evaluates as true. The Otherwise option is used to set up a default set of commands that executes automatically if none of the cases proves to be true. SWITCH structures are often used to evaluate the selection made from a bar menu.

❑ **Loops Structures.** A loop is a structure that repeats a set of commands over and over, so long as a certain condition persists. Loops increase the amount of work done by a script by allowing sections of the script to execute repeatedly.

❑ **WHILE/ENDWHILE.** A WHILE structure creates a loop that repeats a set of command until the specified condition evaluates as false.

❑ **Automatic Loops.** An automatic loop is one that is set to repeat endlessly. Automatic loops require the use of a special command nested inside of a conditional structure to break the execution of the loop.

❑ **TRUE.** The **TRUE** operator (along with **FALSE**) is designed to be used in circumstances where you always want a true (or false) logical expression. **TRUE** is used most commonly with the **WHILE** command to start an automatic loop. Since **TRUE** is always a true value, automatic loops will repeat endlessly unless a break command, such as QUITLOOP, is executed.

❑ **QUITLOOP.** This command will immediately break the execution of a loop whenever it is encountered. **QUITLOOP** is typically used inside an IF THEN/ENDIF structure nested inside an automatic loop in order to break the loop when a specific condition occurs, e.g., user selects **Quit** from menu.

❑ **Subroutines.** A subroutine is a script played as part of another script. Subroutines allow you to modularize your programs by writing small, task-specific scripts and using another script to coordinate those scripts into a single application.

❑ **PLAY.** The **PLAY** commands executes the specified script. When the script is done, control returns to the calling script and the next command, if any, is executed.

❑ **RETURN.** The **RETURN** command causes the current script to stop execution. If the script was executed as a subroutine of another script, control is passed back to the original script where the next command will execute. **RETURN** is usually placed at the end of every script. It can, however, be used at any location in a script.

❑ **Vertical Menus.** A vertical menu is actually a table of values used as a selection list. The **SHOWMENU** command requires the items displayed in the menu to be set at the time the script is written. Selection of items based on the contents of a table field from a bar type of menu would not be accurate if the table was changed. A vertical menu uses the current contents of the table to develop a list of values from which the user can select. Vertical menus combine the flexibility of tables with the selection ease of menus to avoid creating scripts that require direct entry of values.

❑ **WAIT/UNTIL.** This command provides a means by which tables can be integrated into the execution of a script. **WAIT** allows the images on the work area to be visible on the PAL canvas. **WAIT** allows the user limited access to the table. The access to the table continues until the user presses one of the keys specified in the key list.

Scripts

Listing of FIND.SC (1st Version)

```
CLEARALL CLEAR
@ 10,10 ?? ''Total checks written to? ''
ACCEPT ''a20'' TO key
QUERY
```

ck_book	payee	amount	check #
	~key..	calc sum	calc count

```
ENDQUERY
DO_IT!
@ 12,10 ?? "Checks:" @ 12,30 ?? [count of check #]
@ 13,10 ?? "Amount:" @ 13,30 ?? [sum of amount]
@ 24,0 ?? FORMAT("w79,ac","Press any key when done")
x=GETCHAR()
RELEASE VARS ALL
CLEARALL
RETURN
```

Listing of FIND.SC (revised)

```
CLEARALL CLEAR
@ 10,10 ?? "Total checks written to? "
ACCEPT "a20" TO key
QUERY
```

ck_book	payee	amount	check #	deposit
	~key..	calc sum	calc count	calc sum

```
ENDQUERY
DO_IT!
IF [count of check #]=0
THEN
    @ 12,10 ?? "**No records matching "+key+" found.**"
ELSE
    IF UPPER(key)="DEPOSIT"
    THEN
        @ 12,10 ?? "Deposits" @ 12,30 ?? [count of check #]
        @ 13,10 ?? "Amount" @ 13,30 ?? [sum of deposit]
    ELSE
        @ 12,10 ?? "Checks:" @ 12,30 ?? [count of check #]
        @ 13,10 ?? "Amount:" @ 13,30 ?? [sum of amount]
    ENDIF
ENDIF; test for empty Answer table
@ 24,0 ?? FORMAT("w79,ac","Press any key when done")
x=GETCHAR()
```

```
RELEASE VARS ALL
CLEARALL
RETURN
```

Listing of FINDLOOP.SC

```
WHILE true
CLEARALL CLEAR
@ 10,10 ?? "Total checks written to? "
ACCEPT "a20" TO key
QUERY

ck_book | payee  | amount   | check #    | deposit  |
        | ~key.. | calc sum | calc count | calc sum |

ENDQUERY
DO_IT!
IF [count of check #]=0
THEN
   @ 12,10 ?? "**No records matching "+key+" found.**"
ELSE
   IF UPPER(key)="DEPOSIT"
   THEN
      @ 12,10 ?? "Deposits" @ 12,30 ?? [count of check #]
      @ 13,10 ?? "Amount" @ 13,30 ?? [sum of deposit]
   ELSE
      @ 12,10 ?? "Checks:" @ 12,30 ?? [count of check #]
      @ 13,10 ?? "Amount:" @ 13,30 ?? [sum of amount]
   ENDIF
ENDIF; test for empty Answer table
SHOWMENU
"Continue":"Search for another Item",
"Quit":"End Program"
TO program_flow
IF program_flow="Quit"
   THEN QUITLOOP
ENDIF
ENDWHILE; end of automatic loop
```

```
RELEASE VARS ALL
CLEARALL
RETURN
```

Listing of MULTI.SC

```
WHILE true
   SHOWMENU
   ''Balance'':''Summarize checking account'',
   ''Account'':''Summarize by account number'',
   ''Item'':''Summarize by Item'',
   ''Mortgage'':''Calculate Mortgage Payment'',
   ''Quit'':''Exit program''
   TO program
   SWITCH
      CASE program =''Balance'':PLAY ''range1''
      CASE program =''Account'':PLAY ''bar_sum''
      CASE program =''Item'':PLAY ''find''
      CASE program =''Mortgage'':PLAY ''mort''
      OTHERWISE:QUITLOOP
   ENDSWITCH
ENDWHILE
RELEASE VARS ALL
RETURN
```

Listing of VERTMENU.SC (1st version)

```
CLEARALL CLEAR
QUERY

ck_book | payee              |
        | check as Choices   |

ENDQUERY
DO_IT!
CLEARALL
RENAME ''answer'' ''menu''
```

```
VIEW "menu"
MOVETO [choices]
WAIT TABLE
    PROMPT "Select Item to Summarize",
    "Use "+CHR(24)+" or "+CHR(25)+" to position cursor
    "+" then press Enter"
UNTIL "Enter"
key=[choices]
DELETE "menu" CLEAR
@ 10,10 SAY key+ "selected by user"
x=GETCHAR()
RETURN
```

Listing of VERTMENU.SC (complete)

```
CLEARALL CLEAR
QUERY
ck_book | payee            |
        | check as Choices |

ENDQUERY
DO_IT!
CLEARALL
RENAME "answer" "menu"
VIEW "menu"
MOVETO [choices]
WAIT TABLE
        PROMPT "Select Item to Summarize",
        "Use "+CHR(24)+" or "+CHR(25)+" to position cursor
        "+" then press Enter"
UNTIL "Enter"
key=[choices]
CLEARIMAGE CLEAR
@ 10,10 ?? key+" selected by user."
QUERY
ck_book | payee  | amount   | check #    | deposit  |
        | ~key.. | calc sum | calc count | calc sum |

ENDQUERY
DO_IT!
```

```
IF [count of check #]=0
THEN
          @ 12,10 ?? "**No records matching "+key+" found.**"
ELSE
          IF UPPER(key)="DEPOSIT"
          THEN
               @ 12,10 ?? "Deposits" @ 12,30 ?? [count of check #]
               @ 13,10 ?? "Amount" @ 13,30 ?? [sum of deposit]
          ELSE
               @ 12,10 ?? "Checks:" @ 12,30 ?? [count of check #]
               @ 13,10 ?? "Amount:" @ 13,30 ?? [sum of amount]
          ENDIF
ENDIF; test for empty Answer table
@ 24,0 ?? FORMAT("w79,ac","Press any key when done")
x=GETCHAR( )
RELEASE VARS ALL
CLEARALL
RETURN
```

15

Procedural Programming Techniques

In the previous chapters in Part 2 of this book, you learned how to automate operations by writing script programs. Chapter 13 explained the way you can control the information displayed on the screen during a script and how to create scripts that carry on a dialog with the user. Chapter 14 discussed the creation of programs that used special structures such as menus, conditionals, and loops to enhance the look and feel of the user interface as presented by your scripts.

The subject of this chapter is *procedural* programming. The term *procedural* refers to script programs that carry out detailed operations normally left to the built-in features of Paradox. For example, if you want to find the total amount of all the transactions in account 500, you would use a query form command to create an Answer table with the desired values. The exact details of *how* Paradox selects records and calculates values is hidden from you as the user. All you know, and—in most cases—need to know, is that Paradox can supply the desired values in a particular form. Most of the scripts you created rely on powerful built-in functions such as query forms to handle the details of record selection and value summarization. For this reason, your scripts do not have to include many procedural details describing **how** these operations take place.

However, no matter how powerful a feature may be, there are always limitations to its functionality. When you encounter a task that requires a procedure not already built into Paradox, you can use PAL commands and command structures to create your own custom-designed *procedures*.

Custom-designed procedures have the advantage of being able to fit the exact purpose you have in mind. Because they are designed with a specific task in mind, they can often work faster than some built-in procedures that actually do more work than necessary. For example, query form processing always builds a new table, the Answer table, to hold the output of the query. If you only want to display the value on the screen, rather than have it stored on disk in a table, you can create a custom procedure which will eliminate the nonessential aspects of query form processing and return just the type of information needed.

The disadvantage of procedural programming is that you need to learn more about how computers perform tasks such as summarizing field totals, in order to be able to write scripts that use custom-designed procedures.

In this chapter, you will be introduced to an interesting variety of techniques. Some of the techniques can be applied to almost any programming language (e.g., dBASE or FoxBase) with only minor changes in command keywords and syntax. Others are unique to the features built into the PAL language and the Paradox approach to database management.

Scanning a Database Table

In all the scripts you have written up to this point, as well as operations in Part 1, retrieving data from a table has been done by using query forms. The query form is a powerful and flexible tool that is the basis of a wide variety of Paradox operations. However, in many cases, the approach used by query form processing to retrieve data may not fit your exact needs, or may perform more work than is needed to get the desired result. The PAL language makes it possible to create custom-designed data retrieval procedures which focus directly on the source database table. In most cases, you can obtain the desired information faster than you could by using a query form because you avoid writing the data to the disk in the form of an Answer table. If the data is to be displayed on the screen or is printed, and there is no need to have a permanent record of the information, avoiding the creation of the Answer table will improve the overall performance of the script.

One of the basic tools for direct retrieval procedures is the SCAN/ENDSCAN command set. SCAN, like WHILE, creates a loop structure. The main difference is that SCAN is automatically related to the current database table. A loop initiated with a SCAN command will repeat once for each record in the current table. In addition, each time the SCAN loop repeats, the cursor is moved to the next record in the table. When the last record has been reached the SCAN loop terminates.

SCAN loops automatically *walk* through the records in a table, one record at a time. The commands included inside the loop have an opportunity to operate using the data from each one of the records in the table. SCAN loops provide a simple means by which data stored in a table can be manipulated from a script. SCAN loops can create screen displays and printed reports, can update tables, and can perform calculations.

Listing Data

One of the simplest applications of a SCAN loop is to display lists of information stored in tables. While not in and of itself an application that you would commonly use in a script, it will serve to introduce the operation of a SCAN loop. Create a new script called List1 by entering

s e w
list1 ↵

The script shown below will list all the data in the *Check date, Payee*, and *Amount* fields without having to create an Answer table. The single command line **? [check date],[payee],[amount]** will be executed once for each record in the Ck_book table. In addition, each time the loop executes, the cursor position in the table will move down one record. Enter the following script.

```
CLEARALL CLEAR
VIEW "ck_book"
SCAN
    ? [check date],[payee],[amount]
ENDSCAN
CLEARALL
x=GETCHAR()
RETURN
```

Execute the script by entering

[F10] g

The script lists all the data contained in the three fields, Figure 15-1.

Since no formatting was specified, the data is not arranged in columns but simply dumped onto each line. You can improve the appearance of the output by adding formatting commands. Exit the script by entering

↵

Relative Addressing

Data output directly from a table using loop processing can be formatted using the concept of *relative* screen addressing. The @ command has been used to place data at exact screen locations. For example, the command below prints the *Check date* field at row 5, column 10.

```
@ 5,10 ?? [check date]
```

```
1/01/89Deposit0.00
1/22/89Deposit0.00
2/15/89Deposit0.00
2/25/89Deposit0.00
3/22/89Deposit0.00
1/03/89Savings Club71.60
1/03/89Allied Office Furniture750.50
1/04/89Central Office Supplies97.68
1/08/89Western Telephone101.57
1/08/89United Federal Insurance590.00
1/15/89Computer World2245.50
2/10/89Savings Club157.89
2/19/89Western Telephone247.67
3/05/89Fathead Software378.90
3/10/89Interstate Power & Light175.49
3/12/89Central Office Supplies36.89
```

Figure 15-1 Output of SCAN loop.

However, placing a command such as the example inside a SCAN loop would cause each record to print the *Check date* at the same location on the screen overwriting the previous *Check date* each time. What is needed is a way to automatically increment the row location each time the loop displays a new record. This is called *relative* addressing because the actual row or column used is relative to the previous printing. Relative addressing is accomplished through the use of the ROW() and COL() functions. These functions return a numeric value equal to the current row-and-column location of the cursor on the PAL canvas. It is important to keep in mind that the @ command can use a numeric expression, as well as a numeric value, for the row-and-column locations. The command below specifies the row address as **ROW()+1**. This expression uses the current row value and adds 1 to it to determine the row on which to display the *Check date*.

```
@ ROW()+1, 10 ?? [Check date]
```

When the above command is placed into a SCAN loop, it has the effect of displaying each record on a different row.

If you want to display more than one item on a row, simply use ROW() by itself to use the same row number as the previous item. The commands below print all the items on the same row but start each new record on a new row. Note that in order to have the numeric values aligned on the decimal places the FORMAT() function is used to set a uniform width for all *Amounts*.

```
@ ROW()+1, 10 ?? [Check date]
@ ROW() , 20 ?? [payee]
@ ROW() , 45 ?? FORMAT("w12.2,ec",[amount])
```

Load the List1 script into the editor by entering

s e e
list1 ↵

Change the script to read as follows: (Changes in **bold**)

```
CLEARALL CLEAR
VIEW "ck_book"
SCAN
@ ROW()+1, 10 ?? [Check date]
@ ROW() , 20 ?? [payee]
@ ROW() , 45 ?? FORMAT("w12.2,ec",[amount])
ENDSCAN
CLEARALL
x=GETCHAR()
RETURN
```

Execute the script by entering

[F10] g

This time the scanned output is displayed in organized columns, making the results much easier to read, Figure 15-2.

```
1/01/89   Deposit                         0.00
1/22/89   Deposit                         0.00
2/15/89   Deposit                         0.00
2/25/89   Deposit                         0.00
3/22/89   Deposit                         0.00
1/03/89   Savings Club                   71.60
1/03/89   Allied Office Furniture       750.50
1/04/89   Central Office Supplies        97.68
1/08/89   Western Telephone             101.57
1/08/89   United Federal Insurance      590.00
1/15/89   Computer World              2,245.50
2/10/89   Savings Club                  157.89
2/19/89   Western Telephone             247.67
3/05/89   Fathead Software              378.90
3/10/89   Interstate Power & Light      175.49
3/12/89   Central Office Supplies        36.89
```

Figure 15-2 Relative addressing helps organize output.

Exit the script by entering

↵

Pagination

The information displayed as a result of the SCAN loop does not take into consideration what would happen if there were more records in the table than could fit on a single screen. Just as a printed report needs to be broken into pages, screen output needs to be controlled so that output is made one screenful at a time. Breaking a printout into pages is called *pagination*, and the same term can be used to describe the process of breaking up screen lists into screen *pages*.

In order to implement pagination on the screen, you need to add two elements to the script.

❑ **Initialization.** Initialization is a command that sets the starting point on the screen for the first of the relatively addressed lines. If you **CLEAR** the screen just before output, the first line prints on line 1. If you want to start at a lower position on the screen, an @ command which displays at a specific line will mark the line that follows as the starting location.

❑ **Page End Routine.** Inside the SCAN loop an IF THEN/ENDIF structure is needed to determine when the output has reached the lower limit of the screen. The last line on the screen is line 24, but you may set a lower limit at any line you desire. The structure will pause the output for a key press. When the key press is entered, the screen is cleared and the remainder of the records begin to display at the initialization point again.

> *Print pagination, as discussed later in this chapter, uses the same techniques. The only difference is the length of the page and the use of a formfeed instead of a* **CLEAR** *instruction.*

Load the List1 script into the editor by entering

see
list1 ↵

As part of the initialization process, you should display information at the top of the screen that will not change with each screenful of data. Typically, this is information such as a title for display and any column headings that you want touse to identify the data. The important point is that this information should be placed on the screen *before* the SCAN loop begins. The last line of the initialization text will serve as the point at which the SCAN loop will begin to place data on the screen. On line 3, insert the following commands:

```
@ 8,10 ?? "Date"
@ 8,20 ?? "Payee"
@ 8,40 ?? "Amount"
```

Drawing Lines

The screen character-set supported by most MSDOS computers contains a wide variety of characters not found on the keyboard. As mentioned in Chapter 15 you can use the CHR()

function to output these characters as part of your screen display, by concatenating these functions with other text data.

For example, CHR(196) draws a single horizontal line while CHR(205) draws a horizontal double line. You can combine these characters with the FILL() function in order to draw a line across the screen. FILL() repeats a specified character a specified number of times.

FILL(character,repetitions)

Print a line across the screen at line 10 by adding the following command.

```
@ 10,0 ?? FILL(CHR(196),80)
```

Pausing the Scan

The next change to the script takes place at line 11, following the display of the *Amount* field. Before the SCAN loops recycle in order to print the next line, you will want to insert a conditional IF THEN structure which will test to see how far down the screen the cursor has moved. In this example, you will want to stop the display of the records if the cursor has reached row 18. Insert the **IF THEN** command at line 11.

```
IF ROW()=18 THEN
```

If the IF evaluations are true, you will want to draw a line across the bottom of the display and pause the script to allow the user to read the information on the screen. Add the following.

```
@ ROW()+2,0 ?? FILL(CHR(196),80)
@ ROW()+1,0 ?? FORMAT("w79,ac","Press any key")
x=GETCHAR()
```

When the user presses a key, you can assume that he is ready to view another screenful of information. To do that, you need to remove the current information and reposition the cursor at the starting point for a new screen. To reposition the cursor, you can simply repeat the command that drew the line across row 10. Since the information, titles, and column headings, remain the same for all screens there is no need to wipe the entire screen clear. Instead you can use the EOS (end of screen) option with the **CLEAR** command. This option clears the screen, starting at the current cursor position to the end of the screen. Note that this command does not alter the cursor position. Complete the conditional structure by inserting the following.

```
    @ 10,0 ?? FILL(CHR(196),80)
    CLEAR EOS
ENDIF
```

In order to inform the user that he has reached the end of the listing, not just the end of a page, insert the following command at line 20.

```
@ 19,0 ?? FORMAT("w79,ac","* End of Listing *")
```

The full script can be found on pages 614-615. Execute the script by entering

[F10] g

The script displays the first seven records in the table and pauses for the user to press a key, Figure 15-3.

Move to the next screen by entering

↵

The script displays the next group of records on the screen and pauses again. Enter

↵

This time, the message * **End of Listing** * tells you that you have reached the end of the list. Enter

↵

```
Date        Payee                          Amount
-------------------------------------------------
1/01/89     Deposit                          0.00
1/22/89     Deposit                          0.00
2/15/89     Deposit                          0.00
2/25/89     Deposit                          0.00
3/22/89     Deposit                          0.00
1/03/89     Savings Club                    71.60
1/03/89     Allied Office Furniture        750.50
-------------------------------------------------

                  Press any key
```

Figure 15-3 Scan pauses for user to read listing.

Conditional Field Display

If you look at the output of the scan program, you will notice that there is something odd about the first screen, the one that lists the deposits. Since the values for the deposits are actually entered in the *Deposit* field, not the *Amount* field, the values appear as zeros on the display. You can resolve problems like this by adding a conditional IF THEN statement to the script. Load the List1 script into the editor.

s e e
list1 ↵

At line 10, modify the script by adding the commands— shown below in bold—that test the *Payee* field to see if the record is a deposit. Note that the original line 10 is between the ELSE and ENDIF command.

```
IF [payee]=''Deposit'' THEN
    @ ROW() , 45 ?? FORMAT(''w12.2,ec'',[deposit])
ELSE
    @ ROW() , 45 ?? FORMAT(''w12.2,ec'',[amount])
ENDIF
```

Run the script by entering

[F10] g

This time the script uses the *Deposit* field for the deposit records and the *Amount* field for all the rest, Figure 15-4.

Complete the script by entering

↵ (3 times)

```
Date      Payee                             Amount
--------------------------------------------------------
1/01/89   Deposit                         1,700.00
1/22/89   Deposit                           860.00
2/15/89   Deposit                         1,400.00
2/25/89   Deposit                           900.00
3/22/89   Deposit                           875.90
1/03/89   Savings Club                       71.60
1/03/89   Allied Office Furniture           750.50
--------------------------------------------------------
                 Press any key
```

Figure 15-4 Values based on Payee.

Counters and Accumulators

Displaying lists of information is only the most basic task to which SCAN loops can be applied. Of more practical use is the application of SCAN loops for making summary calculations. Summary calculations are created through the special use of memory variables to create *counters* and *accumulators*.

A *counter* is a memory variable that provides a summary count of items such as the number of deposits or the number of checks written in January. A counter is created by entering a command, like the one shown below, into a SCAN loop.

```
kount=kount+1
```

The variable, named *kount* so as not to conflict with the reserved word *count*, is used on both sides of the = sign. If this were an algebraic equation, it would make no sense. But as a PAL language command, it tells Paradox to increase the current value of *kount* by 1. It can be read literally as meaning *let the new value of kount equal the current value of count plus 1*. Placed inside a SCAN loop this command would increment the value of **kount** by one for each record in the table being scanned.

Of course, the real value of counting is that you can count distinct items. Below is an example of how a counter would be used in a loop to count specific items such as deposits and checks. A conditional structure is used to control which of two counters is incremented, based on the *Payee* field.

```
VIEW "ck_book"
count_deps=0
count_checks=0
SCAN
        IF [payee]="Deposit"
                THEN count_deps=count_deps+1
                ELSE count_checks=count_checks+1
        ENDIF
ENDSCAN
```

Note that before the loop begins the counter variables are set to 0. This is called *initialization* of the variable. This is done to ensure that the counting begins at zero and does not continue from some previous use of the variable.

The example is significant because it is able to implement a form of logic that would not be possible with a query form. With a query form, you could count the number of unique items in the *Payee* field. This would give you the correct count for deposits but not for checks, because not all of the checks have the same payee. The conditional structure uses the logic that any transaction that is not a deposit must fall into the checks category. SCAN operations combined with conditional logic can often make summarizations that query forms cannot. This is because query forms depend on the literal information in the fields to group records together.

The conditional logic of PAL command structures allows you to analyze data with more complex logic and create groups of records when the exact field values don't match. One of the most common uses is to group dates by month, something that is quite difficult to do with query forms, since dates must match exactly to be treated as matching values in a query form summary.

An *accumulator* variable is created in a similar way to a counter, with the exception that the name of a field or another variable is used in place of the literal value 1. The command below accumulates the values found in the *Amount* field into a memory variable called *total*.

> *The word* Total *is not a reserved word in PAL, although it is commonly a command name used in other languages such as dBASE.*

```
total=total+[amount]
```

Placed into a SCAN loop, as shown below, the accumulators can draw from selected records just as the counters are controlled by conditional logic.

```
VIEW "ck_book"
count_deps=0
count_checks=0
total_deps=0
total_checks=0
SCAN
     IF [payee]="Deposit"
          THEN count_deps=count_deps+1
               total_deps=total_deps+[deposits]
          ELSE count_checks=count_checks+1
               total_checks=total_checks+[amount]
     ENDIF
ENDSCAN
```

Another advantage of calculating with SCAN loops is that you can perform any number of tasks as you make a single pass through the loop. For example, suppose you wanted to summarize the totals based on two different types of criteria, e.g., deposits or checks and totals by account number. Using query form logic, you would have to perform several query form operations, each one aimed at a particular segment of the table. The main disadvantage of getting the value this way is that each query form will have to make a pass through the entire table. When tables are small, such as the examples used in this book, the time taken for a pass through the table is small, But in larger tables the time is quite significant. Reading data from the disk is by far the slowest process your computer performs, with the exception of printing. For example, it is much faster to perform several calculations on each record in a single scan than it is to perform one calculation each time and perform several scans.

Calculating Values with a Scan Loop

Suppose you wanted to display totals and averages of the checks and deposits at the end of the transaction list produced by the List1 script. That would require the calculation of four values: the totals of checks and deposits and the number of checks and deposits. This can be accomplished by adding accumulators and counters to the SCAN loop. Create a copy of the List1 script called List2 by entering

t c s
list1 ↵
list2 ↵

Load the List2 script into the editor by entering

s e e
list2 ↵

Turn on the insert mode, [Ins] and vertical ruler display, [Ctrl/v].

At the beginning of the script, insert commands that will initialize four variables to the value of zero. To make entry simpler the variables will be TC (total checks), TD (total deposits), CC (count of checks), and CD (count of deposits). Enter

```
tc=0 td=0 cc=0 cd=0
```

The existing SCAN loop already contains a conditional structure that distinguishes between the deposit and check records. All you need to do is insert the counter and accumulator commands into either part of the conditional structure.

At line 13, insert the following commands (on a singe line) which will total and count the deposits.

```
td=td+[deposit] cd=cd+1
```

On line 16, enter the accumulator and counter commands for the checks.

```
tc=tc+[amount] cc=cc+1
```

These commands will calculate the value needed to display the totals and the averages. Move to line 28, a point at which all the records have been displayed. It is here that you can display the values.

The first pair of commands will be used to define the type of numeric formats needed for the display. The most common way to enter format specifications is as a text literal directly in the FORMAT() function. However, when you want to use the same formats in a number of different places, it might be better to assign the format code text to variables and insert the text variables in the FORMAT() function, illustrated below.

```
fmat="w12.2,e$c"
? FORMAT(fmat,[amount])
```

This approach has two advantages. First, you can save time and avoid typos by entering the variable name instead of the entire string. Second, and more important, you can revise the formats of all the items by simply changing the variable definition. For example, suppose you want to increase the width of the numeric formats. If you hadn't used the variable method, you would have to edit every FORMAT() function individually. When you make a change with the variable method, it automatically flows through to all the FORMAT() functions linked to that variable. In this case, there are two styles, one for dollar amounts(FMAT) and one for whole numbers (IMAT).

In addition, the **STYLE** command is used to alter the video attributes of numbers to that they will stand out more on the screen. **STYLE** accepts the options Blink, Reverse, and Intense. Any **?** or **??** issued after a **STYLE** command appear in the style of video specified. **STYLE** used without any options returns the video to normal. Add the following selection beginning at line 28.

```
fmat="w12.2,e$c" imat="w5,ec"
@ 22,10 ?? "Checks"
@ 22,20 STYLE INTENSE ?? FORMAT(imat,cc)
@ 22,40 STYLE REVERSE ?? FORMAT(fmat,tc)
@ 22,60 STYLE ?? FORMAT(fmat,tc/cc)
@ 23,10 ?? "Deposits"
@ 23,20 STYLE INTENSE ?? FORMAT(imat,cd)
@ 23,40 STYLE REVERSE ?? FORMAT(fmat,td)
@ 23,60 STYLE ?? FORMAT(fmat,td/cd)
```

The full listing of the revised script can be found on page 617. Execute the script by entering

[F10] g

Move to the final display screen by entering

↵ ***(2 times)***

The totals, counts, and averages appear at the bottom of the screen, Figure 15-5. Note the effect of the **STYLE** commands on the video. The values were calculated while the SCAN loops were processing the records for display on the screen. Both tasks were accomplished in a single pass through the table, something that could not be done as quickly or as cleanly with query form processing.

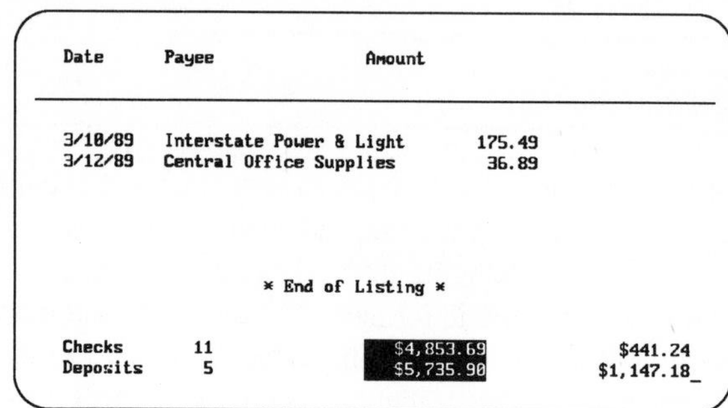

Figure 15-5 Memory variables used as accumulators and counters calculate summary values.

Frequency Distributions

A *frequency distribution* is a type of calculation in which records are divided into classifications. When classifications are made on the basis of numeric values, it is not uncommon that the exact numeric values in each record are unique. However, such values can be classified if you select ranges of values that should be grouped together. For example, all records with values from 0 to 99 might form one group, 100 to 199 a second and so on. In a frequency distribution, you are interested in knowing how many records fall into each range. The ranges are called *bins*, reflecting the way the frequency distributions were done manually.

Frequency distributions are calculated by scanning a database table and analyzing the specified value of each record. The value is then used to increment the value of the bin into which it falls, by one. The final result of the SCAN is a series of bin values that represent the number of records falling into each classification.

Frequency distribution calculations are interesting because they illustrate a special use of the SWITCH structure. Classification by bin ranges would require a fairly complex set of structures, each one having a high and low value used to define the range. However, SWITCH is a shortcut to this type of classification. Recall that the SWITCH structure selects the *first* CASE that evaluates as true. Below is a pseudocode SWITCH structure that selects values 0–100, 101–200, and 201–300. The logical expressions only need to test if the value is less than (or equal to) the high value for each category. This works because SWITCH will select the first true case. For example, the value 150 would be false for CASE {1} but true for CASE {2} and {3}. However, since only the first true case counts in a switch structure, the value would be correctly classified as a CASE {2} value.

```
SWITCH
    CASE variable<=100:.....{1}
    CASE variable<=200:.....{2}
    CASE variable<=300:.....{3}
ENDSWITCH
```

Classifying Values

The following script will put the frequency distribution concept into a concrete form by finding out how many checks fall into various classifications. In this script, there will be five bins:

{1} 0 to 50''
{2} 51 to 100''
{3} 101 to 500''
{4} 501 to 1000''
{5} 1001 & up''

Create a new script called FR by entering

s e w
fr ↵

Begin the script with the usual clearing commands and then add a title printed in the center of the screen. In this case, a new approach to centering using the LEN() function is used. LEN() calculates the total number of characters in an alpha field, variable or literal. To display an item centered on the screen the text is first stored to a memory variable, e.g., **title.** The @ command used to position the cursor for printing the variable uses a formula instead of a numeric value for the column position. The formula is **INT((80-LEN(title))/2)**. The formula takes the length of the text and subtracts that from the width of the screen, 80 columns. That value is divided by 2 to arrive at the position where the text should be printed in order to appear centered. The INT() function is used to truncate the decimal portion of any numbers that do not divide evenly. This is done because Paradox will only accept an integer as a color or row value with the @ command.

The formula may seem a bit complex just to get an item centered, compared to the **FORMAT("w79,ac",<text>)** method. The advantage of the centering formula is that it does not overwrite other items displayed on the same line, which is the case with the FORMAT() method. Add the following section to the new script.

```
CLEARALL CLEAR
title="Analyze Value Distribution"
@ 5,INT((80-LEN(title))/2) STYLE INTENSE ?? title
STYLE
```

With the title displayed, the next task is to get the data items needed for the calculation assembled. This can be done by viewing the Ck_book tables and creating five Memory variables, bin1–bin5, which will serve as the *counters* for each of the 5 classifications.

```
VIEW "ck_book"
bin1=0 bin2=0 bin3=0 bin4=0 bin5=0
```

The next section of the script calculates the distribution by using a SCAN FOR loop to evaluate the *Amount* field in each record. A SWITCH structure, organized as described above, is used to increment the corresponding bin variable based on the value of the *Amount* field. Add the following structure to the script.

```
SCAN FOR [payee]<>"Deposit"
        SWITCH
                CASE [amount]<=50:bin1=bin1+1
                CASE [amount]<=100:bin2=bin2+1
                CASE [amount]<=500:bin3=bin3+1
                CASE [amount]<=1000:bin4=bin4+1
                OTHERWISE:bin5=bin5+1
        ENDSWITCH
ENDSCAN
```

Once the values have been classified, the bin values can be displayed in the form of a table. Complete the script by entering

```
@ 10,10 ?? "0 to 50"
@ 11,10 ?? "51 to 100"
@ 12,10 ?? "101 to 500"
@ 13,10 ?? "501 to 1000"
@ 14,10 ?? "1001 & up"
```

```
@ 10,30 ?? bin1
@ 11,30 ?? bin2
@ 12,30 ?? bin3
@ 13,30 ?? bin4
@ 14,30 ?? bin5
X=GETCHAR()
RELEASE VARS ALL
CLEARALL
RETURN
```

A full listing of the FR script can be found on page 618. Execute the script by entering

[F10] g

The screen display, Figure 15-6, shows that most of the checks written have been in the 101–500 class, with few written for less than 50 or more than 1000.

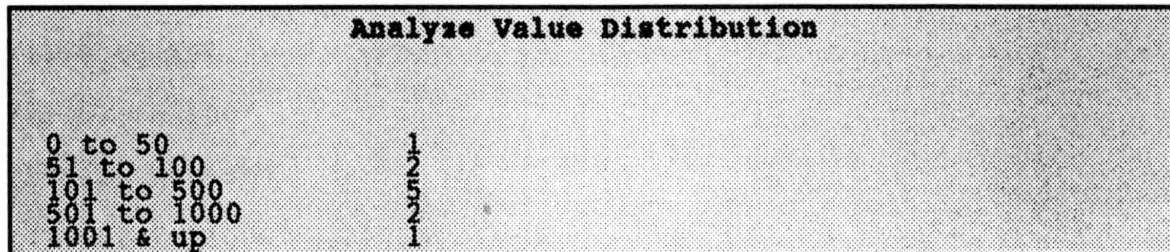

Figure 15-6 Frequency distribution display.

Exit the program by entering

↵

The frequency distribution calculation is an example of a special type of mathematical analysis that can be carried out using a combination of loop and conditional structures. In this case, the SWITCH structure offered a special advantage when it came to distributing values into a series of ranges.

Array Processing

In the previous script a series of five variables, bin1 through bin5, were used to collect data about the distribution of values in the Ck_book table. All five variables functioned in much the same way. They were all the same type, numeric, and were used for the same purpose, counting the number of records that fell into a certain classification.

Once the calculation of the bin counters was complete, it was necessary to print all of the bins to display their values. In the FR script, a specific command (**@ r,c ?? bin#**) was needed in order to display each variable.

It might have been easier to use a command of some type that would tell Paradox to simply *display bins 1 through 5*. The advantage of such a command would be greater the larger the number of bins, i.e., related variables. For example, suppose you wanted to classify records by month. Since there are 12 months in the year, that would mean 12 related variables for each type of value you wanted to calculate. Imagine you wanted to calculate the count and sum for each month. That would be 2 values each for 12 months, a total of 24 variables. If you wanted to keep separate totals for checks and deposits, that would raise the total to 48 variables. This would mean writing 48 @/**??** commands just to display the results, let alone the number of options needed to calculate the value of each variable.

While Paradox does not contain a specific command that allows you to say *display variables 1 through 12* or 1 through 48, it does contain two commands that can greatly simplify the processing of related groups of commands. They are:

❏ **ARRAY.** The **array** command creates an *array* of memory variables. An array is a series of variables that share the same variable name but can be differentiated by the use of a numeric values. For example, the command below creates an array of five memory variables called **bin**.

```
ARRAY bin[5]
```

The variables created by this command would be bin[1], bin[2], bin[3], bin[4], and bin[5]. The individual variables within an array are called **elements**. The advantage of an array is that you can refer to the element by its numeric position in the array. This can be done by using any numeric value, field, variable, or literal to indicate which element in the array you want to reference. The commands below uses the MONTH() function to find the month value(1 through 12) of the date in the *Check date* field. That value is then used to display a corresponding element in the 12-element array **period**.

```
ARRAY period[12]
current_period=MONTH([check date])
? period[current_period]
```

❏ **FOR.** The **FOR** command is used to create a loop structure. This loop structure is different from either the WHILE or SCAN loops in that it is designed to repeat a specified number of times. FOR loops are *counter* loops in that they are designed to move through a range of values, one at a time, until an upper limit is reached. The commands shown below will create a loop in which the value of x will begin at 1 and increment by 1 each time the loop is processed. When the value of x reaches 100, the loop will terminate. The effect of the loop shown below will be to print the numbers 1 to 100.

```
FOR x FROM 1 TO 100
      ? x
ENDFOR
```

Like WHILE loops, you can force a SCAN or FOR loop to terminate by using a ***QUITLOOP*** *command, usually nested inside a conditional structure, within the loop.*

The value used to control the loop, e.g., x, does not need to be included in any of the commands contained within the loop. Its purpose can merely be to define the number of cycles for the loop. The example shown below will print the word *Hello* 100 times.

```
FOR x FROM 1 TO 100
      ? "Hello"
ENDFOR
```

FOR loops do not have to start at 1, nor do they have to increment in steps of 1. The loop shown below counts in a descending order, from 100 to 1 because the step value is -1 instead of the default, $+1$.

```
FOR x FROM 100 TO 1 STEP -1
      ? x
ENDFOR
```

FOR loops can be combined with ARRAY variables in order to reduce the number of commands needed to process a large number of variables. In many cases, an ARRAY/FOR approach allows the same number of commands to process any number of variables. The pseudocode below shows an ARRAY/FOR structure that displays 12 variables. Note that the value designated in the FOR command, **x**, is inserted into the array variable name, **period[x]**. As the value of **x** changes, so will the element of the array which is printed.

```
ARRAY periods[12]
command...
command...
command...
FOR x FROM 1 TO 12
      ? period[x]
ENDFOR
```

Array processing, aided by FOR loops, can be used in a wide variety of situations. Arrays make it much more practical to work with a large number of memory variables. Arrays also make it simpler to revise programs to work with data groups of different sizes. The previous code example requires only two changes to process 48 variables instead of 12.

```
ARRAY periods[48]
command...
command...
command...
FOR x FROM 1 TO 48
          ? period[x]
ENDFOR
```

The primary advantage of ARRAY processing is for the person writing the program. Instead of having to write unique lines of code for each action, array processing allows you to use loop structures to generate variations on a basic command. FOR loops do for array memory variables what SCAN does for processing table records. In fact, the row and column organization of tables has much in common with arrays.

Paradox allows you to create what are called **single** *dimension arrays. In mathematics and in other programming languages, e.g., dBASE IV or FoxBase, you can create two dimensional arrays in which elements can be referred to with a row and column value similar to the way that spreadsheet programs refer to values in row and column cells. This feature is not supported in Paradox 3.5*

Summarizing by Month with Arrays

As an example of how arrays can be used to simplify what would otherwise be a much more complex and tedious programming chore is a program that classifies values by month. In this case, suppose you want to create a display that shows the number and amount of deposits and checks for each month. Create a new script called ARRAY by entering

s e w
array ↵

Although the Ck_book table only had data for three months, the program can be written to account for all twelve months of the year. Begin the script with the usual clearing commands.

```
CLEARALL CLEAR
```

Since there are four data items that you want to calculate for each month, you will need to create a total of 48 variables. However, the variables will be four sets of arrays with twelve elements in each. The ARRAY command will be used to define four arrays: TC (total checks),

CC (count of checks), TD (total deposits), and CD (count of deposits), with 12 elements each. In addition, define two nonarray variables, *depall* and *checkall*, which will be used to calculate the yearly total of checks and deposits.

```
ARRAY tc[12] ARRAY cc[12] ARRAY td[12] ARRAY cd[12]
depall=0 checkall=0
```

The script now contains the necessary arrays.

Initializing the Variables

When an array is created, the elements in the array are not actually defined as full memory variables. Since the array definition does not assign a value to the elements, they must first be initialized. *Initialization* simply refers to assigning each of the elements an initial value. In the arrays used in this script, you will want to define all the elements as having a value of zero to begin the program.

> *Elements in an array do not have to be the same type. A given array can contain date, numeric, and alpha type information in any of the elements.*

The task you have to carry out is to assign zero values to 48 variables. Without array processing, this basic task of initialization would require you to enter 48 commands. However, array processing allows you to use a FOR loop to do most of the work. The command sequence below uses a FOR loop that will count from 1 to 12. The values are assigned to a variable called **element**. Within the loop are four commands, one for each of the four arrays, which assign the element specified by the variable **element** a value of zero. Add the following to the script.

```
FOR element FROM 1 TO 12
    tc[element]=0
    td[element]=0
    cc[element]=0
    cd[element]=0
ENDFOR
```

When the loop has completed, you will have set all 49 array elements to the value of zero.

Referring to Elements by Value

The next part of the script is used to store the deposit and check values into the corresponding elements in each of the four arrays. As in most of the previous programs, a conditional structure is used to separate the deposit records from the check records so that you can get separate tools with the two types of records.

It would also be possible to use a conditional structure, i.e., SWITCH, to separate the check and deposit values by month as well as type of transaction. Using SWITCH to carry out the task, it would be necessary to create two structures, one for deposits and the other for checks, each with 12 cases—one for each month. However, in this instance, it is possible to eliminate the need for these structures. The MONTH() function can extract the number of the month, 1–12, from the date in the *Check date* field. Since each month has a corresponding element in the array, the MONTH() function value can be used to select which element in the array should be used to store the value. This de facto relationship eliminates the need for a conditional structure.

The process begins by placing an image of the Ck_book table on the work area and starting a SCAN loop.

```
VIEW "ck_book"
SCAN
```

The MONTH() function is used to store the month value of the *Check date* in the current record to a variable called **key**.

```
key=MONTH([check date])
```

It is necessary to distinguish between the check and deposit records. Use an **IF** command to test the contents of the *Payee* field.

```
IF [payee]="Deposit" THEN
```

If the record is a deposit, you will want to store the value in the *Deposit* field to the corresponding month element in the TD array.

```
td[key] = td[key] + [deposit]
```

In order to count the number of deposits, increment the corresponding month element in the CD array.

```
cd[key] = cd[key] + 1
```

The **depall** variable will also need to be increased by the value in the *Deposit* field.

```
depall = depall + [deposit]
```

If the record is not a deposit, you need to perform similar tasks using the variables that hold check information by adding the following commands to the script.

```
    ELSE
        tc[key] = tc[key] + [amount]
        cc[key] = cc[key] + 1
        checkall = checkall + [amount]
    ENDIF
ENDSCAN
```

At this point in the script, the only task that remains is to display the information now stored in the array elements. This can be done in a table form. First, display a line of headings which will identify the four columns of elements that you will display.

```
@ 5,5 ?? ''Month''
@ 5,20 ?? ''Deposits''
@ 5,30 ?? ''          Total''
@ 5,50 ?? ''Checks''
@ 5,60 ?? ''          Total''
```

The information in the arrays can be displayed using another FOR loop. Each pass through the loop will print the values from each of the four arrays for that month until all 12 months have been displayed.

You can also take advantage of the loop to create a month label for each row. The MOY() function prints a three-character month abbreviation (Jan, Feb, Mar, etc.) based on a date value. The problem in this case is that you don't have a date value, just a numeric value 1 to 12. This problem can be solved using some additional functions to create a date based on the month value. Note that since you are only displaying the month name, the date which the MOY() function uses can be any date in the corresponding month. If you tack on the characters */1/89* to any month value (e.g., **1**/1/89, **2**/1/89, etc.), you will have text which reads like a date. The text can be converted to an actual date value with the DATEVAL() function. A formula such as **DATEVAL(STRVAL(period) + "/1/89")** would create a date value equal to the first day of the month that corresponds to the value of **period**.

Add the following loop structure to the script.

```
FOR period FROM 1 TO 12
    bmonth=DATEVAL(STRVAL(period)+"/1/89")
    @ 5+period, 5 ?? MOY(bmonth)
    @ 5+period, 20 ?? FORMAT("w5",cd[period])
    @ 5+period, 30 ?? FORMAT("w12.2,ec",td[period])
    @ 5+period, 50 ?? FORMAT("w5",cc[period])
    @ 5+period, 60 ?? FORMAT("w12.2,ec",tc[period])
ENDFOR
```

The final section of the script displays the yearly totals, pauses the script, and then performs the usual end of script housekeeping chores.

```
@ ROW()+2, 5 ?? "Totals"
@ ROW(), 30 ?? FORMAT("w12.2,ec",depall)
@ ROW(), 60 ?? FORMAT("w12.2,ec",checkall)
x=GETCHAR()
RELEASE VARS ALL
CLEARALL
RETURN
```

A full listing of the script can be found on page 619. Run the script by entering

[F10] g

The script displays a table of values, Figure 15-7, that shows the monthly breakdown of transactions.

Month	Deposits	Total	Checks	Total
Jan	2	2,560.00	6	3,856.85
Feb	2	2,300.00	2	405.56
Mar	1	875.90	3	591.28
Apr	0	0.00	0	0.00
May	0	0.00	0	0.00
Jun	0	0.00	0	0.00
Jul	0	0.00	0	0.00
Aug	0	0.00	0	0.00
Sep	0	0.00	0	0.00
Oct	0	0.00	0	0.00
Nov	0	0.00	0	0.00
Dec	0	0.00	0	0.00
Totals		5,735.90		4,853.69

Figure 15-7 Output from Array script.

This script is an example of how arrays can be used to simplify programming tasks that use a large number of memory variables. While arrays cannot be applied in every case, they greatly reduce the amount of PAL commands needed to process data by relying on loops rather than individual instructions.

Array Menus

Because they can be integrated with loop processing so well, arrays make a convenient way to store and retrieve information. Paradox provides a command that can convert text items stored in an array into a Paradox bar menu. The command is called **SHOWARRAY**. It creates the same type of bar menu that **SHOWMENU** does, only it draws the menu items and prompts from arrays. In the previous chapter, you created a script called VERTMENU which used a table as a type of menu. The advantage of the VERTMENU script was that it provided a means by which you could create a menu *on the fly*, based on the current values in a table. In contrast, the **SHOWMENU** command required you to specify the menu options when you were writing the script. In items such as a list of payees, the **SHOWMENU** command was not practical.

However, if you placed the items for the menu into an array, the **SHOWARRAY** command generates a bar type menu using those items. You can create a script that performs the same type of operation as VERTMENU but uses arrays to create a bar menu.

Bar Menus from Arrays

The VERTMENU program used a query form to generate a table which was used as the vertical menu. In this script, you will still use query processing to generate a table of unique values, e.g., a list of payee names, but that table will become the basis of a bar menu. Create a new script called ARRAYMNU by entering

s e w
arraymnu ↵

The first task of this script is to create a query form that generates a list of unique payee names. Since query form processing takes more time than scanning a database table, you might want to display a message on the screen to let the users know that something is going on, rather then letting them look at a blank screen. In this case, display the message *Working...* before you begin the query form processing. The **STYLE** command is used to set the video to blinking, intense. Note that a **STYLE** command without any options follows the display. This command sets the video attributes back to normal so that the next item to be displayed will be in normal video. If you forget to use this command, the rest of the data will be blinking when it is displayed.

```
CLEARALL CLEAR
@ 10,25 STYLE INTENSE,BLINK ?? "Working..."
STYLE
```

The query form will create an Answer table with two fields, *Payee* and *Count of Check #*. Add the query form command to the script.

```
QUERY

ck_book        |payee |check #    |
               |check |calc count |

ENDQUERY
DO_IT!
```

Transferring Fields to Arrays

Once the Answer table has been generated, you will want to transfer the information stored in the fields to arrays. The **SHOWARRAY** command uses two arrays. The values in the first array will be used to generate the menu items. The second array will generate the menu prompts. The arrays used must contain the same number of elements and all of the elements must be alpha type variables.

Before you can copy the information from the table into the array variables, you must create the arrays with the **ARRAY** command. But how will you know the correct number of elements for the arrays? The solution is supplied in the form of the NROW() function. NROWS() returns a numeric value equal to the total number of records in the current table. Since NROWS() is a numeric value, it can be used to determine the number of elements needed in the arrays. The following commands use NROWS() to select the size of two arrays, **items** and **pmts**.

```
ARRAY items[NROWS()]
ARRAY pmts[NROWS()]
```

With the arrays defined, you can transfer the values from the Answer table to the elements of the arrays. The procedure once again involves the use of a SCAN loop to move record by record through the table. During each cycle of the loop the values from the *Payee* and *Count of Check #* fields are transferred to array elements.

In this instance, the order of the items in the table, alphabetical by *Payee*, is the order in which the items should be stored in the array since the **SHOWARRAY** command defines the menu bars in sequence based on the array elements. The RECNO() function provides you with a value equal to the current record number. In the SCAN loop shown below, the RECNO() function is used to specify the element that corresponds to the record number.

Note that all the values in the arrays that will be used to create the menu must be alpha values. Here, the *Count of Check #* field contains numeric values. The values are converted to text and the word *transactions* is added to the number.

```
SCAN
        items[RECNO()]=[payee]
        pmts[RECNO()]=STRVAL([count of check #])+ ''transactions.''
ENDSCAN
```

Once the items have been transferred to the array, the **SHOWARRAY** command can be used to display the menu. The **SHOWARRAY** command uses the array names as parameters. As in the SHOWMENU bar menus, the TO clause assigns the select item to a memory variable, here called **key**.

```
CLEARALL
VIEW ''ck_book''
CLEAR
SHOWARRAY items pmts TO key
```

The remainder of the program is exactly the same as the VERTMENU and FIND scripts. You may want to read the VERTMENU script and edit out the command you don't need.

```
@ 10,10 ?? key+" selected by user."
@ 11,0 STYLE INTENSE ?? FILL(CHR(205),79)
STYLE
total=0 kount=0
SCAN FOR [payee]=key
        IF [payee]="Deposit"
        THEN total=total+[deposit]
        ELSE total=total+[amount]
        ENDIF
        kount=kount+1
ENDSCAN
IF key="Deposit"
THEN @ 12,10 ?? "Deposits:"
ELSE @ 12,10 ?? "Checks:"
ENDIF
@ 13,10 ?? "Amount:"
@ 14,10 ?? "Average:"
@ 12,30 ?? FORMAT("w12",kount )
@ 13,30 ?? FORMAT("w12.2",total)
@ 14,30 ?? FORMAT("w12.2",total/kount)
@ 24,0 ?? FORMAT("w79,ac","Press any key when done")
x=GETCHAR()
RELEASE VARS ALL
CLEARALL
RETURN
```

A full listing of the script can be found on page 620. Execute the script by entering

[F10] g

After flashing the *Working* sign for a few moments, the script displays the bar menu that lists all of the items drawn from the arrays, Figure 15-8.

```
Allied Office Furniture  Central Office Supplies  Computer World  Deposit ►_
1 transactions.
```

Figure 15-8 Menu created from array elements.

Select the Central Office Supplies option by entering

→ ↵

The program summarizes the transactions for that payee. Exit the program by entering

↵

Procedures

In Chapter 14, the concept of modular program design was discussed. *Modular* design refers to the creation of script programs that themselves play other scripts. The scripts executed through the use of the **PLAY** command are called *subroutines*. Subroutines have two major benefits.

❑ **Simplify Program Writing.** Subroutines make it possible to write programs in small, easy-to-write text and to revise modules that can be combined through the use of the **PLAY** command into a larger application. Subroutines allow the logic of any one module to be easier to understand, correct, or change because not all of the detail appears in any one script.

❑ **Allow Several Programs to Use Routines.** Some subroutines contain operations which can be used by many different scripts. When stored as a subroutine, the script can be used by a number of different programs—avoiding the need to duplicate the same code in several scripts.

The reasons for using modular design concepts are very strong. All professional programmers, by education and experience, develop programs in a modular manner. In order to facilitate development of applications in the PAL language, Paradox includes the ability to create **procedures** and **procedure libraries**.

The reasons for creating procedures are the same as for creating subroutines. The only difference between a procedure and a subroutine are technical distinctions that are related to the way in which procedures operate. Procedures are designed to allow users to extend the power of modular design and still achieve better performance than can be achieved with subroutines.

Subroutines versus Procedures

Subroutines and procedures have identical purposes but differ in several respects with regard to the way they are implemented. A subroutine is a script file, SC extension, that is stored on the disk. Each subroutine is stored in a separate file. When a script needs to access a subroutine, a **PLAY** command is issued. Paradox must search the disk and locate the specified script file, load the contents of that script into memory, and execute the commands. The main problem with this method is that reading information from the disk is one of the slowest operations your computer performs. The more scripts called as subroutines to an executing script, the more time will be used up reading the script files of the specified subroutine. This is unfortunate because it means that the more you modularize your application, the greater the amount of wasted time spent in reading each module from the disk. Procedures seek to overcome this weakness by allowing a single script file to be divided into a series of *procedures*. Even though all the commands are stored in a single script file, Paradox treats the procedures as if they were subroutine scripts. However, since all the procedures are loaded when the script is executed, they operate at the same speed as would a script with no subroutines.

Below is a script that uses subroutines to carry out operations selected from a menu bar.

```
SHOWMENU
      "Add":"Add Records",
      "Reports":"Print Reports"
TO choice
SWITCH
      CASE choice="Add":   PLAY "addsub"
      CASE choice="Reports":PLAY "rptsub"
ENDSWITCH
```

The script assumes that there are files ADDSUB.SC and RPTSUB.SC stored on the disk that will execute when the corresponding menu options are selected. Using procedures, all the commands could be placed in a single disk file. Procedures are defined with the commands **PROC <procedure name>** and **ENDPROC**. The pseudocode example below shows how the program would look if procedures instead of subroutines were used.

```
PROC addsub()
commands...
RETURN
ENDPROC

PROC rptsub()
commands..
RETURN
ENDPROC

SHOWMENU
      "Add":"Add Records",
      "Reports":"Print Reports"
TO choice
SWITCH
      CASE choice="Add":   Addsub()
      CASE choice="Reports":Rptsub()
ENDSWITCH
```

The procedures are listed at the beginning of the script file. This is done so that Paradox can read and store the commands in memory before the commands at the end of the script request execution of procedures. When Paradox encounters procedures, the commands are not executed but simply stored in memory for later use. Note that procedure names are always followed by () marks. When a procedure needs to be executed, the name of the procedure is written into the script, e.g., **Addsub()**. It is not necessary to use the **PLAY** command because the procedure commands are already in memory.

Converting Subroutines to Procedures

In Chapter 14, you created a script called MULTI.SC. This script was an example of how a script could use subroutines to carry out various functions coordinated by a master menu. The same results can be obtained, but with greater performance, if the script used procedures rather than subroutines. Begin by creating a new script called MULTIPRO by entering

s e w
multipro ↵

The MULTI script used four scripts (RANGE1, BAR_SUM, FIND, and MORT) as subroutines. You can create procedures for those scripts by reading in the commands contained in those files into the current script and adding the procedure definition command. Begin with the RANGE1 script. Enter the PROC command that will define a procedure called RANGE1. Note that there is no reason why the script and the procedure must have the same name. It is only necessary that the name of the procedure be inserted into the main script wherever a **PLAY <script_name>** command currently exists. In this instance, you will retain the script names as the procedure names for the sake of consistency. Enter

PROC Range1() ↵

Use the **READ** command to load the contents of the RANGE1 script.

[F10] r
range1 ↵

Paradox loads a copy of the RANGE1 script into the current script. To complete the procedure, move the cursor to the end of the command listing by entering

[End] [Ctrl-End] ↵

Add the closing command for the procedure.

ENDPROC ↵ ↵

The process can be repeated for the next script, BAR_SUM, which needs to be defined as a procedure. Enter

PROC Bar_sum() ↵
[F10] r
bar_sum ↵
[End] [Ctrl-End] ↵
ENDPROC ↵ ↵

The procedure should be repeated for the next two scripts, FIND and MORT. Try this on your own. The correct command can be found on page 616 under Exercise 1.

Calling Procedures

The current script now consists of four procedures. The final step is to read in a copy of the script that actually uses procedures. Enter

[F10] r
multi ↵

Move the cursor to the end of the script by entering

[End]

This section of the script into which the MULTI program will be read is different from the other sections previously added because it will not be enclosed with PROC/ENDPROC. This means that, when Paradox reaches that point in the script, the commands begin to be executed as they are encountered. The portion of the script that initiates the actual execution of commands is called the *main line of logic*. The name *main line* refers to the fact that it is these commands that put into play the sequence of operations that activate all the procedures which have been so far defined but not used. The main line will typically contain instructions to execute one or more of the procedures. A command that executes a procedure is known as a *call*. When you execute a procedure, it is designated as *calling* a procedure. In the PAL language, a procedure is *called* when the name of the procedure is encountered in the script. For example, the command shown below shows a CASE that calls the procedure **Find()**.

```
CASE program="Find":Find()
```

The main line section of the current script contains **PLAY** commands that execute subroutine script files. You need to edit this section so that you can replace the **PLAY** commands with calls to the procedures. Edit the script so that the SWITCH structure looks like the one shown below. Changes are shown in **bold.**

```
SWITCH
        CASE program = "Balance": Range1()
        CASE program = "Account": Bar_sum()
        CASE program = "Item": Find()
        CASE program = "Mortgage": Mort()
        OTHERWISE: QUITLOOP
ENDSWITCH
```

Execute the new script by entering

[F10] g

The menu appears as it would with the MULTI script. Execute one of the procedures by making a selection from the menu. For example, suppose you wanted to find the activity in Account 500. Select the Account option by entering

→ ↵

The menu of the account numbers appears immediately. This is because the menu definition is already stored in memory in the BAR_SUM() procedure. In the MULTI script, there would be a delay when the Account option was selected because Paradox had to load the BAR_SUM script before it could display the main menu of that subroutine. Select account 500 by entering

→ ↵

The procedure executes in exactly the same manner as did the subroutines. Exit the script by entering

↵
q

Procedures can be used to execute the same functions as subroutines. In this example, you could see that it was not necessary to modify any of the subroutine files to operate as procedures. Even though they are all stored in a single disk file, they are treated exactly as if they had been stored in five separate files. However, as procedures, they execute much more quickly than would be possible if all of the routines were stored in different files.

User-Defined Functions

Although procedures can duplicate, at a greater speed, all the advantages of subroutines, there are advantages to procedures that go beyond what can be achieved with subroutine scripts. In the previous section, you saw that procedure names look like Paradox functions because they are followed by (). In fact, PAL procedures can be used to create *user-defined* functions. A user-defined function is a special type of procedure designed to return a value. The procedure can be used in a script just as if it were built in PAL functions.

For example, on page 582 a formula was introduced that would calculate the correct column position needed to display a text item as centered on the screen. Below is an example of a procedure that creates a user-defined function called **Center()**, which will calculate the column location.

The user-defined function, **Center()**, pictured in Figure 15-9, requires a parameter. In the example, the parameter is the name of the text item—here, the field *Payee*. When Paradox encounters the user-defined function **Center([payee])**, it searches for a procedure named **Center()**. Note that in the name definition of the procedure it is written as **Center(s)**. The **s** is the name of a variable. When Paradox finds the procedure, it transfers the item found in the user-defined function to the variable name that appears in the procedure name. In other words, Paradox assigns the value of the *Payee* field to the variable named **s**. The procedure then calculates the value and stores it to a variable name **p**. The command **RETURN(p)** tells Paradox to substitute the current value of **p** for the user-defined function **Center([payee])**.

User Defined Function

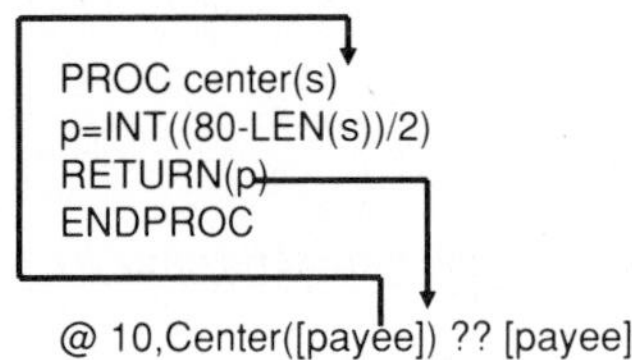

PROC center(s)
p=INT((80-LEN(s))/2)
RETURN(p)
ENDPROC
@ 10,Center([payee]) ?? [payee]

Figure 15-9 User-defined function.

This is exactly how all functions work except that you are not aware of the process when you use the built-in PAL functions. This process is called *passing parameters*. Parameter passing is essential to the creation of user-defined functions because it coordinates the variables in the command with the variables used in the user-defined function routine.

In the **Center()** function, the variable name **s** holds the place in the function routine of some yet-to-be-determined text item. When the function is used in a script, the actual value used as the argument for the function, e.g., Center (**[payee]**), is passed through to the function routine where it is assigned the variable name **s**. The result is that the user-defined function **Center()** can be used with any text item, field, variable, or literal.

> *In this book, in order to distinguish procedures which are user-defined from built-in Paradox PAL commands, PAL commands are entered in UPPER case letters while procedure names are written with the first letter in uppercase and the rest in lowercase, e.g., Center(). This is simply a convention. Paradox does not pay attention to upper and lowercase letters when it executes scripts.*

User-defined functions can have as many parameters as needed. Below is a user-defined function procedure called **Ptax()** that calculates the pre-tax value of amount. The function requires you to enter two parameters: the amount and the rate of tax. The function assigns those parameters to the variables **a** and **r** respectively.

```
PROC ptax(a,r)
rate=r/100
ptax=a-(a/rate)
RETURN(ptax)
ENDPROC

? Ptax([amount],7)
```

When working with user-defined functions that require more than one parameter, you must make sure that the parameters entered into the function are entered in the same order as the variables listed in the PROC command. It is easy to get confused about parameters when you have just created a new function. Since the order in which the parameters are listed is up to the person writing the procedure, you should try to develop consistent habits about the way you use parameters. For example, you may find it more natural to enter percentages, such as a tax rate, as integers rather than decimal. In the **Ptax()** procedure, the command **rate = r/100** converts the integer to the correct decimal value, saving you the trouble of entering **.07** as a parameter. However, if you use integers with some functions but decimals with others, you may find you are confusing yourself about what type of values should be used as parameters. With a little experience, you will begin to find out what approach makes the most sense to you. The sooner you develop these habits, the fewer errors you will encounter.

Creating a User-defined Function

To begin to learn how to create and use procedures create a new script called PROCS1 by entering

s e w
procs1 ↵

Begin with a procedure called **Center()** that will calculate the column position needed to print a given text item in the center of the screen. The procedure is based on the calculation shown on page 582. The advantage of the **Center()** function is that it simplifies the use of this formula by having it entered once in a script and then referenced whenever a line needs to be centered.

Enter the following procedure. Note that the symbol {*blankline*} is inserted into the script listing to indicate that a blank line should be entered. Paradox does not require a procedure to be followed by a blank line, but adding these lines, like indenting, improves the readability of your scripts.

```
PROC center(s)
p=INT((80-LEN(s))/2)
RETURN(p)
ENDPROC
{blankline}
```

With the procedure defined, you can use the function in the main line of logic of your script. In this case, the script simply prints two lines of text and pauses. Note that both lines rely on the **Center()** function to calculate the correct column location.

```
title=''Paradox Procedure Processing''
sub=''Examples of how procedures operate''
STYLE REVERSE @ 5,Center(title) ?? title STYLE
STYLE INTENSE @ 7,Center(sub) ?? sub STYLE
x=GETCHAR()
```

Releasing Procedures

When a procedure is defined by a script, it remains in memory until you exit Paradox or specifically release it from memory. In this respect, procedures are treated like variables—they are retained even after a procedure is terminated, unless the **RELEASE VARS** command is used. Procedures are released with the **RELEASE PROCS** command. You can specify individual procedures or use the word **ALL** to release all of the procedures currently defined in memory. Complete the script by releasing all variables and procedures.

```
RELEASE VARS ALL
RELEASE PROCES ALL
RETURN
```

Execute the script by entering

[F10] g

The procedure displays the two lines of text centered horizontally on the screen display, Figure 15-10.

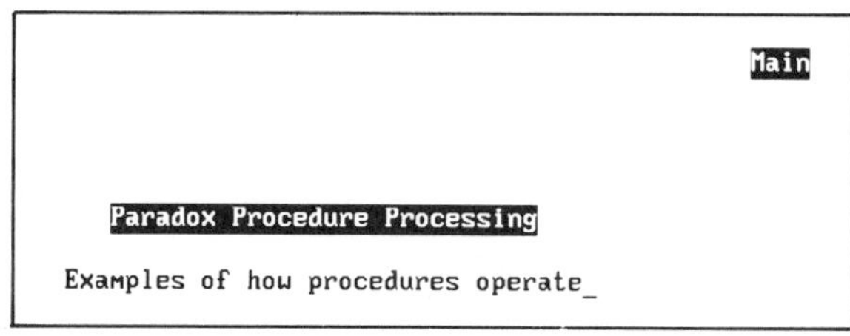

Figure 15-10 User-defined function used in program.

Exit the program by entering

↵

Drawing a Box

User-defined functions and procedures are very useful for extending the PAL language by adding options and routines that are not specifically supported by the basic PAL commands built into Paradox. For example, in the screen form design mode, you have the option of adding single- and double-lined boxes to the screen forms. While these boxes can be used to enhance the look of the screen forms, the PAL language does not have a command that will draw a box on the PAL canvas.

It might be useful to create a procedure routine that would draw these boxes for you. You could then call the procedure whenever you wanted to draw a box on the screen.

How would you go about creating a program that draws a box on the screen? The answer lies in the use of the CHR() function. Recall that CHR() allows you to place characters from the IBM extended character set, not appearing on your keyboard, on the screen. The single- and double-line boxes appearing on the screen are constructed from these characters. Figure 15-11 shows the characters used to create single- and double-line boxes.

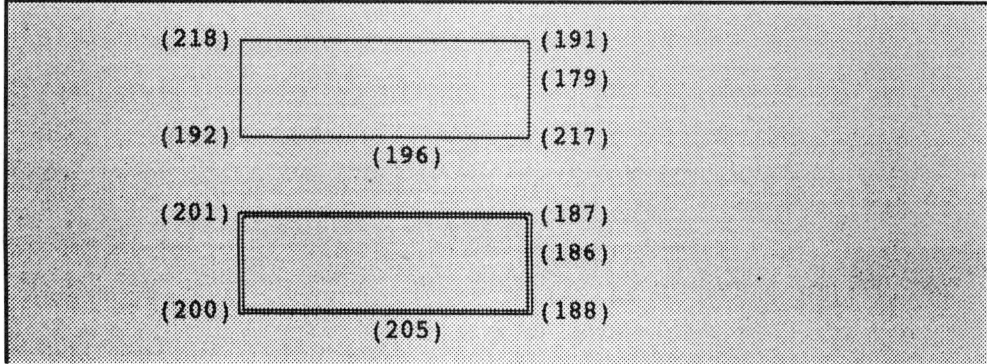

Figure 15-11 Characters used to draw boxes

By displaying the proper characters on the screen, you can draw either a single- or double-lined box.

Drawing a Single-line Box

With the CHR() function you can create a procedure that will draw single-line boxes. Load the PROCS1 script by entering

s e e
proces1 ↵

Turn on the insert mode by entering

[Ins]

Begin by creating the name of the procedure. In this example, the procedure that will draw the box will be called SBOX (single-line box). The procedure will require four parameters: **r** and **c** for the row and column location of the upper left corner of the box, **l** for the length of the box in rows, and **w** for the width of the box in columns.

```
PROC sbox(r,c,l,w)
```

The next section of script assigns each of the six characters needed to draw a single-line box to memory variables. The variables are given the names **hl** (horizontal line), **vl** (vertical line), **ul** (upper left), **ur** (upper right), **ll** (lower left), and **lr** (lower right) to correspond to their placement in the box.

```
hl=CHR(196) vl=CHR(179)
ul=CHR(218) ur=CHR(191)
ll=CHR(192) lr=CHR(217)
```

The next command in the script is **CANVAS OFF**. This command suppresses any updates made to the PAL canvas until a **CANVAS ON** command is encountered. The purpose of this command is to hide the drawing of the box from the user until all the lines and corners have been drawn. The **CANVAS ON** command will then display the completed box on the screen. Without **CANVAS OFF**, the user would see the parts of the box being drawn. The length of time taken for the drawing depends on the speed of your computer, video interface, and monitor. Note that **CANVAS OFF** does not erase characters from the screen. Whatever information is on the screen at the time **CANVAS OFF** is executed remains there until **CANVAS ON** releases Paradox to update the screen.

```
CANVAS OFF
```

The next section of the procedure places the corners of the box. Each corner is printed by using the sum of the four parameters to determine the dimensions of the box.

```
; print corners
@ r,c ?? ul
@ r,c+w ?? ur
@ r+l,c ?? ll
@ r+l,c+w ?? lr
```

When the corners have been placed, you need to draw the vertical and horizontal sides of the box. This can be done with two FOR loops. The first uses the width parameter, **w**, to draw lines at the top and bottom of the box. The expression **c+p** determines the column location of each horizontal line character. The character stops one column before the **w** value since the upper right and lower right corners are already printed at those locations.

```
FOR p FROM 1 TO w-1
        @ r,c+p ?? hl
        @ r+l,c+p ?? hl
ENDFOR
```

The next loop uses the **l** parameter to draw the left and right sides of the box.

```
FOR p FROM 1 to l-1
        @ r+p,c ?? vl
        @ r+p,c+w ?? vl
ENDFOR
```

The box has now been drawn on the screen. Of course, since the CANVAS setting was off, it is not yet visible. Complete the procedure by placing the cursor in the upper left corner of the screen and updating the canvas with **CANVAS ON**.

```
@ 0,0
CANVAS ON
RETURN
ENDPROC
{blankline}
```

You can create an almost identical procedure called Dbox() to draw double-line boxes. The only difference is that Dbox() uses the double-line characters. Add the procedure to the script.

```
PROC dbox(r,c,l,w)
;define characters
hl=CHR(205) vl=CHR(186)
ul=CHR(201) ur=CHR(187)
ll=CHR(200) lr=CHR(188)
CANVAS OFF
; print corners
@ r,c ?? ul
@ r,c+w ?? ur
@ r+l,c ?? ll
@ r+l,c+w ?? lr
FOR p FROM 1 TO w-1
        @ r,c+p ?? hl
        @ r+l,c+p ?? hl
ENDFOR
FOR p FROM 1 to l-1
        @ r+p,c ?? vl
        @ r+p,c+w ?? vl
ENDFOR
@ 0,0
CANVAS ON
RETURN
ENDPROC
```

The procedures can now be called in the program in order to draw the boxes. You need to supply the proper parameters for each procedure as arguments in the procedure call. For example, to draw a single-line box beginning at row 5, column 10, that is 5 lines long and with a width of 60 columns, you would enter **Sbox(5,10,5,60)**. Also keep in mind that parameters that cause the box to go beyond row 24 or column 79 will cause an error.

> *If you desire, you could modify the procedures to truncate boxes with parameters that would fall outside the screen area. Users would then be protected from errors caused by invalid parameters.*

Move the cursor to the end of the script by entering

[End]

You can enhance the main line of logic to include the single- and double-line boxes. Add the commands shown below in **bold** to the script. These commands will draw boxes around the titles.

```
title=''Paradox Procedure Processing''
sub=''Examples of how procedures operate''
dbox(4,10,5,60)
sbox(6,15,2,50)
STYLE REVERSE @ 5,Center(title) ?? title STYLE
STYLE INTENSE @ 7,Center(sub) ?? sub STYLE
```

The full listing of this script can be found on page 621. Execute the script by entering

[F10] g

The Sbox() and Dbox() procedures add single- and double-line boxes to the PAL canvas display, Figure 15-12.

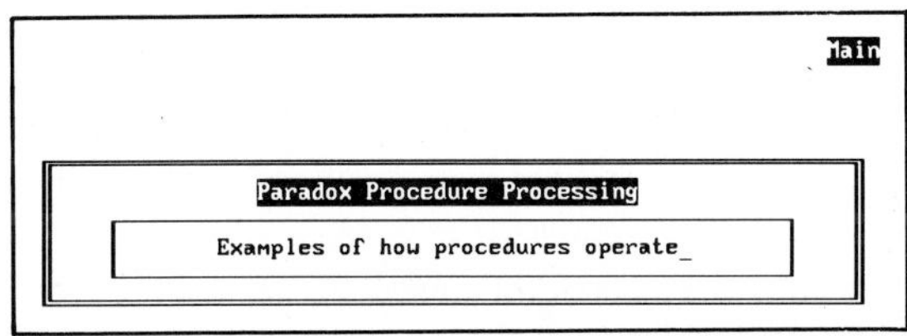

Figure 15-12 Procedures used to draw boxes on PAL canvas.

Exit the script by entering

↵

Libraries

It has been stated that procedures perform the same function as subroutines but have significant advantages. Procedures execute faster than subroutines because they are loaded into memory along with the script in a single step. The script and all the procedures can then execute without having Paradox return to the disk to load additional program segments.

However, page 596 states the second advantage of subroutines is that a given subroutine can be used by many different scripts. If you think about how a procedure is created, it seems to contradict the second advantage of subroutines. If the script and all its procedures are stored in a single file, how can other applications get access to those routines?

For example, the Center(), Sbox(), and Dbox() procedures could be used in any number of scripts because they supply screen formatting options that would be useful, no matter what the nature of the application. However, stored as part of the PROCS1 script, they are available only if you execute the PROCS1 script. The solution to this problem is supplied in the form of Paradox *Procedure Libraries*. A *Procedure Library* is a special type of file whose purpose is to store procedures in a manner that allows all scripts quick access to the procedures.

The Structure of Library Files

At first, the idea of a library file would seem to duplicate the disadvantages of subroutine files. What is the difference between storing a library file instead of a script file? Doesn't Paradox have to search the disk and load the corresponding library file just as it would a subroutine?

On the surface, this would seem to be true. However, library files are different from script files in several important ways. Script files are always stored in ASCII text format. When a script is played, the text file is loaded into memory. However, the commands you write in text must be converted by Paradox into computer-level operation codes. This process of interpreting scans the lines of the script in an attempt to break up the code into actual commands. This process, called *parsing*, refers to a method by which a large item is broken down into smaller parts. It is during this process that Paradox debugs the application. If a command is entered incorrectly, an error is generated. When procedures are placed into a library file, they are stored in interpreted code, not in ASCII text. When a procedure is read from a library file, the process is much faster than reading a normal script file (SC extension).

Library files can contain a large number of individual procedures. Unlike script files, the library files have a file header that enables Paradox to locate specific scripts within the file without having to load the entire library.

The result is that procedures stored in library files have performance advantages over the use of subroutines but still retain their *global* character in that they can be accessed by any number of applications.

In addition, library files have the additional benefit of being written in binary code, not ASCII text, which cannot be read or edited. Procedures stored in library files can be accessed without having the original script files present. This means that you can distribute library files without actually distributing the script files, making your code secure from tampering.

Library Commands

All procedure libraries begin as normal script files. Paradox contains three commands that work with library files.

❑ **CREATELIB.** This command is used to create a new, empty library file. The file will be assigned an LIB file extension.

```
CREATELIB "utils"
```

❑ **WRITELIB.** This command adds one or more procedures currently in memory to an existing library file. Note that you cannot write procedures to a library until you have created that library file. If you write a procedure to a library that already contains a procedure of the same name, the old procedure will be overwritten.

```
WRITELIB "utils" dbox, sbox
```

❑ **READLIB.** This command is used in scripts when you want to access a procedure stored in one of the library files. A procedure must be loaded into memory before it can be executed from a script.

```
READLIB "utils" dbox
```

The Paradox Library

In most cases, you must explicitly read in from a library file using the **READLIB** command any procedures that you wish to execute from a given script, or which are themselves referenced by a procedure which is executing. An attempt in a script to execute a procedure that has not been read into memory will generate an error. However, Paradox does make an exception to this rule. If you create a library with the name PARADOX, file name PARADOX.LIB, in the default directory, Paradox will dynamically load any procedures stored in that file. This means calls made to procedures that have not been loaded will not generate an error if that procedure is stored in PARADOX.LIB. When PARADOX.LIB exists, Paradox will search the procedures in that file automatically if a called procedure is not in memory before it generates an error.

The PARADOX.LIB enables you to store frequently used procedures so that they will be automatically accessed without having to issue a specific **READLIB** command.

Creating a Library File

Suppose you wanted to create a library file that contained the procedures Center(), Sbox(), and Dbox() as defined in the PROCS1 script. Create a copy of the PROCS1 script by entering

t c s
procs1 ↵
lib1 ↵

Load the LIB1 script into the editor by entering

s e e
lib1 ↵

Move the cursor to line 54 of the script. This is the line that contains the command **title=''Paradox Procedure Processing''**.

Erase all the commands in the main line of logic from this script by entering

[Ctrl-y] ***(7 times)***

Place the editor into the insert mode by entering

[Ins]

The script now consists of three procedures but no main-line logic commands to activate the procedures. This is the correct structure for a script whose purpose is to transfer a copy of the procedures into a library file. There are two commands that need to be added to this script in order to carry out that task. The first is a **CREATELIB** command that will create the library file. The second is a **WRITELIB** command that will write the specified procedures into the library file. Insert the following commands.

```
CREATELIB ''utils''
WRITELIB ''utils'' center,sbox,dbox
```

The script you have created is different from most of the other scripts in that its sole purpose is to create a library file with the specified procedures. Once that is done, the file has no purpose except as reference for future modifications to the procedures, should you decide that they are needed. When other programs want to use the procedures, they will access the interpreted versions of these procedures stored in the library file.

Execute the script by entering

[F10] g

If the script has worked correctly, the three procedures have been copied into a file called UTILS.LIB. The script ends with no visible sign that anything has been accomplished. This does not indicate that you have done anything wrong. The actions taken by a script that creates library procedures is not something that places information on the screen.

Using INFOLIB and Miniscript

Unlike script files, which can be examined by loading the information into the editor, library files cannot be directly examined. In order to determine what procedures are stored in a given library file, Paradox includes the **INFOLIB** command. This command places a table on the work area called List that contains a listing of the procedures in the library file.

However, **INFOLIB** is not a Paradox menu command but a PAL language command, which can only be executed from a script. In most cases, a command such as **INFOLIB** would not be used during an actual script program, it would rather be part of the script development process.

One way to obtain the information would be to create a script with a single command, **INFOLIB**.

Paradox includes a command on the PAL menu, [Alt-F10] called **Miniscript** which is designed to simplify just this type of operation. **Miniscript** allows you to enter and execute one or more PAL commands up to a maximum of 175 characters. This command makes it possible to access PAL commands without having to create a script file such as when executing the **INFOLIB** command. To create a miniscript, display the PAL menu by entering

[Alt-F10]

Select the Miniscript option by entering

m

You can enter the commands at the prompt that appears at the top of the screen. In this case, there is only a single command, **INFOLIB.** The miniscript is executed as soon as you press ↵ Enter

infolib "utils" ↵

The **Miniscript** command generates a table called List which shows that the three procedures have been stored in the UTILS library file. See Figure 15-13.

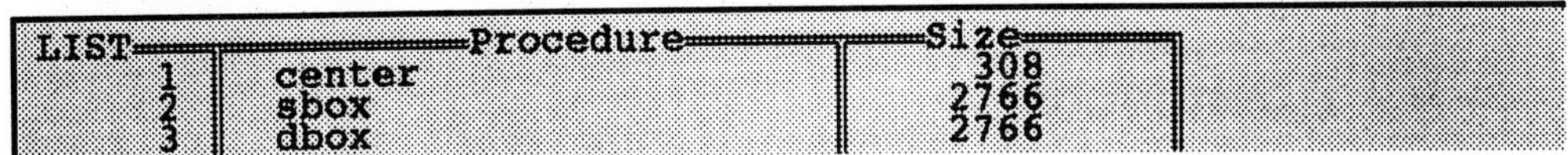

LIST	Procedure	Size
1	center	308
2	sbox	2766
3	dbox	2766

Figure 15-13 Table produced by Infolib command.

Clear the work area by entering

[Alt-F8]

Using Library Procedures

Now that the procedures have been stored in the library, they can be loaded into memory so they can be used with any script you desire. With the library in place, the effect created with the PROCS script can be achieved much more simply. Create a new script called PROCS2 by entering

s e w
proces2 ↵

Begin this script with the usual clearing commands.

```
CLEARALL CLEAR
```

Since this script will need to use the Center(), Sbox(), and Dbox() procedures, they need to be loaded from the library. The READLIB command loads procedures from the specified library.

```
READLIB "utils" center,sbox,dbox
```

The remainder of the script is identical to the main line of logic in the PROCS1 script.

```
title="Paradox Procedure Processing"
sub="Examples of how procedures operate"
dbox(4,10,5,60)
sbox(6,15,2,50)
STYLE REVERSE @ 5,Center(title) ?? title STYLE
STYLE INTENSE @ 7,Center(sub) ?? sub STYLE
x=GETCHAR()
RELEASE VARS ALL
RELEASE PROCS ALL
RETURN
```

Execute the script by entering

[F10] g

The script produces the same result as the PROCS1 script. The performance of this script may be a bit faster since the procedures, which make up the majority of the script, are already interpreted when they are loaded.

Exit the script by entering

↵

Summary

This chapter dealt with the creation of script programs that carried out detailed processing operations. These operations allowed you to achieve results that would have been cumbersome or not directly possible with the built-in data processing features of Paradox, in particular query processing.

❑ **Procedural Programming.** Procedural programming refers to scripts that control, in detail, the operations needed to manipulate data stored in tables. Procedural programming is needed when you want to have more direct control over the details of data manipulation, in contrast to relying on built-in Paradox procedures, such as query form processing. Procedural programming is useful when you want to improve performance by avoiding unnecessary operations, such as the creation of unnecessary Answer tables, or to carry out operations that do not fit the contours of built-in operations. In procedural programming, you must write script commands that handle all the details of the procedure, using loops and conditional structures.

❑ **Relative Addressing.** Relative addressing is used to place information on the PAL canvas relative to the position of other items. The ROW() and COL() functions return the row and column location of the cursor on the PAL canvas. These functions can be used to determine where the next cursor location should be. This approach is useful when processing loops that output data to the screen.

❑ **Counters and Accumulators.** Counters and accumulators are special uses of memory variables to count or sum values. They are used in conjunction with processing loops. The accumulators and counters inserted in the loop can make a number of calculations with only a single pass through the database table. This is in contrast to query form processing which can carry out only one type of logical operation at a time. Since reading tables from the disk is the slowest part of data processing on a computer (with the exception of printing) performances be improved by reducing the number of passes made through the table. The benefit increases as the size of the tables involved increases.

❑ **Arrays.** An array is a series of related memory variables. The variables are all assigned the same name but are differentiated by number. Each numbered variable is called an element. Arrays are important because the elements can be referenced by number, i.e., position in the array, rather than by a unique name. The ability matches up well with loop processing, in particular FOR type loops. The user of variable arrays and loops can reduce the number of commands required to manipulate a large number of memory variables.

❑ **Array Menus.** You can generate bar type menus, using data stored in an array of variables. The **SHOWARRAY** command requires two arrays, one for the menu items, the other for the menu prompts. Array menus make it possible to generate menus on the fly while a script is processing, in contrast to **SHOWMENU** menus which require the number of items to be set before the script is executed.

❑ **Procedures.** A procedure is a script subroutine that can be included within a script file. A procedure is marked with a **PROC** and **ENDPROC** command. When a procedure is encountered in a script, Paradox reads, interprets, and stores the commands in memory but does not execute the commands. The procedure is executed only if it is explicitly called in the main line logic of the script or from within another procedure. Procedures allow you to write modularized scripts without having to create a separate file for each routine.

❑ **User-defined Function.** A user-defined function is a special form of procedure that can be used as if it were a built-in Paradox PAL language function. User-defined functions pass back a value to the calling command, just as a PAL function returns a value.

❑ **Libraries.** Since procedures are written in script files, they would not be available to other scripts. A library is a special type of file in which procedures can be stored and retrieved. The procedures are not stored in ASCII text but in interpreted binary code. This makes loading procedures faster than playing subroutine scripts.

Exercises

Exercise 1 from page 598

```
PROC Find() ↵
[F10] r
find ↵
[End] [Ctrl-End] ↵
ENDPROC ↵ ↵
```

PROC Mort() ↵
[F10] r
mort ↵
[End] [Ctrl-End] ↵
ENDPROC ↵ ↵

Scripts

Listing of Script LIST1.SC

```
CLEARALL CLEAR
VIEW "ck_book"
@ 8,10 ?? "Date"
@ 8,20 ?? "Payee"
@ 8,40 ?? "Amount"
@ 10,0 ?? FILL(CHR(196),80)
SCAN
    @ ROW()+1, 10 ?? [Check date]
    @ ROW() , 20 ?? [payee]
    @ ROW() , 45 ?? FORMAT("w12.2,ec",[amount])
    IF ROW()=18 THEN
        @ ROW()+2,0 ?? FILL(CHR(196),80)
        @ ROW()+1,0 ?? FORMAT("w79,ac","Press any key")
        x=GETCHAR()
        @ 10,0 ?? FILL(CHR(196),80)
        CLEAR EOS
    ENDIF
ENDSCAN
CLEARALL
@ 19,0 ?? FORMAT("w79,ac","* End of Listing *")
x=GETCHAR()
RETURN
```

Listing of Script LIST2.SC

```
tc=0 td=0 cc=0 cd=0
CLEARALL CLEAR
VIEW "ck_book"
```

```
@ 8,10 ?? ''Date''
@ 8,20 ?? ''Payee''
@ 8,40 ?? ''Amount''
@ 10,0 ?? FILL(CHR(196),80)
SCAN
        @ ROW()+1, 10 ?? [Check date]
        @ ROW() , 20 ?? [payee]
        IF [payee]=''Deposit'' THEN
            @ ROW() , 45 ?? FORMAT(''w12.2,ec'',[deposit])
            td=td+[deposit] cd=cd+1
        ELSE
            @ ROW() , 45 ?? FORMAT(''w12.2,ec'',[amount])
            tc=tc+[amount] cc=cc+1
        ENDIF
        IF ROW()=18 THEN
            @ ROW()+2,0 ?? FILL(CHR(196),80)
            @ ROW()+1,0 ?? FORMAT(''w79,ac'',''Press any key'')
            x=GETCHAR()
                        @ 10,0 ?? FILL(CHR(196),80)
            CLEAR EOS
        ENDIF
ENDSCAN
CLEARALL
@ 19,0 ?? FORMAT(''w79,ac'',''* End of Listing *'')
fmat=''w12.2,e$c'' imat=''w5,ec''
@ 22,10 ?? ''Checks''
@ 22,20 STYLE INTENSE ?? FORMAT(imat,cc)
@ 22,40 STYLE REVERSE ?? FORMAT(fmat,tc)
@ 22,60 STYLE ?? FORMAT(fmat,tc/cc)
@ 23,10 ?? ''Deposits''
@ 23,20 STYLE INTENSE ?? FORMAT(imat,cd)
@ 23,40 STYLE REVERSE ?? FORMAT(fmat,td)
@ 23,60 STYLE ?? FORMAT(fmat,td/cd)
x=GETCHAR()
RETURN
```

Listing of Script FR.SC

```
CLEARALL CLEAR
title=''Analyze Value Distribution''
```

```
@ 5,INT((80-LEN(title))/2) STYLE INTENSE ?? title
STYLE
VIEW "ck_book"
bin1=0 bin2=0 bin3=0 bin4=0 bin5=0
SCAN FOR [payee]<>"Deposit"
        SWITCH
              CASE [amount]<=50:bin1=bin1+1
              CASE [amount]<=100:bin2=bin2+1
              CASE [amount]<=500:bin3=bin3+1
              CASE [amount]<=1000:bin4=bin4+1
              OTHERWISE:bin5=bin5+1
        ENDSWITCH
ENDSCAN
@ 10,10 ?? "0 to 50"
@ 11,10 ?? "51 to 100"
@ 12,10 ?? "101 to 500"
@ 13,10 ?? "501 to 1000"
@ 14,10 ?? "1001 & up"
@ 10,30 ?? bin1
@ 11,30 ?? bin2
@ 12,30 ?? bin3
@ 13,30 ?? bin4
@ 14,30 ?? bin5
X=GETCHAR()
RELEASE VARS ALL
CLEARALL
RETURN
```

Listing of Script ARRAY.SC

```
CLEARALL CLEAR
ARRAY tc[12] ARRAY cc[12] ARRAY td[12] ARRAY cd[12]
;initialize array variables
depall=0 checkall=0
FOR element FROM 1 TO 12
        tc[element]=0
        td[element]=0
        cc[element]=0
        cd[element]=0
ENDFOR
```

```
VIEW ''ck_book''
SCAN
        key=MONTH([check date])
        IF [payee]=''Deposit'' THEN
              td[key]=td[key]+[deposit]
              cd[key]=cd[key]+1
              depall=depall+[deposit]
        ELSE
              tc[key]=tc[key]+[amount]
              cc[key]=cc[key]+1
              checkall=checkall+[amount]
        ENDIF
ENDSCAN
@ 5,5 ?? ''Month''
@ 5,20 ?? ''Deposits''
@ 5,30 ?? '' Total''
@ 5,50 ?? ''Checks''
@ 5,60 ?? '' Total''
FOR period FROM 1 TO 12
        bmonth=DATEVAL(STRVAL(period)+''/1/89'')
        @ 5+period, 5 ?? MOY(bmonth)
        @ 5+period, 20 ?? FORMAT(''w5'',cd[period])
        @ 5+period, 30 ?? FORMAT(''w12.2,ec'',td[period])
        @ 5+period, 50 ?? FORMAT(''w5'',cc[period])
        @ 5+period, 60 ?? FORMAT(''w12.2,ec'',tc[period])
ENDFOR
@ ROW()+2, 5 ?? ''Totals''
@ ROW(), 30 ?? FORMAT(''w12.2,ec'',depall)
@ ROW(), 60 ?? FORMAT(''w12.2,ec'',checkall)
x=GETCHAR()
RELEASE VARS ALL
CLEARALL
RETURN
```

Listing of Script ARRAYMNU.SC

```
CLEARALL CLEAR
@ 10,25 STYLE INTENSE,BLINK ?? ''Working...''
STYLE
QUERY
```

```
ck_book |payee  |check #   |
        |check  |calc count|

ENDQUERY
DO_IT!
ARRAY items[NROWS()]
ARRAY pmts[NROWS()]
SCAN
        items[RECNO()] = [payee]
        pmts[RECNO()] = STRVAL(unt of check #]) + "transactions."
ENDSCAN
CLEARALL
VIEW "ck_book"
CLEAR
SHOWARRAY items pmts TO key
@ 10,10 ?? key + " selected by user."
@ 11,0 STYLE INTENSE ?? FILL(CHR(205),79)
STYLE
total = 0 kount = 0
SCAN FOR [payee] = key
        IF [payee] = "Deposit"
        THEN total = total + [deposit]
        ELSE total = total + [amount]
        ENDIF
        kount = kount + 1
ENDSCAN
IF key = "Deposit"
THEN @ 12,10 ?? "Deposits:"
ELSE @ 12,10 ?? "Checks:"
ENDIF
@ 13,10 ?? "Amount:"
@ 14,10 ?? "Average:"
@ 12,30 ?? FORMAT("w12",kount )
@ 13,30 ?? FORMAT("w12.2",total)
@ 14,30 ?? FORMAT("w12.2",total/kount)
@ 24,0 ?? FORMAT("w79,ac","Press any key when done")
x = GETCHAR()
RELEASE VARS ALL
CLEARALL
RETURN
```

Listing of Script PROCS1.SC

```
PROC center(s)
p=INT((80-LEN(s))/2)
RETURN(p)
ENDPROC

PROC sbox(r,c,l,w)
;define characters
CANVAS OFF
hl=CHR(196) vl=CHR(179)
ul=CHR(218) ur=CHR(191)
ll=CHR(192) lr=CHR(217)
; print corners
@ r,c ?? ul
@ r,c+w ?? ur
@ r+l,c ?? ll
@ r+l,c+w ?? lr
FOR p FROM 1 TO w-1
        @ r,c+p ?? hl
        @ r+l,c+p ?? hl
ENDFOR
FOR p FROM 1 to l-1
        @ r+p,c ?? vl
        @ r+p,c+w ?? vl
ENDFOR
@ 0,0
CANVAS ON
RETURN
ENDPROC

PROC dbox(r,c,l,w)
;define characters
CANVAS OFF
hl=CHR(205) vl=CHR(186)
ul=CHR(201) ur=CHR(187)
ll=CHR(200) lr=CHR(188)
; print corners
@ r,c ?? ul
@ r,c+w ?? ur
@ r+l,c ?? ll
```

16

Applications

The term *application* refers to a series of scripts and procedures that create a system which can carry out a wide variety of related tasks. When you design an application in Paradox, you are using the basic Paradox system to create a less general and more specific application. In this book, the example of a checking account database was used to illustrate a wide variety of techniques. Narrowing the scope of a program so that it features areas applied to a specific purpose should have the benefit of making the application easier to learn and use because the options, menus, and reports all relate to the same task.

In this chapter, many of the elements discussed in Part 2 of this book will be pulled together to make a small application that will coordinate many of the checking account tasks. The result will be a script that is an example of how script programming can be used to create a unique database application.

Data Entry and Reports

The application used as an example will be one that creates a unique type of data entry for the checking account database table Ck_book. The goal of the program is to pull all the elements, tables, screen forms, and reports created for Ck_book into a single script program. The program will consist of eight procedures and a main line of logic. The script will also use the Dbox() procedure stored in the Utils library.

Starting the Application

Create a new script file into which to write the application by entering

s e w
ck_app ↵

The Main Menu

The first procedure to be defined is the main program menu. In this case, the main menu consists of three options, Add, Reports, and Quit. The logic could be extended to cover any number of options. The menu will lead to two submenus executed through the Addmnu() and the Rptmnu() procedures.

```
PROC mainmnu()
Showbal()
SHOWMENU
"Add":"Add new checks or deposits",
"Reports":"Print Reports",
"Quit":"Exit Advanced Editing Program"
TO choice
SWITCH
    CASE choice="Add":Addmnu()
    CASE choice="Reports":Reportmnu()
ENDSWITCH
RETURN
ENDPROC
```

The Add Records Menu

Because the Ck_book file holds two different types of related transactions—checks and deposits—the entry routines for each of those items is quite different, using different default values and different screen forms. The Addmnu() procedure displays a menu from which the user can select which type of item he wants to enter.

```
PROC addmnu()
WHILE choice<>"Return"
```

```
        Showbal()
        SHOWMENU
            "Check":"Add new check to database",
            "Deposit":"Add a new deposit to database",
            "Return":"Return to main menu"
        TO choice
        Delay()
        SWITCH
            CASE choice="Check":Addcheck()
            CASE choice="Deposit":Adddep()
        ENDSWITCH
    ENDWHILE
    CLEAR
    RETURN
    ENDPROC
```

The Report Menu

The next procedure displays the Report menu. This procedure contains both the menu structure and the commands to be implemented in order to print reports. Report printing is implemented through the **REPORT** command. **REPORT** requires two parameters. The first is the name of the table and the second is the name of the report to print. Report names correspond to the Report menu numbers displayed on the Report Output menu in Paradox. Note that the report numbers are entered as text values not numeric values.

```
PROC reportmnu()
SHOWMENU
    "Checking":"Checking Account Records",
    "GL":"General Ledger Report"
TO choice
Delay()
SWITCH
    CASE choice="Checking":REPORT "ck_book" "1"
    CASE choice="GL":REPORT "ck_book" "6"
ENDSWITCH
CLEAR
RETURN
ENDPROC
```

Calculating a Running Balance

In the previous procedures, there have been references to a procedure called Showbal(). The procedure is called before the **SHOWMENU** commands in the Addmnu() and Mainmnu() procedures. The purpose of this procedure is to display the current checking account balance at all times. Showbal() itself uses a procedure called Balance() to calculate the current checking account balance. Because Showbal() is executed as part of the Addmnu() procedure, the balance will update after the entry of each new check or deposit.

The first procedure below is the Balance() procedure. It uses a SCAN loop to run though the Ck_book table and accumulate totals for the checks and deposits. Balance() operates as a user-defined function because it returns a value to the calling procedure when it is finished.

```
PROC balance()
VIEW "ck_book"
bal=0
SCAN
     IF [payee]="Deposit"
     THEN bal=bal+[deposit]
     ELSE bal=bal-[amount]
     ENDIF
ENDSCAN
RETURN(bal)
ENDPROC
```

The next procedure, Showbal(), puts the Balance() procedure to use by displaying the value of the user-defined function at row 3, column 61. Note that the information is enclosed in a double-lined box generated with the use of the Dbox() procedure created in the previous chapter and stored in the Utils library file. This implies that you must use **READLIB** to load the Dbox() procedure in order for all this procedure to run properly.

```
PROC showbal()
Dbox(2,60,2,19)
STYLE INTENSE
@ 3,61 ?? "Balance:",Balance()
STYLE
RETURN
ENDPROC
```

Adding Checks

The next procedure is a routine designed for the entry of new checks. In general, data entry operations can be implemented using the built-in Paradox facilities such as the Edit mode, which provides options for using custom-designed screen forms and validity checks.

However, there are some operations that require custom design to implement. For example, Paradox validity checks support the insertion of default values into specified fields whenever a new record is added to a table. However this feature cannot implement *serialized* numbering. *Serialized* numbering refers to automatic consecutive numbering of records. In this example, it would be useful if the check number defaulted to the next check number in the series. This type of serial number is useful in applications such as invoices or purchase orders, which need to be serially numbered.

Although the validity check option cannot implement serial numbering, you can create a procedure that will be able to enter the next number in the series as a default value for each new record.

The first section of the Addcheck() procedure shows how this default value can be found. The procedure begins with a variable, **cn** (check number), set at zero. A SCAN loop processes all the nondeposit records. For each record, the MAX() function is used to compare contents of the *Check #* field to the current value of **cn**. Whichever value is larger is assigned to **cn**. When the scan is complete, **cn** will be equal to the largest value used in the *Check #* field.

```
PROC addcheck()
VIEW ''ck_book''
cn=0
SCAN FOR [payee]<>''Deposit''
     cn=MAX(cn,[check #])
ENDSCAN
```

Once the last check number used in the table has been determined, you are ready to enter the new check. A new record can be added to the table by placing the table in the edit mode, moving the cursor to the end of the table and then moving the cursor down, which creates a new record. Keep in mind that the Edit mode, although activated, is still hidden from the user by the PAL canvas. The table will not become visible until the **WAIT** command is used.

```
EDIT ''ck_book'' END DOWN
```

Setting Defaults

Before the **WAIT** command is used to display the work area so that the user can make entry into the new record, you have the opportunity to insert any default values you desire. In a script, you do not need to rely on the validity-check method to establish default values. Instead, you can directly insert values into the fields using the = command. In most of the previous scripts, the = was used to copy the value of a field into a memory variable.

```
variable=[field_name]]
```

However, the operation can be reversed by reversing the order of the elements in the command. The example below illustrates how the value of a memory variable can be placed into a field in the current record. The memory variable value overwrites the current contents of the field.

```
[field_name]=variable
```

This approach allows you to set the default values in a more flexible way than would be possible with validity checks alone. The first command used below stores the **cn** value plus 1 to the *Check #* field, creating a default value that is the next value in the check number series. The *Check date* field is filled with a date which is one week prior to the current date, TODAY()-7. The idea here is that the user will probably enter the checks and deposits made during the previous week, rather than on a daily basis.

```
[check #]=cn+1
[check date]=TODAY()-7
[deposit]=0
```

Using Forms in Scripts

In Part 1, you created a screen form, form 1, which was designed for check entry. You can take advantage of screen forms in script processing by using the **PICKFORM** command to select an existing screen form.

PICKFORM "1"

Keep in mind that, up to this point, none of the operations has placed information on the PAL canvas. Once the screen form has been selected and default values inserted, the record is ready for editing. The **WAIT** command is used to reveal the Paradox work area which now shows the selected screen form in the edit mode. The **WAIT** command restricts the editing to the current record. This ensures that the application keeps tight control over what records are being accessed. The **WAIT** command allows the user to complete the editing with either [F2] or [Esc].

```
WAIT RECORD
    PROMPT "Adding a check record",
    "Press [F2] when complete or [Esc] to cancel"
UNTIL "F2","Esc"
```

Evaluating a WAIT

When the user enters any of the keys specified in the key list of the **WAIT** command, the wait is terminated and the script continues by executing the next command in the script. It is important to keep in mind that termination of the **WAIT** does not affect the editing mode of the table on the work area. The table remains in exactly the same state it was in before the **WAIT** command was executed— here, the Edit mode. In order to complete the mode, the new record must be saved or the editing changes canceled. In manual operation you would use either **[F2]** or **[F10] c y** to save or cancel the edit mode. You already know that PAL provides the **DO_IT!** command as an equivalent of [F2]. The **CANCELEDIT** PAL command duplicates the **Cancel** on the Edit menu.

However, the tricky part is to determine which key the user pressed to terminate the **WAIT**. PAL automatically stores the text name of the key pressed to a special variable called **retval** (return value). The **retval** variable can be used to determine what key was pressed to end the edit. A conditional structure can then execute the command or commands that correspond to the key pressed.

In addition, a **MESSAGE** command is used to display a message in the lower right corner of the screen, confirming the user's decision to save or cancel the new record.

```
CLEAR
IF retval="F2" THEN
    DO_IT!
    MESSAGE "Check Added to Database"
ELSE
    CANCELEDIT
    MESSAGE "**** Entry Canceled ****"
ENDIF
CLEARIMAGE
RETURN
ENDPROC
```

The procedure ends and the script returns to the Add menu. Recall that before the Add menu appears, the Showbal() procedure will recalculate the account balance ensuring that any new checks or deposits will be automatically reflected in the balance display.

Deposits

The Adddep() procedure is almost identical to the Addcheck() procedure with the exception that a different screen form is used, form 2, and that different default values are inserted into the record. In reference to deposits, you can set the *Payee* field to *Deposit* and the *Acct #* field to 100, since those values are the same for all deposits.

```
PROC adddep()
VIEW "ck_book"
dn=0
SCAN FOR [payee]="Deposit"
      dn=MAX(dn,[check #])
ENDSCAN
EDIT "ck_book" END DOWN
[check #]=dn+1
[payee]="Deposit"
[check date]=TODAY()-7
[acct #]=100
[amount]=0
PICKFORM "2"
WAIT RECORD
    PROMPT "Adding a Deposit Record",
    "Press [F2] when complete or [Esc] to cancel"
UNTIL "F2","Esc"
CLEAR
IF retval="F2" THEN
    DO_IT!
    MESSAGE "Deposit Added to Database"
ELSE
    CANCELEDIT
    MESSAGE "**** Entry Canceled ****"
ENDIF
CLEARIMAGE
RETURN
ENDPROC
```

Delay Messages

When executing a script, it is inevitable that there will be delays while an operation is taking place. In some cases, the user will make a selection from a menu and nothing will appear to happen for a moment or two. While these delays do not affect the logic or design of your program, the person using the program may be disconcerted that there is no immediately visible response to their menu selection.

You can avoid confusion by displaying a message at the very beginning of the task, before any of the time-consuming commands are executed, informing the user that work is being done in the background.

The Delay() procedure is designed to display a blinking message in the center of the screen telling the user that the program is *Working*.

```
PROC delay()
Dbox(8,20,3,40)
STYLE BLINK,INTENSE
@ 9,25 ?? "Working......"
STYLE
ENDPROC
```

The Main Line

The main line of logic in this script consists of a loop that cycles as long as the Quit option is not selected from the main menu. Note that the main line of logic simply initiates the first procedure. The rest of the application simply calls other procedures.

```
;main program logic line
READLIB "utils" Dbox
CLEARALL CLEAR
Choice=" "
WHILE choice<>"Quit"
    Mainmnu()
ENDWHILE
CLEARALL
RELEASE VARS ALL
RELEASE PROCS ALL
RETURN
```

Note that the **REALIB** command at the beginning of the main line loads any procedures from the Utils library that are needed in this application.

When applications are constructed as in this example, it becomes relatively simple to reduce the actual script to just the commands in the main line of logic. Once you have tested all the procedures and are satisfied, you can add the procedures to a library, or create a new library for the procedures. You can then distribute your script application with only two files: the script with the main line of logic and the library with all the procedures needed to carry out the script, e.g., CK_APP.SC and UTILS.LIB. Because the commands in the library file are stored in interpreted form, users with the library version of the application would not be able to modify or read your code.

A full listing of the script can be found on page 631.

Running the Application

You are now ready to execute the application you have just created by entering

[F10] g

The script displays the main menu. In addition, the Showbal() procedure displays the current checking account balance, Figure 16-1.

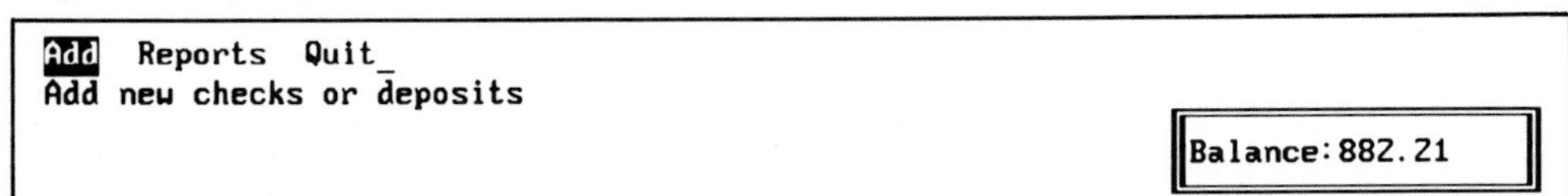

Figure 16-1 Main menu of application with balance displayed.

Select to add a record by entering

a

The Add menu replaces the main menu. This menu allows you to choose between deposit and check entry, Figure 16-2.

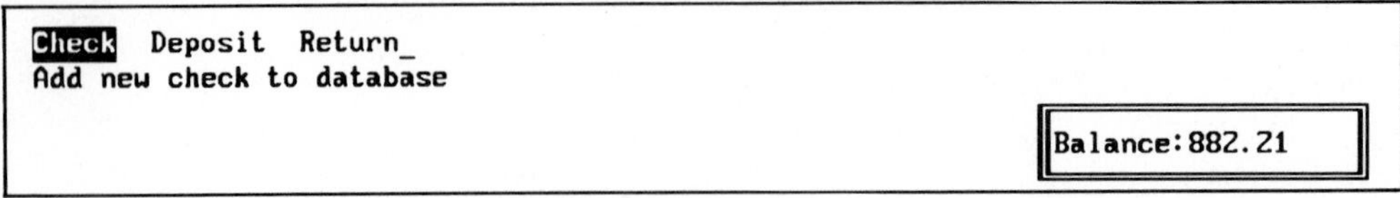

Figure 16-2 Add menu replace main menu on display.

Choose to add a check by entering

c

The *Working* message appears as the program prepares the new record for entry. When ready, the application displays the new record using the check screen form created in Part 1 of this book. Note that the check number is set by default to 1010, which is the next check number in the check numbering series, Figure 16-3.

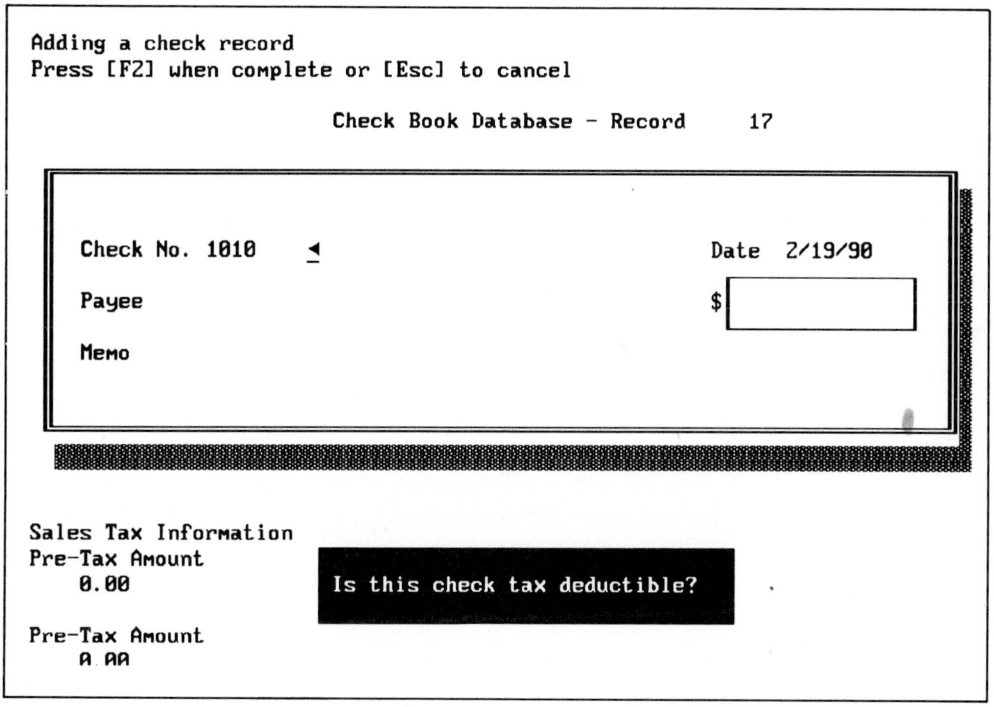

```
Adding a check record
Press [F2] when complete or [Esc] to cancel

                     Check Book Database - Record     17

   Check No. 1010                              Date  2/19/90

   Payee                                       $

   Memo

Sales Tax Information
Pre-Tax Amount
    0.00                Is this check tax deductible?

Pre-Tax Amount
    0.00
```

Figure 16-3 Next check number inserted in new record.

Complete the record by entering

↵(2 times)

LaFish Limited ↵

100

[F2]

The script returns to the add menu with a message at the bottom of the screen confirming that you have just added a new check to the database table. Note that the balance is now $100 less than it was before you entered the new record, demonstrating that the Showbal() procedure will maintain a running balance of the checking account, Figure 16-4.

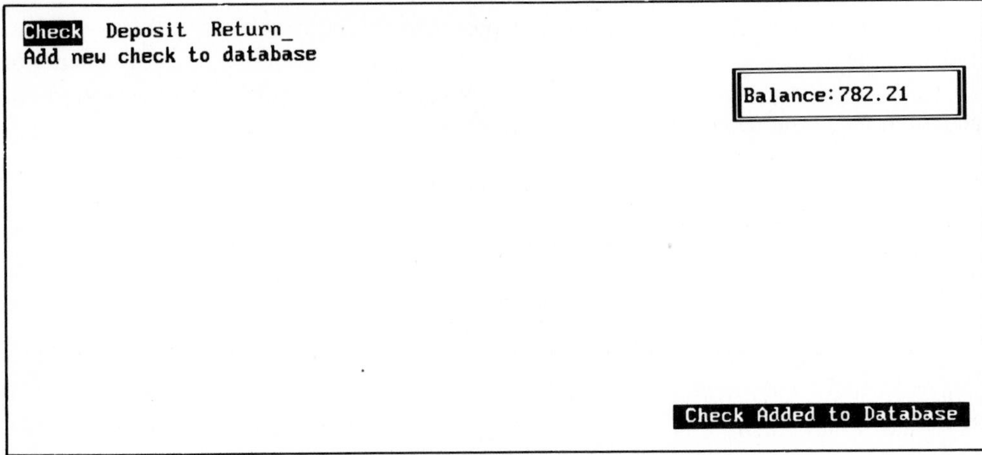

Figure 16-4 Balance adjusts to any new entries.

Exit the application by entering

r q

You can run the script again and explore other aspects of its operation.

The application shows how all the elements discussed in the programming section can be pulled together to form a custom-designed application.

Other Tools

Writing custom applications provides a means by which you can focus the power of Paradox on a specific set of tasks. By focusing the program to a narrow application, you can make the application easier and faster to learn and use than working with Paradox itself. The reason that custom applications are simpler than the full Paradox program is that you are intentionally narrowing the scope of operations. By creating menus that specifically refer to the tasks that you or the other users are familiar with, you create an environment that is easy for individuals to relate to.

The value of customization is that you can make Paradox speak the language of the people who use the application by replacing the general Paradox menus with menus that use terms already familiar to the users.

In examining the basic operations used in database management, you will find that many of the tasks use the same basic program structures with only minor variations caused by differences in table structure or menu terminology.

In order to provide ways of speeding up the development of an application, Paradox provides two additional programs that provide enhanced support for script creation. While it is unfortu-

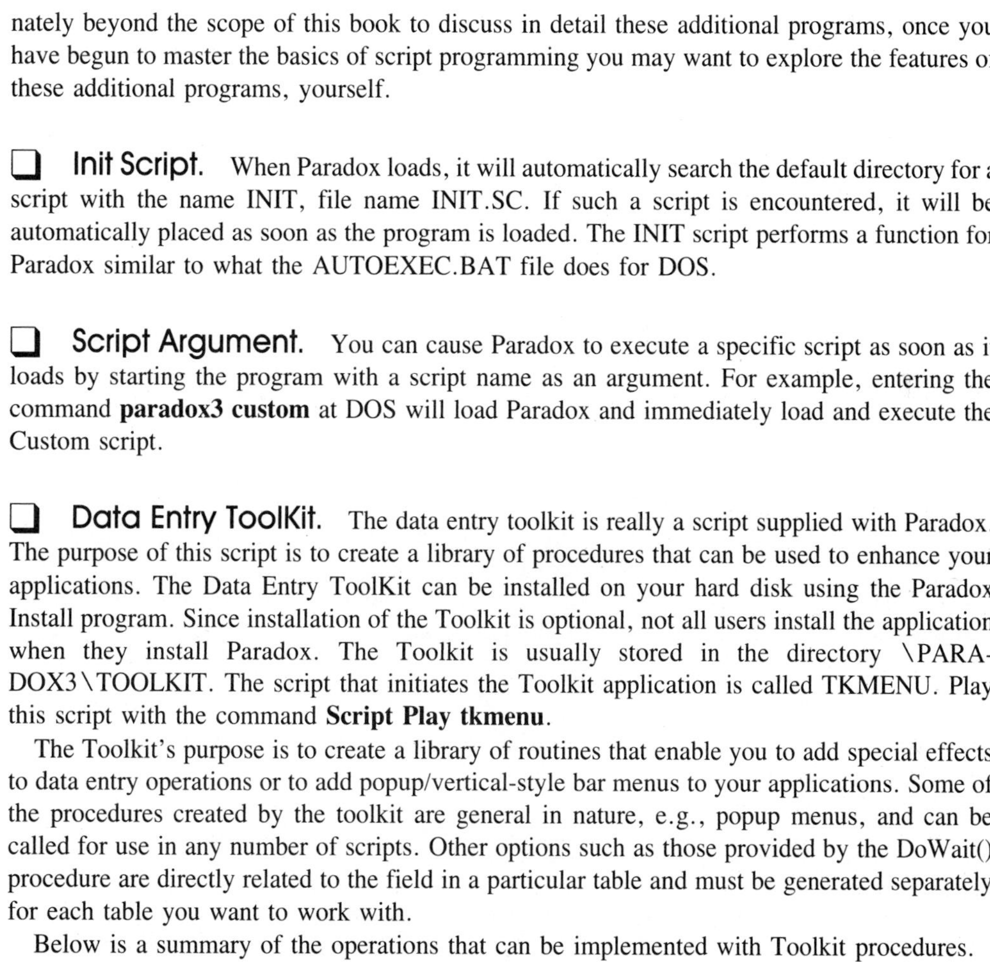

nately beyond the scope of this book to discuss in detail these additional programs, once you have begun to master the basics of script programming you may want to explore the features of these additional programs, yourself.

❑ **Init Script.** When Paradox loads, it will automatically search the default directory for a script with the name INIT, file name INIT.SC. If such a script is encountered, it will be automatically placed as soon as the program is loaded. The INIT script performs a function for Paradox similar to what the AUTOEXEC.BAT file does for DOS.

❑ **Script Argument.** You can cause Paradox to execute a specific script as soon as it loads by starting the program with a script name as an argument. For example, entering the command **paradox3 custom** at DOS will load Paradox and immediately load and execute the Custom script.

❑ **Data Entry ToolKit.** The data entry toolkit is really a script supplied with Paradox. The purpose of this script is to create a library of procedures that can be used to enhance your applications. The Data Entry ToolKit can be installed on your hard disk using the Paradox Install program. Since installation of the Toolkit is optional, not all users install the application when they install Paradox. The Toolkit is usually stored in the directory \PARADOX3\TOOLKIT. The script that initiates the Toolkit application is called TKMENU. Play this script with the command **Script Play tkmenu**.

The Toolkit's purpose is to create a library of routines that enable you to add special effects to data entry operations or to add popup/vertical-style bar menus to your applications. Some of the procedures created by the toolkit are general in nature, e.g., popup menus, and can be called for use in any number of scripts. Other options such as those provided by the DoWait() procedure are directly related to the field in a particular table and must be generated separately for each table you want to work with.

Below is a summary of the operations that can be implemented with Toolkit procedures.

❑ **DoWait Procedures.** DoWait procedures provide a library of procedures that can be used to enhance data entry. DoWait operations fall into a category of programming called *event management*. In normal script programming, you write scripts to handle operations in a sequential fashion. For example, after a menu is displayed you then write commands that will evaluate the menu selection. Event management programming is a style of programming in which you try to anticipate events that may take place during a full-screen entry mode, such as editing a table record. When a **WAIT** command allows the user access to a table record, the script no longer retains control of what the user enters, with the exception of validity checks assigned to the form or the keys in the key list. Event management allows you to establish a set of procedures that will execute immediately if specific events happen during the data editing mode. The DoWait routines are table-specific operations directly related to the structure of the table you are using. DoWait operations can trigger the display of messages, the insertion of default values, validity checks not supported by the ValCheck command, popup selection menus, and other entry enhancements.

❑ **Table or Field Arrive.** You can trigger a DoWait operation when a table or a field is first accessed. For example, you might want to display an explanation of the data entry options when the record is first displayed. You might want to automatically pop up a menu of options when the user moves to a specific field.

❑ **Table or Field Depart.** A DoWait operation can be triggered when the user exits a table record or field. You can specify different actions for a good departure from the field, i.e., a valid entry, or a bad departure, an invalid entry.

❑ **Table Movement.** You can trigger a DoWait operation whenever a cursor movement key is used during an editing session.

❑ **Inactivity.** You can trigger a DoWait action by not entering a keystroke for a specified amount of time. This allows you to set up help screens that display automatically if the user does not make an entry.

❑ **Keys.** A DoWait operation can be triggered by the entry of one or more specific keystrokes.

❑ **Popup Menus.** The toolkit can create two type of procedures that will generate popup-style menus that list options as vertical bars from which the user can select. These popup menu procedures can be used independently of any specific table.

❑ **Passwords.** The Toolkit can produce routines that require the user to enter passwords.

❑ **Personal Programmer.** The Personal Programmer is a separate application supplied with Paradox. The application is run directly from DOS, not as a Paradox script. The Personal Programmer is an application generator. It actually writes scripts and procedures, based on your selections from menus. The programmer assumes that you have created all the database items such as tables, screen forms, reports, and graphs. The programmer then allows you to automatically generate the application scripts by specifying what items should be executed from what menu selection. If you understand the basics of application writing, you can use the Personal Programmer to generate the menus, loops, and other script structures needed to make a complete application. Once one has been created you can make custom modifications, if desired, to the generated scripts.

Summary

This chapter showed an example of how the basic script-writing techniques explained in Part 2 can be brought together to make a custom-designed application. Most applications can be run by executing procedures from a main menu. The design of these applications reduces the main line of logic to a very short program, which displays the main menu. All the rest of the tasks are carried out by procedures stored in the script or in library files.

Script

Listing of Script CK_APP.SC

```
PROC mainmnu()
Showbal()
SHOWMENU
''Add'':''Add new checks or deposits'',
''Reports'':''Print Reports'',
''Quit'':''Exit Advanced Editing Program''
TO choice
SWITCH
    CASE choice=''Add'':Addmnu()
    CASE choice=''Reports'':Reportmnu()
ENDSWITCH
RETURN
ENDPROC

PROC addmnu()
WHILE choice<>''Return''
    Showbal()
    SHOWMENU
        ''Check'':''Add new check to database'',
        ''Deposit'':''Add a new deposit to database'',
        ''Return'':''Return to main menu''
    TO choice
    Delay()
    SWITCH
```

```
            CASE choice=''Check'':Addcheck()
            CASE choice=''Deposit'':Adddep()
        ENDSWITCH
ENDWHILE
CLEAR
RETURN
ENDPROC

PROC reportmnu()
SHOWMENU
    ''Checking'':''Checking Account Records'',
    ''GL'':''General Ledger Report''
TO choice
Delay()
SWITCH
    CASE choice=''Checking'':REPORT ''ck_book'' ''1''
    CASE choice=''GL'':REPORT ''ck_book'' ''6''
ENDSWITCH
CLEAR
RETURN
ENDPROC

PROC balance()
VIEW ''ck_book''
bal=0
SCAN
    IF [payee]=''Deposit''
    THEN bal=bal+[deposit]
    ELSE bal=bal-[amount]
    ENDIF
ENDSCAN
RETURN(bal)
ENDPROC

PROC showbal()
Dbox(2,60,2,19)
STYLE INTENSE
@ 3,61 ?? ''Balance:'',Balance()
STYLE
RETURN
ENDPROC
```

```
PROC addcheck()
VIEW ''ck_book''
cn=0
SCAN FOR [payee]<>''Deposit''
      cn=MAX(cn,[check #])
ENDSCAN
EDIT ''ck_book'' END DOWN
[check #]=cn+1
[check date]=TODAY()-7
[deposit]=0
PICKFORM ''1''
WAIT RECORD
    PROMPT ''Adding a check record'',
    ''Press [F2] when complete or [Esc] to cancel''
UNTIL ''F2'',''Esc''
CLEAR
IF retval=''F2'' THEN
    DO_IT!
    MESSAGE ''Check Added to Database''
ELSE
    CANCELEDIT
    MESSAGE ''**** Entry Canceled ****''
ENDIF
CLEARIMAGE
RETURN
ENDPROC

PROC adddep()
VIEW ''ck_book''
dn=0
SCAN FOR [payee]=''Deposit''
      dn=MAX(dn,[check #])
ENDSCAN
EDIT ''ck_book'' END DOWN
[check #]=dn+1
[payee]=''Deposit''
[check date]=TODAY()-7
[acct #]=100
[amount]=0
PICKFORM ''2''
WAIT RECORD
    PROMPT ''Adding a Deposit Record'',
```

```
    "Press [F2] when complete or [Esc] to cancel"
UNTIL "F2","Esc"
CLEAR
IF retval="F2" THEN
    DO_IT!
    MESSAGE "Deposit Added to Database"
ELSE
    CANCELEDIT
    MESSAGE "**** Entry Canceled ****"
ENDIF
CLEARIMAGE
RETURN
ENDPROC

PROC delay()
Dbox(8,20,3,40)
STYLE BLINK,INTENSE
@ 9,25 ?? "Working......."
STYLE
ENDPROC

;main program logic line
READLIB "utils" Dbox
CLEARALL CLEAR
Choice=" "
WHILE choice<>"Quit"
    Mainmnu()
ENDWHILE
CLEARALL
RELEASE VARS ALL
RELEASE PROCS ALL
RETURN
```

Part 3

Networks

17

Using Paradox on a Network

When Paradox is run on a local area network, the program will automatically implement locking operations that will prevent conflict between users. In this chapter, you will look at how network procedures affect database operations and how Paradox implements database operations in a multiuser environment. In order to discuss how Paradox works in a multiuser environment, you will need to imagine that there is a local area network on which there are at least two users, *Morgan* and *Carolyn*, running Paradox. Both users will have occasion to work with the Ck_book table and its related files as developed in Parts 1 and 2 of the book.

Multiuser Access to Files

In order to understand how Paradox functions in a multiuser environment, you need to understand how a multiuser environment affects basic database operations.

The MSDOS operating system was designed to be used on stand-alone microcomputer systems. In stand-alone systems, there is only a single processing unit that can gain access to any of the devices attached to the computer. Since only a single keyboard is attached to the computer, all commands and data come from a single source.

When computers are connected with a local area network (LAN), the potential exists for users working on different computers to have access to the same files. It is possible that two or more users will attempt to access the same file at the same time. This creates a situation in which conflicts can arise. If changes are made by more than one user, whose changes will be saved and whose discarded? Such conflicts could potentially result in data lost, unless a system is put in place to manage these conflicts. The basic system implemented by the network operating system is to allow file access on a *first come, first served* basis. The first user to gain access to the file locks out all other users from access to that file until the first user has finished and released the file.

If you know in advance that users will never make any changes in the contents of a file, you can use the network operating system to mark that file as **read-only**. A **read-only** file can be accessed by more than one user at a time because no users are permitted to make changes to it. This approach works well for program files. Since you would rarely, if ever, make changes in program files (EXE or COM extensions) you can achieve a measure of sharing by using the **DOS ATTRIB** command to mark programs as read-only. The command shown below marks the file SAMPLE.COM as read-only.

```
ATTRIB +R sample.com
```

The SAMPLE program could then be executed by more than one user without creating a conflict. However, files that contain information such as word processing documents, spreadsheet files, or databases cannot be effectively utilized if they are restricted to read-only access.

Why Databases Are Different

By and large, the system by which the first user gains access to the selected data file applies to the files created by most applications. However, database files have the potential for actual shared access among more than one user at a time. Why are database files different?

The answer is that files created by most applications such as word processing or spreadsheet programs can be accessed in a *random* fashion. In this sense, *random* refers to the fact that when you load a word processing document or a spreadsheet, there is no reason to assume you will access any specific part of the file. In word processing, you may move around to any word, page, or paragraph. In a spreadsheet file, you can move to any of the cells available.

However, database files represent data in a much higher and more clearly defined mode of storage. Database files break up their information into discrete sections called *records*. Most of the operations that change information in a database file operate on one record at a time. This means while you are working on one record, the remainder of the records in the database are not subject to change.

The highly structured makeup of a database file makes it possible and quite logical to allow several users to access records at the same time, so long as no two users access the same record at the same time. In a large database, many users may access the same file at the same time and never select the same records.

Instead of using a file-locking system in which access to the file is granted or denied on an all-or-nothing basis, database programs like Paradox can grant multiple users access to the same database table. The program will lock out each record as it is accessed but permit new users to access any of the records not already in use.

Database files can be subject to a variety of locks—some that affect the file as a whole, and others that effect only individual records within the file.

Types of Locking

When a database table is used in a multiuser environment, users need to be aware that other users have the potential of accessing the same files. Paradox protects tables from corruption by implementing *locks* which control the access to the tables and other related files.

Paradox can implement five different types of locks that affect access to tables.

❑ **Full File Locks.** A full file lock is one that grants the user placing the lock *exclusive* access to the table. While this lock is in place, all other users are refused access to the table. Because selection of a table is the basis for accessing any of the files related to a table such as screen forms or report forms, other users are frozen out completely. A full file lock has the same effect as a DOS file lock.

❑ **Prevent Full File Locks.** This type of lock is designed to prevent a user from placing a full file lock on the specified table. Keep in mind that once any user places a full file lock on a table, no other users can get access. The **prevent** lock tells Paradox not to allow a user to place a full file lock on this table. Placing this prevent lock on a table ensures that other users will be able to gain at least read access to the table. *Read* access is important because it makes it possible for a user who does not have *write* access to the table to gain access to files related to the table, such as report or screen forms.

❑ **Write File Lock.** This type of lock grants the ability to make changes in the table to one user. All other users are restricted to read-only access of the table. Read-only access means that they can display information from the table and gain access to any of the related files, such as report or screen forms.

❑ **Prevent Write File Lock.** This type of lock is used when you want to ensure that no user places a write file lock on the table. When this lock is placed on a table, all users are assured access to any record in the table that is not specifically in use by another user.

❑ **Record Lock.** A record lock grants write access to a specific record to a single user. All other records not locked can be accessed by another user. You can have as many record locks active as there are users active.

Locks and Commands

Why are so many types of locks necessary? The locks are needed because different commands and operations affect tables differently. For example, the modification of the data in a single record has a very limited effect. There is no reason why the changes made in one record should prevent another user from making changes to a different record.

But suppose one user wanted to change the structure of the table? The structure affects all of the records in the table. A user could be permitted to change the structure of a table only if that user had exclusive access, a full file lock, to the entire table. Different commands and operations would require different levels of locks in order to ensure that the activity did not corrupt the data stored in the table.

When a command is executed on a table in a multiuser environment, the goal is to set *the least restrictive* lock possible so that other users have the most opportunity possible to have access to the tables. Applying locks that are too restrictive cuts off users from data and operations that they should be able to carry out without interfering with the other users.

Automatic and Explicit Locks

There are two systems of locking available in Paradox.

❑ **Automatic Locking.** Paradox will automatically implement locks that prevent data corruption. These locks are placed on files or records in response to the activities carried out by various users. The locks are placed on a first come, first served basis. The level of lock applied is based on the activity being carried out. For example, suppose one user is printing a report. There is no reason why other users cannot access and lock individual records while the report is printing. However, if a user is making a copy of a table, other users must be locked out until the copy is made. Allowing some users to edit a table being copied could lead to corruption of the data.

❑ **Explicit Locking.** Explicit locking refers to file or record locks activated directly by the user from the Tools Net menu or through PAL commands in a script. Explicit locks are implemented *before* the user attempts a table operation in contrast to automatic locks generated when a user tries to carry out a table operation. Explicit locks have two advantages. First, you can implement *preventative* locks (prevent file lock or prevent write lock) which limit the types of locks other users can place on a table. Second, you can write script programs that use explicit locking commands to handle user conflicts. These scripts can implement your own custom-designed locking routines designed to fit the way you actually work with certain tables.

The automatic locking system provided by Paradox will prevent data corruption by automatically enforcing locks based on user activities. A Paradox script designed for a stand-alone computer system can run on a multiuser system without modification because the automatic locking system will handle conflicts between users automatically.

However, if you are using a script application—such as the one shown in Chapter 16—to access table data in a multiuser environment you may want to create script procedures that will handle file and record locking in a manner different from the way the automatic system would handle them.

Running Paradox 3 in a Multiuser Environment

As mentioned, MSDOS is inherently a single user operating system. When MSDOS computers are connected by a local area network, a network operating system is used to enhance or replace the MSDOS. This means while all MSDOS computers share the same set of operating system commands, e.g., **COPY, DEL, CD, PATH**, etc., network operating systems will have commands unique to that network operating system. This means installation of Paradox will be different from network to network.

While it is beyond the scope of this book to detail the installation procedures for various network operating systems, it might be useful to touch on some basic points that all networks have in common, keeping in mind that the details may differ from network to network.

Workstation Setup

In a multiuser environment, the Paradox 3.5 program is installed on the file server computers. Other users can access the Paradox 3.5 program and run Paradox from their own computer. In order to run Paradox from a network workstation, the following steps must be taken.

❑ **Update the Number of Users.** Paradox 3.5 has the built-in ability to operate on a local area network. However, Paradox limits the number of users that can access the program at any one time, in order to ensure that only users who have paid for the Paradox program can access the program. The system is implemented through the NUPDATE (network update) program. The NUPDATE program sets the maximum number of network users. When the program is run, you can enter the serial numbers of the Paradox programs and/or Paradox LAN packs you have purchased. Each Paradox program allows one user while each LAN pack allows five users. The total number of simultaneous users is determined by the series numbers you enter. Changes made with the NUPDATE program are stored in a file called PARADOX.SOM which is stored on the file server's disk. The total number of users specified in this file is the maximum number of users that can access Paradox at one time.

❑ **Paths Set.** Access to the Paradox program stored on the file server is accomplished by a *search path* of the workstation. MSDOS was originally designed to access files stored in a

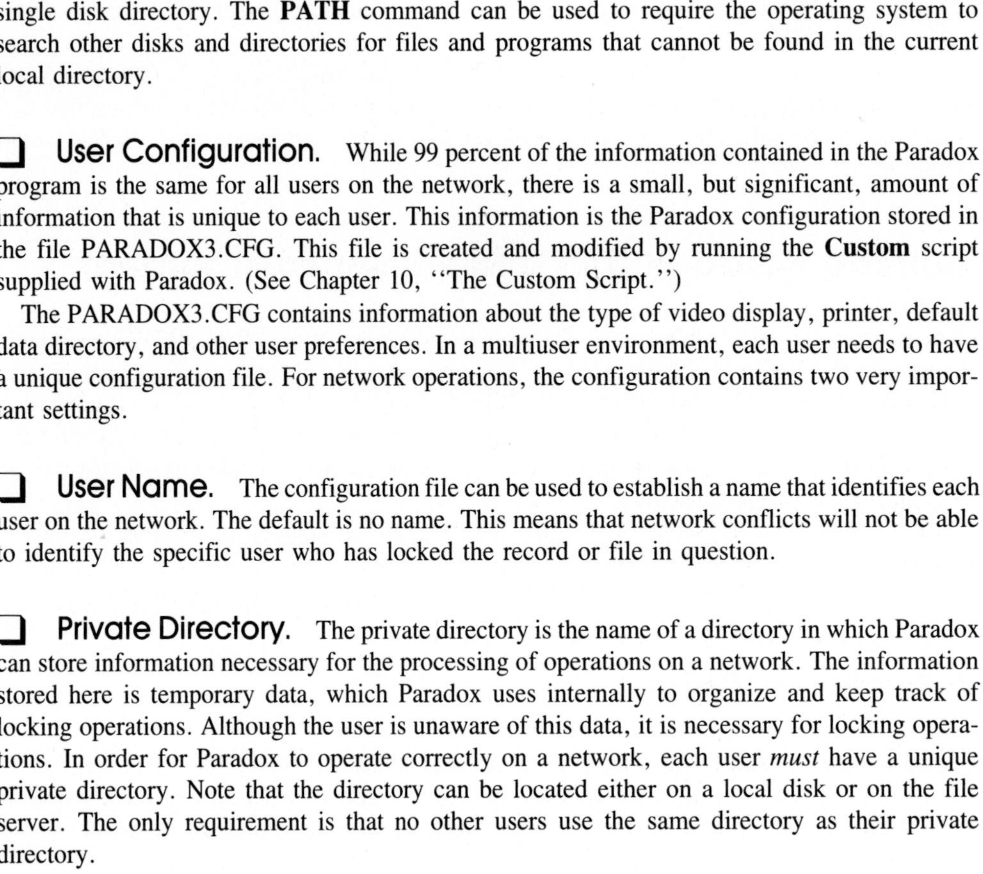

single disk directory. The **PATH** command can be used to require the operating system to search other disks and directories for files and programs that cannot be found in the current local directory.

❑ **User Configuration.** While 99 percent of the information contained in the Paradox program is the same for all users on the network, there is a small, but significant, amount of information that is unique to each user. This information is the Paradox configuration stored in the file PARADOX3.CFG. This file is created and modified by running the **Custom** script supplied with Paradox. (See Chapter 10, ''The Custom Script.'')

The PARADOX3.CFG contains information about the type of video display, printer, default data directory, and other user preferences. In a multiuser environment, each user needs to have a unique configuration file. For network operations, the configuration contains two very important settings.

❑ **User Name.** The configuration file can be used to establish a name that identifies each user on the network. The default is no name. This means that network conflicts will not be able to identify the specific user who has locked the record or file in question.

❑ **Private Directory.** The private directory is the name of a directory in which Paradox can store information necessary for the processing of operations on a network. The information stored here is temporary data, which Paradox uses internally to organize and keep track of locking operations. Although the user is unaware of this data, it is necessary for locking operations. In order for Paradox to operate correctly on a network, each user *must* have a unique private directory. Note that the directory can be located either on a local disk or on the file server. The only requirement is that no other users use the same directory as their private directory.

> *When selecting a private directory, keep in mind the amount of space available on the disk. Since Paradox writes temporary data to this directory, an error can occur if Paradox runs out of space while executing a command. This can happen even if there is still room left on the file server. If you are running a work station from a floppy disk, you may want to use a directory on the file server as the private directory in order to prevent running out of space during a Paradox operation on a large table.*

A Workstation Setup

As an example, suppose that one of the imaginary users, *Morgan*, is using a network work station which has two drives, C: and D:. The Paradox program is stored on the file server which is designated, to Morgan, as drive E:. Morgan will use the root directory of the D: drive as her private directory.

> *Note that drives in this context refers to logical drives. In many cases hard disks with capacities greater than 30 megabytes are partitioned into several parts. These parts are assigned individual drive letters, e.g., C:, D:, E:, etc. even though there is only a single* physical *disk. One reason for this type of partitioning is that DOS versions 3.3 and earlier do not directly support hard disks with capacities greater than 30 megabytes. Multiple logical drive partitions allow these versions of DOS to use drives with capacities greater than 30 megabytes.*

Morgan's first step is to make sure that the paths on her computer are set correctly. She can display the current path setup by entering the following command at DOS.

path ↵

DOS lists the current paths as shown in Figure 17-1.

```
PATH=C:\;C:\DOS;E:\WORD;
```

Figure 17-1 Path listing.

In this example, Morgan needs to add two paths to the current list: **D:** for her private directory and **E:\PARADOX3** for the location of the Paradox 3 program on the file server. The *order* in which these paths appear is *significant*. Morgan intends to place her PARADOX3.CFG file (her personal configuration) in her private directory. This is not required but it makes sense to use the same directory for all Paradox-related files. The directory in which the PARADOX3.CFG file is stored (or will be stored once you create it) *must* precede the path name of the directory in which the Paradox program on the file sever is stored. Morgan can set up the paths by entering the following command. Note that the private directory, D:\, precedes the Paradox directory.

path c:\;c:\dos;d:\;e:\word;e:\paradox3;

Keep in mind that this path setting is temporary and will be lost once the computer is turned off or rebooted. If you include the **PATH** command in the AUTOEXEC.BAT file of the work station, the required paths will be set automatically as part of the boot process.

Creating a Custom Configuration

The PARADOX3.CFG file that contains the custom configuration for each user is created by executing the Custom script program from Paradox. Like all scripts, it must be executed from within the Paradox program. Morgan activates the root directory of her D: drive by entering

d: ↵
cd

Morgan's next action is to run the Paradox program so that she can create her custom configuration. She enters

paradox3 ↵

When Paradox loads, it attempts to find a PARADOX3.CFG file in any of the directories listed in her **PATH** command. At this point, she has not created that file so that Paradox will use the PARADOX3.CFG file found in the PARADOX3 directory of the file server. This configuration may not fit Morgan's setup in some respects, since it probably holds values that match the setup of the file server, e.g., the file server might have a monochrome monitor while the user might have color. These differences can be corrected by running the Custom script.

Changing the Directory

To run the custom script Morgan enters

s p
custom ↵

However, instead of running the script, Paradox displays the message **Cannot find custom script** in the lower right corner of the screen. By default, Paradox uses the *current* directory as the data directory. In this case, the current directory is the local directory D:\. However, the Custom script is stored in the Paradox directory on the file server, in this example E:\PARADOX3. In order to run the Custom script, Morgan must change the active data directory to the Paradox directory on the file server. This is accomplished with the **Tools More Directory** command. Morgan must change the **Script Play** command and then choose **Tools More Directory** by entering

[Esc]*(2 times)*
t m d

Morgan erases the current directory shown, **d:**, and enters the name of the Paradox directory on the file server.

[Ctrl-backspace]
e:\paradox3 ↵
o(the letter O)

Morgan can now execute the Custom script. She reenters the **Script Play** command.

s p
custom ↵

This time, the program is able to load and execute the script. Morgan is asked whether she has a black-and-white monitor. In this case, she enters Y because she has a monochrome monitor.

y

Paradox displays the main menu of the Custom script. Morgan can use the menu to set any of the options she prefers. For example, Morgan knows that the data files she wants to work with, Ck_book etc., are stored in the \PARADOX3 directory on the file server. She decides that she wants to set that directory as the default directory. This means that, even though she starts Paradox from her local drive D:, the program will automatically log into the file server as the data directory. She can accomplish this with the **Defaults SetDirectory** command. She enters

d ↵
s
e
paradox3 ↵

> *When entering the directory path name, Paradox inserts the :\ after you type the drive letter.*

Return to the main menu by entering

r

The Net Menu

The Net menu on the Custom script contains options that relate to network operation. Morgan displays the menu by entering

n

The Net menu lists three options that affect the way Paradox functions on a network, Figure 17-2.

❑ **UserName.** This option allows you to enter a user name that will be used by Paradox to identify Morgan's computer to other users accessing Paradox at the same time. The name is not required to run Paradox on a network but it is useful in understanding how locks are affecting network tasks.

❑ **SetPrivate.** This option is very important because it tells Paradox what directory to use for its temporary files. The directory specified *must* be different for each user on the system in order for the locking system to work properly.

❑ **AutoRefresh.** Paradox will automatically update the screen displays of all users accessing the same tables from time to time. The AutoRefresh setting controls how often Paradox will update your screen displays. The default value is 3. This means that Paradox will update your screen every three seconds with any changes made by other users to the table being accessed by more than one user. You can increase or decrease the time between updates. The smaller the value the faster you will see updates. However, these updates will cause a brief pause while the update process takes place. A longer interval will reduce the frequency of these pauses.

```
UserName  SetPrivate  AutoRefresh  Return
Specify a default user name.
```

Figure 17-2 Net menu.

In this case, Morgan will create a user name and enter her private directory. She selects the UserName option by entering

u

The user name prompt will usually be blank. Note that if the PARADOX3.CFG file loaded from the file server already has been set up for the file server, the user name of the file server may appear. If so, erase it by entering

[Ctrl-backspace]

Morgan enters her user name

Morgan LaFish ↵

Next, Morgan sets her private directory.

s

Delete any directory name that appears and enter the correct directory name, in this case **D:**\.

[Ctrl-backspace]
d ↵
↵

Morgan has now finished her network option selection. She returns to the main menu by entering

r

Saving the Configuration

The final step in setting up a work station is to save the PARADOX3.CFG file which will contain the settings just selected from the menus in the users' directory. The directory that should be used must match the directory specified in the PATH command. In Morgan's case, she could use any of the directories listed in her path command that precede the Paradox file server directory. You will recall that Morgan placed the path D:\ into her path listing before the **E:\PARADOX3** path that leads to the program stored on the file server. This is the directory that should contain the PARADOX3.CFG for Morgan. Note that this is the same directory she has selected for her private directory. This does not have to be the case but it is usually logical to make them the same, so long as storage space is not an issue.

> *If the user boots from a floppy disk, he or she might want to place the PARADOX3.CFG file, which is about 3K in size, on the boot floppy disk, but use a directory on the file server as the private directory to avoid running out of space for temporary files.*

Select the **Do-It!** command from the main menu by entering

→(9 times)↵

Paradox shows two options for saving the configuration, as shown in Figure 17-3. The HardDisk option saves the file in the current directory. The Network option allows you to enter a different directory, i.e., the directory that matches the paths specified on the workstation.

```
HardDisk  Network
Write .CFG file to the directory where the system files are located.
```

Figure 17-3 Select storage location for PARADOX3.CFG file.

In this case, Morgan selects **Network** by entering

n

Paradox inserts the default DOS directory from the user's work station. Since Morgan loaded Paradox from the D:\ directory, that one appears as a default. In this case, Morgan can simply accept that setting since it is the directory she planned to use for the configuration file. She enters

↵

Paradox writes the new configuration file to the specified directory and exits to the operating system.

> *When the Custom script exits to the operating system, the program may display a message such as* **Can't start Paradox: unable to record lock/unlock <path name>\PARADOX.NET You may have insufficient access**. *This message results because the private directory for the current user has not been set up yet. The configuration read from the file server was set up for operating from the file server and does not match the workstation correctly. Don't be concerned, the new configuration file you have stored for the workstation will correct this problem.*

When Paradox exits, it leaves you at the Field server directory, e.g., E:\PARADOX3. To start Paradox from her work station, Morgan needs to change the active drive and path. She enters

d: ↵
cd ↵

She can now run Paradox using her own custom configuration by entering

paradox3 ↵

While Paradox loads, the message **Loading...** appears in the lower right corner. When running the program in a multiuser environment, the message will change to one that reads something like **Count 1 of 6,** Figure 17-4. The message tells you that you are the first user of six possible users. The second user to log into Paradox will see **Count 2 of** , and so on, up to the sixth user. After that, additional users are locked out. Note that the Paradox system does not care which users are logged on, only the total number. For example, a network with twelve work stations can allow all twelve users to access Paradox even though the NUPDATE program has a count of six users. The only restriction is that only six of the twelve can access Paradox simultaneously.

> *The settings made in the configuration file user name, private directory, and auto refresh are default values. You can use the Tools Net menu in Paradox to override these values for the current session if desired.*

Network Operations

Operating Paradox in a network environment is basically the same as operating the program on a stand-alone system. The main difference is that it is possible to encounter locks which are the result of other users' activities that operate on the same tables as you want to use. The conflicts are automatically managed by Paradox, which will display messages informing you when you have encountered a conflict.

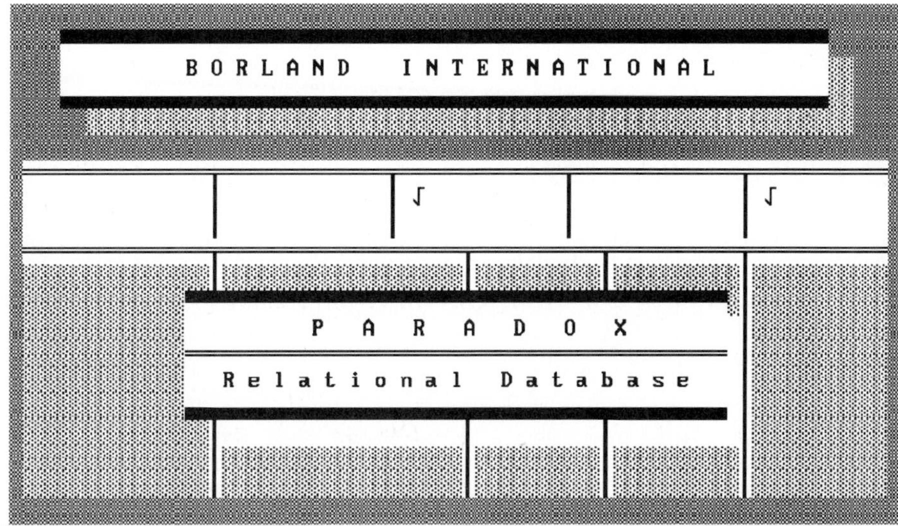

Serial Number: DA233C10639303 Company: Rob Krumm Publications
Contains Licensed Material Copyright (c) Borland International, 1985-1989
All Rights Reserved
Release 3.0 Name: Rob Krumm **User 1 of 6 counts**

Figure 17-4 Count appears when Paradox is loaded from a work station.

To illustrate how Paradox handles multiuser operations, imagine that there are two users, Morgan and Carolyn, accessing the file server that contains the Ck_book table and its related files.

Encountering Locks

To begin her session, Carolyn decides to view the contents of the Ck_book table. She enters

v
ck_book ↵

The Ck_book table is displayed on the work area of Carolyn's computer.
A few moments later, Morgan decides to view the same table. Morgan enters

v
ck_book ↵

The same table appears on Morgan's work area. In this case, there is no conflict between Morgan and Carolyn because **Viewing** a table is a read-only operation, i.e., Paradox does not permit the user to make changes in a table that is displayed on the work area unless she enters the Edit mode. At this point in time, neither user has attempted to edit the table so Paradox allows them both to use the same table at the same time.

Morgan now decides she wants to make some changes. She activates the Edit mode by entering

[F9]

When Morgan's request to edit the table is processed, Paradox finds that Carolyn also is viewing the same table. Since editing would alter the contents of the table, Paradox refuses to allow Morgan to access the table. The program displays a message in the lower right corner telling Morgan that **Ck_book is in use by Carolyn Flynn**, Figure 17-5.

```
Viewing Ck_book table: Record 1 of 17                                   Main

CK_BOOK  Check #    Acct #    Check date    Payee
   1        1        100       1/01/89      Deposit
   2        2        100       1/22/89      Deposit
   3        3        100       2/15/89      Deposit
   4        4        100       2/25/89      Deposit
   5        5        100       3/22/89      Deposit
   6      999        600       1/03/89      Savings Club
   7     1000        500       1/03/89      Allied Office Furniture
   8     1001        600       1/04/89      Central Office Supplies
   9     1002        700       1/08/89      Western Telephone
  10     1003        600       1/08/89      United Federal Insuranc
  11     1004        650       1/15/89      Computer World
  12     1005        600       2/10/89      Savings Club
  13     1006        700       2/19/89      Western Telephone
  14     1007        600       3/05/89      Fathead Software
  15     1008        700       3/10/89      Interstate Power & Ligh
  16     1009        600       3/12/89      Central Office Supplies
  17     1010                  2/19/90      LaFish Limited



                                   Ck book table is in use by Carolyn Flynn
```

Figure 17-5 Morgan is refused edit access to table.

Suppose now Morgan clears the image from her work area by entering

[F8]

Morgan now decides to use the **Ask** command to extract some information from the Ck_book. She enters

a
ck_book ↵

Paradox displays a query form. Morgan selects the *Check date* and *Payee* fields for display by entering

[Tab]*(3 times)*
[F6] [Tab] [F6]

Before Morgan presses the [F2] key to process the query, Carolyn decides she wants to edit the table. She enters

[F9]

Paradox responds by displaying the message **Ck_book is in use by Morgan LaFish**. Why is the table locked for Carolyn? The answer is that even though Morgan is not displaying the Ck_book table, she is working with a query form that will process the data stored in Ck_book. If Carolyn were to make changes in Ck_book, that would affect the results obtained by Morgan when her query is processed. The result is that Carolyn is locked out of the file because Morgan is using a query form related to the same table. Morgan now processes the query by entering

[F2]

The Answer table image is displayed on the work area. Carolyn now attempts to edit the Ck_book table again by entering

[F9]

Carolyn's request to edit the table is still rejected. Recall that so long as the query form is on the work area, the [F2] command will reprocess the query. Carolyn remains locked out of the table in terms of editing. Morgan now decides to remove the query form from the work area. She enters

[F3] [F8]

For the third time, Carolyn attempts to edit the Ck_book table.

[F9]

This time, Carolyn is successful in gaining Edit mode access to the table. Once Morgan removes the query form image from the work area, she has terminated her use of the Ck_book table. The information displayed in the Answer table is separate from the Ck_book table from which it was drawn.

How the Private Directory Works

Morgan now decides to edit the Answer table by entering

[F9]

Morgan has now gained access to the Answer table in the Edit mode. She is free to make any changes she desires. Suppose that Carolyn decides now to process a query on the Ck_book table. She exits the Edit mode and displays a query form by entering

[F2]
[F10] a
ck_book ↵

Carolyn selects the *Payee* and *Amount* fields by entering

[Tab]*(4 times)*
[F6] [Tab] [F6]

Carolyn processes the query by entering

[F2]

The query generates an Answer table. Carolyn decides she wants to edit the Answer table. Morgan enters

[F9]

Note that, at this point, both Carolyn and Morgan are editing the Answer table as shown in Figures 17-6 and 17-7.

How is this possible? How can Paradox allow both users to edit the Answer table at the same time? Previously Paradox rejected attempts by users to edit tables that were displayed by more than one user.

The answer lies in the use of the private directories assigned to each user. Although both users are working from the same data directory, the PARADOX3 directory on the file server, Paradox needs to prevent users from writing files such as Answer tables in that directory or else the queries would overwrite one another. Instead, all temporary tables are written to the private directory specified in each user's configuration file. Since those directories must be unique for each user, Paradox avoids conflict. Even though each user appears to be editing the same table, they are actually two different Answer tables stored in the user's own private directories.

Both users clear their respective work areas by entering

[F2] [Alt-F8]

Coediting

As you have seen, Paradox will automatically prevent any user from editing a file being used by another user. If this were the only way in which Paradox operated, the ability of several users to work with a common database would be extremely limited. In order to allow multiple

```
Editing Answer table: Record 1 of 13                                        Edit  ▲=

CK_BOOK╤═══Check #═══╤═══Acct #═══╤═══Check date═╤═══════════Payee════════
    12 ║    1005     ║       600  ║    2/10/89   ║ Savings Club
    13 ║    1006     ║       700  ║    2/19/89   ║ Western Telephone
    14 ║    1007     ║       600  ║    3/05/89   ║ Fathead Software
    15 ║    1008     ║       700  ║    3/10/89   ║ Interstate Power & Ligh
    16 ║    1009     ║       600  ║    3/12/89   ║ Central Office Supplies
    17 ║    1010     ║            ║    2/19/90   ║ LaFish Limited

ANSWER╤══════════Payee═══════════╤══════Amount═══╗
    1_║ Allied Office Furniture  ║      750.50   ║
    2 ║ Central Office Supplies  ║       36.89   ║
    3 ║ Central Office Supplies  ║       97.68   ║
    4 ║ Computer World           ║    2,245.50   ║
    5 ║ Deposit                  ║        0.00   ║
    6 ║ Fathead Software         ║      378.90   ║
    7 ║ Interstate Power & Light ║      175.49   ║
    8 ║ LaFish Limited           ║      100.00   ║
    9 ║ Savings Club             ║       71.60   ║
   10 ║ Savings Club             ║      157.89   ║
   11 ║ United Federal Insurance ║      590.00   ║
   12 ║ Western Telephone        ║      101.57   ║
   13 ║ Western Telephone        ║      247.67   ║
```

Figure 17-6 Answer table on Carolyn's screen.

users to access the same table, Paradox has a second editing mode called *Coedit*. Coedit is designed to allow multiple users to make changes to the database table at the same time. In order to protect against conflict, Paradox locks individual records as they are edited. When the editing of a given record is complete, Paradox *posts* the changes to the table file. The updated record appears on the screens of all other users working on that table as soon as the auto-refresh cycle executes, by default every three seconds. The Coedit mode can be activated in two ways.

❑ **Modify Coedit.** The **Coedit** command can be selected from the Modify menu.

❑ **[Alt-F9].** The [Alt-F9] key combination will activate the Coedit mode for the table in which the cursor is currently located.

Coedit operates in the same way as the Edit mode with these exceptions.

❑ **Undo.** Since the Coedit post modifies records on a one by one basis, there is no **Cancel** command in the Coedit mode. Paradox does provide the **Undo** command which will restore the last edited record to its previous appearance.

```
Editing Answer table: Record 1 of 17                                    Edit

ANSWER  Check date   Payee
   1     1/01/89     Deposit
   2     1/03/89     Allied Office Furniture
   3     1/03/89     Savings Club
   4     1/04/89     Central Office Supplies
   5     1/08/89     United Federal Insurance
   6     1/08/89     Western Telephone
   7     1/15/89     Computer World
   8     1/22/89     Deposit
   9     2/10/89     Savings Club
  10     2/15/89     Deposit
  11     2/19/89     Western Telephone
  12     2/25/89     Deposit
  13     3/05/89     Fathead Software
  14     3/10/89     Interstate Power & Light
  15     3/12/89     Central Office Supplies
  16     3/22/89     Deposit
  17     2/19/90     LaFish Limited
```

Figure 17-7 Answer table on Morgan's screen.

❑ **ValCheck.** The Coedit mode does not support the creation or modification of validity checks. However, any validity check options established for the table will operate during Coedit.

The Coedit mode will lock a record from use by other users when the following takes place.

❑ **Editing.** If you begin to edit the information in any of the fields in a record, Paradox will attempt to lock that record for the use of the current user. If the record is already locked by another user, the attempt to edit will be rejected. If not, the record is locked for the current user until she saves the changes.

❑ **[Alt-F5].** Using the *field edit* key, [Alt-F5], automatically locks the record unless it is already in use by another user.

A Coediting Session

Morgan begins this session by placing the Ck_book table into the Coedit mode by entering

m c
ck_book ↵

Carolyn displays the Ck_book table on the work area by entering

v
ck_book ↵

Carolyn attempts to place the table into the edit mode by entering

[F9]

The program responds with the message **Ck_book is in use by Morgan LaFish**. Carolyn decides to try the Coedit mode instead. Keep in mind that Carolyn cannot know from the message the exact nature of the conflict with Morgan. For example, had Morgan activated the Edit mode for Ck_book she would see the same message. Carolyn's use of the Coedit mode is only a guess that Morgan is operating in the Coedit mode as well. Carolyn enters

[Alt-F9]

The mode indicator in the upper right corner of the screen changes to Coedit, indicating she is sharing access to the table with Morgan who must also be in the Coedit mode.

Locking Records

When Carolyn and Morgan display the Ck_book table for editing, they notice that record 17 does not have its *Acct #* field filled in. Both of them decide to fill in the missing item of data. Morgan reacts first by entering

[End]
→*(2 times)*

The prompt at the top of the screen reminds Morgan that she can get a list of the accounts by pressing the [F1] key. (The accounts table is linked as a lookup table to this field. See Chapter 9, "Linking Tables to Data Entry.") Morgan enters

[F1]

While Morgan is trying to decide upon the correct account number to insert into the field, Carolyn moves her cursor to the same field by entering

[End]
→*(2 times)*

Carolyn does not bother with the list of account numbers. Being sure that this check should be placed into account 600, she enters

600

```
Coediting Ck_book table: Record 17 of 17                          CoEdit
Press [F1] for help with fill-in
CK_BOOK  Check #    Acct #    Check date    Payee
   1        1        100       1/01/89      Deposit
   2        2        100       1/22/89      Deposit
   3        3        100       2/15/89      Deposit
   4        4        100       2/25/89      Deposit
   5        5        100       3/22/89      Deposit
   6      999        600       1/03/89      Savings Club
   7     1000        500       1/03/89      Allied Office Furniture
   8     1001        600       1/04/89      Central Office Supplies
   9     1002        700       1/08/89      Western Telephone
  10     1003        600       1/08/89      United Federal Insuranc
  11     1004        650       1/15/89      Computer World
  12     1005        600       2/10/89      Savings Club
  13     1006        700       2/19/89      Western Telephone
  14     1007        600       3/05/89      Fathead Software
  15     1008        700       3/10/89      Interstate Power & Ligh
  16     1009        600       3/12/89      Central Office Supplies
  17     1010                  2/19/90      LaFish Limited

                                Record has been locked by Morgan LaFish
```

Figure 17-8 Record lock prevents two users from editing the same record.

With each keystroke that she enters, the program flashes a message in the lower right corner of the screen that reads **Record has been locked by Morgan LaFish**, Figure 17-8.

Morgan now selects account 500 for the transaction by entering

↓ **[F2]**

When the program returns to the main work area, the second line at the top of the screen reads **Record is locked**. The message is now shifted to the right side of the menu area, Figure 17-9.

Morgan has locked the record for her own use. The record will remain locked until the changes she is making are saved. In the Coedit mode those changes will be saved as soon as the cursor is moved to a different record or the [F2] key is pressed. Morgan moves the cursor to previous record by entering

↑

As soon as the cursor moves to a new record, changes occur on both Morgan's and Carolyn's screen. On Morgan's screen, the message **Posted change to record 17** appears in the lower right corner to confirm that the changes have been copied into the disk file, Figure 17-10.

On Carolyn's screen two changes take place a few seconds after Morgan has made her entry. First, the table is updated to show the new value entered for the *Acct #*. Second, a message is displayed in the lower right corner that reads **Current record changed**, Figure 17-11. The message is necessary to inform Carolyn, and any other users, that a change has been made

```
Coediting Ck_book table: Record 17 of 17                           CoEdit
Record is locked                               Press [F1] for help with fill-in
CK_BOOK  Check #      Acct #      Check date    Payee
  1         1          100         1/01/89      Deposit
  2         2          100         1/22/89      Deposit
  3         3          100         2/15/89      Deposit
  4         4          100         2/25/89      Deposit
  5         5          100         3/22/89      Deposit
  6       999          600         1/03/89      Savings Club
  7      1000          500         1/03/89      Allied Office Furniture
  8      1001          600         1/04/89      Central Office Supplies
  9      1002          700         1/08/89      Western Telephone
 10      1003          600         1/08/89      United Federal Insuranc
 11      1004          650         1/15/89      Computer World
 12      1005          600         2/10/89      Savings Club
 13      1006          700         2/19/89      Western Telephone
 14      1007          600         3/05/89      Fathead Software
 15      1008          700         3/10/89      Interstate Power & Ligh
 16      1009          600         3/12/89      Central Office Supplies
 17      1010          500         2/19/90      LaFish Limited
```

Figure 17-9 Screen shows record is locked.

because the changes might have been made to fields not visible on Carolyn's screen at the moment.

When Carolyn sees the update, she believes that Morgan has made a mistake in placing the check into category 500. Because she has been with the company longer, she decides to replace Morgan's entry with her own. She enters

[Ctrl-backspace]

As soon as Carolyn enters her first keystroke, the record, no longer in use by Morgan, is locked for Carolyn's use. The message **Record is locked** appears at the top of the screen to confirm the status. Carolyn now completes her entry.

600

To save the change, Carolyn moves to the beginning of the table by entering

[Home]

Carolyn's screen displays the message **Posted change to record 17**. On the other hand, no message appears on Morgan's screen because she is no longer positioned in the same record. However, the auto-refresh cycle updates her screen to show the corrected record. Carolyn is finished with her editing and exits the Coedit mode by entering

[F2]

```
Coediting Ck_book table: Record 16 of 17                              CoEdit
Press [F1] for help with fill-in
CK_BOOK    Check #         Acct #         Check date        Payee
   1           1             100            1/01/89         Deposit
   2           2             100            1/22/89         Deposit
   3           3             100            2/15/89         Deposit
   4           4             100            2/25/89         Deposit
   5           5             100            3/22/89         Deposit
   6         999             600            1/03/89         Savings Club
   7        1000             500            1/03/89         Allied Office Furniture
   8        1001             600            1/04/89         Central Office Supplies
   9        1002             700            1/08/89         Western Telephone
  10        1003             600            1/08/89         United Federal Insuranc
  11        1004             650            1/15/89         Computer World
  12        1005             600            2/10/89         Savings Club
  13        1006             700            2/19/89         Western Telephone
  14        1007             600            3/05/89         Fathead Software
  15        1008             700            3/10/89         Interstate Power & Ligh
  16        1009             600            3/12/89         Central Office Supplies
  17        1010             500            2/19/90         LaFish Limited

                                                  Posted change to record 12
```

Figure 17-10 Morgan's screen shows changes have been posted to table file.

A moment later, Morgan does the same.

[F2]

Explicit Locks

In looking at the table, Morgan notices something odd. The account number she entered into record 17, account 500, shows 600. She is a bit confused about what is going on. Did she make a typographical error or did another user change her entry? She decides that she will change the entry back to 500. However, she wants to prevent any other users from making changes to that entry until she can check with Carolyn to make sure what the correct entry for that check should be.

Morgan can prevent other users from making changes in the table by placing a write lock on the file. This lock allows other users to view but not change the selected table. This can be done by using the **Lock** command on the Tools Net menu. Morgan enters

[F10] t n

```
Coediting Ck_book table: Record 17 of 17                    CoEdit
Press [F1] for help with fill-in
```

CK_BOOK	Check #	Acct #	Check date	Payee
1	1	100	1/01/89	Deposit
2	2	100	1/22/89	Deposit
3	3	100	2/15/89	Deposit
4	4	100	2/25/89	Deposit
5	5	100	3/22/89	Deposit
6	999	600	1/03/89	Savings Club
7	1000	500	1/03/89	Allied Office Furniture
8	1001	600	1/04/89	Central Office Supplies
9	1002	700	1/08/89	Western Telephone
10	1003	600	1/08/89	United Federal Insuranc
11	1004	650	1/15/89	Computer World
12	1005	600	2/10/89	Savings Club
13	1006	700	2/19/89	Western Telephone
14	1007	600	3/05/89	Fathead Software
15	1008	700	3/10/89	Interstate Power & Ligh
16	1009	600	3/12/89	Central Office Supplies
17	1010	500	2/19/90	LaFish Limited

```
                                              Current record changed
```

Figure 17-11 Carolyn's screen shows new value plus update message.

The menu consists of five options, Figure 17-12. The last three items, SetPrivate, UserName, and AutoRefresh, are the same items that appear in the Net menu of the custom script. You can use these options to override or simply check the default settings. The first two options are used to place explicit locks on tables.

❑ **Lock.** This option allows you to place a full or write lock on a table. Recall that a full lock prevents other users from any access to the table and subsequently any files such as report forms or screen forms related to that table. Write locks allow the table to be viewed (and so allow access to related files) but not edited.

❑ **PreventLock.** Prevent locks are used to keep other users from placing full or write locks on a table.

In this case, Morgan wants to place a write lock on the table. She enters

l

She can select **FullLock** or **WriteLock**. She selects **WriteLock by entering**

w

Paradox asks her to enter the table name.

ck_book ↵

```
Lock  PreventLock  SetPrivate  UserName  AutoRefresh
Lock or unlock a table.
```

Figure 17-12 Tools Net menu.

The next menu displays the options **Set** or **Clear**. The **Set** option establishes a lock and the **Clear** option removes a lock. The menu indicates that, unlike automatic locks which are removed when the user exits the record or table, explicit locks stay in place until the user who placed the lock explicitly removes the lock. Morgan sets the lock by entering

s

The program displays the message **Write lock set** in the lower right corner of the screen. Keep in mind that Morgan can only place the write lock if there are no record or file locks currently active for the specified table.

Morgan can now feel free to change the field back to account 500 by entering

↓
[Alt-F9]
[Ctrl-backspace]
500
[F2]

A few seconds later, Carolyn's screen updates and shows the change in record 17. Carolyn decides to attempt to change the value back to 600. She enters

[Alt-F9]
[End]
→(2] times)
[Ctrl-backspace]

Carolyn is prevented from accessing the field because Morgan has applied a file lock. Carolyn's screen displays the message **Ck_book table is in use by Morgan LaFish** in the lower right corner of the screen. Note that the message is not a record lock message but a file lock.

Morgan and Carolyn now confer about the correct account for record 17. They agree that the entry should be 600. But Carolyn cannot access the table until it is explicitly released by Morgan. Morgan returns to her computer and clears the lock from the table.

[F10] t n l w
ck_book ↵
c

The message in the lower right corner of the screen reads **Write lock cleared**. Carolyn can now complete her entry. She tries again by entering

[Ctrl-backspace]
600
[F2]

The revised field is entered into table. Because Morgan's cursor is still positioned in record 17, the message **Current record changed** appears in the lower right corner of the screen following the refreshing of the display.

To complete the session, both users quit Paradox by entering

[F10] e y

The automatic and explicit locks available in Paradox provide a sensible system by which users can have shared access to database tables on a local area network.

Summary

❑ **Network Configuration.** Paradox can be configured to operate across a Local Area Network. The total number of simultaneous users allowed is determined by the number of Paradox user licenses you own. The serial numbers of these packages increase the user count when added through the NUPDATE program. Access by work stations on the network allow each user to place a configuration file, PARADOX3.CFG, in a unique directory. A path to the user directory and the Paradox directory should be opened with the user directory path always preceding the Paradox directory path.

❑ **User Names.** As part of the network configuration, each user can enter a descriptive name for that user's work station. The name will appear in lock messages generated by Paradox to identify the user who has a lock on a table or record.

❑ **Private Directories.** Many Paradox operations generate files such as Answer tables which always have the same names. In order to avoid conflicts between users on a network, each user must have a unique private directory. Paradox will use that directory to write all temporary files generated during the session in that directory. Note that you should make sure that the private directory is located on a disk with sufficient space to hold the temporary files.

❑ **File Locks.** Tables can be locked in four different ways: file lock, write lock, prevent file lock, and prevent write lock. File locks or prevent file locks include write level locking as well.

❑ **Record Locks.** In order to allow shared access to a given table among more than one user, Paradox permits individual files to be locked by individual users. File locks can only be placed in the Coedit mode.

❑ **Coedit.** The Coedit mode allows editing of records by more than one user at a time. In the coedit mode, a record lock is initiated each time a user makes a change in any field in a record. The lock is released when the user moves to another record or exits the Coedit mode.

❑ **Automatic Locks.** Paradox will automatically implement automatic file and record locks based on the commands issued by individual users.

❑ **Explicit Locks.** Users can place locks that Paradox would not automatically generate by using the Lock and Prevent Lock options on the Tools Net menu. Locks set explicitly from these menus must be explicitly removed or they will remain in force until the user exits Paradox.

18

Programming Scripts on a Network

The automatic locking system built into Paradox will allow many of your scripts to run on a network without modification. However, the PAL language supports multiuser operations with commands that allow you to custom-tailor your script to a multiuser environment.

In this chapter, you will learn the basic issues involved in the design or modification of scripts that are executed on a network.

Checking Table Access

The primary problem presented by a multiuser system is that you cannot begin the script with the assumption that you have full access to the table or the tables that you want to work with. As discussed in Chapter 17, that access can be limited in several ways—depending upon the type of locks placed automatically or explicitly by other users.

Table 18-1 Type of Network Lock

Full File Lock	no shared access
Write File Lock	shared view, no edit
Prevent File Lock	prevents full file lock
Prevent Write Lock	prevents write lock
Record Lock	view record, edit all others

The conflict between the script that you want to execute and the locks placed on tables or records depends on what locks are currently active and what it is that your script is going to do. A lock placed by another user is only significant if it prevents you from performing the task you want to carry out. In some cases, you can carry out the task differently in order to work around a lock.

Calculating Tables on Networks

As an example, begin with a script that is designed to calculate the checking account balance. Create a new script by entering

s e w
mu1 ↵

The primary task of the script is to scan the records in the Ck_book table, add the deposits, and subtract the checks in order to arrive at the current balance.

The actual calculation can be written in the form of a procedure called Balance(). Add the procedure shown below to the script.

```
PROC balance()
b=0
SCAN
    IF [payee]="Deposit"
    THEN b=b+[deposit]
    ELSE b=b-[amount]
    ENDIF
ENDSCAN
RETURN(b)
ENDPROC
```

Note that the Balance() procedure does not contain any special commands related to network operations. Those considerations will be handled in the main line of the program's logic.

Testing for File Locks

The process of calculating the balance does not require full access to the table. In fact, the only problem that the commands in the Balance() procedure would encounter would be if another user had established a full file lock on the Ck_book table.

The first task of the script is to determine if a full file lock exists for the Ck_book. If not you should place a Prevent File Lock type lock on the table to prevent any users coming on line from placing such a lock on the table.

This can be accomplished through the use of the **LOCK** command. The **LOCK** command requires two parameters. The first is the name of the table and the second is the type of lock you want to place on that table. The types of lock are represented by the codes FL (file lock), WL (write lock), PFL (prevent file lock), and PWL (prevent write lock). The names of the tables should be surrounded by quotations but the lock codes are not. The example below attempts to place a prevent file lock on the Ck_book table.

```
LOCK "ck_book" PFL
```

If you want to place more than one type of lock, you can list the locks following a single command. The example below attempts to place a prevent file and a prevent write lock on the Ck_book table.

```
LOCK "accounts" FL, "tax" FL
```

You can attempt to place locks on more than one table if desired. The command below would be used to place full file locks on the Accounts and Tax tables. You would want to perform an action such as this if you were making major changes to these tables, such as changes in table structure.

```
LOCK "ck_book" PFL,"ck_book" PWL
```

It is important to keep in mind that a **LOCK** command indicates an *attempt* to place a lock on a table. In a multiuser environment, there is no guarantee that issuing a **LOCK** command will actually succeed in placing the specified locks.

In most cases, it will be necessary to evaluate the effect of the **LOCK** command immediately after it has been issued in order to determine whether or not the command actually locked the table or tables in the specified manner. This can be done most simply by testing the system's variable **retval**. Immediately following a **LOCK** command, the **retval** variable is set True if the **LOCK** succeeded or False if it did not. Keep in mind that when a **LOCK** command attempts to place multiple locks, the locks will be placed only if all of the specified locks can be implemented. If any one of the locks cannot be placed, none of the locks are placed.

This all-or-nothing approach is designed to eliminate deadlocks. A deadlock could occur if two users each wanted to place the same locks on the same tables. If the locks were executed one at a time, then one of the users might get their first lock while the second got the second lock. They would be deadlocked because neither would have sufficient locks to carry out the task. The all-or-nothing approach would ensure that one of the two got both and the other, none. That way the first user could complete her task and then release the tables for the second user.

As a rule, all the locks needed for an operation, with the exception of record locks, should be executed with a single **LOCK** command so that the results follow the all-or-nothing pattern. If you succeed in placing a lock, keep in mind that it is an explicit lock. This means that it will stay in place until it is specifically removed with the **UNLOCK** command. **UNLOCK** can be used to remove individual locks in a manner similar to the way **LOCK** works. The command below removes two locks from the same table.

```
UNLOCK "ck_book" PFL,"ck_book" PWL
```

You can release all locks by using the All option. The command below removes all locks from all tables previously placed by the current user.

```
UNLOCK ALL
```

In this script, you want to prevent other users from placing a file lock on the Ck_book table. Add the following command to the script.

```
LOCK "ck_book" PFL
```

Once issued, you must *evaluate* the lock in order to know how to proceed. The conditional structure shown below uses the **retval** variable to determine which course of action to take. The command **IF retval THEN** tests the **retval** variable which will be either True or False.

```
IF retval THEN
```

If it is True, you can assume that you can gain at least read-only access to the Ck_book table which is sufficient for calculating the balance. The following series of commands calls the **Balance()** procedure and then displays the results on the screen. Note that the **UNLOCK** is then issued to release the table for other users.

```
VIEW "ck_book"
@ 10,10 ?? "Current Balance = ",Balance()
UNLOCK "ck_book" PFL
CLEARIMAGE
```

The ELSE branch of the IF structure is used if the **retval** variable is False, i.e., a prevent file lock cannot be placed on the table. You can infer from that event that some other user (or conceivably another DOS program such as **COPY**) has locked the file. If that is the case, you cannot carry out your task, i.e., calculating the balance. Your only option is to inform the user and terminate the program.

The **ERRORMESSAGE()** function returns the text of the message that would appear in the lower right corner of the work area when an explicit lock attempt fails. The function provides a simple means of integrating that message in a PAL canvas display. Note that if you only wanted to display the name of the user with whom the lock conflict occurred you would use the **ERRORUSER()** function instead.

```
ELSE
    @ 8,10 ?? "Accurate Account Balance"
    @ 9,10 ?? "Cannot be obtained because"
    @ 10,10 STYLE REVERSE ?? ERRORMESSAGE()
    STYLE
ENDIF
@ 24,79 x=GETCHAR()
RELEASE VARS ALL
RELEASE PROCS ALL
RETURN
```

The full listing of this script can be found on page 685.
Execute the script bu entering

[F10] g

If no locking conflict is encountered, the script will calculate and display the balance. If a conflict does occur, the program will display a message like the one shown in Figure 18-1.

```
Accurate Account Balance
Cannot be obtained because
ck_book table has been locked by Carolyn Flynn
```

Figure 18-1 Message generated when file lock encountered.

Accounting for Record Locks

The previous script approached the problem of gaining access to the table needed for its calculation. However, it is important to keep in mind that the prevent file lock did not prevent other users from locking individual records. The calculation of the balance could proceed even if other users were editing records. Should this be a concern?

In this case, the answer is one which is subject to your personal preference. If other users have been editing individual records, the value drawn from the records as the table is scanned reflects the last saved values. It is, of course, possible that another user is altering the check or deposit value and therefore affecting the account balance.

One way to avoid this problem is to attempt to place a write lock (code WL) at the beginning of the script. If the write lock cannot be placed, then the program terminates. This approach has the drawback of limiting the calculation of the balance to times when no editing is taking place.

Another approach would be to calculate the balance in any event. As a precaution, you might want to count the number of record locks currently in force and display that as a notation displayed along with the balance. For example, if there were three other users that had placed locks on individual records at the time you made your calculation, the program would inform you that three of seventeen, i.e., 18 percent of the table was subject to change. You could then decide to recalculate the balance or not based on the potential accuracy of the values used.

Counting Record Locks

The goal in this script is to carry out the balance calculation and at the same time make note of any records that might be locked. That number would indicate if some or any records were subject to change while the balance was being calculated. Create a new script called MU2 by entering

s e w
mu2 ↵

This script also begins with the **Balance()** procedure. However, in this case, the procedure must count record locks as well as summarize the account balance.

The first change required to achieve this expanded goal is that the table must be placed into the Coedit mode. Record locks can only be placed or checked in that mode. The procedure begins with the activation of the Coedit mode with the **COEDIT** command.

```
PROC balance()
COEDIT "ck_book"
```

In addition to the variable **b** which is used to calculate the balance, a variable called **inuse** is initialized. This variable will be used as a counter for the records which are locked.

```
b=0
inuse=0
```

At this point, you are ready to Scan the table. The first task when the cursor arrives at a record is to test the lock status of the record by attempting to place a record lock on that record. The **LOCKRECORD** command attempts to place a record lock on the current record.

```
SCAN
    LOCKRECORD
```

The result of this command is evaluated with an IF structure. If the record lock can be placed, i.e., **retval** is True, you can infer that the record was not in use by any other users. If it cannot, **retval** is False, the counter **inuse** should be incremented. Note that the **UNLOCKRECORD** command is used to unlock the record once its status has been established.

> *Keep in mind that you can lock as many individual records as you desire at one time. In this case, the* ***UNLOCKRECORD*** *command could be removed. The effect would be that—as each record is scanned—it will be locked until the end of the table is reached. That would ensure that no changes were made to the table until after the balance was displayed. However, if the table is large, this might lock out other users from records until the scan was completed. Keep in mind that all of the record locks would automatically be released once the coedit mode was ended with the* **DO_IT!** *command.*

```
IF retval
    THEN UNLOCKRECORD
    ELSE inuse=inuse+1
ENDIF
```

The next structure calculates the balance.

```
IF [payee]="Deposit"
    THEN b=b+[deposit]
    ELSE b=b-[amount]
ENDIF
```

At the end of the procedure, the **DO_IT**! terminates the Coedit mode. The **inuse** variable is converted to text that represents the percentage of records that were found to be locked by other users.

```
ENDSCAN
DO_IT!
pc_inuse=STRVAL(INT(inuse/NROWS()*100))+"%"
RETURN(b)
ENDPROC
```

The main line of logic of the program begins as did MU1 with a **LOCK** command to test the access to the table on the file lock level. The only change in this action of the script is that a special condition, **IF inuse>0** is added to determine if it is necessary to warn the user that some of the values used in the balance were subject to editing by other users.

```
LOCK "ck_book" PWL, "ch_book" PFL
IF retval THEN
    @ 10,10 ?? "Current Balance = ",Balance()
    IF inuse>0 THEN
    @ 14,10 ?? "Note: "+pc_inuse+" of database in use."
    ENDIF
    UNLOCK "ck_book" PWL, "ck_book" PFL
    CLEARIMAGE
ELSE
    @ 8,10 ?? "Accurate Account Balance"
    @ 9,10 ?? "Cannot be obtained because"
    @ 10,10 STYLE REVERSE ?? ERRORMESSAGE()
    STYLE
ENDIF
@ 24,79 x=GETCHAR()
RELEASE VARS ALL
RELEASE PROCS ALL
RETURN
```

A full listing of this script can be found on page 694. Save and execute the script by entering

[F10] g

If the script encounters records locked by other users it will display a note along with the balance as shown in Figure 18-2.

```
Current Balance = 782.21

Note: 11% of database in use.
```

Figure 18-2 Program calculates balance and number of locked records.

Allowing Options

One of the primary reasons for writing scripts that handle file and record locks is so that you can present the user with information and options that deal with the multiuser access currently taking place on the network.

In the previous program, you calculated the percentage of the table being accessed by other users. This provided the user who was calculating the balance with additional information about the status of the database tables.

Another variation on the same type of summary program would be to give the user the option of checking for record locks or not. Keep in mind that locking each record in a table will slow down the processing of the record a great deal. You might only want to use that option when you wanted to make sure that you understood the reliability of the figures. At other times, you might simply want to get the balance as quickly as possible without concern about editing being performed by other users.

Alternative Selection Methods

The next script combines the approach of MU1 and MU2 and allows the user to select the method desired. Create a new script by entering

s e w
mu3 ↵

The first procedure is called **Balance1()** and it uses the record checking method of calculating the balance created in script MU2.

```
PROC balance1()
COEDIT "ck_book"
b=0
inuse=0
SCAN
    LOCKRECORD
    IF retval
        THEN UNLOCKRECORD
        ELSE inuse=inuse+1
    ENDIF
    IF [payee]="Deposit"
    THEN b=b+[deposit]
    ELSE b=b-[amount]
    ENDIF
ENDSCAN
DO_IT!
pc_inuse=STRVAL(INT(inuse/NROWS()*100))+"%"
RETURN(b)
ENDPROC
```

The second procedure is called **Balance2()** and it uses the non-checking method from MU1.

```
PROC balance2()
VIEW "ck_book"
inuse=0
b=0
SCAN
    IF [payee]="Deposit"
        THEN b=b+[deposit]
        ELSE b=b-[amount]
    ENDIF
ENDSCAN
RETURN(b)
ENDPROC
```

The main line of logic for this program is the same as MU2, except that a menu is added to the script. The purpose of the menu is to offer the user the choice of using the record checking method, which is slower, or the faster method that ignores the lock status of the records.

```
LOCK "ck_book" PWL, "ch_book" PFL
IF retval THEN
     SHOWMENU
     "No Check":"Do not check for editing by other users",
     "Check":"Check for editing by other users"
     TO scan_type
     @ 10,10 ?? "Current Balance = "
     IF scan_type="No Check"
          THEN ?? Balance2()
          ELSE ?? Balance1()
     ENDIF
     IF inuse>0 THEN
          @ 14,10 ?? "Note: "+pc_inuse+" of database in use."
     ENDIF
     UNLOCK "ck_book" PWL, "ck_book" PFL
     CLEARIMAGE
ELSE
     @ 8,10 ?? "Accurate Account Balance"
     @ 9,10 ?? "Cannot be obtained because"
     @ 10,10 STYLE REVERSE ?? ERRORMESSAGE()
     STYLE
ENDIF
@ 24,79 x=GETCHAR()
RELEASE VARS ALL
RELEASE PROCS ALL
RETURN
```

A full listing of the script can be found on page 694. Save and execute the script by entering

[F10] g

The program displays a menu from which the user can select the method of calculation desired, Figure 18-3.

```
No Check  Check_
Do not check for editing by other users
```

Figure 18-3 Menu allows user to select calculation method.

Select the method you prefer. The program will calculate the balance in either case, adding record checking if you select the **Check** option.

Controlling Editing Access

The previous scripts have been concerned with the effect that file locks placed by other users may have on data retrieval operations such as summarizing the account balance of the Ck_book table. The other major category of multiuser operations is the editing of a database table by more than one user at a time. In Chapter 17 you learned that Paradox will automatically implement automatic record locks for all users that are using the Coedit mode to access the same table.

In this section, you will look at a script of about 120 lines that illustrates how you can create routines that will handle record locking and coediting. The advantage of the script is that it offers users wider options for dealing with lock conflicts than does the Paradox automatic locking system.

Multiuser Editing

The script you will create in this section consists of four procedures.

- PROC **Canedit().** This procedure is used to determine if the conditions exist for editing of the specified table. If the table, Ck_book, is locked with a file or write lock, it cannot be edited. In that case, the program has no reason to continue and should terminate.

- PROC **Getrecord().** This routine is a search routine that locates the record you want to edit. In this example, the deposit or record number is used as the key for locating the records. Since the *Check #* field is a key field, this ensures that no two records would have the same key value.

- PROC **Disprecord().** This procedure is used to display the selected record for editing if it is determined that a record lock can be applied to this record.

- PROC **Conflict().** This procedure is activated when the selected record is locked for use by another user. Each procedure demonstrates a different aspect of how network operation can be handled.

The first procedure is the most straightforward. It is used to determine if the specified table can be placed into the Coedit mode. The procedure begins with the **LOCK** command to test, by trying to apply prevent locks, the current lock status of the table. Note that in this script the **LOCK** command is nested inside a WHILE loop. This is done to set up a situation whereby the user can continue to retry access to the table if the table is locked by another user.

```
PROC Canedit()
WHILE true
    LOCK "ck_book" PWL, "ch_book" PFL
```

Following the **LOCK** command, the **retval** variable is tested. In this case, the first test is an IF test to see if the **retval** variable is False, NOT retval. The **ERRORUSER()** function is used to display the name of the user who has placed the lock on the table.

```
IF NOT retval THEN
  @ 10,10 ?? "Required Database not available"
  @ 12,10 ?? "User "+ERRORUSER()+" has exclusive access"
```

Following the message, a menu is displayed. The menu allows the user to retry the locked table in order to gain access or to give up and exit the script program.

The **SETRETRYPERIOD** command determines the amount of time, in seconds, during which Paradox will retry access to the locked file or record. The default value is zero, meaning that Paradox reacts immediately when a resource is locked. In this example, the retry period is set at 10 seconds. Note that during that period, Paradox is no longer under the control of the script.

```
            SHOWMENU
                "Retry Access":"Retry Access to Table",
                "Quit":"Exit Program"
            TO choice
            IF choice="Quit"
                THEN QUIT
                ELSE SETRETRYPERIOD 10
            ENDIF
        ELSE
            SETRETRYPERIOD 0
            QUITLOOP
        ENDIF
ENDWHILE
RETURN
ENDPROC
```

The next procedure is called **Getrecord()**. This procedure is used to locate a record based on the user request. The procedure begins with the display of a prompt at which the user can enter a deposit or check number.

```
PROC Getrecord()
@ 10,10 ?? ''Enter Deposit or Check # ''
ACCEPT ''n'' TO key
```

The table is placed into the Coedit mode. In addition, a variable called **found** is set to the logical value False. This variable will be used to determine if a record with the key value exists in the table. This variable is important, because you do not want the procedure to attempt to lock a record when the desired value cannot be located.

```
COEDIT ''ck_book''
found=False
```

The procedure begins a SCAN loop with a FOR clause. The FOR clause limits the scanned records to those whose *Check #* fields match the key value. Since *Check #* is a key field, and key fields contain unique values, the loop will either locate the desired record or terminate immediately. Thus the script will jump over the command in the loop if the matching record is not located. If the match is found, **LOCKRECORD** is used to test the record for locks by other users.

```
SCAN FOR [check #]=key
    found=True
    LOCKRECORD
```

The next conditional structure executes the **disprecord()** procedure if no record lock conflict is encountered, or the **conflict()** procedure if the record is already in use by another user.

```
IF retval
    THEN disprecord() QUITLOOP
    ELSE conflict() QUITLOOP
ENDIF
```

The remainder of the script will execute if no matching record was found.

```
ENDSCAN
IF NOT found THEN
     DO_IT! CLEARIMAGE
     @ 10,10 STYLE REVERSE
     ?? " No match - Press Key to Continue" STYLE
     x=GETCHAR()
ENDIF
RETURN
ENDPROC
```

The **disprecord()** procedure is the most straightforward one in the program. It shows how a record would be edited once a record lock was established. A conditional structure selects the corresponding screen form and the **WAIT** command gives the user access to the record for editing. Note that the **DO_IT!** command at the end of the procedure exits the Coedit mode. This automatically removes the record lock.

```
PROC disprecord()
IF [payee]="Deposit"
     THEN PICKFORM "2"
     ELSE PICKFORM "1"
ENDIF
WAIT RECORD PROMPT
     'Record Locked for editing",
     "Press [F2] when done"
UNTIL "F2"
DO_IT!
CLEARIMAGE CLEAR
RETURN
ENDPROC
```

The most significant procedure in the program is **conflict()**, because it deals directly with the options given to the user should a record lock be encountered. The procedure offers the user three choices in this situation. First, the user can select to retry access to the record. If the other user has released the record, the current user can gain access. Second, the user can choose to display the data from the record without having editing access. In many cases, this is all that the user needs and the record lock is not needed. The final option is to cancel the attempt to edit the record and to return to the main script menu.

The first section of the procedure starts an automatic loop and displays a menu along with information about the user who is currently editing the record.

```
PROC conflict()
WHILE true
    CLEAR
    @ 10,10 STYLE REVERSE,BLINK
    ?? "Record in use"
    STYLE
    @ 12,10 ?? "User: ",ERRORUSER()
        SHOWMENU
        "Retry":"Retry access for specified period",
        "Display":"Display data - no editing available",
        "Quit":"Cancel attempt to edit record"
    TO choice
```

Once the user makes a selection from the menu, a SWITCH structure is used to carry out the selected option.

The first Case is the retry option. The retry period is extended, in this case to 5 second. Because the application will be out of control for the retry period, the message **Working** is placed on the screen to indicate that the script is carrying out a command. An IF structure evaluates if there has been a change in the lock status during the retry period. If so, **Disprecord()** is activated so that users can get access to editing the record.

```
CLEAR
SWITCH
    CASE choice="Retry":
        SETRETRYPERIOD 5
        @ 10,10 STYLE BLINK ?? "Working..."
        LOCKRECORD
        IF retval THEN
            Disprecord()
            QUITLOOP
        ENDIF
        SETRETRYPERIOD 0
```

If the user selects to display but not edit the record, the script uses the **VIEW** command instead of the **COEDIT** command to display the record. The message from the Wait mode identifies the user who has locked the record.

```
CASE choice="Display":
    current=RECNO()
    DO_IT!
    VIEW "ck_book"
    MOVETO RECORD current
    IF [payee]="Deposit"
        THEN PICKFORM "2"
        ELSE PICKFORM "1"
    ENDIF
    WAIT RECORD PROMPT
        "In use by User:"+ERRORUSER(),
        Press Enter when done"
    UNTIL "enter"
    CLEARIMAGE
    QUITLOOP
```

The final section exits the loop, should the user select to quit.

```
        OTHERWISE:
            DO_IT! CLEARALL QUITLOOP
    ENDSWITCH
ENDWHILE
RETURN
ENDPROC
```

The procedure simplifies the main line of logic. The program first executes **Canedit()** to ensure that there is access to the table. A menu is displayed that allows the user to select to edit a record or quit. All other options are covered by procedures.

```
;main line logic
Canedit()
WHILE true
    CLEAR
    SHOWMENU
```

```
          "Edit":"Find check or deposit to edit",
          "Quit":"Exit Program"
     TO choice
     IF choice = "Edit"
          THEN Getrecord()
          ELSE QUITLOOP
     ENDIF
ENDWHILE
CLEARALL
RELEASE VARS ALL
RELEASE PROCS ALL
RETURN
```

A full listing of the script can be found on page 685. Save the script by entering

[F2]

Running the Script

To illustrate how the script works, imagine the two users Morgan and Carolyn, disscused in Chapter 17. Carolyn begins by placing the Ck_book table into the standard Edit mode by entering

v
ck_book ↵
[F9]

Morgan then executes the MU4 script by entering

s p
mu4 ↵

Morgan immediately encounters a file lock which is the result of Carolyn's using the Edit rather than the Coedit mode, Figure 18-4.

Carolyn now exits the Edit mode and starts up the MU4 script on her computer by entering

[F2]
[F10] s p
mu4 ↵

Morgan decides to retry access to the table by entering

r

Morgan is now able to gain access to the Ck_book table in a shared mode. Her screen now displays the editing menu, Figure 18-5.

```
Retry Access  Quit_
Retry Access to Table



          Required Database not available

          User Carolyn Flynn has exclusive access
```

Figure 18-4 Morgan encounters file lock.

```
Record Locked for editing
Press [F2] when done

                    Check Book Database - Record     14

  Check No. 1007                          Date  3/05/89

  Payee Fathead Software                  $     378.90

  Memo Spreadshee
       t Software


Sales Tax Information
Pre-Tax Amount
  354.11              Is this check tax deductible? Y

Pre-Tax Amount
  24.79
```

Figure 18-5 Morgan gains access to table once Carolyn releases file lock.

Carolyn decides to edit check # 1007. She enters

e
1007

Carolyn's screen shows the selected record in the check screen form, Figure 18-6.

Morgan now attempts to edit the same record by entering

e
1007

However, since Carolyn has access to that record already, Morgan sees a message indicating that the record is in use and a menu of options, Figure 18-7.

In this case, Morgan decides to display the data if she cannot get editing access.

d

The display option shows the record data but does not permit Morgan to change the information. Note that Carolyn is identified at the top of the screen as the user who has locked the record. Any changes made by Carolyn to the record would appear on Morgan's screen, which is automatically updated by the refresh cycle every three seconds.

Carolyn exits the script by entering

[F2]
q

```
Record Locked for editing
Press [F2] when done

                    Check Book Database - Record      14

  Check No. 1007                                Date  3/05/89

  Payee Fathead Software                        $     378.90

  Memo Spreadshee
       t Software

Sales Tax Information
Pre-Tax Amount
  354.11                 Is this check tax deductible? Y

Pre-Tax Amount
  24.79
```

Figure 18-6 Carolyn displays record for editing.

```
Retry  Display  Quit_
Retry access for specified period




              Record in use

              User: Carolyn Flynn
```

Figure 18-7 Morgan encounters locked record.

```
In use by User:Carolyn Flynn
Press Enter when done

                    Check Book Database - Record      14

  Check No. 1007    _                              Date  3/05/89

  Payee Fathead Software                           $     378.90

  Memo Spreadshee
       t Software

Sales Tax Information
Pre-Tax Amount
  354.11                 Is this check tax deductible? Y

Pre-Tax Amount
  24.79
```

Figure 18-8 Morgan selects to display record which is locked by Carolyn.

Morgan tries the record again by entering

↵

e

1007 ↵

This time, she does not encounter a conflict and the script gives her editing access. Morgan exits the script by entering

[F2]
q

Summary

This chapter illustrated how scripts can be adapted to work within the context of the file and record locks that occur on multiuser systems.

❑ **LOCK.** This command can be used to set or test for the presence of file locks, write locks, prevent file, and prevent write locks. **LOCK** can attempt to place one or more locks specified in a list following the command. The locks are applied in an all-or-nothing fashion. The **retval** system variable is True if all locks succeed or False if any one fails to be applied.

❑ **UNLOCK.** This command removes locks applied with the **LOCK** command. You can remove specific locks or use the All option to remove all explicit locks set by the current user.

❑ **LOCKRECORD.** Attempts to place a record level lock on the current record. **Retval** is True if the attempt is successful or False if the record is already locked. This command can only be issued from the Coedit mode.

❑ **SETRETRYPERIOD.** This command controls the amount of time Paradox will spend trying to access a locked record or file. The default is zero, which causes Paradox to move to the next command as soon as a conflict is encountered. Retry times can be increased to allow more opportunity for the application to access the desired resource,

❑ **ERRORMESSAGE().** Returns the text of the error message generated when a lock conflict is encountered.

❑ **ERRORUSER().** Returns the user name of the user who had placed a lock on the desired resource.

❑ **COEDIT.** This command activates the Coedit mode. All record locking operations must take place in the Coedit mode. When the user exits Coedit with the **DO_IT!** command, all record locks are automatically released.

Scripts

Listing of Script MU1.SC

```
PROC balance()
b=0
SCAN
     IF [payee]=''Deposit''
     THEN b=b+[deposit]
     ELSE b=b-[amount]
     ENDIF
ENDSCAN
RETURN(b)
ENDPROC

LOCK ''ch_book'' PFL
IF retval THEN
     VIEW ''ck_book''
     @ 10,10 ?? ''Current Balance = '',Balance()
     UNLOCK ''ck_book'' PWL, ''ck_book'' PFL
     CLEARIMAGE
ELSE
     @ 8,10 ?? ''Accurate Account Balance''
     @ 9,10 ?? ''Cannot be obtained because''
     @ 10,10 STYLE REVERSE ?? ERRORMESSAGE()
     STYLE
ENDIF
@ 24,79 x=GETCHAR()
RELEASE VARS ALL
RELEASE PROCS ALL
RETURN
```

Listing of Script MU2.SC

```
PROC balance()
COEDIT ''ck_book''
b=0
inuse=0
SCAN
```

```
    LOCKRECORD
    IF retval
        THEN UNLOCKRECORD
        ELSE inuse = inuse + 1
    ENDIF
    IF [payee] = ''Deposit''
    THEN b = b + [deposit]
    ELSE b = b-[amount]
    ENDIF
ENDSCAN
DO_IT!
pc_inuse = STRVAL(INT(inuse/NROWS()*100)) + ''%''
RETURN(b)
ENDPROC

LOCK ''ck_book'' PWL, ''ch_book'' PFL
IF retval THEN
    @ 10,10 ?? ''Current Balance = '',Balance()
    IF inuse>0 THEN
        @ 14,10 ?? ''Note: '' + pc_inuse + '' of database in use.''
    ENDIF
    UNLOCK ''ck_book'' PWL, ''ck_book'' PFL
    CLEARIMAGE
ELSE
    @ 8,10 ?? ''Accurate Account Balance''
    @ 9,10 ?? ''Cannot be obtained because''
    @ 10,10 STYLE REVERSE ?? ERRORMESSAGE()
    STYLE
ENDIF
@ 24,79 x = GETCHAR()
RELEASE VARS ALL
RELEASE PROCS ALL
RETURN
```

Listing of Script MU3.SC

```
PROC balance1()
COEDIT ''ck_book''
b = 0
inuse = 0
SCAN
```

```
     LOCKRECORD
     IF retval
          THEN UNLOCKRECORD
          ELSE inuse=inuse+1
     ENDIF
     IF [payee]=''Deposit''
     THEN b=b+[deposit]
     ELSE b=b-[amount]
     ENDIF
ENDSCAN
DO_IT!
pc_inuse=STRVAL(INT(inuse/NROWS()*100))+''%''
RETURN(b)
ENDPROC

PROC balance2()
VIEW ''ck_book''
inuse=0
b=0
SCAN
     IF [payee]=''Deposit''
          THEN b=b+[deposit]
          ELSE b=b-[amount]
     ENDIF
ENDSCAN
RETURN(b)
ENDPROC

LOCK ''ck_book'' PWL, ''ch_book'' PFL
IF retval THEN
     SHOWMENU
     ''No Check'':''Do not check for editing by other users'',
     ''Check'':''Check for editing by other users''
     TO scan_type
     @ 10,10 ?? ''Current Balance = ''
     IF scan_type=''No Check''
          THEN ?? Balance2()
          ELSE ?? Balance1()
     ENDIF
     IF inuse>0 THEN
          @ 14,10 ?? ''Note: ''+pc_inuse+'' of database in use.''
     ENDIF
     UNLOCK ''ck_book'' PWL, ''ck_book'' PFL
```

```
    CLEARIMAGE
ELSE
    @ 8,10 ?? "Accurate Account Balance"
    @ 9,10 ?? "Cannot be obtained because"
    @ 10,10 STYLE REVERSE ?? ERRORMESSAGE()
    STYLE
ENDIF
@ 24,79 x=GETCHAR()
RELEASE VARS ALL
RELEASE PROCS ALL
RETURN
```

Listing of Script MU4.SC

```
PROC Canedit()
WHILE true
    LOCK "ck_book" PWL, "ch_book" PFL
    IF NOT retval THEN
        @ 10,10 ?? "Required Database not available"
        @ 12,10 ?? "User "+ERRORUSER()+" has exclusive access"
        SHOWMENU
            "Retry Access":"Retry Access to Table",
            "Quit":"Exit Program"
        TO choice
        IF choice="Quit"
            THEN QUIT
            ELSE SETRETRYPERIOD 10
        ENDIF
    ELSE
        SETRETRYPERIOD 0
        QUITLOOP
    ENDIF
ENDWHILE
RETURN
ENDPROC

PROC Getrecord()
@ 10,10 ?? "Enter Deposit or Check # "
ACCEPT "n" TO key
COEDIT "ck_book"
found=False
```

```
SCAN FOR [check #]=key
     found=True
     LOCKRECORD
     IF retval
          THEN disprecord() QUITLOOP
          ELSE conflict() QUITLOOP
     ENDIF
ENDSCAN
IF NOT found THEN
     DO_IT! CLEARIMAGE
     @ 10,10 STYLE REVERSE
     ?? " No match - Press Key to Continue" STYLE
     x=GETCHAR()
ENDIF
RETURN
ENDPROC

PROC disprecord()
IF [payee]="Deposit"
     THEN PICKFORM "2"
     ELSE PICKFORM "1"
ENDIF
WAIT RECORD PROMPT
     "Record Locked for editing",
     "Press [F2] when done"
UNTIL "F2"
DO_IT!
CLEARIMAGE CLEAR
RETURN
ENDPROC

PROC conflict()
WHILE true
     CLEAR
     @ 10,10 STYLE REVERSE,BLINK
     ?? "Record in use"
     STYLE
     @ 12,10 ?? "User: ",ERRORUSER()
          SHOWMENU
          "Retry":"Retry access for specified period",
          "Display":"Display data - no editing available",
          "Quit":"Cancel attempt to edit record"
     TO choice
```

```
        CLEAR
        SWITCH
            CASE choice=''Retry'':
                SETRETRYPERIOD 5
                @ 10,10 STYLE BLINK ?? ''Working...''
                LOCKRECORD
                IF retval THEN
                    Disprecord()
                    QUITLOOP
                ENDIF
                SETRETRYPERIOD 0
            CASE choice=''Display'':
                current=RECNO()
                DO_IT!
                VIEW ''ck_book''
                MOVETO RECORD current
                IF [payee]=''Deposit''
                    THEN PICKFORM ''2''
                    ELSE PICKFORM ''1''
                ENDIF
                WAIT RECORD PROMPT
                    ''In use by User:''+ERRORUSER(),
                    ''Press Enter when done''
                UNTIL ''enter''
                CLEARIMAGE
                QUITLOOP
            OTHERWISE:
                DO_IT! CLEARALL QUITLOOP
        ENDSWITCH
    ENDWHILE
    RETURN
    ENDPROC

    ;main line logic
    Canedit()
    WHILE true
        CLEAR
        SHOWMENU
            ''Edit'':''Find check or deposit to edit'',
            'Quit':''Exit Program''
        TO choice
        IF choice=''Edit''
            THEN Getrecord()
```

```
        ELSE QUITLOOP
    ENDIF
ENDWHILE
CLEARALL
RELEASE VARS ALL
RELEASE PROCS ALL
RETURN
```

A

Using PAL Functions

As noted in the introduction to this book, the procedures and techniques discussed will work with all current versions of Paradox including version 3.5 due for release in the second half of 1990. The major changes made to Paradox in version 3.5 involve a new approach to memory management, links to SQL Network Database Servers, and changes in the installation program.

These changes do not affect the Paradox user interface, the command menus, or other tasks described in this book.

One of the minor changes is of significance to a wide variety of users. The change allows screen and report forms used with version 3.5 to include calculated field formulas that use PAL language functions. This change allows you to use some of the sophisticated PAL language functions discussed in Part 2 of the book in the screen and report forms explained in Part 1 of the book.

Below is a list of the PAL functions that can be used in calculated fields.

Time and Date Functions

DATEVAL()	convert a string to a date
DAY()	day of a date as a number
DOW()	day of a date as a string
MONTH()	month as a number
MOY()	month as a three-character string
TIME()	time of day as a text
TODAY()	today's date as a date value
YEAR()	year of a date

Financial Calculations

CNPV()	net present value of a column
FV()	future value of annuity
PMT()	monthly payment for a loan
PV()	present value of an annuity

Mathematical Functions

ABS()	the absolute value of a number
ACOS()	the arc-cosine
ASIN()	the arc-sine
ATAN()	the 2-quadrant arc-tangent
ATAN2()	the 4-quadrant arc-tangent
COS()	the cosine of an angle
EXP()	the natural exponential of a number
INT()	the integer part of a number
LN()	the natural logarithm of a number
LOG()	the base 10 logarithm of a number
MAX()	the maximum of two numbers
MIN()	the minimum of two numbers
MOD()	modular calculation
PI()	the constant pi
POW()	a number raised to a given power
RAND()	pseudo random number
ROUND()	rounds a number to selected digits
SIN()	the sine of an angle
SQRT()	the square root of a number
TAN()	the tangent of an angle

Column-Oriented Statistical Functions

CAVERAGE()	the column average (mean)
CCOUNT()	the count of column values
CMAX()	the column maximum
CMIN()	the column minimum
CSTD()	the column standard deviation
CSUM()	the column sum
CVAR()	the column population variance

Text Functions

ASC()	character to an ASCII value
CHR()	ASCII code value to a character
DATEVAL()	text to a date value
FILL()	string of repeated characters
FORMAT()	set display and output format
LEN()	the length of a text string
LOWER()	text to lower case text
NUMVAL()	text to a number value
SEARCH()	searches for a string within a string
STRVAL()	converts any value to text
SUBSTR()	returns the substring of a string
UPPER()	converts text to upper case
USERNAME()	current network user name

PAL functions allow you to display information on a screen form that you could not have generated using the standard operators available in previous version of Paradox. There are two major advantages provided by PAL functions.

❑ **Special Values.** Many PAL functions provide routines that generate special values based on column information. For example, the DOW() function generates the day of the week, Mon, Tue, Wed, etc., based on a date value. Math functions such as SQRT(), which calculate the square root of a number, generate values that cannot be calculated using the +, -, * and / operations supported in previous version for calculated fields.

❑ **Manipulation.** PAL functions allow you to control the form in which information in a column is displayed. For example, the SUBSTR() function allows you to display only part of the text stored in a column.

Using PAL Functions in Screen Forms

The ability to place PAL functions into the formulas used for calculated fields in report forms greatly expands the type of screen forms you are able to create.

The date functions enable you to use a standard date field to generate date information in many different formats. For example you could display a three character abbreviation for the name of the month using the MOY() function, e.g., **MOY([check date])** or the abbreviation for the day of the week, e.g., **DOW([check date])**.

You can combine more than one function in a formula to produce a wide variety of results. For example, you can produce a month/year display such as **Jan-1990** from a date column by using a formula such as this: **MOY([check date])+"-"+STRVAL(YEAR([check date]))**.

One of the most interesting aspects of this feature is that you can use column summary functions as part of a screen form. This means that even thought the screen form still displays one record at a time, each record can include totals, averages or other statistics that apply to the table as a whole. For example, recall that the *Ck_book* table includes a field called Amount. You could display the total of all of the amounts in all of the records by using the formula **CSUM("ck_book","amount")**. Thus it is possible on a single screen display to present information about an individual record and the entire database table at the same time. In fact, you can create a screen form that shows only summary information about the table. Such as screen form could display totals for the table much faster and simply than outputting a report to the screen or processing a query.

Creating a Sample Screen

As a concrete example of how to apply PAL functions to a screen form design you can create a sample screen form for the *Ck_book* table that uses PAL functions to create special calculated fields. Adding PAL function calculated fields to report forms is done in a similar manner. Begin from the main menu by entering

f d
ck_book ↵
5

Enter the following description for the form.

Form with PAL functions ↵

Displaying the Record Total

While screen forms have a special built in option that will display the current record number the displays did not show the total number of the records in the table, e.g., *Record 1 of 17*, as is the case when you are using the table view mode. The NRECORDS() function allows you to display the total number of records in the table as part of a screen form enabling you to duplicate the displayed used by the Paradox table view display.

Begin by inserting the record number on the form. Enter

[F10] f p #
↵ *(2 times)*

With the record number placed onto the form add the following text.

[spacebar]
of
[spacebar]

The text step is the one that uses the PAL function NRECORDS(). Use the command to insert a calculated field.

[F10] f p c

The formula for this field will be the NRECORD() function. The function requires the name of the table entered as text. Enter

NRECORDS("ck_book")
↵ *(2 times)*

By default Paradox enters a field that extends to the right edge of the screen. Use the ← key to reduce that field to a useable size, in this case 4 digits. The exact number of keystrokes is shown below.

← *(67 times)*
↵

Move the cursor down two lines by entering

↵ *(2 times)*

Date Manipulation

One of the most useful areas for PAL functions is in the area of date manipulation. The information entered into a date fields is a specific day, e.g., 5/14/90. PAL date functions allow you to transform a date into different dates related to items such as the name of the month or the day of the week based on the date stored in the field.

In this case you will create two examples of using PAL date functions in a form. The first is a simple example that uses the DOW() function to print the day of the week along with the date. Place the Check date field onto the form using the **Field Place Regular** command. Enter

Date:
[F10] f p r
→ ***(2 times)***
↵ ***(3 times)***

Next to the date place a calculated field that uses the DOW() function to display a 3 character abbreviation, Mon, Tue, Wed, etc., for the day of the week. The DOW() function requires the name of a field column as its argument. Field names are denoted by surrounding the field name in []. Enter

[spacebar]
[F10] f p c
DOW([check date])
↵ ***(2 times)***

Note that when you insert a calculated formula the display area always stretches to the right edge of the screen. In this case the formula will always yield a 3 character abbreviation. You can use the ← key to shorten the field to 3 characters. The exact keystrokes are shown below.

← ***(60 times)***
↵

Functions in Text Expressions

The previous examples of using PAL functions in calculated fields were simple ones because each formula consisted of a single PAL function. You can use PAL functions in more complicated formulas that generate displays drawn from more than one field or function. For example, in Chapter 6 you created a new field called **Period** so that each record could show a financial period, e.g., 01-Jan, as distinct from the actual check date. You can use formulas with PAL functions to create various kinds of financial period designations by manipulating the elements stored in a date field.

Suppose that you wanted each record to display its financial period in a form such as Jan-90, Feb-90, etc. In order to achieve that display you would have to use two PAL functions.

❑ **MOY().** The MOY()- month of year-function displays a 3 character abbreviation that matches the name of the month, e.g., Jan, Feb, etc.

❑ **YEAR().** The YEAR() function extracts a value equal to the year found in the specified date, e.g., 4/15/90 would yield the value **1990.**

However, the two functions by themselves will not create the desired display for several reasons:

- The YEAR() function returns a four digit value, 1990, not the desired two digits, 90.
- The MOY() functions returns text while the YEAR() function returns a value. In versions earlier than 3.5 you could not create a single formula that contained both text and number information.

Both of these problems can be overcome with PAL functions. The STRVAL() function can convert numeric values into text equivalents allowing the values to be combined with other text and text functions such as MOY(). For example a formula such as **"***"+STRVAL(YEAR([check date]))+"***"** would create a displays such as ****1990****.

The SUBSTR() function allows you to select a section of a text item to be displayed. The SUBSTR() function uses two numbers to indicate the starting character and the number of characters to include. If you wanted to pick out the 90 from 1990 you would use a formula like **SUBSTR("1990",3,2)** which tells the program to start at the third character and include the third and fourth characters. When you combine the SUBSTR() with the previous formula which converts values to text you get a formula that looks like **SUB-STR(STRVAL(YEAR([check date])),3,2)** which will display the last two digits of the year portion of the check date.

> *If you are not familiar with PAL the formulas may seem to be very complex just to solve these simple problems. Be assured that the formulas shown in this section represent a standard approach to data manipulation which would look just about the same in other database languages such as dBASE or Foxbase.*

Add a new field to the form which displays the financial period by entering

[spacebar]
Financial Period:
[spacebar]
[F10] f p c

The formula for this field is a complicated one, **MOY([check date])+"-"+SUBSTR(STRVAL(YEAR([check date])),3,2)**. Take care to enter the proper number and sequence of ().

MOY([check date])+"-"+SUBSTR(STRVAL(YEAR([check date])),3,2)
↵ ***(2 times)***
← ***(35 times)***
↵

Move the cursor down to line 5 of the form by entering

↵ ***(2 times)***

Functions with Column Totals

PAL functions can operate on three levels: table, column, and field orientation. The NRECORDS() function is a table oriented function because it returns information about the overall condition of a specific table. Note that table oriented functions do not have to refer to the table for which the current form is being designed. You might use a formula such as **NRECORDS("account")** which would insert the number of records in the *Accounts* table into a form used by another table.

The date functions, e.g., MOY(), are examples of field oriented functions. These functions draw data from current record in the current table. Each time you display a different record the corresponding data appears in the fields.

Column oriented functions, shown on page 694, allow you to insert statistical information such as sums or averages that include the values in an entire field column into a form or a report. In a screen form this allows you to place summary data onto a screen form. You can use this information to compare record oriented values to the overall total of the column for the table. For example, you might create a formula that calculate what percentage the current check amount is of the total amount of all the checks in the *Ck_book* table.

In a report form, a column oriented function allows you to make similar calculations. Keep in mind that even though report forms generate column and group totals, they do so using accumulators. This means that a summary field in a report contains a zero value at the beginning of the report and accumulates as each record is printed. Conversely, a column oriented function will represent the full column value when ever it appears. This would allow you to print the account balance at the *beginning* of the report instead of only at the end. Also keep in mind that you can draw the statistical data from any table, not just he table for which you are preparing the screen or report.

As an example of how a column oriented function can be combined with record oriented data, add fields to this form that show the current check amount or deposit amount, the total for deposits and checks and the percentage that this check or deposit is of the total. Enter

→ *(18 times)*
Amount
→ *(10 times)*
Deposit ↵
Current

In the amount and deposit columns place the corresponding field.

→ *(6 times)*
[F10] f p r
→ *(3 times)*
↵ *(2 times)*
← *(12 times)*
↵
→ *(4 times)*
[F10] f p r
→ *(7 times)*
↵ *(2 times)*
← *(10 times)*
↵

Move to the next line on the form and label that as the total line. Enter

↵
→ *(8 times)*

Add formulas that use the CSUM() function to sum the *Amount* and *Deposit* field columns. Note that the column statistical commands require that you enter the name of the table and the field in that table you want to operate on. Enter

[F10] f p c
CSUM("ck_book","amount")
↵ *(2 times)*
← *(56 times)*
↵

→ *(4 times)*
[F10] f p c
CSUM("ck_book","deposit")
↵ *(2 times)*
← *(39 times)*
↵

Move to the next line and create a label for Percents.

↵
Percent
→ *(14 times)*

The calculated formula for the percent will use the *Amount* field and compare it with the CSUM() value of the entire *Amount* column. Enter

[F10] f p c
[amount]/CSUM("ck_book","amount")
↵ *(2 times)*
← *(56 times)*
↵

Repeat the process for the *Deposit* column.

→ *(14 times)*
[F10] f p c
[deposit]/CSUM("ck_book","deposit")
↵ *(2 times)*
← *(39 times)*
↵

Save the screen form by entering

[F2]

Display the form by entering

v
ck_book ↵
[F10] i p 5

The screen will look like figure A-1 in which a single screen form shows information about the current records as well as summary calculations that reflect the total of all of the records in the table.

```
Viewing Ck_book table with form F5: Record 1 of 17

    1 of 17

Date: 1/01/89    Sun Financial Period: Jan-89

                    Amount            Deposit
Current             0.00          1,700.00
Total          4953.69        5735.90
Percent              0.0               29.
```

Figure A-1 Summary totals combined with field information.

> *You can use PAL functions to address alignment problems, which occur on screen and report forms. When you want information displayed in columns, you will often find that it is hard to know in advance how the field should be formatted. The FORMAT() function, discussed in Chapter 11 as part of the calculated field formulas, controls the format of the numeric values so that they align vertically.*

Index

A

B

C

D

F

G

H

I

K

L

M

N

Q

R

S